D0861926

Dedication

This report is dedicated to the 11 men who lost their lives on the *Deepwater Horizon* rig on April 20, 2010 and to their families, in hope that this report will help minimize the chance of another such disaster ever happening again.

Jason Anderson

Aaron Dale Burkeen

Donald Clark

Stephen Curtis

Gordon Jones

Roy Wyatt Kemp

Karl Dale Kleppinger, Jr.

Blair Manuel

Dewey Revette

Shane Roshto

Adam Weise

Acknowledgements

We wish to acknowledge the many individuals and organizations, government officials and agencies alike that offered their views and insights to the Commission. We would especially like to express our gratitude to the Coast Guard's Incident Specific Preparedness Review (ISPR) for allowing Commission staff to participate in its interviews and discussions, which was invaluable to the preparation of this report. (A copy of the Coast Guard's ISPR report can be found at the Commission's website at www.oilspillcommission. gov). We would also like to thank Chevron for performing the cement tests that proved so critical to our investigation into the Macondo well blowout.

We also thank the Department of Energy, which served as our supporting agency, and all of the Department employees whose assistance was so essential to the success and functioning of the Commission. In particular, we would like to thank Christopher Smith, Deputy Assistant Secretary for Oil and Natural Gas, who acted as the Commission's Designated Federal Officer, as well as Elena Melchert, Petroleum Engineer in the Office of Oil and Gas Resource Conservation, who served as the Committee Manager.

But most importantly, we are deeply grateful to the citizens of the Gulf who shared their personal experiences as Commissioners traveled in the region, providing a critical human dimension to the disaster and to our undertaking, as well as the many people who testified at the Commission's hearings, provided public comments, and submitted statements to our website. Together, these contributions greatly informed our work and led to a better report. Thank you one and all.

Copyright, Restrictions, and Permissions Notice

Cover Photo: © Steadfast TV

ISBN: 978-0-16-087371-3

Deep Water

The Gulf Oil Disaster and the Future
of Offshore Drilling

Report to the President

National Commission on the BP Deepwater Horizon
Oil Spill and Offshore Drilling

January 2011

Commission Members

Bob Graham, Co-Chair

William K. Reilly, Co-Chair

Frances Beinecke

Donald F. Boesch

Terry D. Garcia

Cherry A. Murray

Fran Ulmer

Table of Contents

Photo: Susan Walsh, Associated Press

Foreword

The explosion that tore through the *Deepwater Horizon* drilling rig last April 20, as the rig's crew completed drilling the exploratory Macondo well deep under the waters of the Gulf of Mexico, began a human, economic, and environmental disaster.

Eleven crew members died, and others were seriously injured, as fire engulfed and ultimately destroyed the rig. And, although the nation would not know the full scope of the disaster for weeks, the first of more than four million barrels of oil began gushing uncontrolled into the Gulf—threatening livelihoods, precious habitats, and even a unique way of life. A treasured American landscape, already battered and degraded from years of mismanagement, faced yet another blow as the oil spread and washed ashore. Five years after Hurricane Katrina, the nation was again transfixed, seemingly helpless, as this new tragedy unfolded in the Gulf. The costs from this one industrial accident are not yet fully counted, but it is already clear that the impacts on the region's natural systems and people were enormous, and that economic losses total tens of billions of dollars.

On May 22, 2010, President Barack Obama announced the creation of the National Commission on the BP Deepwater Horizon Oil Spill and Offshore Drilling: an independent, nonpartisan entity, directed to provide a thorough analysis and impartial judgment. The President charged the Commission to determine the causes of the disaster, and to improve the country's ability to respond to spills, and to recommend reforms to make offshore energy production safer. And the President said we were to follow the facts wherever they led.

This report is the result of an intense six-month effort to fulfill the President's charge.

From the outset, the Commissioners have been determined to learn the essential lessons so expensively revealed in the tragic loss of life at the *Deepwater Horizon* and the severe damages that ensued. The Commission's aim has been to provide the President, policymakers, industry, and the American people a clear, accessible, accurate, and fair account of the largest oil spill in U.S history: the context for the well itself, how the explosion and spill happened, and how industry and government scrambled to respond to an unprecedented emergency. This was our first obligation: determine what happened, why it happened, and explain it to Americans everywhere.

As a result of our investigation, we conclude:

- The explosive loss of the Macondo well could have been prevented.

- The immediate causes of the Macondo well blowout can be traced to a series of identifiable mistakes made by BP, Halliburton, and Transocean that reveal such systematic failures in risk management that they place in doubt the safety culture of the entire industry.

- Deepwater energy exploration and production, particularly at the frontiers of experience, involve risks for which neither industry nor government has been adequately prepared, but for which they can and must be prepared in the future.

- To assure human safety and environmental protection, regulatory oversight of leasing, energy exploration, and production require reforms even beyond those significant reforms already initiated since the *Deepwater Horizon* disaster. Fundamental reform will be needed in both the structure of those in charge of regulatory oversight and their internal decisionmaking process to ensure their political autonomy, technical expertise, and their full consideration of environmental protection concerns.

- Because regulatory oversight alone will not be sufficient to ensure adequate safety, the oil and gas industry will need to take its own, unilateral steps to increase dramatically safety throughout the industry, including self-policing mechanisms that supplement governmental enforcement.

- The technology, laws and regulations, and practices for containing, responding to, and cleaning up spills lag behind the real risks associated with deepwater drilling into large, high-pressure reservoirs of oil and gas located far offshore and thousands of feet below the ocean's surface. Government must close the existing gap and industry must support rather than resist that effort.

- Scientific understanding of environmental conditions in sensitive environments in deep Gulf waters, along the region's coastal habitats, and in areas proposed for more drilling, such as the Arctic, is inadequate. The same is true of the human and natural impacts of oil spills.

We reach these conclusions, and make necessary recommendations, in a constructive spirit: we aim to promote changes that will make American offshore energy exploration and production far safer, today and in the future.

More broadly, the disaster in the Gulf undermined public faith in the energy industry, government regulators, and even our own capability as a nation to respond to crises. It is our hope that a thorough and rigorous accounting, along with focused suggestions for reform, can begin the process of restoring confidence. There is much at stake, not only for the people directly affected in the Gulf region, but for the American people at large. The tremendous resources that exist within our outer continental shelf belong to the nation as a whole. The federal government's authority over the shelf is accordingly plenary, based on its power as both the owner of the resources and in its regulatory capacity as sovereign to protect public health, safety, and welfare. To be allowed to drill on the outer continental shelf is a privilege to be earned, not a private right to be exercised.

"Complex Systems Almost Always Fail in Complex Ways"

As the Board that investigated the loss of the Columbia space shuttle noted, "complex systems almost always fail in complex ways." Though it is tempting to single out one crucial misstep or point the finger at one bad actor as the cause of the *Deepwater Horizon* explosion, any such explanation provides a dangerously incomplete picture of what happened—encouraging the very kind of complacency that led to the accident in the first place. Consistent with the President's request, this report takes an expansive view.

Why was a corporation drilling for oil in mile-deep water 49 miles off the Louisiana coast? To begin, Americans today consume vast amounts of petroleum products—some 18.7 million barrels per day—to fuel our economy. Unlike many other oil-producing countries, the United States relies on private industry—not a state-owned or -controlled enterprise—to supply oil, natural gas, and indeed all of our energy resources. This basic trait of our private-enterprise system has major implications for how the U.S. government oversees and regulates offshore drilling. It also has advantages in fostering a vigorous and competitive industry, which has led worldwide in advancing the technology of finding and extracting oil and gas.

Even as land-based oil production extended as far as the northern Alaska frontier, the oil and gas industry began to move offshore. The industry first moved into shallow water and eventually into deepwater, where technological advances have opened up vast new reserves of oil and gas in remote areas—in recent decades, much deeper under the water's surface and farther offshore than ever before. The *Deepwater Horizon* was drilling the Macondo well under 5,000 feet of Gulf water, and then over 13,000 feet under the sea floor to the hydrocarbon reservoir below. It is a complex, even dazzling, enterprise. The remarkable advances that have propelled the move to deepwater drilling merit comparison with exploring outer space. The Commission is respectful and admiring of the industry's technological capability.

But drilling in deepwater brings new risks, not yet completely addressed by the reviews of where it is safe to drill, what could go wrong, and how to respond if something does go awry. The drilling rigs themselves bristle with potentially dangerous machinery. The deepwater environment is cold, dark, distant, and under high pressures—and the oil and gas reservoirs, when found, exist at even higher pressures (thousands of pounds per square inch), compounding the risks if a well gets out of control. The *Deepwater Horizon* and Macondo well vividly illustrated all of those very real risks. When a failure happens at such depths, regaining control is a formidable engineering challenge—and the costs of failure, we now know, can be catastrophically high.

In the years before the Macondo blowout, neither industry nor government adequately addressed these risks. Investments in safety, containment, and response equipment and practices failed to keep pace with the rapid move into deepwater drilling. Absent major crises, and given the remarkable financial returns available from deepwater reserves, the business culture succumbed to a false sense of security. The *Deepwater Horizon* disaster exhibits the costs of a culture of complacency.

The Commission examined in great detail what went wrong on the rig itself. Our investigative staff uncovered a wealth of specific information that greatly enhances our understanding of the factors that led to the explosion. The separately published report of the chief counsel (a summary of the findings is presented in Chapter 4) offers the fullest account yet of what happened on the rig and why. There are recurring themes of missed warning signals, failure to share information, and a general lack of appreciation for the risks involved. In the view of the Commission, these findings highlight the importance of organizational culture and a consistent commitment to safety by industry, from the highest management levels on down.*

But that complacency affected government as well as industry. The Commission has documented the weaknesses and the inadequacies of the federal regulation and oversight, and made important recommendations for changes in legal authority, regulations, investments in expertise, and management.

The Commission also looked at the effectiveness of the response to the spill. There were remarkable instances of dedication and heroism by individuals involved in the rescue and cleanup. Much was done well—and thanks to a combination of good luck and hard work, the worst-case scenarios did not all come to pass. But it is impossible to argue that the industry or the country was prepared for a disaster of the magnitude of the *Deepwater Horizon* oil spill. Twenty years after the *Exxon Valdez* spill in Alaska, the same blunt response technologies—booms, dispersants, and skimmers—were used, to limited effect. On-the-ground shortcomings in the joint public-private response to an overwhelming spill like that resulting from the blowout of the Macondo well are now evident, and demand public and private investment. So do the weaknesses in local, state, and federal coordination revealed by the emergency. Both government and industry failed to anticipate and prevent this catastrophe, and failed again to be prepared to respond to it.

---

*The chief counsel's investigation was no doubt complicated by the lack of subpoena power. Nonetheless, Chief Counsel Bartlit did an extraordinary job building the record and interpreting what he learned. He used his considerable powers of persuasion along with other tools at his disposal to engage the involved companies in constructive and informative exchanges.

If we are to make future deepwater drilling safer and more environmentally responsible, we will need to address all these deficiencies together; a piecemeal approach will surely leave us vulnerable to future crises in the communities and natural environments most exposed to offshore energy exploration and production.

The Deepwater Drilling Prospect

The damage from the spill and the impact on the people of the Gulf has guided our work from the very beginning. Our first action as a Commission was to visit the Gulf region, to learn directly from those most affected. We heard deeply moving accounts from oystermen witnessing multi-generation family businesses slipping away, fishermen and tourism proprietors bearing the brunt of an ill-founded stigma affecting everything related to the Gulf, and oil-rig workers dealing with mounting bills and threatened home foreclosures, their means of support temporarily derailed by a blanket drilling moratorium, shutting down all deepwater drilling rigs, including those not implicated in the BP spill.

Indeed, the centrality of oil and gas exploration to the Gulf economy is not widely appreciated by many Americans, who enjoy the benefits of the energy essential to their transportation, but bear none of the direct risks of its production. Within the Gulf region, however, the role of the energy industry is well understood and accepted. The notion of clashing interests—of energy extraction versus a natural-resource economy with bountiful fisheries and tourist amenities—misses the extent to which the energy industry is woven into the fabric of the Gulf culture and economy, providing thousands of jobs and essential public revenues. Any discussion of the future of offshore drilling cannot ignore these economic realities.

But those benefits have imposed their costs. The bayous and wetlands of Louisiana have for decades suffered from destructive alteration to accommodate oil exploration. The Gulf ecosystem, a unique American asset, is likely to continue silently washing away unless decisive action is taken to start the work of creating a sustainably healthy and productive landscape. No one should be deluded that restoration on the scale required will occur quickly or cheaply. Indeed, the experience in restoring other large, sensitive regions—the Chesapeake Bay, the Everglades, the Great Lakes—indicates that progress will require coordinated federal and state actions, a dedicated funding source, long-term monitoring, and a vocal and engaged citizenry, supported by robust non-governmental groups, scientific research, and more.

We advocate beginning such an effort, seriously and soon, as a suitable response to the damage and disruption caused by the *Deepwater Horizon* emergency. It is a fair recognition not only of the costs that energy exploitation in the Gulf has, for decades, imposed on the landscape and habitats—and the other economic activities they support—but also of the certainty that Americans will continue to develop the region's offshore energy resources.

For the simple fact is that the bulk of our newly discovered petroleum reserves, and the best prospects for future discoveries, lie not on land, but under water. To date, we have made the decision as a nation to exploit the Gulf's offshore energy resources—ruling much of the Florida, Atlantic, and Pacific coasts out of bounds for drilling. The choice of how aggressively to exploit these resources, wherever they may be found, has profound implications for the future of U.S. energy policy, for our need to understand and assure the integrity of fragile environmental resources, and for the way Americans think about our economy and our security. Although much work is being done to improve the fuel-efficiency of vehicles and to develop alternative fuels, we cannot realistically walk away from these offshore oil resources in the near future. So we must be much better prepared to exploit such resources with far greater care.

The Commission and Its Work

While we took a broad view of the spill, it could not be exhaustive. There is still much we do not know—for instance, the blowout preventer, the last line of defense against loss of well control, is still being analyzed; and the *Deepwater Horizon* itself, after its explosive destruction, remained out of reach during our investigation. The understandable, immediate need to provide answers and concrete suggestions trumped the benefits of a longer, more comprehensive investigation. And as we know from other spills, their environmental consequences play out over decades—and often in unexpected ways. Instead, the Commission focused on areas we thought most likely to inform practical recommendations. Those recommendations are presented in the spirit of transforming America into the global leader for safe and effective offshore drilling operations. Just as this Commission learned from the experiences of other nations in developing our recommendations, the lessons learned from the Deepwater Horizon disaster are not confined to our own government and industry, but relevant to rest of the world.

We wish we could say that our recommendations make a recurrence of a disaster like the Macondo blowout impossible. We do not have that power. No one can eliminate all risks associated with deepwater exploration. But when exploration occurs, particularly in sensitive environments like the Gulf of Mexico or the Arctic, the country has an obligation to make responsible decisions regarding the benefits and risks.

The report is divided into three sections.

Chapters 1 through 3 describe the events of April 20th on the *Deepwater Horizon*, and, more important, the events leading up to it in the preceding decades—especially how the dramatic expansion of deepwater drilling in the Gulf was not met by regulatory oversight capable of ensuring the safety of those drilling operations.

Chapters 4 through 7 lay out the results of our investigation in detail, highlighting the crucial issues we believe must inform policy going forward: the specific engineering and operating choices made in drilling the Macondo well, the attempts to contain and respond to the oil spill, and the impacts of the spill on the region's natural resources, economy, and people—in the context of the progressive degradation of the Mississippi Delta environment.

Chapters 8 through 10 present our recommendations for reforms in business practices, regulatory oversight, and broader policy concerns. We recognize that the improvements we advocate all come with costs and all will take time to implement. But inaction, as we are deeply aware, runs the risk of real costs, too: in more lost lives, in broad damage to the regional economy and its long-term viability, and in further tens of billions of dollars of avoidable clean-up costs. Indeed, if the clear challenges are not addressed and another disaster happens, the entire offshore energy enterprise is threatened—and with it, the nation's economy and security. We suggest a better option: build from this tragedy in a way that makes the Gulf more resilient, the country's energy supplies more secure, our workers safer, and our cherished natural resources better protected.

Our Thanks and Dedication

We thank President Obama for this opportunity to learn thoroughly about the crisis, and to share our findings with the American public. We deeply appreciate the effort people in the affected Gulf regions made to tell us about their experiences, and the time and preparation witnesses before the Commission dedicated to their presentations. We have come to respect the seriousness with which our fellow Commissioners assumed our joint responsibilities, and their diverse expertise and perspectives that helped make its work thorough and productive. On their behalf, we wish to recognize the extraordinary work the Commission's staff—scientists, lawyers, engineers, policy analysts, and more— performed, under demanding deadlines, to make our inquiries broad, deep, and effective; and we especially highlight the leadership contributions of Richard Lazarus, executive director, and Fred Bartlit, chief counsel. Together, they have fulfilled an extraordinary public service.

Finally, to the American people, we reiterate that extracting the energy resources to fuel our cars, heat and light our homes, and power our businesses can be a dangerous enterprise. Our national reliance on fossil fuels is likely to continue for some time—and all of us reap benefits from the risks taken by the men and women working in energy exploration. We owe it to them to ensure that their working environment is as safe as possible. We dedicate this effort to the 11 of our fellow citizens who lost their lives in the *Deepwater Horizon* explosion.

Bob Graham, Co-Chair

William K. Reilly, Co-Chair

Part I

The Path to Tragedy

On April 20, 2010, the 126 workers on the BP *Deepwater Horizon* were going about the routines of completing an exploratory oil well— unaware of impending disaster. What unfolded would have unknown impacts shaped by the Gulf region's distinctive cultures, institutions, and geography—and by economic forces resulting from the unique coexistence of energy resources, bountiful fisheries and wildlife, and coastal tourism. The oil and gas industry, long lured by Gulf reserves and public incentives, progressively developed and deployed new technologies, at ever-larger scales, in pursuit of valuable energy supplies in increasingly deeper waters farther from the coastline. Regulators, however, failed to keep pace with the industrial expansion and new technology—often because of industry's resistance to more effective oversight. The result was a serious, and ultimately inexcusable, shortfall in supervision of offshore drilling that played out in the Macondo well blowout and the catastrophic oil spill that followed. Chapters 1 through 3 describe the interplay of private industry and public oversight in the distinctive Gulf deepwater context: the conditions that governed the deployment of the *Deepwater Horizon* and the drilling of the Macondo well.

Chapter One

"Everyone involved with the job . . . was completely satisfied. . ."

The *Deepwater Horizon*, the Macondo Well, and Sudden Death on the Gulf of Mexico

At 5:45 a.m. on Tuesday, April 20, 2010, a Halliburton Company cementing engineer sent an e-mail from the rig *Deepwater Horizon*, in the Gulf of Mexico off the Louisiana coast, to his colleague in Houston. He had good news: "We have completed the job and it went well."[1]

Outside in the Gulf, it was still dark—beyond the glare of the floodlights on the gargantuan rig, the four decks of which towered above the blue-green water on four huge white columns, all floating on massive pontoons. The oil derrick rose over 20 stories above the top deck. Up on the bridge on the main deck, two officers monitored the satellite-guided dynamic positioning system, controlling thrusters so powerful that they could keep the 33,000-ton *Deepwater Horizon* centered over a well even in high seas. The rig's industrial hum and loud mechanical noises punctuated the sea air as a slight breeze blew in off the water. The crew worked on

Pride of the Transocean fleet of offshore drilling rigs, *Deepwater Horizon* rides calmly on station 40 miles off the Louisiana coast. The $560-million-dollar rig, under lease to BP, was putting the finishing touches on the oil company's 18,000-foot-deep Macondo well when it blew out and escaping methane gas exploded. Eleven workers died in the inferno. According to the government's estimates, by the time the well was sealed months later, over 4 million barrels of oil had spilled into the Gulf.

< *Photo courtesy of Transocean*

the well bore, aiming always to keep the pressure inside the well balancing the force exerted by the surrounding seabed.[2]

By the time the Halliburton engineer had arrived at the rig four days earlier to help cement in the two-and-a-half-mile-deep Macondo well, some crew members had dubbed it "the well from hell."[3] Macondo was not the first well to earn that nickname;[4] like many deepwater wells, it had proved complicated and challenging. As they drilled, the engineers had to modify plans in response to their increasing knowledge of the precise features of the geologic formations thousands of feet below. Deepwater drilling is an unavoidably tough, demanding job, requiring tremendous engineering expertise.

BP drilling engineer Brian Morel, who had designed the Macondo well with other BP engineers including Mark Hafle, was also on board to observe the final stages of work at the well.[5] In an April 14 e-mail, Morel had lamented to his colleagues, "this has been [a] nightmare well which has everyone all over the place."[6] BP and its corporate partners on the well, Anadarko Petroleum and MOEX USA, had, according to government reports, budgeted $96.2 million and 51 days of work to drill the Macondo well in Mississippi Canyon Block 252.[7] They discovered a large reservoir of oil and gas, but drilling had been challenging.

As of April 20, BP and the Macondo well were almost six weeks behind schedule and more than $58 million over budget.[8] The *Deepwater Horizon* was not originally meant to drill Macondo. Another giant rig, the *Marianas*, had initiated work on the well the previous October.[9] Drilling had reached more than 9,000 feet below the ocean surface (4,000 feet below the seabed), with another 9,000 feet to go to "pay zone" (the oil and gas reservoir), when Hurricane Ida so battered the rig on November 9 that it had to be towed in for repair.

Both *Marianas* and *Deepwater Horizon* were semisubmersible rigs owned by Transocean, founded in Louisiana in 1919 as Danciger Oil & Refining Co. and now the world's largest contractor of offshore drilling rigs.[10] In 2009, Transocean's global fleet produced revenues of $11.6 billion.[11] Transocean had consolidated its dominant position in the industry in November 2007 by merging with rival GlobalSantaFe.[12]

Deepwater Horizon, built for $350 million,[13] was seen as the outstanding rig in Transocean's fleet; leasing its services reportedly cost as much as $1 million per day. Since *Deepwater Horizon*'s 2001 maiden voyage to the Gulf, it had been under contract to London-based BP (formerly known as British Petroleum). By 2010, after numerous acquisitions, BP had become the world's fourth-largest corporation (based on revenue)[14] producing more than 4 million barrels of oil daily from 30 countries.* Ten percent of BP's output came from the Gulf of Mexico, where BP America (headquartered in Houston) was the largest producer. But BP had a tarnished reputation for safety. Among other BP accidents, 15 workers died in a 2005 explosion at its Texas City, Texas, refinery; in 2006, there was a major oil spill from a badly corroded BP pipeline in Alaska.

*   *   *   *

---

*A barrel equals 42 gallons.

Deepwater Horizon had arrived at the Macondo lease site on January 31, at 2:15 p.m. It was 55 degrees, chilly and clear—the night of a full moon. About 126 people were aboard: approximately 80 Transocean employees, a few BP men, cafeteria and laundry workers, and a changing group of workers contracted for specialized jobs. Depending on the status of the well, these might include Halliburton cementers, mud loggers from Sperry Sun (a Halliburton subsidiary), mud engineers from M-I SWACO (a subsidiary of Schlumberger, an international oilfield services provider), remotely operated vehicle technicians from Oceaneering, or tank cleaners and technicians from the OCS Group. The offices and living quarters were on the two bottom decks of the rig. Helicopters flew in and out regularly with workers and supplies, landing on the top-deck helipad, and service ships made regular visits.

At its new Macondo assignment, *Deepwater Horizon* floated in 4,992 feet of water just beyond the gentle slope of the continental shelf in the Mississippi Canyon.[15] The seabed far below was near-freezing, visible to the crew only via cameras mounted on the rig's subsea remotely operated vehicle. Another two and a half miles below the seabed was the prize BP sought: a large reservoir of oil and gas from the Middle Miocene era trapped in a porous rock formation at temperatures exceeding 200 degrees.[16] These deepwater hydrocarbon fields, buried far below the seabed—not just in the Gulf, but in other oil-rich zones around the world, too—were the brave new oil frontier. The size of some deepwater fields was so huge that the oil industry had nicknamed those with a billion barrels or more "elephants."[17]

Drilling for oil had always been hard, dirty, dangerous work, combining heavy machinery and volatile hydrocarbons extracted at high pressures. Since 2001, the Gulf of Mexico workforce—35,000 people, working on 90 big drilling rigs and 3,500 production platforms—had suffered 1,550 injuries, 60 deaths, and 948 fires and explosions.[18]

The rig never slept. Most workers on *Deepwater Horizon*, from BP's top "company man" down to the roustabouts, put in a 12-hour night or day shift, working three straight weeks on and then having three weeks off. Rig workers made good money for the dangerous work and long stints away from home and family. Top rig and management jobs paid well into six figures.

On the morning of April 20, Robert Kaluza was BP's day-shift company man on the *Deepwater Horizon*. On board for the first time, he was serving for four days as a relief man for Ronald Sepulvado, a veteran well-site leader on the rig. Sepulvado had flown back to shore April 16 for a required well-control class.[19]

During the rig's daily 7:30 a.m. operations conference call to BP in Houston, engineer Morel discussed the good news that the final cement job at the bottom of the Macondo well had gone fine.[20] To ensure the job did not have problems, a three-man Schlumberger team was scheduled to fly out to the rig later that day, able to perform a suite of tests to examine the well's new bottom cement seal.[21]

According to the BP team's plan, if the cementing went smoothly, as it had, they could skip Schlumberger's cement evaluation. Generally, the completion rig would perform this test when it reopened the well to produce the oil the exploratory drilling had discovered. The decision was made to send the Schlumberger team home on the 11:00 a.m. helicopter, thus saving time and the $128,000 fee. As BP Wells Team Leader John Guide noted, "Everyone involved with the job on the rig site was completely satisfied with the [cementing] job."[22]

At 8:52 a.m., Morel e-mailed the Houston office to reiterate: "Just wanted to let everyone know the cement job went well. Pressures stayed low, but we had full returns on the entire job...We should be coming out of the hole [well] shortly." At 10:14 a.m., David Sims, BP's new drilling operations manager in charge of Macondo, e-mailed to say, "Great job guys!"

*   *   *   *

The rest of the day would be devoted to a series of further tests on the well—positive- and negative-pressure tests—in preparation for "temporary abandonment."* During the positive-pressure test, the drill crew would increase the pressure inside the steel casing and seal assembly to be sure they were intact. The negative-pressure test, by contrast, would reduce the pressure inside the well in order to simulate its state after the *Deepwater Horizon* had packed up and moved on. If pressure increased inside the well during the negative-pressure test, or if fluids flowed up from the well, that would indicate a well integrity problem—a leak of fluids into the well. Such a leak would be a worrisome sign that somewhere the casing and cement had been breached—in which case remedial work would be needed to reestablish the well's integrity.

At 10:43 a.m., Morel, about to leave the rig on the helicopter with the Schlumberger team, sent a short e-mail laying out his plan for conducting the day's tests of the well's integrity and subsequent temporary abandonment procedures. Few had seen the plan's details when the rig supervisors and members of the drill team gathered for the rig's daily 11:00 a.m. pre-tour meeting in the cinema room. "Basically [we] go over what's going to be taking place for today on the rig and the drill floor," said Douglas Brown, chief mechanic.[23]

During the rig meeting, the crew on the drill floor was conducting the Macondo well's positive-pressure test.[24] The positive-pressure test on the casing was reassuring, a success.[25] There was reason for the mood on the rig to be upbeat. Ross Skidmore, a subsea engineer explained, "When you run the last string of casing, and you've got it cemented, it's landed out, and a test was done on it, you say, 'This job, we're at the end of it, we're going to be okay.'"[26]

At noon, the drill crew began to run drill pipe into the well in preparation for the negative-pressure test later that evening.[27] By now, it was a sunny afternoon. Transocean's top men on the rig, Jimmy Harrell and Captain Curt Kuchta, were standing together near the helipad, watching a helicopter gently land. Kuchta had come in from New Orleans just

---

* Temporary abandonment describes the process, after successful exploration, for securing the well until the production platform can be brought in for the purpose of extracting the oil and gas from the reservoir.

that morning to begin his three-week hitch. Harrell was the top Transocean man on the rig when—as now—the well was "latched up." Captain Kuchta, who had served on the *Deepwater Horizon* since June 2008, was in command when the vessel was "unlatched" and thus once again a maritime vessel. [28]

The helicopter landed, the doors opened, and four Houston executives stepped out to begin their 24-hour "management visibility tour."[29] Harrell and Kuchta greeted the VIPs.[30] Two were from Transocean: Buddy Trahan, vice president and operations manager for assets, and Daun Winslow, a one-time assistant driller who had worked his way up to operations manager. BP's representatives were David Sims, the new drilling operations manager (he had sent the congratulatory e-mail about the cement just that morning), and Pat O'Bryan, vice-president for drilling and completions, Gulf of Mexico Deepwater.[31]

At about 4:00 p.m., Harrell began his escorted tour of the *Deepwater Horizon* for the VIPs.[32] He was joined by Chief Engineer Steve Bertone, on board since 2003, and senior toolpusher Randy Ezell, another top man on the rig. [33] Like Harrell, Ezell was an offshore veteran. He had worked for 23 years with Transocean[34] and was now the senior man in charge of the drilling floor. He had been on the rig for years. If any people knew this rig, they were Harrell, Bertone, and Ezell; they showed the VIPs around.

At 5:00 p.m., the rig crew, including toolpusher Wyman Wheeler, began the negative-pressure test.[35] After bleeding pressure from the well, the crew would close it off to check whether the pressure within the drill pipe would remain steady. But the pressure repeatedly built back up. As the crew conducted the test, the drill shack grew crowded.[36] The night crew began arriving to relieve the day shift, and Harrell brought the VIPs through as part of their tour.[37]

"There was quite a few people in there," said Transocean's Winslow. "I tapped Dewey Revette on the shoulder. He was the driller master. I said, 'Hey, how's it going, Dewey? You got everything under control here?'

"And he said, 'Yes, sir.'

"And there seemed to be a discussion going on about some pressure or a negative test. And I said to Jimmy [Harrell] and Randy Ezell, 'Looks like they're having a discussion here. Maybe you could give them some assistance.' And they happily agreed to that."[38] Bertone took over the tour, wandering on to look at the moon pool, down toward the pontoons and the thrusters.[39]

The two shifts continued to discuss how to proceed. It was about 6:00 p.m. Jason Anderson, a tool pusher, turned to Ezell and said, "Why don't you go eat?"[40]

Ezell had originally planned to attend a meeting with the VIPs at 7:00 p.m. He replied, "I can go eat and come back."[41]

Anderson was from Bay City, Texas, and had been on the rig since it was built; he was highly respected as a man who understood the finer points of deepwater well control. This was his final shift on the *Deepwater Horizon*: he had been promoted to teaching in Transocean's well-control school, and he was scheduled to fly out the next day. He told Ezell, "Man, you ain't got to do that. I've got this. Don't worry about it. If I have any problems at all with this test I'll give you a call."[42]

"I knew Jason well," said Ezell, "I've worked with him for all those years, eight or nine years….He was just like a brother. So I had no doubt that if he had any indication of any problem or difficulty at all he would have called me. So I went ahead and ate. I did attend the meeting with the dignitaries."[43]

Wheeler was "convinced that something wasn't right," recalled Christopher Pleasant, a subsea supervisor. Wheeler couldn't believe the explanations he was hearing. But his shift was up.[44]

Don Vidrine, the company man coming on the evening shift, eventually said that another negative test had to be done.[45] This time the crew members were able to get the pressure down to zero on a different pipe, the "kill line," but still not for the drill pipe, which continued to show elevated pressure.[46] According to BP witnesses, Anderson said he had seen this before and explained away the anomalous reading as the "bladder effect."[47] Whether for this reason or another, the men in the shack determined that no flow from the open kill line equaled a successful negative-pressure test.[48]* It was time to get on with the rest of the temporary abandonment process. Kaluza, his shift over, headed off duty.[49]

At 7:00 p.m., after dinner, the VIPs had gathered in the third floor conference room with the rig's leadership. According to BP's Patrick O'Bryan, the *Deepwater Horizon* was "the best performing rig that we had in our fleet and in the Gulf of Mexico. And I believe it was one of the top performing rigs in all the BP floater fleets from the standpoint of safety and drilling performance." O'Bryan, at his new job just four months, was on board in part to learn what made the rig such a stand-out.[50] Despite all the crew's troubles with this latest well,[51] they had not had a single "lost-time incident" in seven years of drilling.[52]

The Transocean managers discussed with their BP counterparts the backlog of rig maintenance. A September 2009 BP safety audit had produced a 30-page list of 390 items requiring 3,545 man-hours of work.[53] The managers reviewed upcoming maintenance schedules and discussed efforts to reduce dropped objects and personal injuries: on a rig with cranes, multiple decks, and complicated heavy machinery, errant objects could be deadly.[54]

Around 9:00 p.m., Transocean's Winslow proposed they all go visit the bridge, which had not been part of their earlier tour. According to David Sims, the bridge was "kind of an impressive place if you hadn't been there…[l]ots of screens…lots of technology."[55] The four

---

* The precise content of this particular conversation is disputed and is considered more fully in Chapter 4.

men walked outside. The Gulf air was warm and the water calm as glass. Beyond the glare of the rig's lights, the night sky glimmered with stars.

*   *   *   *

After concluding that the negative-pressure test was successful, the drilling crew prepared to set a cement plug[56] deep in the well—3,000 feet below the top of the well. [57] They reopened the blowout preventer and began pumping seawater down the drill pipe to displace the mud and spacer* from the riser (the pipe that connected the rig to the well assembly on the seafloor below).[58] When the spacer appeared up at the surface, they stopped pumping because the fluid had to be tested to make sure it was clean enough to dump it in the Gulf, now that it had journeyed down into the well and back. By 9:15 p.m., the crew began discharging the spacer overboard.[59]

*   *   *   *

Inside the bridge, Captain Kuchta welcomed visitors Sims, O'Bryan, Trahan, and Winslow.[60] The two dynamic-positioning officers, Yancy Keplinger and Andrea Fleytas, were also on the bridge.[61] Keplinger was giving the visitors a tour of the bridge while Fleytas was at the desk station.[62] The officers explained how the rig's thrusters kept the *Deepwater Horizon* in place above the well, showed off the radars and current meters, and offered to let the visiting BP men try their hands at the rig's dynamic-positioning video simulator.[63]

Winslow watched as the crew programmed in 70-knot winds and 30-foot seas, and hypothetically put two of the rig's six thrusters out of commission. Then they put the simulator into manual mode and let Sims work the hand controls to maintain the rig's location. Keplinger was advising about how much thrust to use. Winslow decided it was a good moment to go grab a quick cup of coffee and a smoke. He walked down to the rig's smoking area, poured some coffee, and lit his cigarette.[64]

*   *   *   *

Senior Toolpusher Randy Ezell left the evening meeting with BP feeling pleased at their praise "on how good a job we had done...How proud they were of the rig." He stopped in at the galley to get a beverage before continuing to his office. At 9:20, he called Anderson up on the rig floor and asked, "'How did your negative test go?'"[65]

Anderson: "It went good. . . . We bled it off. We watched it for 30 minutes and we had no flow."
Ezell: "What about your displacement? How's it going?"
Anderson: "It's going fine. . . . It won't be much longer and we ought to have our spacer back."

---

* As described more fully in Chapter 4, a "spacer" is a liquid that separates drilling mud used during the drilling operations from the seawater that is pumped in to displace the mud once drilling is complete.

Ezell: "Do you need any help from me?"
Anderson: "No, man. . . . I've got this. . . . Go to bed. I've got it."
Ezell concluded: "Okay."[66]

Ezell walked to his cabin. He had worked with Anderson since the rig came from the shipyard. He had complete confidence in him. "Jason was very acute on what he did. . . he probably had more experience as far as shutting in for kicks than any individual on the *Deepwater Horizon*." So Ezell prepared for bed, called his wife, and then turned off the lights to watch a bit of TV before going to sleep.[67]

*   *   *   *

Up on the bridge, O'Bryan was taking his turn on the simulator.[68] Sims had stepped to the opposite side of the bridge when he felt a distinct high-frequency vibration.[69]

Captain Kuchta looked up and remarked "What's that?" He strode to the port-side door and opened it.[70] Outside, O'Bryan could see the supply vessel *Bankston* glistening with what looked like drilling mud.[71] The captain shut the door "and told everybody to stay inside."[72] Then there began a hissing noise.[73]

*   *   *   *

BP's Vidrine had headed back to his office to do paperwork. He had been there about 10 to 15 minutes when the phone rang. It was Anderson, who reported "they were getting mud back and were diverting to the gas buster." Vidrine grabbed his hard hat and started for the drill floor. By the time he got outside, "[t]here was mud and seawater blowing everywhere, there was a mud film on the deck. I decided not to continue and came back across."[74]

*   *   *   *

Down in Ezell's cabin, he was still watching TV when his phone rang. It was assistant driller Steve Curtis calling, also from the rig floor. "We have a situation. ...The well is blown out. . . . We have mud going to the crown." Ezell was horrified. "Do y'all have it shut in?"[75]

Curtis: "Jason is shutting it in now. . . Randy, we need your help."
Ezell: "Steve, I'll be—I'll be right there."[76]

He put on his coveralls, pulled his socks on, and opened the door to go across the hall to his office for his boots and hard hat. Once in the hall, "a tremendous explosion... blew me probably 20 feet against a bulkhead, against the wall in that office. And I remember then that the lights went out, power went out. I could hear everything deathly calm."[77]

*   *   *   *

Up on the main deck, gantry crane operator Micah Sandell was working with the roustabouts. "I seen mud shooting all the way up to the derrick. . . . Then it just quit. . . I took a deep breath thinking that 'Oh, they got it under control.' Then all the sudden the. . . mud started coming out of the degasser. . . so strong and so loud that it just filled up the whole back deck with a gassy smoke. . . loud enough. . . it's like taking an air hose and sticking it in your ear. Then something exploded. . . that started the first fire...on the starboard side of the derrick."[78]

Sandell jumped up and turned off the crane cab's air conditioner, worried that the gas would come in. "And about that time everything in the back just exploded at one time. It. . . knocked me to the back of the cab. I fell to the floor. . . put my hands over my head and I just said, 'No, God, no.' Because I thought that was it."[79] Then the flames pulled back from his crane and began to shoot straight up, roaring up and over the 20-story derrick.[80]

*   *   *   *

Down in the engine control room, Chief Mechanic Douglas Brown, an Army veteran employed by Transocean, was filling out the nightly log and equipment hours. He had spent the day fixing a saltwater pipe in one of the pontoons. First, he noticed an "extremely loud air leak sound." Then a gas alarm sounded, followed by more and more alarms wailing. In the midst of that noise, Brown noticed someone over the radio. "I heard the captain or chief mate, I'm not sure who, make an announcement to the standby boat, the *Bankston*, saying we were in a well-control situation."[81] The vessel was ordered to back off to 500 meters. [82]

Now Brown could hear the rig's engines revving. "I heard them revving up higher and higher and higher. Next I was expecting the engine trips to take over. . . . That did not happen. After that the power went out." Seconds later, an explosion ripped through the pitch-black control room, hurtling him against the control panel, blasting away the floor. Brown fell through into a subfloor full of cable trays and wires. A second huge explosion roared through, collapsing the ceiling on him. All around in the dark he could hear people screaming and crying for help.[83]

Dazed and buried in debris, he pulled himself out of the subfloor hole. In front of him appeared Mike Williams, chief electronic technician, blood pouring from a wound on his forehead, crawling over the rubble, screaming that he had to get out.[84]

*   *   *   *

Steve Bertone, the rig's chief engineer, had been in bed, reading the first sentence of his book, when he noticed an odd noise. "As it progressively got louder, it sounded like a freight train coming through my bedroom and then there was a thumping sound that consecutively got much faster and with each thump, I felt the rig actually shake."[85] After a loud boom, the lights went out.[86] He leapt out of bed, opening his door to let in the emergency hall light so he could get dressed.[87] The overhead public-address system crackled to life: "Fire. Fire. Fire." [88]

The air smelled and tasted of some kind of fuel. A second explosion roared through, flinging Bertone across his room. He stood up, pulled on his coveralls, work boots, and hard hat, and grabbed a life vest. Out in the hall, clogged with debris from blown-out walls and ceilings, four or five men stood in shock. Bertone yelled to them to go out by the port forward or starboard forward spiral staircases and report to their emergency stations. He ran toward the bridge.[89]

He went to the portside back computer, the dynamic positioning system responsible for maintaining the rig's position. "I observed that we had no engines, no thrusters, no power whatsoever. I picked up the phone which was right there and I tried calling extension 2268, which is the engine control room. There was no dial tone whatsoever." It was then that Bertone looked out to the bridge's starboard window. "I was fully expecting to see steel and pipe and everything on the rig floor." "When I looked out the window, I saw fire from derrick leg to derrick leg and as high as I could see. At that point, I realized that we had just had a blowout."[90]

Fleytas hit the general alarm.[91] The alarm went off: "Report to emergency stations and lifeboats." The rig crew heard: "This is not a drill. This is not a drill."[92] Fleytas, realizing that the rig had not yet issued a Mayday call, sent it out.[93] Out in the dark of the Gulf, three friends on the 31-foot *Ramblin' Wreck* were out on the water for a day of tuna fishing.[94] Around 9:45 p.m., Bradley Shivers trained his binoculars at a brilliant light in the distance and realized it must be an oil rig on fire.[95] On their radio, they heard, "Mayday, Mayday, Mayday, this is the *Deepwater Horizon*. We are on fire."[96] At that moment they "heard and felt a concussive sonic boom."[97] The *Ramblin' Wreck* headed to the scene, their first tuna outing of the year cut short. [98]

Bertone was now back to his station on the bridge, thinking, "The engines should be starting up because in approximately 25 to 30 seconds two engines start up, come online. . . . There was still no power of any kind. No engines starting; no indication of engines starting."[99]

At that moment, the water-tight door to his left banged open and he heard someone say, "The engine room ECR [engine control room] and pump room are gone. They are all gone." Bertone turned around, "What do you mean gone?" The man speaking was so coated in blood Bertone had no idea who he was. Then he recognized the voice. It was Mike Williams. Bertone saw how badly lacerated Williams's forehead was, grabbed a roll of toilet paper from the bathroom, pressed it on the wound to staunch the bleeding, and ordered, "Hold this here."[100]

Then he went back to his station and looked at his screen. "There was still nothing, no engines starting, no thrusters running, nothing. We were still [a] dead ship."[101]

He heard the water-tight door slam again and saw another man soaked in blood, holding a rag to his head, repeating, "I'm hurt. I'm hurt bad, Chief. I'm hurt real bad." It was the voice of Brent Mansfield, a Transocean marine engineer. Bertone pulled back Mansfield's hand holding a rag, saw the head wound, and ran over to the bridge door and yelled down to the life-vessel area, "We need a medic up here now."[102]

*   *   *   *

After the explosion, Randy Ezell lay buried under the blown-out walls and ceilings of the toolpusher's office. The room was dark and smoky, the debris atop him so heavy he could barely move. On the third try, adrenalin kicked in. "I told myself, 'Either you get up or you're going to lay here and die.'" Pulling hard on his right leg, he extricated it and tried to stand up. "That was the wrong thing to do because I immediately stuck my head into smoke. . . .I dropped back down. I got on my hands and knees and for a few moments I was totally disoriented." He wondered which way the door was. He felt air. He crawled through the debris toward the door and realized the "air" was methane. He could feel the droplets. He was crawling slowly atop the rubble in the pitch-black hall when he felt a body.[103]

Ezell then saw a bobbing beam of light. Stan Carden, the electrical supervisor, came round the corner. Carden had a light that bounced off shattered walls and collapsed ceilings in the pitch-black corridor, giving glimpses into rooms on each side wrecked by the power of the blast.[104] Stumbling into what was left of the hall was Offshore Installation Manager Jimmy Harrell, who had been in the shower when the rig exploded;[105] he had donned coveralls, and now was groping his way out of what was left of his room. "I think I've got something in my eyes," Harrell said. He had no shoes. "I got to see if I can find me some shoes."[106]

Carden and Ezell tugged debris off the man they now recognized as Wyman Wheeler. Chad Murray, Transocean's Chief Electrician, also appeared in the hall with a flashlight, and was immediately dispatched to find a stretcher for the injured man.[107]

Believing it would save time to walk Wheeler out, Ezell slung Wheeler's arm around his shoulder. Wheeler groaned, "Set me down . . . . Y'all go on. Save yourself."[108]

Ezell said, "No, we're not going to leave you. We're not going to leave you in here."[109]

Just then, they heard another voice from under the rubble: "God help me. Somebody please help me." Near the ruins of the maintenance office the flashlight picked out a pair of feet jutting from the rubble. It was the visiting Transocean manager, Buddy Trahan, badly injured. By now Murray was there with a stretcher. Ezell, Carden, and Murray dragged away the remains of ceilings and walls trapping Trahan and loaded him on the stretcher. Carden and Murray carried him through the smoke and dark to the bow of the rig and the lifeboats.[110]

Outside, the derrick fire roared upward into the night sky, an inferno throwing off searing heat and clouds of black smoke. The blinding yellow of the flames was the only illumination except for the occasional flashlight. The rig's alarms were going off, while over the public announcement system Keplinger yelled, "THIS IS NOT A DRILL!"[111] As the crew struggled out of the blasted quarters, galley, and offices, in various states of undress, they converged in a chaotic and panicked mass at the lifesaving vessels, putting on life vests.[112]

Sandell, the gantry crane operator, had escaped and come around the port side of the deck to the life vessels. "It was a lot of screaming, just a lot of screaming, a lot of hollering, a lot of scared people, including me, was scared. And trying to get people on boats. It was very unorganized—we had some wounded we was putting in the boat. Had people on the boat yelling, 'Drop the boat, drop the boat,' and we still didn't have everybody on the boat yet. We was still trying to get people on the boat and trying to calm them down enough to—trying to calm them down enough to get everybody on the boat. And there was people jumping off the side. We was trying to get an accurate count and just couldn't get an accurate count because people were just jumping off the boat." [113]

*   *   *   *

On the *Bankston*, Captain Alwin J. Landry was on the bridge updating his log when his mate noticed the mud. Landry stepped out and saw "mud falling on the back half of my boat, kind of like a black rain." He called the *Deepwater Horizon* bridge to say, "I'm getting mud on me." Landry instructed his crew to get inside. The *Deepwater Horizon* called back and told him to move back 500 meters.[114] A crew member noticed a mud-covered seagull and egret fall to the deck.[115] Shortly after, Landry saw the rig explode. Before the ship could move away, his crew had to detach the long mud transfer hose connecting them to the rig.[116]

As they scrambled to disconnect, the *Bankston* slowly moved 100 meters back, then 500 meters. As the rig went dark, and secondary explosions rocked the decks, the *Bankston* turned on its searchlight. Landry could see the *Deepwater Horizon* crew mustering by the portside life vessels. "That's when I seen the first of three or four people jump to the water from the rig."[117]

One of those was Gregory Meche, a compliance specialist. After five minutes of the chaos around the lifeboats, and a series of large explosions, he headed down to the lower deck. He jumped into the water.[118]

Antonio Gervasio, the *Bankston's* relief chief, and two others began launching the ship's fast rescue craft.[119] Within a minute or two of the explosions, they got the boat lowered into the water, and noticed how calm the Gulf was.[120] "I saw the first person jump in the water. So I told one of the guys to keep an eye on him."[121] The rig life jackets were reflective, and as the fast craft made its first sweep round from one side of the burning rig to the other, they hauled Meche and two or three others out of the water.[122]

*   *   *   *

Back on the rig, Transocean's Winslow had made his way from the coffee shop to the lifeboats, surviving the second blast's wave of concussive force, which blew in the corridor's walls and ceilings. On the deck, a firestorm of flames roared in the night sky above the derrick.[123]

Winslow directed the dazed crew toward the covered life-saving vessels, instructing the first arrivals, "We need to make sure we get a good head count." Seeing Captain Kuchta standing at the starboard bridge door, he ran up, and said people should evacuate. Kuchta answered, "Okay." Panic was building as the derrick fire roared. Winslow heard someone yelling that people were jumping overboard. As the lifeboats filled, crew members were screaming to lower the boats.[124] But not everyone was there.[125] Carden and Murray appeared with Trahan on the stretcher and handed him into the vessel, where he was laid out.[126] People in the boat screamed, "We've got to go! We've got to go!"[127]

A man in his life vest was hanging on the rig handrails, preparing to drop overboard. Winslow said, "Hey, where are you going? There's a perfectly good boat here. Do you trust me?" He and another crew member coaxed the man down and into one of the life vessels, where people were still screaming to leave. Down below in the water, the crew could see swaths of burning oil rising and falling with the gentle swell. The jumpers were visibly bobbing and swimming in their life vests shining with fluorescent strips. The *Bankston's* fast rescue craft was hauling them out of the water. [128]

By now, Winslow began to wonder why the derrick was still roaring with flames. Hadn't the blowout preventer been activated, sealing off the well and thus cutting off fuel for the conflagration? He headed to the bridge. Kuchta said, "We've got no power, we've got no water, no emergency generator."[129]

Steve Bertone was still at his station on the bridge and he noticed Christopher Pleasant, one of the subsea engineers, standing next to the panel with the emergency disconnect switch (EDS) to the blowout preventer.[130]

Bertone hollered to Pleasant: "Have you EDSed?"[131]

Pleasant replied he needed permission. Bertone asked Winslow was it okay and Winslow said yes.[132]

Somebody on the bridge yelled, "He cannot EDS without the OIM's [offshore installation manager's] approval."[133]

Harrell, still dazed, somewhat blinded and deafened, had also made it to the bridge, as had BP's Vidrine. [134] With the rig still "latched" to the Macondo well, Harrell was in charge. Bertone yelled, "Can we EDS?" and Harrell yelled back, "Yes, EDS, EDS."[135]

Pleasant opened the clear door covering the panel and pushed the button.
Bertone: "I need confirmation that we have EDSed."
Pleasant: "Yes, we've EDSed."
Bertone: "Chris, I need confirmation again. Have we EDSed?"
Pleasant: "Yes."

Bertone: "Chris, I have to be certain. Have we EDSed?"
Pleasant: "Yes." He pointed to a light in the panel.[136]

By now BP's O'Bryan, who saw red lights on the EDS panel, had put on a life vest. He looked at his colleague, Sims, and said they should head to the lifeboats. Outside, the conflagration continued to rage, a brilliant blinding yellow that threw off a deafening roar and blistering heat. As the fire raged on, new explosions rang out, spewing hot debris. O'Bryan, unsure of which life vessel he should board, recalled being given a notice at his safety orientation listing his boat. He pulled it out of his back pocket: Lifeboat 2. He figured out which one it was, stepped into the dark interior and squeezed into a seat.[137] Some people were screaming, "We've got to go. We've got to go."[138] BP's Robert Kaluza had made his way up from his cabin and had boarded a lifeboat.[139]

Winslow had returned to the lifeboats. He yelled over the noise to the panicked crew members, "We've got plenty of time." Then he looked up at the sky-high flames engulfing the derrick: "Right about that time is when the traveling equipment, the drilling blocks and whatnot on the derrick fell. They were probably 40 to 50 foot in the air, you know, weigh 150,000 pounds, and they didn't make any noise [when they fell]. So at that time, I instructed the boat to my right, which would have been the port survival boat, to depart. They did."[140]

Winslow then helped lower his own life vessel over approximately 125 feet to the Gulf.[141] Winslow discovered the lifeboat windows were obscured by mud.[142] He opened the hatch and pointed the coxswain toward the *Bankston* vessel; he then clambered out onto the outside so that he could grab the rope thrown to him by the *Bankston* crew.[143] The *Bankston* had made radio contact and Captain Landry instructed the vessels to come round to his starboard side, sheltered from the rig.[144]

*   *   *   *

The rig life vessels were not the only small craft fleeing the firestorm. Four high-school buddies out fishing had sailed up to the rig around 7:30 p.m. on their 26-foot catamaran and settled in by the pontoons.[145] The rig's blazing lights attracted small fish, which in turn attracted tuna. About two hours later, the group noticed water flowing out of the rig's pipes, followed by blowing gas. One young man had worked on rigs and began yelling, "Go, go, go, go, GOOOOO!" The owner pointed the boat away from the rig and gunned the engine. Then the lights went out and the rig blew.[146]

*   *   *   *

Back up on the *Deepwater Horizon* bridge, Bertone asked Captain Kuchta's permission to go to the standby generator room to try to manually start it. He assumed that the EDS had worked. "My thinking at that point was the BOP [blowout preventer] had unlatched, what remaining fuel would be in the riser it would burn away and we were going to need power, as well as fire pumps."[147]

As Bertone left, Mike Williams, his head wounds no longer bleeding, said, "You're not going alone, Chief."

"Well, come on."[148]

Paul Meinhart, a motorman, joined them. As Bertone ran to the standby generator room, he looked up at the derrick where the crown should be. "I could see nothing but flames way past the crown." The noise, heat, and smoke were ferocious. The deck was slick, almost an inch and a half deep with something thick like mucus. Bertone thought to himself as he tried not to slip, "Why is all this snot on the deck." They passed the blowout-preventer house, a huge door that seemed 80 to 90 feet tall and 50 feet wide; they looked down into the moon pool and saw only solid flames.[149]

Inside the standby generator room, Bertone flipped the switch from automatic to manual, hitting the reset and the start button. "There was absolutely no turning over of the engine. I tried it again, the reset button and the start. Again, nothing happened." He reset other functions, and turned the switch for the automatic sync on the standby generator to manual. "I ran back to the panel and again, tried the reset and the start. There was no turning over of the engine whatsoever." They made yet another effort using different batteries. Nothing. Bertone yelled, "That's it. Let's go back to the bridge. It's not going to crank."[150]

When they opened the water-tight door to walk back out to the bridge, the heat struck like a blast furnace. The derrick fire roared into the sky, billowing black smoke. The rig had not unlatched from the well. On the bridge, Kuchta was standing with the door open watching the lifeboat station. The first lifeboat had departed, while the second vessel was visible in the burning water just pulling away from the rig.[151]

Bertone returned to the bridge, looked through the open door, and yelled to Williams and Meinhart, "That's it, abandon ship. Let's go." He turned to Keplinger and Fleytas, still manning their radios. He shouted over the noise, "That's it. Abandon ship. Let's go, now."[152]

*   *   *   *

Randy Ezell had stayed with Wyman Wheeler in the blasted-out hallway in the dark. "I told him I wasn't going to leave him and I didn't. And it seemed like an eternity, but it was only a couple of minutes before they [Murray and Carden] came back with the second stretcher. We were able to get Wyman on that stretcher and we took him to the bow of the rig." They emerged from the living quarters to feel the blast of the fire roaring skyward, the sound deafening, the heat roasting. "[T]he first thing I observed is both of the main lifeboats had already been deployed," said Ezell, "and they left. I also looked to my left and I saw Captain [C]urt and a few of his marine crew starting to deploy a life raft. And we continued down the walkway till we got to that life raft and we set the stretcher down."[153] They got a life vest onto Wheeler.[154]

Chief Mate David Young and Bertone "hooked the life raft up and proceeded to crank it up out of its lift, rotated [it] around to the side of the rig and then drop[ped] it—drop[ped] it out so that you could inflate the raft and you could be clear of the rig." A rope attached to a balky shackling device refused to give. Bertone yelled for a knife to cut the rope. Nobody had one. No pocket knives were allowed on the rig. Williams found a gigantic nail-clipper-like device and used it to unscrew the stuck shackle, freeing the rope. The life raft moved out over the side of the rig. Young got in. Behind them, explosions punctuated the heat, noise, and dark. Thick, acrid smoke was rolling over the deck.[155]

Bertone rushed over to the gurney and with Ezell's help maneuvered Wheeler toward the raft. The two men shoved Wheeler off and in. More explosions and searing heat engulfed them. The flames were spreading further up and around the rig toward them. Bertone leaped in the life raft. Even through his leather gloves he could feel the heat. Fleytas jumped in and the raft lurched back and forth. She cried out, "We're going to die. We're going to die." Bertone felt the same way as the raft filled with smoke and the flames leapt closer. "I honestly thought we were going to cook right there." The life raft rocked back and forth in the air between the rig decks, and then began—herky-jerky—to descend. [156]

They touched the water, which was ablaze. Someone yelled, "Where are the paddles?" Bertone jumped out and grabbed the rope and began swimming, pulling the life raft away from the rig. Murray and Minehart jumped into the water to help pull the raft along. Bertone looked up and saw "a tremendous amount of smoke bellowing out from under the rig." At that moment boots appeared out of the smoke: it was Captain Kuchta, jumping into the water. Unable to get into the raft in the confusion, he leaped over 100 feet. He splashed into the Gulf five feet from Bertone. Then a second person came flying through the air, out of the thick smoke, crashing into the water: Keplinger had jumped, too.[157]

By now, Bertone and his men had managed to pull the life raft far enough away from the rig that they could see the circular helipad silhouetted against the flames. Bertone could see someone running at full speed across the helipad deck and then leaping off the rig. It was Mike Williams, the electronics technician.[158] Williams splashed down nearby, resurfaced, and began swimming toward the *Bankston*.[159]

Bertone felt the life raft no longer moving forward.[160] So did Fleytas. She rolled out of the raft into the water and began to swim.[161] Someone hollered, "The painter line is tied to the rig."[162] Bertone could see the painter line go taut. Murray screamed, "Help. We need help over here."[163]

Bertone spotted the *Bankston's* fast rescue craft, its two lights flashing 50 or 60 yards away. The boat had stopped to haul two men from the water. Bertone and others screamed, "We need a knife. We need a knife." As the rescue craft neared, Kuchta swam to get a large foldable pocket knife, swam back, and cut the rope.[164] Heat and smoke boiled out from the rig.

Murray and Carden tied a rope to the fast rescue craft, which towed them to the *Bankston*. Bertone helped lift the injured man (whom he finally learned was Wheeler) onto a stretcher on the flat bottom of the rescue craft.[165] The *Bankston* crew then used its crane to gently lift the stretcher to the deck. By 11:45 p.m., the life boats were empty.

Captain Kuchta went directly to the bridge, where he worked with others "to see who had firefighting capacity," among other matters.[166] Sims and Winslow were already there, organizing BP's and Transocean's response.[167] Harrell remained on the main deck with the traumatized rig crew, many still half dressed, lacerated, or soaked from being in the sea. The crew filled the 260-foot *Bankston's* lounge, galley, and parts of the main deck, including a temporary medical area.[168] Some lay in the bunks.[169] The *Bankston* crew pulled out whatever dry clothes and boots they had, and handed them to the survivors.[170] With both life vessels and the life raft secured to the *Bankston*, the *Deepwater Horizon* leaders could try to take muster.[171] There had been 126 people on the rig when the well blew out.[172] In the confusion, no one yet knew exact counts, but conspicuously missing were those working the drill floor.

*   *   *   *

The *Bankston* was now jammed with the survivors.[173] Some cried, others prayed— grateful to be alive. Bertone went out to the makeshift hospital on the main deck to tend to Mansfield, prostrate on the floor, his head swathed in bandages and gauze, his neck in a brace, his mouth covered with an oxygen mask. Bertone stayed with him, adjusting his oxygen mask and keeping him conscious. On a bed nearby was Buddy Trahan and Bertone talked to him, to keep him awake, too.[174]

When the first Coast Guard helicopter arrived at 11:22 p.m., it lowered a "rescue swimmer" to oversee medical evacuation of the injured.[175] Bertone helped to move Trahan, who was severely injured, onto a gurney.[176] More helicopters would be coming to evacuate the 16 injured crew members to hospitals on the mainland.[177]

On board the *Bankston*, the atmosphere was grim. The crew was forbidden to call home until there was more definitive information.[178] By 11:30 p.m., the managers had taken a final muster and 11 men were missing: Jason Anderson, Dale Burkeen, Donald Clark, Stephen Curtis, Roy Kemp, Gordon Jones, Karl Dale Kleppinger, Blair Manuel, Dewey Revette, Shane Roshto, and Adam Weise.

The survivors sat on the boat in shock and watched the firestorm on the rig rage unabated, its plume of black smoke boiling up high into the night. At 1:30 a.m., the rig listed and rotated in the wake of more secondary explosions. Work boats, which had begun arriving and spraying water on the rig in response to the Mayday call, moved back.[179] By 2:50 a.m., the *Deepwater Horizon* had spun 180 degrees and, its dynamic positioners dead, moved 1,600 feet from the well. By 3:15 a.m., when the U.S. Coast Guard cutter *Pompano* arrived on the scene,[180] the rig was listing heavily. Dennis Martinez realized his dead father's ring, which he removed only when working, was still on the rig.[181]

The three men in the *Ramblin' Wreck* had continued to scour the waters near the rig, looking for survivors or the dead. Several times, they spotted what they thought might be

"I could see nothing but flames way past the crown," chief engineer Steve Bertone recalled of the dramatic moments before he ordered crew members to abandon the rig. Of the 115 survivors, 16 were seriously injured and medevaced to hospitals. Ninety-nine others, including Bertone, were transported to the mainland by the rescue vessel Bankston. Roughly 36 hours after the first explosion, *Deepwater Horizon* sank to the bottom. It was April 22—Earth Day.

Gerald Herbert/Associated Press

a body, only to find it was debris.[182] They heard rumbling sounds coming from deep below the surface of the water—possibly underwater explosions as the rig burned, exploded, listed, and drifted. Frightened, they still kept to their search. After rescue boats came on the scene, they ferried medical supplies between one of those and the *Bankston*. At 3:00 a.m., the three fishermen headed home.

On the *Bankston*, the *Deepwater Horizon* crew deeply wished they could do the same. As the largest boat in the vicinity, the *Bankston* had been ordered by the Coast Guard to stay put while the search and rescue effort unfolded. The search helicopters buzzed overhead, methodically surveying one sector after another. Once the 16 injured were evacuated, said Bertone, "[I] made my way up to one of the upper levels and sat there and watched the rig burn."[183] As oil and gas exploded up and out of the riser, the towering flames set fire to tanks and pipes, sending yet more roiling black smoke high into the sky.

Sitting there hour after hour watching the conflagration with all its cascading smaller explosions was "one of the most painful things we could have ever done," said Randy Ezell. "To stay on location and watch the rig burn. Those guys that were on there were our family. It would be like seeing your children or your brothers or sisters perish in that manner. And that—that put some mental scarring in a lot of people's heads that will never go away. I wish that we could, to the bare minimum, have moved away from the location or something where we didn't just have to sit there and review that many hours. That was extremely painful."[184]

Not until 8:13 that morning, when many boats were on the scene, did the *Bankston* get permission to set sail with the 99 survivors on board for Port Fourchon, Louisiana, the sprawling oil-supply depot that was its home base. The Coast Guard's coordinated search had located no further crew—dead or alive. An hour into the *Bankston's* 114-mile journey back to shore, it stopped at the *Ocean Endeavor* rig to take on two medics.[185] BP's Sims and Transocean's Winslow, along with subsea engineers Mark Hay and Chris Pleasant, debarked to await the *Max Chouest*. They would return to the burning rig and dispatch a remotely operated vehicle down to the burning rig's blowout preventer. The plan was to activate it with a so-called "hot stab" of hydraulic fluid to finally close in the wellhead.[186]

It was a clear spring day as the *Bankston* sailed along through the Gulf, passing the many offshore platforms that dot its blue waters. At 2:09 p.m., the *Bankston* pulled in at the gargantuan Matterhorn production rig to take on more supplies: tobacco, water, and coveralls.[187] Officials from the Coast Guard and Minerals Management Service also boarded. There was still almost a 12-hour journey to Port Fourchon. Officials intended to gather information while memories were still fresh. At 6:35 p.m., the federal officials began conducting interviews, asking each crew member to write a witness statement describing the events they experienced leading up to the blowout and then the abandonment of the rig. The *Bankston* chugged toward the Louisiana coast as night fell. The crew, speaking among themselves, wondered how such a calamity had befallen their rig.

At 1:27 a.m. on Earth Day, Thursday, April 22, 27 hours after the crew had fled the exploding *Deepwater Horizon*, the *Bankston* berthed in slip 1 at the C-Port terminal at Port Fourchon.[188] The exhausted men and women walked on to land. Arrayed before them was a table stacked with forms and surrounded by uniformed officials and company managers. Beyond that stood a long row of portable toilets. As each crew member walked up, he or she was handed a small plastic cup. Per federal regulations, they would all be drug-tested.[189] The investigation of the *Deepwater Horizon* disaster had begun.

Chapter Two

"Each oil well has its own personality"

The History of Offshore Oil and Gas in the United States

March 1938 was an eventful month in the history of oil. Mexico nationalized its oil industry, establishing a precedent. Standard Oil of California (which later became Chevron) completed the first discovery well in Saudi Arabia—still the greatest oil find on record today. And during that same month, the first production of offshore oil took place in the Gulf of Mexico.

Beginning in the 1890s, oil companies had drilled wells in the ocean, but from wooden piers connected to shore. In the 1930s, Texaco and Shell Oil deployed moveable barges to drill in the south Louisiana marshes, protected from extreme conditions in the ocean. In 1937, two independent firms, Pure Oil and Superior Oil, finally plunged away from the shoreline, hiring Texas construction company Brown & Root to build the first freestanding structure in the ocean. It was located on Gulf of Mexico State Lease No. 1, in 14 feet of water, a mile-and-a-half offshore and 13 miles from Cameron, Louisiana, the nearest coastal community. In March 1938, this structure brought in the first well from what was named the Creole Field.[1]

Getting their feet wet for the first time, oil derricks march into the Pacific and the Summerland Oil Field near Santa Barbara, California, at the start of the 20th century. Over the next decades, innovation followed offshore innovation, propelling the industry and helping fuel the nation's remarkable economic expansion. Yet as companies drilled ever deeper and farther from shore, technological hurdles rose ever higher—and risks grew ever greater.

G.H. Eldridge/U.S. Geological Survey

The Creole platform severed oil extraction from land—and did so profitably, setting in motion the march of innovation into ever-deeper waters and new geological environments offshore. The Gulf of Mexico, where offshore drilling began, remained a vital source of oil and gas for the United States. The large, sand-rich depositional system of the Mississippi River that spilled onto the continental margin for tens of millions of years created a world-class petroleum province. The salt domes that pocked the Gulf basin provided excellent traps for hydrocarbons. Prior to 1938, oil hunters had made hundreds of discoveries on domes under the Louisiana and Texas coastal plain. There was no reason to believe that this geology would stop at the shoreline.

The Creole platform highlighted the risks as well as rewards encountered offshore. A hurricane knocked out many of the pilings during construction. The lack of crew quarters on the platform created hardship for workers commuting to and from shore on shrimp boats. Many more challenges lay ahead as the marine environment imposed unique hazards on oil companies trying to adapt land-drilling methods offshore. They would have to squeeze complex drilling and production facilities onto small standing or floating platforms in a region exposed to hurricane-force winds and waves. High costs intensified pressures to find speedy solutions to problems and get the oil flowing. The remoteness of facilities and their space constraints amplified the perils of working under adverse conditions with dangerous equipment and combustible materials. "Nobody really knew what they were doing at that time," recalled a member of Kerr-McGee's earliest offshore drilling crew. "It was blow-by-blow. And it wasn't easy living out there."[2]

As geologists and drillers made discoveries in deeper water, development would stall at a limiting depth, sometimes for several years, until advances were made in production technology to catch up with exploration. Blowouts, drilling-vessel disasters, and platform failures often forced engineers back to the drawing board. Steadily, the offshore industry pioneered ways to meet economic and environmental challenges offshore, first in the Gulf and then around the world. But the risks never went away.

Wading Into Shallow Water

On August 15, 1945, the day after the Japanese surrender in World War II, the U.S. government lifted gasoline and fuel-oil rations. In the first five years after the war, Americans bought an astounding 14 million automobiles, increasing the number of cars in service to 40 million. By 1954, Americans were purchasing 7 million tankfuls of gasoline per day.[3] This booming demand for gasoline, coupled with growing use of home heating oil, vaulted petroleum ahead of coal as the leading source of energy in the United States.

Early Technologies

To meet soaring demand, oil firms embarked on a quest to find new reserves. The intrepid ones returned to the Gulf to drill on leases offered by Louisiana—and made use of wartime technologies and equipment. Sonar and radio positioning developed for warfare at sea proved valuable for offshore exploration. The Navy trained schools of divers in underwater

FIGURE 2.1: Timeline of Major Events

History of Offshore Oil and Gas in the United States

1896	First offshore oil production in the United States—from wooden piers off Summerland, California
1938	First Gulf of Mexico discovery well in state waters; first free-standing production platform in the ocean—Creole field offshore Louisiana
1947	First well drilled from fixed platform offshore out-of-sight-of-land in Federal waters —Kermac 16 offshore Louisiana
1953	Submerged Lands Act & Outer Continental Shelf Lands Act
1954	First federal Outer Continental Shelf lease sale & Maiden voyage of the *Mr. Charlie* submersible drilling vessel, industry's first "day rate" contract
1962	First semi-submersible drilling vessel, *Blue Water 1*, and first subsea well completion
1969	Santa Barbara blowout/oil spill (California)
1978	Shell Oil Company's Cognac production platform (first in 1,000 feet of water) & OCS Lands Act Amendments
1981	First Congressional Outer Continental Shelf leasing moratorium
1982	Creation of the Minerals Management Service (MMS)
1988	Piper Alpha disaster in the North Sea
1994	First production from Shell's Auger tension-leg platform in 2,860 feet of water
1995	Deepwater Royalty Relief Act
1996	First spar production facility in the Gulf of Mexico at the Neptune field
1999	Discovery of BP's Thunder Horse field in 6,000 feet of water; at 1 billion barrels of oil equivalent, the largest discovery in the Gulf of Mexico
2006	Successful test at the Jack 2 field, in 7,000 feet of water and more than 20,000 feet below the seafloor, establishing the viability of the deepwater Lower Tertiary play
2010	Arrival of *Deepwater Horizon* at Macondo well in January

salvage operations and introduced new diving techniques, seeding the diving business that became vital to offshore operations. Construction companies, such as Brown & Root and J. Ray McDermott, and numerous boat operators acquired war-surplus landing craft and converted them to drilling tenders, supply and crew boats, and construction and pipelaying vessels.[4]

In 1947, Kerr-McGee Oil Industries drilled the first productive well "out-of-sight-of-land," on a platform located in 18 feet of water, 10.5 miles off the Louisiana coast in the Ship Shoal area. The Kermac 16 platform used a war-surplus tender barge to house drilling mud and other supplies, plus the workers' quarters, thereby reducing the size and cost of a self-contained drilling and production platform—an important advantage in case of a dry hole. In 1948, Humble Oil (the Texas affiliate of Standard Oil of New Jersey, later renamed Exxon) introduced the concept of latticed steel templates, or "jackets," which provided greater structural integrity than platforms built with individual wood piles.[5]

Drilling Revived

To explore and develop their new leases obtained from the federal government (see Chapter 3 on the origin of federal leasing), oil firms tapped into the Gulf Coast oil-service sector, but they also promoted the formation of a distinct offshore industry by contracting out for specialized services in marine geophysical surveying, offshore engineering and construction, transportation (boats and helicopters), diving, and mobile drilling.[6]

Mobility in drilling was crucial to the offshore industry's long-term viability. The costs of drilling exploratory or "wildcat" wells from fixed platforms, most of which would not discover oil, were prohibitive. In 1954, the Offshore Drilling and Exploration Company capitalized on a novel approach to the quest for mobility, using its $2 million *Mr. Charlie* "submersible" drilling barge. *Mr. Charlie's* hull could rest submerged on the bottom in 30 feet of water for drilling, and then be refloated and moved to other locations, like a bee moving from flower to flower to extract nectar. Working for Shell Oil on the industry's first "day-rate" contract ($6,000 per day), *Mr. Charlie* drilled and developed two of the Gulf Coast's largest oil fields, in the East Bay just off the South Pass outlet of the Mississippi River. "That's a great rig you have there!" exclaimed Shell's New Orleans vice president after the first well. "I can see the day when you will need several more of them."[7]

Giant salt-dome fields discovered offshore Louisiana—Shell's East Bay and West Delta, the California Company's (Chevron) Bay Marchand and Main Pass, Magnolia's (Mobil) Eugene Island, and Humble Oil's Grand Isle, all under less than 30 feet of water—encouraged operators to move farther out in the Gulf. As Offshore Drilling and Exploration expanded its submersible fleet, other companies such as the Zapata Offshore Company (formed in 1954 by future U.S. President George H.W. Bush), experimented with "jack-up" rigs. These rigs jacked their platforms out of the water by extending a series of cylindrical or truss-type legs to the bottom, taking drilling into water depths exceeding 100 feet. By 1957, 23 mobile units were operating along the Gulf and 11 more were under construction.[8]

Drilling offshore was a relatively costly proposition in the 1950s (a Gulf oil executive described it as "a billion-dollar adventure in applied science"[9]), but it was astoundingly successful. In 1956, 26 percent of offshore exploratory wells struck oil and gas, compared to just 11 percent onshore. Of these wells, 1 in 20 discovered fields with more than 50 million barrels of reserves—more than five times the equivalent success rate of onshore wells. By 1957, there were 446 production platforms in federal and state waters. Wells offshore Louisiana and Texas were producing 200,000 barrels a day, feeding the vast refinery complexes that already existed along the Mississippi River between New Orleans and Baton Rouge, in the "Golden Triangle" of coastal East Texas (Beaumont–Port Arthur–Orange), and along the Houston Ship Channel. Offshore wells accounted for 3 percent of total U.S. production, but the percentage was rising.[10]

Pushing Beyond Limits

In the late 1950s, the frantic pace of Gulf offshore exploration slowed. Costs increased significantly in water depths beyond 60 feet (then the definition of "deepwater"). A few jack-up rigs capsized in rough seas. After Glasscock Drilling Company's *Mr. Gus* drilled a $1 million dry hole for Shell in 100 feet of water in 1956, the vessel sank in transit a year later during Hurricane Audrey. Beyond the damage to offshore infrastructure, Audrey destroyed the support center of Cameron, Louisiana, where an estimated 500 people tragically perished. Underwater pipelines, necessary for bringing oil to shore, were expensive and tricky to place in deeper water. A national recession in 1958, an oversupply of crude oil from growing imports, and declining finds in deeper waters tempered enthusiasm for new exploration. At the same time, Louisiana's legal challenge to the state-federal boundary offshore delayed federal lease sales for several years beginning in 1955. Some people in industry thought this did not matter: they believed offshore exploration had reached its limits.[11] Others were more optimistic.

Shell's Frontier Technology and the 1960s Boom

In August 1962, after seven years of research and development, Shell announced it had successfully tested a new kind of "floating drilling platform," redefining the marine geography of commercially exploitable hydrocarbons. The *Blue Water 1* was a converted submersible consisting of three large columns on each side that connected the drilling platform to a submerged hull. Giant mooring lines kept the vessel on position. Until then, companies had been experimenting with ship-shaped vessels called "drillships" to explore in water depths beyond 150 feet, but these could not withstand heavy wave action. Because the *Blue Water 1's* hull could be ballasted to rest safely below wave level, the vessel was remarkably stable. Classified as the first "semisubmersible," the *Blue Water 1* made its successful test in 300 feet of water, and it was equipped to operate in 600 feet. Complementing the new floating platform, Shell tested the first successful subsea wellhead completion using remote controls. As one Shell representative told reporters, "We're looking now at geology first, and then water depths."[12]

The achievement was akin to John Glenn's space orbit the same year. Even more astonishing was Shell's decision, in early 1963, to share its technology with other companies. At its three-week "School for Industry," seven companies and the U.S.

Geological Survey paid $100,000 each to learn about Shell's "deepwater" drilling program—thereby ensuring that suppliers and contractors were up to speed and that there would be at least some competition from other oil companies for deepwater leases (which otherwise would not be awarded at auction). The diffusion of Shell's technology led to the construction of semisubmersibles in Gulf Coast shipyards and enabled the industry to move into deeper water.[13]

Federal policies also helped accelerate offshore exploration and development. Oil import quotas went into effect in 1959 and were tightened in 1962. These measures protected the domestic market for higher-cost offshore oil. In 1960 and 1962, sensing pent-up demand after the hiatus in federal leasing during the late 1950s, the Bureau of Land Management auctioned large swaths of Gulf acreage. The response was overwhelming: in the historic March 1962 sale, 411 tracts, totaling nearly two million acres, were leased—more than in all previous sales combined. The sale opened up new areas off western Louisiana and Texas and extended the average depth of leases to 125 feet. Because so much land was put up for auction, the "cash bonus" price for the average lease was driven down, enabling more companies to participate in the Gulf.[14]

Drilling on that vast inventory of leases set off one of the greatest industrial booms the Gulf Coast had ever seen. By September 1963, nearly 90 drilling operations were in progress. Workers flocked from around the Gulf region to take high-paying jobs offshore or in the growing support centers of New Orleans, Morgan City, Lafayette, Beaumont, and Houston. Although exploratory success offshore Louisiana in the immediate years after 1962 could not match the extraordinary record of the late 1950s, the discovery rate for large fields of 100 million barrels or more was impressive: 155 for offshore Louisiana versus 3,773 for the United States as a whole. By 1968, 14 of the 62 large fields discovered in the United States were offshore Louisiana, and 11 of those 14 lay either wholly or partially within federally administered areas. Total offshore production from the Gulf of Mexico rose from 348,000 barrels per day in 1962 (4.8 percent of total U.S. production) to 915,000 barrels per day in 1968 (8.6 percent of the U.S. total), and most of this increase came from federal areas, especially acreage leased in 1962.[15]

The March 1962 sale had another consequential effect onshore: the $445 million in cash bonuses earned by the government alerted many officials to the importance of outer continental shelf leases as a source of federal revenue. The next year, the Bureau of Land Management opened an office in Los Angeles and offered the first oil and gas leases off the coasts of Oregon and Washington. Three years later, the Bureau offered the first leases in California's Santa Barbara Channel. The federal outer continental shelf leasing program thus took on national scope.[16]

Pushing Technological Frontiers—and Physical Limits

Meanwhile, technological innovations revitalized the Gulf offshore industry and generated interest in other ocean basins. New well designs and well-logging techniques resolved deep subsurface drilling problems and reduced well costs. Drilling experiments in extreme water depths, such as Project "Mohole" funded by the National Science Foundation, set the stage for dramatic advances in future oil exploration. In 1962, Shell equipped the drillship

Eureka with the first automatic dynamic positioning system and embarked on a core-drilling program in 600 to 4,000 feet of water in the Gulf. *Eureka's* cores confirmed for the first time that oil had been generated in the sands that the Mississippi River had deposited over eons in the broad alluvial valley extending beyond the continental shelf into the deep Gulf. Then, beginning in 1968, the Joint Oceanographic Institutions for Deep Earth Sampling project launched the famous voyage of the *Glomar Challenger* drillship, whose core samples gave further evidence of oil generation in extreme ocean depths.[17]

Although exploratory drilling capabilities raced ahead of commercial producing depths—a recurring theme in the history of offshore oil—the industry nevertheless made great advances during the 1960s in all phases of offshore exploration and production. Among other innovations, digital sound recording and processing greatly enhanced the quality of seismic data and fortified geoscientists' ability to interpret subsurface geology. Improvements in soil-boring techniques led to greater understanding of seabed soil mechanics and foundations. Higher-strength steel yielded stronger jacket construction and the use of larger equipment to install larger rigs. Digital computers made possible the three-dimensional modeling of platform jacket designs. Together, these developments moved production operations into 350-foot water depths by 1969.[18]

Toward the end of the decade, however, the cost of bringing in productive leases began to outrun the price of oil, which had remained at $2 to $3 per barrel in the United States since the end of World War II. Many of the large, easy-to-identify structures in the Gulf had been picked over and drilled. Some companies were fooled by geology into making costly mistakes. At a federal offshore Texas sale in 1968, for example, a Humble-Texaco partnership staked $350 million on leases that yielded nothing. Offshore Texas, it turned out, proved to be largely gas-prone, but regulated prices made natural gas less profitable than oil.[19]

Hurricanes wreaked havoc with production. In 1961, Hurricane Carla triggered soil movements in the Mississippi Delta that destroyed a large number of pipelines. Hilda (1964) and Betsy (1965) knocked out 20 platforms and damaged 10 others, as 70-foot wave heights, far exceeding earlier estimates, overwhelmed platform decks. Camille (1969), a Category 5 hurricane, passed directly over 300 platforms, most of which survived the waves, but the storm caused violent mud slides that wiped out three large platforms in 300 feet of water.[20]

On top of the business failures and natural disasters, the sheer technological challenges and the necessity to complete work as quickly as possible compromised safety. Project profitability depended on how soon production could be brought online. Drilling vessels were contracted on day-rates, increasing time pressures. Production processes were highly interdependent: delay in one place could cause delays elsewhere. So there were relentless demands to drill the wells, install the platforms, and get the oil and gas flowing. "When I first started working, they didn't care whether they killed you or not!" remembered one offshore veteran. "In other words, 'we are going to get it done, regardless.' There was no suing like people are suing now. Back then, if you got hurt, they just pushed you to the side and put somebody else in."[21]

Accident rates for mobile drilling vessels remained unacceptably high, especially for jack-ups. Blowouts, helicopter crashes, diving accidents, and routine injuries on platforms were all too common. Facilities engineering on production platforms was a novel concept. Platforms often had equipment squeezed or slapped together on the deck with little concern or foresight for worker safety. Crew quarters, for example, could sometimes be found dangerously close to a compressor building.[22]

Federal oversight followed the philosophy of "minimum regulation, maximum cooperation."[23] Between 1958 and 1960, the U.S. Geological Survey Conservation Division, the regulatory agency then overseeing offshore drilling, issued outer continental shelf Orders 2 through 5, requiring procedures for drilling, plugging, and abandoning wells; determining well productivity; and the installation of subsurface safety devices, or "storm chokes." But the Offshore Operators Committee (representing leaseholders) persuaded regulators to dilute Order 5 to permit waivers on requirements for storm chokes. Significantly, the orders neither specified design criteria or detailed technical standards, nor did they impose any test requirements. Companies had to have certain equipment, but they did not have to test it to see if it worked.[24] In general, as a 1973 National Science Foundation study concluded, "the closeness of government and industry and the commonality of their objectives have worked against development of a system of strict accountability."[25]

Lax enforcement contributed to the lack of accountability. The U.S. Geological Survey freely granted waivers from complying with orders and did not inspect installations regularly. Federal and state regulatory bodies were underfunded and understaffed. In 1969, the Gulf region's lease management office had only 12 people overseeing more than 1,500 platforms. Even those trained inspectors and supervisors often lacked experience in the oil business and a grasp of its changing technological capabilities. "Each oil well has its own personality, is completely different than the next, and has its own problems," observed one consultant in 1970. "It takes good experienced personnel to understand the situation and to cope with it." Too often on drilling structures, he complained, one found inexperienced supervisors; employees who overlooked rules and regulations (the purpose of which they did not understand); and, perhaps most troubling, even orders from bosses to cut corners—all of which created conditions for an "explosive situation."[26]

Explosive Situations

On January 28, 1969, a blowout on Union Oil Company Platform A-21 in the Santa Barbara Channel released an 800-square-mile slick of oil that blackened an estimated 30 miles of California beaches and lethally soaked sea birds in the gooey mess. Although the well's blowout preventer worked, an inadequate well design allowed the hydrocarbons to escape through near-surface ruptures beneath the seafloor. Union Oil had received a waiver from the U.S. Geological Survey to set casing at a shallower depth than required by Order 2, highlighting the lack of accountability that had come to characterize offshore operations.[27] The 11-day blowout spilled an estimated 80,000 to 100,000 barrels of oil[28]—

SANTA BARBARA OIL SPILL

Oil from a ruptured well surrounds a platform six miles off the coast of Santa Barbara. The 1969 spill, an estimated 100,000 barrels, was the largest in U.S. waters prior to 2010. Some 30 miles of shoreline were fouled, and thousands of birds died along with fish, dolphins, and sea lions. The incident drew public outcry and triggered environmental-protection legislation. Today, Platform A-21 is still operating.

Associated Press

the largest offshore drilling accident in American waters until the Macondo blowout. It generated intense opposition to offshore oil in California, but the fallout also reverberated nationally, setting the stage for the passage of the National Environmental Policy Act (NEPA), a symbol of the growing strength of the national environmental movement, as well as a host of other increasingly demanding environmental protection laws throughout the 1970s (See Chapter 3).[29]

Offshore operators suddenly faced a potentially hostile political and regulatory climate. Ten days after the accident, Secretary of the Interior Walter Hickel, with the support of President Richard Nixon, issued a moratorium on all drilling and production in California waters. In April, Secretary Hickel completed a preliminary assessment of the leases affected by the moratorium and allowed 5 of the 72 lessees to resume drilling or production. In August, the Interior Department issued completely revised outer continental shelf Orders 1–7—the first update since the orders were established—with more specific requirements about company plans and equipment for prevention of pollution and blowouts. It also issued new Orders 8 and 9 on the installation and operations of platforms and pipelines. These were the first rules in which the department claimed authority to prohibit leasing in areas of the continental shelf where environmental risks were too high.[30]

The industry protested the new outer continental shelf regulations, but calamities in the Gulf undermined its case. In February 1970, Chevron's Platform C in Main Pass Block 41 blew out and caught fire. The spill forced a postponement of a federal lease sale, damaged wildlife, and drew a $31.5 million suit against the company by Louisiana oyster fishermen and a $70 million suit from shrimp fishermen. Chevron was also fined $1 million for failing to maintain storm chokes and other required safety devices—the first prosecution under the 1953 Outer Continental Shelf Lands Act. The Justice Department also obtained judgments against other major oil and gas companies for similar violations. Then, in December, Shell suffered a major blowout on its Platform B in the Bay Marchand area, killing four men and seriously burning and injuring 37 others. Investigators attributed the accident to human error resulting from several simultaneous operations being performed without clear directions about responsibility. It took 136 days to bring 11 wild wells under control, at a cost of $30 million. The failure or leaking of subsurface-controlled storm chokes contributed to the size of the conflagration.[31]

In the wake of these disasters, the government further strengthened its regulatory program. The Interior Department again revised and expanded outer continental shelf orders to mandate new requirements: surface-controlled storm chokes; the testing of safety devices prior to and in use; more careful control of drilling and casing operations; prior approval of plans and equipment for exploration and development drilling; and updated practices and procedures for installing and operating platforms. To enforce the new regulations, the U.S. Geological Survey tripled its force of inspectors and engineers, ceased using industry-furnished transportation for inspections, and introduced a more systematic inspection program based on newly developed criteria.[32]

In response, the Offshore Operators Committee and the industry's Offshore Safety and Anti-Pollution Equipment Committee worked closely with the U.S. Geological Survey both in advising changes in the outer continental shelf orders and in promptly drafting a new set of American Petroleum Institute (API) "recommended practice" guidance documents for the selection, installation, and testing of safety devices, as well as for platform design. The major offshore operators revamped personnel training for offshore operations, and they formed an organization called Clean Gulf Associates to upgrade oil-spill handling capabilities.[33] Certifying agencies issued new standards and guidelines for mobile drilling.[34] In addition, the industry's annual Offshore Technology Conference, first held in 1969, became an important forum for publishing and sharing technical information that led to safer designs and operations.[35]

The industry's safety record in the Gulf improved significantly after the new regulations and practices were introduced: the reported incidence and rate of fatalities and injuries decreased, as did the rate of fires and explosions.[36] During the 1970s and 1980s, the frequency of blowouts did not decline significantly, but there was a sharp drop in the number of catastrophic blowouts, and fewer casualties and fatalities were associated with them.[37]

Design and equipment problems were steadily being solved. But reducing accidents caused by human error, poor safety management, or simultaneous operations continued to be a vexing challenge.

Constrained Expansion

As new regulations brought more caution to offshore oil development, countervailing forces emerged to speed it up. Domestic oil supply could not keep up with demand. In the postwar period, Americans' consumption of petroleum—largely for operating automobiles—climbed dramatically, rising steadily from 243 gallons of motor gasoline per capita in 1950 to 463 gallons per capita in 1979.[38]

U.S. oil production peaked, however, in 1970. Along with the OPEC oil embargo of 1973 and consequent skyrocketing price of oil products, this event spurred the quest to develop new offshore reserves. With crude oil prices tripling to $10 per barrel, oil companies could justify more expensive offshore drilling and development. Under the mandate of "Project Independence," the Nixon Administration announced a dramatic increase in the pace of leasing in the Gulf and a resumption of sales off the Atlantic, Pacific, and Alaskan coasts. At the March 1974 federal lease sale of offshore Louisiana acreage, the industry spent a record $2.17 billion in cash bonuses for leases covering 522,000 acres, including a few tracts ranging beyond 1,000-foot depths.[39]

The First Deepwater Play

In June 1975, Shell made a monumental discovery on one of those new leases. Shell geophysicists had employed an innovative seismic technique called "bright spot" to lead drillers to an attractive prospect, code-named Cognac, in 1,000 feet of water in the Mississippi Canyon, not far from the mouth of the great river. The drilling uncovered an estimated 100-million-barrel reserve.[40] Cognac pioneered other discoveries in what would come to be known as the "Flex Trend," an area in the Gulf that reaches just beyond the edge of the continental shelf, where there is a flex in the seafloor. The Flex Trend would be the world's first true oil play in 1,000-foot water depths, the modern definition of "deepwater."[41]

When Shell purchased its leases, it did not yet have a design concept for deepwater production. Barges were not big enough to launch a 1,025-foot steel jacket in one piece. Therefore, adapting Exxon's precedent—the company installed its Hondo jacket in 850 feet of water in the Santa Barbara channel in 1976—Shell chose to build the Cognac structure in three pieces and assemble them vertically in place. The complex, nerve-wracking installation inflated total development costs to nearly $800 million. But Cognac was both a technical and commercial success. It won the American Society of Civil Engineers 1980 award for "Outstanding Civil Engineering Achievement," the first ever received by an oil company. Production commenced in 1979, just as the supply shock caused by the Iranian Revolution drove the price of oil to nearly $40 per barrel.[42]

Along with Hondo and major developments in the North Sea pioneered by Phillips, Conoco, and BP, Cognac paved the way for truly enormous offshore engineering-construction projects. In 1976, Brown & Root and J. Ray McDermott opened giant new construction yards at Harbor Island, near Corpus Christi Bay, to accommodate the assembly and load-out of deepwater structures. In these yards, they built jackets lighter and cheaper than Cognac and launched them in single pieces. In the late 1970s, Brown & Root built a 700-foot structure for Chevron's Garden Banks field, and a 650-foot jacket for Atlantic Richfield. In 1980–1981, McDermott built two platforms for Union Oil in the 1,000-foot waters of the East Breaks area, 100 miles south of Galveston. During 1979–1983, Brown & Root built and installed a novel "guyed tower" for Exxon in 1,000 feet of water just southwest of Cognac.[43]

Even as rising oil prices and declining onshore production in the late 1970s spurred them on, Gulf oil operators encountered economic and geological constraints. Bonus bids soared beyond the estimated value of the oil that might be discovered and produced: the September 1980 sale in New Orleans, for example, brought in $2.8 billion in cash bonuses, shattering all previous records. During the 1970s, the bonus paid per barrel of oil equivalent discovered by the largest producing companies increased four- to five-fold, undermining the economics of deepwater.[44] Furthermore, initial production rates from some of the early producing wells in the Flex Trend proved disappointing. Many industry exploration managers came to believe that after 25 years of development, only lean prospects remained in the Gulf. The best hope for increasing national reserves, they concluded, was from other parts of the U.S. outer continental shelf.[45]

Beyond the Shelf

Rising lease bonuses still did not deter major companies (such as Chevron, Exxon, Mobil, and Amoco), along with some of the larger independents (such as Pennzoil, Union, and Tenneco), from drilling and developing fields in the deepwater Flex Trend. But discoveries could not offset overall production declines in the Gulf. Oil production on the shelf had peaked at just above 1 million barrels per day in 1972; by 1978, it had fallen below 800,000 barrels per day. Because discoveries in the Flex Trend play were relatively small, with fairly low flow rates, most Gulf oil and gas still came from shallow water, despite declining overall production there. In 1970, the average production-weighted depth of oil extracted from the Gulf was just 100 feet, and by 1980 it was still less than 200 feet.[46] Many managers had concluded that there would never be economic developments more than 60 miles from shore. Other experts became convinced that significant oil-bearing sands would never be found beyond the continental shelf. "But what conventional wisdom really tells you," as one Shell geophysicist explained, "is that you just don't know what you don't know."[47]

At just that time, some scientists from industry and academia had begun to piece together a regional picture of the geology deep underneath the Gulf by combining information from cores with a regional seismic survey shot out into deepwater. This picture showed that massive salt pillars, or diapirs, had squeezed up from the mother layer of salt deposited beginning 165 million years ago, when the Gulf of Mexico was slowly forming. As the diapirs pinched up, sandstone overlaying the salt slowly subsided, forming cup-shaped "mini-basins" featuring different kinds of configurations for trapping oil. These sandstone formations were named "turbidites" (they had been deposited when ancient underwater rivers, called turbidity currents, channeled huge volumes of sediment onto the continental margin). The structural anomalies in these mini-basins looked similar to productive features on the shelf, but the spotty seismic coverage allowed for only speculative knowledge of their potential, at best. Shell, always the leader in Gulf frontier exploration, had drilled a number of wells in similar rocks along the margin of the continental shelf. Turbidites in deepwater were potentially much larger, less faulted, and might have prolific flow rates. At least in theory, they would require fewer wells, making them more attractive as economically exploitable reservoirs of oil.[48]

During 1978–1980, hoping to test its theories about the regional geology, Shell nominated deepwater tracts for auction. But no other companies seconded its nominations, so the government never selected the tracts for sales.[49] Then, in 1982, the Interior Department announced a new system of area-wide offshore leasing. This policy put into play entire planning areas (e.g., the central Gulf of Mexico) up to 50 million acres, rather than rationing tracts through a tedious nomination and selection process. Companies could bid on any tract they wanted in a lease sale for a given planning area, thus giving them access to far more extensive offshore acreage at significantly less cost.[50]

Strong political opposition to area-wide leasing by some coastal states and environmental organizations stymied its effective use in other parts of the nation (see Chapter 3), but not in the Gulf, where oil companies had long operated. Established infrastructure and abundant geological information there could be put to more flexible use under a more open system. Oil companies responded to area-wide leasing by bidding aggressively for attractive blocks on the continental shelf, while making a number of speculative bids on acreage ranging into 3,000-foot depths beyond the edge of the shelf. The May 25, 1983 sale harvested a record $3.47 billion in high bonus bids. All told, in seven lease sales held from 1983 to 1985, the Interior Department, through the newly formed Minerals Management Service (see Chapter 3), leased 2,653 tracts, more than had been leased in all the federal sales since 1962 combined. About 600 of these tracts lay in deepwater beyond 1,000 feet.[51]

Shell acquired the lion's share of deepwater tracts in the March 1983 sale and immediately started drilling. In 1982, it had leased Sonat Offshore Drilling's *Discoverer Seven Seas*, one of the few vessels rated for 6,000-foot depths. Shell then spent more than $40 million to extend the vessel's depth capability with a larger marine riser, enhanced dynamic positioning, and a new remote-operated vehicle to enable sophisticated work where human divers could not venture. In October 1983, the *Seven Seas* made a major discovery at Shell's Bullwinkle prospect, establishing the deepwater "Mini-Basin Play," which targeted the turbidite sandstones in the basins flanking the salt structures.[52]

In the next central Gulf area-wide sale, in April 1984, many different operators jumped in to compete for deepwater tracts. This prompted Shell to move quickly in deploying the *Shell America*, a $45 million custom-designed, state-of-the-art seismic vessel that provided company geophysicists with high-quality, proprietary seismic data. Armed with these data and other intelligence gained from drilling its 1983 leases, Shell dominated the May 1985 sale, winning 86 of 108 tracts on which it bid, in water depths ranging to 6,000 feet. For

Shell, pushing deeper was an imperative for its operations in the United States, as onshore reserves continued to decline. "Exploration has been called a poker game," explained one Shell official. "But there's more to it than that. In this game, we don't have chips or coins or dollar bills that can change hands over and over again. We're dealing with a declining resource base, and every barrel we find is never going to be found again."[53]

The Era of Uncertainty

The long cycles of oil exploration and development do not always align well with the shorter cycles of the economy. Just as Shell bet heavily on deepwater, the severe recession in 1981 further depressed falling oil demand. For the first time in 34 years, U.S. oil consumption hit a plateau and began declining.[54] The now "forgotten victory" of energy conservation and efficiency measures passed in the mid-1970s, in response to historically high oil prices, reversed the long trend of an increasingly petroleum-intense U.S. economy. During 1985–1986, oil prices collapsed to $10 per barrel, as international producers saturated the global market with crude.[55]

Expensive Gulf development projects were canceled or shelved. Construction of mobile drilling vessels and other kinds of offshore-servicing equipment fell sharply. Unemployed oilfield workers transitioned into new trades, or migrated from southern Louisiana in search of better opportunities. This human and capital flight marked the beginning of what one scholar called "the inevitable disassembly of the offshore system and its onshore support network for the Gulf of Mexico."[56]

The offshore projects that went forward faced intimidating challenges. Shell drilled some dry holes costing more than $10 million apiece. Development stretched the limits of technological and financial resources. To produce oil from the Bullwinkle field, the company installed in 1988 a $500 million fixed platform, 162 stories high—taller than Chicago's Sears Tower (now the Willis Tower), the tallest building in the world at the time. The Bullwinkle platform was the largest and last conventional jacket of its kind. The scale and costs of constructing anything bigger were simply prohibitive.[57]

Moving deeper would require alternative production methods: subsea wells, tension-leg platforms, or floating systems. Operators had put subsea wells to use in the North Sea, but they were still extremely expensive. The tension-leg platform was an innovative concept consisting of a production facility situated on a floating hull held in place by long tendons that kept the hull from bobbing like a cork but allowed some degree of side-to-side motion. In 1984, Conoco installed the first full-scale design of this type in the North Sea, in 485 feet of water, and in 1989 the company placed its Jolliet mini-tension-leg platform in 1,760 feet of water in the Gulf.[58] But tension-leg platforms would have to be scaled up for major projects in deepwater. In 1987–1988, Placid Oil developed a field in 1,500 feet of water with a floating production facility converted from a semisubmersible drilling vessel. But Placid soon abandoned the development, sold the semisubmersible, and sought bankruptcy protection.[59]

Deep Sea Monsters

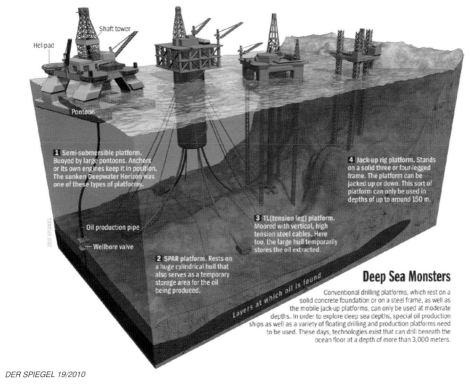

Shaft tower

Helipad

Pontoon

1 Semi-submersible platform. Buoyed by large pontoons. Anchors or its own engines keep it in position. The sunken Deepwater Horizon was one of these types of platforms.

4 Jack-up rig platform. Stands on a solid three or four-legged frame. The platform can be jacked up or down. This sort of platform can only be used in depths of up to around 150 m.

Oil production pipe

Wellbore valve

3 TL(tension leg) platform. Moored with vertical, high tension steel cables. Here too, the large hull temporarily stores the oil extracted.

2 SPAR platform. Rests on a huge cylindrical hull that also serves as a temporary storage area for the oil being produced.

Layers at which oil is found

Deep Sea Monsters

Conventional drilling platforms, which rest on a solid concrete foundation or on a steel frame, as well as the mobile jack-up platforms, can only be used at moderate depths. In order to explore deep sea depths, special oil production ships as well as a variety of floating drilling and production platforms need to be used. These days, technologies exist that can drill beneath the ocean floor at a depth of more than 3,000 meters.

DER SPIEGEL 19/2010

The deepwater costs were matched by the safety and environmental risks. In 1985, an Office of Technology Assessment study of Arctic and deepwater oil drilling highlighted the "special safety risks" of "harsh environments and remote locations." It identified "a need for new approaches to preventing work-related injuries and fatalities in coping with new hazards in the hostile Arctic and deepwater frontiers." It also presciently warned of the glaring deficiencies in safety oversight offshore, observing that "there is no regulatory requirement for the submission of integrated safety plans which address technical, managerial, and other aspects of offshore safety operations."[60]

Setbacks in the Arctic

As the study indicated, deepwater was not the only frontier that captured the industry's interest. In the 1980s, companies also had their sights set on the Arctic region, then thought to have the highest resource potential in the United States. Since the 1960s, major firms had produced oil from Alaska's Kenai Peninsula and Cook Inlet. In 1977, the massive onshore Prudhoe Bay field on the North Slope started pumping oil through the Trans-Alaska Pipeline. Many explorers expected to find the next great oil frontier to the north of Prudhoe Bay, in the Bering, Beaufort, and Chukchi Seas. Although the industry lost a contentious struggle to gain access to the Bering Sea's Bristol Bay, home to the world's largest commercial salmon fishery, they did win the right to lease and drill in the Beaufort and Chukchi Seas.[61]

Everywhere operators drilled offshore Alaska, however, they came up empty. Either they found no source rocks or the deposits they did find were not large enough at that time to turn a profit in the Arctic's forbidding environment. After a costly dry hole at a prospect called Mukluk in the Beaufort Sea and some futile efforts to explore in the Chukchi Sea, the industry temporarily lost its craving for the Arctic. The public-relations fallout from the *Exxon Valdez* oil spill in 1989, which resulted in congressional and presidential moratoriums on leasing in Bristol Bay, contributed to the industry's suspended interest in offshore Alaska.[62]

Renewed Focus on the Gulf of Mexico

The mid-1980s collapse in oil prices also ruined many companies' appetite for further leasing in the deepwater Gulf of Mexico. But Shell and others chose to take a longer-term view—a decision reinforced by the failures in Alaska. Additional reinforcement came in 1987, when the Minerals Management Service reduced the minimum bid for deepwater tracts from $900,000 to $150,000—enabling companies to lock up entire basins for 10 years for only a couple million dollars.[63] During the next five years, despite flat oil and gas prices, the industry acquired 1,500 tracts in deepwater.[64]

Shell's December 1989 announcement of a major discovery at a prospect called Auger, located in the Garden Banks area 136 miles off the Louisiana coast, spurred further interest. Two years earlier, Global Marine's new, giant semisubmersible, the *Zane Barnes*, struck oil for Shell after drilling through 2,860 feet of water and another 16,500 feet beneath the seafloor. Shell kept the discovery quiet as it delineated the extent of the field, which turned out to contain an estimated 220 million barrels of oil equivalent, the company's third-largest offshore discovery in the Gulf. Underpinning Shell's decision to go forward with Auger was the discovery of relatively high flow rates from the turbidite sands at Bullwinkle, where engineers found they could open the wells to 3,500 barrels per day (three times the rate considered good for a well on shallower parts of the Gulf continental shelf). If Auger had similar flow rates, the field could be profitably developed, even in water more than twice as deep as Bullwinkle's. Few people knew that Auger was only one of a number of Shell deepwater discoveries.[65]

As the company formulated an ambitious strategy to launch a series of major platforms, a gloomy economic outlook tempered Shell's euphoria over the Auger discovery and production breakthrough at Bullwinkle. The projected cost of developing Auger exceeded $1 billion. In appraising the next prospect, code-named Mars, Shell's exploration managers looked for ways to save money and offload some of the financial risk; accordingly, in 1988, they brought in British Petroleum (BP) as a partner with a 28.5 percent interest in the project.[66]

At the time, Mars seemed like a risky endeavor, with low probability for a major discovery. Furthermore, BP posed little threat. The company had been kicked out of Iran and Nigeria in 1979 and was struggling with a bloated management structure, poorly performing global assets, and uninspired leadership. Shell viewed BP as merely a banker.[67]

All that changed in 1989, when Sonat's *Discoverer Seven Seas* drilled into Mars. The field, located due south of the mouth of the Mississippi, lay in nearly 3,000 feet of water. The discovery well encountered multiple oil- and gas-bearing layers stacked on top of each other over several hundred meters. Mars was more than twice the size of Auger—the largest field discovered in the Gulf in 25 years. For Shell, Mars promised a big payoff for large bets on deepwater leases. For the industry, Mars confirmed the Mini-Basin trend in the Gulf as a bona fide play. For BP, Mars allowed the company's managers, engineers, and scientists to go to school on Shell's deepwater technology. Perhaps just as importantly, according to BP's chief in the United States, "Mars saved BP from bankruptcy."[68]

During the next several years, major oil companies—and even more significantly, contractors in the offshore service industry—propelled the evolution of technology in innovative new directions. The 1970s revolution in digital, three-dimensional (3-D) seismic imaging, pioneered by Geophysical Services Inc. (GSI), and the 1980s move to computer workstations, which enabled faster processing of the data generated in such surveys, combined to enhance dramatically the industry's accuracy in locating wells for field development—a critical factor when drilling a single well in deepwater could cost as much as $50 million. Beyond development drilling, 3-D seismic imaging boosted the success of wildcat discovery wells from less than 30 percent to 60 or 70 percent. As the major companies began to divest from older producing properties in favor of new deepwater prospects, smaller firms purchased older properties and redeveloped them with significant reserve additions using 3-D seismic imaging. In all, 3-D seismic imaging effectively tripled or even quadrupled the estimated amount of oil and gas reserves in the Gulf of Mexico.[69]

Drilling and subsea engineering advanced in similar fashion. Drilling contractors developed a new generation of vessels that took drilling from 5,000 to 10,000 feet of water, and from 20,000 to 30,000 feet of sub-seafloor depth. New directional drilling techniques, made possible by "downhole steerable motors," allowed engineers to maneuver a well from vertical to horizontal to achieve greater accuracy and more fully exploit reservoirs. Drillers also found ways to obtain information from deep inside wells, using "measurements-while-drilling" tools and sensors that provided position, temperature, pressure, and porosity data while the borehole was being drilled. Improvements in marine risers using lightweight composite materials and tensioners, along with new methods for preventing oil from cooling and clogging in deepwater pipelines, enabled the industry to make long tiebacks between subsea wells and production facilities. To support subsea installation and operations, the industry turned to sophisticated remote-operated vehicles mounted with TV cameras and umbilical tethers containing fiber-optic wire for the transmission of vivid images.[70]

Even as the major operators pushed into deepwater, they outsourced more of the research and development (R&D) of new technologies. The bust of the 1980s had driven the exploration and production companies to decrease internal R&D and adopt policies of buying expertise as needed, rather than cultivating it from within. R&D investments in oil exploration and production by the major companies declined from nearly $1.3 billion in 1982 to $600 million by 1996. According to a National Petroleum Council study, "This 'buy versus build' strategy resulted in a significant reduction in the number of skilled people within operating companies who understood technology development and deployment."[71] Service companies (Schlumberger, Halliburton, Baker Hughes, and Oceaneering) became the major source of technology development. An illustration of this trend was the Texaco-initiated "Deep Star" consortium, established in 1992, through which offshore operators funded contractor-generated R&D.[72]

Rapid technological advances in the early 1990s did not immediately translate into more economically feasible practices. Cost overruns, delays, and strained relationships with contractors plagued the fabrication and installation of Shell's giant tension-leg platform for Auger, the industry's bellwether deepwater project. Further, Shell discovered that crude oil from the Auger field was sour (containing sulfur, which had to be separated out at the refinery) and thus had to be discounted. The company's only salvation on the project depended on Auger's wells flowing at a higher rate than Bullwinkle's.[73]

Auger Pays Off

Fortunately for Shell and the offshore industry, the wells did not disappoint. In the spring of 1994, Shell began to bring in wells at Auger that flowed at more than 10,000 barrels per day. Even with oil prices at $20 per barrel or less, deepwater now promised handsome profits. The Auger wells confirmed the reservoir model for turbidites in deepwater and even exceeded Shell's most optimistic estimates. Engineers designed Auger to handle 42,000 barrels of oil (and 100 million cubic feet of gas) per day from 24 wells, but by July the first three wells were already producing 30,000 barrels per day. "Debottlenecking" efforts eventually raised Auger's capacity to 105,000 barrels of oil and 420 million cubic feet of gas per day by the late 1990s.[74]

Auger's prodigious output also made subsea completions (with the wellhead located on the ocean floor rather than on a surface production platform) economic in the Gulf, as they had been in the North Sea. With tension-leg platforms like Auger, subsea completions became important as a component of an early production system or as a remote subsea development. Large fields or clusters of smaller fields, which otherwise would not justify the expense of multiple or larger platforms, could thus be profitably developed.[75]

Auger's many blessings came at a cost to Shell and the environment. Expanding production at Auger was extremely challenging. At the start of production in April 1994, Shell continuously flared or vented between one and six million cubic feet of natural gas per day, without the required federal permission. The flaring and venting continued for more than four years until the Minerals Management Service announced it had discovered this violation as well as Shell's failure to record and report the releases. In a 2003 civil settlement, Shell agreed to pay $49 million, an amount equivalent to the value of about two weeks of production from Auger. If the company was chastened after having to admit to these serious violations, Shell management also must have been tempted to look at this charge as an incidental cost of doing business in the deepwater Gulf. [76]

AUGER TENSION-LEG PLATFORM

Like a giant alien creature, a scale rendering of a tension-leg drilling platform is superimposed over New Orleans. Built by Shell to tap its Auger deepwater field some 200 miles southwest of the city, the huge platform uses steel mooring cables to stabilize its 3,000-foot legs and can drill 20,000 feet below the seafloor. The platform augured well for Shell in the late 1990s, delivering 100,000 barrels of oil a day.

Courtesy of Shell

Deepwater Treasures

The productivity of the Auger wells made the Gulf of Mexico the hottest oil play in the world. And it was mostly about oil. Deepwater proved to be largely oil-prone. The source rocks for most of the deepwater region are an Upper Jurassic kerogen that generates natural gas only when subjected to very high temperatures. But subterranean thermal gradients and source-rock temperatures in the deep Gulf are quite modest, despite the enormous pressures exerted several miles below the seabed. The massive amounts of salt (see below) has acted like a heat sink, keeping hydrocarbons from getting too hot and thus cooking up large amounts of natural gas.[77]

Despite downward pressure on oil prices in the late 1990s, the promise of prolific production from deepwater was too much to resist. Exploration and production firms with deepwater leases consolidated their positions. Companies that had sat on the sidelines during the 1980s stampeded into unclaimed areas. Newly developing or commercialized exploration and production technologies found vibrant new markets. Contractors all along the Gulf Coast and, indeed, around the world, geared up for a surge of activity. Port Fourchon, Louisiana's southernmost port on the tip of Lafourche Parish, came to life as the jumping-off point for supplying and servicing deepwater operations in the Gulf.[78]

The next landmark on the horizon for deepwater drilling was Mars. In July 1996, Shell began producing from its Mars platform, six months before NASA launched its Pathfinder probe to the planet Mars. At a total cost of $1 billion, Shell's Mars was more than three times as expensive as the Mars Pathfinder, and its remote technologies and engineering systems were arguably more sophisticated. The investment of money and technology paid dividends: the Mars platform tapped into the largest field discovered in the United States since Alaska's Prudhoe Bay. Creating a system to produce the field also established a new paradigm for large projects and revealed how exploration and production strategy was being reshaped in the Gulf.[79]

To reduce costs and avoid the headaches experienced at Auger, Shell introduced a different contracting model at Mars based on "alliances," including the sharing of technology and patents. Shell ended up giving away more than BP, which had little deepwater experience. But the costs and risks were too large to go it alone, as Shell had usually preferred to do. The partners carried the alliance concept over to their relationship with contractors, who built the tension-leg platform hull, fabricated the topsides, and integrated the two. The project team brought in contractors early on to collaborate on developments and share risks and rewards. The key advantage of this approach was that it reduced the so-called "cycle time" of design, bidding, and contracting by an estimated six to nine months.[80] On a platform such as Mars, where the first well came in at 15,000 barrels per day, the time-value of money made at the beginning rather than at the end of the platform's life was quite significant. Shell's contracting model at Mars, replicated on its subsequent tension-leg platforms, established the growing importance of alliance networks for global oil and gas developments in technologically complex frontier regions characterized by high costs and risks.[81]

In the late 1990s, having control of one-third of all Gulf leases in depths greater than 1,500 feet, Shell rolled out one tension-leg platform after the other.[82] In 1997, a Mars "clone" called Ram-Powell, developed in a joint venture with Exxon and Amoco, went on-stream in 3,200 feet of water 80 miles southeast of Mobile, Alabama. In March 1999, Shell and its minority partners, BP, Conoco, and Exxon, started up the massive Ursa, on a lease two blocks to the east of Mars. Nearly double the weight of Mars, Ursa was designed to accommodate astounding initial well-production rates of 30,000 barrels per day; in September 1999, a well at Ursa broke all records with a production rate of nearly 50,000 barrels of oil equivalent per day. Finally, in 2001, Shell brought in production from the Brutus platform, which tapped into a 200-million-barrel field in 3,000 feet of water in the Green Canyon.[83]

Shell's new technologies solidified the company's position as the leader in the Gulf. Its tension-leg platforms, as well as major fixed platforms such as Bullwinkle and West Delta 143, not only produced hydrocarbons from the fields beneath them, but also served as hubs used to take and process oil and gas production from satellite subsea wells, thus extending the life of those platforms once their own production declined. Deepwater output from Shell's platforms and subsea wells, and eventually from other companies in the vicinity, fed into network of Shell-owned or operated crude-oil trunk pipelines, gathering systems, and natural-gas pipelines. Shell also made special arrangements to

FIGURE 2.4: Wells Drilled in the Gulf of Mexico by Water Depth, 1940-2010

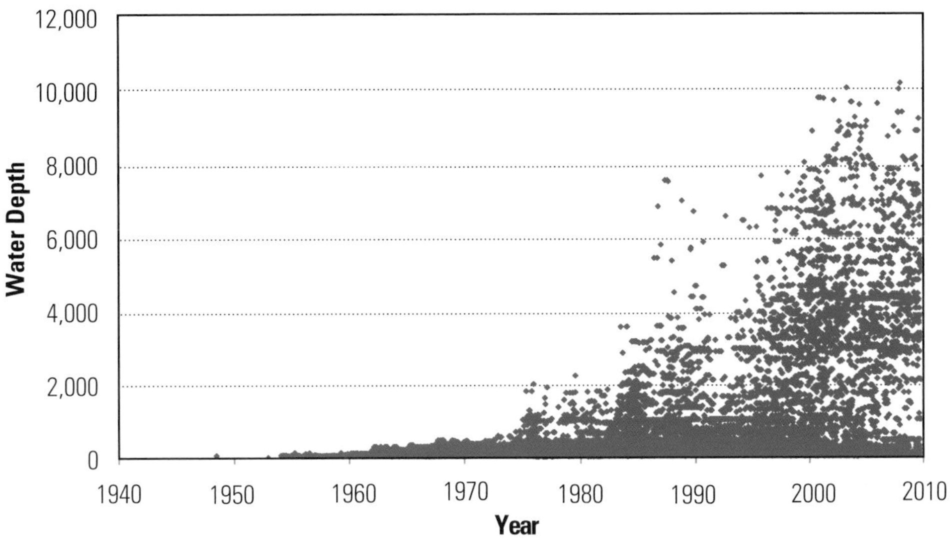

Source: Commission staff, adapted from Bureau of Ocean Energy Management, Regulation and Enforcement

transport crude oil production from its growing deepwater properties into the Clovelly storage facilities owned by the Louisiana Offshore Oil Port in South Louisiana. By 2001, Shell operated 11 of the 16 key oil trunk pipelines servicing deepwater.[84]

Shell's lead in the deepwater Gulf was substantial but not unassailable. During the latter half of the 1990s, many companies gained ground, including a rising percentage of small and midsized independents. But the only company that chased down and eventually overtook Shell was BP.

Deeper Still

In the 1990s, technological breakthroughs in imaging and drilling through massive salt sheets opened a new "subsalt" play, first on the shelf and then ranging into deepwater. Discoveries in at least four different "fold belts" across the Gulf of Mexico extended the search for oil into "ultra-deepwater" and led to another wave of innovation in floating production. In 1990, most oil and gas from the Gulf had still come from shallow water; average production-weighted depth had barely reached 250 feet. By 1998, the weighted average passed the 1,000-foot milestone, at which point deepwater production (at about 700,000 barrels per day of oil and 2 billion cubic feet per day of gas) surpassed that from shallow water for the first time.[85]

As the industry moved deeper, the abandonment and decommissioning of older platforms on the shelf became a thriving business. During the 1990s, 1,264 platforms were removed, more than twice the total prior to 1990; after 2000, removals continued at a rate of 150 per year.[86] Some obsolete platforms found use as "artificial reefs" through a creative program, coordinated by the Minerals Management Service and the states of Texas and Louisiana, to place old platforms in specially designated locations on the sea bottom, where they attracted marine life much like natural reefs.[87]

Meanwhile, another relaxation in the terms of access to Gulf of Mexico leases, in the form of the Deepwater Royalty Relief Act (see Chapter 3), helped sustain the oil industry in deepwater. Deepwater royalty relief no doubt enticed some oil companies, especially non-majors, into deepwater. But judging from the huge upswell in bidding at the May 1995 Central Gulf of Mexico sale, before royalty relief was enacted, the race appeared to be already under way.[88] Oil explorers were clearly gunning for fields like Auger with high flow rates and high ultimate reserves. Many of them were also on the hunt for petroleum in a new geological location: beneath the Gulf's massive sheets of salt.

Subsalt Discoveries

Salt is the dominant structural element in the Gulf of Mexico petroleum system. Oil explorers had long ago discovered oil trapped against the flanks of salt domes or between the salt diapirs in the deepwater mini-basins. But geologists had typically assumed that there could be no oil reservoirs lying beneath any salt they encountered. By the 1970s, advancing knowledge about the basin's regional geology suggested that oil *could* be found under the salt. In many places, the salt pillars that extruded upward into sandstone and shale flowed horizontally in elastic plumes over vast expanses of younger, potentially oil-bearing sediment that extend more than 35,000 square miles across the Gulf. Geologists invented new terminology to describe different kinds of salt formations in the picture they pieced together—canopies, tongues, nappes, egg crates, and turtle domes—and established a special subfield of geology to explain how the salt moves. What they were really interested in, however, was what lay beneath the salt.[89]

The subsalt play began in 1990, when Exxon (with partner Conoco) made the first discovery at a prospect called Mickey. Located in 4,352 feet of water on the Mississippi Canyon 211 lease (about 10 miles northeast of where BP would later drill Macondo), Mickey was not then large enough to put into production.* Two years later, Chevron drilled a well in Garden Banks 165 through almost 7,000 feet of salt and another 5,000 feet of subsalt sediment. The well found no oil, but was a milestone because it demonstrated that the technology existed to drill through an enormous body of salt.[90]

Finally, in 1993, Phillips Petroleum announced the first commercial subsalt oil discovery. Years earlier, Phillips had begun to look systematically for places where salt sheets might be obscuring oil reservoirs. In 1989, the firm acquired 15 leases including one at a location called Mahogany. It was a speculative move. Salt plays tricks with seismic sound waves, which travel through salt at a much higher velocity than through the surrounding sediments and also get refracted, much as the image of a pencil is bent when it is stuck in a glass of water. Obtaining clear images of rocks in their proper location under the salt seemed almost impossible. To get a better focus, Phillips shot a 3-D seismic survey over

* Ten years later, Exxon developed the prospect as a subsea natural gas development called Mica.

the prospect. And to share the substantial expenses of conducting the survey and drilling through the salt—twice the cost of a normal well—the company took on Anadarko and Amoco as partners. Phillips's geophysicists then processed the seismic data with a newly developed computing algorithm, yielding a picture sufficiently improved to make an informed stab at the target. The first well, drilled by a Diamond Offshore semisubmersible, passed through 3,800 feet of salt, at one point encountering unstable rock that threatened to collapse the well. Eventually, the drill hit a 100-million-barrel field. In 1996, Phillips's Mahogany platform began producing at 20,000 barrels per day.[91]

The subsalt play progressed, haltingly, from Mahogany. Drilling through salt involved myriad technical complications. Under high temperature and pressure, salt masses flow, creep, and deform like plastic; this movement can shift the well casing and production tubing. These wells also had to be drilled to great depths, escalating costs. And limitations on computer power made it difficult to obtain reliable seismic images from beneath the salt, adding risk to exploration. Subsalt wells missed hydrocarbons a lot more often than they hit them.[92]

As operators drilled a string of dry holes, the post-Mahogany euphoria ebbed. In the 1995–1997 lease sales, companies began to turn from shallow subsalt prospects, pursuing instead ultra-deepwater (greater than 5,000 feet) prospects, looking for easier-to-image drilling targets in foldbelts formed by the lateral movement of salt and sediment. In 1995, Oryx Energy made a discovery at Neptune, opening a new play in the Western Atwater Foldbelt. The next year Shell announced a strike at its Baha prospect in the far western Gulf. This discovery initiated the Perdido Foldbelt play in more than 8,000 feet of water.[93] A deeper ocean frontier, once again, beckoned the industry.

An Industry Restructured—and Globalized

As geologists and geophysicists in Houston dedicated themselves to solving the riddles presented by depths of the Gulf of Mexico, the world oil industry began a radical restructuring. Oil and gas companies had not yet recovered from the 1980s bust when oil prices swooned again in the late 1990s, driven in large part by the drop in global demand precipitated by the Asian financial crisis. Increased shareholder pressure on oil firms to improve short-term financial results and longer-term profitability spurred one of the greatest merger movements in history. In 1998, BP acquired Amoco. The next year, Exxon merged with Mobil in an $80 billion deal to create the world's largest company. BP-Amoco countered by acquiring ARCO; Total merged with Fina and Elf (renamed Total in 2003); Chevron combined with Texaco; and, finally, Conoco and Phillips joined to create the sixth "super major" (along with Royal Dutch Shell). During these consolidations, many companies relocated staff from New Orleans and elsewhere to Houston, reinforcing that city's claim as the international oil capital.[94]

Mergers boosted results as management pared away overlapping functions and laid off employees, reinforcing the trend toward outsourcing R&D and reducing internal technological expertise. Mergers benefitted the oil industry, on the other hand, by equipping firms with new capital reserves needed to finance long-term growth strategies—some of them dependent on riskier, but potentially higher-return, ventures. The deepwater Gulf figured significantly in the growth strategies of all the "super major" oil companies—albeit as only one among several frontier provinces worldwide. They took renewed interest in Arctic and sub-Arctic regions and began to invest in other deepwater basins from the northeast Atlantic west of the Shetland Islands, to the Campos Basin off Brazil, to West Africa's Gulf of Guinea and offshore Angola, to northwest Australia. By the early 2000s, analysts regarded the three provinces rimming the central Atlantic Ocean—the Gulf of Mexico, Brazil, and West Africa—as the "New Golden Triangle," the place where the largest future reserves were likely to be found.[95]

Echoing the oil companies, consolidation also swept through offshore contractors. After half of the world's seismic crews were idled in 1999 due to a price collapse early in the year, the ensuing shakeout left only handful of seismic contractors, led by Western-Geco, owned by Schlumberger and Baker-Hughes; Petroleum Geo-Services; and CGG and Veritas (which merged in 2007). The major oil-service companies, which provided a variety of drilling, evaluation, well-completion, and production services, began to combine at the same time (notable was the 1998 merger between the oilfield giants, Halliburton and Dresser Industries). Most significantly, the drilling-contractor industry—continuously in the process of mergers, acquisitions, and bankruptcies—consolidated further. In 1999, Sedco-Forex and Transocean, themselves the products of earlier mergers, became Transocean Sedco Forex, later simplified as Transocean. In 2000, it acquired R&B Falcon, whose assets included a semisubmersible under construction in Korea by Hyundai Heavy Industries called the *Deepwater Horizon*. In 2001, Global Marine merged with Santa Fe, and six years later this firm became part of the modern Transocean, by far the largest offshore drilling firm in the world.

During this era, offshore oil exploration and production became an increasingly global enterprise. U.S. operators searched for oil in deepwater basins outside the Gulf of Mexico, and more than ever, companies such as Norway's Statoil, Brazil's Petrobras, and France's Total were drilling in the Gulf. Shipyards along the Gulf Coast—the pioneers in design and construction of mobile offshore drilling units—had by the 1990s almost totally surrendered this work to competitors in Korea and Singapore. Many of the largest offshore engineering, construction, and pipelaying firms (Heerema Marine Contractors, Technip, Worley Parsons, and others) were globally oriented companies based outside the United States.[96]

Offshore contractors headquartered in the Gulf survived by expanding internationally. Morgan City's J. Ray McDermott branched out around the world more aggressively after the 1980s industry depression and eventually moved its headquarters to Houston. Louisiana-based Gulf Island Fabricators, Chet Morrison Contractors, Global Industries, and even Frank's Casing Crew and Rental Tools grew from small, family-owned firms servicing operations in the Gulf to become major offshore contractors active worldwide.

BP's Moment

In the late 1990s, the global company making the biggest news in the Gulf of Mexico was BP. Founded in 1908 and since 1954 named British Petroleum, it had for decades built its business around access to crude oil from Iran and neighboring Middle Eastern countries. In the 1960s and 1970s, BP achieved great success in discovering and developing oil reserves in the North Sea and in Alaska's Prudhoe Bay. By the early 1990s, however, BP had been exiled from the Middle East and Nigeria. Production from Prudhoe and the North Sea were in decline. Billions of dollars had been invested in unprofitable nonpetroleum ventures. And an ambitious exploration program had yet to bear fruit. The company tottered on the brink of bankruptcy.[97]

Sir John Browne, a forceful exploration manager whose father had also worked for BP, orchestrated its stunning turnaround. In the 1980s, as executive vice president of Sohio, BP's American subsidiary, he reined in spending and cut staff in order to place the company on better footing. Returning to London in 1989, he reorganized BP's exploration arm; Browne slashed expenditures, established a rigid—if not ruthless—performance ethic, and refocused on high-risk but potentially high-reward opportunities. Upon becoming chief executive in 1995, he directed a major part of BP's upstream focus to the deepwater Gulf. In the deals he negotiated to acquire Amoco and ARCO, BP emerged with a greatly expanded portfolio of Gulf leases and assets.[98]

In the late 1990s, BP's Gulf exploration team made a series of remarkable deepwater discoveries. Once the fields came online, they vaulted BP ahead of Shell as the Gulf's largest oil producer. BP prided itself as a "fast follower," rather than an "early adopter," in exploiting technological innovations. BP had closely followed Shell at Mars and quickly applied what it had learned to develop the Marlin field with a tension-leg platform in 3,400 feet of water. BP also joined with Exxon in developing deepwater discoveries at the Hoover and Diana fields in the western Gulf. After the string of subsalt dry holes in the mid-1990s, some of BP's competitors began looking for other kinds of plays the Gulf might still present. Shell shifted to managing production from its large number of deepwater developments. But BP sprang faster than anyone to confront the Gulf's nagging exploration challenge—the salt. [99]

In a costly and complex undertaking, BP combined new advances in computer processing for 3-D seismic imaging with new methods of acquiring seismic data from multiple directions to gather a better understanding of the salt history, stratigraphy, and the sources and migration pathways of oil in deepwater. BP's scientists and engineers found geographically promising areas just as large as those discovered and profitably exploited on the shallower continental shelf. Based on their analyses, they began to believe that the deepwater frontier could ultimately hold 40 billion barrels of commercially exploitable oil—four times the prevailing estimates. Said Dave Rainey, BP's deepwater exploration manager, "One of the lessons we have learned about the Gulf of Mexico is never to take it for granted."[100]

FIGURE 2.5: U.S. Crude Oil Production, 1990-2035 (projected)

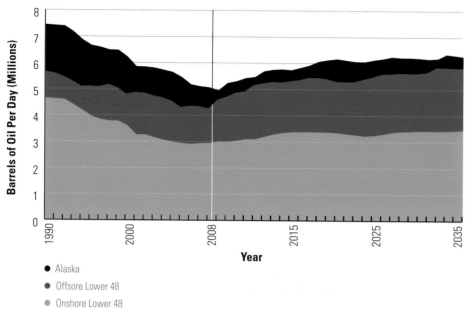

- Alaska
- Offsore Lower 48
- Onshore Lower 48

Source: Commission Staff, Adapted from U.S. Energy Information Administration

As this chart makes clear, overall production of crude oil in the U.S. has been declining for decades. However, production from deepwater wells in the Gulf of Mexico (Offshore Lower 48) is on the rise.

A new generation of drilling vessels coming onto the market, along with advances in drilling, encouraged BP to take the risk to explore those prospects. Outpacing most of the industry by a year, the company shifted its sights to prospects in much deeper waters. Rich rewards followed with a historic string of giant oil finds in subsalt formations ranging out to 7,000 feet of water. In 1998, BP struck oil in the deepwater subsalt of the Green Canyon's Mississippi Fan Foldbelt at Atlantis (minority partner BHP Billiton) and Mad Dog (minority partners BHP Billiton and Chevron), two of the largest fields ever discovered in the Gulf of Mexico. Atlantis's original reserves estimates were 400–800 million barrels of oil equivalent and Mad Dog's were placed at 200–450 million barrels. In 1999, working for BP (and minority partner Exxon) in 6,000 feet of water in the Mississippi Canyon, Transocean's *Discoverer Enterprise* drilled the largest Gulf field of all time, a subsalt prospect called Crazy Horse (subsequently renamed Thunder Horse), containing more than 1 billion barrels of recoverable reserves. That find alone catalyzed yet another rebirth of offshore oil in the Gulf of Mexico.[101]

The discoveries kept coming. A month later, BP made another oil and gas hit at Horn Mountain (150 million barrels of original reserves) in the Mississippi Canyon. In 2000, BP and Shell discovered a major above-the-salt deposit at Holstein (more than 200 million barrels) near the Mad Dog and Atlantis fields in the Green Canyon. The same year, those two partners announced their Na Kika project, a joint subsea development of five independent fields tied back to a central semi-submersible floating production facility, an industry first for the Gulf of Mexico. In 2001, BP found another giant oilfield, containing

500 million barrels, called Thunder Horse North.[102] Also that year, BP and yet another partner, Chevron, discovered a 100 million barrel field in 7,000 feet of water at their Blind Faith prospect in the Mississippi Canyon. (In the harsh glare of hindsight following the Macondo blowout, the executive director of the Natural Resources Defense Council commented that, in the name Blind Faith, "It would be hard to find a more fitting symbol of the oil industry's steady and assertive advance into the Gulf's deep waters, or the corporate thinking behind it."[103])

In August 2002, BP's Browne boldly announced that the company would spend $15 billion during the next decade on drilling and developing these discoveries. BP had become the largest-acreage holder in the deepwater Gulf, with more than 650 tracts in water depths greater than 1,500 feet, and in possession of one-third of all deepwater reserves then discovered. The deepwater Gulf of Mexico, Browne asserted, would be the "central element" of BP's growth strategy.[104] "The question is how they will manage the embarrassment of riches they have," said one analyst at the time. "They have a bunch of projects and they need to coordinate people and contractors. There is the sheer scale of the facilities and the size of the investment required—all this before a drop of oil ever comes out of the ground."[105]

Clouds on the Horizon

After BP's impressive discoveries, the industry dove into deeper waters across the Gulf. From 2001 to 2004, operators found 11 major fields beneath water 7,000 feet deep or more. Most deepwater discoveries were made in relatively young sandstones of the lower Miocene era. But companies increasingly explored down into the deeper and older Paleogene or "Lower Tertiary" strata found in the foldbelts near the edge of the Sigsbee Escarpment, a salt sheet that resembles a near-surface moonscape extending to the base of the continental slope. In 2006, Chevron and its partners Devon Energy and Statoil disclosed promising test results from a two-year-old discovery at its Jack prospect, proving that Lower Tertiary reservoirs could produce oil at pressures encountered at great depths, creating excitement that the Lower Tertiary play might ultimately yield between 3 billion and 15 billion barrels of hydrocarbons—collectively rivaling the size of the great Prudhoe Bay discovery. This implied a future for ultra-deep drilling, ranging out to 10,000-foot water depths and 25,000 feet beneath the seafloor. Reported the *Oil & Gas Journal*, "The Jack-2 test results boost confidence in that potential and highlight the central role technology plays in future supply."[106]

The industry was in need of a confidence booster after the previous three years of development challenges that had sorely tested BP's and the industry's confidence and conviction about deepwater.

BP's decision to develop multiple deepwater fields at once was an incredibly ambitious undertaking. Its program focused on the major fields at Holstein (a discovery above the salt), Mad Dog, Atlantis in the Green Canyon, and Thunder Horse in the Mississippi

BP Thunder Horse Platform

BP's mighty Thunder Horse platform was out-muscled by Hurricane Dennis in 2005 as it was being readied for service. Evacuated crews returned to find the semi-submersible production facility listing badly. After repairs and thorough analysis, additional problems were discovered that put the platform further behind schedule. For BP it was worth the wait: By 2009 Thunder Horse was producing a whopping quarter-million barrels a day.

Getty Images/U.S. Coast Guard photo/PA3 Robert M. Reed/digital version by Science Faction

Canyon—with total potential reserves of 2.5 billion barrels of oil, in water ranging from 4,000 to 7,000 feet deep, requiring wells reaching 30,000 feet in total depth. To produce oil at these places, BP selected "truss spars" for Holstein and Mad Dog, and semisubmersibles (such as the one BP and Shell had introduced at Na Kika), for Thunder Horse and Atlantis.[107]

Beyond about 4,000-foot depths, the weight of tension cables was too great, so BP could not employ tension-leg platforms, the workhorses at Shell's first deepwater projects. The spar, successfully demonstrated in 1996, is a giant buoy consisting of a large-diameter, vertical cylinder supporting a deck for drilling and processing. Its deep-draft floating caisson keeps about 90 percent of the structure underwater, giving the structure favorable motion characteristics. During 2000–2005, Kerr-McGee (acquired by Anadarko in 2006) went on to pioneer several innovations in spar designs.[108]

BP's choice between spars and semisubmersible production facilities depended upon different economic, functional, and safety factors at each field. All four projects would be linked by pipeline to a platform hub, where crude oil would be transferred into a 390-mile pipeline, the Cameron Highway, and transported to refineries at Texas City and Port Arthur. All four projects, as well as Na Kika, also would connect to the BP-operated Mardi Gras transportation system, itself a billion-dollar project that integrated five different

FIGURE 2.6: Deep Discoveries

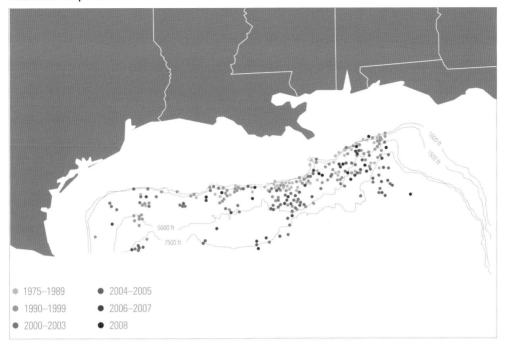

pipelines covering a total of 450 miles, with capacity to transport 1 million barrels of crude and 1.5 billion cubic feet of natural gas per day. The selection and development of technology on all these projects was a major challenge at every step, given the extreme water depths, reservoir conditions, and associated environmental issues. Thunder Horse had an unusually high pressure/high temperature reservoir. Atlantis was located under complex seafloor topography near the steep Sigsbee escarpment, and a large portion of the field was subsalt. Mad Dog lay under a massive salt canopy, causing large uncertainties in describing the actual reservoir. The Holstein geology forced BP to use a spar with wells housed on the platform. As BP production managers admitted in 2004, "None of the projects can be categorized as 'business as usual.'"[109]

The $5 billion Thunder Horse project was especially challenging. A major incident in drilling occurred even before the semisubmersible facility was put in place. In May 2003, the top of the drilling riser on the *Discoverer Enterprise* broke loose from the vessel, ripped apart again 3,000 feet under the surface, and left the lower marine riser package to collapse on and around the top of the blowout preventer, where the riser and drill pipe snapped off. The blowout preventer's blind shear rams were activated and worked as designed, averting any spill. "No one was hurt, and the well was secure," BP reported, "but the initial scene was daunting."[110]

An even bigger scare awaited the Thunder Horse semisubmersible production facility, which was towed to the field and moored on location in April 2005. As work proceeded to connect the predrilled subsea wells and commission all the facilities above and below the water, Hurricane Dennis neared in July, forcing the evacuation of all personnel and leaving the production facility unmanned. "No one could have anticipated the major shock that awaited the first helicopter flights after the storm had passed," according to one official BP account. The columns and other areas of the hull had filled with water, causing the facility to list to one side. Investigations later revealed that a valve in the bilge and ballast system had been installed backward, allowing seawater to move into the hull, a failure exacerbated by electrical pathways that were not watertight. Had BP not arrived when it did, the structure might have been lost. Crisis management crews were able to right the facility within a week, but reworking Thunder Horse's hull systems delayed commissioning for a year. Similar work on the Atlantis semisubmersible production platform pushed its installation back several months, too, until July 2006.[111]

Nor was that the end of BP's major shocks—it discovered that a weld had cracked open on one of the Thunder Horse manifolds that collected oil from the network of satellite subsea wells. The company made the difficult decision to pull out all the manifolds and subsea equipment that had a similar weld configuration— adding hundreds of millions of dollars to the cost of the project. After a lengthy investigation, engineers found that minute cracks had formed in the thermal insulation on the manifold pipe work, leading to reactions that embrittled the weld interface. BP and contractors developed new weld techniques, created more rigorous inspection and assurance procedures, and refurbished all the affected subsea equipment on Thunder Horse and at Atlantis. Thunder Horse finally delivered its first oil on June 2008, three years behind schedule.[112] By March 2009, production ramped up to 250,000 barrels per day, 4.5 percent of total U.S. daily production. (Atlantis went online a year before Thunder Horse, in 2007, but BP has been dogged by accusations that Atlantis has not been in compliance with safety and environmental regulations.[113])

Damaging Hurricanes

BP was not alone confronting environmental challenges. During 2002 and 2004–2005, hurricanes ravaged the Gulf Coast, with major impacts on offshore infrastructure and operations. In September 2002, Hurricane Lili blew into the heart of the Ship Shoal, Eugene Island, and South Marsh Island areas, damaging platforms and pipelines. Two years later, Ivan—a Category 4 storm—swept through the alley east of the Mississippi River delta, causing mudflows and anchor-dragging by mobile drilling units that tore up undersea pipelines. The following year, Hurricane Katrina flooded New Orleans and points east, with horrible effects. Offshore, Katrina destroyed 47 platforms and extensively damaged another 20. The 1,000-ton drilling rig on Shell's Mars platform collapsed, prompting an around-the-clock onsite recovery effort.

A month later, Hurricane Rita, storming farther west, wiped out 66 platforms and broke up another 32. Rita capsized Chevron's Typhoon, an unfortunately named mini-tension-leg platform. The majority of the platforms obliterated in these two storms were from an early generation of Gulf facilities, more than 30 years old. The two hurricanes also damaged more than 70 vessels and nearly 130 oil and natural gas pipelines, as they hit more prolific and sensitive areas than previous storms and, accordingly, caused much more extensive damages. Ominously, the short interval between the two storms exhausted the resources available for normal recovery and overwhelmed support bases.[114]

The Oil Industry and Deepwater Technology at Decade's End

As the end of the decade approached, the offshore industry in the Gulf had recovered from hurricane devastation and pressed on with deepwater and ultra-deepwater developments. Although many independent companies (such as Anadarko, Hess, BHP, Newfield, Marathon, and Mariner) had substantial deepwater leases and were actively exploring and developing them, the edge of the frontier was mainly the playground of the super-majors and firms with partial government ownership, such as Norway's Statoil and Brazil's Petrobras.[115]

In September 2009, Transocean's *Deepwater Horizon* semisubmersible made a historic discovery for BP at the company's Tiber prospect in the Keathley Canyon. Drilling in 4,000 feet of water and to a world-record total depth of 35,055 feet, *Deepwater Horizon* tapped in a pool of crude estimated to contain 4 to 6 billion barrels of oil equivalent, one of the largest U.S. discoveries. Six months later, in March 2010, Shell (with partners Chevron and BP) started production at its Perdido spar in 8,000 feet of water in the Alaminos Canyon. A hub for the development of three fields, Perdido was the world's deepest offshore platform, and the first project to pump oil and gas from the Lower Tertiary. Other Lower Tertiary developments were coming onto the horizon. Later in the year, Petrobras planned to develop the Gulf's first floating production, offloading, and storage facility to produce from Lower Tertiary reservoirs at its Cascade and Chinook prospects. By 2010, the industry had announced 19 discoveries in the Lower Tertiary trend, 14 of them containing more 100 million barrels of oil equivalent.[116]

Technical Tests

The fanfare around these discoveries and developments could not disguise the fact that the technical challenges of ultra-deepwater drilling and production and the subsalt geology remained unique and formidable. Water depths are extreme, down to 10,000 feet. Total well depths, as Tiber demonstrated, can go beyond 30,000 feet. Well shut-in pressures can surpass 10,000 pounds per square inch. Bottom-hole temperatures can exceed 350 degrees Fahrenheit. Salt- and tar-zone formations can be problematic. The sandstone reservoirs are tightly packed, and ensuring hydrocarbon flow through risers and pipelines can be difficult. According to a 2008 report from Chevron engineers for the Society of Petroleum Engineers, all these factors "separate many [Gulf of Mexico] deepwater and ultra-deepwater wells from deepwater and ultra-deepwater wells in other parts of the world."[117]

Drilling in extreme water depths poses special challenges. Risers connecting a drilling vessel to the blowout preventer on the seafloor have to be greatly lengthened, and they are exposed to strong ocean currents encountered in the central Gulf. Managing higher volumes of mud and drilling fluid in these long risers makes drillers' jobs more demanding. Connecting and maintaining blowout preventers thousands of feet beneath the surface can only be performed by remote-operating vehicles. A 2007 article in *Drilling Contractor* described how blowout preventer requirements got tougher as drilling went deeper, because of low temperatures and high pressures at the ocean bottom. The author discussed taking advantage of advances in metallurgy to use higher-strength materials in the blowout preventers' ram connecting rods or ram-shafts. More generally, he suggested "some fundamental paradigm shifts" were needed across a broad range of blowout-preventer technologies to deal with deepwater conditions.[118]

Under such conditions, methane hydrates raised a host of serious problems. Methane gas locked in ice ("fire ice") forms at low temperature and high pressure, and can often be found in sea-floor sediments. Temperature and pressure changes caused by drilling, or even by natural conditions, can activate the release of 160 cubic feet of gas from one cubic foot of methane, collapsing surrounding sediment, and thus destabilizing the drilling foundation. Hydrates can also present well-control problems. As hydrocarbons are produced and transported in cold temperatures and high pressures, hydrates can form and block the flow through deep pipelines and other conduits. Government, academic, and industry research programs on hydrates and associated flow problems begun in the 1990s are continuing.[119]

More broadly, knowledge about localized geology, types of hydrocarbons, and pressure profiles in ultra-deepwater wells is still not thoroughly developed. Geological conditions are complicated and vary from prospect to prospect, and from well to well. Each well, indeed, has its own "personality" that requires maintaining an extremely delicate balance between the counteracting pressures of the subsurface formation and drilling operation. Beneath the salt, pressures in the pores of the sediment are exceedingly hard to predict. Reservoirs in the Lower Tertiary are thicker and with higher viscosity than the fluids found in younger rock. Finally, ultra-deepwater developments are far removed from shore and thus from established infrastructure. As a BP technical paper prepared for the May 2010 Offshore Technology Conference noted, "the trend of deepwater discoveries in the [Gulf of Mexico] is shifting toward one with greater challenges across many disciplines represented by the conditions of Lower Tertiary discoveries."[120]

Nevertheless, the challenges seemed manageable and the rewards appeared worth the perceived risk. The offshore industry had enjoyed a long run in the Gulf without an environmental catastrophe. The hurricanes of mid-decade had caused widespread damage, but not a major offshore spill. In recent years, the industry had touted its relatively clean record in the Gulf as a justification to allow exploration elsewhere. As oil prices climbed from 2003 to 2008, peaking at over $140 per barrel, so did the industry's interest in exploring other frontier areas, especially offshore Alaska. In 2007, Shell and Total bid aggressively for federal leases offered in the Beaufort Sea, and in 2008, Shell spent $2.1 billion for leases in the Chukchi Sea. The following year, however, a lawsuit in a federal appeals court challenging the Minerals Management Service's environmental studies preceding the sale held up applications for permits to drill on these leases.[121]

Still, from 2008 through early 2010, both government and industry were largely bullish about the potential of offshore drilling for the nation's future. Not incidentally, both were earning even greater revenues from ever-more ambitious exploration. In 2008, President George W. Bush and Congress ended the leasing moratoriums on vast stretches of the U.S. outer continental shelf, and Bush proposed opening new areas for exploration. In a March

31, 2010 announcement, President Barack Obama scaled back Bush's plan, but he left open the possibility of expanding offshore leasing beyond the Gulf of Mexico and Alaska. The President defended his position by observing, "oil rigs today generally don't cause spills."[122]

As President Obama spoke, Transocean's *Deepwater Horizon*—fresh from completing BP's spectacular find at Tiber a few months earlier—was busy drilling on BP's Mississippi Canyon 252 lease, in approximately 5,000 feet of water. BP had named the prospect Macondo, after the fictional town in Gabriel Garcia Marquez's novel, *One Hundred Years of Solitude*. The fate of the town of the Macondo, as described in a memorable passage by Marquez, presaged the fate of the Macondo well and summed up the challenges facing the industry as a whole as it plumbed the depths of the Gulf:

> It was as if God had decided to put to the test every capacity for surprise and was keeping the inhabitants of Macondo in a permanent alternation between excitement and disappointment, doubt and revelation, to such an extreme that no one knew for certain where the limits of reality lay.[123]

Chapter Three
"It was like pulling teeth."

Oversight—and Oversights—in Regulating Deepwater Energy Exploration and Production in the Gulf of Mexico

The *Deepwater Horizon* rig sank on April 22, 2010, two days after the Macondo well blowout and explosion that killed 11 workers. Not long after the tragedy, its repercussions shifted to the Minerals Management Service (MMS), the federal agency responsible for overseeing the well's drilling and operation. Nineteen days after the rig sank, Secretary of the Interior Ken Salazar announced his intention to strip MMS's safety and environmental enforcement responsibilities away from its leasing, revenue collection, and permitting functions, and to place the former within a "separate and independent" entity.[1] A week later, he announced MMS would be reorganized into three separate entities with distinct missions: a Bureau of Ocean Energy Management; a Bureau of Safety and Environmental Enforcement; and an Office of Natural Resources Revenue.[2] And, by June 19, the Secretary had discarded the "MMS" name altogether.[3] Like the *Deepwater Horizon*, MMS had ceased to exist.

The rig's demise signals the conflicted evolution— and severe shortcomings—of federal regulation of offshore oil drilling in the United States, and particularly of MMS oversight of deepwater

The often competing goals of energy independence and environmental protection collide at the Department of the Interior, which historically has held broad regulatory authority in both realms. For nearly three decades a single departmental agency, the Minerals Management Service, was at the center of the offshore-oil saga.

Mark Wilson/Getty Images

drilling in the Gulf of Mexico. The regulatory context for the leasing procedures and safety and environmental oversight that led up to the Macondo blowout took shape in the 1970s, when two conflicting priorities dominated the political landscape. The first to appear, in the early 1970s, was the public mandate for environmental protection, which prompted enactment of an extraordinary series of sweeping regulatory laws intended, in the language of the National Environmental Policy Act, to "create and maintain conditions under which man and nature can exist in productive harmony."[4] The second was the nation's drive for energy independence; it led to new policies designed to increase domestic production and decrease American reliance on foreign energy supplies. Oil served as a catalyst for both: the Santa Barbara oil spill in 1969 helped to promote passage of demanding environmental protection mandates, and the OPEC oil embargo of 1973 amplified the urgency of efforts to make the nation more energy self-sufficient.

The federal regulation of offshore drilling awkwardly combined the two priorities, as a series of Congresses, Presidents, and Secretaries of the Interior—responding to competing constituencies in explicitly political ways—sought to reconcile the sometimes conflicting goals of environmental protection, energy independence, and revenue generation. In some offshore regions, oil drilling was essentially banned in response to environmental concerns. Elsewhere, most notably in the Gulf, some environmental protections and safety oversight were formally relaxed or informally diminished so as to render them ineffective, promoting a dramatic expansion of offshore oil and gas production and billions of dollars in federal revenues.

The origins of MMS vividly illustrate that political compromise. Secretary of the Interior James Watt created the agency with great fanfare in January 1982, aiming from the outset to promote domestic energy supplies by dramatically expanding drilling on the outer continental shelf. He combined, in one entity, authority for regulatory oversight with responsibility for collecting for the U.S. Treasury the billions of dollars of revenues obtained from lease sales and royalty payments from producing wells.[5] From birth, MMS had a built-in incentive to promote offshore drilling in sharp tension with its mandate to ensure safe drilling and environmental protection.

Revenue generation—enjoyed both by industry and government—became the dominant objective. But there was a hidden price to be paid for those increased revenues. Any revenue increases dependent on moving drilling further offshore and into much deeper waters came with a corresponding increase in the safety and environmental risks of such drilling. Those increased risks, however, were not matched by greater, more sophisticated regulatory oversight. Industry regularly and intensely resisted such oversight, and neither Congress nor any of a series of presidential administrations mustered the political support necessary to overcome that opposition. Nor, despite their assurances to the contrary, did the oil and gas industry take the initiative to match its massive investments in oil and gas development and production with comparable investments in drilling safety and oil-spill containment technology and contingency response planning in case of an accident.

On April 20, the inherent risks of decades of inadequate regulation, insufficient investment, and incomplete planning were realized in tragic fashion. MMS no doubt can fairly boast of many hardworking individual public servants who have in good faith sought to achieve their agency's important safety mission over sustained industry opposition. But, notwithstanding their individual efforts and accomplishments, the overall picture of MMS that has emerged since April 20 is distressing. MMS became an agency systematically lacking the resources, technical training, or experience in petroleum engineering that is absolutely critical to ensuring that offshore drilling is being conducted in a safe and responsible manner. For a regulatory agency to fall so short of its essential safety mission is inexcusable.

This chapter is divided into three parts. The first part describes the emergence of MMS as the dominant federal regulatory agency responsible for overseeing the offshore oil and gas industry. The second part examines the performance of MMS over time, with particular focus on its efforts to promote drilling safety and the institutional, political, and cultural impediments to its success. Finally, the third part explores in more detail the application of environmental protection requirements to offshore drilling, highlighting the particular ways in which the requirements were effectively diminished or ignored.

Creation of a Cross-Purposes Regulator

The federal government's authority to regulate oil and gas leasing activities on the outer continental shelf is not merely an expression of the government's traditional authority to regulate private activities affecting public health, safety, and welfare. Its authority is even more sweeping in nature and further arises out of the nation's *ownership* of the natural resources on the outer continental shelf and the federal government's corresponding power and responsibility to manage and protect those invaluable resources on behalf of current and future generations of Americans. As described by the Constitution's Property Clause, it is the "power to dispose and make all needful rules and regulations respecting the territory or other property belonging to the United States."[6] The federal government, accordingly, has plenary authority, essentially "without limitations,"[7] "to prescribe the conditions upon which others may obtain rights in" natural resources located on properties that belong to the nation as a whole.[8] Because, moreover, of the national security implications of those resources, especially energy resources, that national power further implicates the President's broad authority as Commander-in-Chief to ensure the maintenance of sufficient energy supplies to keep the nation secure.[9]

Rights and Riches: The Early Skirmishes over the Outer Continental Shelf

The foundations of federal regulation of offshore oil and gas development were laid in the Outer Continental Shelf Lands Act of 1953.[10] That initial legislation gave the Department of the Interior diverse and potentially contradictory responsibilities for offshore mineral development. The vigorous debates preceding enactment of the new law and its early implementation gave the impression that it was all about the money.[11]

The potential windfall from leasing public land offshore to private companies for mineral development provoked an intense dispute between coastal states and the federal government. In 1945, President Harry Truman had proclaimed federal authority over the subsoil of the U.S. continental shelf. California, Texas, and Louisiana defied this proclamation and continued to lease offshore land, prompting suits by the U.S. Department of Justice. The Supreme Court ruled against California in 1947 and against Louisiana and Texas in 1950, declaring that the federal government possessed "paramount rights" that transcended the states' rights of ownership.[12] Offshore leasing and exploration stalled for three years, as Congress and the 1952 presidential candidates postured around proposals to return submerged coastal lands to the states.[13] That conflict was largely resolved in the Submerged Lands Act, passed in 1953, two months before the Outer Continental Shelf Lands Act: states would control three nautical miles out from the shoreline (9 nautical miles for Texas and western Florida due to historic claims).[14] The "outer continental shelf"—seaward of state lands—was claimed by the federal government. Estimates of the value of federal land offshore ranged from $40 billion to $250 billion.[15]

President Truman had called on the nation to postpone mineral development in the federal offshore area, foregoing the revenues immediately available. He argued that setting the federal offshore area aside, in the Naval Petroleum Reserve, would ensure that the oil and gas would be there later when needed for strategic purposes.[16] But the congressional debates in 1953, under President Dwight Eisenhower, focused on what to do with this attractive new source of revenue. Various senators proposed dedicating the funds to deficit reduction or to education. But in the end, the new money from lease sales, rents, and royalties would flow into the general treasury.[17]

The first leases. During the first week of September 1954, Secretary of the Interior Douglas McKay announced the first federal lease sale: rights to explore 748,000 acres off the coast of Louisiana.[18] When the sealed bids were opened on October 13, half the available acreage was leased with winning bids totaling $130 million. The next month, a similar sale off the Texas coast yielded $23 million.[19] The promise of a new stream of federal revenue had come to pass.

The Rise of Environmental Law

At the outset, environmental restrictions on offshore drilling were very limited. The 1953 legislation governing offshore mineral development authorized the Interior Department to prescribe rules "for the prevention of waste and conservation of natural resources" of the outer continental shelf,[20] but "conservation" at that time mostly referred to the desire not to waste the resource physically by destroying the oil and gas reservoir. The Department did announce, however, that the Fish and Wildlife Service would have to approve all offshore drilling in wildlife refuges and that oil and gas leasing there that endangered "rare" wildlife species (like whooping cranes or trumpeter swans) would not be allowed.[21]

Federal offshore leasing policy remained largely unchanged until a Union Oil Company well located in the Santa Barbara Channel blew out on January 28, 1969 (described in Chapter 2). The Interior Department toughened its rules in response to the spill (after first issuing a moratorium on offshore drilling and production in California waters pending those new rules), the first changes since 1953.[22] And, at that time Congress was already taking up legislation in response to heightened awareness of a host of environmental problems, now punctuated by the Santa Barbara spill. Starting with the National Environmental Policy Act (NEPA), signed into law on January 1, 1970,[23] Congress enacted sweeping new environmental protection and resource conservation laws that dramatically changed the federal role in overseeing activities that polluted the air or water or that exploited the nation's natural resources on public lands—including offshore oil and gas development.[24]

Given its bold promises of preserving the environment for future generations, NEPA is often referred to as the *Magna Carta* of the nation's environmental laws. It requires federal agencies to prepare "environmental impact statements" for all proposed "major Federal actions significantly affecting the quality of the human environment" in order to ensure that decisions are based on full consideration of their environmental consequences.[25] Although it is far from clear that either Congress or the President appreciated NEPA's full import, federal courts quickly embraced the law, applying its procedural requirements strictly and enjoining agency actions found to be in violation.[26]

In order to provide the science needed for the environmental reviews and consultations directed by these statutes, the Department of the Interior created the "Environmental Studies Program" in 1973.[27] The program was established to provide information on the geological, physical, biological, and chemical characteristics of offshore oil and gas leasing areas. It was initially focused on scientifically characterizing areas and providing baseline environmental data, but later shifted its focus to research directly linked to resource management decisions by the offshore leasing program.[28]

NEPA was just the first among approximately 20 new laws enacted during the 1970s that aimed to advance environmental protection by curbing pollution of the nation's waters, air, or land; manage commercial activities that sought to exploit the nation's natural resources, including mining and forestry; manage the coastal zone prudently; control noise; regulate toxic substances; and protect endangered species—among other goals.[29] Amid this rapid, extensive transformation of the nation's environmental protection and natural resource management laws, one had particular significance for federal oversight of offshore drilling: the Outer Continental Shelf Lands Act Amendments of 1978. It was the last major natural resource law that Congress passed during the 1970s—and so embodies the shifting nature of national politics from the decade's beginning to its end.

Energy Independence vs. Environmental Protection: Conflicting Aims in High Relief

Although Americans' embrace of environmental protection persisted throughout the decade, the 1973 oil embargo prompted ambitious efforts to promote the nation's energy independence. President Richard Nixon proposed a dramatic expansion of offshore oil and gas development, including in frontier areas around most of the nation's coast. President Jimmy Carter created the Department of Energy in 1977 and secured passage of the National Energy Act of 1978, consisting of five separate laws, some designed to promote development of domestic energy supplies and others to encourage energy conservation.[30]

The Outer Continental Shelf Lands Act Amendments, also enacted that year, not surprisingly reflected the tension between the nation's environmental and energy independence goals. Those skeptical of accelerated offshore leasing—including many coastal states, local governments, fishermen, and environmentalists—sought, to that end, opportunities to ensure that offshore oil and gas leasing complied with strict safeguards and a greater voice in the decisionmaking process. They were concerned about the broad discretion the Act conferred on the Secretary of the Interior over control and management of offshore energy resources.

By contrast, advocates for expanded domestic production wanted to ensure that the new legislation did not allow environmental protection laws to stifle exploration, development, and production of significant offshore oil and gas reservoirs. They were aware that environmental organizations had used NEPA successfully to challenge a proposed lease sale, covering almost 380,000 acres offshore Louisiana and Mississippi, on the grounds that the Interior Department had failed to first prepare an adequate environmental impact statement. The federal courts had agreed and enjoined the sale in January 1972.[31] Coastal states and environmentalists had since launched challenges against other lease sales.

Congress began to hold hearings on revamping the federal offshore leasing program in 1974—just after the oil embargo and not long after those early environmental challenges.[32] The law that emerged in 1978[33] included findings on the need to reduce the nation's dependence on "imports of oil from foreign nations," the potential to increase production of oil and gas on the outer continental shelf significantly "without undue harm or damage to the environment," and the need to review "environmental and safety regulations relating to activities on the Outer Continental Shelf . . . in light of current technology and information."[34] The Act's purposes included "expedited exploration and development of the Outer Continental Shelf" and the "development of new and improved technology for energy resource production which will eliminate or minimize risk of damage to the human, marine, and coastal environments."[35]

The 1978 Act fundamentally transformed federal offshore leasing. The law added detailed procedures governing the leasing of rights to explore, develop, and produce the resources of the outer continental shelf. The offshore program was divided into four distinct stages:
- Development by the Secretary of the Interior of a "schedule of proposed lease sales indicating, as precisely as possible, the size, timing, and location of leasing activity which he determines will best meet national energy needs for the five-year period following its approval or reapproval";[36]
- Lease sales by the Secretary pursuant to that five-year schedule;
- Submission by lessees of exploration plans for the Secretary's approval; and
- Upon discovery of oil and gas in commercial quantities, submission of development and production plans by lessees for the Secretary's approval.

The Act further requires lessees to apply for the Secretary of the Interior's permission prior to drilling *any* wells, pursuant to an approved exploration plan[37] or, in most areas, pursuant to a development and production plan.[38]

FIGURE 3.1: Outer Continental Shelf Oil and Gas Leasing, Exploration & Development Process

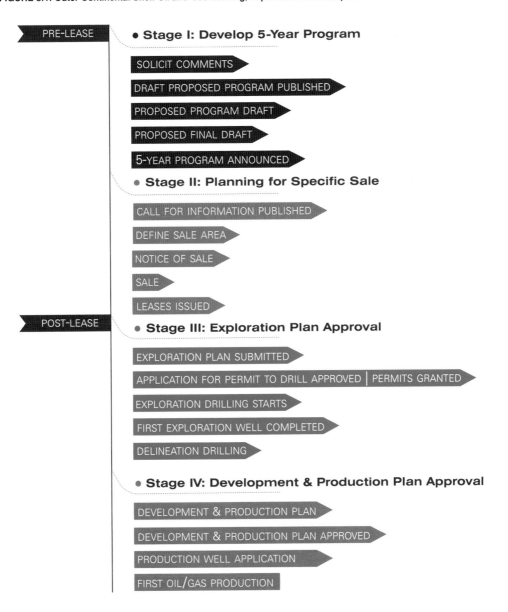

PRE-LEASE

- **Stage I: Develop 5-Year Program**

SOLICIT COMMENTS

DRAFT PROPOSED PROGRAM PUBLISHED

PROPOSED PROGRAM DRAFT

PROPOSED FINAL DRAFT

5-YEAR PROGRAM ANNOUNCED

- **Stage II: Planning for Specific Sale**

CALL FOR INFORMATION PUBLISHED

DEFINE SALE AREA

NOTICE OF SALE

SALE

LEASES ISSUED

POST-LEASE

- **Stage III: Exploration Plan Approval**

EXPLORATION PLAN SUBMITTED

APPLICATION FOR PERMIT TO DRILL APPROVED | PERMITS GRANTED

EXPLORATION DRILLING STARTS

FIRST EXPLORATION WELL COMPLETED

DELINEATION DRILLING

- **Stage IV: Development & Production Plan Approval**

DEVELOPMENT & PRODUCTION PLAN

DEVELOPMENT & PRODUCTION PLAN APPROVED

PRODUCTION WELL APPLICATION

FIRST OIL/GAS PRODUCTION

Four major steps guide the Outer Continental Shelf leasing and development process, from the decision to open an area to drilling, to the operations during oil and gas production. Before a lease is granted, Stage I establishes the "5-Year Program," setting the schedule and possible locations for individual lease sales, and Stage II lays out the details by which each individual lease sale is conducted. After a company acquires a lease, Stage III plans and executes the oil and gas exploration activities, and Stage IV plans and executes the oil and gas development and production operations.

At the same time, the statute also made clear that environmental safeguards are a relevant, important part of the Secretary's decisionmaking. For instance, it charged the Secretary "to obtain a proper balance between the potential for environmental damage, the potential for discovery of oil and gas, and the potential for adverse impact on the coastal zone."[39] The law also expressly required the Secretary to prepare a series of "environmental studies" to assess the environmental impacts of activities on the outer continental shelf,[40] and "the Secretary of the Department in which the Coast Guard is operating" (currently the Department of Homeland Security) to promulgate "safety regulations."[41] Such regulations were to include "the use of the best available and safest technologies which the Secretary [of the Interior] determines to be economically feasible, wherever failure of equipment would have a significant effect on safety, health, or the environment."[42] But this potentially demanding requirement included an exception "where the Secretary determines that the incremental benefits are clearly insufficient to justify the incremental costs of utilizing such technologies."[43]

The Gulf of Mexico exemption. Offsetting the apparent interest in environmental review, the Act reflected a carefully calibrated political compromise designed to promote offshore drilling: it expressly exempted leases in the "Gulf of Mexico" from the law's requirement that development and production pursuant to an oil and gas lease must be based on and consistent with a "development and production plan" submitted by the lessee and approved by the Secretary of the Interior.[44] (No comparable exception applied to "exploration plans," which all lessees were required to submit for approval prior to conducting such drilling, which naturally occurs prior to development and production.[45]) The telling compromise lay in the details: the law specified that a development and production plan must set forth "the environmental safeguards to be implemented"[46] and the Secretary must at least once declare the approval of a development and production plan in any area "to be a major Federal action"—language which triggers NEPA's requirement for an impact statement detailing the environmental consequences of development and production.[47] Therefore, by exempting leases in the Gulf from the required "development and production plan," the Act was also exempting such leases from the related requirement of at least one NEPA impact statement.[48] And the Act included one further bit of congressional horse-trading. It authorized the Secretary of the Interior to reinstate the development and production plan requirements, including NEPA review, for an oil and gas lease located in the *eastern* planning area of the Gulf abutting the western coastline of Florida, leaving only the *central* and *western* Gulf planning areas off limits from such requirements.[49]

The legislative history makes clear that this was a deal brokered between the Carter administration, the oil and gas industry, Congress, and Gulf states. Industry had argued that NEPA and similar requirements could lengthen the interval between leasing and production by three to six years. In response to this concern, Congress amended the bill to draw a distinction between the Gulf of Mexico, where such consultation would not be required, and other offshore areas where it would. The rationale for singling out the Gulf of Mexico for less environmental oversight than other parts of the nation's offshore was that the oil and gas industry in the Gulf was already mature and therefore the environmental risks were already better known than they were in "frontier" areas. This rough geographically-defined generalization took no account of the Gulf's remarkable fisheries, or the economic importance of the region's beaches to the tourism industry. Secretary of the Interior Cecil Andrus sought administrative discretion to require the full environmental review even in some non-frontier areas if drilling in those areas proved to present heightened environmental risks,[50] but the final legislation made that further concession only for a part of the Gulf.[51]

A compromise comes undone. Whatever compromise Congress and President Carter may have thought they had struck in the 1978 legislation quickly unraveled. In the first five-year leasing schedule issued in June 1980, Secretary Andrus offered 55 million acres, and proposed Lease Sale 53 along the Pacific Coast. Unlike previous sales, which had been concentrated on one geographic region, Lease Sale 53 called for nominations of tracts from the Santa Barbara Channel all the way up the California coast to the Oregon border. Fierce opposition immediately greeted the proposed leasing schedule and Lease Sale 53. California and Alaska filed lawsuits challenging the legality of the leasing schedule under the 1978 law. After huge public rallies, Secretary Andrus formally withdrew the entire northern and central California portion of the proposed sale.[52]

The Creation of the Minerals Management Service (MMS)

Against a backdrop of rising inflation, record interest rates, further turbulence in the oil market following the 1979 Iranian revolution, and a severe recession, the politics of offshore drilling became even more volatile early in the administration of President Ronald Reagan, who was inaugurated in January 1981. Perhaps not surprisingly, after the upwelling of new regulatory powers under Presidents Nixon, Ford, and Carter, the new President made clear from the outset his view that government regulation was a leading cause of the nation's problems—a drag on the nation's economy in general and the development of its rich natural resources in particular.

Secretary of the Interior James Watt shared that outlook and focused his early regulatory reform efforts on offshore drilling. He quickly vowed to lease a billion acres of the outer continental shelf—virtually the entire area—for oil and gas exploration.[53] And he made clear his commitment to maintaining that objective, notwithstanding enormous criticism: "If the press is here," he declared during a National Ocean Industries Association meeting in April 1982, "I hope they will write this down. We will offer one billion acres for leasing in the next five years. We will not back away from our plans to have 42 lease sales."[54]

MMS originated in this context, driven by the administration's desire to ensure that it obtained the financial fruits of its plan for this massive expansion in offshore drilling. With the dramatic increase in oil prices over the previous decade, royalties and revenues from federal oil and gas resources had already become the second largest revenue source for the U.S. Treasury. (A September 1980 lease sale in New Orleans had demonstrated the sums potentially at stake, bringing in a record $2.8 billion of cash bonuses, far more than any prior lease sale; see Chapter 2.) Clearly, this was a consequential way to secure revenue without needing to raise taxes.

Revenue collection and regulation, separated. Until this time, the Interior Department's Bureau of Land Management and Bureau of Indian Affairs had been responsible for collecting royalties for mining and drilling on federal and Indian lands, respectively—and regulatory oversight of offshore exploration and energy production had been vested in the U.S. Geological Survey's Conservation Division.

But the department's management of royalties was subjected to frequent criticism. In July 1981, the administration created a Commission on Fiscal Accountability of the

FIGURE 3.2: Federal Revenues from the Outer Continental Shelf, 1955-2010

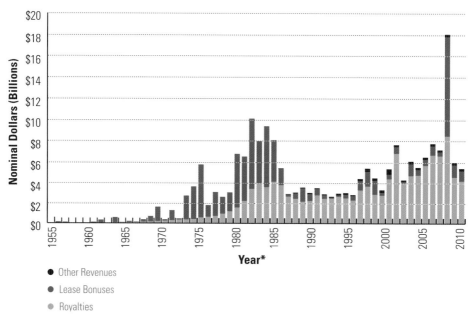

- Other Revenues
- Lease Bonuses
- Royalties

Sources: Minerals Revenue Management, *Total Federal offshore mineral revenue collections, Calendar Years 1953-2000*, 2001, 7, http://www.onrr.gov/Stats/pdfdocs/coll_off.pdf; Office of Natural Resources Revenue, *Total Federal Offshore Reported Royalty Revenues*, http://www.onrr.gov/ONRRWebStats/Home.aspx.

Revenues from lease bonuses can occasionally dwarf royalties. A single 2008 lease sale in the Chukchi Sea, Alaska, brought in a record cash bonus of $2.6 billion.

* Calendar year from 1955-200; fiscal year from 2001-2010

Nation's Energy Resources, charged with reviewing and recommending changes in the system for collecting royalties. Reporting the next January, the commission concluded that "[m]anagement of royalties for the nation's energy resources has been a failure for more than 20 years. . . . [T]he oil and gas industry is not paying all the royalties it rightly owes. The government's royalty recordkeeping . . . is in disarray."[55] It accordingly called for a complete overhaul, including a wholesale reorganization of Interior Department responsibility for overseeing royalty collection from federal and Indian lands.

Mixing oil and water: revenue-collection and regulation combined. Using the discretion conferred on him in the 1978 Outer Continental Shelf Lands Act Amendments, Secretary Watt moved quickly, issuing Secretarial Order No. 3071 on January 19, creating the Minerals Management Service. Moving beyond the commission recommendations for reform of royalty collection, he provided that the new agency would also absorb offshore leasing and oversight responsibilities from the U.S. Geological Survey. There is no available formal record of his reasoning for this further step, but the most likely reasons are revealed by a memorandum written by the Chief of the Conservation Division, Don Kash, dated December 11, 1981, just a few weeks earlier. In that memo, Kash vigorously argued in favor of relocating responsibilities for lease management from the Conservation Division into a new independent agency within the Interior Department—precisely what the Secretary then did.

But Secretary Watt's decision did not fully reflect Kash's concerns. The latter had worried that the controversial politics of lease management were "sullying the [U.S. Geological] Survey's scientific reputation" and threatened its "science ethos" and "scientific virtue." The collision of cultures between those engaged in scientific research and those engaged in lease management was a "continuing source of irritation" and "bitterness" within the U.S. Geological Survey. He was concerned that lease management would increasingly take priority, draining resources from the research that should be the hallmark of the U.S. Geological Survey. Finally, Kash described problems that leasing management would face going forward—foremost among them a tendency toward myopic thinking and inadequately trained personnel. On that last issue, he pointed out that the government could not retain "geologists and geophysicists associated with [outer continental shelf] activities" because they "can move to an industrial or business concern for a substantial increase in pay, almost at will." Kash recommended a series of steps to attract and train personnel capable of overseeing the management of offshore oil and gas activities.[56]

Secretary Watt organized two distinct programs within his newly-minted MMS: the Offshore Energy and Minerals Management program and the Minerals Revenue Management program. (He rejected the General Accounting Office's recommendation, which industry had opposed, that MMS also assume responsibility for *onshore* oil and gas leasing; the Bureau of Land Management retained that regulatory authority.[57]) The result was that the same agency became responsible for regulatory oversight of offshore drilling—and for collecting revenue from that drilling.

The Billion-Acre Leasing Land Rush

It did not take long for Secretary Watt to make sure that his new agency was fully engaged. In July 1982, just after MMS's birth, he issued a new five-year plan that envisioned leasing nearly one billion acres of the outer continental shelf from August 1982 to June 1987—18 times the 55 million acres offered by the first five-year plan of June 1980. To meet this ambitious program, he scheduled 41 sales over the ensuing five years; divided the billion acres into 18 planning areas, ranging in size from 8 million to 133 million acres; and established a streamlined process for leasing in those areas. Under this new process, MMS would no longer lease just those tracts previously designated by industry to be of interest, but would instead offer vast acreage on an "area-wide" basis.[58]

As described in Chapter 2, area-wide leasing promoted significant new discoveries of large oil-bearing formations in contrast to the smaller fields found in shallower depths. Those additional discoveries in fact led to major technological advances and increased exploration of oil and gas reservoirs in Gulf waters. But the federal revenues generated fell short of expectations. With such a large increase in supply, the price offered for leases declined. The Sierra Club claimed that Secretary Watt's plans for accelerated leasing would cost the U.S. Treasury $77 billion over the five-year period.[59] Moreover, the Gulf states persuaded Congress to increase their share of leasing revenues as compensation for physical drainage of oil and gas from reservoirs within state jurisdiction by offshore activities of federal lessees. In 1986, Congress amended the federal law to guarantee that the Gulf states would receive 27 percent of the revenues from leases in the federal zone three nautical miles

Watt and Reagan

In January 1982, President Reagan's Interior Secretary, James Watt, created the Minerals Management Service (MMS) in support of his goal to open unprecedented reaches of U.S. territorial waters to oil and gas exploration. MMS had a conflicting and ultimately disastrous mandate: to both regulate offshore energy leases and collect the revenue they generated.

Frank Johnston/The Washington Post via Getty Images

beyond state waters.[60] Previously the law had provided only that states should receive a "fair and equitable" portion of those revenues, an ambiguous standard that invited disagreement between the federal and state governments concerning what that portion should be.

The Gulf of Mexico's still-more-special status. The distinction first drawn in the 1978 Act between offshore drilling in the Gulf of Mexico and in other parts of the nation was widened further during the 1980s and 1990s. What began as a policy allowing offshore drilling in the Gulf under a more relaxed regulatory regime than applied elsewhere gradually became a policy of allowing offshore drilling, as a practical matter, almost *only* in the Gulf.

Court challenges quickly greeted Secretary Watt's efforts to expand offshore leasing throughout the United States. But decisively, Congress, not court rulings, ended the Secretary's plan and effectively singled out the Gulf for offshore drilling. In a series of recurring one-year moratoriums imposed on the Interior Department's annual budgets, the House Appropriations Committee effectively prohibited everything from new leasing activities to exploration and development on existing leases in areas all over the outer continental shelf outside the Gulf of Mexico and a few sub-regions off of Alaska.[61] From 1982 to 1993, the area covered by these moratoriums expanded from 0.7 million acres to 266 million.[62] The persistent unpopularity of offshore drilling outside the Gulf was underscored by President George H.W. Bush. Despite his background as a former Gulf state (Texan) oil-industry executive, he issued a memorandum in June 1990 that canceled all scheduled sales off of the California, southern Florida,* North Atlantic, Washington, and Oregon coasts and withdrew those areas from leasing until after 2000 (Alaska was not mentioned). At the same time, the President began a process to buy back existing leases in the eastern Gulf of Mexico; he established the proposed Monterey Bay Marine Sanctuary, banning oil and gas leasing there; and he prepared legislation to provide coastal communities directly affected by outer continental shelf development with a greater share of revenues from development and more voice in decisionmaking.[63]

Secretary Watt's promise of offshore drilling throughout the outer continental shelf was never realized. But he succeeded in creating an agency (MMS) and a method of leasing (via area-wide sales) that dramatically expanded the reach of offshore drilling in one place: the Gulf of Mexico. In that one oil- and gas-rich region, that same agency would increasingly struggle to keep up with the pace of industry expansion, while juggling four distinct responsibilities—offshore leasing, revenue collection and auditing, permitting and operational safety, and environmental protection—requiring different skill sets and cultures.

Impediments to Safety Regulation

The federal government has never lacked the sweeping authority required to control whether, when, and how valuable oil and gas resources located on the outer continental shelf are leased, explored, or developed. As described at the outset, the government's authority is virtually without limitation, traceable to both its authority as proprietor and as sovereign, then further bolstered by the President's inherent authority as Chief Executive and Commander-in-Chief to ensure the security of the nation. The root problem has instead been that political leaders within both the Executive Branch and Congress have failed to ensure that agency regulators have had the resources necessary to exercise that authority, including personnel and technical expertise, and, no less important, the political autonomy needed to overcome the powerful commercial interests that have opposed more stringent safety regulation.

* Although Florida's jurisdiction offshore extends to 9 nautical miles, Florida has not joined those other states in favoring significant offshore oil and gas drilling. Florida has instead supported continuing moratoriums on drilling in the outer continental shelf off the Florida coast. Nor has the State sought to promote such drilling within its territorial jurisdiction offshore. Florida's principal reason has been to protect its coast from the potential adverse environmental consequences of drilling activity, including oil spills. See Robert Gramling, *Oil on the Edge: Offshore Development, Conflict, Gridlock* (Albany, NY: SUNY Press, 1996), 13.

Safety on the Outer Continental Shelf: Increasing Risk, Absence of Necessary Regulatory Reform, and Decreasing Government Oversight Capacity

Modern oil and gas drilling rigs and producing platforms are, in effect, enormous floating machines, densely equipped with powerful engines and responsible for keeping within geologic formations large volumes of highly combustible hydrocarbons at high temperatures and pressures. For all their productivity, the rigs expose their crews to the risks of injury or death if not properly operated and maintained—risks compounded for operations conducted in progressively deeper waters, ever farther from shore.

From its creation until the Macondo well blowout, MMS was the federal agency primarily responsible for leasing, safety, environmental compliance, and royalty collection from offshore drilling.* In carrying out its duties, MMS subjected oil and gas activities to an array of prescriptive safety regulations: hundreds of pages of technical requirements for pollution prevention and control, drilling, well-completion operations, oil and gas well-workovers (major well maintenance), production safety systems, platforms and structures, pipelines, well production, and well-control and -production safety training.[64] As required by the 1978 Act, MMS also attempted to conduct both annual and periodic unscheduled (unannounced) inspections of all offshore oil and gas operations to try to assess compliance with those requirements. Agency officials have tried to meet the requirement for annual inspections of the operation of safety equipment designed to prevent blowouts, fires, spills, and other major accidents. In both annual and unannounced inspections, MMS officials used a national checklist, covering categories such as pollution, drilling, well completion, production, crane, electrical, and personal safety. Most inspections tend to cover a subset of the elements on the list. Roughly 20 percent of the matters for inspection (those for the production meters) are not related to safety.[65]

But over time, MMS increasingly fell short in its ability to oversee the offshore oil industry. The agency's resources did not keep pace with industry expansion into deeper waters and industry's related reliance on more demanding technologies. And, senior agency officials' focus on safety gave way to efforts to maximize revenue from leasing and production.

The "Safety Case" and MMS's Inability to Adopt New Practices

By the early 1990s, some MMS officials had begun to rethink the agency's approach to safety oversight of the offshore industry. In the wake of an accumulation of accidents in U.S. waters, and several devastating accidents elsewhere around the globe, they had come to appreciate that a command and control, prescriptive approach to regulation did not adequately address the risks generated by the offshore industry's new technologies and exploration, development, and production activities, including industrial expansion into deeper waters.

In March 1980, the *Alexander Kielland*—built as a drilling rig but under lease to Phillips Petroleum Company to house offshore workers at the Ekofisk Field in the Norwegian North Sea—capsized, killing 123 of the 212 people on board the "flotel." Two years

---

* Other federal agencies, including the United States Coast Guard, Department of Transportation, Occupational Safety and Health Administration, Environmental Protection Agency, and National Oceanic and Atmospheric Administration possess regulatory authority over discrete aspects of oil and gas operations offshore.

later, during preparation for an approaching North Atlantic storm, the *Ocean Ranger* semisubmersible drilling the Hibernia field for Mobil Oil of Canada, sank off the coast of Newfoundland; all 84 crew members were lost in the freezing-cold waters. And in July 1988, the Piper Alpha production platform operated by Occidental Petroleum 120 miles northeast of Aberdeen, Scotland, exploded and sank, killing 167 people, including 2 rescuers.[66] Although the causes of the three accidents varied, they all involved international operations of U.S.-based oil and gas companies. Common contributing factors included inadequate safety assurance, worker training, and evacuation procedures. Poor communication and confusion about lines of authority amplified the death toll in at least two of the accidents.

The Norwegian government responded to the loss of the *Alexander Kielland* by transforming its approach to industry operations. Under the new regime, rather than relying solely on prescribed operational and safety standards, the government required the industry to demonstrate thorough consideration of all risks associated with the structures and operations for a drilling or production plan. The regulator no longer "approved" operations. Shifting the burden of demonstrating safety to the operator, the regulator would instead now "consent" to development activity proceeding only upon the operator's demonstration that sufficient safety and risk management systems were in place.

The Piper Alpha accident and the subsequent investigation led by Lord Cullen had a similar impact on United Kingdom regulation. As in Norway, the previous prescriptive regulatory approach evolved into one where regulations were supplemented with a requirement for companies to demonstrate to the regulator that they had undertaken a thorough assessment of risks associated with an activity and they had adequate safety and risk management systems to address those risks.

All these foreign regulators—the United Kingdom, Norway, and Canada—had previously relied on the kind of prescriptive approach used in the United States, but in the aftermath of these fatal accidents in harsh, remote offshore environments, authorities elsewhere concluded that adding a risk-based approach was essential. They faulted reliance on the "prescriptive regulation with inspection model" for being fundamentally reactive and therefore incapable of driving continuous improvement in policies and practices.[67] According to Magne Ognedal, the Director General of the Norwegian Petroleum Safety Authority, the prescription-only model engendered hostility between the parties and put the risk—legal and moral—onto the *regulator* to accommodate changing technology, geology, and location, rather than onto the *operator*, where the responsibility rightly belonged.[68] Under the new safety-management model, minimum standards for structural and operational integrity (well control, prevention of fires and explosions, and worker safety) remained in place. But the burden now rested on industry to assess the risks associated with offshore activities and demonstrate that each facility had the policies, plans, and systems in place to manage those risks. In the United Kingdom, such risk-management plans were called a "Safety Case."

On March 19, 1989, while the Piper Alpha accident was still under review, a platform operated by ARCO exploded in the South Pass Block 60 off the Louisiana coast. An uncontrolled release of liquid hydrocarbons ignited, destroying the platform and killing seven people. An MMS investigation concluded that poor management of a repair operation was to blame: not only was there an "absence of detailed and coordinated planning for the project," there was a dearth of much-needed "oversight over contractor activities."[69]

After South Pass Block 60, the latest in the series of tragic accidents involving U.S-based companies, MMS convened an internal task force to review its offshore drilling inspection and enforcement program by October 1989. That same year, the agency also commissioned the Marine Board of the National Research Council to make recommendations for overhauling MMS's regulatory program to best fulfill its safety mission at current levels of staffing and budget.[70] The Marine Board's report, delivered in January 1990,[71] concluded that MMS's emphasis on a list of "potential incidents of non-compliance" could lead to an attitude on the part of an operator that compliance with the list equals safety, thereby diminishing "recognition of [the operator's] primary responsibility for safety."[72] The report recommended that MMS place its primary emphasis on the detection of potential accident-producing situations—particularly those involving human factors, operational procedures, and modification of equipment and facilities—rather than scattered instances of noncompliance with hardware specifications.

The Marine Board found that MMS needed to upgrade its program to address changes in the operating environment on the outer continental shelf—including its aging platforms, more complex systems and operations, activities in deeper water at greater distances from shore, and changing characteristics of operating companies. Further, the Board urged continuation of frequent and comprehensive inspections of facilities engaged in drilling and workover operations, including the conduct of the operations themselves, because of "(1) the high frequency of events per unit for these facilities as compared to production facilities, and (2) the large population of workers on each facility. . . ." Overall, the Board recommended that MMS cultivate a more proactive inspector corps and develop a greater focus on identifying emerging safety risks.[73]

Safety reform run aground. Unfortunately, by the time the Marine Board delivered its report, hardly anyone was listening. Five days after the South Pass Block tragedy in March 1989, the *Exxon Valdez* ran aground in Prince William Sound, spilling an estimated 11 million gallons of crude oil on the Alaskan shore. The Board's calls for change were thus presented to a government still preoccupied with cleanup duties in Prince William Sound and to a nation attuned to demands for requiring double-hulled tankers. Ironically, Congress enacted the Oil Pollution Act of 1990, but failed to address *any* of the regulatory deficiencies identified by the Marine Board, while *adding* to MMS's regulatory responsibilities (the agency was charged, under the Act and a supplementary Presidential Executive Order[74] with overseeing offshore pipelines and oil-spill response planning and prevention).[75] The agency's already scarce regulatory resources were stretched even thinner.

MMS nonetheless tried to take the initiative for regulatory reform. In July 1991, in response to the Marine Board report and MMS's own internal task force report, MMS published a notice requesting comments on alternative strategies to promote safety and environmental protection, specifically a requirement that outer continental shelf lessees and/or operators develop, maintain, and implement "a safety and environmental management program (SEMP), similar to the United Kingdom's Formal Safety Assessment or Norway's Concept Safety Evaluation programs."[76] Declaring that lessees and operators already had "full responsibility to plan and prepare for the overall safety and reliability of Outer Continental Shelf operations," MMS asserted that requiring SEMP would help to enhance offshore safety and environmental protection.[77] Acknowledging the difference in scale and scope of the activities between the Gulf of Mexico and the North Sea—as the Gulf consists of many more, but smaller facilities[78]—MMS sought in its request for comments "to determine the degree to which such programs exist and to draw upon that experience in establishing the requirements for a management control program."[79]

Reform indefinitely frozen in time. At the time of the Macondo blowout—almost 20 years after its original proposal—MMS had still not published a rule mandating that all operators have plans to manage safety and environmental risks. The agency's efforts to adopt a more rigorous and effective risk-based safety regulatory regime were repeatedly revisited, refined, delayed, and blocked alternatively by industry or skeptical agency political appointees.[80] MMS thus never achieved the reform of its regulatory oversight of drilling safety consonant with practices that most other countries had embraced decades earlier.

Industry served as an initial impediment to MMS reform efforts—and has largely remained so. In late 1991, the American Petroleum Institute asked the agency to postpone action in order to allow the institute itself to develop an offshore safety standard.[81] MMS agreed, and actively participated in the institute's committee-based process over the next two years. The American Petroleum Institute's "recommended practice" guidance document was published in May 1993—the same month that the UK Safety Case regulations came into force.[82] Missing from the first edition of the Institute's guideline, however, was a key element of standard process safety management[83]—nor did it even cover drilling rigs,[84] clearly an integral element in operating offshore.

MMS announced in June 1994 that it would continue evaluating the new safety concept for two additional years in order to determine whether it should be mandated[85]—a deadline it soon extended by yet another year, delaying a final decision until late 1997.[86] In the meantime, the agency urged companies to adopt safety and environmental management systems voluntarily, and hinted that wide industry participation might prevent a formal rulemaking.[87]

By this time, there appears to have been a working assumption within both the agency and the industry it was charged with overseeing that technological advances had made equipment remarkably reliable. As one MMS official put it in 1996, conceding that the best the agency could do with available resources was to encourage voluntary compliance with SEMP, "We want to approach our relationship with the offshore industry more as a partner than a policeman. We need to create an atmosphere where the primary concern is to fix the problem, not the blame"—an apt characterization for a period of "regulatory reform" in Congress and fiscal restraint nationwide.[88]

Holy Grail or Poisoned Chalice? The MMS voluntary approach to risk assessment was met with skepticism by regulators in the North Sea. At a May 1996 industry forum in Houston, Texas, an official with the UK Health and Safety Executive (HSE) compared the two safety regimes in a presentation titled *US Voluntary SEMP Initiative: Holy Grail or Poisoned Chalice?* "Last year, with the safety cases of most UK rigs already accepted well ahead of the deadline, IADC [the International Association of Drilling Contractors] told us they were pleased to be operating a premium fleet in North Sea and that HSE was not to think of relaxing the safety case requirements." By contrast, he described the voluntary SEMP scheme as an unrealistic halfway position, while noting that "both the US and the UK need more time to find out which way provides the best lasting effect."[89]

Almost a decade later, MMS was no more successful when it tried to resurrect movement toward even a weakened version of a safety and environmental management rule. In May 2006, when MMS finally proposed a rule on "Safety and Environmental Management Systems"—the successor to the long-moribund SEMP initiative—its proposed rule was limited in its reach. The proposal would have required that only 4 of the 12 widely accepted elements of industrial process safety management be put into place. Industry opposition even to this watered-down proposal was swift. And, ultimately, it was only after the Macondo well blowout four years later that the federal agency finalized a more comprehensive, mandatory SEMP rule.

Other MMS regulatory initiatives critical to safety faced strong and effective opposition. In 2003, the White House stiffly opposed MMS's efforts to update its requirements for the reporting of key risk indicators.[90] (MMS had proposed that *all* unintentional gas releases be reported, because even small gas leaks can lead to explosions.[91]) "It was like pulling teeth," one senior MMS official involved with the process told the Commission: "We never got positive cooperation" from either industry or the Office of Management and Budget.[92] The Offshore Operators Committee, an industry association, vehemently objected that the requirement would be too burdensome and not conducive to safety; MMS disagreed, yet the final rule in 2006 mandated that a gas release be reported to MMS only if it resulted in an "equipment or process shut-in," or mechanical closure—a much less complete standard.[93]

Safety Regulation on a Starvation Diet
During the 1990s, the resources available to MMS decreased precipitously just as it faced a dramatic increase in the offshore activity it was charged with overseeing—and matters only deteriorated thereafter. Perversely, MMS's budget reached its lowest point in November 1996,[94] just as major development activities in deepwater were expanding. That December, the *Houston Chronicle* reported with tragic detail an 81 percent increase in offshore fires, explosions, and blowouts in the Gulf since 1992.[95] The oil and gas industry drilled a record number of Gulf wells in 1997—many in deepwater.[96] By 1999, oil production from deepwater eclipsed production from shallow water for the first

FIGURE 3.3: MMS Budget and Gulf of Mexico Crude Oil Production, 1984-2009

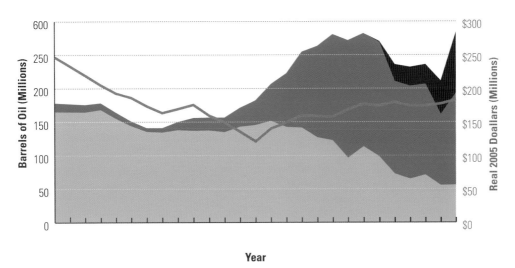

Year

- ● Ultra-Deep (5,000+ ft)
- ● Deep (1,000–4,999 ft)
- ● Shallow (0–999 ft)
- — OEMM Enacted Budget

Sources: "Budget Division: Congressional Budget Justifications," Bureau of Ocean Energy Management, Regulation, and Enforcement, http://www.boemre.gov/adm/budget.html; Minerals Management Service, *Deepwater Gulf of Mexico 2009: Interim Report of 2008 Highlights,* (May 2009), 71-72, http://www.gomr.boemre.gov/PDFs/2009/2009-016.pdf; U.S. Energy Information Administration, *This Week in Petroleum: Production, Proved Reserves and Drilling in the Ultra-Deepwater Gulf of Mexico,* (May 26, 2010), http://www.eia.gov/oog/info/twip/twiparch/100526/twipprint.html.

In the last twenty years, MMS's leasing, environmental, and regulatory budget decreased or remained static while deepwater oil production in the Gulf of Mexico boomed. Note: OEMM (Office of Energy and Minerals Management) has responsibility for renewable energy, leasing and environmental, resource evaluation, regulatory, and information management programs. It does not include revenue management or general administration.

time.[97] Oil production in the Gulf grew from 275 million barrels in 1990 (when only 4.4 percent of that volume came from deepwater wells) to 567 million barrels in 2009 (when deepwater wells yielded more than 80 percent of the total).[98]

Changing technology and changing industry structure outpacing regulations. As MMS's resources lagged behind the industry's expansion into deepwater drilling—with its larger-scale and more demanding technology, greater pressures, and increasing distance from shore-based infrastructure and environmental and safety resources—the agency's ability to do its job was seriously compromised.[99] Of particular concern, MMS was unable to maintain up-to-date technical drilling-safety requirements to keep up with industry's rapidly evolving deepwater technology. As drilling technology evolved, many aspects of drilling lacked corresponding safety regulations. The regulations increasingly lagged behind industry and what was happening in the field.

When industry contended that blowout-preventer stacks—the critical last line of defense in maintaining control over a well—were more reliable than the regulations recognized, warranting less frequent pressure testing, MMS conceded and halved the mandated

Drill Pipe

Waiting their turn, lengths of colored drill pipe stack up aboard a Transocean rig. Independent studies suggest that failures of crucial blowout preventer components could be caused in part by industry-driven changes to drill-pipe strength and configuration.

Derick E. Hingle/Bloomberg via Getty Images

frequency of tests.[100]* Soon afterward, a series of third-party technical studies raised the possibility of high failure rates for the blowout preventers' control systems, annular rams, and blind-shear rams under certain deepwater conditions and due to changes in the configuration and strength of drill pipe used by industry.[101] Two studies commissioned by MMS found that many rig operators, by not testing blowout preventers, were basing their representations that the tool would work "on information not necessarily consistent with the equipment in use."[102] Yet, MMS never revised its blowout-preventer regulations nor added verification as an independent inspection item in light of this new information.[103]

Nor did MMS adapt its regulatory framework in response to significant ways in which the oil and gas industry has changed over time. In particular, the industry has witnessed a rise in specialized service contractors, such as Halliburton and Transocean that serviced BP at the Macondo well. When the lessee directly regulated by the government is itself not performing many of the activities critical to well safety, that separation of functions poses heightened challenges for the regulator. But there was no apparent effort by MMS to respond to those challenges by making the service companies more accountable.

Permit "shopping." With increasing industry activity, MMS regulators could not possibly keep pace. The oil and gas industry works 24/7, but MMS regulators generally work regular office hours, requiring "on-call" responsibility to be assigned to individual senior engineers. Those engineers, however, work at a marked disadvantage because they cannot gain access to the permit database from off-site locations due to security concerns.[104] Even during normal business hours, the Gulf of Mexico office lacks a sufficient number of engineers to process permit reviews with necessary scrutiny. From 2005 to 2009, the number of applications for drilling permits in just the MMS New Orleans District increased 71 percent: from 1,246 to 2,136.[105] Without enough engineers in the Gulf of Mexico district office to process all the applications, some operators literally "shop around." They "contact district offices outside the appropriate jurisdictional area . . . to find an engineer who will eventually give approval."[106]

Inspections forgone. Not surprisingly, with diminished resources, MMS inspections became less effective, as the Interior Department's Inspector General reported in 1999.[107]

FIGURE 3.4: MMS Inspections in the Gulf of Mexico, 1990-2009

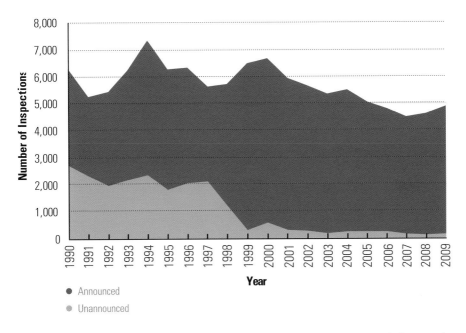

Source: Bureau of Ocean Energy Management, Regulation, and Enforcement data upon National Commission Staff request to the Department of the Interior.

"Unannounced" or surprise inspections of offshore oil and gas activity grew increasingly rare over time. Less than 3% of MMS inspections conducted in 2009 were unannounced.

The frequency of unannounced inspections plummeted.[108] Although the raw incident data are online, MMS last produced an analysis of offshore incidents—critical data for promoting the safety of offshore operations—for calendar year 2000.[109] And MMS's progressive reduction in oversight relative to the level of industry activity occurred just as the industry struggled to find highly trained staff needed to work the expanding population of deepwater drilling rigs.[110] Precisely when the need for regulatory oversight intensified, the government's capacity for oversight diminished.

Overlaps and "underlaps." The lack of resources extended beyond MMS. The United States Coast Guard is responsible for regulating the "safety of life and property on Outer Continental Shelf (OCS) facilities, vessels, and other units engaged in OCS activities."[111] Because most drilling rigs and even some production platforms fall under the definition of "vessels," part of the responsibility for regulating their safe operation (and full authority for certifying their seaworthiness) is within the jurisdiction of the Coast Guard.[112] But just when the need for Coast Guard oversight increased during the 1990s—as industry drilled in deeper waters farther offshore and used more ambitious floating drilling and production systems—it, too, faced more severe budgetary restraints. Accordingly, the Coast Guard failed to update its marine-safety rules—the last major revision was in 1982[113]—to reflect the industry's new technology. The resource plight worsened further following the terrorist attacks of September 11, 2001, given the nation's overriding need to focus on border and port security. The Coast Guard's "solution"—to transfer much of its responsibility for fixed platform safety to MMS in 2002[114]—eerily echoed earlier cycles of expanding MMS's mandate in the face of inadequate resources, stretching its capabilities thinner still. The practical effect of the Coast Guard and MMS's shared responsibility for offshore safety has been the presence of "overlaps" in jurisdiction that have required the renegotiation of informal interagency agreements ever since 1989—the continuance of which has left MMS with "underlaps" in resources.[115]

The Culture of Revenue Maximization

When Interior Secretary Watt moved regulatory oversight of offshore energy exploration and production to a new entity that was also responsible for collecting revenue from the activity it regulated, he created a new agency that inexorably came to be dominated by its focus on maximizing that revenue.

For at least the past 15 years, every former MMS Director has freely acknowledged that the royalty issues have taken most of the Director's time—at the expense of offshore regulatory oversight.[116] In 1995, as the United States faced global competition for oil exploration and development capital during a period of low prices, Congress enacted the Deep Water Royalty Relief Act.[117] It provided a suspension of royalty payments on a portion of new production from deepwater operations.

But when prices and volumes increased, the sheer amount of money at stake—literally billions of dollars (MMS total onshore and offshore revenues for 2008 were $23 billion[118])—compelled even greater attention, as the White House, members of Congress, and certainly the states each advanced competing notions of how those sums might best be spent.* Litigation, new regulations, and legislation designed to increase one party's relative share of such massive sums have been a constant feature of managing the flow of royalties from onshore and offshore energy production. Such disputes have invariably been controversial, politically sensitive, and time-consuming for MMS decisionmakers.[119]

Agency leadership and technical expertise. Agency personnel naturally look to agency leadership to signal what constitutes their primary mission, including the expertise and experience that such leaders bring with them. In the case of MMS, those signals were profoundly disturbing, yet nonetheless consistent over time. No one who has led MMS since it was created almost 30 years ago has possessed significant training or experience in petroleum engineering or petroleum geology, or any significant technical expertise related to drilling safety.

In the absence of a clear statement from the top about the necessity for such expertise to ensure drilling safety, it should be no surprise that MMS personnel have suffered from the loss of essential expertise throughout their ranks. Indeed, the lack of requisite training is abysmal. According to a recent survey conducted at the request of the Secretary of the Interior, "[a]lmost half of the [MMS] inspectors surveyed do not believe they have received sufficient training." MMS, unlike Interior's Bureau of Land Management (which

---

* Because of a bureaucratic mistake within Interior, however, federal lease sales held in 1998 and 1999 failed to include price thresholds in each lease, meaning that those lessees received relief from royalty payments even though higher oil prices made such relief wholly unnecessary. The Government Accountability Office has estimated that the error could cost the government at least $10 billion and perhaps as much as $80 billion. Government Accountability Office, "Oil and Gas Royalties – Royalty Relief Will Likely Cost the Government Billions, but the Final Costs Have Yet to Be Determined" (January 18, 2007), 3, 5.

inspects onshore oil and gas drilling operations), has no "oil and gas inspection certification program" and no exam "is required of each inspector in order to be certified." MMS "does not provide formal training specific to the inspections process, and does not keep up with changing technology. Some inspectors noted that they rely on industry representatives to explain the technology at a facility."[120]

The Macondo well blowout makes all too clear the cost of such a departure from the standards of excellence that the nation expects from its public servants. As described in Chapter 4, the MMS personnel responsible for reviewing the permit applications submitted to MMS for the Macondo well were neither required nor prepared to evaluate the aspects of that drilling operation that were in fact critical to ensuring well safety. The regulations did not mandate that MMS regulators inquire into the specifics of "rupture disks," "long string" well designs, cementing process, the use of centralizers, lockdown sleeves, or the temporary abandonment procedures (see Chapter 4). And, no doubt for that same reason, the MMS personnel responsible for deciding whether the necessary drilling permits were granted lacked the expertise that would have been necessary in any event to determine the relative safety of the well based on any of these factors.*

Agency integrity and pockets of corruption. The preoccupation with revenues did not merely divert MMS leaders' attention from drilling safety. It also allowed the ethical culture to degenerate in a few isolated offices, leading to serious charges of abuse of government authority and even charges of criminal misconduct by a few individuals. This conduct was far removed from the daily work of almost all those agency personnel who performed regulatory oversight of offshore drilling. But the conduct of a few working elsewhere in the agency unfairly cast a cloud over the agency as a whole, especially in the immediate aftermath of the Macondo well blowout, providing a ready reminder of the critical importance of public trust in the management of the nation's resources.

The most notorious example arose from the "royalty in kind" program, based in Denver, Colorado. Under the program, MMS exercised its option to accept royalty payments "in kind" rather than in cash.† A September 2008 Inspector General's report implicated more than a dozen employees in the Denver royalty-in-kind office in unethical and criminal conduct.[121] Those MMS staff had also socialized with, and received a wide array of gifts from, companies with whom they were conducting business. The Inspector General further acknowledged that although "99.9 percent of [Interior] employees are hard-working, ethical, and well-intentioned[,] . . . the conduct of a few has cast a shadow on an entire bureau."[122]

Nor was unethical conduct limited to MMS's revenue collections. It extended to some of those who worked on overseeing offshore oil and gas activities in the Gulf of Mexico. An Inspector General's investigation in 2010 revealed that prior to 2007, "a culture of

---

* See, *e.g.*, Written submission to the National Commission from MMS permitting official, November 5, 2010 ("I did not know they were using nitrogen foamed cement. . . . [I]t would not have mattered under the regulations. We do not do any evaluations of types of cement."); *id.* ("I do not recall them informing me as to why they decided not to drill to that length. . . . We do not need an explanation as to why a well is not drilled to the proposed depth.").; *id.* ("At the time I reviewed the APD [drilling permit application], my knowledge of rupture disks was limited to what I had learned from the previous drilling engineer when working with him learning the review process."); *id.* ("I did not receive training on lock down sleeve setting procedures.").

†The royalty-in-kind program allowed MMS to market the natural gas or oil to establish a reference against which it could evaluate industry reports of their market value.

accepting gifts from oil and gas companies was prevalent throughout the MMS Lake Charles[, Louisiana] office." "[A] number of MMS employees at th[at] district office admitted to attending sporting events prior to 2007 in which oil and gas production companies sponsored teams, as well as receiving lunches and accepting gifts." The investigation found that one employee had conducted inspections on a company's oil platforms while in the process of negotiating (and later accepting employment) with the company.[123] Here again, the actions of a few damaged the reputation of the agency as a whole, and demoralized the vast majority of MMS employees who avoided such conflicts.[124] In January 2009, only days after taking office, Secretary Salazar met with MMS employees and announced an ethics reform initiative in response to the problems identified at MMS and elsewhere in the agency.[125]

Mismanagement and Misdirection

Perhaps because of the cumulative lack of adequate resources, absence of a sustained agency mission, or sheer erosion of professional culture within some offices, MMS came progressively to suffer from serious deficiencies of organization and management: the fundamental traits of any effective institution. According to the Outer Continental Shelf Safety Oversight Board,* MMS lacks "a formal, bureau-wide compilation of rules, regulations, policies, or practices pertinent to inspections, nor does it have a comprehensive handbook addressing inspector roles and responsibilities." As a result, the Board concluded, "policies and enforcement mechanisms vary among the [Gulf of Mexico] districts and the regions, and there is no formal process to promote standardization, consistency, and operational efficiency."[126]

The Safety Oversight Board singled out MMS's handling of inspections for pointed criticism. For example, management promoted inspections by single inspectors in order to increase the total number of inspections, even though "most inspectors interviewed said that two-person teams would increase efficiencies, eliminate reliance on an operator representative for observations on safety tests, improve the thoroughness of the inspection, and reduce the ability of operators to successfully pressure an inspector not to issue [a citation]." The Board's interviews revealed "staff concerns regarding a perceived emphasis on the quantity rather than quality of inspection."[127]

The agency's management shortcomings were underscored, and compounded, by lack of communication and inconsistencies among its three regional offices for the Gulf of Mexico, the Pacific, and Alaska. The directors of each regional office naturally adapted practices to best suit the specific characteristics and needs of the region. But by acting in parallel fashion, with little coordination in decisionmaking and resource allocation, program implementation, regulatory interpretation, and enforcement policies became inconsistent, undermining the integrity of MMS's work.[128] For example, the Safety Oversight Board found that "the Pacific Region employs 5 inspectors to inspect 23 production facilities—a ratio of 1 inspector for every 5 facilities. By contrast, the [Gulf of Mexico Region] employs 55 inspectors to inspect about 3,000 facilities—a ratio of 1 inspector for every 54 facilities." [129]

---

* Secretary Salazar created the Outer Continental Shelf Safety Oversight Board in the immediate aftermath of the Macondo well blowout and charged the Board with reviewing the effectiveness of MMS's management. The Board issued its report on September 1, 2010.

Ultimately, MMS was unable to ensure that its staffing capabilities and competencies kept pace with the changing risks and volume of offshore activity. As the Safety Oversight Board concluded, the Gulf of Mexico "district offices did not have a sufficient number of engineers to efficiently and effectively conduct permit reviews."[130] As the Chief of the U.S. Geological Survey's Conservation Division had warned nearly 30 years earlier,[131] salaries—for engineers stuck in the midranges of the federal pay scale—were far too low to attract individuals possessing the experience and expertise needed to oversee the increasingly complicated oil and gas drilling activities in the deepwater Gulf.[132] At the most elementary level, MMS frequently lacked defined qualifications that new employees must meet before they start performing their jobs, or clear procedures for on-the-job training. The Board report further observed that the "amount of time and the structure of this training vary from office to office and from inspector to inspector," and it concluded that the on-the-job training "does not address the need for substantive, consistent training in all aspects of the job."[133]

An Environment Unfavorable to Responsible Drilling

Erosion of Environmental-Protection Safeguards in the Gulf of Mexico

Even as oversight of drilling safety became less effective while the industry pursued more demanding deepwater plays in the Gulf of Mexico, environmental safeguards eroded, too—putting the rich natural resources of the Gulf waters and the surrounding coasts at increasing risk.

The legislative promise. The 1978 Outer Continental Shelf Lands Act Amendments promised full consideration of concerns for environmental protection. The Act provides that "[m]anagement of the outer Continental Shelf shall be conducted in a manner which considers economic, social, and environmental values of the renewable and nonrenewable resources contained in the outer Continental Shelf, and the potential impact of oil and gas exploration on other resource values of the outer Continental Shelf and the marine, coastal, and human environments."[134] It further requires that the timing and location of exploration, development, and production of oil and gas take environmental factors into consideration, including: existing ecological characteristics; an equitable sharing of development benefits and environmental risks among the regions; the relative environmental sensitivity and marine productivity of areas; and relevant environmental and predictive information.[135] Based on an evaluation of these and other factors, the Act directs the Secretary of the Interior to select the "timing and location of leasing, to the maximum extent practicable, so as to obtain a proper balance between the potential for environmental damage, the potential for the discovery of oil and gas, and the potential for adverse impact on the coastal zone."[136]

A host of other laws, many enacted by Congress during the 1970s surge of environmental legislation, buttress these promised priorities. Of particular relevance to oil and gas leasing on the outer continental shelf is the National Environmental Policy Act requirement that federal agencies prepare environmental impact statements for all major federal actions significantly affecting the human environment.[137] Those detailed statements must include not only discussion of the immediate adverse impacts on the natural environment that might result from the federal action, but also the "socio-economic"* effects of those impacts.[138] The Magnuson-Stevens Fishery Conservation and Management Act requires agencies to analyze the potentially adverse impacts of oil and gas activities on fish habitat and populations, and provide conservation measures to mitigate those impacts.[139] The Endangered Species Act requires federal agencies to determine the potential adverse impact of oil and gas activities on endangered and threatened species, limits activities that harm individual members of such species, and bars altogether activities that place such species in jeopardy.[140] The Marine Mammal Protection Act imposes limits on activities that injure or even harass marine mammals.[141] The National Marine Sanctuaries Act requires consultations to guard against harm to marine sanctuary resources from oil and gas leasing activities.[142] The federal Clean Water Act imposes permitting requirements on any discharge of pollutants into navigable waters from such activities.[143] And, the Oil Pollution Act of 1990,[144] supplemented by a Presidential Executive Order,[145] imposes a panoply of oil-spill planning, preparedness, and response requirements on fixed and floating facilities engaged in oil and gas exploration, development, and production on the outer continental shelf.

Promise vs. practice. But some of these apparent statutory promises dim upon closer examination. The Outer Continental Shelf Lands Act routinely requires consideration of environmental protection concerns in leasing location and timing—but ultimately gives the Secretary of the Interior tremendous discretion in deciding what weight to give those concerns.[146] The balance ultimately struck depends largely on the politics of the moment. The Secretary can assign significant weight to environmental protection concerns—or not.

And in fact, parts of the 1978 Act arguably stack the deck *against* full consideration of environmental concerns. For instance, the law provides that the Secretary must approve a lessee's exploration plan within 30 days of submission.[147] If environmental review is to occur after plan submission, that timetable effectively precludes the kind of exacting review necessary to ensure that the Act's environmental safeguards can be achieved. It would, in effect, be a statement by Congress that the rush to energy exploration is too important to be delayed.

The Act also expressly singles out the Gulf of Mexico for less rigorous environmental oversight under NEPA. As a result of political compromise with oil and gas interests, the Act exempts lessees from submitting development and production plans (which include environmental safeguards) for agency approval. Accordingly, Gulf leases, unlike those applicable to other offshore areas, are not subject to the requirement of at least one NEPA environmental impact statement for development plans for a particular geographic area.[148]

None of the other statutes includes such a stark exception, but their effects still are more limited than it might at first seem. For instance, both the Endangered Species Act and the

---

* As the Macondo well blowout makes clear, the socio-economic effects of an oil spill are hardly an incidental concern. As described in Chapter 6, the economic costs of the spill to the Gulf states can be measured in the billions of dollars. Yet absent careful NEPA review, there are no assurances that these potential consequences of a decision to lease, explore, develop, or drill in any given location will be carefully considered by the governmental decisionmaker before the decision is made.

Clean Water Act impose tough substantive limits on activities. But each has only a narrow, discrete focus and statutory trigger: threats to endangered or threatened species or their critical habitat under the Endangered Species Act or, under the Clean Water Act, only the incidental aspects of oil and gas activities that discharge pollutants into navigable waters (unless, of course there is an oil spill).

Neither the Magnuson-Stevens Act nor the Marine Sanctuaries law imposes any mandatory substantive limitation on oil and gas activities offshore. Each instead authorizes the National Oceanic and Atmospheric Administration (NOAA) to make recommendations to MMS about possible adverse environmental impacts (to fish habitat and marine sanctuaries) and appropriate conservation measures. Congress clearly assigned NOAA this central role because it is the federal agency most expert on ocean science and has a clear mission to serve as the steward safeguarding the nation's ocean resources. But, notwithstanding that assignment, neither law provides any corresponding obligation on the part of MMS to heed NOAA's advice. MMS can, and has, on occasion given little or no weight to NOAA's views; according to NOAA officials, that causes some NOAA scientists to expend fewer resources on generating such views.

As a result, although the various laws create the potential for comprehensive environmental protection in oil and gas drilling on the outer continental shelf, neither alone nor in combination do any of the laws come close to *ensuring* a reasonable level of overall environmental protection applicable to all aspects of oil and gas activities on the outer continental shelf. Whether they have achieved their statutory objectives has therefore historically depended instead entirely on the discretionary determinations of MMS officials.

Limiting NEPA. The Department of the Interior and MMS also took a series of steps that further limited the potential for NEPA to ensure government decisions were based on full consideration of their environmental consequences. Erosion of NEPA's application to offshore oil and gas activities began, as noted, when Congress exempted a category of leasing activities in the Gulf of Mexico from NEPA review. The Interior Department, however, subsequently took that legislative exemption and unilaterally expanded its scope beyond those original legislative terms.

Although the 1978 Act exempted only the Interior Department's review of a lessee's "development and production plan" from the environmental impact statement process, Interior unilaterally extended that exemption. In January 1981, the Department promulgated final rules declaring that exploration plans in the central and western Gulf of Mexico were "categorically excluded" from NEPA review.* At that same time, the Department also categorically excluded from NEPA review applications to drill wells (for exploration or subsequent development and production of oil and gas) "when said well and appropriate mitigation measures are described in an approved exploration plan, development plan, or production plan."[149] In 1986, MMS scaled back the categorical

---

* The President's Council on Environmental Quality, which is responsible for the administration of NEPA, has promulgated a regulation that permits agencies to create "categorical exclusions" from NEPA review for categories of minor activities that can be reasonably assumed in advance not to have significant environmental impacts. See 40 C.F.R. § 1508.4.

exclusion to account for the possibility that NEPA review would be needed for these activities in certain narrowly defined "extraordinary circumstances." Extraordinary circumstances include those actions that have highly uncertain and potentially significant environmental effects or involve unique or unknown environmental risks.[150]

But because MMS personnel were apparently reluctant to conclude that such extraordinary circumstances were present, the rule in practice in the Gulf of Mexico was the categorical *exclusion*—rather than the *exception* to that exclusion. MMS staff have reported that leasing coordinators and managers discouraged them from reaching conclusions about potential environmental impacts that would increase the burden on lessees, "thus causing unnecessary delays for operators." The Safety Oversight Board also noted that "[s]ome [MMS] environmental staff also reported that environmental assessments for smaller operators may be minimized if the [Regional Office of Field Operations] manager determines that implementing the recommendation may be too costly."[151]

With regard to NEPA specifically, some MMS managers reportedly "changed or minimized the [MMS] scientists' potential environmental impact findings in [NEPA] documents to expedite plan approvals." According to several MMS environmental scientists, "their managers believed the result of NEPA evaluations should always be a 'green light' to proceed." In some cases, there may also have been built-in employee financial incentives that "distort[ed] balanced decision-making" to the extent that "[e]mployee performance plans and monetary awards [were] . . . based on meeting deadlines for leasing or development approvals."[152]

Finally, just as a matter of sheer practicality, MMS personnel plainly lacked the substantial resources that would have been required to engage in meaningful NEPA review in light of the extraordinary expansion of leasing activity in the Gulf. There were literally hundreds of exploration, development, and production plans, as well as individual permit drilling applications to be processed. No President ever sought for MMS the level of resources that would have been required to prepare individual assessments concerning whether each of those activities required an environmental impact statement, let alone such a statement for those that did. Nor did Congress. It should be no surprise under such circumstances that a culture of complacency with regard to NEPA developed within MMS, notwithstanding the best intentions of many MMS environmental scientists.

The Macondo Well

The gap between the protections promised by environmental statutes and regulations and actual practice is fully illustrated in the review and permitting of the Macondo well itself. MMS engaged in no NEPA review of the well's permitting, and neither MMS nor other federal agencies gave significant attention to the environmental mandates of other federal laws.

NEPA. MMS performed no meaningful NEPA review of the potentially significant adverse environmental consequences associated with its permitting for drilling of BP's exploratory Macondo well. MMS categorically excluded from environmental impact review BP's initial and revised exploration plans—even though the exploration plan could have qualified for an "extraordinary circumstances" exception to such exclusion, in light of the abundant deep-sea life in that geographic area and the biological and geological complexity of that same area.[153] MMS similarly categorically excluded from any NEPA review the multiple applications for drilling permits and modification of drilling permits associated with the Macondo well. The justification for these exclusions was that MMS had already conducted NEPA reviews for both the Five-Year Program and the Lease Sale that applied to the Macondo well. The flaw in that agency logic is that both those prior NEPA reviews were conducted on a broad programmatic basis, covering huge expanses of leased areas of which the Macondo well was a relatively incidental part. Neither, moreover, included a "worst case analysis" because the President's Council on Environmental Quality had eliminated the requirement for such analysis under NEPA for all federal agencies in 1986.[154] As a result, none of those prior programmatic reviews carefully considered site-specific factors relevant to the risks presented by the drilling of the Macondo well.*

Fishery conservation and management. Under the Magnuson-Stevens Fishery Conservation and Management Act, federal agencies must consult with NOAA on all activities (or proposed activities) authorized, funded, or undertaken by the agency that may adversely affect essential fish habitat. For the Gulf of Mexico, accordingly, NOAA prepared a "programmatic" Essential Fish Habitat Consultation for the entire Gulf.[155] To similar effect, MMS complied with the Magnuson-Stevens consultation requirement by preparing Essential Fish Habitat Assessments that looked at offshore oil and gas leasing activities in the Gulf broadly.[156] Neither NOAA nor MMS considered the possible adverse impacts of any one well, such as the Macondo well, in isolation. Nor would it have been practical for them to do so in light of their understandable focus on possible cumulative impacts on fish populations from many offshore leasing activities. What is more telling, however, is that to the extent that the MMS Assessment identified potential threats to essential fish habitat and marine fishery resources from oil spills, both NOAA and MMS ultimately relied exclusively on conservation measures included in oil-spill response plans prepared by the oil and gas industry pursuant to the Oil Pollution Act of 1990 to address those threats.[157] For the Macondo well, both agencies assumed that BP's plan would adequately address those threats and therefore there was no need to seek to do so directly through the Magnuson-Stevens Act. There was, however, little reason to assume that those plans were in fact up to the task.

Oil Pollution Act of 1990 and Oil Spill Response Plans. Under the Oil Pollution Act of 1990, as supplemented by a Presidential Executive Order, MMS is responsible for oil-spill planning and preparedness as well as select response activities for fixed and floating facilities engaged in exploration, development, and production of liquid hydrocarbons and for certain oil pipelines. The agency requires all owners or operators of offshore oil-handling, storage, or transportation facilities to prepare Oil Spill Response Plans. MMS regulations detail the elements of the response plan (an emergency-response action plan, oil-spill response equipment inventory, oil-spill response contractual agreements, a

---

* For instance, bluefin tuna are both commercially vital and biologically significant as predators in the Gulf. But in the relevant Five-Year (2007–2012) Programmatic Environmental Impact Statement on the entire offshore leasing program—covering the *entire* outer continental shelf of the United States—MMS discusses potential impacts of leasing activities on bluefin tuna in one sentence. Subsequent MMS environmental impact statements for lease sales within the Gulf of Mexico contained *no* significant or geographically-focused analysis of the potential impacts on bluefin tuna. And, in finally permitting the drilling of the Macondo well, MMS categorically excluded the action from any NEPA review, and thus conducted no analysis of the potential impacts of drilling on bluefin tuna, based on the rationale that it had already adequately reviewed environmental impacts in its prior reviews.

calculation of the worst-case discharge scenario, plan for dispersant use, in-situ burning plan, and information regarding oil-spill response training and drills).[158] The emergency-response plan is supposed to be the core of the overall plan, and in turn is required to include information regarding the spill-response team; the types and characteristics of oil at the facilities; procedures for early detection of a spill; and procedures to be followed in the case of a spill.[159]

But neither BP, in crafting its Oil Spill Response Plan for the Gulf of Mexico applicable to the Macondo well, nor MMS in approving it, evidenced serious attention to detail.[160] For instance, the BP plan identified three different worst-case scenarios that ranged from 28,033 to 250,000 barrels of oil discharge and used identical language to "analyze" the shoreline impacts under each scenario.[161] To the same effect, half of the "Resource Identification" appendix (five pages) to the BP Oil Spill Response Plan was copied from material on NOAA websites, without any discernible effort to determine the applicability of that information to the Gulf of Mexico. As a result, the BP Oil Spill Response Plan described biological resources nonexistent in the Gulf—including sea lions, sea otters, and walruses.*

Even more troubling, the MMS Gulf of Mexico Regional Office approved the BP plan without additional analysis. There is little in that approval to suggest that BP and MMS gave close scrutiny to the contents of the Oil Spill Response Plan. The Regional Office's routine practice was to review and approve oil-spill response plans within 30 days of their receipt. Absent any legal requirement to do so, the office did not distribute submitted plans to other federal agencies for review or comment, nor did it seek public review or comment.

The inescapable conclusion is striking, and profoundly unsettling. Notwithstanding statutory promises of layers of required environmental scrutiny—by NEPA, the Magnuson-Stevens Act, the Outer Continental Shelf Lands Act, and the Oil Pollution Act—and the potential application of some of the nation's toughest environmental restrictions—the Endangered Species Act and Clean Water Act—*none* of these laws resulted in site-specific review of the drilling operations of the Macondo well. The agency in charge, MMS, lacked the resources and committed agency culture to do so, and none of the other federal agencies with relevant environmental expertise had adequate resources or sufficient statutory authority to make sure the resulting gap in attention to environmental protection concerns was filled.†

Federal oversight of oil and gas activities in the Gulf of Mexico—almost the only area where substantial amounts of drilling were taking place—took a generally minimalist approach in the years leading up to the Macondo explosion. The national government failed to exercise the full scope of its power, grounded both in its role as owner of the natural resources to be developed and in its role as sovereign and responsible for ensuring the safety of drilling operations. Many aspects of national environmental law

---

* The BP plan does not appear to be an aberration. It was prepared by a contractor who also prepared the Gulf of Mexico plans for Chevron, ConocoPhillips, ExxonMobil, Shell, and other companies operating in the Gulf. The result is four nearly identical plans that repeat the same mistakes found in the BP plan applicable to the Macondo well.

† The President's decision in March 2010 to expand offshore oil and gas leasing is a more recent example of the absence of full consideration of environmental protection concerns. According to their testimony before the Commission in August 2010, the White House did not ask either the Chair of the President's Council on Environmental Quality or the Administrator of NOAA to be directly involved in reviewing the plans before the President's decision. See Testimony of The Honorable Nancy Sutley, Chair, Council on Environmental Quality, and The Honorable Jane Lubchenco, Administrator, NOAA, Hearing before the National Commission, August 25, 2010.

were ignored, resulting in less oversight than would have applied in other areas of the country. In addition, MMS lacked the resources and technical expertise, beginning with its leadership, to require rigorous standards of safety in the risky deepwater and had fallen behind other countries in its ability to move beyond a prescription and inspection system to one that would be based on more sophisticated risk analysis.

In short, the safety risks had dramatically increased with the shift to the Gulf's deepwaters, but Presidents, members of Congress, and agency leadership had become preoccupied for decades with the enormous revenues generated by such drilling rather than focused on ensuring its safety. With the benefit of hindsight, the only question had become not whether an accident would happen, but when. On April 20, 2010, that question was answered.

Part II

Explosion and Aftermath: The Causes and Consequences of the Disaster

The loss of control of the Macondo well; the resulting explosion, fire, and destruction of the *Deepwater Horizon* rig; and the ensuing spill of nearly 5 million barrels of oil before the well was capped on July 15 reflect specific decisions about well design, construction, monitoring, and testing. The Commission's detailed analysis (Chapter 4) explains those actions in the context of this specific reservoir and subsurface geology as well as the regulatory framework and practices that affected those business decisions. Once the rig was destroyed and the uncontrolled flow of oil began leaking into the Gulf, industry and government struggled to contain and respond to the spill—prompting important questions about public and private authority, technical capability and capacity, and the current state of the art in addressing such crises. Understanding of the Gulf ecosystem and the regional economy underlies an early assessment of the spill's impacts and how to restore damaged natural resources, respond to economic losses, and address adverse impacts on human health. Chapters 4, 5, 6, and 7 address the related issues of containment and response, impact assessment, recovery, and restoration.

Chapter Four

"But, who cares, it's done, end of story, [we] will probably be fine and we'll get a good cement job."

The Macondo Well and the Blowout

In March 2008, BP paid a little over $34 million to the Minerals Management Service for an exclusive lease to drill in Mississippi Canyon Block 252, a nine-square-mile plot in the Gulf of Mexico. Although the Mississippi Canyon area has many productive oil fields, BP knew relatively little about the geology of Block 252: Macondo would be its first well on the new lease. BP planned to drill the well to 20,200 feet, both to learn more about the geology of the area and because it thought—based on available geological data—that it might find an oil and gas reservoir that would warrant installing production equipment at the well.[1] At the time, BP would have had good reason to expect that the well would be capable of generating a large profit.

Little more than two years later, however, BP found itself paying out tens of billions of dollars to

Fighting a losing battle, fireboats pour water onto the doomed rig in the hours after the Macondo well blowout. The tragic loss of the *Deepwater Horizon* at the close of the complex drilling project resulted from a series of missteps and oversights and an overall failure of management.

< *U.S. Coast Guard photo*

contain a blowout at the Macondo well, mitigate the damage resulting from the millions of gallons of oil flowing from that well into the Gulf of Mexico, and compensate the hundreds of thousands of individuals and businesses harmed by the spill. And that is likely just the beginning. BP, its partners (Anadarko and MOEX), and its key contractors (particularly Halliburton and Transocean) face potential liability for the billions more necessary to restore natural resources harmed by the spill.

The well blew out because a number of separate risk factors, oversights, and outright mistakes combined to overwhelm the safeguards meant to prevent just such an event from happening. But most of the mistakes and oversights at Macondo can be traced back to a single overarching failure—a failure of management. Better management by BP, Halliburton, and Transocean would almost certainly have prevented the blowout by improving the ability of individuals involved to identify the risks they faced, and to properly evaluate, communicate, and address them. A blowout in deepwater was not a statistical inevitability.

The Challenges of Deepwater Drilling at the Macondo Well

High Pressures and Risk of a Well Blowout

Oil forms deep beneath the Earth's surface when organic materials deposited in ancient sediments slowly transform in response to intense heat and pressure. Over the course of millions of years, these materials "cook" into liquid and gaseous hydrocarbons. The transformed materials can flow through porous mineral layers, and tend to migrate upward because they are lighter than other fluids in the pore spaces. If there is a path that leads to the surface, the hydrocarbons will emerge above ground in a seep or tar pit. If an impermeable layer instead blocks the way, the hydrocarbons can collect in porous rock beneath the impermeable layer. The business of drilling for oil consists of finding and tapping these "pay zones" of porous hydrocarbon-filled rock.

Pore Pressure and Fracture Gradient

Pore pressure is the pressure exerted by fluids in the pore space of rock. If drillers do not balance pore pressure with pressure from drilling fluids, hydrocarbons can flow into the wellbore (the hole drilled by the rig, including the casing) and unprotected sections of the well can collapse. The pore-pressure gradient, expressed as an equivalent mud weight, is a curve that shows the increase of pore pressure in a well by depth.

Fracture pressure is the pressure at which the geologic formation is not strong enough to withstand the pressure of the drilling fluids in a well and hence will fracture. When fracture occurs, drilling fluids flow out of the wellbore into the formation instead of circulating back to the surface. This causes what is known as "lost returns" or "lost circulation." The fracture gradient, expressed as an equivalent mud weight, is a curve that shows the fracture pressure of rocks in a well by depth.

The weight of the rocks above a pay zone can generate tremendous pressure on the hydrocarbons. Typically, the deeper the well, the higher the pressure—and the higher the pressure, the greater the challenges in safely tapping those hydrocarbons. The first oil wells were drilled on land and involved relatively low-pressure oil reservoirs. As oil companies drilled farther offshore, they encountered large hydrocarbon deposits, often in more porous and permeable geologic formations, and, like at the Macondo well, at ever-higher pressures.

The principal challenge in deepwater drilling is to drill a path to the hydrocarbon-filled pay zone in a manner that simultaneously controls these enormous pressures and avoids fracturing the geologic formation in which the reservoir is found. It is a delicate balance. The drillers must balance the reservoir pressure (pore pressure) pushing hydrocarbons into the well with counter-pressure from inside the wellbore. If too much counter-pressure is used, the formation can be fractured. But if too little counter-pressure is used, the result can be an uncontrolled intrusion of hydrocarbons into the well, and a discharge from the well itself as the oil and gas rush up and out of the well. An uncontrolled discharge is known as a blowout.

Drill Pipe, Mud, Casing, Cement, and Well Control

Those drilling in deepwater, just like those drilling on land, use drill pipe, casing, mud, and cement in a series of carefully calibrated steps to control pressure while drilling thousands of feet below the seafloor to reach the pay zone. Drilling mud, which is used to lubricate and cool the drill bit during drilling, plays a critical role in controlling the hydrocarbon pressure in a well. The weight of the column of mud in a well exerts pressure that counterbalances the pressure in the hydrocarbon formation. If the mud weight is too low, fluids such as oil and gas can enter the well, causing what is known as a "kick." But if the mud weight is too high, it can fracture the surrounding rock, potentially leading to "lost returns"—leakage of the mud into the formation. The rig crew therefore monitors and adjusts the weight (density) of the drilling mud as the well is being drilled—one of many sensitive, technical tasks requiring special equipment and the interpretation of data from difficult drilling environments.

Drilling Terminology

Drilling through the seafloor does not differ fundamentally from drilling on land. The crews on any drilling rig use rotary drill bits that they lubricate and cool with drilling mud—an ordinary name for what is today a sophisticated blend of synthetic fluids, polymers, and weighting agents that often costs over $100 per barrel. The rig crews pump the mud down through a drill pipe that connects with and turns the bit. The mud flows out holes in the bit and then circulates back to the rig through the space between the drill pipe and the sides of the well (the annulus), carrying to the surface bits of rock called cuttings that the drill bit has removed from the bottom of the well. When the mud returns to the rig at the surface, the cuttings are sieved out and the mud is sent back down the drill string. The mud thus travels in a closed loop.

As the well deepens, the crew lines its walls with a series of steel tubes called *casing*. The casing creates a foundation for continued drilling by reinforcing upper portions of the hole as drilling progresses. After installing a casing string, the crews drill farther, sending each successive string of casing down through the prior ones, so the well's diameter becomes progressively smaller as it gets deeper. A completed deepwater well typically telescopes down from a starting casing diameter of three feet or more at the wellhead to a diameter of 10 inches or less at the bottom.

Casing strings, which are a series of steel tubes installed to line the well as the drilling progresses, also help to control pressures. First, they protect more fragile sections of the well structure outside the casing from the pressure of the mud inside. Second, they prevent high-pressure fluids (like hydrocarbons) outside the casing from entering the wellbore and flowing up the well. To secure the casing, crews pump in cement to seal the space between the casing and the wellbore. If a completed well can yield economically valuable oil and gas, the crews can initiate production by punching holes through the casing and surrounding cement to allow hydrocarbons to flow into the well.

Designed and used properly, drilling mud, cement, and casing work together to enable the crew to control wellbore pressure. If they fail, the crew can, in an emergency, close powerful blowout-preventer valves that should seal off the well at the wellhead.

Deepwater Horizon Arrives and Resumes Drilling the Well

After purchasing the rights to drill in Block 252, BP became the legal "operator" for any activities on that block. But BP neither owned the rigs, nor operated them in the normal sense of the word. Rather, the company's Houston-based engineering team designed the well and specified in detail how it was to be drilled. A team of specialized contractors would then do the physical work of actually drilling the well—a common industry practice. Transocean, a leading owner of deepwater drilling rigs, would provide BP with a rig and the crew to run it. Two BP "Well Site Leaders" (the "company men") would be on the rig at all times to direct the crew and contractors and their work, and would maintain regular contact with the BP engineers on shore.

BP actually used two Transocean rigs to drill the Macondo well. The *Marianas* began work in October 2009 and drilled for 34 days, reaching a depth of 9,090 feet, before it had to stop drilling and move off-site to avoid Hurricane Ida. As described in Chapter 1, the storm nevertheless damaged the rig badly enough that BP called in the *Deepwater Horizon* to take over.

While the *Marianas* had been anchored in place with huge mooring chains, the *Deepwater Horizon* was a dynamically positioned mobile offshore drilling unit (MODU).[2] It relied on thrusters and satellite-positioning technology to stay in place over the well. Once the rig arrived on January 31, 2010, and began drilling operations, Transocean's Offshore Installation Manager Jimmy Harrell took over responsibility as the top Transocean employee on the rig.

When the *Deepwater Horizon* arrived, its first task was to lower its giant blowout preventer (BOP) onto the wellhead that the *Marianas* had left behind. The BOP is a stack of enormous valves that rig crews use both as a drilling tool and as an emergency safety device. Once it is put in place, everything needed in the well—drilling pipe, bits, casing, and mud—passes through the BOP. Every drilling rig has its own BOP, which its crew must test before and during drilling operations. After a week of surface testing, the *Deepwater*

FIGURE 4.1: Macondo Well Schematic

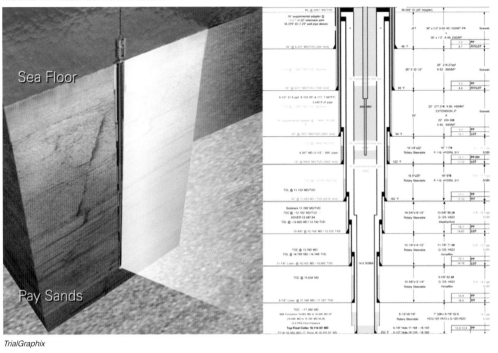

TrialGraphix

Horizon rig crew lowered the 400-ton device down through a mile of seawater and used a remotely operated vehicle (ROV) to guide it so that it could be latched onto the wellhead below.

The *Deepwater Horizon*'s blowout preventer had several features that could be used to seal the well. The top two were large, donut-shaped rubber elements called "annular preventers" that encircled drill pipe or casing inside the BOP. When squeezed shut, they sealed off the annular space around the drill pipe. The BOP also contained five sets of metal rams. The "blind shear ram" was designed to cut through drill pipe inside the BOP to seal off the well in emergency situations. It could be activated manually by drillers on the rig, by an ROV, or by an automated emergency "deadman system." A casing shear ram was designed to cut through casing; and three sets of pipe rams were in place to close off the space around the drill pipe.

Below the wellhead stretched four telescopic casing strings installed by the *Marianas* to reinforce the hole it had begun drilling. The *Deepwater Horizon* crew proceeded to drill deeper into the Earth, setting progressively smaller-diameter casing strings along the way as required. (Figure 4.1) They cemented each new string into place, anchoring the well to—and sealing the well off from—the surrounding rock.

"Lost Circulation" Event at the Pay Zone, and a Revised Plan for the Well

By early April, the *Deepwater Horizon* crew had begun to penetrate the pay zone—the porous hydrocarbon-bearing rock that BP had hoped to find. But on April 9, they suffered a setback. At 18,193 feet below sea level, the pressure exerted by the drilling mud exceeded the strength of the formation. Mud began flowing into cracks in the formation instead of returning to the rig. The rig had to stop drilling until the crew could seal the fracture and restore mud circulation.[3]

Lost circulation events are a fact of life in the oil business. The crew responded with a standard industry tactic. They pumped 172 barrels of thick, viscous fluid known as a "lost circulation pill" down the drill string, hoping it would plug the fractures in the formation.[4] The approach worked, but BP's on-shore engineering team realized the situation had become delicate. They had to maintain the weight of the mud in the wellbore at approximately 14.0 pounds per gallon (ppg) in order to balance the pressure exerted by hydrocarbons in the pay zone.[5] But drilling deeper would exert even more pressure on the formation, pressure that the BP team measured in terms of equivalent circulating density (ECD). The engineers calculated that drilling with 14.0 ppg mud in the wellbore would yield an ECD of nearly 14.5 ppg—enough of an increase that they risked further fracturing of the rock and more lost returns.

Equivalent Circulating Density (ECD)
A column of fluid will exert an amount of pressure on its surroundings that can be calculated if one knows the height of the column and the density of the fluid. If one pumps the fluid to make it circulate through the column, it will exert even more pressure. Equivalent circulating density or ECD is used to describe the total effective pressure that a column of drilling mud exerts on a formation as it is circulated through the drill string and back up the wellbore. To pump a given fluid faster or through narrower restrictions, it has to be pumped at greater pressure, and this, in turn, increases the ECD.

The engineers concluded they had "run out of drilling margin": the well would have to stop short of its original objective of 20,200 feet.[6] After cautiously drilling to a total depth of 18,360 feet, BP informed its lease partners Anadarko and MOEX that "well integrity and safety" issues required the rig to stop drilling further.[7]

At that point, Macondo was stable. Because the column of drilling mud in the wellbore was heavy enough to balance the hydrocarbon pressure, BP and its contractors, including Transocean, were able to spend the next five days[8] between April 11 and 15 "logging" the open hole with sophisticated instruments. Based on the logging data, BP concluded that it had drilled into a hydrocarbon reservoir of sufficient size (at least 50 million barrels[9]) and pressure that it was economically worthwhile to install a final "production casing" string that BP would eventually use to recover the oil and gas.

Preparing the Well for Subsequent Production

The engineers recognized that the lost circulation problems and delicacy of the rock formation at the bottom of the well would make it challenging to install the production casing.[10] After the rig crew lowered the casing into its final position, Halliburton would cement it into place. Halliburton would pump a specialized cement blend down the inside of the casing string; when it reached the end of the casing, cement would flow out the bottom and up into the annular space between the casing and the sides of the open hole. Once cured, the cement would bond to the formation and the casing and—if all went

FIGURE 4.2: "Long String" vs. "Liner"

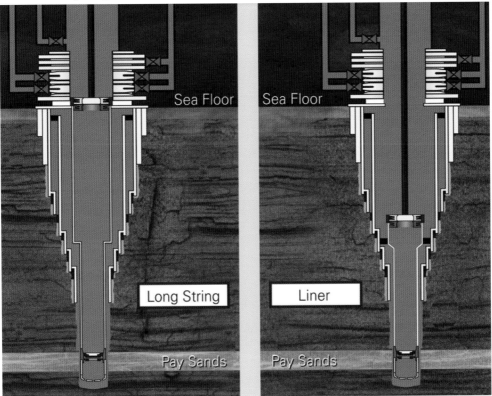

Two options for the Macondo production casing.

TrialGraphix

well—seal off the annular space. BP and Halliburton had cemented the previous casing strings at Macondo, and this cement job would be particularly important. The first attempt at cementing any casing string is commonly called the primary cement job. For a primary cement job to be successful, it must seal off, or "isolate," the hydrocarbon-bearing zone from the annular space around the casing and from the inside of the casing itself.

The Engineers Select a "Long String" Casing

BP's design team originally had planned to use a "long string" production casing—a single continuous wall of steel between the wellhead on the seafloor, and the oil and gas zone at the bottom of the well. But after the lost circulation event, they were forced to reconsider. As another option, they evaluated a "liner"—a shorter string of casing hung lower in the well and anchored to the next higher string. (Figure 4.2) A liner would result in a more complex—and theoretically more leak-prone—system over the life of the well. But it would be easier to cement into place at Macondo.

On April 14 and 15, BP's engineers, working with a Halliburton engineer, used sophisticated computer programs to model the likely outcome of the cementing process. When early results suggested the long string could not be cemented reliably, BP's design team switched to a liner. But that shift met resistance within BP.[11] The engineers were encouraged to engage an in-house BP cementing expert to review Halliburton's recommendations. That BP expert determined that certain inputs should be corrected. Calculations with the new inputs showed that a long string could be cemented properly. The BP engineers accordingly decided that installing a long string was "*again* the primary option."[12]

Centralizers and the Risk of Channeling

Installing the agreed-upon casing was a major job. Even moving at top speed, the crew on the *Deepwater Horizon* needed more than 18 hours just to lower a tool, such as a drill bit, from the rig floor to the bottom of the well, 18,000 feet below sea level. Assembling the production casing section-by-section and lowering the lengthening string down into the well below would require roughly 37 hours.[13]

As the crew gradually assembled and lowered the casing, they paused several times to install centralizers (Figure 4.3) at predetermined points along the casing string. Centralizers are critical components in ensuring a good cement job. When a casing string hangs in the center of the wellbore, cement pumped down the casing will flow evenly back up the annulus, displacing any mud and debris that were previously in that space and leaving a clean column of cement. If the casing is not centered, the cement will flow preferentially up the path of least resistance—the larger spaces in the annulus—and slowly or not at all in the narrower annular space. That can leave behind channels of drilling mud that can severely compromise a primary cement job by creating paths and gaps through which pressurized hydrocarbons can flow.

BP's original designs had called for 16 or more centralizers to be placed along the long string.[14] But on April 1, team member Brian Morel learned that BP's supplier (Weatherford) had in stock only six "subs"[15]—centralizers designed to screw securely into

FIGURE 4.3: Centralizer Sub

Centralizer "subs" screw into place between sections of casing.

Weatherford

place between sections of casing. The alternative was to use "slip-on" centralizers—devices that slide onto the exterior of a piece of casing where they are normally secured in place by mechanical "stop collars" on either side. These collars can either be welded directly to the centralizers or supplied as separate pieces. The BP team—and Wells Team Leader John Guide in particular—distrusted slip-on centralizers with separate stop collars because the pieces can slide out of position or, worse, catch on other equipment as the casing is lowered.[16]

Shortly after the BP team decided on the long string, Halliburton engineer Jesse Gagliano ran computer simulations using proprietary software called OptiCem, in part to predict whether mud channeling would occur. OptiCem calculates the likely outcome of a cement job based on a number of variables, including the geometry of the wellbore and casing, the size and location of centralizers, the rate at which cement will be pumped, and the relative weight and viscosity of the cement compared to the mud it displaces. Gagliano's calculations suggested that the Macondo production casing would need more than six centralizers to avoid channeling.

Gagliano told BP engineers Mark Hafle and Brett Cocales about the problem on the afternoon of April 15.[17] With de facto leader John Guide out of the office, Gregory Walz, the BP Drilling Engineering Team Leader, obtained permission from senior manager David Sims to order 15 additional slip-on centralizers—the most BP could transport immediately in a helicopter. That evening, Gagliano reran his simulations and found that channeling due to gas flow would be less severe with 21 centralizers in place. Late that night, Walz sent an e-mail to Guide explaining that he and Sims felt that BP needed to "honor the [OptiCem] modeling to be consistent with our previous decisions to go with the long string."[18]

When Guide learned the next day of the decision to add more centralizers, he initially deferred, but then challenged the decision. Walz had earlier assured Guide that the 15 additional centralizers would be custom-designed one-piece units that BP had used on a prior well and would limit the potential for centralizer "hang up."[19] But when the centralizers arrived, BP engineer Brian Morel, who happened to be out on the rig, reported that the centralizers were of conventional design with separate stop collars. Morel e-mailed BP drilling engineer Brett Cocales to question the need for additional centralizers.[20] Cocales responded that the team would "probably be fine" even without the additional centralizers and that "Guide is right on the risk/reward equation."[21]

Guide pointed out to Walz that the new centralizers were not custom-made as specified.[22] "Also," he noted, "it will take 10 hrs to install them." He complained that the "last minute addition" of centralizers would add 45 pieces of equipment to the casing that could come off during installation, and concluded by saying that he was "very concerned." In the end, Guide's view prevailed; BP installed only the six centralizer subs on the Macondo production casing.

Lowering the Casing String Into Position

Early on the morning of April 18, with a centralizer plan in hand, the rig crew finally began assembling and lowering the long string into position. The leading end of the casing,

FIGURE 4.4: Shoe Track

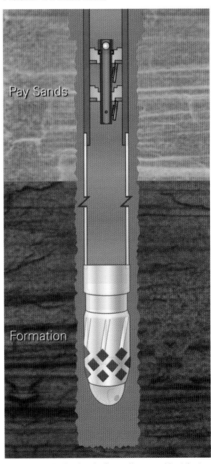

Pay Sands

Formation

The shoe track, showing the float collar assembly at the top and the reamer shoe at the bottom.

TrialGraphix

the "shoe track," began with a "reamer shoe"—a bullet-shaped piece of metal with three holes designed to help guide the casing down the hole. (Figure 4.4) The reamer shoe was followed by 180 feet of seven-inch-diameter steel casing. Then came a Weatherford-manufactured "float collar," a simple arrangement of two flapper (float) valves, spaced one after the other, held open by a short "auto-fill tube" through which the mud in the well could flow. As the long string was lowered down the wellbore, the mud passed through the holes in the reamer shoe and auto-fill tube that propped open the float valves, giving it a clear flow path upward.

Preparation for Cementing—and Unexpected Pressure Anomalies in the Well

The long string was installed in its final position early on the afternoon of April 19. With the top end of the string seated in the wellhead and its bottom end located just above the bottom of the wellbore, the crew's next job was to prepare the float-valve system for cementing. During the cementing process, fluids pumped into the well should flow in a one-way path: *down* the center of the last casing string, *out* the bottom, and *up* the annulus (between the exterior of the steel casing and the surrounding rock formations). To ensure unidirectional flow, the crew needed to push the auto-fill tube downward, so it would no longer prop open the float valves. With the tube out of the way, the flapper valves would spring shut and convert from two-way valves into one-way valves that would allow mud and cement to flow *down* the casing into the shoe track, but prevent any fluid from reversing direction and coming back *up* the casing. Once the float valves had converted, Halliburton could pump cement down through the casing and up around the annulus; the valves would keep cement from flowing back up the casing once the crew stopped pumping.

To convert the float valves, that evening the crew began pumping mud down through the casing. Based on Weatherford's specifications, the valves should convert once the rate of flow though holes in the auto-fill tube had reached roughly 6 barrels per minute (bpm), causing a differential pressure on the tube of approximately 600 pounds per square inch (psi).[23] But the crew hit a stumbling block. They pumped fluids into the well, eventually pressuring up to 1,800 psi, but could not establish flow.

Well Site Leader Bob Kaluza and BP engineer Morel[24] called Guide, their supervisor on shore. In consultation with Guide and Weatherford staff, the rig team decided to increase the pump pressure in discrete increments, hoping eventually to dislodge the auto-fill tube.[25] On their ninth attempt, pump pressure peaked at 3,142 psi and then suddenly dropped as mud finally began to flow. Significantly, however, the pump rate of mud into the well and through the shoe track thereafter never exceeded approximately 4 bpm.[26]

BP's team concluded that the float valves had converted, but noted another anomaly. The drilling-mud subcontractor, M-I SWACO, had predicted that it would take a pressure of 570 psi to circulate mud after converting the float valves.[27] Instead, the rig crew reported that circulation pressure was much lower: only 340 psi. BP's Well Site Leader Bob Kaluza expressed concern about low circulating pressure.[28] He and the Transocean crew switched circulating pumps to see if that made a difference, and eventually concluded that the pressure gauge they had been relying on was broken.[29] Believing they had converted the float valves and reestablished mud circulation in the well, BP was ready at last to pump cement down the production casing and complete the primary cement job.

The Inherently Uncertain Cementing Process

Cementing an oil well is an inherently uncertain process. To establish isolation across a hydrocarbon zone at the bottom of a well, engineers must send a slug of cement down the inside of the well. They then pump mud in after it to push the cement down until it "turns the corner" at the bottom of the well and flows up into the annular space. If done properly, the slug of cement will create a long and continuous seal around the production casing, and will fill the shoe track in the bottom of the final casing string. But things can go wrong even under optimal conditions. If the cement is pumped too far or not far enough, it may not isolate the hydrocarbon zones. If oil-based drilling mud contaminates the water-based cement as the cement flows down the well, the cement can set slowly or not at all. And, as previously noted, the cement can "channel," filling the annulus unevenly and allowing hydrocarbons to bypass cement in the annular space. Given the variety of things that can go wrong with a cement job, it is hardly surprising that a 2007 MMS study identified cementing problems as one of the "most significant factors" leading to blowouts between 1992 and 2006.[30]

Even following best practices, a cement crew can never be certain how a cement job at the bottom of the well is proceeding as it is pumped. Cement does its work literally miles away from the rig floor, and the crew has no direct way to see where it is, whether it is contaminated, or whether it has sealed off the well. To gauge progress, the crew must instead rely on subtle, indirect indicators like pressure and volume: they know how much cement and mud they have sent down the well and how hard the pumps are working to push it. The crew can use these readings to check whether each barrel of cement pumped into the well displaces an equal volume of drilling mud—producing "full returns." They can also check for pressure spikes to confirm that "wiper plugs" (used to separate the cement from the surrounding drilling mud) have landed on time as expected at the bottom of the well. And they can look for "lift pressure"—a steady increase in pump pressure signifying that the cement has turned the corner at the bottom of the well and is being pushed up into the annular space against gravity.

While they suggest generally that the job has gone as planned, these indicators say little specific about the location and quality of the cement at the bottom of the well. None of them can take the place of pressure testing and cement evaluation logging (see below).

The Cementing Design: Critical Decisions for a Fragile Formation

In the days leading up to the final cementing process, BP engineers focused heavily on the biggest challenge: the risk of fracturing the formation and losing returns. John Guide explained after the incident that losing returns "was the No. 1 risk."[31] He and the other BP engineers worried that if their cementing procedure placed too much pressure on the geologic formation below, it might trigger another lost-returns event similar to the one on April 9. In this case, critical cement—not mud—might flow into the formation and be lost, potentially leaving the annular space at the bottom of the well open to hydrocarbon flow.

The BP team's concerns led them to place a number of significant constraints on Halliburton's cementing design. The first compromise in BP's plan was to limit the circulation of drilling mud through the wellbore before cementing. Optimally, mud in the wellbore would have been circulated "bottoms up"—meaning the rig crew would have pumped enough mud down the wellbore to bring mud originally at the bottom of the well all the way back up to the rig. There are at least two benefits to bottoms up circulation. Such extensive circulation cleans the wellbore and reduces the likelihood of channeling. And circulating bottoms up allows technicians on the rig to examine mud from the bottom of the well for hydrocarbon content before cementing. But the BP engineers feared that the longer the rig crew circulated mud through the casing before cementing, the greater the risk of another lost-returns event. Accordingly, BP circulated approximately 350 barrels of mud before cementing, rather than the 2,760 barrels needed to do a full bottoms up circulation.[32]

BP compromised again by deciding to pump cement down the well at the relatively low rate of 4 barrels or less per minute.[33] Higher flow rates tend to increase the efficiency with which cement displaces mud from the annular space. But the increased pump pressure required to move the cement quickly would mean more pressure on the formation (ECD) and an increased risk of lost returns. BP decided to reduce the risk of lost returns in exchange for a less-than-optimal rate of cement flow.

BP made a third compromise by limiting the volume of cement that Halliburton would pump down the well. Pumping more cement is a standard industry practice to insure against uncertain cementing conditions: more cement means less risk of contamination and less risk that the cement job will be compromised by slight errors in placement. But more cement at Macondo would mean a higher cement column in the annulus, which in turn would exert more pressure on the fragile formation below. Accordingly, BP determined that the annular cement column should extend only 500 feet above the uppermost hydrocarbon-bearing zone (and 800 feet above the main hydrocarbon zones), and that this would be sufficient to fulfill MMS regulations of "500 feet above the uppermost hydrocarbon-bearing zone."[34] However, it did *not* satisfy BP's own internal guidelines, which specify that the top of the annular cement should be 1,000 feet above the uppermost hydrocarbon zone.[35] As designed, BP would have Halliburton pump a total of approximately 60 barrels of cement down the well—a volume that its own engineers recognized would provide little margin for error.[36]

Finally, in close consultation with Halliburton, BP chose to use "nitrogen foam cement"—a cement formula that has been leavened with tiny bubbles of nitrogen gas, injected into the cement slurry just before it goes down the well. This formula was chosen to lighten the resulting slurry from approximately 16.7 ppg to 14.5 ppg—thereby reducing the pressure the cement would exert on the fragile formation. The bubbles, in theory, would also help to balance the pore pressure in the formation and clear the annular space of mud as the cement flowed upward. Halliburton is an industry leader in foam cementing, but BP appears to have had little experience with foam technology for cementing production casing in the Gulf of Mexico.[37]

The Cement Slurry: Laboratory Analyses

A cement slurry must be tested before it is used in a cement job. Because the pressure and temperature at the bottom of a well can significantly alter the strength and curing rate of a given cement slurry—and because storing cement on a rig can alter its chemical composition over time—companies like Halliburton normally fly cement samples from the rig back to a laboratory shortly before pumping a job to make sure the cement will work under the conditions in the well. The laboratory conducts a number of tests to evaluate the slurry's viscosity and flow characteristics, the rate at which it will cure, and its eventual compressive strength.

When testing a slurry that will be foamed with nitrogen, the lab also evaluates the stability of the cement that results. A stable foam slurry will retain its bubbles and overall density long enough to allow the cement to cure. The result is hardened cement that has tiny, evenly dispersed, and unconnected nitrogen bubbles throughout. If the foam does not remain stable up until the time the cement cures, the small nitrogen bubbles may coalesce into larger ones, rendering the hardened cement porous and permeable.[38] If the instability is particularly severe, the nitrogen can "break out" of the cement, with unpredictable consequences.

On February 10, soon after the *Deepwater Horizon* began work on the well, Jesse Gagliano asked Halliburton laboratory personnel to run a series of "pilot tests" on the cement blend stored on the *Deepwater Horizon* that Halliburton planned to use at Macondo.[39] They tested the slurry[40] and reported the results to Gagliano. He sent the laboratory report to BP on March 8 as an attachment to an e-mail in which he discussed his recommended plan for cementing an earlier Macondo casing string.[41]

The reported data that Gagliano sent to BP on March 8 included the results of a single foam stability test. To the trained eye, that test showed that the February foam slurry design was unstable. Gagliano did not comment on the evidence of the cement slurry's instability, and there is no evidence that BP examined the foam stability data in the report at all.

Documents identified after the blowout reveal that Halliburton personnel had also conducted another foam stability test earlier in February. The earlier test had been conducted under slightly different conditions than the later one and had failed more severely.[42] It appears that Halliburton never reported the results of the earlier February test to BP.

Halliburton conducted another round of tests in mid-April, just before pumping the final cement job. By then, the BP team had given Halliburton more accurate information about the temperatures and pressures at the bottom of the Macondo well, and Halliburton had progressed further with its cementing plan. Using this information, the laboratory personnel conducted several tests, including a foam stability test, starting on approximately April 13. The first test Halliburton conducted showed once again that the cement slurry would be unstable.[43] The Commission does not believe that Halliburton ever reported this information to BP. Instead, it appears that Halliburton personnel subsequently ran a second foam stability test, this time doubling the pre-test "conditioning time" to three hours.[44]

The evidence suggests that Halliburton began the second test at approximately 2:00 a.m. on April 18.[45] That test would normally take 48 hours. Halliburton finished pumping the cement job just before 48 hours would have elapsed.[46] Although the second test at least arguably suggests the foam cement design used at Macondo would be stable, it is unclear whether Halliburton had results from that test in hand before it pumped the job. Halliburton did not send the results of the final test to BP until April 26, six days after the blowout.[47]

Evaluating the Cementing Job

Transocean's rig crew and Halliburton's cementers finished pumping the primary cement job at 12:40 a.m. on April 20.[48] Once the pumps were off, a BP representative and Vincent Tabler of Halliburton performed a check to see whether the float valves were closed and holding. They opened a valve at the cementing unit to see whether any fluid flowed from the well. If more fluid came back than expected, that would indicate that cement was migrating back up into the casing and pushing the fluids above it out of the top of the well. Models had predicted 5 barrels of flow back. According to Brian Morel, the two men observed 5.5 barrels of flow, tapering off to a "finger tip trickle."[49] According to Morel, 5.5 barrels of flow-back volume was within the acceptable margin for error.[50] Tabler testified that they watched flow "until it was probably what we call a pencil stream," which stopped, started up again, and then stopped altogether.[51] While it is not clear how long the two men actually watched for potential flow, they eventually concluded the float valves were holding.

With no lost returns, BP and Halliburton declared the job a success. Nathaniel Chaisson, one of Halliburton's crew on the rig, sent an e-mail to Jesse Gagliano at 5:45 a.m. saying, "We have completed the job and it went well."[52] He attached a detailed report stating that the job had been "pumped as planned" and that he had seen full returns throughout the process.[53] And just before leaving the rig, Morel e-mailed the rest of the BP team to say "the Halliburton cement team . . . did a great job."[54]

Cement Evaluation Tools

Cement evaluation tools (including "cement bond logs") test the integrity of cement in the annular space around a casing. The tools measure whether and to what extent cement has bonded to the outside of the casing and formation, and the location and severity of any channels through the cement. Although a modern cement evaluation combines several different instruments, the primary approach is to analyze the casing's response to acoustic signals. Just as a muffled bell sounds different than a free-swinging bell, a well casing will respond differently depending on the volume and quality of cement around it. Cement evaluation tools do have important limits. Among other things, they work better after the cement has had time to cure completely. They also cannot evaluate cement in the shoe track of a casing, or in the annular space below the float valves.

At the 7:30 a.m. morning meeting with contractors on the rig, the BP team concluded the cement job went well enough to send home a team of technicians from Schlumberger who had been standing by on the rig for at least one day already[55] waiting to perform a suite of cement evaluation tests on the primary cement job, including cement bond logs.[56] The BP team relied on a "decision tree" that Guide and BP engineers had prepared beforehand. The

FIGURE 4.5: Temporary Abandonment

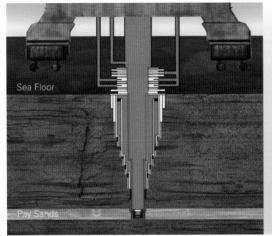
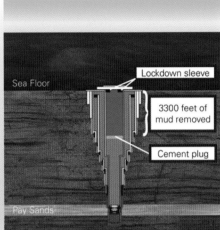

Lockdown sleeve

3300 feet of
mud removed

Cement plug

Sea Floor

Sea Floor

Pay Sands

Pay Sands

End of Cement Job   Temporarily Abandoned

The status of the well before and after temporary abandonment.

TrialGraphix

primary criterion BP appears to have used to determine whether to perform the cement evaluation test was whether there were "[l]osses while cementing [the] long string."[57] Having seen no lost returns during the cement job, BP sent the Schlumberger team home and moved on to prepare the well for temporary abandonment.

Temporary Abandonment and Preparing to Move On to the Next Job

Once BP decided to send the Schlumberger team home, *Deepwater Horizon*'s crew began the final phase of its work. Drilling the Macondo well had required a giant offshore rig of *Deepwater Horizon*'s capabilities. By contrast, BP, like most operators, would give the job of "completing" the well to a smaller (and less costly) rig, which would install hydrocarbon-collection and -production equipment. To make way for the new rig, the *Deepwater Horizon* would have to remove its riser* and blowout preventer from the wellhead—and before it could do those things, the crew had to secure the well through a process called "temporary abandonment."

Four features of the temporarily abandoned well are worth noting. First is the single 300-foot-long cement plug inside the wellbore. MMS regulations required BP to install a cement plug as a backup for the cement job at the bottom of the well. Second is the location of the cement plug: BP planned to put it 3,300 feet below the ocean floor, or "mud line" (which was deeper than MMS regulations allowed without dispensation, and deeper than usual).[58] Third is the presence of seawater in the well below the sea floor: BP planned to replace 3,000 feet of mud in the wellbore above the cement plug with much

---

* The riser is the piping that connects the drilling rig at the surface with the BOP at the wellhead on the seafloor.

lighter seawater (seawater weighs roughly 8.6 ppg, while the mud in the wellbore weighed roughly 14.5 ppg). Fourth is the lockdown sleeve—a mechanical device that locks the long casing string to the wellhead to prevent it from lifting out of place during subsequent production operations. (Figure 4.5)

At 10:43 a.m., Morel e-mailed an "Ops Note" to the rest of the Macondo team listing the temporary abandonment procedures for the well.[59] It was the first time the BP Well Site Leaders on the rig had seen the procedures they would use that day. BP first shared the procedures with the rig crew at the 11 a.m. pre-tour meeting that morning.[60] The basic sequence was as follows:

Lockdown Sleeve

Before the Macondo blowout, a *lockdown sleeve* was not generally considered a safety mechanism or barrier to flow prior to the production phase of the well. Drilling rigs did not generally set lockdown sleeves. Rather, completion or production rigs did so after the drilling phase. BP decided to have the Deepwater Horizon set the lockdown sleeve because the Horizon could do the job more quickly than the completion rig. Based on the Macondo event, and given early concerns that upward forces during the blowout had approached or exceeded the force needed to lift the production casing up out of its seat in the wellhead, the Commission believes operators should consider installing a lockdown sleeve or other device to lock the casing hanger in place as part of drilling operations (or, at the very least, at the outset of temporary abandonment).

---

1. Perform a positive-pressure test to test the integrity of the production casing;
2. Run the drill pipe into the well to 8,367 feet (3,300 feet below the mud line);
3. Displace 3,300 feet of mud in the well with seawater, lifting the mud above the BOP and into the riser;
4. Perform a negative-pressure test to assess the integrity of the well and bottom-hole cement job to ensure *outside* fluids (such as hydrocarbons) are not leaking *into* the well;
5. Displace the mud in the riser with seawater;
6. Set the surface cement plug at 8,367 feet; and
7. Set the lockdown sleeve.[61]

The crew would never get through all of the steps in the procedure.

BP's Macondo team had made numerous changes to the temporary abandonment procedures in the two weeks leading up to the April 20 "Ops Note." For example, in its April 12 drilling plan, BP had planned (1) to set the lockdown sleeve before setting the surface cement plug and (2) to set the surface cement plug in seawater only 6,000 feet below sea level (as opposed to 8,367 feet). The April 12 plan did not include a negative-pressure test.[62] On April 14, Morel sent an e-mail entitled "Forward Ops" setting forth a different procedure, which included a negative-pressure test but would require setting the surface cement plug in mud before displacement of the riser with seawater.[63] On April 16, BP sent an Application for Permit to Modify to MMS describing a temporary abandonment procedure that was different from the procedure in either the April 12 drilling plan, the April 14 e-mail, or the April 20 "Ops Note."[64] There is no evidence that these changes went through *any* sort of formal risk assessment or management of change process.

Countdown to Blowout

The first step in the temporary abandonment was to test well integrity: to make sure there were no leaks in the well.

The Positive-Pressure Test

The positive-pressure test evaluates, among other things, the ability of the casing in the well to hold in pressure. MMS regulations require a positive-pressure test prior to temporary abandonment.[65] To perform the test at Macondo, the *Deepwater Horizon*'s crew first closed off the well below the BOP by shutting the blind shear ram (there was no drill pipe in the well at the time).[66] Then, much like pumping air into a bike tire to check for leaks, the rig crew pumped fluids into the well (through pipes running from the rig to the BOP) to generate pressure and then checked to see if it would hold.

The crew started the positive-pressure test at noon.[67] They pressured the well up to 250 psi for 5 minutes, and then pressured up to 2,500 psi and watched for 30 minutes. The pressure inside the well remained steady during both tests, showing there were no leaks in the production casing through which fluids could pass from inside the well to the outside. The drilling crew and BP's Well Site Leader Bob Kaluza considered the test successful. Later in the afternoon, Kaluza showed visiting BP executive Pat O'Bryan the pressure chart from the test; O'Bryan remarked, "Things looked good with the positive test."[68]

The Negative-Pressure Test: Unexpected Pressure Readings

The negative-pressure test checks not only the integrity of the casing, like the positive-pressure test, but also the integrity of the bottomhole cement job. At the Macondo well, the negative-pressure test was the *only* test performed that would have checked the integrity of the bottomhole cement job.

Instead of pumping pressure into the wellbore to see if fluids leak out, the crew *removes* pressure from inside the well to see if fluids, such as hydrocarbons, leak in, past or through the bottomhole cement job. In so doing, the crew simulates the effect of removing the mud in the wellbore and the riser (and the pressure exerted by that mud) during temporary abandonment. If the casing and primary cement have been designed and installed properly, they will prevent hydrocarbons from intruding even when that "overbalancing" pressure is removed.[69] First, the crew sets up the well to simulate the expected hydrostatic pressure exerted by the column of fluids on the bottom of the well in its abandoned state. Second, the crew bleeds off any pent-up pressure that remains in the well, taking it down to 0 psi. Third, the crew and Well Site Leaders watch to make sure that nothing flows up from and out of the well and that no pressure builds back up inside of the well. If there is no flow or pressure buildup, that means that the casing and primary cement have sealed the well off from external fluid pressure and flow. A negative-pressure test is successful if there is no flow out of the well for a sustained period and if there is no pressure build-up inside the well when it is closed at the surface.

To conduct a proper negative test at Macondo, BP would have to isolate the well from the effect of the 5,000-foot-plus column of drilling mud in the riser and a further 3,300-foot column of drilling mud below the seafloor. Those heavy columns of mud exerted much more pressure on the well than the seawater that would replace them after temporary abandonment. Specifically, the pressure at the bottom of the well would be approximately 2,350 psi *lower* after temporary abandonment than before.[70] Once this pressure was removed, the downward force of the column of fluids in the well would be less than the pressure of the hydrocarbons in the reservoir, so the well would be in what is called an "underbalanced" state. It was therefore critical to test and confirm the ability of the well (including the primary cement job) to withstand the underbalance. If the test showed that hydrocarbons would leak into the well once it was underbalanced, BP would need to diagnose and fix the problem (perhaps remediating the cement job) before moving on, a process that could take many days.

The crew began the negative test of Macondo at 5:00 p.m. Earlier in the day, the crew had prepared for the negative test by setting up the well to simulate the planned removal of the mud in the riser and 3,300 feet of drilling mud in the wellbore. The crew ran the drill pipe down to approximately 8,367 feet below sea level and then pumped a "spacer"—a liquid mixture that serves to separate the heavy drilling mud from the seawater—followed by seawater down the drill pipe to push (displace) 3,300 feet of mud from below the mud line to above the BOP. (Figure 4.6)

While drilling crews routinely use water-based spacer fluids to separate oil-based drilling mud from seawater, the spacer BP chose to use during the negative pressure test was unusual. BP had directed M-I SWACO mud engineers on the rig to create a spacer out of two different lost-circulation materials left over on the rig—the heavy, viscous drilling fluids used to patch fractures in the formation when the crew experiences lost returns.[71] M-I SWACO had previously mixed two different unused batches, or "pills," of lost-circulation materials in case there were further lost returns.[72] BP wanted to use these materials as spacer in order to avoid having to dispose of them onshore as hazardous waste pursuant to the Resource and Conservation Recovery Act, exploiting an exception that allows companies to dump water-based "drilling fluids" overboard if they have been circulated down through a well.[73] At BP's direction, M-I SWACO combined the materials to create an unusually large volume of spacer that had never previously been used by anyone on the rig or by BP as a spacer, nor been thoroughly tested for that purpose.[74]

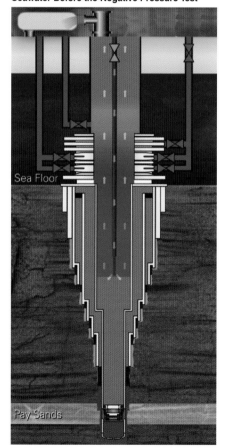

FIGURE 4.6: Displacing Mud With Spacer and Seawater Before the Negative Pressure Test

Seawater (blue) displaces mud (brown) from wellbore and riser, with spacer fluid separating the two.

TrialGraphix

Once the crew had displaced the mud to above the BOP, they shut an annular preventer in the BOP, isolating the well from the downward pressure exerted by the heavy mud and spacer in the riser. The crew could now perform the negative-pressure test using the drill pipe: it would open the top of the drill pipe on the rig, bleed the drill pipe pressure to zero, and then watch for flow. The crew opened the drill pipe at the rig to bleed off any pressure that had built up in the well during the mud-displacement process. The crew tried to bleed the pressure down to zero, but could not get it below 266 psi. When the drill pipe was closed, the pressure jumped back up to 1,262 psi.

Around this time, the driller's shack was growing crowded. The night crew was arriving in preparation for the 6:00 p.m. shift change, which meant that both toolpushers—Wyman Wheeler and Jason Anderson—and both Well Site Leaders—Bob Kaluza and Don Vidrine—were present. In addition, a group of visiting BP and Transocean executives entered as part of a rig tour escorted by Transocean Offshore Installation Manager Jimmy Harrell.[75] It was apparent to at least one member of the tour that the crew was having a "little bit of a problem."[76]

The crew had noticed that the fluid level inside the riser was dropping, suggesting that spacer was leaking down past the annular preventer, out of the riser, and into the well (Figure 4.7). Harrell, who stayed behind in the drill shack as the tour continued, ordered the annular preventer closed more tightly to stop the leak.[77] Harrell then left the rig floor.

With that problem solved, the crew refilled the riser and once again opened up the drill pipe and attempted a second time to bleed the pressure down to 0 psi. This time, they were able to do so. But when they shut the drill pipe in again, the pressure built back up to at least 773 psi. The crew then attempted a third time to bleed off the pressure from the drill pipe, and was again able to get it down to 0 psi. When the crew shut the well back in, however, the pressure increased to 1,400 psi. At this point, the crew had bled the drill-pipe pressure down three times, but each time it had built back up. For a successful negative-pressure test, the pressure must remain at 0 psi when the pipe is closed after the pressure is bled off.

The Transocean crew and BP Well Site Leaders met on the rig floor to discuss the readings. In addition to Kaluza, Vidrine, and Anderson, Dewey Revette (Transocean's on-duty driller) and BP Well Site Leader trainee Lee Lambert were there. According to post-incident statements from both Well Site Leaders, Anderson said that the 1,400 psi pressure on the drill pipe was being caused by a phenomenon called the "bladder effect."[78] According to Lambert, Anderson explained that heavy mud in the riser was exerting pressure on the annular preventer, which in turn transmitted pressure to the drill pipe. Lambert said that he did not recall anyone agreeing or disagreeing with Anderson's explanation.[79]

According to Harrell, after a lengthy discussion, BP Well Site Leader Vidrine then insisted on running a second negative-pressure test, this time monitoring pressure and flow on the kill line rather than the drill pipe. (The kill line is one of three pipes, each approximately 3 inches in diameter, that run from the rig to the BOP to allow the crew to circulate fluids into and out of the well at the sea floor.) The pressure on the kill line during the negative-pressure test should have been identical to the pressure on the drill pipe, as both flow

FIGURE 4.7: Fluids Leak Past Annular Preventer

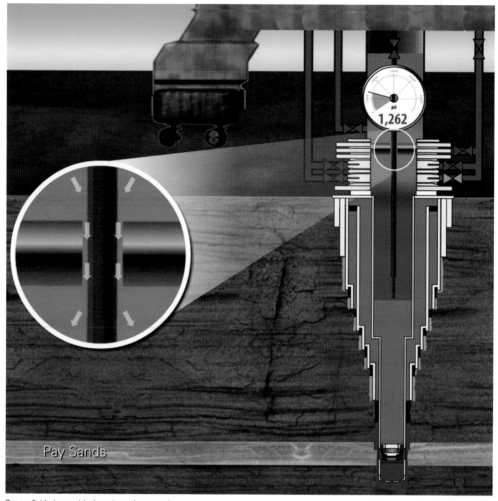

Spacer fluids (orange) leak past annular preventer.

TrialGraphix

paths went to the same place (and both should have been filled with seawater). Vidrine apparently insisted the negative test be repeated on the kill line because BP had specified that the test would be performed on the kill line in a permit application it submitted earlier to MMS.[80]

For the second test, the crew opened the kill line and bled the pressure down to 0 psi. A small amount of fluid flowed, and then stopped.[81] Rig personnel left the kill line open for 30 minutes but did not observe any flow from it. The test on the kill line thus satisfied the criteria for a successful negative pressure test—no flow or pressure buildup for a sustained period of time. But the pressure on the drill pipe remained at 1,400 psi throughout. The Well Site Leaders and crew never appear to have reconciled the two different pressure readings.[82] The "bladder effect" may have been proposed as an explanation for the anomaly—but based on available information, the 1,400 psi reading on the drill pipe could *only* have been caused by a leak into the well. Nevertheless, at 8 p.m., BP Well Site Leaders, in consultation with the crew, made a key error and mistakenly concluded the second negative test procedure had confirmed the well's integrity. They declared the test a success and moved on to the next step in temporary abandonment.

Displacing Mud from the Riser—and Mounting Signs of a Kick

At 8:02 p.m., the crew opened the annular preventer and began displacing mud and spacer from the riser. Halliburton cementer Chris Haire went to the drill shack to check on the status of the upcoming surface cement plug job. Revette and Anderson told him the negative-pressure test had been successful and that Haire should prepare to set the surface cement plug.[83]

Revette sat down in his driller's chair to monitor the well for kicks—any unplanned influxes of gas or fluids—and other anomalies. As gaseous hydrocarbons in a kick rise up the wellbore, they expand with ever-increasing speed—a barrel of natural gas at Macondo could expand over a hundredfold as it traveled the 5,000 feet between the wellhead and the rig above.[84] And as the gas expands, it pushes mud upward faster and faster, reducing the pressure on the gas and increasing the speed of the kick—making it imperative that rig crews recognize and respond to a kick as early as possible.

The individuals responsible for detecting kicks on a rig include the driller, assistant drillers, and the mudlogger.[85] Dewey Revette was the driller on duty at the time; the two assistant drillers on duty were Donald Clark and Stephen Curtis. Joseph Keith of Sperry Sun was the mudlogger.

These individuals look for kicks by monitoring real-time data displays in the driller's shack, mudlogger's shack, and elsewhere on the rig. They watch two primary parameters. The first, and most reliable when available, is the volume of mud in the active pits. The volume of mud sent from the active pits into the well should equal the volume of mud returning to the active pits from the well. An increase in volume is a powerful indicator that something is flowing into the well.

Second, under normal circumstances, the volume and rate of flow of fluids coming from the well should equal the volume and rate of flow of fluid pumped into the well. If flow out of the well is greater than flow into the well, it is a strong indicator that a kick may be under way.

> **Active Pit System**
> Rigs contain multiple mud pits. The Deepwater Horizon had 20 in all. Various fluids can be stored in these pits, including drilling mud. The *active pit system* is a subset of the mud pits that the driller selects for monitoring purposes.

In addition to these two primary parameters, the crew can perform visual "flow checks." There were a number of cameras and stations on the *Deepwater Horizon* where the driller, mudlogger, and others could observe whether fluids were flowing from the well. When the pumps are shut off and mud is no longer being sent into the well, flow out of the well should stop. Visual flow checks are a reliable way to monitor for kicks when pumps are off and are often used to confirm other kick indicators.

Finally, the driller and mudlogger also monitor drill-pipe pressure, but it is a more ambiguous kick indicator than the other parameters because there can be many reasons for a change in drill pressure. If drill-pipe pressure *decreases* while the pump rate remains constant, that may indicate that hydrocarbons have entered the wellbore and are moving up the well past the sides of the drill pipe. The lighter-weight hydrocarbons exert less downward pressure, meaning the pumps do not need to work as hard to push fluids into the well. If drill-pipe pressure *increases* while the pump rate remains constant, that may indicate that heavier mud is being pushed up from below (perhaps by hydrocarbons) and displacing lighter fluids in the well adjacent to the drill pipe. Unexplained changes in drill-pipe pressure may not always indicate a kick, but when observed should be investigated. The crew should shut down the pumps and monitor the well to confirm it is static; if they are unable to do so, they should shut in the well until the source of the readings can be determined.

The *Deepwater Horizon* had two separate systems for collecting and displaying real-time data. The "Hitec" system, owned by Transocean, was the source on which the *Deepwater Horizon*'s drilling crew typically relied for monitoring the well. The "Sperry Sun" system—installed and operated by a Halliburton subsidiary at BP's request—sent data back to shore in real time, allowing BP personnel to access and monitor this data from anywhere with an Internet connection.* Individuals on the rig could monitor data from the Sperry Sun system as well.

Once the crew began displacing the riser with seawater at 8:02 p.m., they confronted the challenge of dealing with all of the returning mud. The driller repeatedly rerouted the mud returns from one pit to another in order to accommodate the incoming volume.[86] During that time, the crew also sent mud from other locations into the active pit system.[87] It is not clear whether the driller, assistant drillers, or mudlogger could adequately monitor active pit volume (or flow-in versus flow-out) during that time given all the activity.

Nevertheless, things appear to have been relatively uneventful until 9:00 p.m. Drill-pipe pressure was slowly but steadily decreasing over that time as lighter seawater displaced heavy drilling mud in the riser, lowering the pressure in the well and making it progressively easier to push seawater down into the well through the drill pipe.[88]

At approximately 9:01 p.m., however, drill-pipe pressure (shown by the red line in Figure 4.8) began slowly *increasing*, despite the fact that the pump rate remained constant.[89] Over the next seven minutes, it crept slowly upward from 1,250 to 1,350 psi.[90] While the

---

* It is difficult, if not impossible, to know precisely what the driller, assistant drillers, and mudloggers were doing and what data they were looking at between 8:00 p.m. and the first explosion at 9:49 p.m. Both the Hitec and Sperry Sun displays can be customized, and each operator typically has his own preferred set-up. Moreover, the full Hitec data set sank with the rig, leaving only the Sperry Sun subset of the data behind. Because the Sperry Sun data are all that is now available, the Commission focuses upon that data while recognizing that it is at best an approximation of what the driller, mudlogger, and others on the rig may have been looking at in the hours and minutes leading up to the blowout.

FIGURE 4.8: Increasing Drill-Pipe Pressure

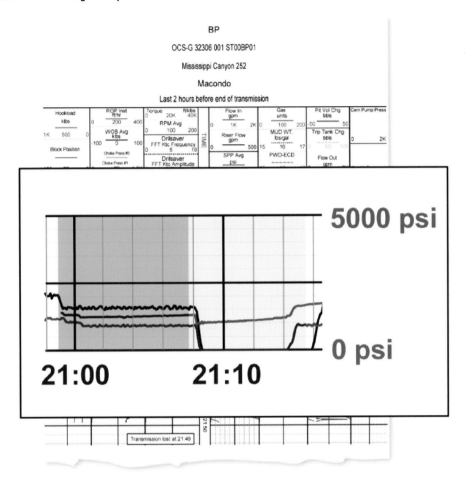

Sperry Sun drill-pipe pressure data (in red).

magnitude of the increase may have appeared only as a subtle trend on the Sperry Sun display, the change in direction from decreasing to increasing was not. [91]

Had someone noticed it, he would have had to explain to himself how the drill-pipe pressure could be increasing while the pump rate was not. One possible reason might have been that hydrocarbons were flowing into the well and pushing heavy drilling mud up past the drill pipe.

The crew may have been distracted by other matters. At about that time, the last of the mud in the riser was arriving at the rig.[92] After that point, the next returning fluid would be the 400-plus barrels of spacer the crew had pumped into the well during the negative-pressure test. BP planned to dump that spacer overboard, but, according to regulations, would first have to run a test to make sure that it had removed all of the oil-based mud from the riser.[93]

At 9:08 p.m., the crew shut down the pumps to perform this "sheen test."[94] They closed a valve on the flow line that had been carrying fluids from the well to the pit system.[95] Mud engineer Greg Meche sampled the fluid and had it tested. Well Site Leader Vidrine waited for confirmation that there was no oily "sheen" on the returning spacer.[96] And mudlogger Joseph Keith performed a visual flow check to ensure the well was not flowing while the pumps were off. According to Keith, there was no flow.[97]

The pumps were shut down for 6 minutes, from 9:08 p.m. to 9:14 p.m. Meche took a sample of the returning fluid from the shaker house* and went to the mud lab to run the test.[98] He then returned to the shaker house, weighed the sample, and spoke with another of the mud engineers about the results.[99] When Vidrine learned the results, he signed off on the test and the crew turned the pumps back on.[100]

What nobody appears to have noticed during those six minutes (perhaps as a result of all of the activity) was that drill-pipe pressure was increasing again. With the pumps off, the drill-pipe pressure (red line in yellow box in Figure 4.8) should have stayed constant or gone down. Instead, it went up by approximately 250 psi.[101] This increase in pressure was clear in the Sperry Sun data, and likely would have been clearer on the Hitec display. Had someone noticed it, he would have recognized this as a significant anomaly that warranted further investigation before turning the pumps back on. But by 9:14 p.m., the crew turned the pumps back on, obscuring the signal. Drill-pipe pressure increased, but so did the pump rate.[102]

Four minutes later, a pressure-relief valve on one of the pumps blew.[103] Revette organized a group of crewmembers to go to the pump room to fix the valve. The group included derrickhand Wyatt Kemp, floorhands Shane Roshto and Adam Weise, and possibly one of the assistant drillers.[104] These men were still attending to the repair at the time of the first explosion.[105]

At about 9:20 p.m., senior toolpusher Randy Ezell called the rig floor and asked Jason Anderson about the negative-pressure test. Anderson responded that, "It went good." Ezell then asked about the displacement. Anderson reassured Ezell, "It's going fine. . . . I've got this."[106]

Shortly before 9:30 p.m., Revette noticed an odd and unexpected pressure difference between the drill pipe and the kill line. At roughly 9:30 p.m., the crew shut off the pumps to investigate.[107] At about that time, Chief Mate David Young arrived at the rig floor to discuss the upcoming cement plug job with Revette and Anderson.[108] Young witnessed Revette and Anderson having a calm discussion about a "differential pressure."[109] Anderson informed Young that the cement plug would be delayed.[110]

The drill-pipe pressure initially decreased after the pumps were turned off, but then increased by 550 psi over a 5.5 minute period.[111] (Figure 4.9) Meanwhile, the pressure on the kill line remained significantly lower. At approximately 9:36 p.m., Revette ordered

---

* The "shaker house" is a room or small separate structure on the rig for "shale shakers"—sieves and shakers that remove cuttings from the mud as it comes out of the well.

FIGURE 4.9: Fluctuating Drill-Pipe Pressure

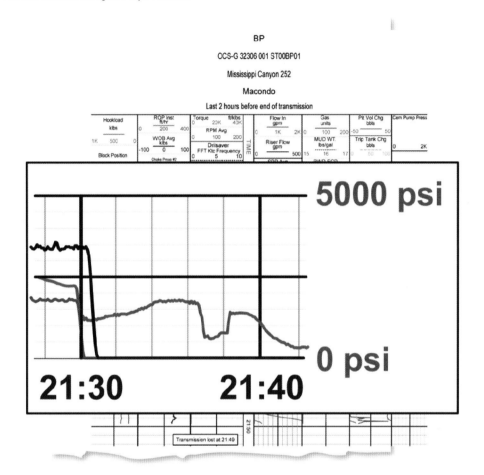

Sperry Sun drill-pipe pressure data (in red).

floorhand Caleb Holloway to bleed off the drill-pipe pressure, in an apparent attempt to eliminate the difference.[112] The drill-pipe pressure initially dropped off as expected, but immediately began climbing again.[113] Young and Anderson left the rig floor.[114] Despite the mounting evidence of a kick, however, neither Revette nor Anderson performed a visual flow check or shut in the well.

At 9:39 p.m., drill-pipe pressure shifted direction and started decreasing.[115] In retrospect, this was a very bad sign. It likely meant that lighter-weight hydrocarbons were now pushing heavy drilling mud out of the way up the casing past the drill pipe.

Diversion and Explosion

Sometime between 9:40 and 9:43 p.m., drilling mud began spewing from the rotary onto the rig floor. This appears to have been the first moment Revette or others realized that a kick had occurred. At about that time, Anderson and assistant driller Stephen Curtis returned to the rig floor.[116]

The men took immediate action. First, they routed the flow coming from the riser through the diverter system, deciding to send it into the mud–gas separator rather than overboard into the sea (which was another option).[117] Second, they closed one of the annular preventers on the BOP to shut in the well.[118] At roughly 9:45 p.m., assistant driller Curtis called senior toolpusher Ezell to tell him that the well was blowing out, that mud was going into the crown on top of the derrick, and that Anderson was shutting the well in.[119]

Their efforts were futile. By the time the rig crew acted, gas was already above the BOP, rocketing up the riser, and expanding rapidly. At the Commission's November 8, 2010, hearing, a representative from Transocean likened it to "a 550-ton freight train hitting the rig floor," followed by what he described as "a jet engine's worth of gas coming out of the rotary."[120] The flow from the well quickly overwhelmed the mud–gas separator system. Ignition and explosion were all but inevitable. The first explosion occurred at approximately 9:49 p.m. On the drilling floor, the Macondo disaster claimed its first victims.

The Well is Not Sealed by the Blowout Preventer

The BOP is designed to contain pressure within the wellbore and halt an uncontrolled flow of hydrocarbons to the rig. The *Deepwater Horizon*'s BOP did not succeed in containing the Macondo well.

Diverter System

The *diverter system* provides two alternate paths for gas or gas-bearing mud returning to the rig from the well. The first path is through the mud-gas separator ("MGS"). The MGS consists of a series of pipes, valves, and a tank configured to remove gas entrained in relatively small amounts of mud. The gas is then vented from an outlet valve located high on the derrick. The MGS cannot accommodate substantial rates of mud flow. The second path is overboard. The diverter system has two 14-inch pipes, one starboard and one portside, through which flow can be sent overboard on the downwind side of the rig.

Witness accounts indicate that the rig crew activated one of the annular preventers around 9:41 p.m., and pressure readings suggest they activated a variable bore ram (which closes around the drill pipe) around 9:46 p.m.[121] Flow rates at this point may have been too high for either the annular preventer or a variable bore ram to seal the well. (Earlier kick detection would have improved the odds of success.)

After the first explosion, crewmembers on the bridge attempted to engage the rig's emergency disconnect system (EDS). The EDS should have closed the blind shear ram, severed the drill pipe, sealed the well, and disconnected the rig from the BOP.[122] But none of that happened. Amid confusion on the bridge, and initial hesitancy from Captain Kuchta, subsea supervisor Chris Pleasant rushed to the main control panel and pushed the EDS button.[123] Although the panel indicators lit up, the rig never disconnected.[124] It is possible that the first explosion had already damaged the cables to the BOP, preventing the disconnect sequence from starting.

Even so, the BOP's automatic mode function (the "deadman" system) should have triggered the blind shear ram after the power, communication, and hydraulics connections between the rig and the BOP were cut. But the deadman failed too. Although it is too early to tell at this point, this failure may have been due to poor maintenance. Post-incident testing of the two redundant "pods" that control the deadman revealed low battery charges in one pod and defective solenoid valves in the other. If those problems existed at the time of the blowout, they would have prevented the deadman system from working.[125*]

The Immediate Causes of the Macondo Well Blowout

As this narrative suggests, the Macondo blowout was the product of several individual missteps and oversights by BP, Halliburton, and Transocean, which government regulators lacked the authority, the necessary resources, and the technical expertise to prevent. We may never know the precise extent to which each of these missteps and oversights in fact caused the accident to occur. Certainly we will never know what motivated the final decisions of those on the rig who died that night. What we nonetheless do know is considerable and significant: (1) each of the mistakes made on the rig and onshore by industry and government increased the risk of a well blowout; (2) the cumulative risk that resulted from these decisions and actions was both unreasonably large and avoidable; and (3) the risk of a catastrophic blowout was ultimately realized on April 20 and several of the mistakes were contributing causes of the blowout.

The immediate cause of the Macondo blowout was a failure to contain hydrocarbon pressures in the well. Three things could have contained those pressures: the cement at the bottom of the well, the mud in the well and in the riser, and the blowout preventer. But mistakes and failures to appreciate risk compromised each of those potential barriers, steadily depriving the rig crew of safeguards until the blowout was inevitable and, at the very end, uncontrollable.

Cementing

Long string casing vs. liner. BP's decision to employ a long string was not unprecedented. Long strings are used with some frequency by other operators in the Gulf of Mexico, although not very often at wells like Macondo—a deepwater well in an unfamiliar geology requiring a finesse cement job.[126] It is not clear whether the decision to use a long string well design contributed directly to the blowout:[127] But it did increase the difficulty of obtaining a reliable primary cement job in several respects,[128] and primary cement failure was a direct cause of the blowout. The long string decision should have led BP and Halliburton to be on heightened alert for any signs of primary cement failure.

Number of centralizers. The evidence to date does not unequivocally establish whether the failure to use 15 additional centralizers was a direct cause of the blowout. But the process

---

* The Commission has not yet determined whether the BOP failed to operate as designed or whether any of the factors discussed contributed to such a failure. The Commission believes it is inappropriate to speculate about answers to those questions at this time. Test records of critical emergency backup systems have not yet been made available. More importantly, a government-sponsored forensic analysis of the BOP is still under way; when completed, that should shed light on why the BOP failed to shut in the Macondo well.

by which BP arrived at the decision to use only six centralizers at Macondo illuminates the flaws in BP's management and design procedures, as well as poor communication between BP and Halliburton.

For example, it does not appear that BP's team tried to determine before April 15 whether additional centralizers would be needed. Had BP examined the issue earlier, it might have been able to secure additional centralizers of the design it favored. Nor does it appear that BP based its decision on a full examination of all potential risks involved. Instead, the decision appears to have been driven by an aversion to one particular risk: that slip-on centralizers would hang up on other equipment.

BP did not inform Halliburton of the number of centralizers it eventually used, let alone request new modeling to predict the impact of using only six centralizers.[129] Halliburton happened to find out that BP had run only six centralizers when one of its cement engineers overheard a discussion on the rig.[130]

Capping off the communication failures, BP now contends that the 15 additional centralizers the BP team flew to the rig may, in fact, have been the ones they wanted. BP's investigation report states that BP's Macondo team "erroneously believed" they had been sent the wrong centralizers.[131] To this day, BP witnesses provide conflicting accounts as to what type of centralizers were actually sent to the rig.

BP's overall approach to the centralizer decision is perhaps best summed up in an e-mail from BP engineer Brett Cocales sent to Brian Morel on April 16. Cocales expressed disagreement with Morel's opinion that more centralizers were unnecessary because the hole was straight, but then concluded the e-mail by saying

> But, who cares, it's done, end of story, [we] will probably be fine and we'll get a good cement job. I would rather have to squeeze [remediate the cement job] than get stuck above the WH [wellhead]. So Guide is right on the risk/reward equation.[132]

Float-valve conversion and circulating pressure. Whether the float valves converted, let alone whether "unconverted" float valves contributed to the eventual blowout, has not yet been, and may never be, established with certainty. But, what is certain is that BP's team again failed to take time to consider whether and to what extent the anomalous pressure readings may have indicated other problems or increased the risk of the upcoming cement job.

BP's team appears not to have seriously examined *why* it had to apply over four times the 750 psi design pressure to convert the float valves. More importantly, the team assumed that the sharp drop from 3,142 psi meant the float valves had in fact converted. That was not at all certain. The auto-fill tube was designed to convert in response to *flow-induced* pressure. Without the required rate of flow, an increase in *static* pressure, no matter how great, will not dislodge the tube.

While BP's Macondo team focused on the peak pressure reading of 3,142 psi and the fact that circulation was reestablished, it does not appear the team ever considered whether sufficient mud flow rate had been achieved to convert the float valves. They should have considered this issue. Because of ECD concerns, BP's engineers had specified a very low circulating pump rate—lower than the flow rate necessary to convert the float valves. BP does not appear to have accounted for this fact.

Cement evaluation log decision. The BP team erred by focusing on full returns as the sole criterion for deciding whether to run a cement evaluation log. Receiving full returns was a good indication that cement or other fluids had not been lost to the weakened formation. But full returns provided, at best, limited or no information about: (1) the precise location where the cement had ended up; (2) whether channeling had occurred; (3) whether the cement had been contaminated;[133] or (4) whether the foam cement had remained stable. Although other indicators—such as on-time arrival of the cement plugs and observation of expected lift pressure—were reassuring, they too provided limited information. Other cement evaluation tools could have provided more direct information about cementing success.

Cement evaluation logs plainly have their limitations, particularly at Macondo. But while many companies do not run cement evaluation logs until the completion phase, BP should have run one here—or sought other equivalent indications of cement quality in light of the many issues surrounding and leading up to the cement job. BP's own report agrees.[134]

Foam cement testing. As explained in an October letter written by the Commission's Chief Counsel, independent cement testing conducted by Chevron strongly suggests the foam cement slurry used at Macondo was unstable.[135] As it turned out, Chevron's tests were consistent with several of Halliburton's own internal test results, some of which appear never to have been reported to BP.

Halliburton's two February tests both indicated that the foam cement slurry would be unstable, which should have prompted the company to reconsider its slurry design.[136] It is irrelevant that the February tests were performed on a slightly different slurry than was actually pumped at Macondo or that assumptions about down-hole temperatures and pressures in February had changed by April 19. Under the circumstances, Halliburton should have examined why the February foam cement slurry was unstable, and should have highlighted the problematic test results for BP.

The two April foam stability tests further illuminate problems with Halliburton's cement design process. Like the two February tests, the first April test indicated the slurry was unstable.[*] This should have prompted Halliburton to review the Macondo slurry design *immediately*, especially given how little time remained before the cement was to be pumped. There is no indication that Halliburton *ever* conducted such a review or alerted BP to the results. It appears that Halliburton personnel responded instead by modifying the

---

[*] Halliburton contends that its lab personnel performed this test improperly, but has not yet produced adequate evidence to support this assertion.

test conditions—specifically, the pre-testing conditioning time—and thereby achieving an arguably successful test result.

Halliburton has to date provided nothing to suggest that its personnel selected the final conditioning time based on any sort of disciplined technical analysis of the Macondo well conditions.[137] Moreover, Halliburton has not yet provided the Commission with evidence to support its view that cement should be "conditioned" for an extended time before stability testing. Given the apparent importance of this view, it should have been supported by careful pre-incident technical analysis and actual physical testing. At present, it appears only to be an unconfirmed hypothesis.

Even more serious, Halliburton documents strongly suggest that the final foam stability test results indicating a stable slurry may not even have been available before Halliburton pumped the primary cement job at Macondo.[138] If true, Halliburton pumped foam cement into the well at Macondo at a time when all available test data showed the cement would be, in fact, unstable.

Risk evaluation of Macondo cementing decisions and procedures. BP's fundamental mistake was its failure—notwithstanding the inherent uncertainty of cementing and the many specific risk factors surrounding the cement job at Macondo—to exercise special caution (and, accordingly, to direct its contractors to be especially vigilant) before relying on the primary cement as a barrier to hydrocarbon flow.

Those decisions and risk factors included, among other things:
- Difficult drilling conditions, including serious lost returns in the cementing zone;
- Difficulty converting float equipment and low circulating pressure after purported conversion;
- No bottoms up circulation;
- Less than recommended number of centralizers;
- Low rate of cement flow; and
- Low cement volume.

Based on evidence currently available, there is nothing to suggest that BP's engineering team conducted a formal, disciplined analysis of the combined impact of these risk factors on the prospects for a successful cement job. There is nothing to suggest that BP communicated a need for elevated vigilance after the job. And there is nothing to indicate that Halliburton highlighted to BP or others the relative difficulty of BP's cementing plan before, during, or after the job, or that it recommended any post-cementing measures to confirm that the primary cement had in fact isolated the high-pressure hydrocarbons in the pay zone.

Negative-Pressure Test

Even when there is no reason for concern about a cement job, a negative-pressure test is "very important."[139] By sending Schlumberger's cement evaluation team back to shore, BP chose to rely entirely on the negative-pressure test to directly evaluate the integrity of the primary cement at Macondo.

It is now undisputed that the negative-pressure test at Macondo was conducted and interpreted improperly. For instance, BP used a spacer that had not been used by anyone at BP or on the rig before, that was not fully tested, and that may have clogged the kill line.[140] The pressure data were not ambiguous. Rather, they showed repeatedly that formation fluids, in this case hydrocarbons, were flowing into the well. The failure to properly conduct and interpret the negative-pressure test was a major contributing factor to the blowout.

Given the risk factors surrounding the primary cement job and other prior unusual events (such as difficulty converting the float valves), the BP Well Site Leaders and, to the extent they were aware of the issues, the Transocean crew should have been particularly sensitive to anomalous pressure readings and ready to accept that the primary cement job could have failed.[141] It appears instead they started from the assumption that the well could not be flowing, and kept running tests and coming up with various explanations until they had convinced themselves their assumption was correct.[142]

The Commission has identified a number of potential factors that may have contributed to the failure to properly conduct and interpret the negative pressure test that night:

- First, there was no standard procedure for running or interpreting the test in either MMS regulations or written industry protocols. Indeed, the regulations and standards did not require BP to run a negative-pressure test at all.

- Second, BP and Transocean had no internal procedures for running or interpreting negative-pressure tests, and had not formally trained their personnel in how to do so.

- Third, the BP Macondo team did not provide the Well Site Leaders or rig crew with specific procedures for performing the negative-pressure test at Macondo.

- Fourth, BP did not have in place (or did not enforce) any policy that would have required personnel to call back to shore for a second opinion about confusing data.

- Finally, due to poor communication, it does not appear that the men performing and interpreting the test had a full appreciation of the context in which they were performing it. Such an appreciation might have increased their willingness to believe the well was flowing. Context aside, however, individuals conducting and interpreting the negative-pressure test should always do so with an expectation that the well might lack integrity.

Temporary Abandonment Procedures

Another factor that may have contributed to the blowout was BP's temporary abandonment procedure.

First, it was not necessary or advisable for BP to replace 3,300 feet of mud below the mud line with seawater. By replacing that much heavy drilling mud with much lighter seawater, BP placed more stress on the cement job at the bottom of the well than necessary. BP's stated reason for doing so was its preference for setting cement plugs in seawater rather than mud.[143] While industry experts have acknowledged that setting cement plugs in seawater can avoid mud contamination and that it is not unusual for operators to set cement plugs in seawater,[144] BP has provided no evidence that it or another operator has ever set a surface cement plug so deep in seawater (particularly without additional barriers). The risks BP created by its decision to displace 3,300 feet of mud with seawater outweighed its concerns about cement setting better in seawater than in mud. As BP has admitted, cement plugs *can* be set in mud.[145] BP also could have set one or more non-cement bridge plugs (which work equally well in mud or seawater).[146] No evidence has yet been produced that the BP team ever formally evaluated these options or the relative risks created by removing 3,300 feet of mud.

It was not necessary to set the cement plug 3,300 feet below the mudline. The BP Macondo team chose to do so in order to set the lockdown sleeve last in the temporary abandonment sequence to minimize the chances of damage to the sleeve. Setting the lockdown sleeve would require 100,000 pounds of force. The BP Macondo team sought to generate that force by hanging 3,000 feet of drill pipe below the sleeve—hence the desire to set the cement plug 3,000 feet below the mud line. BP's desire to set the lockdown sleeve last did not justify the risks its decision created. BP could have used other proven means to protect the lockdown sleeve if set earlier in the process. It also did not need 3,000 feet of space to generate 100,000 pounds of force.[147] Merrick Kelley, the individual at BP in charge of lockdown sleeves in the Gulf of Mexico, told Commission staff that he had recommended setting the plug roughly 1,300 feet below the mud line (using heavier drill pipe), rather than 3,300 feet down. That would have significantly increased the margin of safety for the well.[148]

The most troubling aspect of BP's temporary abandonment procedure was BP's decision to displace mud from the riser before setting the surface cement plug or other barrier in the production casing.[149] During displacement of the riser, the BOP would be open, leaving the cement at the bottom of the well (in the annulus and shoe track) as the *only* physical barrier to flow up the production casing between the pay zone and the rig.[150] Relying so heavily on primary cement integrity put a significant premium on the negative-pressure test and well monitoring during displacement, both of which are subject to human error.

BP's decision under these circumstances to displace mud from the riser before setting another barrier unnecessarily and substantially increased the risk of a blowout. BP could have set the surface cement plug, or a mechanical plug, before displacing the riser.[151] BP could have replaced the mud in the wellbore with heavier mud sufficient to overbalance the well.[152] It is not apparent why BP chose not to do any of these things.

Kick Detection

The drilling crew and other individuals on the rig also missed critical signs that a kick was occurring. The crew could have prevented the blowout—or at least significantly reduced its impact—if they had reacted in a timely and appropriate manner. What is not now clear is precisely why the crew missed these signals.

The Sperry Sun data available to the crew from between 8:00 p.m. and 9:49 p.m. reveal a number of different signals that if observed, should at least have prompted the driller to investigate further, for instance, by conducting a visual flow check, and then shutting in the well if there were indications of flow. For instance, the increasing drill-pipe pressure after the pumps were shut down for the sheen test at 9:08 p.m. was a clear signal that something was happening in the well. Similarly, at roughly 9:30 p.m., the driller and toolpusher recognized an anomalous pressure difference between the drill pipe and kill line.[153] Both of these signals should have prompted action—especially the latter: it was clearly recognized by the crew and echoed the odd pressure readings observed during the negative-pressure test. The crew should have done a flow check and shut in the well immediately upon confirmation of flow.

Why did the crew miss or misinterpret these signals? One possible reason is that they had done a number of things that confounded their ability to interpret signals from the well. For instance, after 9:08 p.m., the crew began sending fluids returning from the well overboard, bypassing the active pit system and the flow-out meter (at least the Sperry Sun flow-out meter). Only the mudlogger performed a visual flow check.[154]

It was neither necessary nor advisable—particularly where the cement at the bottom (in the annulus and shoe track) was the only barrier between the rig and pay zone—to bypass the active system and flow-out meter or to perform potentially confounding simultaneous operations during displacement of the riser. For instance, the crew could have routed the seawater through the active pit system before sending it into the well.

In the future, the instrumentation and displays used for well monitoring must be improved. There is no apparent reason why more sophisticated, automated alarms and algorithms cannot be built into the display system to alert the driller and mudlogger when anomalies arise. These individuals sit for 12 hours at a time in front of these displays. In light of the potential consequences, it is no longer acceptable to rely on a system that requires the right person to be looking at the right data at the right time, and then to understand its significance in spite of simultaneous activities and other monitoring responsibilities.

Diversion and Blowout Preventer Activation

The crew should have diverted the flow overboard when mud started spewing from the rig floor. While that ultimately may not have prevented an explosion, diverting overboard would have reduced the risk of ignition of the rising gas. Considering the circumstances, the crew also should have activated the blind shear ram to close in the well. Diverting the flow overboard and/or activating the blind shear ram may not have prevented the explosion, but likely could have given the crew more time and perhaps limited the impact of the explosion.

There are a few possible explanations for why the crew did neither:

- First, they may not have recognized the severity of the situation, though that seems unlikely given the amount of mud that spewed from the rig floor.

- Second, they did not have much time to act. The explosion occurred roughly six to eight minutes after mud first emerged onto the rig floor.

- Finally, and perhaps most significantly, the rig crew had not been trained adequately how to respond to such an emergency situation. In the future, well-control training should include simulations and drills for such emergencies—including the momentous decision to engage the blind shear rams or trigger the EDS.

The Root Causes: Failures in Industry and Government

Overarching Management Failures by Industry

Whatever irreducible uncertainty may persist regarding the precise contribution to the blowout of each of several potentially immediate causes, no such uncertainty exists about the blowout's root causes. The blowout was not the product of a series of aberrational decisions made by rogue industry or government officials that could not have been anticipated or expected to occur again. Rather, the root causes are systemic and, absent significant reform in both industry practices and government policies, might well recur. The missteps were rooted in systemic failures by industry management (extending beyond BP to contractors that serve many in the industry), and also by failures of government to provide effective regulatory oversight of offshore drilling.

The most significant failure at Macondo—and the clear root cause of the blowout—was a failure of industry management. Most, if not all, of the failures at Macondo can be traced back to underlying failures of management and communication. Better management of decisionmaking processes within BP and other companies, better communication within and between BP and its contractors, and effective training of key engineering and rig personnel would have prevented the Macondo incident. BP and other operators must have effective systems in place for integrating the various corporate cultures, internal procedures, and decisionmaking protocols of the many different contractors involved in drilling a deepwater well.

BP's management process did not adequately identify or address risks created by late changes to well design and procedures. BP did not have adequate controls in place to ensure that key decisions in the months leading up to the blowout were safe or sound from an engineering perspective. While initial well design decisions undergo a serious peer-review process[155] and changes to well design are subsequently subject to a management of change (MOC) process,[156] changes to drilling procedures in the weeks and days before implementation are typically *not* subject to any such peer-review or MOC process. At Macondo, such decisions appear to have been made by the BP Macondo team in *ad hoc* fashion without any formal risk analysis or internal expert review.[157] This appears to have been a key causal factor of the blowout.

A few obvious examples, such as the last-minute confusion regarding whether to run six or 21 centralizers, have already been highlighted. Another clear example is provided by the temporary abandonment procedure used at Macondo. As discussed earlier, that procedure changed dramatically and repeatedly during the week leading up to the blowout. As of April 12, the plan was to set the cement plug in seawater less than 1,000 feet below the mud line after setting the lockdown sleeve. Two days later, Morel sent an e-mail in which the procedure was to set the cement plug in mud before displacing the riser with seawater. By April 20, the plan had morphed into the one set forth in the "Ops Note": the crew would remove 3,300 feet of mud from below the mud line and set the cement plug after the riser had been displaced.

There is no readily discernible reason why these temporary abandonment procedures could not have been more thoroughly and rigorously vetted earlier in the design process.[158] It does not appear that the changes to the temporary abandonment procedures went through any sort of formal review at all.

Halliburton and BP's management processes did not ensure that cement was adequately tested. Halliburton had insufficient controls in place to ensure that laboratory testing was performed in a timely fashion or that test results were vetted rigorously in-house or with the client. In fact, it appears that Halliburton did not even have testing results in its possession showing the Macondo slurry was stable until *after* the job had been pumped. It is difficult to imagine a clearer failure of management or communication.

The story of the foam stability tests may illuminate management problems within BP as well. By early April, BP team members had recognized the importance of timely cement testing.[159] And by mid–April, BP's team had identified concerns regarding the timeliness of Halliburton's testing process.[160] But despite their recognition that final changes to the cement design (made to accommodate their concerns about lost returns) might increase the risks of foam instability,[161] BP personnel do not appear to have insisted that Halliburton complete its foam stability tests—let alone report the results to BP for review—before ordering primary cementing to begin.

BP, Transocean, and Halliburton failed to communicate adequately. Information appears to have been excessively compartmentalized at Macondo as a result of poor communication. BP did not share important information with its contractors, or sometimes internally even with members of its own team. Contractors did not share important information with BP or each other. As a result, individuals often found themselves making critical decisions without a full appreciation for the context in which they were being made (or even without recognition that the decisions *were* critical).

For example, many BP and Halliburton employees were aware of the difficulty of the primary cement job. But those issues were for the most part *not* communicated to the rig crew that conducted the negative-pressure test and monitored the well. It appears that

BP did not even communicate many of those issues to its own personnel on the rig—in particular to Bob Kaluza, who was on his first hitch as a Well Site Leader on the *Deepwater Horizon*. Similarly, it appears at this time that the BP Well Site Leaders did not consult anyone on shore about the anomalous data observed during the negative-pressure test.[162] Had they done so, the Macondo blowout may not have happened.

Transocean failed to adequately communicate lessons from an earlier near-miss to its crew. Transocean failed to adequately communicate to its crew lessons learned from an eerily similar near-miss on one of its rigs in the North Sea four months prior to the Macondo blowout. On December 23, 2009, gas entered the riser on that rig while the crew was displacing a well with seawater during a completion operation. As at Macondo, the rig's crew had already run a negative-pressure test on the lone physical barrier between the pay zone and the rig, and had declared the test a success.[163] The tested barrier nevertheless failed during displacement, resulting in an influx of hydrocarbons. Mud spewed onto the rig floor—but fortunately the crew was able to shut in the well before a blowout occurred.[164] Nearly one metric ton of oil-based mud ended up in the ocean. The incident cost Transocean 11.2 days of additional work and more than 5 million British pounds in expenses.[165]

Transocean subsequently created an internal PowerPoint presentation warning that "[t]ested barriers can fail" and that "risk perception of barrier failure was blinkered by the positive inflow test [negative test]."[166] The presentation noted that "[f]luid displacements for inflow test [negative test] and well clean up operations are not adequately covered in our well control manual or adequately cover displacements in under balanced operations."[167] It concluded with a slide titled "Are we ready?" and "WHAT IF?" containing the bullet points: "[h]igh vigilance when reduced to one barrier underbalanced," "[r]ecognise when going underbalanced—heightened vigilance," and "[h]ighlight what the kick indicators are when not drilling."[168]

Transocean eventually sent out an "operations advisory" to some of its fleet (in the North Sea) on April 14, 2010, reiterating many of the lessons learned and warnings from the presentation. It set out "mandatory" actions to take, acknowledging a "Lack of Well Control preparedness during completion phase," requiring that "[s]tandard well control practices must be maintained through the life span of the well" and stating that "[w]ell programs must specify operations where a single mechanical barrier . . . is in effect and a warning must be included to raise awareness. . . ."[169]

The language in this "advisory" is less pointed and vivid than the language in the earlier PowerPoint. Moreover, according to Transocean, neither the PowerPoint nor this advisory ever made it to the *Deepwater Horizon* crew.[170]

Transocean has suggested that the North Sea incident and advisory were irrelevant to what happened in the Gulf of Mexico. The December incident in the North Sea occurred during the completion phase and involved failure of a different tested barrier. Those are largely

FIGURE 4.10: Examples of Decisions That Increased Risk At Macondo While Potentially Saving Time

Decision	Was There A Less Risky Alternative Available?	Less Time Than Alternative?	Decision-maker
Not Waiting for More Centralizers of Preferred Design	Yes	Saved Time	BP on Shore
Not Waiting for Foam Stability Test Results and/or Redesigning Slurry	Yes	Saved Time	Halliburton (and Perhaps BP) on Shore
Not Running Cement Evaluation Log	Yes	Saved Time	BP on Shore
Using Spacer Made from Combined Lost Circulation Materials to Avoid Disposal Issues	Yes	Saved Time	BP on Shore
Displacing Mud from Riser Before Setting Surface Cement Plug	Yes	Unclear	BP on Shore
Setting Surface Cement Plug 3,000 Feet Below Mud Line in Seawater	Yes	Unclear	BP on Shore (Approved by MMS)
Not Installing Additional Physical Barriers During Temporary Abandonment Procedure	Yes	Saved Time	BP on Shore
Not Performing Further Well Integrity Diagnostics in Light of Troubling and Unexplained Negative Pressure Test Results	Yes	Saved Time	BP (and Perhaps Transocean) on Rig
Bypassing Pits and Conducting Other Simultaneous Operations During Displacement	Yes	Saved Time	Transocean (and Perhaps BP) on Rig

cosmetic differences. The basic facts of both incidents are the same. Had the rig crew been adequately informed of the prior event and trained on its lessons, events at Macondo may have unfolded very differently.[171]

Decisionmaking processes at Macondo did not adequately ensure that personnel fully considered the risks created by time- and money-saving decisions. Whether purposeful or not, many of the decisions that BP, Halliburton, and Transocean made that increased the risk of the Macondo blowout clearly saved those companies significant time (and money).[*]

There is nothing inherently wrong with choosing a less-costly or less-time-consuming alternative—as long as it is proven to be equally safe. The problem is that, at least in regard to BP's Macondo team, there appears to have been no formal system for ensuring that alternative procedures were in fact equally safe. None of BP's (or the other companies') decisions in Figure 4.10 appear to have been subject to a comprehensive and systematic risk-analysis, peer-review, or management of change process. The evidence now available does not show that the BP team members (or other companies' personnel) responsible for these decisions conducted *any* sort of formal analysis to assess the relative riskiness of available alternatives.

---

[*] The Commission cannot say whether any person at BP or another company at Macondo consciously chose a riskier alternative because it would cost the company less money.

Corporations understandably encourage cost-saving and efficiency. But given the dangers of deepwater drilling, companies involved must have in place strict policies requiring rigorous analysis and proof that less-costly alternatives are in fact equally safe. If BP had any such policies in place, it does not appear that its Macondo team adhered to them. Unless companies create and enforce such policies, there is simply too great a risk that financial pressures will systematically bias decisionmaking in favor of time- and cost-savings. It is also critical (as described in greater length in Chapter 8) that companies implement and maintain a pervasive top-down safety culture (such as the ones described by the ExxonMobil and Shell CEOs at the Commission's hearing on November 9, 2010) that reward employees and contractors who take action when there is a safety concern even though such action costs the company time and money.[172]

Of course, some decisions will have shorter timelines than others, and a full-blown peer-reviewed risk analysis is not always practicable. But even where decisions need to be made in relatively short order, there must be systems in place to ensure that some sort of formal risk analysis takes place when procedures are changed, and that the analysis considers the impact of the decision in the context of all system risks. If it turns out there is insufficient time to perform such an analysis, only proven alternatives should be considered.

Regulatory Failures

Government also failed to provide the oversight necessary to prevent these lapses in judgment and management by private industry. As discussed in Chapter 3, MMS regulations were inadequate to address the risks of deepwater drilling. Many critical aspects of drilling operations were left to industry to decide without agency review. For instance, there was no requirement, let alone protocol, for a negative-pressure test, the misreading of which was a major contributor to the Macondo blowout. Nor were there detailed requirements related to the testing of the cement essential for well stability.

Responsibilities for these shortfalls are best not assigned to MMS alone. The root cause can be better found by considering how, as described in Chapter 3, efforts to expand regulatory oversight, tighten safety requirements, and provide funding to equip regulators with the resources, personnel, and training needed to be effective were either overtly resisted or not supported by industry, members of Congress, and several administrations. As a result, neither the regulations nor the regulators were asking the tough questions or requiring the demonstration of preparedness that could have avoided the Macondo disaster.

But even if MMS had the resources and political support needed to promulgate the kinds of regulations necessary to reduce risk, it would still have lacked personnel with the kinds of expertise and training needed to enforce those regulations effectively. The significance of inadequate training is underscored by MMS's approval of BP's request to set its temporary abandonment plug 3,300 feet below the mud line. At least in this instance, there was a MMS regulation that potentially applied. MMS regulations state that cement plugs for temporary abandonment should normally be installed "no more than 1,000 feet below the mud line," but also allow the agency to approve "alternate requirements for subsea wells case-by-case."[173] Crucially, alternate procedures "must provide a level of safety and environmental protection that equals or surpasses current MMS requirements."[174]

BP asked for permission to set its unusually deep cement plug in an April 16 permit application to MMS.[175] BP stated that it needed to set the plug deep in the well to minimize potential damage to the lockdown sleeve, and said it would increase the length of the cement plug to compensate for the added depth. An MMS official approved the request in less than 90 minutes.[176] The official did so because, after speaking with BP, he was persuaded that 3,000 feet was needed to accommodate setting the lockdown sleeve, which he thought was important to do. It is not clear what, if any, steps the official took to determine whether BP's proposed procedure would "provide a level of safety . . . that equal[ed] or surpass[ed]" a procedure in which the plug would have been set much higher up in the well.

MMS's cursory review of the temporary abandonment procedure mirrors BP's apparent lack of controls governing certain key engineering decisions. Like BP, MMS focused its engineering review on the initial well design, and paid far less attention to key decisions regarding procedures during the drilling of the well. Also like BP, MMS did not assess the full set of risks presented by the temporary abandonment procedure. The limited scope of the regulations is partly to blame. But MMS did not supplement the regulations with the training or the processes that would have provided its permitting official with the guidance and knowledge to make an adequate determination of the procedure's safety.

*   *   *   *

Deepwater drilling provides the nation with essential supplies of oil and gas. At the same time, it is an inherently risky business given the enormous pressures and geologic uncertainties present in the formations where oil and gas are found—thousands of feet below the ocean floor. Notwithstanding those inherent risks, the accident of April 20 was avoidable. It resulted from clear mistakes made in the first instance by BP, Halliburton, and Transocean, and by government officials who, relying too much on industry's assertions of the safety of their operations, failed to create and apply a program of regulatory oversight that would have properly minimized the risks of deepwater drilling. It is now clear that both industry and government need to reassess and change business practices to minimize the risks of such drilling.

The tragic results of that accident included the immediate deaths of 11 men who worked on the rig, and serious injury to many others on the rig at the time of the explosion. During the next few hours, days, weeks, and ultimately months, BP and the federal government struggled with their next great challenge: containing the spill and coordinating a massive response effort to mitigate the threatened harm to the Gulf of Mexico and to the Gulf coast. They faced the largest offshore oil spill in the nation's history—and the first from a subsea well located a mile beneath the ocean's surface.

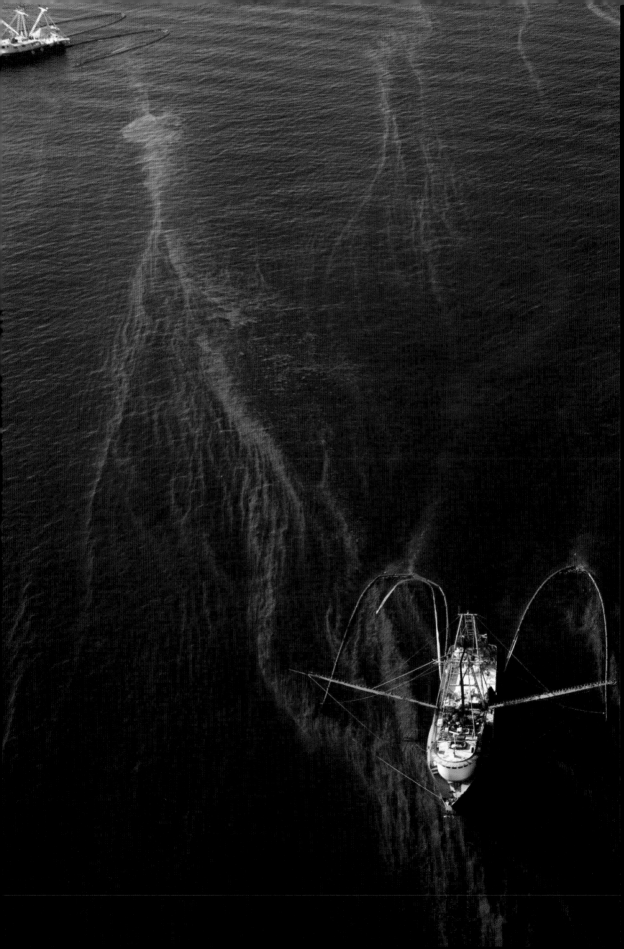

Chapter Five
"You're in it now, up to your neck!"

Response and Containment

No single story dominated newspaper headlines on April 21 and 22. America's most-read papers led with articles about the progress of financial reform legislation; the Supreme Court's 8–1 ruling in a case about video depictions of animal cruelty and the First Amendment; the death of civil rights leader Dorothy Height; and the Food and Drug Administration's plans to target sodium content in packaged foods.[1] Editors appear to have viewed these as slow news days. The *New York Times*, for example, ran a front-page story on April 22 about how travelers in Europe were coping with flight cancellations caused by volcanic ash, titled "Routine Flights Become Overland Odysseys, Minus Clean Socks."[2]

A reader who flipped 12 more pages into the *Times* would have encountered a less lighthearted headline: "11 Remain Missing After Oil Rig Explodes Off Louisiana."[3] *USA Today* and the *Wall Street Journal* covered the *Deepwater Horizon* explosion on their front pages on April 22.[4] The articles described the tragic accident and ensuing search-and-rescue operation—*USA Today* said it "could be one of the worst offshore drilling accidents in U.S. history"[5]—but did not discuss the potential for environmental calamity. As the *Los Angeles Times* put it, "Coast Guard experts worked to assess any environmental cleanup that may be necessary. . .

Shrimp boats skim oil off the coast of Louisiana in mid-May. At its peak, the response to the spill involved over 45,000 people and thousands of watercraft, including private "vessels of opportunity" put to work by BP. The well was finally capped on July 15—87 days after the explosion.

< *Tyrone Turner/Photo courtesy of National Geographic*

[b]ut the main focus was on the missing workers."[6] Other dimensions of the disaster would emerge in the days that followed.

The Early Response (April 20–28)

On the night of April 20, as the *Deepwater Horizon* burned and the rig's survivors huddled on the *Bankston*, the response began. Coast Guard helicopters from the Marine Safety Unit in Morgan City, Louisiana searched for missing crew members. The first Coast Guard cutter to join the search was the *Pompano*, with others to follow. An offshore supply vessel found two burned life rafts. Coast Guard responders knew that approximately 700,000 gallons of diesel fuel were on the rig and could spill into the Gulf. By 10:00 the next morning, planes involved in the search for survivors reported a variably-colored sheen, two miles long by half a mile wide, on the water.

The Captain of the Marine Safety Unit, Joseph Paradis, directed these preliminary efforts. He became the first Federal On-Scene Coordinator under what is known as the National Contingency Plan, a set of federal regulations prescribing the government's response to spills and threatened spills of oil and other hazardous materials.* Under the Plan, when a spill occurs in coastal waters, the Coast Guard has the authority to respond.[7]

As the search and rescue continued on April 21, the oily sheen grew, more Coast Guard personnel and resources became involved, and Rear Admiral Mary Landry took over as Federal On-Scene Coordinator. The commander of Coast Guard District 8 (which includes, among other regions, the Gulf coast from Texas to the Florida panhandle), she would remain Federal On-Scene Coordinator until June 1. While the firefighting efforts continued, she told reporters, "We are only seeing minor sheening on the water. . . . We do not see a major spill emanating from this incident."[8] At this point, Admiral Landry's concern was the fuel oil that could spill from the rig, though she cautioned, "We don't know what's going on subsurface."[9]

As Coast Guard vessels continued the search and rescue operation, private offshore supply vessels sprayed water on the fire. Transocean hired Smit Salvage Americas, a salvage company, to try to save the rig. There was confusion about whether Transocean, the Coast Guard, the salvage company, or anyone at all was directing the firefighting operations.† Captain James Hanzalik, Chief of Incident Response in District 8, would later say that the Coast Guard, which was focused on the search and rescue and then on the spreading oil, "monitored what was going on, but [was] not directing any firefighting resources."[10] By the morning of April 21, the rig was listing. At 11:53 that evening, it shifted and leaned even more.

At 10:22 a.m. on April 22, the rig sank, taking with it the diesel fuel still on board. By that time, the Coast Guard had established an Incident Command Post in a BP facility in Houma, Louisiana. BP had formed a command post in its corporate headquarters in

---

* Created in 1968, the National Contingency Plan has been amended and expanded in the years since. The Oil Pollution Act of 1990 substantially expanded the Plan in response to the *Exxon Valdez* spill.
† The Coast Guard/Bureau of Ocean Energy Management, Regulation, and Enforcement *Deepwater Horizon* Joint Investigation Team, which plans to issue a report in March 2011, is examining the firefighting efforts.

Houston, Texas shortly after the explosion, and the Coast Guard established an Incident Command Post there as well.

These Incident Command Posts, along with one in Mobile, Alabama, and others established later, would become the centers of response operations, with their activities directed by the Federal On-Scene Coordinator as part of the government's Unified Command. The latter is a command structure, created and implemented by the National Contingency Plan, which integrates the "responsible party" (here, BP) with federal and state officials "to achieve an effective and efficient response."[11] The Coast Guard established a Unified Area Command— headquarters for the regional spill response—on April 23 in Robert, Louisiana, later moving it to New Orleans. It eventually included representatives from the federal government, Louisiana, Alabama, Mississippi, Florida, and BP.

Other federal agencies—including the National Oceanic and Atmospheric Administration (NOAA) and Minerals Management Service (MMS)*—immediately sent emergency responders to the Unified Area Command and Incident Command Posts. A host of senior officials, including Secretary of the Interior Ken Salazar and Secretary of Homeland Security Janet Napolitano, briefed the President on their departments' efforts on the afternoon of April 22.[12] Members of the National Response Team, drawn from the 16 federal agencies responsible for coordinating emergency preparedness and response to oil- and hazardous-substance-pollution incidents,[13] began conducting daily telephone meetings.

Even before the rig sank, BP and Transocean directed their attention to the 53-foot-tall blowout preventer (BOP) stack sitting atop the Macondo well. At about 6:00 p.m. on April 21, BP and Transocean began using remotely operated vehicles to try to close the BOP and stop the flow of oil and gas fueling the fire.

These early operations primarily attempted to activate the BOP's blind shear ram and seal off the well. During the attempts, MMS officials were embedded, as observers, in the operations centers at Transocean and BP headquarters in Houston. Because of the emergency, on-scene personnel from BP, Transocean, and Cameron (the company that manufactured the BOP) made decisions without the need for government approvals. Beginning on April 21 and continuing throughout the effort to control the well, Secretary Salazar received daily updates through conference calls with BP's technical teams.

The initial news was encouraging. On April 23, Admiral Landry told the press that, according to surveillance by remotely operated vehicles, the BOP, although "[i]t is not a guarantee," appeared to have done its job, sealing off the flow of oil and preventing any leak.[14] The good news did not last. The Coast Guard suspended its search for the 11 missing workers later that day. And, when Admiral Landry spoke, remotely operated vehicles had not yet surveyed the entire length of the broken riser pipe—previously

---

* On June 18, 2010, Secretary of the Interior Ken Salazar ordered that the Minerals Management Service be officially renamed the Bureau of Ocean Energy Management, Regulation, and Enforcement. For consistency, throughout this chapter, we refer to the agency as the Minerals Management Service (MMS), its name at the time of the April 20 blowout.

Oil spews unchecked from the *Deepwater Horizon's* severed riser in this video frame taken May 26. When the rig sank, the riser broke off, settling on the sea floor.

© BP p.l.c

connecting the well to the now-sunk *Deepwater Horizon*—that still jutted out of the top of the BOP. By mid-afternoon on April 23, the vehicles had discovered that oil was leaking from the end of the riser, where it had broken off from the *Deepwater Horizon* when the rig sank. By the next morning, the vehicles had also discovered a second leak from a kink in the riser, located above the BOP. On April 24, Unified Command announced that the riser was leaking oil at a rate of 1,000 barrels per day.[15] This number appears to have come from BP, although how it was calculated remains unclear.[16]

As BP realized that the early efforts to stop the flow of oil had failed, it considered ways to control the well other than by triggering the BOP. A primary option was to drill a relief well to intersect the Macondo well at its source and enable a drilling rig to pump in cement to stop the flow of oil. While it could take more than three months to drill, a relief well was the only source-control option mentioned by name in BP's Initial Exploration Plan.[17] Industry and government experts characterized a relief well as the only likely and accepted solution to a subsea blowout.[18] BP had begun looking for available drilling rigs on the morning of April 21; it secured two, and began drilling a primary relief well on May 2 and a back-up well insisted upon by Secretary Salazar on May 17.[19]

Responders, meanwhile, shifted their focus to the release of large amounts of oil. Although the National Contingency Plan requires the Coast Guard to supervise an oil-spill response in coastal waters, it does not envision that the Coast Guard will provide all, or even most, of the response equipment. That role is filled by private oil-spill removal organizations, which contract with the oil companies that are required to demonstrate response capacity. BP's main oil-spill removal organization in the Gulf is the Marine Spill Response Corporation, a nonprofit created by industry after the *Exxon Valdez* disaster to respond to oil spills. The Marine Spill Response Corporation dispatched four skimmers within hours of the explosion.[20] BP's oil-spill response plan for the Gulf of Mexico claimed that response vessels provided by the Marine Spill Response Corporation and other private oil-spill removal organizations could recover nearly 500,000 barrels of oil per day.[21]

Despite these claims, the oil-spill removal organizations were quickly outmatched. While production technology had made great advances since *Exxon Valdez* (see Chapter 2), spill-response technology had not. The Oil Pollution Act of 1990, by requiring double hulls in oil tankers, had effectively reduced tanker spills.[22] But it did not provide incentives for industry or guaranteed funding for federal agencies to conduct research on oil-spill response. Though incremental improvements in skimming and boom had been realized in the intervening 21 years, the technologies used in response to the *Deepwater Horizon* and *Exxon Valdez* oil spills were largely the same.[23]

If BP's response capacity was underwhelming, some aspects of its response plan were embarrassing. In the plan, BP had named Peter Lutz as a wildlife expert on whom it would rely; he had died several years before BP submitted its plan. BP listed seals and walruses as two species of concern in case of an oil spill in the Gulf; these species never see Gulf waters. And a link in the plan that purported to go to the Marine Spill Response Corporation website actually led to a Japanese entertainment site.[24] (Congressional investigation revealed that the response plans submitted to MMS by ExxonMobil, Chevron, ConocoPhillips, and Shell were almost identical to BP's—they too suggested impressive but unrealistic response capacity and three included the embarrassing reference to walruses.[25] See Chapter 3 for more discussion of these plans.)

By April 25, responders had started to realize that the estimated spill volume of 1,000 barrels per day might be inaccurate. Dispersants applied to break up the surface slick were not having the anticipated effect. Either the dispersants were inexplicably not working, or the amount of oil was greater than previously suspected. Between April 26 and April 28, BP personnel within Unified Command reportedly said that they thought 1,000 to 6,000 barrels were leaking each day.[26]

To alert government leadership that the spill could be larger than 1,000 barrels per day, a NOAA scientist created a one-page report on April 26 estimating the flow rate at roughly 5,000 barrels per day. He based this estimate on other responders' visual observations of the speed with which oil was leaking from the end of the riser, as well as the size and color of the oil slick on the Gulf's surface.[27] Both methodologies, the scientist recognized, were highly imprecise: he relied on rough guesses, for example, of the velocity of the oil as it left the riser and the thickness of the surface slick. He told a NOAA colleague in Unified Command that the flow could be 5,000 to 10,000 barrels per day.[28] At a press conference on April 28, Admiral Landry stated, "NOAA experts believe the output could be *as much as* 5,000 barrels" (emphasis added).[29]

Although it represented a five-fold increase over the then-current figure, 5,000 barrels per day was a back-of-the-envelope estimate, and Unified Command did not explain how NOAA calculated it. Nevertheless, for the next four weeks, it remained the official government estimate of the spill size.

The Response Ramps Up (April 29–May 1)
At the peak of the response, more than 45,000 people participated.[30] In addition to deploying active-duty members to the Gulf, the Coast Guard called up reservists. Some 1,100 Louisiana National Guard troops served under the direction of Unified Command.[31] The Environmental Protection Agency (EPA), NOAA, and other federal agencies shifted hundreds of responders to the region.

Consistent with the Unified Command framework, BP played a major role from the outset. Most Coast Guard responders had a BP counterpart. For instance, Doug Suttles, BP's Chief

In a joint press briefing, BP Chief Operating Officer of Exploration and Production Doug Suttles takes the podium alongside Federal On-Scene Coordinator and Coast Guard Rear Admiral Mary Landry. The Coast Guard considered BP a co-combatant in the effort to battle the oil.

U.S. Coast Guard photo/Petty Officer 3rd Class Cory J. Mendenhall

Operating Officer of Exploration and Production, was the counterpart to the Federal On-Scene Coordinator. BP employees were scattered through the command structure, in roles ranging from waste management to environmental assessment. Sometimes, a BP employee supervised Coast Guard or other federal responders.

The preference under the National Contingency Plan is for the Federal On-Scene Coordinator to supervise response activities while the responsible party conducts—and funds—them. When a spill "results in a substantial threat to public health or welfare of the United States," the Plan requires the Federal On-Scene Coordinator to direct all response efforts.[32] The Coast Guard also has the option to "federalize" the spill—conducting and funding all aspects of the response through the Oil Spill Liability Trust Fund, and later seeking reimbursement from the responsible party.[33] But in most spills, especially when the responsible party has deep pockets and is willing to carry out response activities, federalizing is not preferred. Coast Guard leaders, shaped by their experience implementing the National Contingency Plan through a unified command system, viewed the responsible party as a co-combatant in the fight against the oil. From their perspective, BP took its role as responsible party seriously and had an open checkbook for response costs.* That did not mean BP was happy to pay. Tony Hayward, the Chief Executive Officer of BP, reportedly asked board members, "What the hell did we do to deserve this?"[34]

Though willing to fund and carry out the response, BP had no available, tested technique to stop a deepwater blowout other than the lengthy process of drilling a relief well. Forty years earlier, the government had recognized the need for subsea containment technology. In 1969, following the Santa Barbara Channel spill, the Nixon administration had issued a report recommending, in part, that "[u]nderwater methods to collect oil from subsea leaks should be developed."[35] For deepwater wells, however, such development had never occurred. Within a week of the explosion, BP embarked on what would become a massive effort to generate containment options, either by adapting shallow-water technology to the deepwater environment, or by designing entirely new devices. Different teams at BP's Houston headquarters focused on different ways either to stop the flow of oil or to collect it at the source. Each team had what amounted to a blank check. As one contractor put it, "Whatever you needed, you got it. If you needed something from a machine shop and you couldn't jump in line, you bought the machine shop."[36]

While the Coast Guard oversaw the response at the surface, MMS primarily oversaw source-control operations. BP would draft detailed procedures describing an operation it wished to perform around the wellhead. MMS and Coast Guard officials in Houston participated in the drafting process to help identify and mitigate hazards, including risks to worker safety. At Unified Area Command, Lars Herbst, MMS Gulf of Mexico Regional Director, or his deputy, Mike Saucier, would review and approve the procedures, before the Federal On-Scene Coordinator gave the final go-ahead. This hierarchy of approvals remained in place throughout the containment effort.

MMS was the sole government agency charged with understanding deepwater wells and related technology, such as BOPs. But its supervision of the containment effort was limited, in line with its role in overseeing deepwater drilling more generally. Its staff did not attempt to dictate whether BP should perform an operation, determine whether it had a significant likelihood of success, or suggest consideration of other options. This limited role stemmed in part from a lack of resources. At most, MMS had four to five employees in Houston trying to oversee BP's efforts. One employee described his experience as akin to standing in a hurricane.

Interviews of MMS staff members involved in the containment effort also suggest that the agency did not view itself as capable of, or responsible for, providing more substantive oversight. One MMS employee asserted that BP, and industry more broadly, possessed 10

---

*   The day the rig exploded, the emergency reserve available to the Federal On-Scene Coordinator in the Oil Spill Liability Trust Fund and not obligated to other ongoing response actions amounted to $18,600,000. In contrast, by November 11, 2010, BP had paid $580,977,461 to the federal government for response costs. BP's total expenditures on the response also included payments to states and to contractors it hired directly. Paul Guinee, e-mail to Commission staff, November 16, 2010; BP, *Claims and Government Payments Gulf of Mexico Oil Spill Public Report* (November 11, 2010).

times the expertise that MMS could bring to bear on the complex problem of deepwater spill containment. Another pointed out that MMS had trouble attracting the most talented personnel, who are more likely to work in industry where salaries are higher. A third MMS employee stated that he could count on one hand the people from the agency whom he would trust to make key decisions in an effort of this magnitude. Perhaps most revealingly, two different MMS employees separately recalled being asked—one by Secretary Salazar, and the other by Assistant Secretary Tom Strickland—what they would do if the U.S. government took over the containment effort. Both said they would hire BP or another major oil company.

Though the Coast Guard and MMS believed they had to work closely with BP, others in government did not share this view of the relationship with the responsible party. At an April 29 press conference with several senior administration officials, Coast Guard Rear Admiral Sally Brice O'Hara referred to BP as "our partner," prompting Secretary Napolitano to emphasize, "They are not our partner."[37] Secretary Salazar later said on *CNN* that the government would keep its "boot on the neck" of BP.[38]

While struggling to explain its oversight role to the public, the federal government increased its commitment to the spill response. On April 29, a week after the rig sank and a day after the flow-rate estimate rose to 5,000 barrels per day, the Coast Guard designated the disaster a "Spill of National Significance"[39]—the first time the government had used that designation. A Spill of National Significance is one "that due to its severity, size, location, actual or potential impact on the public health and welfare or the environment, or the necessary response effort, is so complex that it requires extraordinary coordination of federal, state, local, and responsible party resources to contain and clean up the discharge."[40] The designation permitted a National Incident Commander to "assume the role of the [Federal On-Scene Coordinator] in communicating with affected parties and the public, and coordinating federal, state, local, and international resources at the national level."[41] Other than the quoted sentence, the National Contingency Plan is silent on the role of the National Incident Commander, who can fill the position, and what tasks he or she will handle. As a result, there is no clear line between the National Incident Commander's responsibilities and those of the Federal On-Scene Coordinator. During the *Deepwater Horizon* spill response, the National Incident Commander coordinated interagency efforts on the wide variety of issues responders faced, and dealt with high-level political and media inquiries, while the Federal On-Scene Coordinator generally retained oversight of day-to-day operations. More than anyone else, the National Incident Commander became the face of the federal response. When President Obama visited the Gulf on May 2, a fisherman asked who would pay his bills while he was out of work; the President responded that the National Incident Commander would take care of it.[42]

On May 1, Secretary Napolitano announced that Admiral Thad Allen, the outgoing Commandant of the Coast Guard and then its only four-star Admiral, would serve as National Incident Commander.[43] Admiral Allen was well known in the Gulf. He had previously overseen the ocean rescue and return to Cuba of Elian Gonzalez in 1999; the Coast Guard's work securing harbors along the Eastern Seaboard after the attacks of September 11, 2001; and the federal response to Hurricanes Katrina and Rita, after the

Surrounded by orange containment boom, National Incident Commander Admiral Thad Allen speaks to the press in Venice, Louisiana. The outgoing Coast Guard Commandant postponed his retirement to assume the post, drawing on his experience leading the federal response to Hurricane Katrina and overseeing oil-spill readiness exercises in the Gulf.

Steven Johnson/Miami Herald/MCT via Getty Images

Bush Administration asked him to replace the stumbling director of the Federal Emergency Management Agency, Michael Brown, as the lead federal official.[44] His leadership during Katrina was widely considered a success. A Baton Rouge *Advocate* editorial published near the end of his time in the Gulf highlighted his local popularity and thanked him for his service.[45] Less celebrated in the media, but no less important for the task facing him as National Incident Commander, was Admiral Allen's role overseeing a 2002 simulation that tested the readiness of the Coast Guard and other agencies to respond to a Spill of National Significance off the coast of Louisiana.[46] As Commandant, Admiral Allen was already participating in the response, and he put off his scheduled retirement when he became National Incident Commander.

As the National Incident Command took shape in early May, BP's efforts to stop the flow of oil continued to focus on actuating the BOP, which BP still believed was the best chance of quickly shutting in the well. These efforts were plagued by engineering and organizational problems. For instance, it took nearly 10 days for a Transocean representative to realize that the stack's plumbing differed from the diagrams on which BP and Transocean were relying, and to inform the engineers attempting to trigger one of the BOP's rams through a hydraulic panel that they had been misdirecting their efforts.[47] (Without properly recording the change, Transocean had reconfigured the BOP; the panel that was supposed to control that ram actually operated a different, "test" ram, which could not stop the flow of oil and gas.[48] BP Vice President Harry Thierens, who was BP's lead on BOP interventions, stated afterward that he was "quite frankly astonished that this could have happened."[49]) While this and other problems delayed BP's efforts, the flow of oil and sand continued to wear down the BOP's parts, making closure more difficult.[50]

BP stopped trying to close the BOP on May 5.[51] By May 7, it had concluded that "[t]he possibility of closing the BOP has now been essentially exhausted."[52] In mid-May, at the suggestion of Secretary of Energy Steven Chu, BP undertook gamma-ray imaging of the BOP, which lacked instrumentation to show the position of its rams.[53] The imaging indicated that, although the blind shear ram had closed at least partially, oil continued to flow past it.

The "Social and Political Nullification" of the National Contingency Plan (April 29–May 1)

The hurricane-stricken Gulf states are all too familiar with emergency response; all are among the top dozen states in number of declared major disasters.[54] State and local officials in the Gulf are accustomed to setting up emergency-response structures pursuant to the Stafford Act, under which the federal government provides funding and assists state and local governments during a major disaster.[55] In contrast, the National Contingency Plan, which governs oil spills, gives the Federal On-Scene Coordinator the power to direct all response actions.[56] Thus, while the Stafford Act envisions a state-directed (though in part federally funded) response, the National Contingency Plan puts federal officials in charge.

State and local officials chafed under federal control of the response. Louisiana Governor Bobby Jindal's advisors reportedly spent days trying to determine whether the Stafford Act or the National Contingency Plan applied.[57] On April 29, Governor Jindal declared a state of emergency in Louisiana, authorizing the director of the Governor's Office of Homeland Security and Emergency Preparedness to undertake any legal activities deemed necessary to respond and to begin coordinating state response efforts.[58] These efforts took place outside of the Unified Command framework. The Governors of Mississippi, Alabama, and Florida followed suit, declaring states of emergency the next day.[59]

At the outset of the spill, the pre-designated State On-Scene Coordinators for Louisiana, Alabama, and Mississippi participated in Unified Command.[60] These individuals were career oil-spill responders: familiar with the National Contingency Plan, experienced in responding to spills, and accustomed to working with the Coast Guard. Some had participated in the 2002 spill exercise run by Admiral Allen. They shared the Coast Guard's view that the responsible party is an important ally, not an adversary, in responding to a spill.

During this spill, however, the Governors and other state political officials participated in the response in unprecedented ways, taking decisions out of the hands of career oil-spill responders. These high-level state officials were much less familiar with spill-response planning. In addition to the National Contingency Plan, each Coast Guard sector is an "Area" with an Area Contingency Plan created by relevant state and federal agencies. When confronted with a contingency plan setting out how the federal and state governments were supposed to run an oil-spill response, one high-level state official told a Coast Guard responder that he never signed it. According to the Coast Guard officer, the state official was not questioning whether his signature appeared on the document, but asserting that he had not substantively reviewed the plan.[61] State and local officials largely rejected the pre-spill plans and began to create their own response structures.

Because the majority of the oil would come ashore in Louisiana, these issues of control mattered most there. Louisiana declined to empower the officials that it sent to work with federal responders within Unified Command, instead requiring most decisions to go through the Governor's office. For example, the Louisiana representative at Unified Area Command could not approve the daily agenda of response activities.[62] Responders worked around this problem, but it complicated operations.

Local officials were even less familiar with oil-spill planning, though they had robust experience with other emergencies. Under Louisiana law, Parish Presidents exercise substantial authority—mirroring that of the Governor—during hurricanes and other natural disasters.[63] The parishes wanted to assert that same control during the spill, and many used money distributed by BP to purchase their own equipment and establish their own operating centers outside of Unified Command. Eventually, the Coast Guard assigned a liaison officer to each Parish President, who attempted to improve relationships with the parishes by providing information and reporting back to Unified Command on local needs.

Local resentment became a media theme and then a self-fulfilling prophesy. Even those who privately thought the federal government was doing the best it could under the circumstances did not say so publicly.[64] Coast Guard responders watched Governor Jindal—and the TV cameras following him—return to what appeared to be the same spot of oiled marsh day after day to complain about the inadequacy of the federal response, even though only a small amount of marsh was then oiled. When the Coast Guard sought to clean up that piece of affected marsh, Governor Jindal refused to confirm its location.[65] Journalists encouraged state and local officials and residents to display their anger at the federal response, and offered coverage when they did. Anderson Cooper reportedly asked a Parish President to bring an angry, unemployed offshore oil worker on his show. When the Parish President could not promise the worker would be "angry," both were disinvited.[66]

As the media coverage grew more frenzied, the pressure increased on federal, state, and local officials to take action and to avoid being seen as in league with BP. What Admiral Allen would later call "the social and political nullification" of the National Contingency Plan, which envisions "unity of effort" between the federal government, state governments, and the responsible party, was well underway.[67]

Spill Impacts and Efforts To Help

Effects on the Gulf economy, environment, and way of life increased as the spill dragged on and oil crept closer to shorelines. Concerns about fisheries took hold immediately. The

Gulf of Mexico is home to crab, shrimp, oyster, and finfish fisheries, all of which were affected by the oil. The Louisiana Department of Wildlife and Fisheries and the Department of Health and Hospitals began closing fisheries and oyster grounds in state waters— three miles or less from shore—on April 30. State fishery closures continued piece by piece, beginning on June 2 in Alabama, June 4 in Mississippi, and June 14 in Florida.[68] NOAA's Office of Response and Restoration began conducting flyovers and modeling the movement of the oil beginning April 23.[69] Responders used these daily trajectory forecasts to anticipate where oil would be over the next 24- and 48-hour periods. Based on the forecasts, as well as sampling in or near affected areas, the federal fishery closures began on May 2. Through an emergency rule, NOAA's National Marine Fisheries Service first closed an area spanning approximately 6,817 square miles, or 3 percent of the Gulf federal fishing zone.[70] On May 7, NOAA increased the closed area to 4.5 percent of that zone.[71] A week later, it extended the closures indefinitely.[72] NOAA continued to close additional areas, and on June 2—at the peak of the closures—it prohibited all fishing in nearly 37 percent of the Gulf zone.[73]

Although unable to fish, many fishermen were not content to lay idle. As contractors and subcontractors set up camp in towns across the Gulf to carry out response activities, residents viewed them with suspicion. People in Lafourche Parish, for example, worried about the out-of-state oil-spill-response contractors who took over their shores bringing crime and taking away spill-related job opportunities.[74] Parish Presidents pushed BP and Unified Command to give clean-up jobs to residents and, in the newly out-of-work fishermen, saw a fleet of experienced captains who were more familiar with the intricate shoreline than any out-of-state oil-spill responders.

The Vessels of Opportunity program was BP's answer, and a way for BP to provide some income to affected residents outside of the formal claims process. Through the program, BP employed private vessels to conduct response efforts such as skimming, booming, and transporting supplies. Vessels of opportunity made between $1,200 and $3,000 per day, depending on the size of the boat. Individual crew members made $200 for an eight-hour day.[75] But the program had delays and problems. BP and the Coast Guard were slow to develop eligibility requirements (such as an operable VHF-FM radio) for boats.[76] Initially, there was not enough work. Later, residents and Parish Presidents complained that BP was not sufficiently targeting out-of-work fishermen at whom the program was ostensibly directed, and that wealthy or non-local boat owners were taking advantage of poor oversight to gain spots in the program. Eventually, BP established a verification process that prioritized boats registered with the state before March 2010 and that accepted only one boat per owner.[77] The group that may have lost out the most on the program was the large population of Vietnamese-American fishermen. Many had arrived in the region as refugees and struggled with the lack of Vietnamese-language training.[78] (Chapter 6 discusses the impacts of the spill on minority fishing communities.)

Angry that BP was deploying non-local boats in his parish waters, Craig Taffaro, President of St. Bernard Parish, started his own program using the commercial fishing fleet based there. He submitted invoices to BP, which it paid. The State of Louisiana also began its own program, as did Plaquemines and Jefferson Parishes.[79] Unified Command struggled to coordinate this floating militia of independent vessels and to give them useful response tasks. Having hundreds of vessels look for oil did not contribute significantly to the response, because aircraft were more effective at spotting oil.[80] Placing boom requires skill and training, and responders differed in their judgments of how much the vessels contributed.

In addition to overseeing the Vessels of Opportunity program, Unified Command needed to ensure that all workers, whether on boats or on shore, were adequately trained and taking safety precautions. The Occupational Safety and Health Administration (OSHA) began working with Unified Command at the end of April; under the National Contingency Plan, all response actions must comply with OSHA's training and safety requirements.[81] OSHA established rules regarding protective equipment and, because the response relied in part on untrained workers, a shortened training course.[82] Residents were eager to take on clean-up jobs, but some worried that, notwithstanding OSHA's involvement, response-related work would affect their health.[83] (Chapter 6 discusses the impacts of response activities on health.)

Health issues for non-workers were thornier. The Centers for Disease Control and Prevention represents the Department of Health and Human Services on the National Response Team and had participated in recent spill training exercises. The Centers for Disease Control, however, had not foreseen that an oil spill could affect the health of the broader population and had not fully considered the role health agencies might play in a spill response.[84] Others in the Department, including the Assistant Secretary for Preparedness and Response, had not either.[85] Consequently, the Department had to consider during the disaster how it would fund spill-related activities, because BP would have to pay only for those deemed response measures by Unified Command. The Department was concerned that neither the Oil Spill Liability Trust Fund nor BP would reimburse it for activities such as long-term health surveillance, and negotiations over what costs qualified for reimbursement took time.[86] At the request of Unified Command, Health and Human Services eventually, in June, sent a Senior Health Policy Advisor to support the National Incident Commander on public health issues.[87]

The spill affected wildlife health as well. On April 30, the *Times-Picayune* reported the recovery of the first oiled bird.[88] From then on, crude-covered animals were a fixture in the media coverage and public perceptions of the disaster. The U.S. Fish and Wildlife Service, NOAA's Fisheries Service, state wildlife agencies, and academic organizations oversaw animal response and rehabilitation efforts.[89] Wildlife responders took recovered animals to one of several treatment centers, washing, monitoring, and then releasing them.[90] According to the Audubon Society, more than 12,000 volunteers signed up to help with these efforts during a single week in early May.[91] Not all offers of assistance were accepted. Some groups that could have provided skilled wildlife responders, such as the National Wildlife Federation, felt discouraged from helping; in their view, there was no effective process for integrating skilled volunteers into the response structure.[92] Would-be volunteers worried that animal mortality was greater than it would have been had more rescuers been out looking for oiled animals.[93] (Chapter 6 discusses impacts on wildlife in detail.)

Free once more, a pair of pelicans test their wings in Aransas National Wildlife Refuge after being de-oiled and nursed back to health. Taking part in the release are veterinarian Sharon Taylor and Refuge manager Dan Alonso. Over a thousand birds affected by the spill were rehabilitated; thousands of others were not so fortunate.

U.S. Coast Guard photo/Petty Officer 3rd Class Robert Brazzell

Along with volunteering for wildlife rescue, members of the general public submitted to BP and the Coast Guard numerous ideas for how to clean up the oil or plug the well. For instance, movie star Kevin Costner argued for the use of his oil-water separator, and BP eventually purchased 32 units.[94] Citizens without Costner's resources had more trouble getting their ideas reviewed. On June 4, the Coast Guard established the Interagency Alternative Technology Assessment Program to receive, acknowledge, and evaluate ideas.[95] The program received about 4,000 submissions.[96] Most of the proposals were not viable or required too much time for development into operational response tools.* As ideas came in, the Coast Guard screened them and sent the most promising to the Federal On-Scene Coordinator, who ended up testing about a dozen during the course of the spill. None was implemented on a large scale, but the Coast Guard plans to use some of the proposals in its spill-response research.[97]

Foreign companies and countries also offered assistance in the form of response equipment and vessels. The Coast Guard and National Incident Command accepted some of these offers and rejected others.[98] News reports and politicians alleged that the federal government turned away foreign offers of assistance because of the Jones Act, a law preventing foreign vessels from participating in trade between U.S. ports.[99] While decisionmakers did decline to purchase some foreign equipment for operational reasons—

---

* Although intellectual property concerns prohibit the Coast Guard from disclosing the proposals actually submitted, news outlets reported that individuals suggested ideas like dumping popcorn from airplanes; soaking up the oil with packing peanuts, sawdust, kitty litter, and air conditioning filters; and using liquid nitrogen to freeze the oil. Julie Schmit, "After BP Oil Spill, Thousands of Ideas Poured in for Cleanup," *USA Today,* November 15, 2010; John W. Schoen, "BP's Suggestion Box Is Spilling Over," MSNBC, May 14, 2010.

for example, Dutch vessels that would have taken weeks to outfit and sail to the region, and a Taiwanese super-skimmer that was expensive and highly inefficient in the Gulf—they did not reject foreign ships because of Jones Act restrictions.[100] These restrictions did not even come into play for the vast majority of vessels operating at the wellhead, because the Act does not block foreign vessels from loading and then unloading oil more than three miles off the coast.[101] When the Act did apply, the National Incident Commander appears to have granted waivers and exemptions when requested.[102]

In the end, the response technology that created the most controversy was not a mechanical tool like a skimmer or oil-water separator, but a chemical one.

Initial Dispersant Decisions (April 30–May 10)

Even before they were certain that oil was spilling into the Gulf, responders had readied planes full of dispersants to use in a potential response. Dispersants include surfactants that break down oil into smaller droplets, which are more likely to dissolve into the water column.[103] On April 24, once Unified Command knew a leak existed and coastal impacts were possible, Admiral Landry told reporters: "We have one-third of the world's dispersant resources on standby. . . . Our goal is to fight this oil spill as far away from the coastline as possible."[104] Faced with what one Coast Guard captain called a "tradeoff of bad choices" between spraying chemicals on the water or watching more oil reach the shore,[105] responders would wield dispersants in the battle against oil for the next 12 weeks, using novel methods and unprecedented volumes.

Dispersants do not remove oil from the water altogether. Energy from wind and waves naturally disperses oil, and dispersants accelerate this process by allowing oil to mix with water. Dispersed oil is diluted as it mixes vertically and horizontally in the water column.[106] Using dispersants has several potential benefits. First, less oil will reach shorelines and fragile environments such as marshes.[107] Second, animals and birds that float on or wade through the water surface may encounter less oil.[108] Third, dispersants may accelerate the rate at which oil biodegrades.[109] Finally, responders to an oil spill can use dispersants when bad weather prevents skimming or burning. But dispersants also pose potential threats. Less oil on the surface means more in the water column, spread over a wider area, potentially increasing exposure for marine life. Chemically dispersed oil can be toxic in both the short and long term. Moreover, some studies have found that dispersants do not increase biodegradation rates—or may even inhibit biodegradation.[110]

At the direction of the Federal On-Scene Coordinator, responders first sprayed dispersants on the surface oil slick on April 22.[111] Long before the spill, interagency "Regional Response Teams" had evaluated and preauthorized the use of specific dispersants in the Gulf of Mexico, with limits as to geographic areas where the chemicals could be applied, but not on overall volume or duration of use.[112] The teams included representatives from relevant state governments and from federal agencies with authority over oil spills, including the Coast Guard, EPA, the Department of the Interior, and NOAA. Preauthorization, requiring the concurrence of the Team, allows the Federal On-Scene Coordinator to employ dispersants immediately following a spill.[113] Timing matters, because the chemicals are most effective when oil is fresh, before it has weathered and emulsified.[114] Without preauthorization, responders can still use dispersants during a spill if EPA and state authorities approve.[115] With the permission of the Federal On-Scene Coordinator, BP and its contractors applied 14,654 gallons of the dispersant Corexit on the surface during the week of April 20 to 26.[116]

Under the terms of the preauthorization, Corexit was a permissible dispersant because EPA listed it on the National Contingency Plan Product Schedule. EPA obtains toxicity data from the manufacturer before placing a dispersant on that schedule.[117] Some toxicologists have questioned the reliability and comparability of the testing by manufacturers.[118] Moreover, the required testing is limited to acute (short-term) toxicity studies on one fish species and one shrimp species;[119] it does not consider issues such as persistence in the environment and long-term effects.

Dispersant use increased during the first weeks of the spill. From April 27 to May 3, responders applied 141,358 gallons to the surface. The following week, they applied 168,988 gallons. The Coast Guard and other responders had often deployed dispersants to respond to spills, but never in such volumes; during the *Exxon Valdez* spill, responders sprayed about 5,500 gallons, and that use was controversial.[120]

Faced with high-volume dispersant use, Gulf residents became concerned that the chemicals were just as bad as the spilled oil itself. Some workers reported nausea and headaches after coming into contact with dispersants.[121] However, OSHA found no evidence of unsafe dispersant exposure among responders.[122] Environmental groups pressured Nalco, the company that manufactures Corexit, to disclose its formula. Although it had given the formula to EPA during the pre-listing process, Nalco declined to make the formula public, citing intellectual property concerns.[123] This decision did not reassure the citizens of the Gulf.

As the volume of dispersants sprayed on the surface grew, BP raised the idea of applying dispersants directly at the well, rather than waiting for the oil to reach the surface a mile above.[124] Responders had never before applied dispersants in the deep sea. Within Unified Command, some scientists were cautiously optimistic. They hoped that, in addition to reducing shoreline impacts, subsea application would mean less dispersants used overall, because they would be more effective in the turbulent subsea environment. Responders would later conclude that subsea dispersant application also helped to protect worker health by lowering the concentrations of volatile organic compounds at the surface.[125]

But responders were concerned about the absence of information on the effects of dispersants in the deepwater environment. No federal agency had studied subsea dispersant use and private studies had been extremely limited.[126] BP's Hayward was less than helpful; he told a British newspaper, "The Gulf of Mexico is a very big ocean. The amount of volume of oil and dispersant we are putting into it is tiny in relation to the total water volume."[127] While federal officials did not possess the scientific information they needed to guide their choices, they had to make choices nevertheless.

From April 30 to May 10, scientists within Unified Command worked intensively to create a monitoring protocol for subsea dispersant use that would detect adverse environmental effects and provide criteria for when the use was appropriate. It was unclear whether the preauthorizations by the Regional Response Teams covered subsea dispersant use. EPA believed they did not and wanted to make decisions about such use at a high level within the agency. But it had trouble establishing clear and rapid communication, both internally and outside the agency.[128] This slowed creation and review of the testing protocols, while Coast Guard responders and NOAA scientists chafed at the delay.

On May 10, after several rounds of testing and revision, EPA adopted a testing protocol created by NOAA and BP scientists as its directive regarding subsea dispersant use. The directive, as later amended by EPA, limited subsea application to 15,000 gallons per day and required monitoring and compliance with environmental toxicity guidelines.[129] Administrator Lisa Jackson ultimately gave EPA's approval for subsea dispersant use and would later call it the hardest decision she ever made.[130] Observed toxicity levels never exceeded the guidelines in EPA's directive, and responders continued to apply dispersants at the source until BP capped the well.

Deploying the Containment Dome (May 6–8)
While scientists tried to determine if subsea dispersant use was even possible, BP engineers simultaneously worked to contain and recover oil until they could kill the well. Within days of discovering the leaks from the broken riser on the sea floor, they began to consider use of a large containment dome. The idea was to place the dome, also known as a cofferdam, over the larger of the two leaks, with a pipe at the top channeling oil and gas to the *Discoverer Enterprise*, a ship on the surface. BP already had several cofferdams, which it had used to provide safe working space for divers repairing leaks from shallow-water wells following Hurricanes Katrina and Rita.[131] By May 4, BP had finished modifying for deep-sea use and oil collection a preexisting dome that was 14 feet wide, 24 feet long, and 40 feet tall.[132] Following an MMS inspection of the *Discoverer Enterprise*, BP began to lower the 98-ton dome to the sea floor late in the evening of May 6.[133]

The likelihood of collecting oil with the cofferdam was uncertain. BP's Suttles publicly cautioned that previous successful uses had been in much shallower water.[134] BP recognized that chief among potential problems was the risk that methane gas escaping from the well would come into contact with cold sea water and form slushy hydrates, essentially clogging the cofferdam with hydrocarbon ice.[135] Notwithstanding the uncertainty, BP, in a presentation to the leadership of the Department of the Interior, described the probability of the containment dome's success as "Medium/High."[136] Others in the oil and gas industry were not so optimistic: many experts believed the cofferdam effort was very likely to fail because of hydrates.[137]

The effort did fail, for that reason. Although BP had a plan to deal with hydrates once the cofferdam was in place, it had not planned to mitigate hydrate formation during installation.[138] When crews started to maneuver the cofferdam into position on the evening of May 7, hydrates formed before they could place the dome over the leak, clogging the opening through which oil was to be funneled.[139] According to Richard Lynch, a vice president overseeing the effort, BP never anticipated hydrates developing this early.[140]

Because hydrocarbons are lighter than water, the containment dome became buoyant as it filled with oil and gas while BP tried to lower it. BP engineers told Lynch that they had "lost the cofferdam" as the dome, full of flammable material, floated up toward the ships on the ocean surface. Averting a potential disaster, the engineers were able to regain control of the dome and move it to safety on the sea floor.[141] In the wake of the cofferdam's failure, one high-level government official recalled Andy Inglis, BP's Chief Executive Officer of Exploration and Production, saying with disgust, "If we had tried to make a hydrate collection contraption, we couldn't have done a better job."[142]

Inaccurate estimates of the well's flow also affected the cofferdam effort. According to Suttles, during this time, no one at BP believed the flow was greater than 13,000 to 14,000 barrels per day.[143] The government's then-current estimate of the flow was 5,000 barrels per day. The far larger volume of the actual flow—about 60,000 barrels per day, according to the government's now-current estimate—may be part of the reason hydrates formed more quickly than expected.[144] Moreover, BP had publicly predicted that the cofferdam would remove about 85 percent of the oil spilling into the sea.[145] But the ship it planned to connect to the cofferdam was capable of processing a maximum of 15,000 barrels per day.[146] While BP may have misjudged the probability of success, its decision to deploy the dome instead of another containment device appears to have turned more on timing than on perceived effectiveness: the dome was largely off-the-shelf and therefore ready to use in early May, before other equipment.[147]

With the failure of the cofferdam highlighting the shortage of viable options to contain and control the well, somewhat outlandish suggestions filled the void. In mid-May, a Russian newspaper suggested detonating a nuclear weapon deep within the well to stop the flow of oil, as the former Soviet Union had done on a number of occasions.[148] BP moved on: a little over a week after giving up on the cofferdam, on May 16, it was able to deploy a new collection device. Named the Riser Insertion Tube Tool, the device was a tube, four inches in diameter, that fit into the end of the riser and carried oil and gas up to the *Discoverer Enterprise*. This tool, BP's first effective means of containment, collected approximately 22,000 barrels of oil over its nine days of use.

Flow-Rate Estimates Creep Up (May 27)

After Unified Command announced its best estimate of the flow rate as 5,000 barrels per day on April 28, a number of independent scientists began to register their disagreement. BP had contacted scientists at the Woods Hole Oceanographic Institution on May 1 about undertaking diagnostic work on the BOP and measuring the flow using a remotely operated vehicle with sonar and acoustic sensors. But BP cancelled the Woods Hole project on May 6 to instead deploy the containment dome.[149] Based on satellite imagery of the surface slick, other non-government scientists arrived at estimates in late April and early May ranging from 5,000 to 26,500 barrels of oil per day.[150] Using the appearance of oil on the surface to assess flow from a source 5,000 feet below is inherently unreliable, but the outside scientists had no other data. That changed on May 12, when BP released a 30-second video of oil and gas streaming from the end of the broken riser. Within 24 hours, independent scientists had seized on this information and published three new estimates of the combined flow of oil and gas that ranged from 20,000 to 100,000 barrels per day.[151] On May 18, BP released another video, this time of the leak at the kink. Combining estimated flow from the two sources, a non-government scientist, Steve Wereley, testified before Congress that approximately 50,000 barrels of oil per day were flowing into the Gulf.[152]

BP dismissed these new estimates, with spokesman Bill Salvin stating, "We've said all along that there's no way to estimate the flow coming out of the pipe accurately."[153] The government disagrees with Salvin's claim: according to Marcia McNutt, Director of the U.S. Geological Survey, if a similar blowout occurs in the future, the government will be able to quickly and reliably estimate the flow rate using the very oceanographic techniques that Woods Hole was prepared to use on May 6.[154*] At the time, the government responded to the independent estimates by devoting greater resources to the question of flow rate. On May 19, the National Incident Command created an interagency Flow Rate Technical Group and charged it with generating a preliminary flow rate as soon as possible and, within two months, a final estimate based on peer-reviewed methodologies. On May 23, at Secretary Salazar's recommendation, the National Incident Command appointed McNutt the leader.

The Group consisted of both government and non-government scientists, and included subgroups using different methodologies. It published its first estimate on May 27, stating: "The only range of flow rates that is consistent with all 3 of the methods considered by the [the Group] is 12,000 to 19,000 barrels per day. Higher flow rates [of up to 25,000 barrels per day] are consistent with the data considered by [one subgroup]."[155] The Group released little additional information about its calculations. A few days later, it issued a two-page report stating that the 12,000 to 25,000 barrel range represented the "lower bound" of one subgroup's estimates, and that this subgroup had chosen not to release its "upper bound" estimates, deeming them speculative because of "unknown unknowns."[156]

Responders uniformly contended that they were responding to the oil as it appeared on the water's surface, and that the problems with quantifying the flow from the source did not affect their ability to respond. In response to a congressional inquiry later in the summer about dispersant use, however, Admiral Allen indicated that early dispersant decisions were based on the 5,000 barrels per day figure, and that the higher estimate from the Flow Rate Technical Group "spurred responders to consider reassessing the strategy for the use of dispersants as well as other oil recovery methods."[157]

Later studies would conclude that 12,000 to 25,000 barrels a day was still a significant underestimate of the amount of oil streaming into the Gulf.

---

* At the behest of the Coast Guard, Woods Hole used its sonar and acoustic technology on May 31 to gather data that later yielded a flow-rate estimate of 58,000 barrels per day. On June 21, Woods Hole, again with the support of the Coast Guard, collected source samples, which initially demonstrated that 43.7 percent of the total flow was oil, while the remainder was gas. (Woods Hole has since revised this figure to 42.8 percent.)

Top government officials work on source control out of BP's Houston headquarters. At center is Secretary of Energy Steven Chu, flanked by Secretary of the Interior Ken Salazar (right) and Director of Sandia National Laboratories Tom Hunter.

Unified Area Command, Deepwater Horizon Response

The Top Kill and Junk Shot (May 26–28)

Throughout May, the federal government increased its presence in Houston, the hub of the well-control effort. In early May, scientists and engineers from three Department of Energy national laboratories began to work on-site with BP on containment. On May 7, Secretary Salazar asked McNutt, who had traveled to the Gulf with him on May 4, to remain in Houston. Finally, on May 10, President Obama directed Secretary Chu to form a team of government officials and scientists to work with BP on source control.[158] On May 11, Secretary Chu called several prominent scientists and asked them to join him the next morning for a meeting in Houston.[159]

The May 12 meeting signified the beginning of an oversight role for Secretary Chu and his team of science advisors. Secretary Chu is a Nobel Prize-winning physicist who had previously directed the Lawrence Berkeley National Laboratory, where he had led an effort to expand research into synthetic biofuels.[160] Though well known for his wide-ranging intelligence, Secretary Chu was not an oil and gas or drilling expert. During the following weeks, he immersed himself in the finer points of petroleum engineering and became intimately involved in decisionmaking with respect to containment of the well.

Although they were highly respected within their fields of study, the members of the advisory team had limited experience with well control and varying levels of experience with petroleum engineering generally. Secretary Chu assumed—correctly—that BP had already hired a host of containment experts, and he wanted advisors known for creative thinking. His principal deputy on the team, Tom Hunter, was about to retire from his position as Director of Sandia National Laboratories. Along with McNutt, Hunter served as a link between the on-site government scientists and engineers and the rest of Secretary Chu's science advisors, who were for the most part based elsewhere. Another team member, Richard Garwin, helped design the world's first hydrogen bomb and had worked to extinguish oil fires in Kuwait following the first Gulf War. Alexander Slocum, an MIT professor who holds about 70 patents, had done some previous work on drilling design. George Cooper had been the head of the Petroleum Engineering Program at the University of California, Berkeley.

The role of both the national laboratories scientists and Secretary Chu's advisors took time to evolve from helping BP diagnose the situation—for instance, using gamma-ray imaging to show the position of the BOP's rams—to substantively overseeing BP's decisions on containment. In part, this was because the Secretary of Energy, his team of advisors, and the national laboratories personnel lacked a formal role within Unified Command. Their supervision was informally grafted onto the command framework.

In addition, the national laboratories team did not immediately integrate itself into the existing source-control structure, led by MMS and the Coast Guard. While MMS, the Coast Guard, and McNutt worked out of offices on the third floor of BP's Houston headquarters, the national laboratories team sat on the eighteenth floor.[161] One MMS staff member who was in Houston from late April through early July said that he never interacted with the national laboratories team: they never reached out to him, and he had no idea what they were working on. Perhaps because the lines of authority were unclear, BP's sharing of data with the government science teams was uneven at first. BP gave information when asked, but not proactively, so government officials had to know what data they needed and ask for it specifically.[162] Finally, both the national laboratories team and the science advisors had to educate themselves on the situation, and on deepwater petroleum engineering, before they knew enough to challenge BP and participate in high-level decisionmaking.[163]

With more substantive government oversight on the way but not yet in place, BP moved toward its first attempt to kill the well completely, via procedures called the "top kill" and "junk shot." Those names were fodder for late night comics: Jay Leno suggested that the top kill "sound[ed] like some bad Steven Seagal movie from the '80s."[164] In fact, both procedures are standard industry techniques for stopping the flow from a blown-out well (though they had never been used in deepwater[165]). A top kill—also known as a momentum or dynamic kill—involves pumping heavy drilling mud into the top of the well through the BOP's choke and kill lines, at rates and pressures high enough to force escaping oil back down the well and into the reservoir. A junk shot complements a top kill. It involves pumping material (including pieces of tire rubber and golf balls) into the bottom of a BOP through the choke and kill lines. That material ideally gets caught on obstructions within the BOP and impedes the flow of oil and gas. By slowing or stopping the flow, a successful junk shot makes it easier to execute a top kill.

BP's top-kill team began work in the immediate aftermath of the initial efforts to trigger the BOP.[166] In planning the operation, both BP and federal engineers modeled different scenarios based on different rates at which oil might be flowing from the well. National laboratories engineers used the then-current flow-rate estimate of 5,000 barrels per day.[167] Paul Tooms, BP's Vice President of Engineering, recalled that given the planned pumping rates, the top kill was unlikely to succeed with flow rates greater than 15,000 barrels of oil per day.[168] A senior administration official similarly recalled being told by a BP engineer that the top kill would not work if the flow rate exceeded 13,000 barrels per day.[169]

With the approval of the Federal On-Scene Coordinator, the top kill began on the afternoon of May 26. Secretary Chu and some members of his science team were in the command center in Houston.[170] During three separate attempts over three consecutive days, BP pumped mud at rates exceeding 100,000 barrels per day and fired numerous shots of junk into the BOP.[171] During each effort, pressures within the well initially dropped, but then flattened, indicating that the top kill had stopped making progress.[172] After the third unsuccessful attempt, BP and the government agreed to discontinue the strategy.[173]

As with the cofferdam, BP struggled with public communications surrounding the top kill. At the time, both industry and government officials were highly uncertain about the operation's probability of success. One MMS employee estimated that probability as less than 50 percent, while a BP contractor said that he only gave the top kill a "tiny" chance to succeed.[174] But BP's Hayward told reporters, "We rate the probability of success between 60 and 70 percent."[175] After the top kill failed, that prediction may have lessened public confidence in BP's management of the effort to control the well.

The Federal Role Increases (Late May)

By late May, the competence and effectiveness of the federal response was under assault. Polls showed that 60 percent of adults thought the government was doing a poor job of handling the spill.[176] News articles chronicled local anger that BP appeared in charge of clean-up efforts.[177] The government's estimate of the flow rate was climbing and, with the failure of the top kill, no end to the spill was in sight.

On May 28, President Obama made his second trip to the region to see response efforts and meet with state and local leaders. Plaquemines Parish President Billy Nungesser would later claim, incorrectly, that he had not been invited to this important meeting.[178] He told the *Plaquemines Gazette* that he had smuggled himself and another Parish President across bays and bayous and through an armada of state boats, gaining access only after threatening to call Anderson Cooper.[179]

The meeting with the President occurred at the Coast Guard station in Grand Isle, Louisiana, and included, among others, Governor Jindal, Florida Governor Charlie Crist, Alabama Governor Bob Riley, Louisiana Senators David Vitter and Mary Landrieu, Louisiana Congressman Charlie Melancon, New Orleans Mayor Mitch Landrieu, Lafourche Parish President Charlotte Randolph, and Parish President Nungesser.[180] President Obama emphasized the seriousness with which the government was treating the spill, announcing at a press conference after the meeting that he would triple the federal manpower and equipment involved in the response.[181] Though Coast Guard responders believed they were already dedicating every available resource to the spill, and did not see across-the-board "tripling" as the best use of resources, they dutifully attempted to triple the personnel engaged and boom deployed. They chronicled their progress in Louisiana in a report titled "Status on Tripling."[182]

While in Grand Isle, President Obama also received an "earful" about Louisiana's proposal to build massive offshore sand berms as a physical obstacle to oil, which

Under fire, President Barack Obama meets with dissatisfied state and local officials in Grand Isle, Louisiana on May 28, during his second visit to the Gulf since the spill began. Visible clockwise from the President: Plaquemines Parish President Billy Nungesser, Louisiana Governor Bobby Jindal, New Orleans Mayor Mitch Landrieu, Grand Isle Mayor David Camardelle, and Florida Governor Charlie Crist.

David Grunfeld/The Times-Picayune. Photo © 2010 The Times-Picayune Publishing Co., all rights reserved. Used with permission of The Times-Picayune.

the National Incident Command had declined to approve in its entirety.[183] Parish President Nungesser, seated immediately to the President's left, was the first attendee to speak at the meeting and was adamant about the need for the entire berms project. Governor Jindal echoed him. In line with the federal government's effort to be more responsive to local demands, President Obama turned to Admiral Allen and asked him, in front of the berms' strongest proponents, to figure out a solution.[184]

The "tripling" order and promise to promptly reevaluate the berms project were only two of many actions at the end of May by which the federal government attempted to demonstrate its focus on the *Deepwater Horizon* disaster and commitment to the communities in the Gulf. The President signed the Executive Order creating this Commission on May 21.[185] On May 27, he announced a moratorium on offshore deepwater drilling and held a press conference about the administration response.[186] The same day, Elizabeth Birnbaum, the head of MMS, resigned—"on her own terms and on her own volition," according to Secretary Salazar.[187] Most symbolically, the federal government stopped holding joint press conferences with BP. From June 1 on, Admiral Allen gave his own daily press briefing.[188] But local officials continued to attack the adequacy of the federal response and to assert that that BP was running the response effort.

The Battles over Boom and Berms (May to June)
While the response had many dimensions, local communities fixated on the deployment of boom to prevent oil from washing ashore. Although not the most effective response tool, boom is a measurable, physical object that visibly stops oil. Residents could not see source-control efforts on the ocean floor or skimming far out in the Gulf, but they could see boats laying ribbons of bright orange or yellow floating boom to protect their shorelines. According to one Terrebonne Parish resident, boom was eye candy—seeing it gave him a sense of satisfaction (even if it did not do much).[189]

The Moratorium

On May 27, after a 30-day interagency examination of deepwater drilling operations, Secretary Salazar directed MMS to issue a six-month moratorium on all drilling at a water depth of more than 500 feet in the Gulf of Mexico and the Pacific Ocean. Department officials justified the moratorium as providing time for this Commission to do its work and for MMS to undertake needed safety reforms. The moratorium took effect on May 30 and halted work on 33 offshore deepwater rigs in the Gulf.

The oil and gas industry, local communities, and elected officials from the region immediately criticized the action. Senator Landrieu testified before this Commission in July that the moratorium was "unnecessary, ill-conceived and has actually created a second economic disaster for the Gulf Coast that has the potential to become greater than the first." On July 30, BP established a $100 million charitable fund to assist rig workers experiencing economic hardship because of the moratorium.

The federal government concluded that the moratorium's impact would be less severe. On September 16, a federal interagency report stated that the moratorium "may temporarily result in up to 8,000 to 12,000 fewer jobs in the Gulf Coast," with these losses attributed mostly to small businesses. Louisiana elected officials criticized the report's methodology and the decision to conduct this analysis after, instead of before, the moratorium began.

A group of companies that provide support services for deepwater drilling vessels challenged the moratorium in federal district court in Louisiana. On June 22, the court ruled that the moratorium violated the Administrative Procedure Act and enjoined its continued enforcement. The federal government asked the Fifth Circuit Court of Appeals to stay the district court's ruling, but the Fifth Circuit denied that request on July 8. The Department of the Interior then issued a revised moratorium on July 12, which limited drilling based on the equipment a rig used rather than the depth of the wellhead. Neither the first nor the second moratorium provided a company with the option of avoiding the bar on drilling by proving the safety of its rig operations to the government. A second group of offshore support companies challenged the revised moratorium. Before the district court could rule on this new lawsuit, the Department lifted the moratorium on October 12, seven weeks ahead of its scheduled November 30 expiration.

On September 30, a few weeks before lifting the moratorium, the Department promulgated new regulations on topics such as well casing and cementing, blowout preventers, safety certification, emergency response, and worker training. Compliance with the new rules is a prerequisite for both shallow and deepwater drilling permits. Some companies called these new requirements a "de facto moratorium" because of the time needed to meet them and for the Department to verify compliance.

A vessel places containment boom in Louisiana's Barataria Bay. Hundreds of miles of boom were deployed along the Gulf coast, but politicians clamored for more of the highly visible barriers.

U.S. Coast Guard photo/Petty Officer 3rd Class Ann Marie Gorden

Boom became a symbol of federal responsiveness to local communities. NOAA scientists worked through the night, every night, to prepare oil trajectory forecasts for federal responders to review as they began their days.[190] Responders used those forecasts to plan their actions, including where to place boom. Federal responders thought that officials and residents complaining about lack of boom did not understand their strategy for deployment; officials and residents thought that federal responders were inattentive to local needs.[191] The National Incident Command was not deaf to these complaints and gave an unofficial order to "keep the parishes happy."[192] Coast Guard responders distributed many miles of boom according to political, rather than operational, imperatives. They felt hamstrung by the outrage that resulted when a parish or state felt slighted by allocation decisions, so they placed boom wherever they could.[193]

Every Governor wanted more boom. When the oiling risk was highest in Louisiana, the Coast Guard directed boom there. Governor Riley of Alabama contended that this decision left his state's shoreline in danger.[194] At a press conference in mid-May, Governor Jindal said that the containment boom provided to Louisiana by the Coast Guard and BP was inadequate, while local officials behind him held up pictures of oil-coated pelicans.[195] Florida Department of Environmental Protection Secretary Mike Sole told reporters, "A lot of the decisions about Florida are being made in Mobile." He said he had warned the Federal On-Scene Coordinator, "Florida is important. We have 770 miles of shoreline to protect. I'm concerned that we're not getting enough focus on Florida."[196]

The competition for boom occurred at the parish and town levels as well. St. Bernard Parish had its own contractor bring in boom; it then sought to make the Coast Guard purchase and deploy that boom locally.[197] Some parishes reportedly ordered boom directly from suppliers and told them to "send the bill to BP."[198] Lafourche Parish kept demanding more boom—until it realized that certain skimmers were more effective and began demanding those skimmers instead.[199] Unified Command struggled to track how much boom was deployed and where.

Initially, responders made booming decisions based on their knowledge of the region's geography, the location of environmentally sensitive areas, and NOAA's oil trajectory forecasts. The oil-spill planning documents did not lay out a specific booming map, because the coastal ecosystem, particularly in the marshes, frequently changes. Unified Command eventually brought the Parish Presidents together to review boom plans that each parish had created. Some were infeasible—for instance, requesting that boom be placed in tidal passes where currents would drive oil under the boom or else damage it. In addition to worrying about useless or unnecessary boom, responders were concerned that storms could blow it into delicate marsh habitat. They deployed boom based on local pressures only to pull it away during bad weather.[200]

Once parishes had boom, they did not want to let it go. On July 22, Parish President Nungesser threatened to blow out the tires of trucks carrying away boom as the Coast Guard prepared for Tropical Storm Bonnie. Though he claimed that he was joking, the FBI called to reprimand him.[201] Other Parish Presidents issued orders prohibiting the removal of response equipment from their parishes and threatened Coast Guard responders with arrest.[202] Officials asked responders to measure "feet of boom deployed"—a statistic that was time-consuming to generate and had little value in assessing response efforts.[203] All of these problems distracted responders from their focus on cleaning up the spill.

The boom wars never reached a resolution. Responders knew that in deploying boom they were often responding to the politics of the spill rather than the spill itself. And the miles of boom along the coastline still did not prevent oil from washing up on the shore.

The boom wars were relatively civil, however, compared to the struggle among the State of Louisiana, the Army Corps of Engineers, the National Incident Command, and, ultimately, the White House over berms. Reinforcing barrier islands had long been a component of Louisiana's and Plaquemines Parish's coastal restoration plans.[204] But by early May, Governor Jindal and Parish President Nungesser had seized on an idea (originally proposed by Deltares, a Dutch independent research institute, together with Van Oord, a Dutch dredging and marine contractor) to construct massive, linear sand berms along Louisiana's barrier islands for spill response, to guard the coastline from oil.[205] The berms project presented an opportunity for Louisiana to take the lead on a large-scale response measure—with BP footing the bill. Moreover, after the spill ended, the berms' purpose could "pivot" from response to coastal restoration.[206]

On May 11, Louisiana's Office of Coastal Protection and Restoration applied to the Corps for an emergency permit to construct berms to "enhanc[e] the capability of the islands to

Voices from the Gulf
"If I was a mom, what would I do?"

Michelle Rolls-Thomas/Associated Press

Sheryl Lindsay, Orange Beach
Weddings, Orange Beach AL

When Sheryl Lindsay picked up the April 21 Mobile *Press-Register* and read the headline, "At least 11 workers sought after gulf rig explosion," she recalled, "My heart went out to the workers on that rig, the victims and their families. I couldn't believe what had happened." The newspaper reported that six of the *Deepwater Horizon* survivors had been flown to a Mobile, Alabama, trauma unit.

For six years, Lindsay had been president of Orange Beach Weddings, which coordinated and arranged "The Wedding of Your Dreams" on Alabama's Gulf Coast near the Florida line. Her offices on Perdido Boulevard overlooked the pristine white sand beaches of Orange Beach, Alabama—one of her firm's specialties was elegant beach ceremonies and festivities. Her busy season was starting, with 73 weddings booked for 2010. She worked with numerous contractors, from wedding planners and caterers to ministers and photographers. She knew that BP's Macondo well was now spewing oil; "But I never thought it would affect us here."

On April 30, the day after the U.S. Coast Guard declared the Macondo blowout a "spill of national significance," Lindsay was in her office when the phone rang. It was her first cancellation. "When the bride called to cancel, she said it was because of the spill. She didn't want her guests coming down to find oil on the beaches. She didn't want to come if they couldn't swim or eat the seafood. That's when I knew."

In the wake of the oil spill, "Every time the phone rang, all we got was another cancellation—or someone asking how bad it was down here. I became a counselor for these brides. Orange Beach is a popular spot for destination weddings, and many of my brides come from out of state. But if girls' weddings were still a few months out, they still had time to change plans and move the wedding somewhere else. A lot of girls asked me what they should do—they were worried about the smell, whether the guests could swim and the quality of the seafood." She continued, "This was their big day. It was tough. And you think, 'If I was a mom, what would I do?'"

"What's funny," Lindsay said, "is we only had about three bad weeks where oil was washing on shore and BP was staging clean-up on the beach. That was in June. The rest of the summer the beaches were pretty much clean but folks still didn't come down." As the spill gushed on, Lindsay began to realize she had no idea what the next year would look like, but it didn't look good. She did not think she could afford to renew her office lease. In 2009, she had taken out a small business loan from the local bank for $55,000 to expand her firm, but now she began to fear she could not meet those payments as her business diminished.

reduce the inland movement of oil from the BP Deepwater Horizon Oil Spill."[207] Colonel Alvin Lee, two months shy of the end of his three-year tour as the Commander of the Corps for the District of New Orleans, cancelled a long-scheduled vacation, and the Corps immediately sought comments on the proposal from relevant federal and state agencies.[208]

The patience of Louisiana officials quickly wore thin. On May 17, Governor Jindal's office summoned Colonel Lee to the New Orleans airport for a meeting that included three Parish Presidents, the Chairman of the Office of Coastal Protection and Restoration, the Adjutant General for Louisiana, and the Governor himself. The group's message to Colonel Lee was clear: approve the berms project, and do it quickly.[209] The entire Louisiana congressional delegation wrote Colonel Lee on May 20, to "implore [him] to immediately approve the emergency authorization request" for the Louisiana berms.[210] In a May 21 letter to President Obama, Senator Vitter asked the President to stop the "tragic bureaucratic stranglehold" and to "make this happen now."[211]

The Corps reviewed agency comments, conducted its own evaluation of the project, and engaged in dialogue with state officials. On May 27—just 16 days after it had received Louisiana's application—the Corps approved the issuance of an emergency permit for a significantly scaled-back berms project: six "reaches" totaling 39.5 miles in length.[212] During the review process, commenting agencies expressed skepticism that the berms could be constructed in time to be effective for spill response and concern that partially completed berms would do more environmental harm than good.[213] The Corps' job, however, was to analyze the "feasibility and environmental impacts" of the berms. The National Incident Commander had the task of determining whether the berms would be "effective. . . in combating the oil spill."[214] That determination was necessary to make BP pay for the project as a response measure.

The same day the Corps approved the six reaches, Admiral Allen authorized one of the six as a prototype oil-spill response mechanism.[215] Earlier in May, an interagency task force had advised the National Incident Command that the project would not be an effective spill-response measure, in part because the berms could not be constructed in time to fight the spill.[216] But public and political pressure had been unyielding. In an attempt to balance both sets of concerns, on May 22, Admiral Allen e-mailed an idea to his deputy: "What are the chances we could pick a couple of no brainer projects and call them prototypes to give us some trade space on the larger issue and give that to Jindal this weekend?"[217] Five days later, the National Incident Command announced its approval of one prototype berm, to cost $16 million.[218] The accompanying press release promised that additional berms could be constructed if the approved section proved effective. Building even one prototype segment would take months, however, and the segment would then need to be analyzed. Any further construction therefore would not begin until the fall.

But because of the meeting in Grand Isle on May 28, where Parish President Nungesser and Governor Jindal urged President Obama to approve the entire project, the National Incident Command would change course. At the meeting, the President turned to Admiral Allen and, in front of the assembled Governors and other leaders, asked him to assemble a group of experts to examine the merits of Louisiana's proposal as a spill-response measure.

Admiral Allen replied that this might take some time. It was the Friday afternoon before Memorial Day weekend. But the President pushed, asking, "Can you do it next week?" Admiral Allen, put on the spot, pledged to do his best.[219]

After the meeting, Governor Jindal immediately announced that the President had "agreed that work on the first segment must begin immediately" and that the federal government would decide "within two to three days" whether the additional five segments should proceed.[220] Parish President Nungesser told a similar story to Anderson Cooper on *CNN* that evening, saying "The President committed by early next week, we will have an answer and I believe that he's going to task BP."[221]

On June 1, Admiral Allen convened a summit in New Orleans "which included members of academia [one from Louisiana State University and a second from the University of New Orleans], federal trustees, fish and wildlife service and NOAA," as well as Governor Jindal and Parish President Nungesser. Although some experts at the summit expressed concern about causing harm to the environment, the discussion focused on the berms' potential to protect marshlands.[222] The politics of the project remained close at hand: Parish President Nungesser walked out, calling the meeting a "Dog and Pony Show,"[223] only to return in time to speak at the end. Governor Jindal continued to express his frustration and pressed for approval of all six reaches covered by the Corps permit.[224] In the face of the spill and in front of the Louisiana politicians, no one directly opposed the berms, and a "preponderance of opinion" at the summit suggested the berms would be an effective response measure.[225]

That evening, following the summit, Admiral Allen and BP's Hayward had dinner together in New Orleans to discuss the berms.[226] The following afternoon, Admiral Allen gave the go-ahead to all six reaches approved by the Corps, to be funded by BP.[227] BP estimated the cost to be $360 million, double the entire amount it had spent as of early June in "helping the region respond to the oil spill."[228] The Corps pegged the cost at $424 million.[229]

Louisiana awarded contracts for the project to Shaw Group, a Baton Rouge–based engineering, construction, and environmental services firm, and C.F. Bean LLC, a dredging contractor based in Plaquemines Parish.[230] Shaw estimated that five of the six berm reaches would be completed by November 1, and that the sixth would be completed by the end of November.[231] The National Incident Command estimated that the construction time for all six reaches would be six to nine months.[232] Even if those estimates had been correct, the project would have been nowhere close to complete by the time the government expected BP to kill the Macondo well with a relief well. As it happened, all of the estimates were far too rosy. Only a fraction of the planned reaches would be finished before the spill ended, and very little oil would be captured.

From Containment to Collection (Late May to Early July)

Following the unsuccessful top kill, BP teams in Houston met through the night of May 28 to assess the operation.[233] Some meetings occurred behind closed doors, without government participation. At one point, Herbst of MMS and Admiral Kevin Cook, who had been dispatched by Admiral Allen to be his representative in Houston, entered a meeting and stated that they had a right to be present. Apparently, government officials had not previously insisted on joining these types of meetings, and BP personnel were surprised by the interruption.[234] The failure of the top kill marked a turning point for the government science teams, with the government significantly increasing its oversight of the containment effort.

The next morning, BP presented its analysis of why the top kill failed to stop the flow of oil. The analysis focused on the well's 16-inch casing, the outermost barrier between the well and the surrounding rock for more than 1,000 vertical feet. That casing was purposely fabricated with three sets of weak points, called rupture disks. During the well's production phase, the hot oil coursing through the production casing, which is inside the 16-inch casing, would lead to a buildup of pressure in the well. If the pressure buildup was too high, it could cause the collapse of one of the two casings. The disks were designed to rupture and relieve this potential buildup of pressure before a casing collapsed.

The disks could rupture in two ways. If pressure between the 16-inch casing and the production casing were too high, the rupture disks would *burst outward* before the production casing collapsed. If pressure outside the 16-inch casing were too high, the rupture disks would *collapse inward* before the casing itself collapsed.[235] Once ruptured, the disks would create small holes in the 16-inch casing, bleeding built-up pressure off into the rock. According to BP's top-kill analysis, pressures created by the initial blowout could have caused the rupture disks to collapse inward, compromising the well's integrity.[236] BP believed that the mud it had pumped down the well during the top kill could have gone out into the rock through the rupture disks, instead of staying within the well and pushing oil back down into the reservoir as intended.[237]

Collapse of the rupture disks was only one of BP's possible explanations for the unsuccessful top kill.[238] But the company presented it to the government as the most likely scenario.[239] Although the government science teams did not fully accept BP's analysis of what happened to the mud, they agreed that the rupture disks could have collapsed during the blowout, and that the integrity of the well had to be considered in future containment efforts.[240] In retrospect, government officials have suggested that the top kill likely failed because the rate at which oil was flowing from the well was many times greater than the then-current 5,000 barrels-per-day estimate. Because BP did not pump mud into the well at a rate high enough to counter the actual flow, oil and gas from the well pushed mud back up the BOP and out of the riser.[241]

BP had previously said that, if the top kill failed, its next step might be to install a second BOP on top of the existing one to shut in the well.[242] But now, the company engineers viewed the possibility that the rupture disks had collapsed as a reason to discard capping the well as an option.[243] If BP shut the well in, oil and gas could flow out the rupture disks and into the rock surrounding the well in a "broach" or "underground blowout." From there, the hydrocarbons could rise through the layers of rock and flow into the ocean from many points on the sea floor. This would make containment nearly impossible, at least until the completion of a relief well. Thus, in the aftermath of the top kill, BP and the government focused on trying to collect the oil, with the relief wells still providing the most likely avenue for killing the well altogether.[244]

Transocean's huge drill ship the *Discoverer Enterprise*, its derrick towering 400 feet above the sea, and Helix's *Q4000* (foreground) sit over the gushing wellhead. Together the vessels were able to recover up to 25,000 barrels of oil per day.

Julie Dermansky ©2010

BP had a team ready to proceed with new collection tools almost immediately.[245] On May 29, the company and the government announced that BP would attempt to cut off the portion of the riser still attached to the top of the BOP and install a collection device—the "top hat"—which would then be connected via a new riser to the *Discoverer Enterprise* above.[246] BP began installing the device on June 1, and had the top hat in place and functioning by 11:30 p.m. on June 3. Having learned from its cofferdam experience, BP injected methanol to prevent formation of hydrates. By June 8, the *Discoverer Enterprise* was collecting nearly 15,000 barrels of oil per day.

BP also developed a system to bring oil and gas to the surface through the choke line on the BOP. BP outfitted the *Q4000*, a vessel involved in the top-kill effort, with collection equipment, including an oil and gas burner imported from France. After it became operational on June 16, the *Q4000* system was able to process and burn up to 10,000 barrels of oil per day.[*]

On occasion, BP was overly optimistic about the percentage of the oil it could remove or collect. On June 1, Suttles said that he expected the top hat, when connected to the *Discoverer Enterprise*, to be able to collect the "vast majority" of the oil.[247] Within days, it became apparent that the top hat and *Discoverer Enterprise* were inadequate. On June 6, Hayward told the *BBC* that, with the *Q4000* in place, "we would very much hope to be containing the vast majority of the oil."[248] But when the *Q4000* came online in mid–June, the two vessels' joint capacity of 25,000 barrels per day was still insufficient.

---

[*] Over the course of June and early July, BP worked on further expanding its containment system, which it asserted would eventually be able to collect up to 90,000 barrels of oil per day. BP never used the complete system, based around two freestanding risers connected to the choke and kill lines on the BOP, because it succeeded in capping the well on July 15.

It is unclear whether BP could have increased its collection capacity more rapidly than it did. BP's Lynch said that the speed at which the company brought capacity online was limited solely by the availability of dynamically positioned production vessels.* One senior Coast Guard official challenged BP's definition of availability: he suggested that BP did not consider options such as procuring ships on charter with other companies until the government pushed it to do so. Obtaining another production vessel might have enabled BP to collect oil through the BOP's kill line at a rate comparable to that of the *Q4000*.[249]

Continued Conflict about Dispersant Use (May 10–July 14)

Because of the insufficient collection capacity, oil continued to flow into the Gulf. Though the subsea use of dispersants proved helpful in preventing huge surface slicks, it did not initially have the predicted effect of reducing the total volume of dispersants applied. At a May 24 press conference, EPA Administrator Jackson announced that the government was instructing BP to "take immediate steps to significantly scale back the overall use of dispersants" and expressed EPA's belief that "we can reduce the amount of dispersant applied by as much as half, and I think probably 75 percent, maybe more."[250] A Coast Guard–EPA letter and joint directive issued two days later instructed BP to "eliminate the surface application of dispersants," except in "rare cases when there may have to be an exemption."[251]

Despite this directive, surface use of dispersants continued. When surveillance aircraft spotted oil and no other method of cleaning it up was available in the area, BP would ask for an exemption from the Federal On-Scene Coordinator, who would then seek EPA's approval. The Coast Guard could not unilaterally allow the exemption; EPA had the final vote.

EPA expressed frustration that BP sought regular exemptions, and it repeatedly asked for more robust explanations of why BP could not use mechanical recovery methods, such as skimming and burning, instead of dispersants.[252] Coast Guard responders, who viewed dispersants as a powerful tool to protect the coastline, wondered why EPA wanted to cast aside the advance planning that went into the preauthorization of surface dispersant use.[253]

These different perspectives on dispersants led to conflicts between EPA and the Coast Guard. For example, on June 7, BP requested permission to spray dispersants on several large slicks. Despite Federal-On Scene Coordinator Rear Admiral James Watson's statement that he had "determined aerial dispersant the best and only way to mitigate the pending landfall effect of the oil spotted," EPA would not approve the exemption.[254] The Coast Guard captain leading the majority of front-line operations was furious. "It would be a travesty," he wrote, "if the oil hits the beach because we did not use the tools available to fight this offshore. This responsibility needs to be placed squarely in EPA's court if it does hit the shoreline."[255] Later that day, without having received responses to its requests for additional data, EPA threatened to issue a directive "to stop the use of all dispersants."[256]

* Dynamically positioned vessels have computer-controlled systems that maintain the vessel's exact position and direction, despite external factors such as wind, waves, and current.

The working relationship between the agencies improved over time, with more complete justifications for dispersant use included in the daily requests for exemptions.[257] But disagreements came to a boil again in mid–July. By this point, EPA had finally installed a senior official, Assistant Administrator for Solid Waste and Emergency Response Mathy Stanislaus, on the ground at Unified Area Command.[258] On July 13, BP's head of dispersant operations made a request to apply 10,000 gallons to slicks.[259] The request ultimately went to Stanislaus, who denied it, noting that skimming in particular had been extremely effective over the past few days.[260] The Federal On-Scene Coordinator (by this time Rear Admiral Paul Zukunft) replied that he could not "take the dispersant tool out of my kit when" oil threatened to hit environmentally sensitive areas in Louisiana. "We spent over a month cleaning Barataria Bay with over 1500 people and 600 vessels," he added, "and still incurred significant wildlife kills while exposing these clean-up crews to extreme heat conditions. That is the trade-off option where dispersants come into play. . . ."[261] The back-and-forth continued, with BP ultimately prohibited from using dispersants on July 14.[262] The capping of the well the next day tabled the conflict.

Months later, Admiral Allen and Administrator Jackson would say that they had cooperated closely, nearly attained the goal of a 75 percent reduction in dispersant use, and were satisfied with the use of dispersants to mitigate the spill.[263]

The Well Is Finally Capped (Late June to July 15—and Beyond)

Meanwhile, in Houston, the government continued to develop a more effective structure for oversight of well control. The basic elements of the structure were in place by mid-May, and the roles of the different government teams were better defined by mid-June. MMS and the Coast Guard continued to focus on identifying hazards in BP's technical procedures; personnel from the national laboratories and the U.S. Geological Survey provided information and analyses to the science advisors and BP; and the science advisors conducted their own independent analyses and helped inform the government's ultimate decisionmakers, including Secretary Chu, Secretary Salazar, McNutt, Hunter, Carol Browner (Director of the White House Office of Energy and Climate Change Policy), and Admiral Allen.[264]

Following the failure of the top kill, BP began presenting its source-control plans for review by these government teams. The science advisors would question BP's assumptions, forcing it to evaluate worst-case scenarios and explain how it was mitigating risks.[265] The government saw its pushback as essential because BP would not, on its own, consider the full range of possibilities.[266] According to one senior government official, before the increased supervision, BP "hoped for the best, planned for the best, expected the best."[267] BP often found the supervision frustrating. Tooms, BP's Vice President of Engineering, believed that the government science advisors unnecessarily slowed the containment effort, arguing that scientists consider risk differently than engineers and that BP had expertise in managing risk.[268] BP, however, was not in the best position to tout that expertise: its well had just blown out.

In mid- to late June, the government teams also began to seek more frequent input from other oil companies, primarily through large conference calls of 30 or more people.

Although BP had previously turned to others in industry for advice, it had generally asked discrete questions about aspects of source control. The government teams, by contrast, asked other companies to comment on BP's overall plans and to help force BP to consider contingencies. BP, which believed its competitors suffered from a conflict of interest, did not appreciate the increased industry involvement. After one meeting in which BP's competitors aggressively challenged its plans, BP refused to meet with them again, forcing the government teams to schedule separate meetings.[269]

The conference calls were somewhat disorganized, with no agenda and participants sometimes not knowing who was speaking. One industry participant recalled an instance when he was chagrined to learn he had been talking to Secretary Chu without realizing it.[270] A senior government official noted that some colleagues viewed BP's conflict-of-interest concerns as valid and took the competitors' advice "with a grain of salt."[271] But government personnel generally found the industry participation helpful.

The science advisors' oversight increased substantially during June. On June 18, Secretary Chu sent an e-mail to the advisory team as well as some national laboratories scientists, describing their expanded role. The e-mail cited a scene from the classic World War II movie *The Guns of Navarone*, and quoted the character played by Gregory Peck: "[Y]our bystanding days are over! You're in it now, up to your neck! They told me that you're a genius with explosives. Start proving it!" Recognizing that there were "[p]robably no shaped charges to be used on this mission," Secretary Chu wrote that "the rest rings true." He enclosed a directive that Admiral Watson, the Federal On-Scene Coordinator, would issue the next day, formally requiring BP to submit any "pending decision" on containment to the government "for review."[272]

The role of the science advisors and the on-site scientists increased just as the source-control effort approached a critical phase. By late June, BP was well on its way toward deploying a "capping stack," which, once installed on top of the BOP, would enable BP to shut in the well. The capping stack was essentially a smaller version of a BOP, similarly designed to stop the flow of oil and gas. BP had internally discussed installing a tight-sealing cap within a week of the blowout.[273] Following the top kill, however, BP and the government had shelved the idea of shutting in the well, in part because of concerns that the rupture disks in the well's 16-inch casing had collapsed, potentially allowing oil to flow out of the well into the rock. The government and BP had to take these concerns into account when planning for use of the capping stack.

Secretary Chu and Hunter briefed the President on the capping stack in late June or early July, and he approved its use. The government appears to have delayed installation for a few days, however, to continue analyzing the significant risks of shutting in the well.[274] One critical analysis involved the geology surrounding the Macondo well. The government's scientific Well Integrity Team concluded that it would take a total of approximately 100,000 barrels of oil flowing through the rupture disks into the surrounding rock for oil to create paths through the rock to the sea floor. The Team further concluded that such paths were likely to close or "heal" *if* BP and the government detected oil flow into the rock and reopened the capping stack with sufficient speed. To spot any

Voices from the Gulf
"This unnatural, unnatural catastrophe. . . ."

The Louisiana Seafood Marketing
and Promotion Board

Al & Sal Sunseri, P&J Oyster Company, New Orleans, LA

Al and Sal Sunseri are co-owners of P&J Oyster Company, their family's 134-year-old business in the French Quarter of New Orleans. P&J processes and sells some 60,000 Louisiana oysters to the city's best restaurants and local oyster bars on a typical day. When Al first heard about the *Deepwater Horizon* rig accident, he recalled thinking, "'What a terrible thing for those people.'" He added, "I didn't think more about it because the Coast Guard and everyone said it would be limited."

Al's routine remained unchanged in the days after the *Deepwater Horizon* blowout and fire: early mornings bustling with deliveries, the din of his skilled shuckers pounding and prying open oysters, preparing orders. Then, on Saturday, April 24, the Sunseris and the rest of America heard that oil was leaking from the rig's broken riser. With each passing day, the news only got worse.

P&J oysters are an institution in New Orleans, a celebrated brand proudly listed on local menus as a promise of taste and quality. P&J specializes in Louisiana oysters; most of their suppliers farm in the Barataria Basin, west of the Mississippi River. P&J had survived floods, the Great Depression, and even Hurricane Katrina. But now, the Sunseri family and the staff were all at the mercy of a runaway oil spill, with no end in sight.

Throughout May, the Macondo well gushed on unchecked, and by early June, the government had closed Louisiana oyster beds. The Sunseris had taken over from their father 25 years earlier. Now, for the first time, they had to lay off 11 skilled shuckers. "These ladies here, those guys—I grew up with them," Al said. "We were in our twenties when we started." Longtime employee Wayne Gordon, 42, had been shucking at P&J since he was 18: "Twenty-four years. I cannot imagine not being here." As the shuckers worked their way through what was to be the final pile of succulent Louisiana shellfish, the owner of a nearby restaurant appeared with a breakfast buffet of scrambled eggs, fried ham, grits, and biscuits. "After a funeral, we bring food," said the restaurateur, a longtime customer.

Al's son Blake, 24, has spent the past three years learning the business, intent on becoming the sixth family generation to run it. "This is a real devastating event for me," he said. "This is my home, it feels like I don't really have a say in what's going on around me." He could have been speaking for millions of his fellow Americans, all along the Gulf of Mexico coast, who suddenly found themselves and their worlds facing ruin from what his uncle, Sal, called "this unnatural, unnatural catastrophe."

problem quickly enough to avoid lasting damage, the Team recommended monitoring shut-in pressure at the BOP as well as visual, seismic, sonar, and acoustic data.[275] Because shutting the capping stack would increase the pressure inside the well, the government was also concerned about bursting either the rupture disks (if they had not already collapsed) or another weak point in the casings. One industry executive recalled discussing this issue on a conference call with the science advisors; he expressed his view that allowing the pressure to climb above the level recorded during the top kill would be traveling into uncharted territory, with uncertain risks.

On July 9, as analysis of these risks continued, Admiral Allen authorized BP to install the capping stack, but not to close it.[276] The extremely complicated operation began the next day. After removing the top hat from the top of the riser, remotely operated vehicles had to unbolt the stub of riser connected to the top of the *Deepwater Horizon* BOP stack, remove this stub, look for any pieces of drill pipe sticking up through the top of the BOP stack, slide the capping stack into place, and bolt it to the BOP stack. The process went smoothly, and BP finished installing the capping stack without incident by July 12. Suttles described this installation as the best operation of the entire source-control effort.[277]

BP next prepared to temporarily close the capping stack in a planned "well integrity test," to determine whether the well had been compromised and oil could flow into the rock formation. In a July 12 letter, Admiral Allen formally authorized the test to begin.[278] But it did not. About two hours before the test was supposed to start, the government teams met with BP and industry representatives, including from Exxon (in person) and Shell (by phone). Secretary Chu and Admiral Allen were both present in person. BP faced significant criticism of the wisdom of attempting the test, with Exxon and Shell raising concerns associated with shutting in the well that had yet to be considered by BP or the government.[279] In the most extreme scenario, one industry expert suggested that an underground blowout could cause the sands around the wellhead to liquefy and the entire BOP to disappear into the sea floor.[280] Because Secretary Chu and the science advisors believed that these risks required further study, Admiral Allen delayed the test to allow for 24 hours of additional analysis.[281]

Overnight, the government science teams reached out to industry and academia for help. By 10:00 the next morning, experts had reassured the government that catching a leak early enough would prevent catastrophic consequences.[282] With the government teams satisfied, Admiral Allen reauthorized the well integrity test. The test was to last from 6 to 48 hours, and BP had to monitor pressure, sonar, acoustic, and visual data continuously, as recommended by the Well Integrity Team.[283] Secretary Chu required BP to dedicate two remotely operated vehicles to visually monitor for leaks at the wellhead.

Although the Well Integrity Team had calculated that it would take a leak of approximately 100,000 barrels for oil and gas to reach the sea floor, the government was prepared to permit a leak of only 20,000 barrels before requiring the capping stack to be reopened.[284] Using an estimate for the expected pressure at shut-in derived from BP's modeling of the reservoir, the Team developed guidelines for the length of the test.[285] If the pressure at shut-in was less than 6,000 pounds per square inch, major well damage was likely—BP would

FIGURE 5.1: Protocol for Well Integrity Test

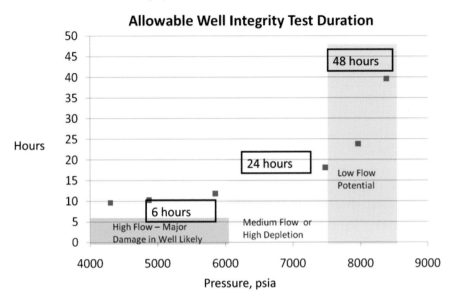

Allowable Well Integrity Test Duration

- Duration (in hours) calculated by National Labs flow analysts using estimated flow rates at varying BOP (PT-B) pressures and maximum allowable flow into formation of 20,000 bbls.

have to terminate the test within six hours and reopen the well. If the shut-in pressure was greater than 7,500 pounds per square inch, the risk of a leak was low, and the test could proceed for the full 48 hours. Finally, if the shut-in pressure was between 6,000 and 7,500 pounds per square inch, the risk of a leak was uncertain—either there was a medium-sized leak or the reservoir was highly depleted. Under this scenario, the test could proceed for 24 hours. (See Figure 5.1.) If the pressure was too high, there was also the risk of causing a new rupture.

After a 24-hour delay to repair a minor leak, BP shut the stack and began the well integrity test at about 2:25 p.m. on July 15.[286] For the first time in 87 days, no oil flowed into the Gulf of Mexico. Initial wellhead pressure readings were just over 6,600 pounds per square inch—in an uncertain middle range that one senior administration official termed "purgatory"—and rising slowly.[287] Later that afternoon, the science advisors, including McNutt and Hunter, met with Secretaries Salazar and Chu to determine whether to keep the well shut in. Based on the early pressure data, the group appears to have been firmly in favor of reopening the well. Garwin, who had opposed even undertaking the well integrity test, voiced the strongest opinion, arguing BP ought to stop the test immediately and wondering whether it was already too late. No one at the meeting appears to have argued in favor of keeping the well closed.[288]

Following the science team meeting, Admirals Allen and Cook, Browner, Secretaries Chu and Salazar, and McNutt had a series of conversations to determine how to proceed. Keeping the capping stack shut could cause an underground blowout and, in the worst case, loss of a significant portion of the 110-million-barrel reservoir into the Gulf.[289] This risk had to be balanced against the benefit of stopping the spill, a continuing environmental disaster. The government decisionmakers recognized that the public wanted the well plugged and the flow of oil into the Gulf stopped, but the risk of causing greater harm was real.

Admiral Cook made the argument that eventually prevailed. He reminded the others that, before the test began, BP and the government had considered the possibility of pressure measurements like those being observed. Both had agreed that, in such a case, the test should last 24 hours, with consultation between the parties before reopening the well.[290] The government leaders decided that they should follow this protocol: the stack would stay closed overnight.

This additional time proved critical. Using a single cell-phone photograph of the plot of initial pressure readings, Paul Hsieh, a U.S. Geological Survey scientist then in Menlo Park, California, worked overnight to develop an explanation of the results of the test, including the lower-than-expected shut-in pressure. Pre-test expectations had been based on an incomplete understanding of the reservoir's geometry and on pressure readings from a single gauge at the bottom of the BOP, which was only accurate to plus or minus 400 pounds per square inch and functioning sporadically. At the government's behest, BP had equipped the capping stack with pressure gauges.[291] Following the shut-in of the well, those gauges provided accurate pressure data for the first time. Using that data along with a flow-rate estimate of 55,000 barrels per day and BP's estimate that the reservoir contained 110 million barrels of oil, Hsieh was able to generate a model that predicted the observed shut-in pressure without having to assume a significant oil and gas leak into the rock formation.[292]

The next morning, the government principals and the science advisors—who had been convinced that reopening the stack was necessary—hosted a meeting. Both BP and Hsieh made presentations explaining the observed pressures at shut-in, with BP arguing that the well should remain capped.[293] Participants had different recollections as to whether Hsieh's or BP's presentation carried more weight. But the outcome of the meeting was clear: the stack would stay shut, with the government reevaluating that decision every six hours.

While it went unrealized at the time, a critical point had passed. As intense monitoring of the area around the wellhead continued over the next several days, Hsieh's model continued to predict the behavior of the well, and a leak into the formation became progressively less likely.[294] Although the well integrity test had originally been scheduled to last a maximum of 48 hours, Admiral Allen began to extend it in 24-hour increments beginning on July 17. At his July 24 press briefing, he stated what was by then plain: "our confidence [in the capping stack] is increasing and we have better integrity in the well than we may have guessed."[295]

Meanwhile, on July 19, BP publicly raised the possibility of killing the well before completing a relief well, through a procedure called a "static kill."[296] Like the top kill, the static kill involved pumping heavy drilling mud into the well in an effort to push oil and gas back into the reservoir. But because the oil and gas were already static, the pumping rates required for the static kill to succeed were far lower than for the top kill.

The primary concern with the static kill was the pressure it would put on the well. On July 28, BP received an unsolicited letter from Pat Campbell, a Vice President at Superior Energy Services, which owned BP contractor Wild Well Control, recommending in no uncertain terms that the static kill not proceed. Campbell, who had worked with legendary well-control expert Red Adair, reiterated a point already raised by others in the industry: that the only pressure the well could withstand for certain was the current shut-in pressure (approximately 6,920 pounds per square inch at the time he wrote).[297]

Despite these issues, after some delays caused by weather and work on the first relief well, the government approved the plan for the static kill on August 2.[298] A mud injection test began on August 3, and pressure at the wellhead increased only slightly before beginning to drop.[299] Based on the positive results of the test, BP began slowly pumping more drilling mud into the well later that same day. By 11:00 p.m., the static kill had succeeded.[300] The following evening, Admiral Allen authorized BP to follow the mud with cement.[301] BP finished cementing the next day. On August 8, Admiral Allen reported that the cement had been pressure-tested and was holding.[302]

The Fate of the Oil (August 4)

On August 4, the same day it announced the static kill's success, the federal government released a 5-page report titled *BP Deepwater Horizon Oil Budget: What Happened to the Oil?*, as well as a 10-page supporting document titled *Deepwater Horizon MC252 Gulf Incident Oil Budget.*[303] The "Oil Budget" provided the government's first public estimate of the total volume of oil discharged during the spill—roughly 4.9 million barrels. The government arrived at this number using its current flow-rate estimate, which ranges from 62,200 barrels per day on April 22 to 52,700 barrels per day on July 14, just before the capping stack stopped the flow.[304] * The Oil Budget also described the efficacy of different response methods.

The Oil Budget was originally an operational tool, intended as a guide for responders, not as the basis for a scientific report on what happened to the oil. Nonetheless, in late July, the White House decided to publicly release the Oil Budget and asked NOAA to take the lead on drafting a short report to introduce the tool.[305] The Budget cleared the interagency review process in time for its August 4 release.†

The White House's Browner appeared on six morning newscasts on August 4 to discuss both the successful static kill and the Oil Budget report. On *NBC*, *MSNBC*, and *ABC*, she told viewers that, according to the report, "the vast majority," or approximately three-quarters, of the oil "is gone" or "appears to be gone."‡ The Budget, however, did not

---

* The government's estimate, which is current as this report goes to press, has an uncertainty factor of ±10 percent. It is the Commission's understanding that the government's Flow Rate Technical Group will issue a final report in January 2011. In a peer-reviewed paper published in *Science Express* on September 23, 2010, Timothy Crone and Maya Tolstoy of Columbia University's Lamont-Doherty Earth Observatory estimated that the total release was roughly 5.2 million barrels—slightly higher than the government's estimate. While BP has not released its own flow-rate figures, it has suggested that the government's estimate of the total amount of oil released from the Macondo well is 20 to 50 percent too high.

† During the review process, EPA expressed concerns about the pie chart's potential to obscure the uncertainty of the government's estimates. Lisa Jackson, e-mail to Jane Lubchenco, July 31, 2010. For example, EPA recommended that NOAA combine chemically and naturally dispersed oil into a single category because there was not enough information to accurately distinguish between the two mechanisms. Bob Perciasepe, e-mail to Jane Lubchenco and others, July 31, 2010; Bob Perciasepe, e-mail to Stephen Hammond and others, August 1, 2010. NOAA disagreed. Administrator Jane Lubchenco asserted that combining the two categories would not decrease any uncertainty and that "'[c]hemically dispersed' is part of the federal response and 'naturally dispersed' is not, and there is interest in being able to sum up the federal response efforts." Jane Lubchenco, e-mail to Bob Perciasepe and others, August 1, 2010.

‡ On the other three shows, Browner similarly stated that "what the scientists are telling us is that the vast majority of the oil has been cleaned, it's been captured, it's been skimmed, it's been burned, mother nature has done its part" (*Fox News*); "our scientists are telling us that the vast majority of the oil has been contained, it's been burned, it's been cleaned" (*CBS*); and "our scientists and external scientists believe that the vast majority of the oil has now been contained, it's been skimmed, mother nature has done its part, it's been evaporated" (*CNN*).

FIGURE 5.2: August 4 Oil Budget

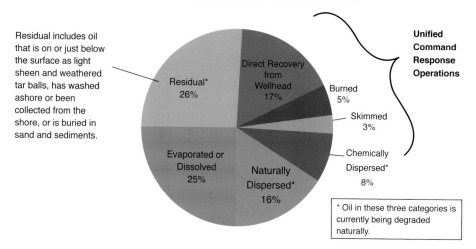

Deepwater Horizon Oil Budget
Based on estimated release of 4.9m barrels of oil

Residual includes oil that is on or just below the surface as light sheen and weathered tar balls, has washed ashore or been collected from the shore, or is buried in sand and sediments.

Residual* 26%

Direct Recovery from Wellhead 17%

Burned 5%

Skimmed 3%

Evaporated or Dissolved 25%

Naturally Dispersed* 16%

Chemically Dispersed* 8%

Unified Command Response Operations

* Oil in these three categories is currently being degraded naturally.

show that most of the oil was gone. The three-quarters of the oil not in the "remaining" category included "dissolved" and "dispersed" oil that was potentially biodegrading, but not necessarily gone. By 9:00 a.m., NOAA Administrator Jane Lubchenco e-mailed Browner's deputy and other officials to express her concern "that the oil budget is being portrayed as saying that 75% of the oil is gone": "It's not accurate to say that 75% of the oil is gone. 50% of it is gone—either evaporated or burned, skimmed or recovered from the wellhead." Lubchenco asked the officials to "help make sure" the error was corrected.[306]* She had made the same point to the White House before the Budget rollout; a July 30 e-mail to Browner's deputy had emphasized that Lubchenco opposed grouping dispersed oil with recovered oil because the former was "still out there or [was] being degraded."[307]

At a press briefing that afternoon, Browner said that the report had "been subjected to a scientific protocol, which means you peer review, peer review, and peer review." Earlier in the same briefing, Lubchenco had said "[t]he report was produced by scientific experts from a number of different agencies, federal agencies, with peer review of the calculations that went into this by both other federal and non-federal scientists."[308] The Budget, however, was not "peer-reviewed" as the scientific community uses that term. Many of the outside scientists listed as reviewers had not even seen the final report.

The rollout of the Oil Budget drew immediate criticism, with scientists pointing out that Browner's optimism about the percentage of the oil that was gone was unsupported, especially because of the uncertain rate of biodegradation.[309] Moreover, after a summer of ever-increasing official estimates of the spill's size, the public was dubious of the government's conclusions. As a *Times-Picayune* editorial noted, "From the start of the

---

* The U.S. Geological Survey, which had also been involved in developing the Oil Budget tool and editing the report, expressed similar misgivings about the portrayal of the report. At 11:00 a.m., U.S. Geological Survey scientist Mark Sogge told a colleague, "We need to keep in mind, and make it clear to others, that this is NOT a [U.S. Geological Survey] product." Mark Sogge, e-mail to Stephen Hammond, August 4, 2010.

disaster. . . the government has badly underestimated the amount of oil spewing from the runaway well. That poor track record makes people understandably skeptical of [the Oil Budget] report."[310] Lubchenco has since acknowledged that she was "in error" when claiming that the Oil Budget had been peer-reviewed.[311] NOAA has emphasized that the report's "purpose was to describe the short-term fate of the oil and to guide immediate efforts to respond to the emergency" rather than to "provide information about the impact of the oil" or "indicate where the oil is now."[312]

NOAA supplied these explanations on November 23, when it released a new version of the Oil Budget: *Oil Budget Calculator Technical Documentation*, a peer-reviewed report of over 200 pages that gave the formulas used and updated the percentages in the original budget.[313] The new version's biggest change was its estimate of the amount of oil chemically dispersed, which doubled from 8 percent to 16 percent. Of this additional 8 percent, 3 percent came from the "naturally dispersed" category, 2 percent from the "evaporated or dissolved" category, and 3 percent from the "residual" category. (These changes brought the total amount of "residual" oil down from 26 to 23 percent.)

As a tool for responders, the Oil Budget indicated that response and containment operations collected, eliminated, or dispersed about 41 percent of the oil, with containment ("direct recovery from wellhead") the most effective method, and chemical dispersants breaking down a substantial fraction. Response technology (skimming or burning) removed—as opposed to dispersed—only 8 percent of the oil. Dispersion of the oil before it reached the surface limited the amount that responders could skim, burn, or disperse at the surface. Nevertheless, responders considered burning an important success: it had never before been attempted on this scale, and burning techniques advanced during the spill.[314] Skimming was less of a success: despite the participation of hundreds of ships and thousands of people, it collected only 3 percent of the oil.

The least effective response technology was the berms, which the Oil Budget documents do not even mention. By the time BP capped the well on July 15—day 44 of the berm construction project—Louisiana's contractor estimated that 10 percent of one reach—6 percent of the total project—had been completed.[315] In late May, Governor Jindal had asserted that "[w]e could have built 10 miles of sand [berms] already if [the Corps] would have approved our permit when we originally requested it."[316] In fact, it took five months to build roughly 10 miles of berms, at a cost of about $220 million.[317] Estimates of how much oil the berms collected vary, but none is much more than 1,000 total barrels.[318] On November 1, Governor Jindal announced plans to convert the berms into part of a long-term coastal restoration project, which BP would continue to fund. In his recently released book, the Governor maintained that the berms were "one of the most effective protection measures" against oil reaching the Louisiana coast.[319]

The End of the Well, but Not the End of the Response

In mid-September, the first relief well—which BP had begun drilling in early May—finally intercepted the Macondo well, allowing BP to pump in cement and permanently seal the reservoir. On September 19, 152 days after the blowout, Admiral Allen announced: "the Macondo 252 well is effectively dead."[320]

But fears about health and safety did not die with the well. Some Gulf residents continued to believe that BP had used dispersants onshore, nearshore, at night, and without government approval, and that it had continued using them after it capped the well. The Commission has not seen credible evidence supporting these claims. NOAA reopened one-third of the area closed to fishing on July 22 and continued to reopen additional sections based on a testing and sampling protocol developed and implemented with the Food and Drug Administration.[321] But some scientists questioned the protocol, while some fishermen were hesitant to give up income from the Vessels of Opportunity program and return to their regular jobs in the midst of public concern about Gulf seafood.[322] (Chapter 6 discusses seafood safety.)

Residents also had to cope with the miles of used boom and other debris. Despite the typical spill-responder uniform of rubber gloves and protective coveralls, BP planned to send the thousands of tons of oily debris generated over the summer to ordinary municipal landfills.[323] Wastes from oil exploration and production are classified as non-hazardous by law and do not require specialized disposal.[324] Although the federal government generally does not supervise the disposal of non-hazardous waste, on June 29, the Coast Guard and EPA issued a directive requiring BP to test its waste for hazardous elements, publicize the results, and consult with the communities where the waste was to be stored.[325] In addition, EPA announced it would conduct its own twice-monthly testing of the debris and would post the results online.[326] BP was initially slow to release its testing data. After receiving a sternly-worded letter from Federal On-Scene Coordinator Admiral Zukunft on July 24, however, it started regularly posting the results on its website.[327] EPA began sampling the waste and posting the test data as well, after some criticism and delay.[328] As of November 17, EPA's tests had not shown any of the waste to be hazardous.[329]

As BP and EPA implemented the waste directives, environmental justice activists argued that BP was dumping the debris disproportionately in poor and non-white communities.[330] Residents of Harrison County, Mississippi fiercely opposed the disposal of oiled waste in their Pecan Grove landfill, and BP agreed not to use it.[331] Environmental justice advocate and scholar Robert Bullard contended that the racial makeup of Harrison County was a factor, and EPA objected to BP's decision.[332] The Federal On-Scene Coordinator instructed BP to follow the approved waste plan, noting that "[a]llowing one community to reject acceptance of waste. . . may complicate remaining waste disposal efforts." BP began to use the site for waste staging, though not for disposal.[333]

With the well sealed, the number of responders in the Gulf decreased. The National Incident Command officially stood down on October 1.[334] Admiral Allen turned over the remaining tasks to Federal On-Scene Coordinator Admiral Zukunft and finally retired. BP started to shut down some of its programs, and Coast Guard responders started to head to their next posts. The spill and the emergency response had ended. Figuring out the extent of the damage, and how to repair it, had begun.

Voices from the Gulf
"I don't know what to do with myself."

Dean Blanchard, Dean Blanchard Seafood Inc., Grand Isle, LA

Dean Blanchard runs Louisiana's biggest shrimp business, on Grand Isle—a Mississippi River Delta barrier island 50 miles south of New Orleans, fully exposed to the Gulf of Mexico. During the warm months of a typical shrimp season, Blanchard Seafood and its extensive network of bayside wharves are a frenetic cacophony of languages and accents—Spanish, Vietnamese, a smattering of Cajun French, and the various Deep South dialects—as more than a thousand fishermen offload the catch from their shrimping vessels. The shrimp are sorted by size and dispatched into the world.

During 30 years in business, Blanchard had become one of the nation's principal suppliers—and a multi-millionaire. In season, he bought as much as 500,000 pounds of shrimp daily from more than a thousand fishermen. The cold 2009-2010 winter had raised high hopes: "Every 10 years, when you get a cold winter, you get a really good shrimp crop," he explained. "We were licking our chops."

But with the Macondo well gushing more than 50,000 barrels of oil a day, and no end in sight, the brown shrimp season had been canceled just as it was about to start. By mid-May, tar balls and oil had started washing up onto Grand Isle's wetlands and beaches. By mid-June, Blanchard figured, "I've lost $15 million of sales in the last 50 days. That would have been $1 million in my pocket." The usually busy docks were quiet, the only activity the occasional coming and going of boats and crews working for BP cleaning and containing the oil. "I don't know what to do with myself," Blanchard explained. "I built all this over the last 30 years, and now for what?" "We've got 1,400 vessels that go and catch shrimp, come to our facility." Now, he continued, "basically we've lost all our customers because we can't supply them."

For decades, oil and seafood had mixed comfortably in Louisiana's coastal culture. Each year Morgan City hosted the annual Shrimp and Petroleum Festival, a rollicking celebration of the state's two high-profile economic mainstays. Oil has long provided the region's best-paying jobs, and the revenue to finance everything from state roads to free school books. The maritime world of seafood has deeper cultural roots, and provides a living and a way of life along the gulf coast, one of the nation's most productive fishing waters. Many families had members in both worlds. Indeed, Blanchard's own grandfather had made a fortune servicing the offshore oil industry.

But now those two worlds had collided—and everything seemed at risk.

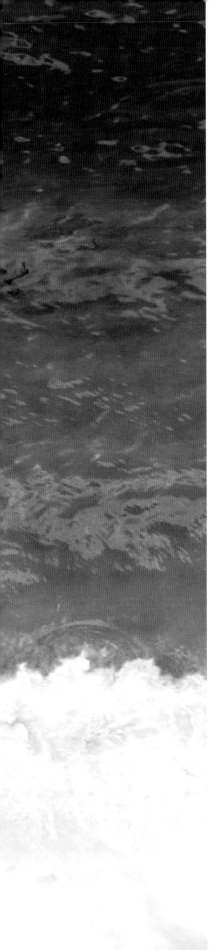

Chapter Six

"The worst environmental disaster America has ever faced."

Oiling a Rich Environment: Impacts and Assessment

When President Barack Obama addressed the nation from the Oval Office on June 15—nearly two months after the Macondo well began gushing crude oil and one month before engineers subdued it—he said:

> Already, this oil spill is the worst environmental disaster America has ever faced. And unlike an earthquake or a hurricane, it's not a single event that does its damage in a matter of minutes or days. The millions of gallons of oil that have spilled into the Gulf of Mexico are more like an epidemic, one that we will be fighting for months and even years.[1]

The *Deepwater Horizon* blowout produced the largest accidental marine oil spill in U.S. history,[2] an acute human and environmental tragedy. Worse still, as discussed in Chapter 7, it occurred in the midst of environmental disasters related to land-based pollution and massive destruction of coastal wetlands—chronic crises that proceed insidiously and will require not months but decades of national effort to address and repair.

A lone beachgoer encounters bands of oil along Alabama's Orange Beach. Though wind and currents helped keep most of the spilled oil offshore, all told some 650 miles of Gulf Coast habitat were oiled to one degree or another— Louisiana was hardest hit—impacting ecosystems, the economy, and human health.

< Tyrone Turner/Photo courtesy of National Geographic

Laws guide resolution of damages from the spill itself. There is a suite of policies and programs aimed at improving discrete environmental issues within the Gulf and along its coast. The law also provides compensation for direct economic impacts. This chapter analyzes these immediate impacts, not only on the natural environment but also on the economy and on human health in the affected region. Unfortunately, the human–health effects are the least-recognized fallout from the spill, and those least-well addressed in existing law and policies.

The Impact on Nature

The *Deepwater Horizon* oil spill immediately threatened a rich, productive marine ecosystem. To mitigate both direct and indirect adverse environmental impacts, BP and the federal government took proactive measures in response to the unprecedented magnitude of the spill.[3] Unfortunately, comprehensive data on conditions before the spill—the natural "status quo ante" from the shoreline to the deepwater Gulf—were generally lacking.[4] Even now, information on the nature of the damage associated with the released oil is being realized in bits and pieces: reports of visibly oiled and dead wildlife, polluted marshes, and lifeless deepwater corals. Moreover, scientific knowledge of deepwater marine communities is limited, and it is there that a significant volume of oil was dispersed from the wellhead, naturally and chemically, into small droplets.[5] Scientists simply do not yet know how to predict the ecological consequences and effects on key species that might result from oil exposure in the water column, both far below and near the surface.[6]

Much more oil might have made landfall, but currents and winds kept most of the oil offshore, and a large circulating eddy kept oil from riding the Loop Current toward the Florida Keys.[7] Oil-eating microbes probably broke down a substantial volume of the spilled crude, and the warm temperatures aided degradation and evaporation[8]—favorable conditions not present in colder offshore energy regions.[9] (Oil-degrading microbes are still active in cold water, but less so than in warmer water.) However widespread (and in many cases severe) the natural resource damages are, those observed so far have fallen short of some of the worst expectations and reported conjectures during the early stages of the spill.[10] So much remains unknown that will only become clearer after long-term monitoring of the marine ecosystem. Government scientists (funded by the responsible party) are undertaking a massive effort to assess the damages to the public's natural resources. Additionally, despite significant delays in funding and lack of timely access to the response zone, independent scientific research of coastal and marine impacts is proceeding as well.

A rich marine ecosystem. Particularly along the Louisiana coast, the Gulf of Mexico is no stranger to oil spills.[11] But unlike past insults, this one spewed from the depths of the ocean, the bathypelagic zone (3,300–13,000 feet deep). Despite the cold, constant darkness and high pressure (over 150 atmospheres), scientists know that the region has abundant and diverse marine life. There are cold-water corals, fish, and worms that produce light like fireflies to compensate for the perpetual night. Bacteria, mussels, and tubeworms have adapted to life in an environment where oil, natural gas, and methane seep from cracks in the seafloor. Endangered sperm whales dive to this depth and beyond to feed on giant squid and other prey.[12]

Elmer's Island in Grand Isle, La.

A dark tongue of oil invaded sensitive wetlands last May near Grand Isle, Louisiana, despite the presence of booms deployed to stop it. In a hopeful development over the summer, scientists found new plant growth in similarly oiled marshes, indicating that oil had not penetrated into root systems.

Patrick Semansky/Associated Press

Higher up the water column, light and temperature gradually increase and the ascending sperm whales—and Macondo well oil—encounter sharks, hundreds of fish species, shrimp, jellyfish, sea turtles, and dolphins. As the sperm whales surface for air at the bright and balmy Gulf surface, they pass through multitudes of plankton, floating seaweed beds, and schools of fish. Some of these fish species spend their early lives in the coastal waters and estuaries; others travel along annual migration routes from the Atlantic Ocean to the Gulf. The floating seaweed beds (sargassum), fish larvae, and plankton drift with the surface currents and are driven by the wind—as is the oil rising from below. The critical sargassum habitats lure sea turtles, tuna, dolphins, and numerous game fish to feed on the snails, shrimp, crabs, and juvenile species that seek shelter and food in the seaweed.[13]

Overhead are multitudes of seabirds—among them brown pelicans, northern gannets, and laughing gulls—that in turn feed in the ocean and coastal estuaries.[14] Dozens of bird species fly the Mississippi migration route each year, a major attraction for bird watchers, who flock to coastal Louisiana and Texas to catch a glimpse of migrating and resident shorebirds and nesting seabirds. Some of these birds feed on estuarine shrimp, fish, and crabs; others depend on shellfish and other small organisms that populate the expansive mudflats. Larger wading birds stalk their prey in the shallow water of mangroves, marshes, and other habitats that shelter fish and frogs. Raptors, including ospreys, bald eagles, and peregrine falcons, also pluck their prey from any of these environments and carry it to their perches.

As the unprecedented volume of oil gushing from the Macondo blowout reached the surface, it had the potential to affect all of these marine and coastal organisms and to wash into the salt marshes, mudflats, mangroves, and sandy beaches—each in its way an

Oiled Sargassum

Wildlife biologist Mark Dodd surveys a raft of oil-soaked sargassum, also known as gulfweed. The floating beds are home to snails, shrimp, crabs, and other small creatures that—oiled or not—are ingested by turtles, dolphins, tuna, and game fish.

Blair Witherington/FWC

essential habitat at one or more stages of many species' lifecycles.[15] And these marine and coastal species are so interdependent that a significant effect on any one has the potential to disturb several existing populations in this complex food web.[16]

Encountering oil. Organisms are exposed to oil through ingestion, filtration, inhalation, absorption, and fouling.[17] Predators may ingest oil while eating other oiled organisms or mistaking oil globules for food. Filter feeders—including some fish, oysters, shrimp, krill, jellyfish, corals, sponges, and whale sharks—will ingest minute oil particles suspended in the water column. Surface-breathing mammals and reptiles surrounded by an oil slick may inhale oily water or its fumes. Birds are highly vulnerable to having their feathers oiled, reducing their ability to properly regulate body temperature.[18] Moderate to heavy external oiling of animals can inhibit their ability to walk, fly, swim, and eat. Similarly, oiling of plants can impede their ability to transpire and conduct photosynthesis, and oiling of coastal sediments can smother the plants they anchor and the many organisms that live below.

Americans watched as the oil eventually came to rest along intermittent stretches of the Gulf coast. Before it arrived, scientists rushed to collect crucial baseline data on coastal and water-column conditions. Some of the oil propelled up from the wellhead was dispersed by natural and chemical means (as described in Chapter 5), creating a deep-ocean plume of oil droplets and dissolved hydrocarbons.[19] A portion of the oil that rose to the surface was also naturally and chemically dispersed in the shallow water column.[20]

The oil that made landfall was fairly "weathered," consisting of emulsions of crude oil and depleted of its more volatile components. More than 650 miles of Gulf coastal habitats—

salt marsh, mudflat, mangroves, and sand beaches—were oiled; more than 130 miles have been designated as moderately to heavily oiled. Louisiana's fragile delta habitats bore the brunt of the damage, with approximately 20 additional miles of Mississippi, Alabama, and Florida shorelines moderately to heavily oiled.[21] Light oiling and tar balls extended east to Panama City, Florida. Except for occasional tarballs, *Deepwater Horizon* oil never reached Texas or the tourism centers along the southwest Florida coast.[22]

Assessing the mixture of oil and life at the water's edge. The most biologically productive area along a sandy beach occurs where seaweed and other organic materials wash up just above the high tide line in the "wrack zone." Here, shorebirds forage for insects and other small organisms. As oil moves onto a beach with the rising tide, it is deposited in the wrack zone. Removing oiled wrack is the most prudent means of removing the oil—but doing so removes the living community, too. As the response to the spill proceeded, the Audubon Society evaluated wrack density along shorelines; it found that the wrack density on beaches east of the Mississippi River, where cleanup activities occurred, was "nearly absent," indicating "diminished habitat quality."[23]

Few beachgoers realize that millions of microscopic organisms live in the Gulf's soggy sands between high and low tide. By comparing samples taken before and after beaches were oiled, Holly Bik of the University of New Hampshire's Hubbard Center for Genome Studies, together with scientists at Auburn University and the University of Texas, hopes to determine the impact on this understudied community of sediment-dwelling microfauna.[24]

Tidal mudflats, generally devoid of vegetation and exposed at low tide, are more sensitive to pollutants than beaches.[25] The Louisiana delta and the estuarine bays of Mississippi and Alabama have large expanses of tidal mudflats, which support dense populations of burrowing species (vulnerable to smothering), foraging birds, crabs, and other organisms.[26] As oil settles on the flats, crabs and other burrowing animals help mix the oil into the sediment layer (an ecological process called bioturbation), extending the potential damage below the surface.[27]

Salt marsh and mangroves are both highly productive and sensitive habitats. Marsh grasses tolerate surface coating by weathered oil fairly well, but they will die if oil penetrates the saturated sediments and is absorbed by the root system.[28] When that happens, the plants' root systems degrade, making the marsh much more susceptible to erosion and threatening the habitat on which a wide variety of animals depend. People and equipment deployed in response to the spill can themselves damage the marsh; for example, summer storms pushed boom (used to corral waterborne oil) deep into the marshes, from which it could only be removed by intrusive methods that caused additional harm to the marsh topography.[29] Scientists working in oiled marshes observed new plant growth during the summer of 2010—a positive sign that oil had not penetrated into the rich, organic soils and inhibited root systems.[30] Professor Eugene Turner of Louisiana State University's Coastal Ecology Institute plans to study the effects of oil on the local salt marshes for at least the next year. His preliminary observations, through the fall of 2010, indicate some stress resulting in loss of marsh along its edge, but the estimated loss "pales in comparison" to the annual loss associated with dredging and flood protection (described in Chapter 7).[31]

The marine impacts. When water temperatures warm in the late spring, female oysters release millions of eggs into the water column. The timing of the Macondo oil spill may have been detrimental to oyster reproduction and the spawning of many other species.[32] Submerged oil floating in the nearshore water column poses potential threats to diverse shellfish and fish species. Although the impacts are not yet known, the presence of oil in the nearshore environment has been documented. Oil that reached the Gulf's estuarine waters forced closures of and likely damaged substantial tracts of Louisiana oyster beds.[33] Oyster mortality observed in the highly productive areas of Barataria Bay and Breton Sound, estuaries that flank the lower Mississippi River, appear to be due, in large part, to the flood of fresh water introduced through river diversions in what many believe was a futile attempt to keep oil from entering the estuarine areas.[34]

Beyond their commercial import, oysters are a keystone species—an organism that exerts a shaping, disproportionate influence on its habitat and community.[35] A single adult oyster can filter more than one gallon of water per hour, effectively removing impurities—including oil—from the water column.[36] Oyster reefs established on an estuary's muddy bottom can increase the surface area fifty-fold, creating intricate habitats for crabs, small fish, and other animals, which in turn sustain larger species.[37]

Harriet Perry, Director of the Center for Fisheries Research and Development at the University of Southern Mississippi, and scientists at Tulane University are studying the potential effects of oil on larvae of blue crabs, another keystone species. The slick from the Macondo oil spill ultimately covered about 40 percent of the offshore area used by larvae of the northern Gulf's estuarine-dependent species.[38] The Gulf coast's blue crab population had already declined considerably during the past 8 to 10 years as a result of a regional drought.[39] Perry and other scientists raced to take samples before the oil arrived and then after, hoping to be able to separate the oil-related impacts on wildlife from climate-related changes.[40]

Many large fish species are dependent on the health of the estuarine and marine habitats and resources. The National Oceanic and Atmospheric Administration (NOAA) noted that species with "essential fish habitat"[41] near the oil spill include scalloped hammerhead, shortfin mako, silky, whale, bigeye thresher, longfin mako, and oceanic whitetip sharks; and swordfish, white marlin, blue marlin, yellowfin tuna, bluefin tuna, longbill spearfish, and sailfish. Other important Gulf fish include red snapper, gag grouper, gray triggerfish, red drum, vermilion snapper, greater amberjack, black drum, cobia and dolphin (mahi-mahi); coastal migratory open-water species, such as king and Spanish mackerel; and open-water sharks.[42]

Oil in the water column affects fish and other marine organisms through dermal contact, filtration, or ingestion. How much oil they accumulate depends on its concentration in food, water, and sediments they encounter, time and exposure, and the characteristics of each species—particularly the extent of their fatty tissue. Although oil is not very soluble

Voices from the Gulf
"I have to make house payments and boat payments."

Claire Luby

Ve Van Nguyen,
Oysterman, Buras, LA

Ve Van Nguyen was an oystermen working for one of the suppliers to P&J Oyster Company. A Vietnamese refugee who fled his homeland with his wife and young family in a boat in 1978, Van Nguyen had made it to the United States. He eventually settled in Buras, located in Plaquemines Parish in 1983, joining a large Vietnamese and Cambodian community that found limited English skills no impediment to earning a living fishing and shrimping. He had been a fisherman in Vietnam, and as he explained in his native language, "I grew up near the sea and I'm used to eating seafood. I wanted to live where there's lots of seafood." He and his wife had both worked on the water, and in recent years they had purchased two specially outfitted oystering boats, in addition to two other boats used for gill fishing. They had loans to repay. In 2009, when they had $80,000 in income from harvesting oysters, that was not a problem. Their four children were grown, with one still at home.

When Van Nguyen heard on television about the oil spill, he recalls, "I felt that I was going crazy and was really worried that I can't work anymore. I was afraid that the oil would spread and people can't eat what we catch so I wouldn't be able to work. So I was going through a mental crisis." Louisiana has about 25,000 Vietnamese Americans.

All through May, the Macondo well gushed oil as the government was closing Louisiana oyster beds. Ve Van Nguyen and his wife both found interim work using their boats to install booms against the spreading oil slicks, as part of BP's clean up. But he made nowhere near as much money as he would have harvesting oysters. Like so many others around the Gulf, he said, "I worry about myself and my wife. I don't know how we can make it." He had received some BP payments, but wondered how long those would go on? "I have to make house payments and boat payments." At age 60, he was no longer young, but certainly expected to continue oystering. But now, if BP does not compensate him for an amount similar to the lost income, "I can't do anything except for applying for welfare and food stamps." He had had his four boats towed back to his house. The future? "Everyone is worried and scared about that. They are scared of poisoning so we have to rely on the government to take care of it. I don't know what will happen."

Turtle in East Grande Terre Island, LA

Sad testament to the spill, a sea turtle lies dead beside the black tide that took its life along East Grand Terre Island in Louisiana. As of November 2010, the carcasses of more than 600 of the endangered reptiles had been collected. Countless others undoubtedly perished.

Benjamin Lowy/Edit by Getty Images

in water, oil and lipids do mix very well, so high concentrations of petroleum can be found in the fat-rich tissues of the liver, brain, kidneys, and ovaries. Muscle generally has the lowest lipid concentrations, but fish with fatty flesh can accumulate more oil than leaner species.[43] Oil constituents can be transferred through the food chain: heavier hydrocarbons can be passed from water to phytoplankton and then to zooplankton, or from sediments to polychaete worms and eventually to fish.[44] Because animals that are several steps up the food chain, like small fish, have the capability to metabolize hydrocarbons fairly rapidly, their predators will actually not accumulate much from eating them. Accordingly, bioaccumulation of toxic oil components does occur in fish, but biomagnification, with increasingly higher concentrations in animals at each level, does not occur.[45]

It would be impossible to sample and assess each of the thousands of marine fish and other species inhabiting the open-ocean water column. But scientists monitoring the spill along the shorelines and aboard research vessels have sampled plankton, shellfish, fish, water, sediment, and other environmental media to better understand the potential impacts on all terrestrial and marine organisms.[46] Tens of thousands of samples have been collected. They will likely analyze the samples to determine concentrations of oil and dispersants, and combine that information with existing data on species populations and distributions to model the potential impact of contamination in the water column on different species. In addition, large fish—like bluefin tuna and whale sharks (the world's largest fish)— mammals, and turtles are being tagged with tracking devices so scientists can follow their movements in the hope of learning how they have been affected by the spill.[47] By overlaying maps of the extent of the oil spill, derived from satellite images from the European Space Agency, with simulations of bluefin tuna spawning grounds and models of larval development, the Ocean Foundation estimated that the spill could have affected 20 percent of the 2010 season's population of bluefin tuna larvae, further placing at risk an already severely overfished species.[48]

Birds, mammals, turtles. Oiled birds are often the most visually disturbing and widely disseminated images associated with a major oil spill—as in the landmark Santa Barbara accident of 1969.[49] Through November 1, 2010, wildlife responders had collected 8,183 birds, 1,144 sea turtles, and 109 marine mammals affected by the spill—alive or dead, visibly oiled or not.[50] Given the effects of hiding, scavenging, sinking, decomposition, and the sheer size of the search area, many more specimens were not intercepted.[51] Therefore, scientists will assess the estimated total damage by applying a multiplier to the final observed number of casualties, and will likely issue separate estimates of sub-lethal effects and the impact of the spill on future populations.

In September 28 testimony before the Commission, Jane Lyder, Deputy Assistant Secretary of the Department of the Interior for Fish and Wildlife and Parks, said that "With more than 60 percent of the data verified, the three most affected [bird] species appear to be Brown Pelicans, Northern Gannets, and Laughing Gulls." She added that "The fall migration is underway. Songbirds and shorebirds began their migration to the Gulf coast in July. Waterfowl began arriving in late August and early September. We know there are significant impacts to marsh and coastal wetland habitats along sections of the Louisiana coast, particularly near Grand Isle, Louisiana. We are continuing to monitor what the full impact will be to migratory birds and other wildlife."[52]

The potential impact on marine mammals and sea turtles is harder to assess. Tim Ragen, Executive Director of the federal Marine Mammal Commission, testifying before a House of Representatives subcommittee on June 10, 2010, could only conclude, "Unfortunately, the scientific foundation for evaluating the potential effects of the *Deepwater Horizon* spill on many marine mammals inhabiting the Gulf is weak."[53]

According to NOAA, "Of the 28 species of marine mammals known to live in the Gulf of Mexico, all are protected, and six (sperm, sei, fin, blue, humpback and North Atlantic right whales) are listed as endangered under the Endangered Species Act." Also of note, "At least four species of threatened/endangered sea turtles (Kemp's ridley, green, leatherback, and loggerhead) are residents of the northern Gulf of Mexico and are represented by all life stages. A fifth species, the hawksbill turtle, can be found in the southern Gulf. The only nesting beaches in the world for Kemp's ridley turtles are in the western Gulf of Mexico."[54] As of November 1, the Unified Area Command reported that nine marine mammals had been collected alive (and three were released).[55] One hundred mammals were collected dead, though only four of those were visibly oiled. Most of the marine mammal mortalities were bottlenose dolphins.[56] Also among the dead was one juvenile sperm whale; it was found floating more than 70 miles from the source of the spill, reportedly unoiled.[57] More than 600 dead sea turtles were collected.[58]

Deepwater plumes of dispersed oil. The highly visible damage to wildlife aside, public and scientific concern about the *Deepwater Horizon* spill—at unprecedented water depths—has for some time focused on the impacts of an invisible subsurface "plume," or more accurately "clouds" of minute oil droplets moving slowly over the seabed. As of November 2010, three independent, peer-reviewed studies[59] confirmed the presence of a deepwater plume of highly dispersed oil droplets and dissolved gases at between 3,200 and 4,200 feet deep and extending for many miles, primarily to the southwest of the wellhead.

How will such substances affect the deepwater environment? One concern centered on decomposition and the resulting depletion of the oxygen supply on which aquatic species depend. Bacterial decomposition begins quickly for the light hydrocarbon gases, propane and ethane, but more slowly for the heavier hydrocarbons typically present in a liquid form and for the predominant gas, methane. The blooms of bacteria stimulated by lighter hydrocarbons prime the populations for degradation of other hydrocarbons. The degradation rates are sufficient to reduce the dissolved oxygen concentrations in the plume, but not to harmfully low levels associated with dead zones, where aquatic species cannot survive.[60] Subsequent mixing with adjacent, uncontaminated waters by slow-flowing currents appears to have been sufficient to prevent any further depletion of dissolved oxygen in the aging plumes.[61] These findings do not rule out potential impacts of deepwater oil and dispersant concentrations on individual species.[62] Chemical analyses of water samples taken from the established deepwater plume in May 2010 suggest that hydrocarbon concentrations were high enough at the time to cause acute toxicity to exposed organisms,[63] although concentrations declined over several miles from the well as the plume mixed with the surrounding water.

Federal scientists have estimated that about 15 percent of the oil escaping the wellhead was physically dispersed by the fluid turbulence around the flow of oil and gas. The deepwater plume would have formed even if chemical dispersants had not been injected at the wellhead. But the addition of 18,379 barrels of dispersants to the discharging oil and gas stream may have increased the volume of oil in the deepwater plumes to a degree comparable to that from physical dispersion alone.[64] As of late 2010, there have been unconfirmed reports of oil deposited on the seafloor in the vicinity of the Macondo well.[65] If confirmed by chemical analyses, this would not be particularly surprising because oil droplets can become entrained in denser particulate matter, including the flocks of organic matter (referred to by scientists as "marine snow") that characterize open-ocean waters, and settle on the ocean floor. There have also been recent reports of dead or dying deepwater corals living on rock outcrops that could have been impinged by the deep plumes.[66]

Because the *Deepwater Horizon* spill was unprecedented in size, location, and duration,[67] deepwater ecosystems were exposed to large volumes of oil for an extended period. It will take further investigation and more time to assess the impacts on these ecosystems, their extent and duration. Unfortunately, except for studies that have focused on rare and specialized communities associated with rocky outcrops or seeps, scientific understanding of the deepwater Gulf ecosystem has not advanced with the industrial development of deepwater drilling and production.[68]

Figure 6.1: Assessment Categories for Natural Resource Damage Assessment

WATER COLUMN AND SEDIMENTS
- Water quality surveys
- Transect surveys to detect submerged oil
- Oil plume modeling
- Sediment sampling

TURTLES AND MARINE MAMMALS
- Aerial surveys
- Tissue sampling
- Acoustic monitoring
- Satellite tagging

SHORELINES
- Aerial surveys
- Ground surveys
- Observations of the quality of habitat
- Measurements of subsurface oil near the shore

TERRESTRIAL AND AQUATIC SPECIES
- Ground surveys
- Observations of the quality of habitat

HUMAN USE
- Aerial surveys
- Ground surveys

FISHERIES
- Plankton surveys
- Invertebrate surveys
- Adult fish surveys
- Larval fish surveys

AQUATIC VEGETATION
- Aerial surveys
- Field surveys in large beds of aquatic vegetation

BIRDS
- Aerial surveys
- Ground surveys
- Nearshore boat surveys
- Offshore boat surveys
- Radio telemetry

SHELLFISH
- Oyster surveys
- Tissue and sediment sampling
- Mussel collection
- Shrimp collection

CORALS
- Coral surveys
- Tissue collections
- Contaminant surveys

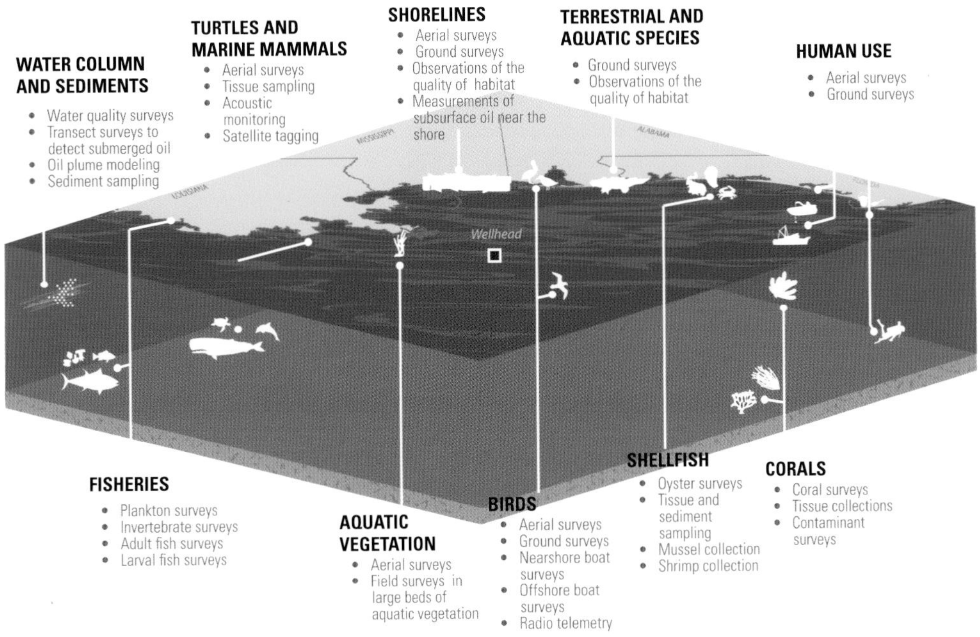

This figure represents the various natural resource categories being assessed as part of the Deepwater Horizon Natural Resource Damage Assessment. Such an assessment, which always follows an oil spill, is used to make the public whole for ecological damages caused by a spill. This graphic illustrates the three-dimensional challenges that an assessment of a deep sea blowout presents.

NOAA (adapted)

Natural Resource Damage Assessment

The federal Oil Pollution Act (OPA or the Act) creates a process for assessing the damages caused by an oil spill and then the expenditure of monies collected to address those damages. To that end, the Act formally designates "natural resource trustees," who are responsible for assessing the "natural resources damages" of the spill.[69] (Figure 6.1) The trustees accordingly prepare a "natural resource damage assessment" that seeks to quantify oil-spill damages to: (1) public natural resources; (2) the services they provide (e.g., oysters provide water filtration); and (3) the public's lost use of those resources.[70] For the Macondo spill, NOAA and the Department of the Interior are leading the effort as trustees on behalf of the federal government.[71] The Department of Defense will also participate on behalf of affected military property along the Gulf coast.[72] The federal representatives will be joined by natural resource trustees from the five Gulf States.[73]

Identifying and quantifying damages, particularly where complex ecosystems are involved, present enormous challenges. Developing sound sampling protocols that cover adequate time scales, teasing out the effects of other environmental disturbances, and scaling the damages to the appropriate restoration projects often takes considerable time. A typical damage assessment can take years. Two sets of determinations—one concerning the baseline conditions against which damages to each species or habitat will be assessed and another concerning the quantification of those damages—are particularly difficult and consequential in terms of the overall results.

The goal of a natural resource damage assessment is "to make the environment and public whole for injuries to natural resources and services resulting from [an oil spill]."[74] The injury is quantified by reference to baseline conditions: "the condition of the natural resources and services that would have existed had the incident not occurred."[75] But making this determination is often inherently difficult and highly contentious. Without well-established baseline conditions, there can be inaccurate quantification of damages or required restoration. Given that the ecological baseline can vary seasonally, annually, and over much longer time scales, it can be difficult to pinpoint the exact condition of an ecosystem prior to a spill. Because long-term historical data are often nonexistent or discontinuous, natural resource trustees are likely to be disadvantaged by a lack of sufficient information to fully characterize the condition of relevant ecosystems prior to the incident in question.[76]

As OPA regulations indicate, "baseline" for purposes of damage assessment is generally considered to be the condition of the resource just prior to the spill.[77] The precise application of this definition has particular importance in the Gulf of Mexico context, where many coastal habitats have been substantially degraded over decades—even centuries—under the pressure of ever-expanding industrial, commercial, and residential development. The natural resource damage assessment regulations, as generally applied, require that BP and other potentially responsible parties restore Gulf resources to their functioning level as of April 19, 2010—by which point the Gulf ecosystem in April 2010 was already weakened.[78] In this context, effective long-term restoration will require the stabilization and eventual reversal of a number of long-standing, damaging trends.

The effort to thoroughly address the ecological impacts of this historic pollution event is unprecedented in scale. Thousands of samples have been collected from dozens of research cruises. Hundreds of miles of coastline have been observed and sampled.[79] Marine mammals and turtles are being observed aerially and monitored by satellite or radio tracking devices.[80] The assessment of natural resources damages is the largest and most complex that the government has ever undertaken to assess oil spill impacts.

Supporting independent scientific research. Apart from these governmental efforts, independent scientists have also sought to study the spill's impacts. But funding for academic and other scientists in the days and weeks immediately after the spill was limited.[81] As a result, the nation lost a fleeting opportunity to maximize scientific understanding of how oil spills—particularly in the deep ocean—adversely affect individual organisms and the marine ecosystem. Such research depends on sampling, measurements, and investigations that can be accomplished only during and right after the spill. The National Science Foundation tried to fill the gap by funding studies under its Grants for Rapid Response Research (RAPID) Program, aimed at better understanding potential impacts to coastal and marine habitats and resources.[82] Through September 2010, the Foundation funded 167 *Deepwater Horizon* research projects totaling $19.4 million.[83] The Foundation became practically the sole provider of emergency funding for independent scientists as the disaster unfolded. Nevertheless, the Program was not a panacea—because individual RAPID grants cannot exceed $200,000 per year, many scientists were left to seek additional funding to pay for the necessary, costly chemical analyses of their environmental samples.

In May, BP committed to provide $500 million for independent research on ecosystem assessment, impacts, and recovery efforts. Unfortunately, for multiple procedural and political reasons, by late November 2010 BP had only allocated a small portion of that money.[84] BP has since announced that it intends to work through the Gulf of Mexico Alliance, an organization led by the five Gulf coast governors, to implement this research program.[85] Here too, meaningful scientific inquiry will need to include long-term monitoring of the impacts of the spill on the Gulf's marine and coastal ecosystems.

With numerous studies under way through both the government's damage-assessment process and independent scientific research, the published literature regarding environmental impacts from the Macondo blowout can be expected to grow substantially. Major research commitments, totaling hundreds of millions of dollars, have already been made.[86]

Economic Impacts

The *Deepwater Horizon* oil spill put at risk two enormous economic engines that rely on it. Tourism and fishing, the industries affected as collateral damage, were highly sensitive to both direct ecosystem harm and, indirectly, public perceptions and fears of tainted seafood and soiled beaches. For this reason, whatever uncertainty may exist about the immediate and long-term adverse environmental impacts of the oil spill, no such uncertainty exists in terms of the significant adverse economic effects—especially from loss of confidence in commercial fishing.[87] The Gulf coast's economy depends heavily on commercial fisheries, tourism, and energy production[88]—each directly and immediately affected by the oil gushing from the Macondo well. Federal and state closures of commercial fisheries—a precautionary public-health measure—at once suspended much of the fishing and processing industry;[89] public concern nationwide that seafood was not safe to eat further compounded the economic impact along the Gulf.[90] Similarly, public perception that otherwise clean beaches were, or would become, oiled or that air quality during peak vacation season was impaired led to declines in hotel bookings, restaurant seatings, and a wide array of coastal activities.[91] Claims for losses have been submitted by real-estate agents and developers,[92] fishing charters,[93] and even an Alabama dentist who alleged a loss of summer customers.[94] And the Gulf oil and gas industry, its workers, and the regional economy were affected as the federal government imposed a moratorium (described in Chapter 5) on deepwater drilling intended to prevent another disastrous spill while the causes and consequences of the blowout were evaluated.[95]

That BP agreed to place in escrow a $20 billion fund to help address financial losses, at President Obama's urging, indicates the magnitude of the economic impact from the loss of control of this one deepwater well.[96] In its first eight weeks of operation, as of November 23, the independently administered Gulf Coast Claims Facility had paid out more than $2 billion to approximately 127,000 claimants.[97] By comparison, during its two-year

Figure 6.2: Annual Tourism & Fishing Revenue: Economic Activity by County

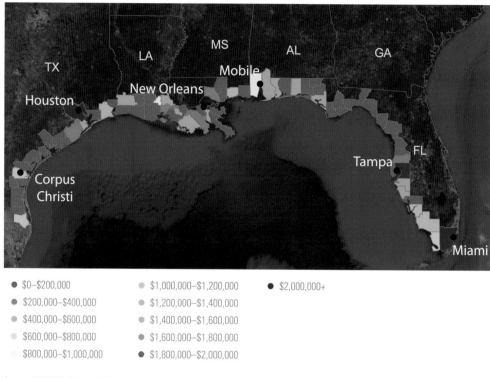

- $0–$200,000
- $200,000–$400,000
- $400,000–$600,000
- $600,000–$800,000
- $800,000–$1,000,000
- $1,000,000–$1,200,000
- $1,200,000–$1,400,000
- $1,400,000–$1,600,000
- $1,600,000–$1,800,000
- $1,800,000–$2,000,000
- $2,000,000+

Source: 2007 U.S. Economic Census
Note: Tourism includes: sporting goods stores, scenic/sightseeing transport (water), fishing clubs/guides, hunting/fishing reserves, camps, boat rentals, hotels, casinos, and nature parks. Fishing inlcudes: finfish, shellfish, other seafood, canning, frozen seafood, seafood markets and wholesalers.

lifespan, the September 11th Victim Compensation Fund awarded just over $7 billion to 5,560 individual claimants.[98]

It is currently not clear, however, the extent to which the enormous indirect economic impacts associated with loss of consumer confidence and injuries to the Gulf coast "brand" will ultimately be deemed compensable and that resulting uncertainty has generated intense debate among diverse government entities, local communities, interest groups, and BP. The federal Oil Pollution Act, for instance, does expressly recognize the appropriateness of compensation for "loss of profits or impairment of earning capacity resulting from property loss or natural resource injury."[99] But there is no easy legal answer to the question of how closely linked those lost profits or earnings must be to the spill before they should be deemed compensable. The search for such a rational endpoint for liability has already stymied the Gulf Coast Claims Facility in its processing of claims.[100] The absence of clear and fair procedures for systematically evaluating such claims deserves focused attention as the lessons from the *Deepwater Horizon* oil spill are learned.

The major industries in the "hardest working basin." Florida State University oceanographer Ian McDonald has called the Gulf of Mexico "the hardest working of our ocean basins."[101] The southern coast of the United States produces more than one-third of the nation's domestic seafood supply,[102] including most of the shrimp, crawfish, blue crabs, and oysters.[103] It produces one-third of all domestic oil,[104] and claims four of the top seven trading ports by tonnage.[105] The northern Gulf also provides diverse fish nursery and feeding grounds in the form of expansive marshes, mangrove stands, swamp forests, and seagrass beds, and boasts some of best beaches and waters in the United States for recreation and tourism.[106] Coastal tourism and commercial fisheries generate more than $40 billion of economic activity annually in the five Gulf States.[107] (Figure 6.2)

In 2008, according to NOAA, Gulf commercial fishermen harvested 1.27 billion pounds of finfish and shellfish that earned $659 million in total landings revenue.[108] Other contributors to the total Gulf fishing economy are seafood processors, warehouses, distributors, and wholesalers. Gulf fishermen land 73 percent of the nation's shrimp—half from Louisiana waters. Louisiana accounts for 67 percent of the nation's oyster production and 26 percent of the blue crab production.[109]

As described in Chapter 5, NOAA and state fisheries agencies responded to the *Deepwater Horizon* spill by closing huge portions of the Gulf to commercial and recreational fishing. At the most extensive point, 88,522 square miles of the Gulf of Mexico were closed to fishing[110]—one-third of the U.S. portion of the Gulf of Mexico, an area larger than the six New England states. In mid-June, NOAA and the Food and Drug Administration (FDA) released a protocol for reopening fisheries that would apply consistently to state and federal waters while striking a balance between keeping tainted seafood from market and unnecessarily crippling the seafood industry.[111] What ensued was likely the most rigorous seafood-testing campaign in U.S. history.

By late September, when nearly 32,000 square miles of the Gulf were still closed to fishing,[112] government officials made strong statements about the safety of seafood caught in reopened areas. "The shrimp, fish, and crabs are perfectly safe to eat," claimed Bob Dickey, Director of Seafood Science and Technology at the FDA.[113] Bill Walker, Executive Director of the Mississippi Department of Marine Resources, pronounced that "based on credible scientific data collected using federally-approved sampling and analytical techniques, Mississippi seafood has been safe and healthy to eat throughout the entirety of this event."[114] NOAA Administrator Jane Lubchenco stated, "I have confidence in our protocols and have enjoyed Gulf seafood each trip I've made to the region."[115]

But despite these assurances, some citizens continue to doubt the safety of Gulf seafood. "Everybody's credibility has been damaged by all this," said Ian MacDonald. He continued, "[The] many changes of course that NOAA took. The great concern about [the Environmental Protection Agency] and the licensing of dispersant use. The fact of the way it was handled has undermined public confidence."[116] Florida journalist Travis Pillow asked, "If people couldn't believe [the government's] estimates of how much oil was gushing into the Gulf, how could they believe their reassurance that beaches were clean or seafood was safe?"[117]

Constant media coverage about the spill also plainly shaped citizens' perception of the risks to public health. According to Timothy Fitzgerald, Senior Policy Analyst for the

Vendor Sign at Taste of Chicago

Perception is reality for the Gulf seafood industry. The economic calamity that descended when commercial fisheries were closed as a health-safety precaution should have been alleviated when they reopened, but the public still wasn't buying. Fact: After a rigorous testing campaign, most commercial species appear untainted.

Albert Ettinger

Environmental Defense Fund's Ocean Program, "Most people have very little connection to, or understanding of, the fish they buy,"[118] increasing their reliance on mass media to inform their decisions.[119] Scott Dekle, general manager of the VersaCold Atlas seafood warehouse, noted that news of the spill "got plastered all over the local and national media day after day after day. No one sees Anderson Cooper now standing outside Southern Seafood saying, 'This is great.'"[120] As a result, the public has come to associate Gulf seafood with oil. In August, Jonah Berger, a marketing professor at the University of Pennsylvania's Wharton School, said of Gulf seafood, "[R]ight now, the only association is a negative one, and so it's going to be much harder for that association to disappear."[121]

Most commercial Gulf seafood species seem to have emerged from the oil spill without any clear evidence of taint or contamination.[122] The real impact here is the reputational damage to Gulf seafood as a safe brand. Continued government testing, improvements in public outreach, and a coordinated marketing campaign may be needed to expedite its recovery. After several requests over several months, BP relented in early November and agreed to give Louisiana $48 million and Florida $20 million for seafood testing and marketing.[123] As of early December, BP is considering a similar request from Alabama.[124]

Voices from the Gulf
"We were called liars when we said we didn't have oil on the beaches"

Joe Mayer

Patricia Denny, Destin, FL

On May 2, 1985, Patricia Denny took a job as a secretary in a brand new real estate company in Destin, Florida, a small Emerald Coast family beach town proud of its white beaches and green waters. She married, had two girls, and worked hard at Holiday Isle Properties, rising to General Manager, where she managed 177 vacation rentals. In 2009, her longtime boss retired and Denny became the owner. "I was beyond excited. My dream was coming true—all the late hours, 7-day work weeks. Something I felt so passionate about was finally happening."

In her 24 years as a property manager, Denny has weathered some tough years: "I truly never thought things could be worse than 2004-5. Not only did the real estate market come to an abrupt halt, we had hurricane after hurricane. . . . But we rebounded on our own—no hand-outs, no help from government or our insurance company."

In late April 2010, when Denny saw the news on TV about the *Deepwater Horizon* explosion, "I remember thinking, 'How awful,' but the news reported that BP was going to stop the oil from spewing and all would be well. . . . Then NOAA predicted a shift in the weather and that impact from the oil was imminent. I was devastated. I couldn't sleep, I couldn't eat. It was the worst time of my life. Everything was at risk—my home, my income, my children's education, my three employees who are like a family to me."

In early May, to show that their pristine beaches were still sugary white, "We started filming daily and sometimes twice daily a video for YouTube called Shore Shots. It involved one of my employees standing in front of the camera and showing the Gulf of Mexico and the lack of oil despite being told otherwise. . . . It was not always well received. We were called liars when we said we didn't have oil on the beaches and told we were poisoning people with Corexit for our own greedy gain. It was definitely tough.

"By July the oil was here. No way I could prevent it from coming on – revenue dropped significantly. By August it was awful. No one, I mean no one, believed that we weren't covered in oil similar to the *Exxon Valdez*."

Denny's older daughter was a junior and biology major at the University of Alabama in Birmingham. As the cancellations rolled in, the young woman withdrew from college in July for what would have been her senior year. She moved home to help her mother run the company." It breaks my heart to see her do this," says Denny. "I am hoping she can go back sometime in the future but at this time I don't know when that is."*

*In early December 2010, Denny received compensation for her losses from the Gulf Coast Claims Facility, administered by Kenneth Feinberg and funded by BP.

Public Health Precautions

PUBLIC HEALTH PRECAUTIONS

This beach has been impacted by the oil spill in the Gulf of Mexico.

Oil may come and go at any time and it may not be visible.

If you see oil in the water, you are cautioned not to enter.

- Do not handle tar balls.

- Avoid contact with the oil.

- If you get oil or tar balls on your skin, wash with soap and water.

- If you get oil on your clothing, launder as usual.

- Do not use harsh detergents, solvents or other chemicals to wash oil from skin or clothing; they may promote absorption of the oil through the skin.

- If the odor causes nausea, vomiting, headache or breathing problems, leave the affected area.

FOR MORE INFORMATION CONTACT:
Alabama Department of Public Health _ _ _ _ _ _ _ _ _ 1.866.264.4073
Report oiled wildlife   _ _ _ _ _ _ _ _ _ _ _ _ _ _ _ _ 1.866.557.1401
Report odor_ 1.800.424.8802

ADVISORIES WILL BE POSTED AS NECESSARY.   **ADPH.ORG**
07.30.10

A sign of the times is posted at a public beach in Alabama. Long viewed strictly as environmental disasters, major oil spills can be hazardous to human health, beyond direct fatalities or injuries. Many Gulf Coast residents have complained of respiratory problems and headaches, and depressive illness has skyrocketed.

Rocky Kistner/NRDC

Coastal tourism. The Gulf coast generates an estimated $19.7 billion of tourism activity annually.[125] Florida accounts for more than 50 percent of the total[126] and, accordingly, attributes enormous actual and potential losses in tourism-related revenue to the oil spill. Quantifying such losses and the value of reputational damage may be even more difficult than assigning a value to the indirect losses suffered by the Louisiana fishing industry. Furthermore, responsibility for compensating those who may have suffered the indirect financial losses poses challenges of law, administration, and equity.

Floridians expressed frustrations with the news coverage of the oil spill—not all of it accurate. As described by Keith Overton, Chairman of the Florida Restaurant and Lodging Association and Chief Operating Officer of the TradeWinds Island Resorts in St. Pete Beach, in testimony before the Commission in July 2010, "These losses have occurred in our area, in the Tampa Bay area, without a single drop of oil ever reaching our beach and that is true for most of Florida. Pensacola has had some oil but the rest of the Panhandle is in pretty good shape right now. But you wouldn't know that if you looked at the national news media or you read the newspaper each day."[127] With dismay, he described a newscast that showed footage of President Obama walking along an unoiled Pensacola beach in mid-June, but with superimposed oil dripping down the screen behind him.

Just as the potential extent of the spill's impact was coming into focus, Michael Hecht, President of Greater New Orleans, Inc., a regional economic alliance in southeast Louisiana, testified in July that "going forward . . . this perception, this brand issue, is incredibly important."[128] A Louisiana-commissioned national poll conducted in early August 2010 found that 29 percent of respondents who were planning to visit the state said they were actively canceling or postponing their visits because of the oil spill.[129] Overton noted that the downturn in hotel reservations through June 2010 in unoiled Pinellas County had cost roughly $70 million and could total in the billions for the Florida Panhandle.

Human Health

Because oil spills have historically been viewed as environmental disasters, affecting nature, the Oil Pollution Act of 1990 and related policies offer fewer tools for addressing the human dimensions of such accidents. But in the case of the Macondo blowout—of unprecedented size, affecting a broad area, and the entire regional economy—assessment of impacts must also include the effects on human health, mental and physical. The *Deepwater Horizon* crew of course bore the immediate, devastating effects of the rig's destruction: 11 deaths, 17 injuries, and the unquestioned trauma of losing colleagues; the terror of the explosions and fires, the harrowing rescue, and the sense of involvement in the wider damages that ensued; and the rigors of the investigations and recovery efforts since.

But the tangible human health effects are more widespread. It was certainly a cruel, added misfortune that the Macondo spill bore down most heavily on southern Louisiana, less than five years after Hurricane Katrina ravaged the Louisiana and Mississippi coast, ruined much of New Orleans, killed hundreds, drove some of the population away permanently (including essential medical professionals), devastated the local economy, and shocked the nation with images of disorder and suffering. An unfortunate lesson of the oil spill is

Figure 6.3: Recent Changes in Emotional Well Being Along the Gulf Coast

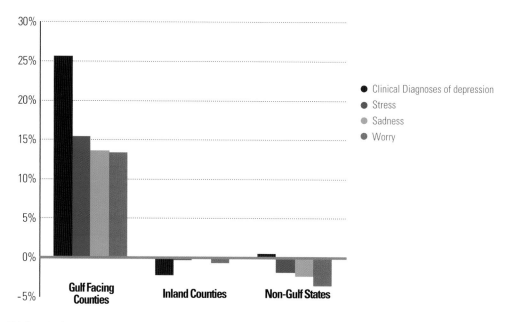

This figure depicts the recent changes in emotional well-being along the Gulf coast, as indicated in the Gallup Survey conducted April 21 to August 6, 2010.

Gaullup-Heathways Well-Being Index Change Since April 20th 2010

that the nation was not well prepared for the possibility of widespread, adverse effects on human health and mental well-being, especially among a particularly vulnerable citizenry. Gulf communities have long-time residents with strong roots to the region. Of coastal Louisiana residents surveyed after the spill, 60 percent of respondents reported living in their communities their entire lives and another 21 percent had lived there at least 20 years.[130] This context of regional and cultural ties to their communities exacerbates the worry and stress caused by the oil spill. Nearly 60 percent of respondents reported feeling worried almost constantly during the week prior to being surveyed because of the spill.[131] Louisiana shrimper Donald Johnfroe, Jr., said, "Everything I'm making now is going to pay off debt from this summer. I'm behind on my child-support payments, house payments. I need money."[132] Residents are worried about the economy, their way of life, and the stability of their communities. All of these factors play a role in affecting their health.

During the Commission's first public hearing in New Orleans on July 12–13, representatives of community groups focused on the psychological impacts. "Our people are used to tragedies and pulling themselves up from their bootstraps . . . but no one is saved from depression and fear," said Sharon Gauthe, Executive Director of Bayou Interfaith Shared Community Organizing. Grace Scire, Gulf coast Regional Director for Boat People SOS, told the Commission about her experiences working with the Vietnamese, Laotian, and Cambodian communities in the Gulf: "People are so dejected—it's not even the word for that—they're still recovering from Katrina."[133] Both speakers emphasized the need for additional community mental health services.

Industry and government responders did not adequately anticipate or address the magnitude of potential health impacts. Meanwhile, many citizens were coping with physical ailments (e.g., respiratory problems, headaches) and stress. Though health agencies eventually issued personal protective equipment guidelines for response workers and created a registry of these newly trained personnel, they missed the crucial window for screening their baseline physical health before the workers were directly exposed to oil products.[134]

Although many of the behavioral and psychological effects of the oil spill remain unknown, a Gallup survey of nearly 2,600 residents revealed that medical diagnoses of depressive illness had increased by 25 percent since the rig explosion.[135] The "well-being index" included in the Gallup study showed that coastal residents reported being stressed, worried, and sad more often than their inland counterparts (Figure 6.3).

There is also an indication that domestic violence increased. Between April and June 2010, the Administration for Children and Families observed a spike in calls to the National Domestic Violence Hotline from Gulf coast states, most notably in Louisiana.[136] Such broad community impacts suggest the need to monitor and respond to longer-term effects as warranted, and to pay special attention to especially vulnerable populations along the Gulf coast, including children, minority fishing communities, and Indian tribes.

Children and families. Children are particularly vulnerable to disruption in social, familial, and community stability as a result of disaster. A study conducted after Katrina found that children exposed to the hurricane were five times more likely to suffer from serious emotional disturbances than they were before the hurricane.[137] Although the direct impacts of the oil spill of course cannot be compared to the utter devastation wrought on entire communities by Katrina, some studies have already begun to document the spill's impact on children and families. A telephone survey of more than 900 coastal Louisiana adults two months after the spill began indicated that 46 percent felt they were unable to take care of their families as well as they would like.[138] In another survey of more than 1,200 adults living within 10 miles of the coast, parents from Louisiana and Mississippi reported that more than one-third of their children were suffering mental or physical health effects as a result of the oil spill. The most significant health impact was reported among families earning less than $25,000 annually.[139]

Exactly what proportion of health symptoms is attributable to the oil spill? Meaningful measurement is difficult at best. The preliminary findings of one academic study reported an "exposure differential" between exposed and non-exposed subjects.[140] Adults and children who were directly exposed to oil were, on average, twice as likely to report new physical or mental health issues as those who were not.[141]

Minority fishing communities. Another sensitive community is the 40,000 Southeast Asian immigrants who live along the Gulf coast (primarily Vietnamese, but also Laotians and Cambodians, many of them refugees from the decades-long wars in that region), one-fifth of who are fishermen.[142] Most of these families suffered direct, grievous harm from the 2005 hurricanes[143] and now face the spill-related loss of their livelihoods for an uncertain duration. Many of the fishermen speak little or no English, making their access to the Gulf Coast Claims Facility especially challenging[144] and posing difficulties in finding work outside the fishing industry. As the Commission heard in July, the cultural stigma associated with mental health problems in some of these communities complicates efforts to help those in need.[145]

Tribal communities. According to Brenda Robichaux, former principal Chief of the United Houma Nation, tribal communities on the coast are paying "the ultimate price" for both the mismanagement of the Mississippi River Delta over the past half-century (see discussion in Chapter 7) as well as the development of the offshore oil industry.[146] Both activities have contributed to the loss of wetlands and the destruction of barrier islands, which play crucial roles in protecting the tribes from major storms. Just as they began to recover from four hurricanes in three years, many members of Gulf coastal tribal communities for whom fishing is a lifestyle and a livelihood, suffered directly from the oil spill and face a difficult future.

Long-term health effects. The long-term health impacts of oil spills remain largely uncertain, but research conducted in the wake of other disasters provides some insight. A survey conducted one year after *Exxon Valdez* found that cleanup workers classified as being subjected to "high exposure" were 3.6 times as likely to have a generalized anxiety disorder and 2.9 times as likely to have post-traumatic stress disorder as members of an unexposed group.[147] Alaska Natives were particularly prone to effects of chemical exposure and, for cultural reasons, less likely to seek mental health services.[148] Unlike natural disasters, where mental health consequences generally dissipate relatively quickly, technological disasters are known to have chronic impacts on affected individuals and communities—a problem that is worsened as issues of fault and compensation are negotiated or litigated over an extended period.[149] Important symptoms include depression, substance abuse, domestic violence, psychological disorders, and disruption of family structures.[150] Evidence of these effects, as noted, has already appeared in the Gulf coast communities most directly influenced by the oil spill.[151]

To date, the Gulf Coast Compensation Fund has maintained that it will not pay damages for mental illness caused by the spill. According to its administrator, Kenneth Feinberg: "If you start compensating purely mental anguish without a physical injury—anxiety, stress—we'll be getting millions of claims from people watching television. You have to draw the line somewhere."[152] The affected Gulf coast states' health departments (excluding Texas) received $42 million for mental health from BP, and the Substance Abuse and Mental Health Administration received $10 million.[153]

Because no biological specimens were taken at the outset of the response, the study of future health effects will be constrained by a lack of baseline data. No biological samples were taken from cleanup workers before or immediately after their exposure to oil. More generally, given the unreliability of surveillance in the days and weeks after the spill, the quality of any baseline data for studies on long-term health effects was compromised. For future emergency response efforts, the government should have enhanced authority to ensure adequate baseline data and surveillance measures.[154] In the meantime, at a minimum, long-term monitoring of *Deepwater Horizon* responders' health and of community health in the most affected coastal areas is warranted and scientifically important.

However, the focus on long-term research cannot overshadow the need to provide immediate medical assistance to affected communities, which have suffered from limited access to healthcare services.[155] In the years following Hurricane Katrina, many of the damaged healthcare facilities were not rebuilt or replaced, including the major provider of indigent care, Louisiana State University Charity Hospital.[156] This left coastal communities vulnerable and lacking adequate access to care.[157] The greatest damage to Louisiana's health-services infrastructure was in Region One (Orleans, Jefferson, St. Bernard, and Plaquemines Parishes).[158] A year after the storm, New Orleans had been federally designated as a health professional shortage area (HPSA) for primary care, mental healthcare, and dental care. By 2008, 86 percent of Louisiana's parishes were HPSA-designated, with Medicaid and uninsured residents hardest hit.[159] Resources including federal Primary Care Access Stabilization Grants were made available to the state[160] and by August 2010, five years after Katrina, substantial progress had been made in restoring healthcare resources through a redesigned primary-care safety net.[161]

*   *   *   *

Assessing the environmental, economic, and human health damages from the *Deepwater Horizon* oil spill is, of course, only the threshold challenge. The even larger challenge now facing the Gulf is how to achieve its restoration, notwithstanding years of failed efforts to recover from past destruction.

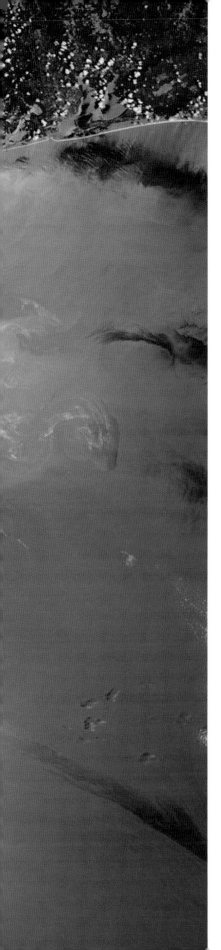

Chapter Seven

"People have plan fatigue . . . they've been planned to death"

Recovery and Restoration

Whatever the final tally of shorelines oiled, fishing days lost, and waterfowl killed, the *Deepwater Horizon* oil spill touched virtually every aspect of life on the Gulf of Mexico coast— and far beyond. Tens of thousands of residents draw fish and seafood from the Gulf's waters, which supply much of the nation. Many thousands more produce oil and gas from its buried stores. Gulf coast ports handle enormous volumes of grain and freight leaving American farms and factories and goods arriving from abroad. Vacationers come from across the country and around the globe to sun and swim on Gulf coast beaches.

But even before the highly visible damages caused by the spill became clear, many of those crucial Gulf resources faced long-term threats. Indeed, the Louisiana coast—that essential borderland and nursery to the nation's richest fisheries—has hit a dark trifecta. First, more than 2,300 square miles[1] of coastal wetlands (an area larger than the State of Delaware) have been lost to the Gulf since the United States raised the massive levees along the lower Mississippi River after the devastating Great Flood of 1927. Exceptionally powerful hurricanes, always a threat to the region, struck the coast in

Satellite-eye views of the Gulf a month after the Macondo blowout reveal the extent of the spill. Oil appears lighter or darker in the photograph depending on the relative angles of sun and camera.

< *NASA/GSFC, MODIS Rapid Response*

FIGURE 7.1: Maximum Extent of Oil

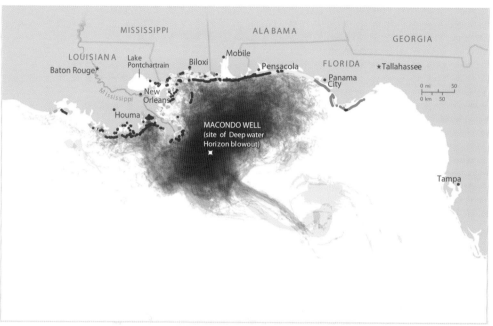

Oil	Tarballs	Surface Oil*
● Very Light Oiling	● Light Tarballs	○ 1 to 10 Days
● Light Oiling	● Medium Tarballs	● 10 to 30 Days
● Medium Oiling	● Heavy Tarballs	● More than 30 Days
● Heavy Oiling		

Surface Oiling Surveys: May 17 - July 25
Shoreline Oiling: Most severe oiling observed through November

Map courtesy of National Geographic (surface oil) and modified by Commission staff, NOAA/Coast Guard SCAT map (shoreline oiling)

2005 (Katrina and Rita) and 2008 (Gustav and Ike), causing even more wetland loss and erosion. Second, low-oxygen bottom waters were in the process of forming a massive "dead zone" extending up to 7,700 square miles during the summer of 2010. Referred to as hypoxia, this phenomenon has intensified and expanded since the early 1970s[2] as a result of nutrient pollution, mainly from Midwestern agriculture. And finally, the *Deepwater Horizon* disaster made matters worse: 11 rig workers killed in the explosion and 17 injured;[3] many thousands of people out of work; birds and sea animals killed and significant habitats damaged or destroyed.

These three protracted tragedies—coastal land loss, hypoxia, and the oiling itself—set up the central question for recovery from the spill: can or should such a major pollution event steer political energy, human resources, and funding into solutions for a continuing, systemic tragedy? The spill itself is a regional issue, but the slow-motion decimation of the Gulf of Mexico's coastal and marine environment—created by federal and state policies, and exacerbated by energy infrastructure and pollution—is an unmet national challenge.

Beyond these acute effects, the wider American public might not understand (and certainly has not given high priority to addressing) the root problems affecting the interrelated Mississippi River–Gulf of Mexico system that extends into the nation's heartland. Absent a comprehensive approach and national commitment to the Gulf coastal ecosystems, there are insufficient authorities and inadequate funds available to address the costly and progressive environmental losses now underway. In the aftermath of the *Deepwater Horizon* spill, state and federal authorities have moved to link spill recovery to more comprehensive reforms that were already in progress.[4]

A comprehensive response to the oil spill (and preparedness for the future) requires a national vision for restoring the waters, land, and their ecosystems to health. "Restoration" is the term of art for attempting to bring natural resources back after a spill. It also describes the recovery of large ecosystems by addressing the longstanding environmental problems that have caused their deterioration. The goal of any such effort is not necessarily to rebuild wetlands and barrier islands so that the coast looks like it did 100 years ago, but rather to reintroduce elements of the natural system so that the Mississippi River Delta—the epicenter of the threatened coastal region—can begin to heal itself.[5]

To that end, conversations about repairing the Gulf coast and marine ecosystems increasingly aim at restoring the region's natural "resilience."[6] Prior to the spill, Gulf states and federal authorities were already in various stages of restoring parts of the Gulf. Numerous ecosystem challenges now face the regions of the Gulf coast affected by the *Deepwater Horizon* spill. Barrier islands and shorelines are eroding from Florida to Texas. Essential habitats in coastal bays and estuaries have been lost to or degraded by pollution, energy or other development, changes in freshwater inflows, and overfishing.[7]

The largest and most formidable challenges, however, are to bring balance and efficiency to the Gulf's shared marine resources, and to address the rapid and continuous loss of wetlands, barrier islands, and shorelines comprising the Mississippi Delta and associated Chenier Plain of southwestern Louisiana. While many areas along the Gulf Coast require such restoration, the Mississippi Delta and the Gulf itself requires special attention.

Advancing Restoration Options for Offshore Ecosystems and Resources

Beyond restoration of Delta and other coastal ecosystems, a broader restoration effort—guided by new research and an understanding of what long-term damages may be resulting from the spill—seeks to improve the environmental quality of the marine habitat. These issues link a complex web of problems (including the annual appearance of the low-oxygen dead zone in waters of the Louisiana-Texas continental shelf) with the continued efforts to conserve the biodiversity and resources of offshore ecosystems.

Implementing the Gulf Hypoxia Action Plan. Hypoxia kills or excludes most marine animals over vast areas of the continental shelf. Scientific investigations have shown that such extensive and severe hypoxia is a recent phenomenon, fueled by the increased loads of nutrients carried down the Mississippi and Atchafalaya rivers, largely as a result of fertilizers used to support intense agriculture within the river basin.[8] Phytoplankton bloom thanks to the nutrients, and the process of their decay depletes oxygen over thousands of

FIGURE 7.2: Coastal Marine Users

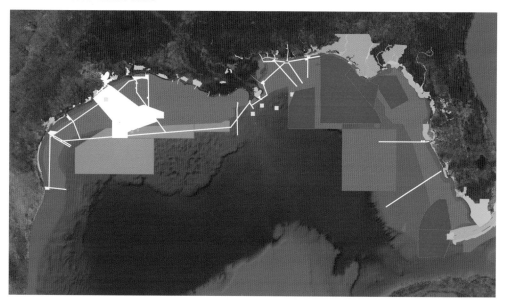

Industrial	Preservation	Manage	Other
○ Shipping	● Marine Sanctuary	● Fisheries Management Area	● Research Area
● Military	● Coastal Preserve	● Water Magagement Area	● Archeological
● Oil Lighting Area	● National Wildlife Refuge & Shoreline	● Wildlife Magagement Area	
• Oil Platform		● State Magagement Area	

NOAA

square miles of seabed. These hypoxic seafloor habitats could become prime candidates for restoration efforts in the aftermath of the *Deepwater Horizon* disaster.

A plan of action produced in 2001 and updated in 2008 by the Mississippi River Gulf of Mexico Watershed Nutrient Task Force* outlines how to proceed.[9] The Action Plan aims to reduce the average extent of the hypoxic zone to less than 5,000 square kilometers (1,930 square miles), or about one-fourth the area affected in 2010, by reducing the discharges of nitrogen and phosphorus into the Gulf. The original target date for achieving this goal was 2015, but implementation has languished. As part of a comprehensive restoration program, regulations that limit discharges under the Clean Water Act could be more rigorously applied, and federally-authorized conservation programs could be better targeted to achieve greater results. Hypoxia abatement should also be integrated with coastal ecosystem restoration in order to optimize nutrient removal by river diversions and to reduce the risks of injecting greater nutrient loads into the waters of the continental shelf.

Marine spatial planning. The U.S. part of the Gulf of Mexico is already as compartmentalized as any water body in the world. The Department of the Interior divides

---

* The Task Force consists of state and natural resources agencies and federal agencies, including NOAA, EPA, the Departments of Agriculture and of the Interior, and the Army Corps of Engineers.

the northern Gulf into a grid for administrative purposes. Oil and gas companies lease individual blocks within this grid for exploration and production.[10] Other entities manage the Gulf to maximize their own benefit—for fishing, tourism, or conservation.

All this activity also makes the Gulf a crowded space administratively, with coordination insufficient to resolve potential conflicts among oil and gas development, fishing, navigation, and military operations. The *Deepwater Horizon* disaster occurred at a time when U.S. policy toward its waters was under significant revision. The National Oceans Council, created by Executive Order in July 2010,[11] is authorized to set and manage executive-branch marine policy and to implement recommendations of a task force appointed by President Obama in 2009.[12]

Among the most significant initiatives are steps that would reorganize—or in some cases organize—how Americans benefit from resources in federal waters. Scientists and policy advocates use the phrase "coastal and marine spatial planning" to describe a suite of technologies, best practices, and inter-industry networking to optimize the use of resources for all.[13] In the Gulf of Mexico, where the oil and gas industry has a very large presence, marine spatial planning can help lead to better oversight, and in the event of an accident, better communication among all users. Massachusetts and Rhode Island recently formalized this approach to their state waters.[14] Norway has implemented planning in its crowded northern waters, an area which includes oil and gas infrastructure.[15]

More a management or governance strategy than a discrete program, marine spatial planning is evolutionary in nature. The Department of the Interior is already charged to manage energy resources on the outer continental shelf in a way that is, among other requirements, "consistent with the need . . . to balance orderly resource development with protection of the human, marine, and coastal environments."[16] Proponents expect federal and statewide marine spatial planning to bring together agencies, jurisdictions, and communities to share information and best practices—and in so doing, better balance the many interests on and beneath the water.[17]

Marine protected areas. Within the context of coastal and marine spatial planning, there are opportunities for protection and restoration of resources harmed not only by the present oil spill, but also by oil and gas development generally and other commercial activities. Marine protected areas have been effective as a means to conserve marine biodiversity and enhance the resilience of fish stocks in the face of harvest pressures.[18] Strategically selected and designated marine protected areas could be an effective way to restore offshore ecosystems within the framework of a comprehensive restoration program. Modern management tools can go a long way toward making Gulf fisheries more robust by preventing overfishing. The *Deepwater Horizon* disaster delayed the start of a new National Oceanic and Atmospheric Administration (NOAA) fisheries management policy. On November 4, 2010, the "NOAA Catch Share Policy" went into effect. The policy divides the total allowable catch in a fishery into shares held by individuals and various entities. The holders of the catch shares must cease fishing once they have reached their limit. This is one step toward protecting the health of commercial and recreational fisheries.

FIGURE 7.3: Coastal Vulnerability Index

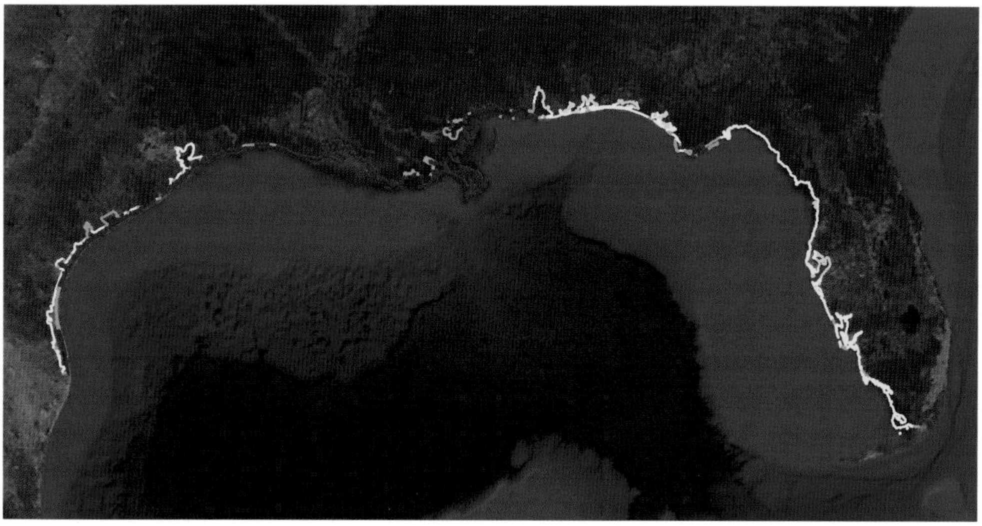

Coastal Vulnerability Index (CVI)

- Very High
- High
- Moderate
- Low

USGS National Assessment of Coastal Vulnerability to Future Sea-Level Rise –Open File Report 00-179

Toward a Functioning Delta

The Delta difference. The land at the mouth of the Mississippi River differs from that of neighboring regions: the underlying rock is hundreds of feet below the surface,[19] buried by mud deposited over many millennia. River-borne sediment has, literally, created the land—a coastal habitat of remarkable biological productivity, and a buffer that protects the densely settled land upriver from the full force of battering waves. But the sea constantly carries that coastal land away.

The Mississippi River, extending some 2,300 miles upstream to Minnesota, runs through the heart of the third largest watershed in the world (after the Amazon and the Congo). Water enters its basin from 31 states. Water from the northern reaches of the basin can take a month to reach the Gulf. About two weeks after the historic rains that flooded Nashville and killed at least 31 people across the southeast in May 2010, the water flowed past New Orleans; when it entered the Gulf, that freshwater swell may have helped keep oil-covered offshore waters away from marshes in the spill's early days.[20]

As the Mississippi meanders south, it picks up silt, sand, and organic materials. Under largely natural conditions (before the 1930s), the river cast this sediment across the wetland plain before draining into the Gulf. The accumulating material attracts the microbes and marsh grasses that undergird the coastal ecosystem. During the 7,000 to 8,000 years since the end of the last ice age, the Mississippi has shaped and reshaped its delta—even, on occasion, carving wholly new routes to the Gulf.

Voices from the Gulf

"Louisiana is paying a grave price for what the rest of the country is enjoying."

Dennis Woltering

Brenda Dardar Robichaux,

Former Chief of the United Houma Nation, Raceland, LA

Brenda Dardar Robichaux could not help noticing as the local coastline, ditched for oil-related navigation and pipeline corridors, progressively disappeared all through Terrebonne, Lafourche, Jefferson, St. Mary, St. Bernard and Plaquemines parishes. As Principal Chief (from 1997 until 2010) of the 17,000-member United Houma Nation, whose people lived in and made their livelihoods from the coastal lands of southeastern Louisiana, she said, "We have seen small canals turn into large bayous; we have watched hundreds of acres of wetlands wash away; we have seen freshwater bayous turn into saltwater." And her people have become exposed to severe risks: "Hurricanes Gustav and Ike destroyed our community on Isle de Jean Charles because we no longer have the barrier islands protecting us. Today Isle de Jean Charles is just a sliver of what it once was. The length of the island is still several miles, but the width is maybe an acre. When I was little there were fields that we [the Houma People] raised cattle and horses on. We had gardens and the kids played baseball. Now there is no such thing. The backyards are water."

Former Chief Robichaux initially saw some possible good coming from the spill: serious attention being paid to coastal restoration. "The spill certainly adds another level of awareness to the problem—like Katrina did—but we need major change now, and not just little projects. When the oil spill happened, I was hopeful that all the attention it was bringing might finally wake people up. I was optimistic. I was thinking if we're ever going to get vision for coastal restoration off the ground, now is the time. But I don't see that happening."

For centuries, the United Houma Nation's culture and economy have been entwined with the bounty of the gulf. "Our people follow the seasons," Robichaux explained. "In the summer we catch shrimp, crabs, and garfish. In the winter we harvest oysters and trap nutria, muskrat, and otters…Houma fishermen are intimately familiar with the lakes and bayous of our region. They know the stories of how these places got their names. They know how the tides flow and the winds blow… All of these traditions are in danger of disappearing."

Like all Americans, she knew well the nation's dependence on oil: "Louisiana is paying a grave price for what the rest of the country is enjoying, whether it's seafood or what oil and gas provide. But our tribal citizens are paying the ultimate price, because we live along the coast of southeast Louisiana. We as a nation, not only people in Louisiana, not just people on the coast, but the nation, need to evaluate our dependency on oil and gas. We need to re-evaluate our entire lifestyle. It's not just a Gulf Coast issue."

Beginning late in the nineteenth century, the Atchafalaya River in southern Louisiana captured an increasing share of Mississippi waters, greatly reducing flow into the lower part of the Mississippi.[21] Were nature left to itself, the flow would have diverted over time primarily to the Atchafalaya, which provides a much shorter route to the Gulf. This change would have been catastrophic to communities and industry along the lower river, leaving the port of New Orleans on a silted-in bayou without a freshwater supply. To forestall that switch in river channels, the U.S. Army Corps of Engineers built the Old River Control Structures: a series of dams, completed in 1963, that ensure 70 percent of Mississippi waters flow past New Orleans and 30 percent reach the Gulf through the Atchafalaya. All other distributaries of the great river have been closed.[22]

Managing the river for human ends—to improve navigation and control flooding with artificial levees—accelerates the natural deterioration of coastal wetlands and landforms. Flooding is the process that feeds this landscape, causing the accretion of sediments through which nature constructed the Delta. Under human control, the river now carries that sediment out into the Gulf, where it is deposited beyond the reach of natural deltaic processes, breaking the Delta's means for self-preservation. Managing the flow down the Atchafalaya was only the most recent intervention that has disrupted the natural mechanisms at work in the Delta. Addressing the central issue of the Delta's functioning lies at the core of strategies for long-term restoration.

The sediment problem. The re-engineering of the Mississippi River system—resulting in the "sediment starvation" of the Delta—began even before the Great Flood of 1927, when 145 levees failed, at least 246 people died, and floodwaters throughout the river basin caused the modern equivalent of $2 billion to $5 billion in damage.[23] It accelerated after that flood, when the Flood Control Act of 1928 authorized an epic levee-building program.[24] The Mississippi River and Tributaries Project engaged the Corps in building levees to contain floods, constructing strategic floodways, improving the river channels for shipping and floodwater carrying capacity, and reconstructing tributary basins for flood control. The Corps now manages the resulting protective system, with 2,203 miles of levees.[25]

As flooding decreased, and improved river traffic and long-distance shipping allowed local communities to grow, the closure of the Mississippi's crevasses, flood plains, and distributaries had the unforeseen consequence of endangering the very communities that enjoyed those benefits. In written remarks to the Commission, Senator Mary Landrieu decried the "strangulation" of nature: "For more than a century, the federal government has mismanaged critical water-resource projects, placing delicate ecosystems like the Mississippi River Delta at extreme risk of complete and utter collapse."[26] The loss of protective wetlands, like a catastrophic oil spill, is a manmade disaster.

In effect, the system built by the Corps is causing southern Louisiana to disappear (even though the Corps has, during the past 20 years, begun taking steps to offset these unforeseen consequences).[27] The annual sediment load reaching the Delta has decreased from 400 million metric tons before 1900 to 145 million metric tons in recent years. And very little of that reaches wetlands.[28]

FIGURE 7.4: Louisiana Coastal Erosion

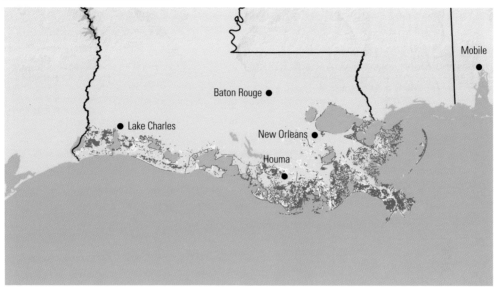

Mobile

Baton Rouge ●

● Lake Charles

New Orleans ●

Houma

- Land Loss 1932–2000
- Land Gain 1932–2000
  Projected Land Loss 2000–2050
- Projected Land Gain 2000–2050

USGS Open File Report 2009-11-0408

Rising waters. Even as the altered river delivers less sediment to replenish the Delta, the relative sea level is rising in southern Louisiana—the net result of land subsidence and actual sea level rise.[29] Subsidence is a critical problem in the Gulf region, which naturally sinks 1 to 5 millimeters per year. In some places near the outer Delta, subsidence is nearly 10 millimeters per year, largely from manmade impacts.[30] It is particularly intense in the Delta, where the Gulf has swallowed more than 2,300 square miles of coastal wetlands since the early part of the twentieth century.[31] Explanations for the phenomenon vary. One is that sediment rich in organic material behaves like a sponge: squeeze out the water and it shrinks.[32] Another relates to deep tectonic faulting.[33] A third correlates hydrocarbon extraction with subsidence-driven wetland loss.[34] Whatever the reason, the channeling of river sediment into the Gulf is interrupting natural land generation, and the region cannot keep pace with relative sea level rise.

Navigation and channeling the wetlands. Relative sea level rise endangers marsh grasses and other swamp trees as they become subject to inundation by the salty Gulf. At the same time, the growing oil and gas industry dredged 10,000 miles of canals through Louisiana's wetlands in order to move in drilling barges or lay pipelines, leaving arrow-straight channels through what had been a convoluted maze.[35] Dredged sediment lines the canal: artificial banks change water flow and prevent flooding, so sediment mobilized by tidal flows cannot replenish the land. Water forms pools behind the banks, submerging marsh. And the channels admit saltwater flow into brackish and freshwater environments, jeopardizing the overall ecosystem. Researchers have reached no solid consensus on how much wetland loss to attribute to the canals' direct and indirect effects, although some scientists attribute 35 percent to the canals' indirect effects.[36] In 2009, a Minerals Management Service study concluded, "The construction of outer continental shelf-related pipelines through coastal ecosystems can cause locally intense habitat changes, thereby contributing to the loss of critically important land and wetland areas" through their conversion to open water, or from freshwater marsh into saltwater marsh.[37]

Congress and the Corps put the most well known of the navigation canals out of business in 2008. The Corps in 1968 finished the Mississippi River Gulf Outlet—affectionately, or derisively, called "Mr. Go" (MRGO)—a straight shot from the Gulf to the Port of New Orleans. This canal's story is emblematic of the larger problem of wetland canals' environmental impacts. The 66-mile outlet shortened and simplified ships' approach to the port. Heralded as a boon to economic development, the project never proved transformative—except environmentally. Construction destroyed the existing ecosystems and excavated more than 270 million cubic yards of material—slightly more than was removed to build the Panama Canal.[38] The project converted about 3,350 acres of fresh or intermediate marsh and 8,000 acres of cypress swamps into brackish marsh. Nearly 20,000 acres of brackish marsh and swamp became saline marsh. More than 5,000 acres of marsh next to the channel had disappeared by 1996.[39] Maintenance costs increased significantly over the years, including costs related to hurricanes—even as shipping through the canal declined. The Corps estimated that the canal would require $22.1 million per year in dredging, or about $12,657 per ship every day. By the late 1990s, multiple stakeholders had pressed the Corps to close the canal.[40]

That was before Katrina. As the hurricane approached Louisiana's eastern coast, its storm surge pushed into the shipping channel, breaching levees, thereby contributing to the flooding of New Orleans.[41] Congress de-authorized the Mississippi River Gulf Outlet canal in 2008 and a contractor sealed off its southern entrance with rock fill in 2009.[42] Congress has undertaken no similar effort to address the ongoing harm caused by vast network of canals and infrastructure built into the wetlands—incursions that have hastened by decades the demise of the already sediment-starved Delta.

Planning without end. By the early 1950s, Gulf coast researchers had become aware of gaps in understanding how coasts naturally worked. In 1952, Louisiana State University created a Coastal Studies Institute. Scientists there and elsewhere sought to explain the relationship between floods breaching natural levees and the health of marshland and barrier islands fed by the sediment.[43]

The U.S. Fish and Wildlife Service in 1959 sent the Corps a memorandum suggesting that the declining health of oyster reefs caused by increasing salinity might be addressed by diverting fresh water from the Mississippi into discrete areas.[44] The first diversion, at Caernarvon, was authorized in 1965, and two years later Congress instructed the Corps to develop a strategy "in the interest of hurricane protection, prevention of saltwater intrusion, preservation of fish and wildlife, [and] prevention of erosion."[45] A 1973 report to the Corps suggested diversions to deliver sediment and lower salinity.[46] A 1979 study examined the economic impacts of wetland loss, with guidelines that "center on avoiding the disruption of wetland hydrology," and found that land loss was greater than previously measured.[47] Eight years later, a new group called the Coalition to Restore Coastal Louisiana suggested the same strategy: fix the hydrology.[48] In the 20 years since, a few small-scale programs and many reports have directed the state and federal governments to fix the hydrology. None approach the necessary scale for meaningful restoration[49], although they have provided smaller successes and helpful organizational models.

Simulations predict that, at the current rate of land loss, much of southern Louisiana will disappear by 2100. The region will transition from marshy lowlands to a fully aquatic system because of erosion and submergence,[50] leaving New Orleans an expensive island fortress.

Among efforts to identify and begin to address the problem are these highlights:

- Louisiana Act 6. In 1989, the Louisiana legislature passed Act 6, establishing a wetlands authority and an executive office to prioritize and manage a restoration strategy and projects.

- The Coastal Wetlands, Planning, Protection and Restoration Act. The following year, Congress enacted the so-called Breaux Act, named for its sponsor, Louisiana Senator John Breaux. It authorizes civil works aimed at marsh regeneration, shoreline protection, barrier-island reconstruction, hydrologic engineering, and the use of dredged material for restoration purposes. The Act has a dedicated funding source, the Sport Fish Restoration and Boating Trust Fund, which receives taxes on gasoline for motorboats and other small engines, and on sport-fishing equipment.[51] The taxes have yielded between nearly $30 million and $80 million per year.[52] Programs under the Act, which involve collaboration among Louisiana and five federal agencies including the Corps, have been credited with protecting 110,000 acres of wetlands.[53]

  In 1998, more ambitiously, the Breaux Act agencies agreed to the recommendations of Coast 2050, an 18-month feasibility study for coastal restoration. The report was based upon original research and 65 public meetings, and was supported by 20 coastal parishes. The report's recommendations were aimed at allowing healthy flows of sediment into the Mississippi, preserving salinity levels and land critical to sensitive habitats, and diverting sediment-rich fresh water to replenish starving marsh.[54]

  In 2004, the Corps produced its Louisiana Coastal Area Comprehensive Coastwide Ecosystem Restoration report, a package of projects meant to meet the coastal challenges. This led to creation of the Louisiana Coastal Area Ecosystem Restoration Program under the 2007 Water Resources Development Act. After the Office of Management and Budget opposed the high price tag of a more comprehensive proposal—about $14 billion—the Corps slimmed its initial implementation down to 15 projects that would together cost more than $2 billion.[55]

Katrina's aftermath. Weeks after Hurricane Katrina ravaged much of coastal Louisiana and Mississippi, the Louisiana legislature established a Coastal Protection and Restoration Authority that combined responses to wetland loss and hurricane risk—related goals separated in state bureaucracy. In September 2006, Louisianans approved a constitutional amendment that explicitly ties state revenues from oil and gas activities in federal waters to storm protection and rebuilding wetlands.[56]

The relative priority of the two goals is not yet certain. Although one rule of thumb for the Louisiana coast holds that each 2.7 square miles of marshland reduces a hurricane's storm surge by one foot,[57] the relationship has not been easy to precisely quantify. In the meantime, construction for storm protection is tangible and has been readily funded. The Corps has been able to fast-track building new levees to protect New Orleans from the projected "100-year storm"; the project should be completed in 2011—just five years after it began. By contrast, direct instructions and guaranteed funding have mostly eluded restoration efforts. The state has engaged the Corps to design and build two new, large levee systems, but their effects on southern Louisiana communities and wetland survival are still being studied.[58] Traditional flood protection usually involves "hard-engineering," essentially levee-building. Part of the promise of the state's newly organized approach is in protective "soft-engineering," or regenerating wetlands and barrier islands for the dual purposes of ecosystem restoration and storm protection.

Congress also asked the Corps to develop comprehensive statewide hurricane-protection options after Hurricanes Katrina and Rita. The Department of Defense Appropriation Act of 2006 directed the Corps to design a suite of improvements to the Louisiana and Mississippi coasts, including improvements for "hurricane and storm damage reduction, prevention of saltwater intrusion, preservation of fish and wildlife, prevention of erosion, and other related water resource purposes at full Federal expense."[59] A September 2009 Chief of Engineers' report suggested 12 projects for Mississippi, costing more than $1 billion, that would help restore barrier islands, beaches, sensitive habitats, and coastal ecosystems. Congress has appropriated $439 million to implement Mississippi's program so far.[60] The Corps has also drafted a counterpart Louisiana Coastal Protection and Restoration Final Technical Report,[61] but the future of the Louisiana program is uncertain, as the report includes a wide range of options rather than a specific plan.

Other sources of funding for sustained restoration efforts include the State of Louisiana's Coastal Protection and Restoration Fund, about $25 million a year from state mineral income plus budget surpluses in 2007–2009;[62] the federal Coastal Impact Assistance Program, which authorizes $250 million split among six states in each fiscal year from 2007–2010 to fund natural resources recovery, conservation, and protective measures;[63] and the federal Gulf of Mexico Energy Security Act, in which participating Gulf states (all but Florida) share 37.5 percent of federal offshore revenue from new lease areas for use in coastal protection, including onshore infrastructure projects that mitigate the impacts of outer continental shelf energy activities.[64]

Voices from the Gulf

"An entire culture being washed away by crude oil and chemicals"

Claire Luby

Clarence R. Duplessis,
Commercial Fisherman, Davant, LA

When Clarence R. Duplessis was born in 1945 in the small Gulf Coast fishing community of Davant, just north of Pointe-a-la-Hache, he became the seventh generation of his family to live in Plaquemines Parish, Louisiana. After high school, Duplessis, joined the U.S. Marine Corps, served a tour of duty in Vietnam, and met his wife, Bonnie, who served in the Navy.

Upon their return to Louisiana, Mr. Duplessis found work at the Kaiser Aluminum plant in Chalmette, La. In 1989, when the plant shut, he says, "I had a young family to feed, clothe, and educate. This. . . was a problem with a solution. I was still young and had experience with shrimping and oystering. I had salt water in my veins at birth. I went fishing and my children paid their college tuition by working as deckhands.

"In 2005, Hurricane Katrina hit us with a crippling blow. Wow! A major problem!. . . My wife and I lost everything we owned in Hurricane Katrina. . . Even then, though the entire region was wiped out and the insurance companies packed their bags and left us, there was still a solution…The fishing communities and people of South Louisiana are some of the hardest working, defiant yet kindest people on God's earth. After the storm we faced the difficult task of rebuilding, but that was the solution.

"Now, five years later we are facing the *Deepwater Horizon* oil spill. This is the worst of our problems because we have no answers, no solutions, only questions. As we watch our livelihood and even an entire culture being washed away by crude oil and chemicals that no one knows the long term effects of, we ask: [W]ill we have the mortgage payment next month? . . . How long will this last? Will I be able to go oystering next year or ever again? How long will it take the fisheries to recover?. . . Will BP do what is right or will they pack their bags and leave us like the insurance companies did? What can I do to survive?…I have a thousand questions and no answers. Now, I hope you can understand why this problem is the worst of my life!"

Toward coordinated strategies and action. In the fall of 2009, President Obama directed the Council on Environmental Quality and the Office of Management and Budget to co-chair a Louisiana-Mississippi Gulf Coast Ecosystem Restoration Working Group, made up of federal agency and state representatives.[65] Six months later—about six weeks before the *Deepwater Horizon* exploded—the group presented a "road map" for federal-state collaboration and set out 2010–2011 deadlines for advancing policymaking.[66] The President's fiscal year 2011 budget requested $19 million for construction, sediment use, and river diversions and $16.6 million for studies of eventual restoration projects.

After the spill, the President in June commissioned Secretary of the Navy and former Governor of Mississippi Ray Mabus to study Gulf coast recovery and propose ways to address chronic Gulf marine and coastal issues. The resulting "Mabus report," published on September 28, 2010, analyzed ecosystem restoration, human health, economic recovery, and the nonprofit sector.[67] A week later, the President issued Executive Order 13554, creating a Gulf Coast Ecosystem Restoration Task Force comprised of federal agency and state representatives to "coordinate intergovernmental responsibilities, planning, and exchange of information so as to better implement Gulf Coast ecosystem restoration and to facilitate appropriate accountability and support throughout the restoration process."[68]

In the course of his work, Secretary Mabus repeatedly referred to the rising public impatience with plans unaccompanied by action. As he put it in June, "I also understand that people have plan fatigue, that they've been planned to death."[69] In the meantime, at current erosion rates, an area of the Delta the size of a football field is consumed by Gulf waters every hour.[70]

Identifying options for funding and governance. The twentieth-century re-engineering of the Mississippi River basin, and subsequent piecemeal efforts to restore its nourishing flows of water and sediment, teach important lessons about any future, comprehensive approach to coastal management. Many of the re-engineering projects have provided only incremental gains.[71] Discrete restoration projects, moreover, are unable to reverse the loss of Delta land and habitats in the aggregate. The many layers of federal, state, and local authorities—some overlapping and conflicting—make it difficult as a practical matter to devise, implement, and make mid-course corrections to a strategy for restoration. And secure, sustained sources of funding on the scale required to do the necessary work are not now in place.[72] The contrast with the reconstruction of the protective hurricane levees around New Orleans from 2006 through 2011 could not be clearer.

Estimates of the cost of Gulf restoration, including but not limited to the Mississippi Delta, vary widely, but according to testimony before the Commission, full restoration of the Gulf will require $15 billion to $20 billion: a minimum of $500 million annually for 30 years.[73] Current funding sources do not approach those figures. Beginning in 2017, Phase II of the Gulf of Mexico Energy Security Act,[74] which governs sharing of oil-related revenues, will begin to bring large amounts of money to the Gulf States. Much of this could be directed to restoration.

The *Deepwater Horizon* disaster provides a significant opportunity to begin funding restoration sooner. It will generate monies that can be directed to jumpstart key Gulf restoration projects. And it can provide the basis for launching a long-needed federal-state entity capable of managing the restoration effort over the longer term, guided by a clear set of principles.

In the aftermath of the spill, the responsible party (or parties) will be liable for damages in the amount necessary for "restoring, rehabilitating, replacing, or acquiring the equivalent of" natural resources harmed by the spill.[75] The responsible party will also pay fines if found in violation of federal laws. The maximum civil penalties under the Clean Water Act could range from $4.5 billion to $21 billion, depending upon findings of negligence and the calculation of barrels discharged. The Act provides for a civil penalty for unpermitted discharges of up to $37,500 per day of violation or up to $1,100 per barrel of oil discharged. In the case of an operator's gross negligence or willful misconduct, the penalty becomes not less than $140,000 and not more than $4,300 per barrel of oil discharged.[76] Criminal fines could be large, as well.[77] A negligent violation of the Clean Water Act's criminal provision is subject to a fine of between $2,500 and $25,000 per day of violation for a first violation and up to $50,000 per day for subsequent violations.[78] For knowing violations of the Act, criminal fines range between $5,000 and $50,000 per day of violation for a first conviction, and up to $100,000 per day for subsequent violations.[79] Civil and criminal fines are both deposited in the Oil Spill Liability Trust Fund, established after the *Exxon Valdez* spill to help pay for cleanup and certain damages after a spill, but use of that Fund is restricted.[80]

The Mabus report, as well as regional members of Congress and Governors from the Gulf, have proposed directing a significant amount of the penalty funds to long-term ecosystem restoration in the Gulf (and in the case of the Mabus report, to economic and health recovery as well). Secretary Mabus recommended that the President urge Congress to pass legislation to dedicate some of the penalties for those purposes.

Legislative proposals to establish a coordinating and decisionmaking council, as recommended in Secretary Mabus's report,[81] call for a state-federal governing entity that has authority to prioritize restoration projects based on a comprehensive strategic plan. Although the details of early proposals varied, most recognized the need for a single, Gulf-wide decisionmaking authority and a strong leadership commitment to fund only those projects that conform to an agreed-upon vision for long-term restoration.

Planning and program design for any comprehensive Gulf restoration effort will have to be based on sound science. In different circumstances, the *Exxon Valdez* Trustee Council Science Panel reviewed all proposed projects both for technical merit and for consistency with the overall restoration goals (as set forth in the Restoration Plan) and annual work plans.[82] This effort, although encompassing projects of a different nature and scope than those in the Gulf, enabled effective scientific communication with the Trustee Council.[83]

A successful Gulf-wide scientific process would likewise be structured to allow meaningful and timely input by scientists into the decisionmaking process. Ideally, it would provide a science program with the resources to evaluate individual projects for consistency with a comprehensive plan; to research long-term restoration issues; and to develop and apply performance measures and indicators of long-term restoration that allow decisionmakers to adjust the plan based on new science or changed circumstances. Particularly with respect to long-term research issues, the diverse resources and expertise of the federal government should be brought to bear.

Finally, no authority will succeed without the confidence and support of the citizens of the region. Leaders of restoration efforts emphasize the importance of gaining the support of those most directly affected by restoration projects. Local citizen support is important for several reasons: it can reduce delay of projects due to litigation or other opposition; it contributes to political support for overall goals and funding, in the short and long terms; and it contributes to overall trust in government, which results in support for local projects.[84] Any structure should therefore include a citizens' advisory council to provide formal advice and a direct line to citizens' concerns.

Putting Restoration on the Agenda

Speaking to the nation in June 2010 from the Oval Office, President Obama clearly linked spill recovery and long-term stewardship: "The oil spill represents just the latest blow to a place that's already suffered multiple economic disasters and decades of environmental degradation that has led to disappearing wetlands and habitats. And the region still hasn't recovered from Hurricanes Katrina and Rita. That's why we must make a commitment to the Gulf Coast that goes beyond responding to the crisis of the moment."[85] In mid-July, Louisiana Governor Bobby Jindal announced his "Agenda for Revitalizing Coastal Louisiana," which extols Louisianans' resilience both in general and in recovering from the 2005 and 2008 storms: "There is not a doubt in my mind that we will recover and restore our coast and our wetlands to not only be Sportsman's Paradise again, but to be an even more plentiful source of abundant natural resources than ever before."[86]

"Restoration" itself has several specified meanings. NOAA defines post-spill restoration under the Oil Pollution Act as "the goal of a natural resource damage assessment, which involves rehabilitating, replacing, or acquiring the equivalent of injured natural resources and the services they provided."[87] In some cases after an oil spill, natural resource trustees—such as the involved state and federal agencies—and the party responsible for the spill can alter the charge. For example, the concept of "enhancement" that emerged after *Exxon Valdez* gave trustees additional latitude in restoring Prince William Sound and its ecological region.[88] This addition enabled planners to strive for improvements, rather than returning to a baseline.

Nature has no baseline: natural systems change and evolve continuously. "Restoration" therefore should have another, broader meaning. In the Gulf, it must encompass reversing the progressive erosion of coastal land and habitats that buffer human communities from storms and sustain the area's biological productivity. In this context, restoration does not imply returning landforms to a particular map, but rather making the river,

Delta, and Gulf coastal and marine systems more resilient. The economies of the Gulf—fisheries, energy, and tourism—are as rooted in the environment as any in the developed world. Restoration, or restored resilience, represents an effort to sustain these diverse, interdependent activities and the environment on which they depend for future generations.

Part III

Lessons Learned: Industry, Government, Energy Policy

The private oil and gas industry is the lead actor in exploration and production of Gulf energy resources. In the wake of the BP *Deepwater Horizon* disaster—a crisis that was unanticipated, on a scale for which companies had not prepared to respond—changes in safety and environmental practices, safety training, drilling technology, containment and clean-up technology, preparedness, corporate culture, and management behavior will be required if deepwater energy operations are to be pursued in the Gulf—or elsewhere. Maintaining the public trust and earning the privilege of drilling on the outer continental shelf requires no less. As Chapter 8 explains, some of the required responses are under way; for other measures, there are useful precedents from other industries. Beyond the oil and gas industry's response, the inadequacies in permitting and regulatory standards, practices, and oversight revealed by the crisis have already caused significant changes in the federal rules and procedures for deepwater drilling. But further action, including the creation of an independent safety authority, is clearly warranted, as described in Chapter 9.

Finally, the interplay of public incentives, security considerations, energy conservation and use, and alternative energy sources, among other factors, will shape future deepwater drilling in the Gulf and in other frontier areas, as discussed in Chapter 10. Because some of those frontiers are defined by greater well depths and pressures, and others are in settings as yet untapped (the Arctic, in particular)—with economies, environmental resources, and community characteristics different from those tested so severely in and along the Gulf Coast—learning the right lessons from the BP *Deepwater Horizon*, and adapting them to different contexts, must thoroughly inform the future of America's offshore oil policy.

Chapter Eight
"Safety is not proprietary."

Changing Business as Usual

The *Deepwater Horizon* blowout, explosion, and oil spill did not have to happen. Previous chapters have explained the immediate and root causes for why they nonetheless did. The American public, government, and the oil and gas industry need to understand what went wrong so they can pursue the changes required to prevent such devastating accidents from recurring.

This chapter examines how petroleum companies have been managing the risks associated with finding and producing oil and how they can do it better, individually and as a responsible industry overall. The record shows that without effective government oversight, the offshore oil and gas industry will not adequately reduce the risk of accidents, nor prepare effectively to respond in emergencies. However, government oversight, alone, cannot reduce those risks to the full extent possible. Government oversight (see Chapter 9) must be accompanied by the oil and gas industry's internal reinvention: sweeping reforms that accomplish no less than a fundamental transformation of its safety culture. Only through such a demonstrated transformation will industry—in the aftermath of the *Deepwater Horizon* disaster—truly earn the privilege of access to the nation's energy resources located on federal properties.

Even as Deepwater Horizon burns, oil from the blown out well begins to spread across the Gulf. Preventing such disasters in the future will take more effective government oversight. Most crucial, however, will be the oil and gas industry's commitment to fundamentally transform its own safety culture.

< Gerald Herbert/Associated Press

Offshore oil and gas exploration and production are risky. But even the most inherently risky industry can be made much safer, given the right incentives and disciplined systems, sustained by committed leadership and effective training. The critical common element is an unwavering commitment to safety at the top of an organization: the CEO and board of directors must create the culture and establish the conditions under which everyone in a company shares responsibility for maintaining a relentless focus on preventing accidents. Likewise, for the entire industry, leadership needs to come from the CEOs collectively, who can apply pressure on their peers to enhance performance.

Properly managed, the presence of risk does not mean that accidents have to happen. As Magne Ognedal, Director General of Norway's Petroleum Safety Authority, put it: "risk must be managed at every level and in every company involved in this business. . . . In this way, risk in the petroleum sector can be kept at a level society is willing to accept. And we can reduce the probability that major accidents will hit us again."[1]

BP's Safety Culture

BP has proclaimed the importance of safety for its vast worldwide operations. "Our goal of 'no accidents, no harm to people and no damage to the environment' is fundamental to BP's activities," stated the company's Sustainability Review 2009. "We work to achieve this through consistent management processes, ongoing training programmes, rigorous risk management and a culture of continuous improvement." It added that "creating a safe and healthy working environment is essential for our success. Since 1999, injury rates and spills have reduced by approximately 75%."[2]

Yet despite the improvement in injury and spill rates during that decade, BP has caused a number of disastrous or potentially disastrous workplace incidents that suggest its approach to managing safety has been on individual worker occupational safety but not on process safety. These incidents and subsequent analyses indicate that the company does not have consistent and reliable risk-management processes—and thus has been unable to meet its professed commitment to safety. BP's safety lapses have been chronic.

Safety Culture

The United Kingdom Health and Safety Executive formally defines the **safety culture** of an organization as "the product of individual and group values, attitudes, and perceptions, competencies, and patterns of behavior that determine the commitment to, and the style and proficiency of, an organisation's health and safety management." A more popular description is that safety culture means doing the right thing even when the no one is watching. There are two kinds of safety: **occupational safety**, which refers to keeping people safe, and **process safety,** which refers to the procedures for minimizing risk more generally.

Refinery accidents. Between May 29 and June 10, 2000, BP's Grangemouth Complex on Scotland's Firth of Forth suffered three potentially life-threatening accidents: a power-distribution failure leading to the emergency shutdown of the oil refinery; the rupture of a main steam pipe; and a fire in the refinery's fluidized catalytic cracker unit (which turns petroleum into gasoline).[3] The U.K. Health and Safety Executive investigated the incidents. About the power loss, it said: "Subsequent investigations revealed a number of weaknesses in the safety management systems on-site over a period of time which contributed to the succession of events that resulted in the power distribution failure."[4]

It made virtually the same comment about the other two incidents.[5] The Executive's wider conclusions included:

- "BP Group policies set high expectations but these were not consistently achieved because of organisational and cultural reasons;
- "BP Group and Complex Management did not detect and intervene early enough on deteriorating performance;
- "BP failed to achieve the operational control and maintenance of process and systems required by law;
- "The BP Task Force findings and recommendations properly addressed the way forward to ensure safe and reliable operations at the Complex."[6]

North Sea platforms. It was not only BP's refineries that had problems. In November 2003, a gas line ruptured on BP Forties Alpha platform in the North Sea, flooding the platform with methane. It was a windy day and there was no spark to ignite the gas,[7] so the platform avoided the fate of the Piper Alpha (operated by Occidental Petroleum), where a blown gas line led to explosions that killed 165 crew members and 2 rescuers in 1988 (see Chapter 3).[8] BP admitted breaking the law by allowing pipes to corrode on the Forties Alpha and paid a $290,000 fine.[9]

On the platform that Thursday, November 27, 2003, was a BP engineer named Oberon Houston, who later resigned from the company. He told the Commission that BP focused heavily on personnel safety and not on maintaining its facilities. He added that BP was preparing to sell the depleted field, and was running it at minimum cost: "The focus on controlling costs was acute at BP, to the point that it became a distraction. They just go after it with a ferocity that is mind-numbing and terrifying. No one's ever asked to cut corners or take a risk, but it often ends up like that."[10]

The Texas City refinery explosion: a deficient safety culture. On March 23, 2005, a blast at BP's Texas City refinery—the third largest refinery in the United States—killed 15 people and injured more than 170.[11] A U.S. Chemical Safety Board report on the Texas City refinery explosion found a recurring pattern. It concluded that "BP Group did not systematically review its refinery operations and corporate governance worldwide to implement needed changes identified in the Health and Safety Executive report and in its own Task Force report, even though the Group Chief Executive told staff in October 2000 edition of BP's in-house magazine that BP would learn lessons from Grangemouth and other incidents."[12]

Testifying in 2007 about the Texas City event before a U.S. Senate Subcommittee, Carolyn W. Merritt, Chairman and CEO of the Chemical Safety Board, described the equipment that caused the blast as "1950s-era" and "unsafe," and stressed that it was equipment that "many companies around the world ha[d] long since eliminated. . . ."[13] Merritt added that BP had in fact considered eliminating the equipment in 2002, which had by then already

Explosion at BP's Texas City Refinery

BP is no stranger to serious accidents. In March 2005, an explosion rocked the company's Texas City refinery near Houston; 15 workers lost their lives. One year later a BP pipeline on Alaska's North Slope ruptured, spilling more than 200,000 gallons of oil onto the fragile tundra. Yet, the report notes, in recent years the company's safety record in the Gulf of Mexico has been excellent.

William Philpott/AFP/Getty Images

resulted in "a number of serious releases," but had ultimately declined to do so "[f]or a variety of reasons—including cost pressures" and BP's ability to take advantage of "the existence of an exemption under [U.S. Environmental Protection Agency] air regulations. . . ."[14]

The Safety Board's report on Texas City noted that "while most attention was focused on the injury rate, the overall safety culture and process safety management program had serious deficiencies. Despite numerous previous fatalities at the Texas City refinery (23 deaths in the 30 years prior to the 2005 disaster) and many hazardous material releases, BP did not take effective steps to stem the growing risks of a catastrophic event."[15] The report added: "Cost-cutting and failure to invest in the 1990s by Amoco (who merged with BP in 1998) and then BP left the Texas City refinery vulnerable to a catastrophe. BP targeted budget cuts of 25 percent in 1999 and another 25 percent in 2005, even though much of the refinery's infrastructure and process equipment were in disrepair. Also, operator training and staffing were downsized."[16]

The Safety Board further singled what it characterized as the "organizational causes embedded in the refinery's culture," including:

*   "BP Texas City lacked a reporting and learning culture. Reporting bad news was not encouraged, and often Texas City managers did not effectively investigate incidents or take appropriate corrective action.
*   "BP Group lacked focus on controlling major hazard risk. BP management paid attention to, measured, and rewarded personal safety rather than process safety.
*   "BP Group and Texas City managers provided ineffective leadership and oversight. BP management did not implement adequate safety oversight, provide needed human and economic resources, or consistently model adherence to safety rules and procedures.
*   "BP Group and Texas City did not effectively evaluate the safety implications of major organizational, personnel, and policy changes." [17]

At the Chemical Safety Board's instigation, BP established its own independent panel to review its safety procedures and find ways to improve them.[18] That panel, chaired by former U.S. Secretary of State James Baker III, issued its report a few months before the Chemical Board report in 2007. The Baker panel was no more charitable in its assessment. The panel found that BP management had not distinguished between occupational safety—concern over slips, sprains, and other workplace accidents—and process safety: hazard analysis, design for safety, material verification, equipment maintenance, and process-change reporting. And the panel further concluded that BP was not investing leadership and other resources in managing the highest risks.[19]

The Baker panel especially faulted BP for failing to learn the lessons of Grangemouth by repeating them in the events leading up to the Texas City refinery explosion. According to the panel, "in its response to Grangemouth, BP missed an opportunity to make and sustain company-wide changes that would have resulted in safer workplaces for its employees and contractors."[20] Underscoring the depth of the organizational problem facing BP, the panel singled out for criticism BP's overall approach to accident analysis: "BP's investigation system has not instituted effective root cause analysis procedures to identify systemic causal factors."[21]

Prudhoe Bay pipeline leak. In March 2006—one year after the Texas City refinery explosion and one year before the Chemical Safety Board report on it—BP had yet another significant industrial accident. Its network of pipelines in Prudhoe Bay, Alaska, leaked 212,252 gallons of oil into the delicate tundra environment—the worst spill ever recorded on the North Slope.[22] The leak went undetected for as long as five days. [23] Upon analysis, the pipes were found to have been poorly maintained and inspected.[24] BP paid more than $20 million in fines and restitution.[25]

Progress in follow-up on the safety recommendations. The Baker panel report contained 10 recommendations "intended to promote significant, sustained improvements in BP's process safety performance."[26] Recommendation nine advocated that BP establish an independent expert to monitor and report on its progress in executing the panel's other recommendations in its U.S. refineries, in refining management, and at the BP board and executive management levels.[27] In the executive summary of the third annual report of that expert, covering January–December 2009, he remarked that:

> Delivery against milestones related to implementation of the Recommendations remains a critical performance objective for the U.S. refineries. Virtually all of the milestones in the U.S. Refining's 2009 plans were delivered on schedule.

> "While significant gaps have been closed and most of the new systems, processes, standards, and practices required for continued process safety improvements have been developed, much work remains to be done to fully implement them. BP must now demonstrate improved capability for systematic management of these systems, processes, standards, and practices so it can accelerate the overall pace of implementing the Recommendations.[28]

The independent expert also noted, apropos of the Baker panel report's final recommendation that BP use the lessons learned from the Texas City tragedy to transform the company into a recognized industry leader in process safety management:

> BP is striving to transform the company into a recognized industry leader in process safety . . . and . . . has made significant improvements each year in response to all Recommendations. However, much work remains to fully implement the Recommendations. . . . BP will be an industry leader when its process safety performance is superior to that of its peers, and its peers recognize BP as a true leader to emulate.[29]

In recent years in the Gulf of Mexico, BP's safety offshore drilling record was reportedly excellent.[30]

Deepwater Horizon

BP's safety culture failed on the night of April 20, 2010, as reflected in the actions of BP personnel on- and offshore and in the actions of BP's contractors. As described in Chapter 4, BP, Halliburton, and Transocean did not adequately identify or address risks of an accident—not in the well design, cementing, or temporary abandonment procedures. Their management systems were marked by poor communications among BP, Transocean, and Halliburton employees regarding the risks associated with decisions being made. The decisionmaking process on the rig was excessively compartmentalized, so individuals on the rig frequently made critical decisions without fully appreciating just how essential the decisions were to well safety—singly and in combination. As a result, officials made a series of decisions that saved BP, Halliburton, and Transocean time and money—but without full appreciation of the associated risks.

BP conducted its own accident investigation of *Deepwater Horizon*, but once again kept its scope extremely narrow.[31] Professor Najmedin Meshkati of the University of Southern California, Los Angles—a member of the separate National Academy of Engineering committee investigating the oil spill—criticized BP's accident report for neglecting to "address human performance issues and organizational factors which, in any major accident investigation, constitute major contributing factors." He added that BP's investigation also ignored factors such as fatigue, long shifts, and the company's poor safety culture.[32]

Upon reading the BP report, this Commission's Chief Scientific and Engineering Advisor, Richard Sears, commented that "it appeared that for BP, the accident happened at 9:49 p.m. on April 20; whereas in some ways, the blowout began in early 2009 when they initially designed the well."[33]

The Culture on the Rig

BP was operator of the Macondo well and in that capacity had both the overall responsibility for everything that went on and was in the best position to promote a culture of safety on the rig, including in the actions of its two significant contractors, Halliburton and Transocean. But the extensive involvement of those contractors in the mistakes that caused the Macondo well blowout underscores the compelling need for a fundamental shift in industry culture that extends beyond BP. As described in Chapter 2, offshore drilling and energy production involve a complex interrelationship among companies. No single company—not even at the major integrated oil companies—performs the full panoply of activities required for oil and gas drilling. All contract out for the services of other companies for critical aspects of their operations. For this same reason, whatever the specific contractual relationships, operating safely in this environment clearly demands a safety culture that encompasses every element of the extended drilling services, and operating industry.

Transocean, for instance, was a major contractor for the Macondo well and is the world's largest operator of offshore oil rigs, including the *Deepwater Horizon*; Transocean personnel made up the largest single contingent on the rig at the time of the accident, and 9 of the 11 men who died on April 20 worked for the company. As described in Chapter 4, a number of the mistakes made on the rig can be directly traced to Transocean personnel, including inadequate monitoring of the Macondo well for problems during the temporary abandonment procedures and failure to divert the mud and gas away from the rig during the first few minutes of the blowout.

A survey of the Transocean crew regarding "safety management and safety culture" on the *Deepwater Horizon* conducted just a few weeks before the accident hints at the organizational roots of the problem.[34] The research, conducted at Transocean's request, involved surveys and interviews with hundreds of employees onshore and on four rigs, including *Deepwater Horizon*, which was surveyed from March 12 to March 16. The reviewers found *Deepwater Horizon* "relatively strong in many of the core aspects of safety management."[35] But there were also weaknesses. Some 46 percent of crew members surveyed felt that some of the workforce feared reprisals for reporting unsafe situations, and 15 percent felt that there were not always enough people available to carry out work safely.[36] Some Transocean crews complained that the safety manual was "unstructured," "hard to navigate," and "not written with the end user in mind"; and that there is "poor distinction between what is required and how this should be achieved."[37] According to the final survey report, Transocean's crews "don't always know what they don't know. [F]ront line crews are potentially working with a mindset that they believe they are fully aware of all the hazards when it's highly likely that they are not."[38]

Halliburton, BP's other major contractor for the Macondo well, is one of the world's largest providers of products and services to the energy industry.[39] It has offices in 70 countries, and Halliburton-affiliated companies have participated in the majority of producing deepwater wells and contributed to most of the world's deepwater well completions.[40] Yet notwithstanding its clear experience and expertise in cementing—a $1.7 billion business for the company in 2009[41]—Halliburton prepared cement for the Macondo well that had repeatedly failed Halliburton's own laboratory tests (see Chapter 4). And then, despite those test results, Halliburton managers onshore let its crew and those of Transocean and BP on the Deepwater Horizon continue with the cement job apparently without first ensuring good stability results.

Halliburton also was the cementer on a well that suffered a blowout in August 2009, in the Timor Sea off Australia. The *Montara* rig caught fire and a well leaked tens of thousands of barrels of oil over two and a half months before it was shut down.[42] The leak occurred because the cement seal failed, the government report into the accident found. However, the report said it would not be appropriate to criticize Halliburton, because the operator "exercised overall control over and responsibility for cementing operations."[43] The inquiry concluded that "Halliburton was not required or expected to 'value add' by doing more than complying with [the operator's] instructions."[44] In this, *Montara* offers yet another example of a lack of communication between operators and service providers and of the gaps between the silos of expertise that exist in the deepwater oil and gas industry.

Absence of Adequate Safety Culture in the Offshore U.S. Oil and Gas Industry

As noted, the offshore oil and gas industry is inherently risky, beginning with the initial exploratory activities and continuing through the transportation of oil and gas produced from the wells. The drilling rigs are themselves dangerous places to work, dense with heavy equipment, hazardous chemicals, and flammable oil and gas—all surrounded by the open-sea environment far from shore, where weather and water conditions can change rapidly and dramatically. The seriousness of these risks to worker safety and the environment are underscored by the sheer number of accidents, large and small, that have occurred in oil and gas drilling activities in the Gulf, even in the absence of a major spill since the 1979 Ixtoc spill, until the Macondo blowout (see graphic).[45] No operator or lessee is immune from these safety challenges.

But the pervasive riskiness of exploring for and producing offshore oil and gas does not explain the extent to which approaches to safety differ among companies, nor why they differ within companies depending on where they are working. From 2004 to 2009, fatalities in the offshore oil and gas industry were more than four times higher per person-hours worked in U.S. waters than in European waters, even though many of the same companies work in both venues.[46] This striking statistical discrepancy reinforces the view that the problem is not an inherent trait of the business itself, but rather depends on the differing cultures and regulatory systems under which members of the industry operate.

The American Petroleum Institute: expert or advocate? In the United States, the American Petroleum Institute (API) has played a dominant role in developing safety standards for the oil and gas industry.[47] And it clearly possesses significant, longstanding technical expertise. API produces standards, recommended practices, specifications, codes, technical publications, reports, and studies that cover the industry and are utilized around the world.[48] In conjunction with API's Quality Programs, many of these standards form the basis of API certification programs.[49] And the U.S. Department of the Interior has historically adopted those recommended practices and standards, developed by technical experts within API, as formal agency regulations.[50]

Based on this Commission's multiple meetings and discussions with leading members of the oil and gas industry, however, it is clear that API's ability to serve as a reliable standard-setter for drilling safety is compromised by its role as the industry's principal lobbyist and public policy advocate. Because they would make oil and gas industry operations potentially more costly, API regularly resists agency rulemakings that government regulators believe would make those operations safer, and API favors rulemaking that promotes industry autonomy from government oversight.[51]

According to statements made by industry officials to the Commission, API's proffered safety and technical standards were a major casualty of this conflicted role. As described by one representative, API-proposed safety standards have increasingly failed to reflect "best industry practices" and have instead expressed the "lowest common denominator"—in other words, a standard that almost all operators could readily achieve. Because, moreover, the Interior Department has in turn relied on API in developing its own regulatory safety standards, API's shortfalls have undermined the entire federal regulatory system.[52]

As described in Chapter 4, the inadequacies of the resulting federal standards are evident in the decisions that led to the Macondo well blowout. Federal authorities lacked regulations

FIGURE 8.1: Loss of Well Control Accidents

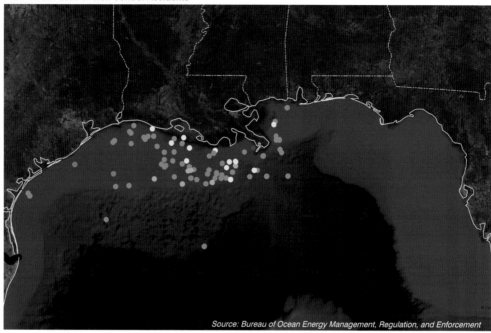

Source: Bureau of Ocean Energy Management, Regulation, and Enforcement

Loss of Well Control Accidents and Resulting Consequences

- Loss of Well Control
- Panel Investigation
- Fire or Explosion
- Fatalities
- Fire or Explosion with Fatalities or Injuries

Between 1996 and 2009, in the U.S. Gulf of Mexico, there were 79 reported loss of well control accidents—when hydrocarbons flowed uncontrolled either underground or at the surface.

The regulator considers the following three factors when determining whether or not an accident will undergo a panel investigation: the actual and potential severity of the incident; the complexity of the incident; and, the probability of similar incidents occurring.

Loss of Well Control Accidents & Consequences		
Date	Company	Consequence Code
01/24/96	Oryx Energy Company	
11/10/96	Norcen Explorer, Inc.	
11/27/96	Tana Oil and Gas Corporation	
12/03/96	Amoco Production Company	
01/10/97	BHP Petroleum, Inc.	
03/04/97	Shell Offshore, Inc.	
04/01/97	American Exploration Company	
05/31/97	Houston Exploration Company	
10/20/97	Freeport-McMoRan Resource Partners	
01/06/98	Hall-Houston Oil Company	
01/16/98	Chevron U.S.A., Inc.	
04/30/98	Vastar Resources Inc.	
07/08/98	Newfield Exploration Company	
11/22/98	Ocean Energy Inc.	
12/09/98	Petrobras America Inc.	
02/10/99	Union Pacific Resources Company	

08/11/99	Freeport McMoran Sulphur Inc.	
09/09/99	Newfield Exploration Company	
12/02/99	Apache Corporation	
12/05/99	Freeport McMoran Sulphur LLC	
01/02/00	Callon Petroleum Operating Company	
01/05/00	Apache Corporation	
01/12/00	Murphy Exploration & Production Company	
02/28/00	Murphy Exploration and Production Company	
03/22/00	Forcenergy Inc.	
04/07/00	Union Oil Company of California	
08/15/00	Houston Exploration Company	
11/18/00	Houston Exploration Company	
03/01/01	Forest Oil Corporation	
04/02/01	Newfield Exploration Company	
04/04/01	Matrix Oil & Gas, Inc.	
05/10/01	Devon Energy Production Company	
05/24/01	BHP Petroleum (Americas) Inc.	
07/06/01	Tri-Union Development Corporation	
07/13/01	William G. Helis Company	
10/24/01	Argo, L.L.C.	
11/21/01	BP Amoco Corporation	
01/12/02	BP Amoco Corporation	
08/08/02	BP Exploration & Oil Inc	
09/07/02	El Paso Production Oil & Gas Company	
10/03/02	Murphy Exploration & Production Co.	
11/14/02	BP Exploration & Production Inc.	
12/06/02	Kerr McGee Corporation	
03/08/03	Anadarko E&P Company	
04/12/03	Helis Oil & Gas Corporation	
04/22/03	ChevronTexaco Corporation	
09/02/03	Manti Operating Company	
12/04/03	Walter Oil & Gas Corporation	
02/09/04	Energy Partners, Ltd.	
02/17/04	Orca Energy (Dunhill), L.P.	
02/22/04	ATP Oil & Gas Corporation	
10/21/04	Amerada Hess Corporation	
03/08/05	Hunt Oil Company	
05/28/05	W & T Offshore, Inc.	
11/30/05	W & T Offshore, Inc.	
12/01/05	Chevron USA.	
02/20/06	Forest Oil Corporation	
11/18/06	Dominion Exploration & Production, Inc.	
01/23/07	Fairways Offshore Exploration, Inc.	
03/16/07	East Cameron Partners, LP	
06/24/07	Stone Energy Corporation	
08/22/07	Apache Corporation	
09/07/07	Eni US Operating Co. Inc.	
11/20/07	BP Corporation North America Inc.	
12/03/07	Rooster Petroleum, LLC	
02/14/08	Apache Corporation	
04/23/08	Apache Corporation	
04/26/08	LLOG Exploration Offshore, Inc.	
05/06/08	Mariner Energy, Inc.	
08/19/08	Energy Resource Technology GOM, Inc.	
10/31/08	Chevron U.S.A. Inc.	
11/01/08	Union Oil Company of California	
12/20/08	El Paso E&P Company, L.P.	
04/19/09	LLOG Exploration Offshore, Inc.	
04/23/09	Stone Energy Corporation	
05/27/09	Stone Energy Corporation	
08/26/09	Stone Energy Corporation	
12/22/09	Not Listed	
12/29/09	Murphy Exploration & Production Company	

FIGURE 8.2: Fatalities from Offshore Oil and Gas Operations

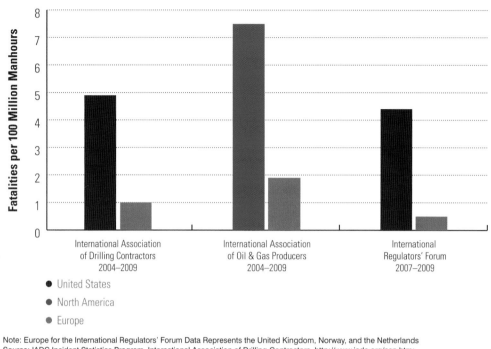

Note: Europe for the International Regulators' Forum Data Represents the United Kingdom, Norway, and the Netherlands
Source: IADC Incident Statistics Program, International Association of Drilling Contractors, http://www.iadc.org/asp.htm;
    Safety Performance Indicators, International Association of Oil & Gas Producers, http://www.ogp.org.uk/;
    IRF Country Performance Measures, International Regulators' Forum,
    http://www.irfoffshoresafety.com/country/performance/.

covering some of the most critical decisions made on the *Deepwater Horizon* that affected the safety of the Macondo well. For instance, notwithstanding the enormously important role cementing plays in well construction—especially in the high-pressure conditions often present in deepwater drilling—there were no meaningful regulations governing the requirements for cementing a well and testing the cement used. Nor were there regulations governing negative-pressure testing of the well's integrity—a fundamental check against dangerous hydrocarbon incursions into an underbalanced well. On many of these critical matters, the federal regulations either failed to account for the particular challenges of deepwater drilling or were silent altogether.

For years, API also led the effort to persuade the Minerals Management Service not to adopt a new regulatory approach—the Safety and Environmental Management System (SEMS)—and instead has favored relying on voluntary, recommended safety practices.[53] Safety and environmental management systems are used in similar forms in other parts of the world and many credit them with the better safety records achieved outside U.S. waters (see Chapter 3). Beginning early in the last decade, the trade organization steadfastly resisted MMS's efforts to require all companies to demonstrate that they have a complete safety and environmental management system[54] in addition to meeting more traditional, prescriptive regulations—despite the fact that this is the direction taken in other countries in response to the Piper Alpha rig explosion in the late 1980s.[55] Indeed, many operators in the Gulf were used to this safety-based approach on their rigs in the North Sea and Canada. It was not until this past September—after the Macondo blowout—that the Department of the Interior was finally able to announce a new, mandatory Safety and Environmental Management System:[56] almost two decades after the approach was adopted in the United Kingdom, where it is called the "safety case."[57] Moreover, API opposed revisions to the incident reporting rule that would have helped better identify safety risks.[58]

Decreasing safety-related research and development. Safely managing industrial hazards for oil and gas drilling requires experience and knowledge: knowing not only which actions to perform at various points on a checklist during a procedure, but also basic knowledge of the interactions of oil, gas, cement, drilling mud, sand, rock, and salt water that enables correct decisions when unexpected events occur. Yet such knowledge and experience within the industry may be decreasing.

The chair of the University of Texas's Department of Petroleum and Geosystems Engineering, Tad Patzek, testified before Congress in 2010 that "the oil and gas industry has eliminated most of its research capabilities, which three decades ago allowed it to rapidly expand deepwater production."[59] "Academic research has been important but small in scale and permanently starved of funding," Patzek continued. "The depletion of industry research capabilities and the starvation of academia that educates the new industry leaders have resulted in a scarcity of experienced personnel that can grasp the complexity of offshore operations and make quick and correct decisions."[60] Nor, Patzek stressed, could industry depend upon contractors to fill the safety gap: "The individual contractors have different cultures and management structures, leading easily to conflicts of interest, confusion, lack of coordination, and severely slowed decision-making."[61]*

Hazardous Industries Can Become Safer

Even inherently risky businesses can be made much safer, given the right motivations and systems-safety management practices. Civil aviation and nuclear-fueled electric power are two good examples of industries that have had to manage the risk of catastrophic failures and losses. In the public sector, the United States Navy also faced the challenge of improving safety in its nuclear-power vessels—and did so.

The primary motivation for improving safety in each instance is that neither the public (as consumers and as voters) nor the government would allow such enterprises to operate if they suffered many accidents. People would not board planes if an unacceptable number crashed. The reaction to the contained partial core meltdown at the Three Mile Island power plant in 1979 has kept the industry from expanding in the United States for more than three decades.[62] And, nuclear submarines carry highly skilled crews and are enormously expensive to build (not to mention carrying a fuel source that would pose wide dangers in case of a leak)—all factors that compel the Navy to put a premium on safe practices.

---

* According to Michael Bromwich, Director of the Interior Department's Bureau of Ocean Energy Management, Regulation and Enforcement, the chairs of university departments of petroleum engineering whom he recently visited "expressed great concern about the level of R&D in the private sector into drilling and drilling safety."

Civil aviation. The airline industry, for instance, is well aware that the industry as a whole suffers if the public lacks trust in the safety of any one company. The Federal Aviation Administration (FAA) is responsible for the safety of civil aviation,[63] and the airline industry lends resources to bolster government oversight.[64] The government enhances its oversight abilities by relying heavily on private Designated Engineering Representatives— either consultants or employees of aircraft manufacturers such as Boeing.[65] These engineers work for their employers and may approve, or recommend approval of, technical data provided to the FAA for the company.[66] It is a good example of industry and government "sharing" experts.[67]

Boeing itself has worked closely with the FAA to improve safety performance.[68] In the 1950s, only 20 percent of Americans were willing to fly, and there were 14 to 15 major accidents a year.[69] Boeing had a strong incentive to improve performance, and attitudes toward aviation, if it were to grow its commercial business. Despite an enormous increase (ten- to twentyfold) in airline flight operations between 1955 and 1991, the number of accidents fell to approximately four to five per year, one-fourth the annual rate in the 1950s.[70]

The nuclear Navy. Turning from the skies to the sea, between 1915 and 1963, the U.S. Navy lost about one submarine every three years to noncombat causes.[71] In 1963, when the nuclear-powered *USS Thresher* was lost during a deep test dive, 112 naval personnel and 17 civilians perished.[72] The Navy investigation found that a deficient silver-braze joint in a piping system had failed, flooding the engine room.[73] The investigation went far beyond immediate causes and "found deficient specifications, shipbuilding practices, and maintenance practices, along with inadequate documentation of construction and maintenance actions and deficient operational procedures."[74] After the *Thresher* loss, Admiral Hyman Rickover, then head of the nuclear Navy, told his staff to establish a system to ensure that such an accident would never recur.[75] The new SUBSAFE system was established within 54 days of the loss of the *Thresher*, and no SUBSAFE-certified submarine has since been lost.[76]

SUBSAFE has two goals, both crucial for submarines: maintaining the watertight integrity of the hull, and maintaining operability and integrity of critical systems that allow control and recovery from a flooding hazard.[77] The system covers the administrative, organizational, technical, design, material-control, fabrication, testing, work-control, auditing, and certification aspects of submarine development and operations (see sidebar).[78] As important as procedures, SUBSAFE establishes a mindset—in this case, a questioning attitude and what the officers call *chronic uneasiness*, summarized in the saying, "Trust, but verify."[79]

Another critical component of SUBSAFE is a separation of powers—no simple achievement in an organization as homogeneous and hierarchical as the Navy. In fact, there is always a dynamic tension among the Platform Program Managers (responsible for the costs, schedule, and quality of ships under their control), the Independent Technical Authority, and the Independent Safety and Quality Assurance Authority—the nuclear Navy's "three-legged stool."[80] The Platform Managers can select only from a set of acceptable design options, to ensure that safety is not traded off for performance.[81] The Technical Authority approves these acceptable options.[82] The Safety Authority is responsible for administering SUBSAFE and enforcing compliance.[83]

> **Principles of the Naval "SUBSAFE" System**
> - Top management commitment to safety
> - Clear and written safety requirements
> - Education, not just training
> - Regular rewriting of requirements
> - Separation of powers and assignment of responsibilities
> - Emphasis on rigor, technical compliance, and work discipline
> - Documentation capturing what is done and why it is done
> - Participatory audit approach, and requirements for objective quality evidence
> - Program based on written procedures, not personality-driven
> - Continual certification of a facility
> - Accountability and accompanying responsibility
> - Special efforts to be vigilant against complacency

SUBSAFE involves a great deal of certification (of design, materials, fabrication, and testing), and the overall SUBSAFE certification must be maintained through the life of the vessel.[84] Audits assure compliance, and the audits are treated not so much as exams by outsiders but as constructive learning experiences.[85] Continuous training and education of personnel are emphasized.[86] Many of the civilian contracting companies that service the nuclear Navy also service the offshore oil and gas industry and seem to cope well with the rigorous nature of the SUBSAFE system.[87]

Learning from Accidents: Exxon, Shell, and Bhopal

The Navy learned from the loss of the *USS Thresher* and set up an effective safety system. The American oil and gas industry must learn from the loss of the *Deepwater Horizon* and do the same today.

The *Exxon Valdez* aftermath. Among oil and gas companies, ExxonMobil's wake-up call came in 1989, when its *Exxon Valdez* tanker struck a reef in Prince William Sound, Alaska, and spilled approximately 11 million gallons of crude oil.[88] Until the *Deepwater Horizon* disaster, this was the biggest spill in U.S. waters.[89] The spill covered thousands of miles of pristine waters and coastal areas, killing marine mammals, fish, and seabirds, and damaging the livelihoods of the people who lived and worked in the region.[90] A fatigued and overworked crew, inadequate safety escort vessels, and a single hulled tanker have been cited among the causes of the accident.[91] Exxon spent approximately $2.1 billion in clean-up costs, and, pursuant to a settlement with the United States and Alaska, agreed to pay a criminal fine of $150 million ($125 million of which was forgiven in light of its cleanup efforts), $100 million in criminal restitution, and $900 million to settle civil claims, subject to a reopener provisions allowing for an additional $100 million.[92]*

---

* A private civil lawsuit has been under way for the past two decades. A jury initially awarded the plaintiffs $287 million in actual damages and $5 billion in punitive damages, but the Supreme Court subsequently ruled that punitive damages could not exceed twice actual damages, or $507.5 million. Exxon Shipping Co. v. Baker, 554 U.S. 471 (2008).

Exxon Valdez Oil Spill

The crippled tanker *Exxon Valdez* lies atop Bligh Reef off the coast of Alaska two days after running aground on March 24, 1989. More than a quarter-million barrels of oil leaked into Prince William Sound, wreaking environmental havoc and becoming the largest spill in U.S. waters until the *Deepwater Horizon* disaster.

Natalie B. Fobes/National Geographic/Getty Images

Following the spill, both government policy and industry practice changed dramatically. Congress enacted the Oil Pollution Act of 1990 and Exxon introduced its Operations Integrity Management System (OIMS) in 1992.[93] ExxonMobil CEO Rex Tillerson told the Commission's November 9 hearing that "OIMS is a rigorous 11-point set of elements designed to identify management and hazard risks. Its framework covers all aspects of safety, including management leadership and accountability; design, construction and maintenance of facilities; emergency preparedness; management of change; assessment of performance; and, of course, thorough inquiries into accidents and incidents."[94]

"OIMS guides the activities of each of ExxonMobil's more than 80,000 employees," he continued, "as well as our third-party contractors around the world. Over time it has become embedded into everyday work processes at all levels. Through OIMS, ExxonMobil monitors, benchmarks, and measures aspects of our safety performance. Its structure and standards are shared and communicated the world over."[95] "Safety is not proprietary," Tillerson added. "And for this reason ExxonMobil shares its best practices within our industry and across other industries. We seek to learn from others."[96] The reported improvements in the company's safety and environmental performance have been impressive. In 2009, the company reported that it had received a rating of 10 out of 10 from GovernanceMetrics International, placing it among the top one percent of companies rated.[97]* It also reported that it had had no spills from a marine vessel between 2006 and 2009, and that in 2009 it continued to lead the industry with combined employee and contractor workforce lost-time incident rates at best-ever levels.[98]

Shell's safety response. Shell, a long-time leader in Gulf of Mexico operations (before BP surpassed it, as described in Chapter 2), has had its own safety problems. Two men died in a gas leak on the company's Brent Bravo platform in 2003; former Shell senior manager Bill Campbell, who had earlier led a safety review, said after the accident that his 1999 warnings had been ignored by the company.[99] Shell denied that it operated at high levels of risk.[100]

Shell subsequently tightened and simplified its safety rules.[101] Shell also has promoted the use of the "safety case" worldwide (a risk-management approach to regulation described in Chapter 3).[102] It has adopted the safety-case approach even in the United States, where it is not required to do so, and has promoted it for the industry more broadly.[103] Marvin Odum, president of Shell Oil Company and director of Shell's Upstream Americas business, told the Commission's November 9 hearing that "the safety case in deepwater drilling shows how we identify and assess the hazards on a rig; how we establish the barriers to prevent and control those hazards; how we assign the critical activities needed to maintain the integrity of these barriers."[104]

Odum said that Shell also encourages workers to call for work to stop when they suspect that something is proceeding improperly, and gives awards to these "Goal Zero Heroes" (referring to the corporate goal of zero accidents).[105] He added that audits are key to system safety and that "in 2009, DuPont administered its safety and culture survey in our drilling organization, comparing us to the world's best across a range of industries. While we ranked world-class overall, improvement areas were identified."[106]

Bhopal and Responsible Care. The chemical industry's Responsible Care initiative was developed in Canada and launched in 1985 after the disastrous 1984 chemical leak in Bhopal, India.[107] It operates in 53 countries and describes itself as "the chemical industry's global voluntary initiative under which companies, through their national associations, work together to continuously improve their health, safety and environmental performance, and communicate with stakeholders about their products and processes in the manufacture and supply of safe and affordable goods that bring real benefits to society."[108] The American Chemistry Council can expel member firms for non-compliance with Responsible Care.[109] Subsequent analysis, however, suggests that the program's success has turned less on the availability of such formal sanctions and more on informal disciplinary mechanisms such as peer pressure and institutional norms of compliance: "Executives from leading firms pressure their non-compliant counterparts at industry meetings to adopt and adhere to the industrial codes."[110]

Of course, in drawing lessons from prior accidents, it is essential that they be projected beyond the particular circumstances of the accident at hand, to guide present and future

---

* Governance Metrics International (GMI) is an independent governance research and ratings firm providing institutional investors an objective way of assessing corporate governance risk as well as governance leaders in their portfolios.

performance, lest government regulators and industry leaders make the classic mistake of "preparing to fight the last war." As discussed in Chapters 3 and 5, despite the steps taken in the aftermath of *Exxon Valdez* to enhance transportation safety and oil spill response from a tanker spill, too little effort was made to take those lessons and apply them more broadly to the risks associated with the future of offshore drilling, in the deepwater of the Gulf.

Industry Self-Policing as a Supplement to Government Regulation

One of the key responsibilities of government is to regulate—to direct the behavior of individuals and institutions according to rules. Many businesses and business groups are involved in internal standard-setting, evaluation, and other activities that constitute self-policing or self-regulation. Such oversight can be conducted by a private entity established and supported by an industry to ensure safe operations by individual members (among other purposes), often because industry leaders recognize that a misstep by any one member necessarily has significant repercussions for them all. But even in industries with strong self-policing, government also needs to be strongly present, providing oversight and/or additional regulatory control—responsibilities that cannot be abdicated if public safety, health, and welfare are to be protected.

The logic of self-policing. Industry-standard setting and self-policing organizations are widespread in the United States and in most industrialized nations—typically for operations marked by technical complexity, such as the chemical, nuclear power, civil aviation, and oil and gas industries, where government oversight is also present. These processes coexist where there are, as a practical matter, relatively limited numbers of people with the requisite expertise and experience, making it hard for government to be able to rely solely on its own personnel (especially when government cannot compete with private-sector salaries for those experts). Support for standard-setting and self-policing also arises in industries whose reputations depend on the performance of each company, and where significant revenues are at stake—witness both the airline industry's private Designated Engineering Representatives (discussed above) and the Institute of Nuclear Power Operations (see below). Though the Navy is a government organization, SUBSAFE is also an example of self-policing to help assure the safety of its nuclear submarines.

The limits of unregulated self-policing. Industry self-policing is not a substitute for government but serves as an important supplement to government oversight. And the cost of forgetting that essential premise can be calamitous. In the financial sector, for example, the Securities and Exchange Commission's Consolidated Supervised Entities Program had, in 2004, delegated regulatory risk assessment of global investment bank conglomerates to the banks themselves.[111] The program was designed to cover a regulatory gap left by Congress amid changes in global finance, but it was entirely voluntary.[112] Four years later, Securities and Exchange Commission Chairman Christopher Cox ended the program, declaring it a failure—indeed "fundamentally flawed"—after companies like Bear Sterns failed to adequately assess the risk of a sharp downturn in housing prices on their large, leveraged investments in mortgage-backed securities.[113]

A second cautionary tale involves an environmental disaster. When political opposition stymied federal and state regulation of toxic coal ash and other residues from power generation, the electric utilities that had opposed regulations deferred to the Utilities Solid Wastes Activities Group's voluntary "Action Plan" to manage such wastes.[114] The U.S. Environmental Protection Agency stepped back from regulating such hazards.[115] And, in 2008, an earthen dam containing coal ash gave way in eastern Tennessee, releasing more than a billion gallons of coal ash across a large portion of Roane County and polluting rivers that carried the hazardous wastes farther afield.[116]

The Nuclear Model

The risk-management challenges presented by nuclear power are in some respects analogous to those presented by deepwater drilling: the dependence on highly sophisticated and complex technologies, the low probability/catastrophic consequences nature of the risks generated, and the related tendency for a culture of complacency to develop over time in the absence of major accidents. For the nuclear power industry, it took a crisis— the partial meltdown in 1979 of the radioactive core in Unit Two at the Three Mile Island Nuclear Generating Station—to prompt a transformation of its safety culture.[117] But that is what industry accomplished and reportedly with significant, positive results.[118] For that reason, the nuclear power industry's method of transforming business-as-usual practices offers a useful analogue as the oil and gas industry now seeks to do the same more than 30 years later.

The first recommendation of the President's Commission that investigated the root causes of the Three Mile Island accident was directed to industry, and made clear the extent to which the industry need to transform its safety culture:

> [T]he nuclear industry must dramatically change its attitudes toward safety and regulations. The Commission has recommended that the new regulatory agency prescribe strict standards. At the same time . . . the industry must also set and police its own standards of excellence to ensure the effective management and safe operation of nuclear power plants.[119]

Two months later, in December 1979, the nuclear power industry created the Institute of Nuclear Power Operations (INPO), a nonprofit organization with the ambitious mission "to promote the highest levels of safety and reliability—to promote excellence—in the operation of commercial nuclear power plants."[120]

INPO's structure more closely resembles the utilities it "regulates" than it does the Nuclear Regulatory Commission (NRC), the federal regulatory agency whose work INPO is designed to complement. INPO's president answers to a board of directors, consisting of senior industry executives—mainly CEOs.[121] A few years after its founding, INPO established its own inspection process, based on its studies of what needed inspecting and how to do so.[122] Today, nuclear power plant inspections are thorough, but not adversarial. Because many INPO inspectors are nuclear employees drawn from other power plants, a great deal of cross-fertilization of knowledge occurs, and strong peer relationships are created.[123] INPO's normative system establishes a structured way of thinking about plant operations by translating these matters into the language of responsibility as it spells out what it means to occupy a particular role and what it means to behave in a manner appropriate to that position.[124]

Inspection teams and procedures. INPO inspection teams usually number about 20 people: one-third are permanent, full-time inspectors; one-third are on loan from the industry for 18 to 24 months; and the remainder are peer evaluators on loan just for that particular inspection (but these cannot be from the utility being inspected).[125]

Each of the 66 nuclear sites (encompassing 104 reactors, operated by 26 utilities) is inspected every 24 months.[126] Inspectors rotate through assignments; each inspector averages 4 to 5 inspections per year. (Besides the major inspection of each site every two years, INPO performs a series of other evaluations and provides other safety-oriented services throughout the year. For example, utilities' training programs are evaluated and accredited every 24 months.)[127] Importantly, INPO is not the sole source of plant inspections, but instead serves as a significant supplement. Nuclear insurers, the Occupational Safety and Health Administration, and the NRC also conduct inspections; INPO coordinates with the NRC and other inspectors to avoid schedule conflicts.[128]

Nor is there anything casual about an INPO inspection. It is thorough and careful, extending for five to six weeks: two weeks of preparation and analysis of pre-delivered data from the site, two weeks on the site, a week of internal review and report writing by functional and cross-functional sub-teams, and perhaps another week reviewing with the INPO president.[129] Any lessons learned that are deemed valuable to the rest of the industry are posted on INPO's private online portal, but the name of the site is scrubbed from the text.[130] All plants respond to INPO's assessment reports by documenting actions planned to address any reported problems. A poorly performing plant will receive higher attention from INPO to see if the plant's responsive actions are on track. INPO will also work to give them help or coordinate help from other stations.[131] Furthermore, assessment results are never revealed to anyone other than the utility CEOs and site managers, but INPO formally meets with the NRC four times a year to discuss trends and information of "mutual interest." And if INPO has discovered serious problems associated with specific plants, it notifies the NRC.[132]

The performance evaluation. INPO considers at each plant such metrics as consistency of operations, safety-system performance, and workers' collective radiation exposure.[133] But its Plant Performance Assessments are the real backbone of its work. These exercises figuratively deconstruct and reconstruct the plants, looking into all aspects of operations, maintenance, and engineering. The inspection teams evaluate processes and behaviors that cross organizational boundaries such as safety culture, self-assessment, corrective action, operating experience, human performance, and training. The performance of operations and training personnel during simulator exercises is included in each evaluation. Where possible, observations of plant startups, shutdowns, and major planned changes are also included.[134]

INPO strongly discourages a rule-bound, compliance-oriented approach that would encourage a mentality of ticking boxes—and in fact its reports are not in checklist form.[135] Many of the risk factors that nuclear companies must deal with are beyond their control. One issue that is clearly within the industry's control is standardization: of design requirements, resulting advanced designs, and operations. The industry has devoted significant time and resources to this issue over the past few decades.[136] "Good practice" documents are written with an eye toward processes that are applicable across the industry.[137]

From the control room to the CEO. INPO directly connects those responsible for the day-to-day operations of nuclear plants with senior management.[138] Two INPO Industry Review Groups, which act in an advisory capacity to senior management, enable lower-level employees involved in plant operations to communicate with vice presidents and division directors.[139] Review groups also assess INPO programs and evaluate INPO's performance itself.[140] The existence of these groups reflects INPO's commitment to tie together senior management and lower-level, operational employees.

INPO's influence. In addition to its individual site evaluations, INPO hosts an industry "CEO Conference," usually each November, which includes numerous speakers from nuclear organizations and also some non-nuclear companies, with a focus on nuclear safety.[141] During this conference, the INPO president gathers only the 26 utility CEOs in a private room to reveal to all the executives the grades for each site, based on the assessments.[142] These grades range from one (most favorable) to five. Approximately 40 percent of the grades are INPO 1, 40 to 50 percent are INPO 2, and 10 to 15 percent are INPO 3 or 4. (The last time any site was given a grade of 5 was in the late 1980s.)[143] An INPO 5 indicates a site with significant operational problems, triggering a shutdown. And a grade of INPO 4 requires a verbal explanation by the affected CEO on the spot.[144] This meeting is not intended to shame or punish, but to put the facts on the table. CEOs with low-rated plants typically will describe to their peers what comprehensive actions they are undertaking to address the causes of the problems. All CEOs recognize that it is in everybody's interest to help lower performers operate better. At the larger dinner, with all conference attendees present, INPO announces and congratulates only the INPO 1 plants.[145] A former Chief Nuclear Officer of a major utility described INPO 1 as equivalent to receiving an Academy Award.[146]

Presentation of relative standings before the rest of the industry produces a high level of peer pressure; as one CEO put it, "You get the whole top level of the utility industry focused on the poor performer."[147] It also gives the industry the ability to "clean out" poor management. Because INPO's directors are industry peers, CEOs may become aware of a company taking too much risk and offer to loan people to help the "underperformer" come up to speed.[148]

The impact on insurance premiums. Although the Price-Anderson Act limits the liability of those who operate nuclear power plants in the case of an accident, owners of nuclear plants insure through Nuclear Electric Insurance Limited, an industry mutual insurance company, against losses associated with on-site problems such as power interruptions, decontamination, and physical property damage.[149] Nuclear Electric Insurance Limited is allowed to visit INPO's office at least once a year to view the assessment ratings (but they are not provided with copies).[150] And, like any other insurance company, Nuclear Electric Insurance Limited sets insurance premiums based on its assessment of risk. Sites with top INPO ratings are charged lower premiums than stations with lower ratings.[151] NEIL requires that license holders be active members of INPO or that they notify NEIL formally and promptly if they stop being a member – and they must show NEIL how they will accomplish a level of oversight equivalent to what INPO provides. This has never occurred. In reality, NEIL's board would quickly discuss removal of insurance coverage should a member choose to drop out of INPO activities.[152] So utilities have a tremendous financial incentive to carry out INPO's recommendations.[153]

Compensation competitive with industry. INPO has about 400 employees, including about 60 on long-term loan from its member utilities. Of the total staff and management cadre, 250 are nuclear technical personnel.[154] INPO can do its job only if its employees possess technical expertise at least equal to that possessed by those in the industry INPO is charged with overseeing. To a certain extent, INPO achieves that standard by relying on experts on loan from industry for extended periods of time.[155] But to ensure that INPO's own full-time personnel possess the requisite qualifications, industry salaries are benchmarked, and INPO provides its employees comparable compensation.[156] INPO has therefore not suffered from the expertise gap too often evident with government inspectors (witness the issue raised at the founding of the Minerals Management Service, as discussed in Chapter 3). INPO can pay these higher salaries because it is not subject to the same budgetary constraints faced by a public agency. Each utility contributes to INPO's budget based on the number of reactors it owns. Budgets are approved by INPO's board each autumn. (INPO's fiscal year 2010 budget was $99 million, with more than $100 million budgeted for 2011.)[157]

INPO "clout" and industry acceptance. INPO's ability to achieve widespread acceptance within the nuclear power industry was not preordained. The new self-policing enterprise had to earn the necessary reputation for fairness and integrity over time.[158] A formative moment in gaining the necessary stature occurred in 1988, when INPO helped bring about the firing of a utility's corporate leadership following a plant shutdown.[159] Beginning in December 1984, INPO inspectors reported pervasive safety problems at Philadelphia Electric's Peach Bottom nuclear plant—including incidents of employees literally sleeping on the job. When INPO was dissatisfied with the plant's response to these concerns, it scheduled more inspections and meetings with Philadelphia Electric officials, and sent letters further detailing the depth of its concerns. These concerns prompted the NRC to order a shutdown of the plant, and when Philadelphia Electric submitted a recovery plan to the Commission to restart the plant, an INPO-convened industry panel sharply condemned the plan as seriously flawed. INPO and the NRC worked closely and cooperatively, with INPO so harshly criticizing Philadelphia Electric's management that several top executives ultimately lost their jobs. From then on, the message within the industry was clear: "INPO has a great deal of clout" and Peach Bottom became a symbol of INPO's new power. [160]

Although INPO has its detractors,* it does appear to have helped the nuclear power industry improve and maintain performance and safety during the past three decades. INPO has helped the industry measure its progress in improving safety standards and has served as a vehicle for making advances in control-room design, plant and personnel performance, training and qualification, self-regulation, emergency response, maintenance, and radiation protection, among other areas.[161] During the past 30 years, the nuclear industry has improved plant efficiency, significantly reduced the number of automatic emergency reactor shutdowns per year, and reduced collective radiation accident rates by a factor of six compared to the 1980s.[162] The industry has achieved these milestones, in part, through INPO's role in promoting a strong nuclear safety culture and presenting performance objectives and criteria to help the industry strive for and surpass safety goals.[163]

An INPO for Oil?

In the aftermath of the *Deepwater Horizon* spill, could the oil and gas industry similarly improve its safety culture by creating a self-policing entity like INPO as a supplement to government oversight? There are clear parallels that would strongly support such an effort, but also some equally clear differences between the oil and gas industry and the nuclear power industry that at least caution against wholesale adoption of the INPO model.

Similarities: Need, incentive, and means. The reason the INPO model holds promise is because the oil and gas industry, like the nuclear power industry after Three Mile Island, has both the substantial economic resources and the necessary economic incentive to make it happen. INPO was formed because doing so was in industry's self-interest.[164] As the *Deepwater Horizon* disaster made unambiguously clear, the entire industry's reputation, and perhaps its viability, ultimately turn on its lowest-performing members.† If any one company is involved in an accident with widespread and potentially enormous costs, like those that followed the Macondo blowout, everyone in the industry—companies and employees—suffers, as do regional economies and the nation as a whole. No one, in industry or in government, can afford a repeat of the Macondo explosion and spill. Also, as the enormous sums that BP was willing and able to expend to contain and respond to the Gulf spill make clear (see Chapter 5), the oil and gas industry possesses the financial means to fund a very healthy and effective self-policing organization akin to INPO.

A second fundamental parallel is that no one in the oil and gas industry has the unilateral right to engage in offshore drilling on the outer continental shelf any more than a utility has the right to construct and operate a nuclear power plant absent federal governmental approval. Indeed, the extent of governmental authority is even greater in the offshore context. The oil and gas industry does not own the valuable energy resources located on the outer continental shelf, which belong to the American people and are managed by the federal government on their behalf. As described in Chapter 3, the government accordingly

---

* The Union of Concerned Scientists has on occasion faulted INPO (and the Nuclear Regulatory Commission) for not inspecting some plants with sufficient rigor and skepticism, and has pointedly raised the issue whether the fact that industry pays for INPO's services presents a conflict of interest that compromises its essential impartiality.
† This was also the case in the INPO context; in part, industry mobilized to unify "in reaction to a mutual internal threat, unsafe nuclear utilities." Joseph Rees, *Hostages of Each Other* (Chicago: The University of Chicago Press 1994), 44.

possesses sweeping authority to dictate the terms of private access to those resources in its lease agreements with private parties. And, in particular, government could decide to condition such access, either directly or indirectly, on participation with an industry safety institute.

A third clear parallel is the possibility in both contexts—offshore drilling and nuclear power—for industry self-policing to supplement government regulation.[165] As described in Chapter 3, government regulators need to improve their in-house technical expertise dramatically,[166] but they are unlikely ever to possess technical expertise truly commensurate with that of private industry. The salary differential, combined with the sheer depth of industry expertise on a wide variety of topics critical to understanding and managing offshore drilling operations, would make that goal illusory. Such expertise is, however, a prerequisite for the thorough, rigorous inspections required to ensure safe operation of dozens of deepwater exploration rigs and production platforms (the former operating in multiple locations and different geologies each year)[167]—a number that rises sharply if installations in shallower Gulf waters are included. By supplementing governmental oversight, with the kind of self-policing accomplished by INPO for nuclear power, that gap in expertise can be sharply narrowed. Government can never abdicate its ultimate responsibility to ensure drilling safety, but it can effectively take advantage of industry expertise to meet that objective.

Differences that warrant modifying the INPO model. But there are also clear differences between the two industries that would require a differently defined self-policing entity for offshore oil and gas. For instance, the U.S. nuclear power industry is based at a limited number of fixed sites, using a small number of known technological designs, and operated by an industry subject to comprehensive public regulation[168]—from permission to construct facilities through detailed oversight of design, operations, and maintenance. The oil and gas industry is structured much differently. As described by ExxonMobil's Tillerson, his industry "is moving to different locations, different environments, evolving, all kinds of technologies being introduced."[169] For this reason, he explained, while the oil and gas industry can "look at the principles around INPO in terms of how do you share best practices, how do you assess where the companies are operating at certain levels of competency?"[170], he appeared to suggest there would be limits in the application of every aspect of the INPO model to offshore drilling for oil and gas.

The oil and gas industry is more fragmented and diversified in nature—from integrated global oil companies to independent exploration and drilling enterprises—and therefore less cohesive than the nuclear power operators who joined to establish INPO.* As a result, it could be more challenging to create an INPO-like organization. And oil and gas executives would need assurances that any industry-wide efforts to promote better safety did not subsequently serve as the basis for claims that industry had violated antitrust laws. Finally, concerns about potential disclosure to business competitors of proprietary information might make it harder to establish an INPO-like entity in the oil and gas

---

* Prior to the Three Mile Island accident, however, the nuclear power industry was reportedly far less cohesive than it became after that accident. See Rees, *Hostages of Each Other*, 42 ("when officials describe the pre-TMI nuclear industry, a collective portrait emerges in which each nuclear utility behaved like an 'island unto itself' or 'independent barony.' In short, the industry was *fragmented*.") (emphasis in original).

industry. Technology and design apparently are more uniform in nuclear power than in offshore drilling. For this reason, Michael Bromwich, Director of the Bureau of Ocean Energy Management, Regulation, and Enforcement (the successor to MMS), cautioned that an INPO-like approach might run into problems if companies perceived the potential for inspections of offshore facilities to reveal "technical and proprietary and confidential information that companies may be reluctant to share with one another."[171]

Essential Features of a Self-Policing Safety Organization for the Oil and Gas Industry

Like the nuclear power industry in 1979—in the immediate aftermath of the Three Mile Island accident—the nation's oil and gas industry needs now to embrace the potential for an industry safety institute to supplement government oversight of industry operations. Akin to INPO, such a new safety institute can provide the nation with the assurances of safety necessary to allow the oil and gas industry access to the nation's energy resources on the outer continental shelf. To be sure, the significant differences between the two types of industries warrant significant differences in the precise structure and operation of their respective industry safety institutes. But, as elaborated below, the basic, successful principles upon which the INPO model is premised can serve as the touchstones for the oil and gas industry in establishing its own.

Credibility. To be credible, any industry-created safety institute would need to have complete command of technical expertise available through industry sources—and complete freedom from any suggestion that its operations are compromised by multiple other interests and agendas. As a consensus-based organization, the American Petroleum Institute (API) is culturally ill-suited to drive a safety revolution in the industry. For this reason, it is essential that the safety enterprise operate apart from the API. As described above and in Chapter 3, API's longstanding role as an industry lobbyist and policy advocate—with an established record of opposing reform and modernization of safety regulations—renders it inappropriate to serve a self-policing function. In the aftermath of the *Deepwater Horizon* tragedy, the Commission strongly believes that the oil and gas industry cannot persuade the American public that it is changing business-as-usual practices if it attempts to fend off more effective public oversight by chartering a self-policing function under the control of an advocacy organization.

An industry-wide commitment to rigorous auditing and continuous improvement. The INPO experience makes clear that any successful oil and gas industry safety institute would require in the first instance strong board-level support from CEOs and boards of directors of member companies for a rigorous inspection and auditing function. Such audits would need to be aimed at assessing companies' safety cultures (from design, training, and operations through incident investigation and management of improvements) and encouraging learning about and implementation of enhanced practices. As at INPO, the inspection and auditing function would need to be conducted by safety institute staff, complemented by experts seconded from industry companies, able to analyze the full range of technologies and practices, and designed to promote cross-company learning and shared responsibility while protecting proprietary information.

There would also need to be a commitment to share findings about safety records and best practices within the industry, aggregate data, and analyze performance trends, shortcomings, and needs for further research and development. Accountability could be enhanced by a requirement that companies report their audit scores to their boards of directors and insurance companies.

The main goal is to drive continuous improvement in every company's standards and performance, measured against global benchmarks. The means, to that end, include the safety auditor's reviews; insurer evaluations of risk; and management recognition of and incentives for effective behavior. Senior leadership would be accountable to the company's board of directors, who in turn would be accountable to investors.

In a broader sense, the industry's safety institute could facilitate a smooth transition to a regulatory regime based on systems safety engineering and improved coordination among operators and contractors—the principles of the U.K.'s "safety case" that shifts responsibility for maintaining safe operations at all times to the operators themselves. It should drive continuous improvement in standards and practices by incorporating the highest standards achieved globally, including (but not exclusively) those set by the API.

An initial set of standards and scope of operation. The industry needs to benchmark safety and environmental practice rules against recognized global best practices. The Safety and Environmental Management Program Recommended Practice 75 (API RP 75) developed in 1993 by the API and incorporated by reference in the Department of the Interior's new workplace safety rules, adopted in October 2010, is a reasonable starting point.[172] Updates to those safety rules are needed immediately, but a new industry safety institution could make a credible start by requiring members to adopt all safety standards promptly—and mandating that the companies, in turn, require that their contractors and service providers comply with the new safety rules.

Because the number of offshore drilling operations subject to potential inspection is much greater than the number of nuclear sites INPO must review (although the number of exploratory rigs on the outer continental shelf is comparable to the number of nuclear plant sites), any new oil and gas industry safety institution will likely need, as a practical matter, to phase in its inspections over time. Accordingly, the safety institute will need to identify those operations that present the greatest risks because of the type of drilling (for example, deepwater or ultra-deepwater), the challenges of drilling in a particular kind of or less-well-known geologic formation, or the location of the operation in a remote frontier area where containment and response resources may be fewer.* Over time, the safety institute might move to cover more offshore operations to reduce the risk of accidents that can lead to loss of life or property, or environmental damage.

---

* Given the speed with which companies are moving into ever deeper, less well understood geologic formations, the institute will have to move quickly.

FIGURE 8.3: Schematic of the Marine Well Containment System

Courtesy of the Marine Well Containment Company LLC

Industry Responsibilities for Containment and Response

Industry's responsibilities do not end with efforts to prevent blowouts like that at the Macondo well. They extend to efforts to contain any such incidents as quickly as possible and to mitigate the harm caused by spills through effective response efforts. As described in Chapter 5, once a spill occurs, the government must be capable of taking charge of those efforts. But government depends upon the resources and expertise of private industry to contain a blown-out well and to respond to a massive subsea oil spill. Chapter 5 also explains how woefully unprepared both government and industry were to contain or respond to a deepwater well blowout like that at Macondo. All parties lacked adequate contingency planning, and neither government nor industry had invested sufficiently in research, development, and demonstration to improve containment or response technology. Notwithstanding its promises in the aftermath of *Exxon Valdez* that industry would commit significant funds to support more research and development in response technology—through the "Marine Spill Response Corporation," for example—those commitments were soon forgotten as memories dimmed.[173]

From now on, the oil and gas industry needs to combine its commitment to transform its safety culture with adequate resources for containment and response. Large-scale rescue, response, and containment capabilities need to be developed and demonstrated—including equipment, procedures, and logistics—and enabled by extensive training, including full-scale field exercises and international cooperation.

To that end, at least two industry spill containment initiatives have emerged that build on ideas and equipment that were deployed in response to the Macondo blowout and spill. The nonprofit Marine Well Containment Company, created in July 2010 by four of the five major, integrated oil and gas companies (with BP subsequently announcing its intention to join), is a significant step toward improving well containment capability in the Gulf of Mexico.[174] The four founding companies have committed $1 billion for startup costs to develop the Marine Well Containment Company's rapid-response system, which includes modular containment equipment that can be used to collect oil flowing from a blown-out deepwater well. The system is designed to mobilize within 24 hours and be operational within weeks, ready to contain spills 10,000 feet below the surface, at volumes up to 100,000 barrels per day.[175] Although many of the details surrounding the company's governance and membership structure have not yet been finalized, membership is open to all oil and gas operators in the Gulf of Mexico. Nonmembers will be able to gain access through service contracts.[176]

The second spill containment initiative is being coordinated by Helix Energy Solutions Group, which played a major role in the Macondo well containment efforts. Helix is seeking industry participation to make permanent modifications to the equipment it used in responding to the Macondo blowout and spill. It offers more modest containment capacity than the Marine Well Containment Company—less than the 100,000 barrels per day without additional investment—but at a lower cost. Although Helix maintains that it is not in competition with the Marine Well Containment Company,[177] its system appears to be attracting the interest of many of the independent oil and gas producers in the Gulf, who have expressed concerns about cost of and access to the Marine Well Containment Company.[178]

The Marine Well Containment Company and Helix spill containment proposals are promising, but they have at least two fundamental limitations. First, the systems are not designed to contain all possible catastrophic failures, only the next *Deepwater Horizon*-type spill. For instance, while both systems are designed to contain quickly the kind of blowout that happened at Macondo, they would not be able to contain a spill of the type that occurred in the Gulf of Mexico in 1979 during the Ixtoc oil spill, where the rig collapsed on top of the well. In addition, neither the Marine Well Containment Company's planned capabilities nor Helix's go past 10,000 feet despite the fact that current drilling technology extends beyond this depth.

Second, and perhaps most important, it seems that neither the Marine Well Containment Company nor the Helix system is structured to ensure the long-term ability to innovate and adapt over time to the next frontiers and technologies. What resources, if any, either initiative will dedicate to research and development going forward are unclear. The Marine Well Containment Company, in particular, could become another Marine Spill Response Corporation (as described in Chapter 5)—an industry nonprofit initiative created in response to a major oil spill that becomes underfunded and fails to innovate over time—if it does not implement specific policies and procedures to monitor and guarantee its long-term readiness as well as funding and investment levels.

The primary long-term goal of a spill containment company or consortia should be to ensure that an appropriate containment system is readily available to contain quickly spills in the Gulf of Mexico with the best available technology. Any spill containment company or consortia should ensure that it remains focused on this goal, even when doing so potentially conflicts with the short-term interests of its founding companies, in the case of Marine Well Containment Company, or the parent company, in the case of Helix. An independent advisory board, with representatives from industry, the federal government, state and local governments, and environmental groups could help keep any spill containment initiative focused on innovative, adaptive, effective spill response over the long term.

As next-generation equipment is developed, industry must ensure that its containment technology is compatible with its wells. For instance, it may be useful to consider design modifications to blowout preventer stacks that would allow for more expeditious hook-ups of injection and evacuation networks and hoses, reducing the capital costs and increasing the flexibility of the spill containment companies or consortia. Capping and containment options should also be developed in advance to contain blowouts from platform wells.

Managing Liability

The market has a financial mechanism for encouraging risk-managing behaviors: the cost of insurance. In the wake of *Deepwater Horizon* oil spill, early reports indicated that insurance premiums rose by as much as 15 to 25 percent in shallow waters and up to 50 percent for deepwater rigs.[179] An energy underwriter predicted that premiums for deepwater operations would rise 25–30 percent and by 100 percent for deepwater drilling.[180] Companies insure for many perils, and a major reinsurer has represented to the Commission that there is ample additional coverage for most risks. The significant exception is third-party liability, about which there remains considerable uncertainty.[181]

The liability cap. Under the Oil Pollution Act of 1990 (the Act), responsible parties, including the lessees of offshore facilities, are strictly liable for removal costs and certain damages resulting from a spill.[182] Compensable damages are defined in the Act.[183] Removal costs themselves are unlimited, but there is a cap on liability for damages: for offshore facilities, $75 million.[184] The cap does not apply in cases of gross negligence, violation of an applicable regulation, or acts of war, and does not limit the amount of civil or criminal fines that might be imposed for violations of federal law, such as the Clean Water Act, nor does it limit damages under state law.[185]

As it became apparent that the damages from the *Deepwater Horizon* oil spill were likely to be orders of magnitude greater than the existing cap, Congress began to consider raising that cap significantly (to as much as $10 billion) or even eliminating it altogether.[186] The arguments in favor of such a change are straightforward. The amount of potential damage caused by a major spill clearly exceeds the existing caps, and one cannot fairly assume that the responsible party causing a future spill will, like BP, have sufficient resources to fully compensate for that damage. Nor should the spill's victims or federal taxpayers have to pay the bill for industry's shortcomings. Increasing liability limits would also serve as a powerful incentive for companies to pay closer attention to safety, including investing more in technology that promotes safer operations.

Notwithstanding these arguments in favor of at least raising the liability cap, legislative efforts quickly stalled when members of Congress learned more about the potential impact on the structure of the oil and gas industry. A substantial portion of the offshore industry in the Gulf is made up of smaller, independent operators who fear that they would be unable to afford the dramatically higher insurance premiums that would result from a significant raising or elimination of the cap.[187] The concern is that lifting the liability cap immediately could have a harmful, anticompetitive impact on the independents and their thousands of employees and other commercial interests. Both large and small firms argue that the result would be detrimental, among other reasons, because the independent producers develop many smaller and end-of-life oil fields that the larger firms find uneconomic.

Apart from the handful of major companies, like BP, none in the oil and gas industry have the ability to self-insure against a major accident. But under current law, no company operating in the Gulf has had to demonstrate financial capacity to cover liabilities amounting to anything close to the cost of the BP spill—extending into the tens of billions of dollars.[188] Analysts have suggested that the insurance industry could adjust over time to the demand for capacity.[189] In fact, Munich Re announced on September 12, 2010, that it has developed a new concept for insuring offshore oil drilling, which has the potential to create coverage on the order of $10–20 billion per drilling operation.[190] Other proposals include mutual insurance funds that would pool risks.[191] The effectiveness of such mechanisms is currently unknown.[192] Congress and industry are considering a series of more nuanced measures that, while raising the cap, also seek to anticipate and mitigate the potentially adverse impact on the smaller, independent operators in the Gulf without distorting incentives to avoid accidents to begin with, or to be adequately prepared to respond to and contain spills that do occur. None of these proposals had been enacted by the end of 2010.

The Challenge of Change

Changing institutional culture and behavior is rarely easy. Business interests naturally prefer stable laws and market conditions that allow planning and investments (which can run into the billions of dollars for extensive deepwater operations in the Gulf) based on a clear understanding of what the future holds. But in the aftermath of the *Deepwater Horizon* spill, the operating environment and legal regime have been in constant flux. Beginning with a drilling moratorium, the industry has been struggling since the spring to recover from the nation's loss of trust in the safety of its operations, especially in the deepwater Gulf.

The oil and gas industry needs now to regain that trust, but doing so will require it to take bold action to make clear that business will no longer be conducted as usual in the Gulf. Industry must seize the opportunity to demonstrate that it is fully committed to subjecting its own internal operations to fundamental change and not merely because it is being forced to do so. Underscoring the sincerity and depth of their commitment to embracing a new safety culture, company leaders will need to lead the effort to guarantee that risk management improves throughout the industry to ensure that the mistakes made at the Macondo well are not repeated. And those leaders must also demonstrate an equal commitment to ensuring adequate containment and response technology and resources in case another spill happens. Only then will the oil and gas industry truly demonstrate that it is ready, willing, and able to engage in the kind of responsible offshore drilling practices upon which the nation's basic energy supplies depend.

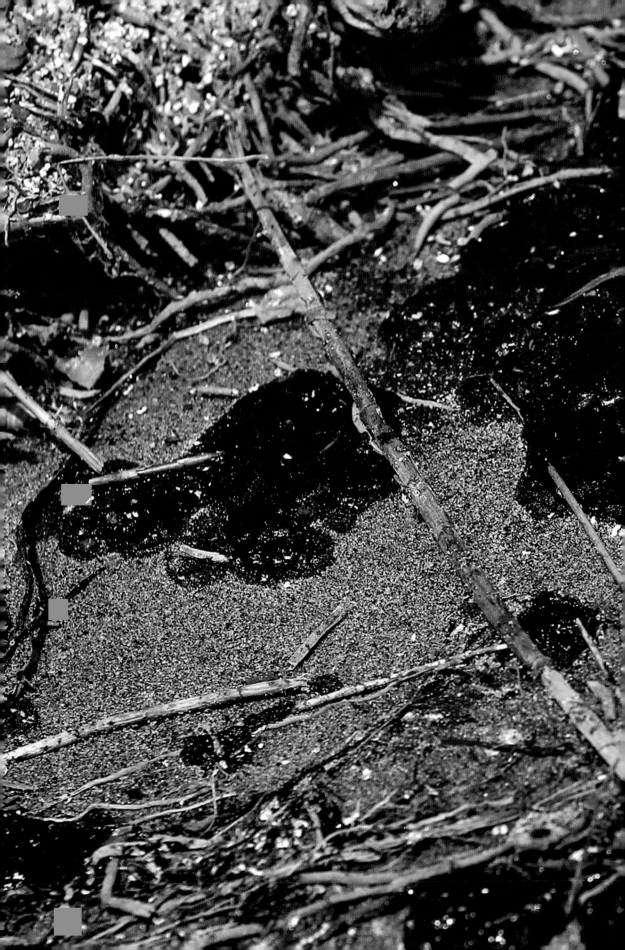

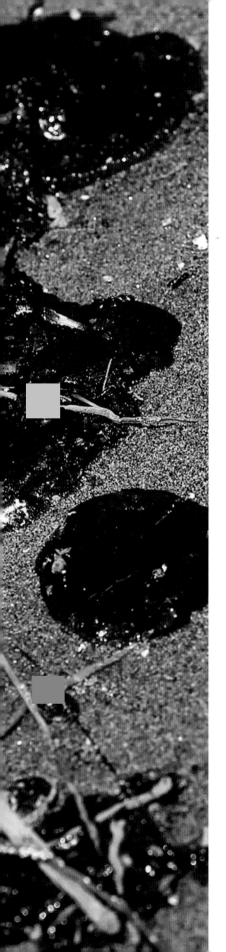

Chapter Nine

"Develop options for guarding against, and mitigating the impact of, oil spills associated with offshore drilling."

Investing in Safety, Investing in Response, Investing in the Gulf

Introduction

The President asked this Commission to "develop options for guarding against, and mitigating the impact of, oil spills associated with offshore drilling"[1] in recognition of the compelling need to balance the nation's interest in offshore energy resources with protection of our rich marine and coastal environments. To that end, previous chapters of this report have detailed the complex web of decisions, actions, and circumstances

Ugly fallout from the spill, tarballs foul a beach near Venice, Louisiana. The report sets out a broad array of recommendations for action by the federal government to better manage and protect the nation's offshore energy resources. Two overarching and convergent goals: minimize the risk of another major spill along with its economic and environmental consequences—and be prepared when it happens.

< Win McNamee/Getty Images

that set the stage for the BP *Deepwater Horizon* disaster. Among the chief actors in that web was the government itself, which played a key role both in setting the policies that shaped offshore oil and gas activities in the Gulf over the course of many decades, and in overseeing responses to the spill once it began.

This chapter presents the Commission's recommendations for addressing the causes and consequences of the spill with a focus on the government's role (recommendations targeted to industry are presented in Chapter 8). The recommendations reflect the government's sweeping sovereign authority as both owner of the seabed and water column and as the regulator of activities, with the overriding responsibility to manage and protect the valuable resources of the Outer Continental Shelf (OCS) on behalf of current and future generations of Americans. They are grouped in seven distinct areas:

A. Improving the Safety of Offshore Operations
B. Safeguarding the Environment
C. Strengthening Oil Spill Response, Planning, and Capacity
D. Advancing Well-Containment Capabilities
E. Overcoming the Impacts of the *Deepwater Horizon* Spill and Restoring the Gulf
F. Ensuring Financial Responsibility
G. Promoting Congressional Engagement to Ensure Responsible Offshore Drilling

The sections that follow summarize the context and rationale for each of the Commission's specific recommendations. Other chapters of this report, as well as staff working papers published by the Commission and available at www.oilspillcommission.gov,* provide additional detail and further support for the recommendations. Chapter 10 presents additional recommendations concerning the future of offshore drilling, including prospective drilling in the Arctic.

A. Improving the Safety of Offshore Operations

As detailed in Chapters 3 and 4, and in staff working papers, federal efforts to regulate the offshore oil and gas industry have suffered for years from cross-cutting purposes, pressure from political and industry interests, a deepening deficit of technical expertise, and severely inadequate resources available to the government agencies tasked with the leasing function and regulation. In the aftermath of the *Deepwater Horizon* oil spill, the Department of the Interior has already taken a series of significant and important steps to improve regulatory oversight of offshore drilling. But given the deep-rooted problems that had existed at the Department's Minerals Management Service (MMS) before the spill occurred, and the near certainty that the oil and gas industry will seek to expand into ever more challenging environments in the years ahead, a more comprehensive overhaul of both leasing and the regulatory policies and institutions used to oversee offshore activities is required. The necessary overhaul, to be successful, must address three core issues: (1) reducing and managing risk more effectively using strategies that can keep pace with a technologically

---

complex and rapidly evolving industry, particularly in high-risk and frontier areas; (2) assuring the independence and integrity of government institutions charged with protecting the public interest; and (3) securing the resources needed to provide a robust capability to execute the leasing function and adequate regulatory oversight.

1. The Need for a New Approach to Risk Assessment and Management

As described in Chapter 3 and staff working papers, neither the industry's nor the federal government's approaches to managing and overseeing the leasing and development of offshore resources have kept pace with rapid changes in the technology, practices, and risks associated with the different geological and ocean environments being explored and developed for oil and gas production. Nor do these approaches reflect the significant changes that have occurred in the structure of the oil and gas industry itself—especially the rise of specialized service contractors and the general trend toward outsourcing multiple functions. When the operator directly regulated by the government does not itself perform many of the activities critical to well safety, regulators face additional challenges due to the separation of these functions. However, MMS did not change its regulatory oversight to respond to these industry changes by making the service companies more accountable. In other countries, operators of drilling are required to demonstrate to the regulators their own fitness and risk management systems.

Also missing has been any systematic updating of the risk assessment and risk management tools used as the basis for regulation. MMS attempted under several administrations to promulgate regulations that would have required companies to manage all of their activities and facilities, and those of their contractors, under a documented Safety and Environmental Management System (SEMS). But, in the face of industry opposition, MMS did not adopt such a requirement until September 2010, after the BP *Deepwater Horizon* disaster. Industry objections also derailed a past MMS proposal to expand data reporting requirements as part of an effort to track and analyze offshore incidents and to identify safety trends and lagging and leading indicators. The proposal was abandoned when the Office of Management and Budget agreed with industry complaints about compliance cost (industry also complained about the potential for overlap with Coast Guard reporting requirements). As a result, there has historically been no legal requirement that industry track or report instances of uncontrolled hydrocarbon releases or "near misses"—both indicators that could point to a heightened potential for serious accidents. The United States has the highest reported rate of fatalities in offshore oil and gas drilling among its international peers, but it has the lowest reporting of injuries. This striking contrast suggests a significant under-reporting of injuries in the United States and highlights the need for better data collection to ensure needed attention to worker safety.

Government agencies that regulate offshore activity should reorient their regulatory approaches to integrate more sophisticated risk assessment and risk management practices into their oversight of energy developers operating offshore. They should shift their focus from prescriptive regulations covering only the operator to a foundation of augmented prescriptive regulations, including those relating to well design and integrity, supplemented by a proactive, risk-based performance approach that is specific to individual facilities, operations, and environments. This would be similar to the "safety case"[*] approach that is used in the North Sea, which requires the operator and drilling rig owners to assess the risks associated with a specific operation, develop a coordinated plan to manage those risks, integrate all involved contractors in a safety management system, and take responsibility for developing and managing the risk management process.

To accomplish these goals of creating a new approach to risk assessment and management, the Commission offers the following three recommendations:

Recommendations

A1: The Department of the Interior should supplement the risk-management program with prescriptive safety and pollution-prevention standards that are developed and selected in consultation with international regulatory peers and that are at least as rigorous as the leasing terms and regulatory requirements in peer oil-producing nations.

A2: The Department of the Interior should develop a proactive, risk-based performance approach specific to individual facilities, operations and environments, similar to the "safety case" approach in the North Sea.

A3: Working with the International Regulators' Forum and other organizations, Congress and the Department of the Interior should identify those drilling, production, and emergency-response standards that best protect offshore workers and the environment, and initiate new standards and revisions to fill gaps and correct deficiencies. These standards should be applied throughout the Gulf of Mexico, in the Arctic, and globally wherever the international industry operates. Standards should be updated at least every five years as under the formal review process of the International Organization for Standardization (ISO).

More specifically, the following actions are needed to truly transition to a proactive, risk-based performance approach:

- Engage a competent, independent engineering consultant to review existing regulations for adequacy and "fit for purpose" as a first step toward benchmarking U.S. regulations against the highest international standards. Following this review, develop and implement regulations for safety and environmental protection that are at least as rigorous as the regulations in peer oil-producing nations. A new regulatory entity for safety and environment (as described below) should ensure that while engaged in petroleum activities all drilling and production platforms are certified and operating at the highest level of international regulatory practice.

- Require operators to develop a comprehensive "safety case" as part of their exploration and production plans—initially for ultra-deepwater (more than 5,000

---

[*] The term "safety case" is a shorthand expression for a comprehensive and structured set of safety documentation that provides a basis for determining whether a risk management system for a specific vessel or equipment is adequately safe for a given application in a given environment.

feet) areas, areas with complex geology, and any other frontier or high-risk areas—such as the Arctic. In addition, for lease sales in those and other areas, prospective lessees should be required to demonstrate competence, based on experience, financial capacity, and expertise, as a prequalification for bidding.

• Expand Safety Environmental Management System requirements to include regular third-party audits at three- to five-year intervals and certification. These plans should be expanded for frontier areas to encompass the full range of risk assessment and management.

• For both new and transferred leases, require the operator to participate in a new safety institute or agree to expert audits, and to contribute to safety and environmental research and development. Approval to transfer leases sold prior to this requirement should be conditioned on the new requirements based on risk factors related to the specific requirements of the lease. The lease stipulation should also include the requirement that the operator possess adequate capability to contain and respond to an oil spill, and sufficient financial capacity to compensate for damages caused by a spill.

• To cultivate and maintain government expertise on offshore drilling safety:

(1) Establish a process under the auspices of the National Academy of Engineering to identify criteria for high-risk wells and develop methodology to assess those risks. This process should include, to the extent that the National Academy deems appropriate, input from experts in the U.S. Geological Survey, the Department of Energy, NOAA, and academia. Furthermore, the Department of the Interior should develop in-house competence to perform such sophisticated risk assessments. Such evaluations could guide the transition to a system where all operators and contractors are required to demonstrate an integrated, proactive, risk management approach prior to leases being granted or receiving permits for exploration wells and major development projects. As noted above, these efforts should initially focus on areas with complex geology, ultra-deep water, and any other frontier or high-risk areas—such as the Arctic.

(2) Establish a coordinated, interagency research effort to develop safer systems, equipment, and practices to prevent failures of both design and equipment in the future. The federal government has relevant expertise in areas such as the application of remote sensing and diagnostics, sensors and instrumentation, and command electronics that could and should be transferred to the offshore industry.* The Ultra-Deepwater and Unconventional Natural Gas and Other Petroleum Resources Program, an existing research and development program created by statute and managed by the Secretary of Energy, should be refocused toward mitigating the risks of offshore operations.

---

* Secretary of Energy Steven Chu advised the Commission on the capacity within the Department of Energy, the Nuclear Regulatory Commission, the Federal Aviation Administration and elsewhere in the federal government to undertake sophisticated risk and technology assessments. The Department of Energy and the national laboratories have the depth and breadth of research and technical experience in such areas as high-performance computing, image processing, mechanical/structural stress analysis, complex fluid flow simulations, and other areas that proved instrumental in diagnosing the state of the Macondo well blowout preventer and in assessing plans to stop the leak.

- Develop more detailed requirements for incident reporting and data concerning offshore incidents and "near misses." Such data collection would allow for better tracking of incidents and stronger risk assessments and analysis. In particular, such reporting should be publicly available and should apply to all offshore activities, including incidents relating to helicopters and supply vessels, regardless of whether these incidents occur on or at actual drilling rigs or production facilities. In addition, Interior, in cooperation with the International Regulators Forum, should take the lead in developing international standards for incident reporting in order to develop a consistent, global set of data regarding fatalities, injuries, hydrocarbon releases, and other accidents. Sharing information as to what went wrong in offshore operations, regardless of location, is key to avoiding such mistakes.

- Lead in the development and adoption of shared international standards, particularly in the Gulf of Mexico and the Arctic. Transparent information and data sharing within the offshore industry and among international regulators is critical to continuous improvement in standards and risk management practices. The United States shares the waters of the Gulf of Mexico and its sub-surface resources with Cuba and the Republic of Mexico. After many decades of declining investment and production in the Mexican part of the Gulf by PEMEX, the national oil company, a recent Mexican Supreme Court ruling has created the opportunity for U.S. and other foreign oil and gas companies to enter Mexican waters. PEMEX has indicated its intention to auction deepwater contracts beginning in 2012. Separately, Cuba has already leased blocks 50 miles off the coast of Florida with reported plans for seven exploration wells by 2014. Agreement on standards for operations should be part of any negotiation to define the maritime boundary between the United States, Mexico, and Cuba in the eastern Gulf of Mexico. The need for international standards for activities in the Arctic is also unquestioned: the United States has already awarded leases in the region and now it is incumbent on the United States to push for such standards.

- Provide protection for "whistleblowers" who notify authorities about lapses in safety. All offshore workers have a duty to ensure safe operating practices to prevent accidents. To ensure all workers, regardless of employer, will take appropriate action whenever necessary, Congress should amend the Outer Continental Shelf Lands Act or specific safety statutes to provide the same whistleblower protection that workers are guaranteed in other comparable settings.

2. The Need for a New, Independent Agency

As described in detail in Chapter 3, primary responsibility for regulating the offshore oil and gas industry prior to the *Deepwater Horizon* accident was consolidated in a single agency, MMS. MMS was not only responsible for offshore leasing and resource management; it also collected and disbursed revenues from offshore leasing, conducted environmental reviews, reviewed plans and issued permits, conducted audits and inspections, and enforced safety and environmental regulations. And though the revenue management and resource management functions of MMS were separated into two distinct divisions, the mingling of distinct statutory responsibilities—each of which required different skill sets and fostered different institutional cultures—led inevitably to internal tensions and a confusion of goals that weakened the agency's effectiveness and made it more susceptible to outside pressures.

At the core of this tension was a trade-off between, on the one hand, promoting the "expeditious and orderly development" of offshore resources, as mandated by the Outer Continental Lands Act of 1978, while also ensuring, on the other hand, that offshore development proceeded in a manner that protected human health, safety, and the environment. Over the course of many years, political pressure generated by a demand for lease revenues and industry pressure to expand access and expedite permit approvals and other regulatory processes often combined to push MMS toward elevating the former goal over the latter. At the same time, the fact that MMS lacked either a clearly articulated mission or adequate guidance for balancing its different missions led to inefficient management and a tendency to defer to industry, which successfully sought congressional and political intervention to shorten time frames for plan and permit reviews, blocked royalty valuation rulemakings, and advocated to delay and weaken rules aimed at improving the safety management of operations.

All of these problems were compounded by an outdated organizational structure, a chronic shortage of resources, a lack of sufficient technological expertise, and the inherent difficulty of coordinating effectively with all the other government agencies that had statutory responsibility for some aspect of offshore oil and gas activities. Besides MMS, other offices of the Department of the Interior as well as the Departments of Transportation, Commerce, Defense, and Homeland Security, and the Environmental Protection Agency (EPA) were involved in some aspect of the industry and its many-faceted facilities and operations, from workers on production platforms to pipelines, helicopters, drilling rigs, and supply vessels.

Not surprisingly, the Macondo well failure in April 2010 turned a harsh spotlight on all these bureaucratic inadequacies and shortcomings. And shortly after the accident, Interior Secretary Ken Salazar renamed MMS the Bureau of Ocean Energy Management, Regulation and Enforcement (BOEMRE) and announced a plan to split its responsibilities into three separate offices.[*]

Although the proposed reorganization of Interior's offshore leasing, safety, and revenue management program represents a significant improvement, it does not adequately address the deeper problem of fully insulating the Department's safety and environmental protection functions from the pressures to increase production and maximize lease revenues.

---

[*] The use of "BOEMRE" will be limited here to actions since MMS was renamed.

Recommendations

A4: Congress and the Department of the Interior should create an independent agency within the Department of the Interior with enforcement authority to oversee all aspects of offshore drilling safety (operational and occupational), as well as the structural and operational integrity of all offshore energy production facilities, including both oil and gas production and renewable energy production.

A5: Congress and the Department of the Interior should provide a mechanism, including the use of lease provisions for the payment of regulatory fees, for adequate, stable, and secure funding to the key regulatory agencies—Interior, Coast Guard, and NOAA—to ensure that they can perform their duties, expedite permits and reviews as needed, and hire experienced engineers, inspectors, scientists, and first responders. (See Recommendation G2.)

The roles and responsibilities of the former MMS should be separated into three entities with clearly defined statutory authorities. One entity would be responsible for offshore safety and environmental enforcement; another would perform functions related to leasing and environmental science; and the third would manage natural resource revenues. The safety and environment enforcement authority or entity, in particular, should have primary statutory responsibility for overseeing the structural and operational integrity of all offshore energy-related facilities and activities, including both oil and gas offshore drilling and renewable energy facilities.

- A new office of safety should consolidate responsibility for safety—including infrastructure and operational integrity, as well as spill prevention and response—for all offshore fossil fuel and renewable resource development activities, structures, and workers. It should be an independent agency housed at the Department of the Interior to facilitate coordination with a new office for leasing and environmental science. Congress should enact an organic act to establish its authorities and responsibilities, consolidating the various responsibilities now under the Outer Continental Shelf Lands Act, the Pipeline Safety Act, and Coast Guard authorizations. The new office should have primary authority over facilities, structures, and units for offshore oil and gas drilling, production, and renewable energy that are engaged in energy-related activities, including authority to establish and enforce specific safety and environmental protection requirements for these units as well as requirements for operators who may be leasing the facilities.

- Congress should review and consider amending where necessary the governing statutes for all agencies involved in offshore activities to be consistent with the responsibilities functionally assigned to those agencies. The safety-related responsibilities of the new offshore safety agency should be included in a separate statute. (Further specifics regarding the Commission's recommended organizational structure for new offices to regulate safety and leasing are discussed below).

- To ensure that Interior has the ability to provide adequate leasing capabilities and regulatory oversight for the increasingly complex energy-related activities being undertaken on the OCS, budgets for these new offices as well as existing agencies should come directly from fees paid by the offshore industry, akin to how fees charged to the telecommunications industry pay for the expenses of the Federal Communications Commission, which is essentially fully funded by such regulated industry payments. Through this mechanism, Congress, through legislation, and Interior, through lease provisions,[2] could expressly oblige lessees to fund the regulation necessary to allow for private industry access to the energy resources on the OCS, including renewables. Under existing law, the oil and gas industry already pays inspection fees that currently amount to about $10 million per year or about 3 percent of BOEMRE's annual budget, but this amount can and should be increased significantly. (See Recommendation G2.)

Implementing the Commission's recommendation to reorganize the former MMS into three offices and to enhance these offices' technical capacities will require a sustained effort over a period of years. The President or Interior Secretary should effect this reorganization to the extent possible administratively and request congressional enactment to confirm its permanence and provide for the statutory recognition of a term of office for the director of safety and environmental regulation.

PROPOSED REORGANIZATION OF THE FORMER MINERALS MANAGEMENT SERVICE

Offshore Safety Authority: This office would exercise independent statutory authority over technical and operational safety in all phases of OCS energy resource development projects, including the planning, designing, constructing, operating, and decommissioning of facilities and projects, and will have overall responsibility for fostering safe and environmentally sound offshore energy operations. The new agency would oversee all non-economic aspects of the operations and structures involved in drilling and production of oil and gas, pipelines, and wind towers, wave, tidal, and other renewable technologies located on the federal offshore zone. The new safety and environment authority would also have the lead coordination role in relation to other regulators with independent authority over offshore oil and gas activities, including EPA, NOAA and the Coast Guard.

Key responsibilities include:

- Reviewing and approving (or denying) all permits under exploration, development, and production plans.

- Inspecting all offshore operations by expert teams through scheduled and unannounced inspections.

- Auditing or otherwise requiring certification of operator health, safety, and environmental management systems.

- Evaluating eligibility for lessees based on safety and environmental qualifications.

- Reviewing and approving the safety and feasibility of any environmental mitigation activities prescribed by National Environmental Policy Act (NEPA) documents and other environmental consultations, authorization, or permits in addition to enforcing such requirements over the duration of an operation.

- Collecting and analyzing leading and lagging indicators from all active parties for full risk evaluation.

- Promulgating all structural integrity, process, and workplace safety rules and regulations in order to create a foundation of prescriptive regulations to supplement performance-based ("safety case") regulations.

- Providing technical review and comment on the five-year leasing program and individual lease sales.

- Providing technical review of spill response and containment plans.

- Reviewing and approving all spill response and containment plans and advising the new safety authority on environmental considerations.

- Investigating all accidents and other significant events that could have potentially turned catastrophic.

The organization and staffing composition should be decided during a transition period, when the areas and activities are analyzed and categorized by risk. The director of the new organization should be a qualified executive with a relevant engineering or technical background, and should be appointed by the President for a five- to six-year term and confirmed by the Senate. In addition, the new agency should have classifications and salary scales for engineering and technical staff and inspectors similar to those of the Nuclear Regulatory Commission.

Leasing and Environmental Science Office: This office would act as the leasing and resource manager for conventional and renewable energy and other mineral resources on the OCS. Charged with fostering environmentally responsible and efficient development of the OCS, the office would ensure that the American people both receive fair market value for the rights conveyed and that the nation's rich marine environment remains protected. The United States cannot afford a repetition of the kind of contractual drafting mistake that, as described in Chapter 3, is literally costing the nation tens of billions of dollars in lost revenues.

Key responsibilities include:

- Conducting OCS resource planning processes, including the five-year leasing program and individual lease sales.

- Conducting individual lease sales for oil, gas, and renewable energy facilities offshore.

- Promulgating rules and regulations with respect to lease terms, resource access, and use.

- Approving non-engineering or operations aspects of exploration, development, and production plans, subject to review by the new safety authority to ensure no conflicts with permitting requirements for infrastructure and operations.

- Reviewing and approving all spill response and containment plans and advising the new safety authority on environmental considerations.

- Making resource management decisions, such as those related to timing of reservoir abandonment and shared reservoir issues, unitization, commingling, and optimizing oil and gas recovery.

- Reviewing and approving permits for seismic activities.

- Conducting NEPA reviews at all relevant phases and coordinating other environmental reviews when appropriate

- Administering the Environmental Studies Program.

The leasing and environmental science office would include two distinct divisions: a leasing and resource evaluation division and an environmental science division. To provide an important and equitable voice for environmental concerns during the five-year planning process and lease awards, the environmental science division would be structured with a separate line of reporting to the Assistant Secretary overseeing offshore drilling and the environmental science division would be led by a Chief Scientist. The Chief Scientist's responsibilities would include, but not be limited to, conducting all NEPA reviews and coordinating other environmental reviews when appropriate and administering the Environmental Studies Program. The Chief Scientist's expert judgment on environmental protection concerns would be accorded significant weight in the leasing decision-making process, including on questions concerning whether and where leasing should occur and what environmental protection and mitigation conditions should be placed on leases that are issued. The new organization and process would also include enhanced review of environmental decisions and enforcement by the safety authority. It should track all mitigation efforts from NEPA documents and other environmental reviews to assist the new safety authority in its environmental enforcement duties.

Office of Natural Resources Revenue (ONRR): Revenue collection and auditing functions would remain with the Assistant Secretary for Policy, Management, and Budget as per the recent re-organization implemented by Secretary Salazar.

B. Safeguarding the Environment

The adequacy of the existing regulatory regime to assure the environmental safety of offshore drilling (as distinct from worker or occupational safety) has come under a great deal of scrutiny since the *Deepwater Horizon* incident. In its work on this question, the Commission focused on two issues: (1) the application of NEPA requirements to the offshore leasing process and (2) the need for better science and greater interagency consultation to improve decision-making concerning the management of offshore resources.

1. The Need to Revise and Strengthen NEPA Policies and Practices in the Offshore Drilling Context

The Commission has reviewed the leasing and permitting processes that MMS followed in the Gulf of Mexico before the *Deepwater Horizon* incident. The results lead the Commission to conclude that the breakdown of the environmental review process for OCS activities was systemic and that Interior's approach to the application of NEPA requirements in the offshore oil and gas context needs significant revision. In particular, the application of tiering, the use of categorical exclusions, the practice of area-wide leasing, and the failure to develop formal NEPA guidance for the agency all contributed to this breakdown.

Tiering. Under MMS, the NEPA process for offshore oil and gas leasing relied heavily on "tiering"—a practice under which a broad environmental impact statement was used to cover "general matters" across a large area, while issues specific to a particular site or smaller area were addressed through "subsequent narrower statements of environmental analyses."[3] Tiering was meant to encourage more thorough reviews at each subsequent stage of the offshore leasing process, and to avoid the duplication of general information that would have been covered in previous environmental reviews. As applied by MMS, however, tiering was not always consistent with its original purpose: instead, it created a system where deeper environmental analysis at more geographically targeted and advanced planning stages did not always take place.

Categorical Exclusions. The Council on Environmental Quality's implementing regulations for NEPA define "categorical exclusions" as "a category of actions which do not individually or cumulatively have a significant effect on the human environment . . . and for which, therefore, neither an environmental assessment nor an environmental impact statement is required."[4] MMS has historically applied categorical exclusions to both Exploration Plans and Development Operations Coordination Documents[5] in the Gulf of Mexico. Although there are legitimate differences between the Gulf and other regions of the OCS, the basis for such a wide disparity in the use of categorical exclusions is questionable. And in the aftermath of the BP *Deepwater Horizon* spill, it is difficult to argue that deepwater drilling is an activity that does not present at least some potentially significant risk of harm to the environment of the Gulf. That is no doubt why, prompted by a comprehensive review of MMS's use of categorical exclusions by the Council on Environmental Quality, Interior announced in August 2010 that it would restrict its use of categorical exclusions for offshore oil and gas development "to activities involving limited environmental risk," while it undertakes a comprehensive review of its NEPA process.[6]

Area-Wide Leasing. OCS lease sales cover such large geographic areas that meaningful NEPA review is difficult. A decision to dramatically increase the size of lease sales—known as area-wide leasing—was made over 20 years ago at the request of industry; it has necessitated environmental analyses of very large areas at the lease sale stage. For example, the Final Environmental Impact Statement for the 2007–2012 multi-lease sales in the Gulf of Mexico covered more than 87 million acres,[7] while the Final Environmental Impact Statement for Chukchi Sea Lease Sale 193 covered about 34 million acres.[8] Given that 2008 lease sales in the Central Gulf of Mexico and the Chukchi Sea attracted almost $3.7 billion and almost $2.7 billion in high bids, respectively, it is appropriate to conduct environmental reviews on a finer geographic scale before private-sector commitments of this magnitude are made to purchase leases.

NEPA Guidance. Though expected to prepare a handbook on NEPA requirements,[9] MMS never developed formal NEPA guidance. As the Government Accountability Office noted in a review of the MMS Alaska Region Office: "The lack of a comprehensive NEPA guidance handbook, combined with high staff turnover, leaves the process for meeting NEPA requirements ill-defined for the analysts charged with developing NEPA documents."[10] BOEMRE is currently in the process of developing an internal NEPA guidance document—a step that should ensure a higher level of NEPA consistency and transparency across regions.

Recommendation

B1: The Council on Environmental Quality and the Department of the Interior should revise and strengthen the NEPA policies, practices, and procedures to improve the level of environmental analysis, transparency, and consistency at all stages of the OCS planning, leasing, exploration, and development process.

Interior should take the following steps to strengthen NEPA review of the offshore leasing process:

- The new office of leasing and environmental science should, in consultation with the Council on Environmental Quality, develop and make public a formal NEPA handbook within one year. The handbook should address the issue of tiering and provide guidelines for applying NEPA in a consistent, transparent, and appropriate manner to decisions affecting OCS oil and gas activities.

- Interior should require, through this formal NEPA handbook, environmental impact statements for both the Five-Year Plan and for specific lease sales before plans for exploration, development, and production are approved in areas with complex geology, in ultra-deepwater, and in the Arctic and other frontier areas. Exploration plans and development and production plans in all other areas should be subject to NEPA review consistent with the Council on Environmental Quality's implementing regulations.

- In less well-explored areas, Interior should reduce the size of lease sales so their geographic scope allows for a meaningful analysis of potential environmental impacts and identification of areas of ecological significance. A bidder on tracts in these areas and all other areas should be able to demonstrate, in addition to financial prequalification and ability to contain a maximum-size spill, experience operating in similar environments and a record of safe, environmentally responsible operation— either in the United States or as verified by a peer regulator for another country. The distinction between the OCS and less well-explored areas in the Gulf should be defined by the new entity in charge of leasing and environmental science.

- Congress should amend the Outer Continental Shelf Lands Act to extend the 30-day deadline for approving exploration plans to 60 days. In addition, MMS should not consider such plans officially "submitted" until all of the required content, necessary environmental reviews, and other analyses are complete and adequate to provide a sound basis for decision-making. Exploration and development plans would be considered higher-level plans for purposes of agency review and approval under a reorganized regulatory structure. The office of safety and environment, separate from the office (or division) of leasing, would be responsible for permitting and approving well designs, drilling plans, and any structures.

2. The Need for Greater Interagency Consultation

Under OCSLA, it is up to the Secretary of the Interior to choose the proper balance between environmental protection and resource development. In making leasing decisions, the Secretary is required to solicit and consider suggestions from any interested agency, but he or she is not required to respond to the comments or accord them any particular weight. Similar issues arise at the individual lease sale stage and at the development and production plan stage. As a result, NOAA—the nation's ocean agency with the most expertise in marine science and the management of living marine resources—effectively has the same limited role as the general public in the decisions on selecting where and when to lease portions of the OCS. A more robust and formal interagency consultation process is needed—with the goal of identifying precise areas that should be excluded from lease sales because of their high ecological importance or sensitivity. In addition to NOAA, other federal agencies that should be involved include the U.S. Fish and Wildlife Service and EPA.

Strengthened interagency coordination on offshore oil and gas activities will also be important in implementing the final recommendations of the Interagency Ocean Policy Task Force. These recommendations, adopted by President Obama by Executive Order on July 19, 2010, mandate a new national ocean policy that includes a framework for coastal and marine spatial planning, as well as a comprehensive, adaptive, integrated, transparent, ecosystem- and science-based process for analyzing current and anticipated uses of ocean, coastal, and Great Lakes areas.[11] Coastal and marine spatial planning applies a multi-sector approach in an effort to simultaneously reduce user conflicts and environmental impacts associated with ocean and coastal activities. Integrating five-year leasing plans and associated leasing decisions with the coastal and marine spatial planning process will be an important step toward assuring the sustainable use of ocean and coastal ecosystems. It could also reduce uncertainty for industry and provide greater predictability for potential users of different areas.

To ensure that offshore oil and gas development and production proceed in ways that minimize adverse impacts to the natural and human environment, decisions about these activities must be grounded in strong science. With respect to funding the necessary science, the Outer Continental Shelf Lands Act requires Interior to study the "assessment and management of environmental impacts on the outer Continental Shelf and coastal areas that might be affected by oil and gas or other mineral developments. . . ."[12] Initiated in 1973, funding for the Environmental Studies Program at Interior peaked in 1976 at roughly $55 million, but had fallen to less than $20 million during most of the 1990s and 2000s. It was only recently increased to approximately $30 million.[13]

Future research must be conducted in a systematic way that strategically enhances understanding of the impacts of oil and gas activities and provides regulators with the timely and scale-appropriate information required for sound decisions. Long-term studies that provide critical scientific information on OCS frontier or lesser known areas,* or systematic efforts to fill data gaps in areas with existing oil and gas activity, can help ensure that the selection of new leasing areas is informed by a full understanding of potential impacts on important ecological resources. In frontier areas, it will be important to collect data on prevailing environmental conditions on a broad geographic scale, not just at individual lease sites. Additionally, post-development ecological monitoring is critical to understanding the impacts of oil and gas activities and to facilitate an adaptive approach to environmental management. Expanded coordination and cooperation on scientific research efforts with NOAA, the U.S. Geological Survey, and other agencies with relevant expertise can improve the quality of science available for OCS decision-making. Much of this research will also be relevant to other offshore activities, including the development of offshore wind resources.

Recommendations

B2: The Department of the Interior should reduce risk to the environment from OCS oil and gas activities by strengthening science and interagency consultations in the OCS oil and gas decision-making process.

---

* The term "frontier areas" include areas of the OCS that either have never been leased, or have not been leased in many years. It includes the Arctic (Beaufort and Chukchi Seas) and the Atlantic and portions of the Pacific.

B3: Congress, by enacting legislation, and the Department of the Interior, through its lease provision, should require the oil and gas industry to pay fees that support environmental science and regulatory review related to OCS oil and gas activities to enable cooperating agencies to carry out these responsibilities. (See Recommendation G2.)

Several actions are needed to implement these recommendations:

- Congress should amend the Outer Continental Shelf Lands Act to provide NOAA with a formal consultative role during the development of five-year lease plan and lease sale stages. Consultation should occur no later than 60 days in advance of final Department of the Interior decisions on lease plans and sales. Specifically, NOAA should provide comments and recommendations concerning specific geographic areas that should be excluded from the leasing program or treated in a specific manner due to their ecological sensitivity or for other reasons relevant to NOAA's ocean and coastal science expertise. Interior must adopt NOAA's recommendations unless the Department determines that doing so would be inconsistent with important national policy interests. Moreover, Interior must publish in writing its rationale for rejecting NOAA's recommendation.

- The Department of Energy, NOAA, the U.S. Geological Survey, and other interested agencies should establish a joint research program to systematically collect critical scientific data, fill research gaps, and provide comprehensive, ecosystem-based scientific reviews of OCS areas that are currently or will likely be open for oil and gas leasing, and for offshore areas being considered for the siting of sources of renewable energy such as wind power. This program should build on existing data; should aim to supplement data collected from individual lease sites by industry to develop information for broader geographic areas; and should engage the non-federal scientific community through such mechanisms as the National Oceanographic Partnership Program. The research should outline and develop the necessary data for: (1) decision-making related to future leasing, exploration, and development; (2) measuring and monitoring impacts on ecological resources; and (3) providing necessary data for natural resource damage assessment should an oil spill occur.

- The National Academy of Sciences should regularly evaluate the government's studies program in this area, preferably at five-year intervals.

- Together with NOAA, the new division of environmental science under the direction of the Chief Scientist in the Office of Leasing and Environmental Science should develop an environmental monitoring program or set of protocols to be implemented by oil and gas companies at lease sites once exploration and development and production activities begin. Areas of ecological interest and areas where data gaps exist should be targeted for monitoring programs. In addition, monitoring should be conducted in a way that is independently verifiable and allows for comparisons across individual sites. Companies should provide all monitoring data to the federal government.

- NOAA and other federal agencies with appropriate expertise should be encouraged to act as cooperating agencies in NEPA reviews of offshore energy production activities, including exploration and development plans and drilling permit applications. Federal agencies that submit comments to Interior as part of a NEPA process should receive a written response indicating how the information was applied and if it was not included, why it was not included.

C. Strengthening Oil Spill Response, Planning, and Capacity

Just as the events of April 20, 2010 exposed a regulatory regime that had not kept up with the industry it was responsible for overseeing, the events that unfolded in subsequent weeks and months made it dismayingly clear that neither BP nor the federal government was prepared to deal with a spill of the magnitude and complexity of the *Deepwater Horizon* disaster. This section discusses the Commission's recommendations in the area of oil spill response and planning. Broadly speaking they address three critical issues or gaps in the government's existing response capacity: (1) the failure to plan effectively for a large-scale, difficult-to-contain spill in the deepwater environment or potentially in the Arctic; (2) the difficulty of coordinating with state and local government officials to deliver an effective response; and (3) a lack of information and understanding concerning the efficacy of specific response measures, such as dispersants and berms.

1. The Need for Improved Oil Spill Response Planning

Oil spill response planning and analysis across the government needs to be overhauled in light of the lessons of the *Deepwater Horizon* blowout. A common interagency approach to analyzing oil spill risks and a common understanding of the issues and impacts involved are needed and must be consistently incorporated in environmental reviews, consultations, and authorizations. Environmental review and spill planning currently occurs at different levels within the government and industry, and these reviews and plans have not been sufficiently coordinated to ensure either searching review of industry plans or adequate preparation.

One of the common threads that runs through many of the environmental review documents prepared for Gulf of Mexico oil and gas activities in the years leading up to the *Deepwater Horizon* spill was their reliance on MMS oil spill risk and impact analyses. To the extent that any of these documents contained errors or incomplete information, those gaps and errors carried through to subsequent environmental reviews by other agencies.

The government's spill-response planning occurs largely outside of MMS. The National Contingency Plan, mandated by the Clean Water Act, prescribes the nationwide response structure for spills of oil or releases of hazardous substances and creates a tiered planning process. Regional Response Teams include representation from federal agencies and state governments, and develop Regional Contingency Plans as well as preauthorization protocols for certain response strategies. The Area Committees, which develop Area

Contingency Plans, similarly include federal and state representatives but are led by the Coast Guard. (The Coast Guard and EPA co-chair the regional teams.) The Area Contingency Plans are the most specific and the most relied-upon during the response to a spill.

While industry spill response plans must "be consistent with the requirements of the National Contingency Plan and Area Contingency Plans,"[14] those industry plans presently require only the approval of BOEMRE.[15] Its regulations outline what needs to be included in these plans and direct the company to include information about a worst case scenario, including how to calculate the volume of oil, determine its trajectory, and a response strategy.[16] As noted above, MMS oil spill risk and impacts modeling formed the basis of the required analysis. These response plans were not distributed to any federal agencies for review and comment outside of MMS. Additionally, only a small number of the plans developed for the Gulf were sent to the existing Office of Leasing and Environment for detailed environmental review within MMS or shared with other federal agencies with relevant expertise, such as NOAA or the Coast Guard. Finally, no provision was made for any form of public review or comment, and plans were not available to the public after they received MMS approval.

Recommendation

C1: The Department of the Interior should create a rigorous, transparent, and meaningful oil spill risk analysis and planning process for the development and implementation of better oil spill response.

Several steps are needed to implement a rigorous, transparent, and meaningful oil spill risk analysis and planning process:

- Interior should review and revise its regulations and guidance for industry oil spill response plans in light of the lessons learned from the *Deepwater Horizon* experience.

- A new process for reviewing spill response plans is needed. This process should ensure that all critical information and spill scenarios are included in the plans, including oil spill containment and control methods to ensure that operators can deliver the capabilities indicated in their response plans. In addition, the new entity within Interior that is charged with overseeing offshore safety and environmental protection will have to verify operator capability to perform according to the plans.

- Interior must ensure that adequate technical expertise exists within the staff responsible for reviewing and approving spill response plans.

- In addition to the Department of the Interior, other agencies with relevant scientific and operational expertise should play a role in evaluating spill response plans to verify that operators can conduct the response and containment operations detailed in their plans. Specifically, oil spill response plans, including source-control measures, should be subject to interagency review and approval by the Coast Guard, EPA, and NOAA. Other parts of the federal government, such as Department of Energy national laboratories that possess relevant scientific expertise, could be consulted. This would help remedy the past failure to integrate multiple area, regional, and industry response plans, by involving the agencies with primary responsibility for government spill response planning in oversight of industry planning. Plans should also be made available for a public comment period prior to final approval and response plans should be made available to the public following their approval.

- Interior should incorporate the "worst-case scenario" calculations from industry oil spill response plans into NEPA documents and other environmental analyses or reviews. This does not mean that Interior would be required to conduct a "worst-case scenario analysis" under NEPA, but it does mean that Interior would use industry's worst-case estimates for potential oil spill situations in its environmental analyses.

2. The Need for a New Approach to Handling Spills of National Significance

The Macondo well blowout caused the largest accidental oil spill in history—one that presented an unprecedented challenge to the response capability of both government and industry. Clearly, neither was adequately equipped: In fact it was quickly evident that even the response capacity indicated in industry's spill response plans did not exist. Though the National Contingency Plan permitted the government to designate the spill as one of "national significance," this designation did not trigger any procedures other than allowing the federal government to name a National Incident Commander.

The spill's magnitude calls into question whether the National Contingency Plan establishes an appropriate relationship between the federal government and the responsible party, as the public demanded in the weeks and months following the *Deepwater Horizon* spill that the government demonstrate control of the response. The responsible party that caused the spill is clearly legally responsible for containing the spill and mitigating its harmful consequences. The federal government, not the responsible party, must be in charge of those efforts. As this spill demonstrated, the government unfortunately lacked both the expertise and the capacity to oversee aspects of the response at the outset of the spill—particularly the effort to control the well. Only as the full scope of the disaster unfolded and the government gathered and focused its resources from a variety of agencies was the government ultimately able to take charge.

Recommendation

C2: EPA and the Coast Guard should establish distinct plans and procedures for responding to a "Spill of National Significance."

Under existing law, EPA is the federal agency responsible for developing a National Contingency Plan, which is the federal government's blueprint for responding to both oil spills and hazardous substances releases. In light of the *Deepwater Horizon* oil spill, EPA should amend or issue new guidance on the National Contingency Plan to add distinct plans and procedures for Spills of National Significance. In those amendments, EPA should:

- Increase government oversight of the responsible party, based on the National Contingency Plan's requirement that the government "direct" the response where a spill poses a substantial threat to public health or welfare.[17]

- Augment the National Response Team and Regional Response Team structures to establish additional frameworks for providing interagency scientific and policymaking expertise during a spill. Further, EPA, NOAA, and the Coast Guard should develop procedures to facilitate review and input from the scientific community—for example, by encouraging disclosure of underlying methodologies and data.

- Create a communications protocol that accounts for participation by high-level officials who may be less familiar with the National Contingency Plan structure and create a communications center within the National Incident Command—separate from the joint information center established in partnership with the responsible party—to help transmit consistent and complete information to the public.

3. The Need to Strengthen State and Local Involvement

The response to the *Deepwater Horizon* disaster showed that state and local elected officials had not been adequately involved in oil spill contingency planning, though career responders in state government had participated extensively in such planning. Before the *Deepwater Horizon* spill, state and local elected officials were not regular participants in Area Committee meetings or familiar with local Area Contingency Plans. The Coast Guard and Area Committee member agencies had done little to reach out to state and local elected officials. These state and local officials were more familiar with hurricane response under the Stafford Act, in which the federal government provides funding and supports state and local governments, but does not control emergency response operations. As a result, state and local political officials had incorrect expectations about their roles. They understandably wanted to be responsive to citizens who were concerned about the spill and, regardless of the official response plans, sought state and local governmental assistance.

Unfamiliarity with, and lack of trust in, the federal response manifested itself in competing state structures and attempts to control response operations that undercut the efficiency of the response overall. Federal responders improved their relationship with state and local officials as the response progressed—but had better coordination and communication existed sooner, that relationship could have been more productive in the early days of the spill response. Moreover, increased citizen involvement before a spill occurs could create better mechanisms to utilize local citizens in response efforts, provide an additional layer of review to prevent industry and government complacency, and increase public trust in response operations.

Recommendation

C3: EPA and the Coast Guard should bolster state and local involvement in oil spill contingency planning and training and create a mechanism for local involvement in spill planning and response similar to the Regional Citizens' Advisory Councils mandated by the Oil Pollution Act of 1990.

EPA and the Coast Guard, as the chair and vice-chair of the National Response Team, should issue policies and guidance for increased state and local involvement in oil spill contingency planning and training. This guidance should provide protocols to:

- Include local officials from areas at high risk for oil spills in training exercises.

- Establish liaisons between the Unified Command and affected local communities at the outset of a spill response.

- Add a local on-scene coordinator position to the Unified Command structure.

- Provide additional clarification and guidance to federal, state, and local officials on the differences between emergency response under the Stafford Act and under the National Contingency Plan.

In addition, a mechanism should be created for ongoing local involvement in spill planning and response in the Gulf. In the Oil Pollution Act of 1990, Congress mandated citizens' councils for Prince William Sound and Cook Inlet. In the Gulf, such a council should broadly represent the citizens' interests in the area, such as fishing and tourism, and possibly include representation from oil and gas workers as ex-officio, non-voting members. The citizens' group could be funded by Gulf lease holders. The Commission further recommends that federal regulators be required to consult with the council on relevant issues, that operators provide the council with access to records and other information, and that entities (either in industry or in government) declining the council's advice submit their reasons to the council in writing.

4. The Need for Increased Research and Development to Improve Spill Response

The technology available for cleaning up oil spills has improved only incrementally since 1990. Federal research and development programs in this area are underfunded: In fact, Congress has never appropriated even half the full amount authorized by the Oil Pollution Act of 1990 for oil spill research and development. In addition, the major oil companies have committed minimal resources to in-house research and development related to spill response technology. Oil spill removal organizations are underfunded in general and dedicate few if any resources to research and development. Though some commentators and industry representatives have argued that more research and development would not have allowed for a more effective spill response because no technology will ever collect more than a fraction of spilled oil, the fact is that neither industry nor government has made significant investments in improving the menu of response options or significantly improved their effectiveness. Thus any argument about the limited potential of response technology is speculative. After the *Deepwater Horizon* spill, agencies, industry, and entrepreneurs focused attention on developing new response technologies for the first time in 20 years, and a number of promising options emerged within a relatively short period of time—including beach-cleaning machines, subsea dispersant delivery systems, and new in situ burning techniques.

Recommendation

C4: Congress should provide mandatory funding for oil spill response research and development and provide incentives for private-sector research and development.

Specifically, Congress should provide mandatory funding (i.e. funding not subject to the annual appropriations process) at a level equal to or greater than the amount authorized by the Oil Pollution Act of 1990 to increase federal funding for oil spill response research by agencies such as Interior, the Coast Guard, EPA, and NOAA—including NOAA's Office of Response and Restoration. To be sure, such mandatory appropriations are rarely done, but they are not unprecedented. Congress has included such a provision when, as here, Congress seeks to target appropriations to support a discrete category of activities where Congress perceives that the need is high and the concern is great that the desired activity will otherwise go unfunded over a sustained period of time. For instance, Congress has provided for an annual mandatory appropriation of $100 million for emergency highway repairs for those damaged by natural disasters or catastrophic failures.[18] Congress also provided for mandatory funding for five years for several farm conservation programs in the Farm Security and Rural Investment Act of 2002.[19] By similarly removing oil spill research and development funding from the ordinary appropriations process, Congress can avoid the experience that followed the *Exxon Valdez* spill, when support for response research and development decreased over time. Moreover, Congress can comply with its pay-as-you-go rules by supporting increased research and development funding with a fee on offshore lessees. (See Recommendation G2.)

An advisory board, made up of experts from relevant offices of the Department of the Interior, U.S. Geological Survey, Department of Energy, EPA, and NOAA, as well as from professional societies, academia, industry, and non-governmental organizations, should be established to develop a research agenda and roadmap. In addition, to promote increased research investments by industry, the Coast Guard should revise its Effective Daily Recovery Capacity regulations to encourage the development and use of more efficient oil recovery equipment. At the same time, EPA should revise its oiled-water discharge regulations and streamline its permitting process for open-water testing. Finally, Congress and the Administration should encourage private investment in response technology more broadly, including through public-private partnerships and a tax credit for research and development in this area.

5. The Need for New Regulations to Govern the Use of Dispersants

The decision to use dispersants involves difficult tradeoffs: If dispersants are effective, less oil will reach shorelines and fragile marsh environments, but more dispersed oil will be spread throughout the water column. Prior to the *Deepwater Horizon* incident, the federal government had not adequately planned for the use of dispersants to address such a large and sustained oil spill, and did not have sufficient research on the long-term effects of dispersants and dispersed oil to guide its decision-making. Officials had to make decisions about dispersant use without important relevant information or the time to gather such information. Under the circumstances, however, the Commission believes that the National Incident Commander, Federal On-Scene Coordinators, and EPA Administrator made reasonable decisions regarding the use of dispersants at the surface and in the subsea environment.

Recommendation

C5: EPA should update and periodically review its dispersant testing protocols for product listing or pre-approval, and modify the pre-approval process to include temporal duration, spatial reach, and volume of the spill.

EPA should update its dispersant testing protocols and require more comprehensive testing prior to listing or pre-approving dispersant products. The Coast Guard and EPA, as co-chairs of the Regional Response Teams and leaders of the Area Contingency Plan drafting process, should modify pre-approvals of dispersant use under the National Contingency Plan to establish procedures for further consultation based on the temporal duration, spatial reach, or volume of the spill and volume of dispersants that responders are seeking to apply. EPA and NOAA should conduct and encourage further research on dispersants, including research on the impacts of high-volume and subsea use of dispersants, the long-term fate and effects of dispersants and dispersed oil, and the development of less toxic dispersants.

6. The Need to Re-evaluate the Use of Offshore Barrier Berms in Spill Response

Offshore barrier berms generally do not constitute a viable spill response measure for several reasons. These reasons include the time and cost of construction, and the highly variable and dynamic marine environment that limit effectiveness and pose the potential for negative environmental impacts resulting from dredging and filling. Thus, for instance, barrier berms constructed off the shores of Louisiana in response to the *Deepwater Horizon* spill could not be considered a success. Only a fraction of the project (approximately 6 percent) was completed by the time the well was capped, and no estimate of the amount of oil trapped by the berms is much more than 1,000 total barrels. In fact, the Louisiana berms project stands out as the most expensive and perhaps most controversial response measure deployed to fight the *Deepwater Horizon* spill. The decision to approve the project as one of the oil spill response techniques to be funded by the responsible party was based primarily on the demands of local and regional interests rather than on a scientific assessment of its likely efficacy.

Recommendation

C6: The Coast Guard should issue guidance to establish that offshore barrier berms and similar dredged barriers generally will not be authorized as an oil spill response measure in the National Contingency Plan or any Area Contingency Plan.

D. Advancing Well-Containment Capabilities

As described in Chapter 5, the most obvious, immediately consequential, and plainly frustrating shortcoming of the oil spill response set in motion by the events of April 20, 2010 was the simple inability—of BP, of the federal government, or of any other potential intervener—to contain the flow of oil from the damaged Macondo well. Clearly, improving the technologies and methods available to cap or control a failed well in the extreme conditions thousands of feet below the sea is critical to restoring the public's confidence that deepwater oil and gas production can continue, and even expand into new areas, in a manner that does not pose unacceptable risks of another disaster. Better technology and methods are also needed to gather accurate information in the event of an accident or failure. This section discusses the Commission's recommendations for advancing well-containment capabilities in the wake of the Macondo well blowout.

1. The Need for Government to Develop Greater Source-Control Expertise

As described in Chapter 5, at the time of the Macondo well blowout on April 20, the U.S. government was unprepared to oversee a deepwater source-control effort. Though the public expected federal authorities to take charge once the accident occurred, neither MMS nor the Coast Guard had the expertise or resources to supervise BP's well-containment efforts. Once the Secretary of Energy's science team, the U.S. Geological Survey, the national laboratories, and other sources of scientific expertise became involved, the government was able to substantively supervise BP's decision-making, forcing the company to fully consider contingencies and justify its chosen path. The government's oversight effort was assisted by outside industry experts, although their involvement also raised some concerns (about conflicts of interest, sharing of proprietary information, and potential liability for participants) that were never resolved.

Recommendation

D1: The National Response Team should develop and maintain expertise within the Federal government to oversee source-control efforts.

The National Response Team should create an interagency group—including representation from the Department of the Interior, Coast Guard, and the Department of Energy and its national laboratories—to develop and maintain expertise in source control, potentially through public-private partnerships. The proposed Ocean Energy Safety Institute at the Department of the Interior could play a role in developing such expertise.

In addition, EPA should amend the National Contingency Plan to:

- Define and institutionalize the role of federal agencies and the national laboratories that possess relevant scientific expertise in source-control.

Create a mechanism for involving outside industry experts in source-control design and oversight.

2. The Need to Strengthen Industry's Spill Preparedness

Beyond attempting to close the blowout preventer stack, no proven options for rapid source control in deepwater existed when the blowout occurred. BP's Initial Exploration Plan for the area that included the Macondo prospect identified only one response option by name: a relief well, which would take months to drill. Although BP was able to develop new source-control technologies in a compressed timeframe, the containment effort would have benefited from prior preparation and contingency planning.

Recommendation

D2: The Department of the Interior should require offshore operators to provide detailed plans for source control as part of their oil spill response plans and applications for permits to drill.

Consistent with the enhanced planning process described above in Recommendation C1, oil spill response plans should be required to include detailed plans for source control. These plans should demonstrate that an operator's containment technology is immediately deployable and effective. (BOEMRE has recently issued a Notice to Lessees requiring operators to demonstrate, as part of the spill response planning process, that they have "access to and can deploy surface and subsea containment resources that would be adequate to promptly respond to a blowout or other loss of well control."[20] In enforcing this Notice, BOEMRE must ensure that operators provide detailed descriptions of their technology and demonstrate that it is deployable and effective.)

In applications for permits to drill, the Department of the Interior should require operators to provide a specific source-control analysis for each well. The analysis must demonstrate that an operator's containment technology is compatible with the well. (The Department of the Interior could implement this requirement through amendments to existing regulations[21] or through a Notice to Lessees.[22] The latter option could be implemented more quickly, though the former might be more permanent.)

As with oil spill response plans, source-control plans should be reviewed and approved by agencies with relevant expertise, including the Department of the Interior and the Coast Guard.

3. The Need for Improved Capability to Develop Accurate Flow Rate Estimates

As described in Chapter 5, early flow rate estimates were highly variable and difficult to determine accurately. However, the understated estimates of the amount of oil spilling from the Macondo well appear to have impeded planning for and analysis of source-control efforts like the cofferdam and especially the top kill. U.S. Geological Survey Director Marcia McNutt stated that if a similar blowout occurs in the future, the government will be able to quickly and reliably estimate oil flow using the oceanographic techniques that eventually provided an accurate estimate of the flow rate from the Macondo well.[23]

Recommendation

D3: The National Response Team should develop and maintain expertise within the federal government to obtain accurate estimates of flow rate or spill volume early in a source-control effort.

The National Response Team should create an interagency group—including representation from the Department of the Interior, the Coast Guard, the national laboratories, and NOAA—to develop and maintain expertise in estimating flow rates and spill volumes, potentially through consultation with outside scientists.

In addition, EPA should amend the National Contingency Plan to create a protocol for the government to obtain accurate estimates of flow rate or spill volume from the outset of a spill. This protocol should require the responsible party to provide the government with all data necessary to estimate flow rate or spill volume.

4. The Need for a More Robust Well Design and Approval Process

Among the problems that complicated the Macondo well-containment effort was a lack of reliable diagnostic tools. The *Deepwater Horizon* blowout preventer had one pressure gauge accurate to plus or minus 400 pounds per square inch. This meant BP and the government could not get accurate pressure readings, which in turn hampered their ability to estimate the oil flow rate, undertake reservoir modeling, and plan for source control operations. In addition, the blowout preventer lacked a means of indicating whether and to what extent its rams and annular preventers had closed. Without such instruments, the government and BP expended significant resources on basic data-collection such as obtaining gamma-ray images of the blowout preventer and adding pressure sensors to the top hat after it was deployed. Meanwhile, the presence of rupture disks in the Macondo well's 16-inch casing led to concerns about well integrity that further complicated the source-control effort. BP had not considered the impact of these disks on post-blowout containment when it designed the well.[24]

Recommendation

D4: The Department of the Interior should require offshore operators
seeking its approval of proposed well design to demonstrate that:

- Well components, including blowout preventer stacks, are equipped with
  sensors or other tools to obtain accurate diagnostic information—for example,
  regarding pressures and the position of blowout preventer rams.

- Wells are designed to mitigate risks to well integrity during post-blowout
  containment efforts.

E. Overcoming the Impacts of the *Deepwater Horizon* Spill and Restoring the Gulf

As described in Chapters 6 and 7, even before the Macondo well was finally capped and
oil stopped flowing, major efforts were underway to mitigate and begin to repair the
environmental and economic harm caused by the spill. Those efforts are continuing—and
likely will for years. Nevertheless, any effort to draw lessons learned from the *Deepwater
Horizon* spill for the purpose of developing options (as the Commission's charter states) to
"guard against, and mitigate the impact of, any oil spills associated with offshore drilling
in the future" would necessarily be incomplete without an early appraisal of progress
toward longer-term restoration in the Gulf. This section describes the actions and initiatives
that have been launched to assess and overcome the impacts of the spill, and presents the
Commission's recommendations for steps that should be taken to ensure the following
three goals are met:

- The environment and the economy of the Gulf region recovers as completely and as
  quickly as possible, not only from the direct impacts of the spill, but from the decades
  of degradation that preceded it;
- The people of the Gulf are fairly compensated for the direct and indirect impacts of
  the spill; and
- Lessons learned from restoration efforts in the Gulf—including advances in scientific
  understanding, data collection, mitigation technologies and techniques, planning,
  and institutional coordination—result in enhanced capacity to remedy the impacts of
  future offshore oil spills and better manage the myriad economic, environmental, and
  social interests that must be balanced in the Gulf and other critical offshore areas.

1. The Need for Improved Understanding of Oil Spill Impacts, Particularly in the Deepwater Environment

A sophisticated understanding of the full range of impacts from a large-scale oil spill is
critical to effective recovery and restoration efforts. Because, however, the concentration
and toxicity of oil dissipate rapidly within the first few days to weeks of exposure to the
elements, the window of opportunity to collect data in the aftermath of an accident is

narrow. For this reason, advance planning and rapid response mechanisms, are essential to capitalize on research opportunities.

Independent scientists, many of who are long-time scholars of the Gulf ecosystem or have unique capabilities, were eager to study the spill and contribute to the injury assessment. However, the independent science community's ability to participate early on was hampered by a lack of timely access to the response zone. This had the effect of diminishing what was learned from the spill.

Recommendation

E1: The Coast Guard, through the Federal On-Scene Coordinator, should provide scientists with timely access to the response zone so that they can conduct independent scientific research during an oil spill response and long-term monitoring in the future.

The National Science Foundation, in consultation with the new National Ocean Council, should expand on its RAPID grant program to create a framework under which independent science during a spill can be coordinated, with an emphasis on data-sharing, communication, and timely access within the response zone. By ensuring that independent scientists can receive expedited funding after an oil spill, government will gain a more complete understanding of spill-related environmental impacts. A demonstrated commitment to independent science will also serve to bolster public confidence and trust. The rush to study the impacts of the *Deepwater Horizon* spill put a strain on existing scientific resources in the Gulf. Independent, industry, and government scientists all wrangled for funding, equipment and vessels, often duplicating efforts in the process. A program that effectively coordinates research initiatives and resources will provide a significant added value to the scientific community under exigent conditions.

2. The Need for Fair, Transparent Compensatory Restoration Based on Natural Resource Damage Assessments

As described in Chapter 6, the *Deepwater Horizon* spill caused substantial damage to natural resources and habitats across the Gulf coast and in the deepwater offshore environment. Damages to natural resources are formally assessed subject to regulations established under the Natural Resource Damage Assessment provisions of the Oil Pollution Act. The Act requires that the public be compensated for injury to and lost use of public resources. The regulation provides that compensation should be "in-place" and "in-kind" wherever possible, thereby favoring restoration measures with a connection to oil spill impacts. The *Deepwater Horizon* spill is unprecedented in that five Gulf States were affected, each with its own restoration agenda, even though most of the damage occurred in Louisiana. The damage offshore is unprecedented and unknown. The Trustees* responsible for the damage assessment are under pressure to approve projects with an "equitable" (i.e., each state

---

* The Natural Resource Damage Assessment regulation provides for the designation of affected state, federal, and tribal Trustees to conduct the damage assessment of natural resources, achieve agreement on restoration goals, and design and implement restoration projects to meet those goals. In this case, the Trustees comprise designated federal and state officials who are encouraged to work together and achieve consensus on restoration goals and projects though a Trustee Council. While the regulation supports cooperation, it does not explicitly require consensus by the Trustees. If certain Trustees disagree with the direction of the Natural Resource Damage Assessment process, they are free to break away from the Council and seek reimbursement for natural resource damages on their own.

receives an equal portion) allocation of resources that may not be entirely consonant with the "in-place, in-kind" requirement.

Another challenge for the Trustees is assessing and providing compensatory restoration for the potentially significant marine and deepwater impacts associated with this spill. Historically, most applications of the Natural Resource Damage Assessment process have focused on coastal restoration, but the Macondo well, which spilled oil 5,000 feet below the surface, may have damaged organisms in the water column or on the sea floor for which there should be compensation as well.

Recommendation

E2: The Trustees for Natural Resources should ensure that compensatory restoration under the Natural Resource Damage Assessment process is transparent and appropriate.

Restoration decisions must be transparent, appropriate, and apolitical. The Trustees should appoint an independent scientific auditor to ensure that projects are authorized on the basis of their ability to mitigate actual damages caused by the spill, with special care taken to assess and compensate poorly understood marine impacts. Further, any potential settlement agreement between the responsible party and the Trustees should provide for long-term monitoring of affected resources for a period of at least three to five years, as well as "enhancement"* beyond the baseline. By hewing closely to the "in-place" and "in-kind" principles that underpin Natural Resource Damage Assessment regulations, Trustees will help ensure that injured public resources, and the communities that rely on them, are made whole to the fullest extent possible, regardless of state and federal boundaries. A focus on ocean impacts will provide an invaluable opportunity—missed during the Ixtoc spill of 1979—to assess and remediate damage to marine ecosystems after an oil spill.

3. The Need to Address Human Health Impacts, Especially Among Response Workers and in Affected Communities

As described in Chapter 6, the National Contingency Plan overlooks the need to respond to widespread concerns about human health impacts. For smaller oil spills, the response effort is generally carried out by trained oil spill response technicians, but given the scale of the response to the *Deepwater Horizon* spill and the need to enlist thousands of previously untrained individuals to clean the waters and coastline, many response workers were not screened for pre-existing conditions. This lack of basic medical information, which could have been collected if a short medical questionnaire had been distributed, limits the ability to draw accurate conclusions regarding long-term physical health impacts. Additionally, residents of coastal communities may believe that they suffered adverse health consequences resulting from both chemical exposure from the spill itself and the mental stress occasioned by the spill's assault on their livelihoods.

---

* "Enhancement" is a term coined during settlement negotiations after the *Exxon Valdez* oil spill of 1989. It requires the responsible party to fund restoration beyond that needed merely to return injured resources to baseline conditions. Rather, any funding should be sufficient to ensure that restoration leaves the affected system better off than before a spill.

Adequate funding and resources were not in place to deal with claims of physical and mental illness among Gulf coast residents resulting from, or exacerbated by, the spill, response actions, and the resulting impacts. Whether allegations that the spill created health problems for responders and Gulf Coast residents are warranted does not change the perception among some that government has not been responsive to health concerns.

The National Contingency Plan contains no specific guidance for responding to public health impacts of an oil spill or hazardous substances release. By contrast, the National Response Framework—which provides the structure for a national response to terrorist attacks, major disasters, and other kinds of emergencies—incorporates a protocol for responding to public health exigencies.

Recommendation

E3: EPA should develop distinct plans and procedures to address human health impacts during a Spill of National Significance.

EPA should amend the National Contingency Plan to add distinct procedures to address human health impacts during a Spill of National Significance. Spills of this magnitude necessarily require a significant clean-up effort, potentially exposing workers to toxic compounds in oil and dispersants. Additionally, residents of coastal communities may suffer adverse health consequences due to both chemical exposure from the spill itself, and the mental stress occasioned by the assault on their livelihoods or way of life. With respect to worker health and safety, existing authorities[25] should be strengthened to ensure consistent application of medical screening and surveillance procedures for both formal response contractors and ad hoc citizen responders. Regarding public health, a medical services protocol similar to the Public Health and Medical Services Annex of the National Response Framework should be incorporated to ensure emergency medical care, timely dissemination of public health information,[26] and medical monitoring and surveillance.[27]

Furthermore, a public health protocol requiring the collection of adequate baseline data and long-term monitoring would allow researchers to assess the human dimensions of oil spills with greater accuracy. Without sound data on the causal or correlative relationships between chemical (i.e., oil and dispersants) exposure and human health, a number of response methods may be used inappropriately—including the provision of appropriate protective gear for cleanup workers.[28]

4. The Need to Restore Consumer Confidence

As described in Chapter 6, images of spewing oil and oiled beaches in newspapers and on television set the stage for public concern regarding the safety of Gulf seafood. Additional factors contributed to the lingering impression that the public could not trust government assurances that the seafood was safe: the unprecedented volumes of dispersants used, confusion over the flow rate and fate of the oil, frustration about the government's relationship with BP in spill cleanup, and lawsuits filed by fishermen contesting the government's assurance of seafood safety. The economic blow to the Gulf region associated with this loss of consumer confidence is sizable. BP gave Louisiana and Florida $68 million for seafood testing and marketing, as well as money to assess impacts on tourism and fund promotional activities. As of early December, BP was considering a similar request from Alabama.

In future spills, however, there is no guarantee that a responsible party will have the means or the inclination to compensate such losses. Such indirect financial harms are currently not compensable under the Oil Pollution Act. Nevertheless, losses in consumer confidence are real and Congress, federal agencies, and responsible parties should consider ways to restore consumer confidence in the aftermath of a Spill of National Significance.

Recommendation
E4: Congress, federal agencies, and responsible parties should take steps to restore consumer confidence in the aftermath of a Spill of National Significance.

5. The Need for a Long-Term Restoration Effort that Is Well Funded, Scientifically Grounded, and Responsive to Regional Needs and Public Input
As described in Chapter 7, a lack of sustained and predictable funding, together with failed project coordination and long-term planning, have resulted in incomplete and often ineffective efforts to restore the Gulf's natural environment. Currently, no funding source exists to support regional restoration efforts. Estimates of the cost of Gulf restoration vary widely, but according to testimony before the Commission, fully restoring the Gulf will require $15 billion–$20 billion, or a minimum of $500 million per year, over 30 years. While a number of different sources currently provide funding to individual states for restoration, none of these sources provides funds for Gulf-wide coastal and marine restoration and none is sufficient to support the sustained effort required. Most policymakers agree that without a reliable source of long-term funding, it will be impossible to achieve restoration in the Gulf.

Several Gulf States and the federal government have filed or are expected to file suit against BP and other companies involved in the spill, which will likely create opportunities to direct new restoration funds to the region. In some cases, congressional action will be required to ensure that funds are directed to this purpose. Meanwhile, Congress has already begun considering other potential funding sources, including a higher per-barrel tax on oil production, increased royalties or fees, and direct appropriations for Gulf-wide restoration through the normal federal budget process. Although many of these proposals face political hurdles, the fact remains that resources are needed if progress on coastal restoration is to continue. Inaction is a prescription for further degradation: since many Gulf ecosystems were already fragile and deteriorating before the spill, maintaining the status quo amounts to accepting their continued decline, with the longer-term risks and vulnerabilities this entails.

In order for funding to be most efficiently directed at long-term restoration, a decision-making body is needed that has authority to set binding priorities and criteria for project funding. The Gulf Coast Ecosystem Restoration Task Force is now in place; it was recommended by a September 2010 report on restoration from Secretary of the Navy Ray

Mabus to the President and subsequently established by Presidential Executive Order.[29] According to the language of the Executive Order, the job of the Task Force is to begin coordinating the different restoration projects being undertaken by various jurisdictions in the Gulf, coordinating related science activities, and engaging stakeholders. However, as many in Congress and the Administration have suggested, the Task Force lacks some features necessary to effectively direct long-term restoration efforts in the Gulf—most importantly the ability to set binding goals and priorities. A number of critical issues remain to be addressed, including how to allocate funding in a way that addresses the relative restoration needs of individual states; how to balance the roles and interests of the state and federal governments; how to ensure that decisions are made efficiently and quickly; how to incorporate good science without unduly slowing valuable projects; and how to incorporate meaningful public input.

Recommendations

E5: Congress should dedicate 80 percent of the Clean Water Act penalties to long-term restoration of the Gulf of Mexico.

E6: Congress and federal and state agencies should build the organizational, financial, scientific, and public outreach capacities needed to put the restoration effort on a strong footing.

The Commission's recommendations share much common ground with those outlined in Secretary Mabus's report this past September. For instance, the Commission recommends that Congress—recognizing that dedicated, sustained funding is necessary to accomplish long-term Gulf of Mexico ecosystem restoration—should direct 80 percent of Clean Water Act penalties to support implementation of a region-wide restoration strategy. Directing such payments to the Gulf could, for the next 10 years, provide significant funding. If litigation arising from the spill results in civil or criminal penalties, a global settlement of litigation should include supplemental environmental projects* and community service projects that direct payments to the Gulf. Should Clean Water Act penalties not be redirected toward Gulf ecosystem restoration, Congress should consider other mechanisms for a dedicated funding stream not subject to annual appropriations.

The Commission recommends that Congress establish a joint state-federal Gulf Coast Ecosystem Restoration Council. The structure of the *Exxon Valdez* Oil Spill Trustee Council should inform the structure of the Gulf Coast Council on the question of the relative representation of the federal and state governments on the council. The Gulf Coast Council should implement a restoration strategy for the region that is compatible with existing state restoration goals. This strategy should set short- and long-term goals with criteria for selecting projects for funding. Key criteria should include (1) national significance; (2) contribution to achieving ecosystem resilience; and (3) the extent to which national policies such as related to flood control, oil and gas development, agriculture, and navigation directly contributed to the environmental problem.

---

* "Supplemental environmental projects" are projects that a defendant agrees to undertake as part of a settlement with government of an enforcement action and that are above and beyond those necessary to comply with applicable legal requirements.

Experience in major restoration endeavors, including those in the Gulf, has shown that, absent binding goals to drive the process, restoration projects are insufficiently funded, focused, or coordinated. Establishing a region-wide council to coordinate agency activities represents a necessary first step, but without authority to set priorities and resolve conflicts, such a council will be hampered in its ability to achieve environmental goals. The Commission recommends that a region-wide council for the Gulf be given authority to set priorities that will govern the expenditure of funds and resolve any conflicts regarding eligibility of projects. The council should further define specific categories of projects that could meet each of the three criteria listed above. Projects could be categorized in a number of ways—for example, by habitat (key estuaries, sea grass, wetlands, coral reefs); by goal (biological productivity and ecosystem function, improving resilience, restoring fisheries); or by specific project type (river diversion, beach nourishment).

The Commission believes that having a comprehensive, binding strategy to guide the restoration effort is critical to success. By elaborating on the goals set by the governing entity and by providing specific milestones and restoration objectives, such a strategy would focus the overall effort and help ensure that projects are not duplicative. The strategy could also include a map that ties projects to specific places and provide a useful mechanism for public involvement. Congress should also ensure that the priorities and decisions of the Gulf Coast Council are informed by input from a Citizens Advisory Council that represents diverse stakeholders.

Finally, but essentially, restoration decisions must be rooted in science. An approach that draws heavily on information and advice from scientists will result in project selection and funding allocations that are more likely to lead to an effective region-wide restoration strategy. It will also advance transparency in decision-making and enhance credibility with the public. The Commission accordingly recommends the establishment of a Gulf Coast Ecosystem Restoration Science and Technology Program that would address these issues in three ways: 1) by creating a scientific research and analysis program, supported by the restoration fund, that is designed to support the design of scientifically sound restoration projects; 2) by creating a science panel to evaluate individual projects for technical effectiveness and consistency with the comprehensive strategy; and 3) by supporting adaptive management plans based on monitoring of outcomes scaled both to the strategy itself and to the individual projects or categories of projects included in it.

6. The Need for Better Tools to Balance Economic and Environmental Interests in the Gulf

Federal agencies charged with managing activities within the U.S. Exclusive Economic Zone have tended to work largely in isolation from one another. Responsive to the recommendations of the 2004 U.S. Commission on Ocean Policy, President Obama in June 2009 directed two dozen federal departments and agencies to provide in-depth recommendations about how federal policy can address inefficiencies in the nation's traditionally ad hoc management of its seas. The Interagency Ocean Policy Task Force reported in the summer of 2010; its recommendations were subsequently included in a Presidential Executive Order, issued on July 15, 2010, that created a new National Ocean Council to coordinate federal marine policy.

Prominent recommendations included a requirement that key regional and federal authorities develop and implement coastal and marine spatial planning, for ocean users and the public. This system is designed to optimize marine productivity. More broadly, scientific advice grounded in peer-reviewed empirical research inform strategy and decision-making in ocean management, including for energy, shipping, national defense, sustainable fisheries, and conservation.

Recommendation

E7: The appropriate federal agencies, including EPA, Interior, and NOAA, and the Trustees for Natural Resources should better balance the myriad economic and environmental interests concentrated in the Gulf region going forward. This would include improved monitoring and increased use of sophisticated tools like coastal and marine spatial planning. Many of these tools and capacities will also be important to manage areas of the OCS outside the Gulf.

The Commission recommends that as a part of management and restoration efforts in the marine environment greater attention should be given to new tools for managing ocean resources, including monitoring systems and spatial planning. Marine scientists have emerged from the *Deepwater Horizon* incident with more precise questions to investigate and a better sense of monitoring needs in the Gulf of Mexico, which because of its multiple uses and economic value should be a national priority. To that end, the National Ocean Council should work with the responsible federal agencies, industry and the scientific community to expand the Gulf of Mexico Integrated Ocean Observing System, including the installation and maintenance of an in situ network of instruments deployed on selected production platforms. Participation in this system by industry should be regarded as a reasonable part of doing business in nation's waters.

Coastal and marine spatial planning has the potential to improve overall efficiency and reduce conflicts among ocean users. Congress should fund grants for the development of regional planning bodies at the amount requested by the President in the fiscal year 2011 budget submitted to Congress. Ocean management should also include more strategically sited Marine Protected Areas, including but not limited to National Marine Sanctuaries, which can be used as "mitigation banks" to help offset harm to the marine environment. Given the economic and cultural importance of fishing in the Gulf region—and the importance of Gulf seafood to the rest of the country—scientifically valid measures, such as catch share programs, should be adopted to prevent overfishing and ensure the continuity of robust fisheries.

Marine spatial planning was designed to ensure that myriad ocean management decisions are compatible and consistent, that they make sense. In the decades since marine protection began, scientists have developed a much more robust understanding of the Gulf's physical and ecological processes. Now, for example, Marine Protected Areas can be used—and should be used—to ensure the continuity and robustness of fisheries into the future. Rationalizing ocean use around this much improved scientific understanding—for example, by identifying which parts of the ocean are appropriate (or inappropriate) for certain uses—should serve to maximize the productivity of natural systems and end inefficient or harmful practices that have accumulated over time.

F. Ensuring Financial Responsibility

As described in Chapter 6, oil spills cause a range of harms, both economic and environmental, to individuals and ecosystems. The Oil Pollution Act makes the party responsible for a spill liable for compensating those who suffered as a result of the spill—through property damage, lost profits, and other economic injuries—and for restoring injured natural resources. The Act also provides an opportunity to make claims for compensation from a dedicated Oil Spill Liability Trust Fund. The Oil Pollution Act, however, imposes limits on both the amount for which the responsible party is liable, and the amount of compensation available through the trust fund. In the case of the *Deepwater Horizon* spill, BP (a responsible party) has placed $20 billion in escrow to compensate private individuals and businesses through the independent Gulf Coast Claims Facility. But if a less well capitalized company had caused the spill, neither a multi-billion dollar compensation fund nor the funds necessary to restore injured resources, would likely have been available.

It is critical that compensation to victims be paid in full, and that the process for receiving compensation is swift and efficient. The Commission offers recommendations that would increase assurances that responsible parties are able to compensate victims (and at the same time strengthens incentives to prevent accidents in the first place), and that the Oil Spill Liability Trust Fund provide any compensation not provided by responsible parties. It also recommends a close review of the Gulf Coast Claims Facility process to determine its effectiveness in adjudicating compensation claims and its value as a model for future Spills of National Significance.

1. The Need to Increase Existing Limitations on Responsible Party Liability

Liability for damages from spills from offshore facilities is capped under the Oil Pollution Act at $75 million, unless it can be shown that the responsible party was guilty of gross negligence or willful misconduct, violated a federal safety regulation, or failed to report the incident or cooperate with removal activities, in which case there is no limit on damages (see Chapter 8). Claims up to $1 billion above the $75 million cap for certain damages can be made to, and paid out of, the Oil Spill Liability Trust Fund, which is currently supported by an 8-cent per-barrel tax on domestic and imported oil.

The Oil Pollution Act also requires responsible parties to "establish and maintain evidence of financial responsibility," generally based on a "worst-case discharge" estimate. In the case of offshore facilities, necessary financial responsibility ranges from $35 million to $150 million. The financial responsibility requirement provides a direct link between the Oil Pollution Act and insurance, as the Act provides that financial responsibility may be "established by any one, or by any combination, of the following methods" if determined by the Secretary of the Interior to be acceptable: "evidence of insurance, surety bond, guarantee, letter of credit, qualification as a self-insurer, or other evidence of financial responsibility."

There are two main problems with the current liability cap and financial responsibility dollar amounts:

- Lack of Adequate Safety Incentives: A threshold problem with any damages cap that limits liability well below levels that may actually be incurred is that such a cap distorts the incentives of industry participants to adopt cost-effective safety precautions. Decisions regarding safety precautions are made for a variety of reasons, some of which cannot be influenced by policy measures. The relatively modest liability cap and financial responsibility requirements provide little incentive for oil companies to improve safety practices.

- Inadequate Damages Compensation: BP's damages from the *Deepwater Horizon* spill will total in the tens of billions of dollars. The company has already paid claims that measure in the billions, and has waived the statutory $75 million cap. But there is no guarantee that other companies in the future will agree to waive the cap. And if an oil company with more limited financial means than BP had caused the *Deepwater Horizon* spill, that company might well have declared bankruptcy long before paying fully for all damages. In the case of a large spill, the Oil Spill Liability Trust Fund would likely not provide sufficient backup. Thus, a significant portion of the injuries caused to individuals and natural resources, as well as government response costs, could go uncompensated.

Any discussion of increasing liability caps and financial responsibility requirements must balance two competing public policy concerns: first, the goal of ensuring that the risk of major spills is minimized, and in the event of a spill, victims are fully compensated; and second, that increased caps and financial responsibility requirements to do not drive competent independent oil companies out of the market. A realistic policy solution also requires an understanding of the host of complex economic impacts that could result from increases to liability caps and financial responsibility requirements.

Recommendation

F1: Congress should significantly increase the liability cap and financial responsibility requirements for offshore facilities.

To address both the incentive and compensation concerns noted above, Congress should significantly raise the liability cap. Financial responsibility limits should also be increased, because if an oil company does not have adequate resources to pay for a spill, the application of increased liability has little effect: Should a company go bankrupt before fully compensating for a spill, its liability is effectively capped. If, however, the level of liability imposed and the level of financial responsibility required are set to levels that bear some relationship to potential damages, firms will have greater incentives to maximize prevention and minimize potential risk of oil spills[30] and also have the financial means to ensure that victims of spills do not go uncompensated.

Legislative attempts to raise the cap and financial responsibility requirements to significantly higher levels have been met with the argument that these changes will cause insurance carriers to drop oil pollution coverage, leading to an exodus of small and independent companies from the offshore drilling market. The counter-argument is that oil companies should bear the social costs of their activities, and if those costs are too large or unpredictable to be insurable, then it is appropriate that these companies exit the market.

There is legitimacy to aspects of both arguments. A company should not be able to cause billions of dollars of damage and walk away, simply because its operations contribute to the economy of the Gulf. Nor should smaller companies that can demonstrate the ability to drill safely and to pay for damages resulting from a large spill be forced out of the market. However, smaller companies that cannot demonstrate financial responsibility and meet risk requirements set and monitored by the Department of the Interior or a third party should not be allowed to make others pay for the costs of their accidents.

One option for keeping competent independents in the market is a mutual insurance pool. Under such an arrangement, individual companies engaged in offshore drilling would pay premiums into a pool, which would pay out damages caused by a company as a result of a spill. A possible downside is that the mutual pool could have the effect of undercutting incentives individual firms might otherwise have to improve safety practices—but this problem could be addressed, for example, by tying premium levels to the financial and safety risk posed by an individual company's activities. This option would allow companies to demonstrate financial responsibility for the cost of spills, at least to the limit paid out by the pool.

Another option would be to phase in increases in the liability cap and financial responsibility requirements, which would allow the insurance industry a period of adjustment. Although any increase in liability limits and financial responsibility requirements would test the capacity of the offshore drilling insurance market, over time such a change would almost certainly stimulate an increase in insurance capacity. A phased-in approach would allow Congress to re-assess any concerns about limited capacity in the insurance industry in light of actual experience.

Finally, regardless of how insurance is provided, smaller firms could be encouraged to partner with firms with greater financial resources. It should be noted that "joint ventures" between larger and smaller companies already exist; thus a policy change may not be necessary to encourage such arrangements.

2. The Need to Increase Limitations on Payments from the Oil Spill Liability Trust Fund

If liability and financial responsibility limits are not set at a level that will ensure payment of all damages for spills, then another source of funding will be required to ensure full compensation. The federal government could cover additional compensation costs, but this approach requires the taxpayer to foot the bill. Therefore, Congress should raise the Oil Spill Liability Trust Fund per-incident limit because the current limits are clearly inadequate.

Recommendation

F2: Congress should increase the limit on per-incident payouts from the Oil Spill Liability Trust Fund.

Raising the Oil Spill Liability Trust Fund's per-incident limit will require the Fund to grow through an increase of the per-barrel tax on domestic and imported oil production. An alternative would be to increase the Trust Fund through a surcharge by mandatory provisions in drilling leases triggered in the event that there are inadequate sums available in the Fund. An increase in the Oil Spill Liability Trust Fund's per-incident limit would not provide an incentive to offshore facilities to mitigate risks, because risks are pooled and the Oil Spill Liability Trust Fund is funded by parties other than those who engage in offshore drilling activities. But raising the limit would help ensure that victims have access to compensation without the need to seek further specific funding from Congress, or otherwise burdening the taxpayer.

3. The Need for Better Auditing and Monitoring of Risk

The Interior Department currently determines financial responsibility levels based on potential worst-case discharges, as required by the Oil Pollution Act. Although the agency's analysis to some degree accounts for the risk associated with individual drilling activities, it does not fully account for the range of factors that could affect the cost of a spill, and thus the level of financial responsibility that should be required. Interior should analyze a host of specific, risk-related criteria when determining financial responsibility limits applicable to a particular company, including, but not limited to: geological and environmental considerations, the applicant's experience and expertise, and applicable risk management plans. This increased scrutiny would provide an additional guard against unqualified companies entering the offshore drilling market.

Recommendation

F3: The Department of the Interior should enhance auditing and evaluation of the risk of offshore drilling activities by individual participants (operator, driller, other service companies). The Department of the Interior, insurance underwriters, or other independent entities should evaluate and monitor the risk of offshore drilling activities to promote enhanced risk management in offshore operations and to discourage unqualified companies from remaining in the market.

If liability and financial responsibility limits are raised, increased liabilities will be borne by insurance carriers, which will have a strong incentive to promote new safety techniques and methods, as well as to monitor risk. Insurance carriers might insist on certification of operators by an independent entity devoted to identifying best safety practices and monitoring risk, such as a self-policing safety organization for the oil and gas industry, as recommended in Chapter 8. Insurers or a self-policing safety organization for the industry also could provide a guard against unqualified companies entering the offshore drilling market.

4. The Need for Assessment of the Existing Claims Process

The Oil Pollution Act holds the responsible party liable for private claims brought by individuals or businesses for removal costs and certain damages. All claims must first be presented to the responsible party, but if the responsible party denies a claim, the claimant may pursue an in-court action or present an uncompensated claim for payment to the Oil Spill Liability Trust Fund. The Gulf Coast Claims Facility (Claims Facility), which is independently administered on behalf of BP (the responsible party), has established a claims processing mechanism that attempts to resolve claims against the responsible party outside of the courts.[31] Kenneth Feinberg, formerly Special Master for the September 11th Victim Compensation Fund, administers the $20 billion escrow account through the Claims Facility. Eligible claims include: (1) removal and clean-up costs; (2) physical damages to real or personal property; (3) lost profits or impairment of earning capacity; (4) loss of subsistence use of natural resources; and (5) physical injury or death. The Facility does not pay claims brought by the government, or related to real estate, the moratorium, or the Vessel of Opportunity program.[32]

To date, some claimants have been dissatisfied with decisions to deny certain claims and with the amount and timeliness of compensation received from approved claims, which has required Feinberg to reconsider the rules and processes in place for reimbursement. The United States Department of Justice sent a letter to Feinberg on September 17, 2010, urging expediency.[33] In response, the Claims Facility noted that the large number of fraudulent and undocumented claims have slowed the process.[34] Nonetheless, after the September 17 letter, Feinberg made several adjustments to the program including streamlining processing time and removing geographic proximity to the oil spill as bar against payment, Feinberg also extended the timeframe within which claimants could receive interim payments without waiving their right to pursue litigation.[35] As of December 11, 2010, the Claims Facility has paid more than $2.4 billion in claims to more than 164,000 claimants.[36] The Commission believes it would be useful to evaluate the effectiveness of the Claims Facility as a means of informing the compensation process in future large spills.

Recommendation

F4: The Department of Justice's Office of Dispute Resolution should conduct an evaluation of the Gulf Coast Claims Facility once all claims have been paid out, in order to inform claims processes in future Spills of National Significance. The evaluation should include a review of the process, the guidelines used for compensation, and the success rate for avoiding law suits.

G. Promoting Congressional Engagement to Ensure Responsible Offshore Drilling

The Commission's recommendations in this report include some directed to Congress for specific legislation, and others directed to various specific federal agencies, responsible parties, and the oil and gas industry in general. The several recommendations directed to Congress, however, also highlight a further lesson: the need for Congress to engage more systematically in ensuring the safety of drilling in the OCS and environmental protection. This includes more active congressional oversight, and also includes congressional action to ensure that those in government responsible for safety oversight and environmental protection review have the resources necessary to do their jobs. To that end, this final set of recommendations addresses the need for Congress itself to take affirmative steps to ensure responsible offshore drilling.

1. The Need for Congressional Awareness and Engagement

In the years between the *Exxon Valdez* spill and the spring of 2010, Congress, like much of the nation, appears to have developed a false sense of security about the risks of offshore oil and gas development. Congress showed its support for offshore drilling in a number of ways, but did not take any steps to mitigate the increased perils that accompany drilling in ever-deeper water. Until the *Deepwater Horizon* exploded, 11 rig workers lost their lives, and millions of barrels of oil spilled into the Gulf of Mexico, Congress had not introduced legislation to address the risks of deepwater drilling.

The congressional committee structure makes it much harder to focus on safety and environmental issues associated with offshore oil and gas development. In the 111th Congress, multiple committees in both chambers claimed jurisdiction over offshore energy development. The House Natural Resources Committee, for example, had jurisdiction over "mineral land laws and claims and entries there under" and "mineral resources of public lands." Its Subcommittee on Energy and Mineral Resources was specifically charged with oversight of "conservation and development of oil and gas resources of the Outer Continental Shelf." But the House Committee on Energy and Commerce oversaw "exploration, production, storage, supply, marketing, pricing, and regulation of energy resources, including all fossil fuels," as well "national energy policy generally." Similarly, the jurisdiction of the Senate Committee on Energy and Natural Resources included "extraction of minerals from oceans and Outer Continental Shelf lands," and its Subcommittee on Energy was responsible for oversight of "oil and natural gas regulation" generally. By contrast, the Senate Committee on Environment and Public Works claimed oversight over "environmental aspects of Outer Continental Shelf lands." Yet, during the 110th and 111th Congresses, none of the subcommittees of environment and public works claimed oversight specifically over OCS lands issues.

In neither the House nor the Senate are any of these committees charged with directly overseeing the safety and environmental impacts of offshore development, separate from the conflicting goal of resource development and royalties. The House Committee on

Education and Labor and the Senate Committee on Health, Education, Labor, and Pensions both emphasize occupational safety and health. But neither committee appears to focus on process safety—the vital approach identified by this Commission's investigation that encompasses procedures for minimizing adverse events such as effective hazard analysis, management of risk, communication, and auditing. Finally, no oversight of any of these matters has been conducted by any of the several House or Senate committees or subcommittees responsible for the nation's tax policies or overall appropriations process, notwithstanding the significant impact those policies and appropriations have on both the extent of energy industry activities on the OCS and the government's ability to oversee that activity effectively.

After the *Deepwater Horizon* explosion and resulting oil spill, numerous committees took an interest in offshore safety and environmental issues and held hearings. In short, it took a catastrophe to attract congressional attention.

Recommendation

G1: Increase and maintain congressional awareness of the risks of offshore drilling in two ways. First, create additional congressional oversight of offshore safety and environmental risks. Second, require the appropriate congressional committees to hold an annual oversight hearing on the state of technology, application of process safety, and environmental protection to ensure these issues receive continuing congressional attention.

- The House and Senate Rules Committee should each assign a specific committee or subcommittee to oversee process safety and environmental issues related to offshore energy development. These committees should also be given the task of overseeing the Offshore Safety Authority, the creation of which this Commission has separately recommended.

- Congress should require the Secretary of the Interior to submit an annual public report on energy offshore development activities to the applicable congressional committees. This report should focus on the Department's progress in improving its prescriptive safety regulations; steps taken by industry and the Department to improve facility management; the Department's progress in implementing a stronger environmental assessment program, including developing improved NEPA guidelines; and on any other steps taken by industry or the Department to address safety and environmental concerns offshore. The report should also detail the industry's safety and environmental record during the previous 12 months. Finally, the report should highlight any areas in which the Department believes industry is not doing all that it can to promote safety and the environment and any areas where additional legislation could be helpful to the Department's efforts.

- Congress should require the Department of the Interior's Office of Inspector General to submit an independent annual public report to the applicable congressional committees. The report should provide an independent description of the Offshore

Safety Authority's activities over the previous 12 months, including its efforts to improve offshore safety and to investigate accidents and other significant offshore incidents. The report should also include the Inspector General's evaluation of the Authority's efforts and the Inspector General's recommendations for improvement.

2. The Need for Adequate Funding for Safety Oversight and Environmental Review

Many of the earlier recommendations require adequate congressional funding in order to be implemented effectively. For instance, the new Offshore Safety Authority at Interior cannot be expected to succeed in meaningfully overseeing the oil and gas industry if Congress does not ensure it has the resources to do so. Agencies cannot conduct the scientific and environmental research necessary to evaluate impacts of offshore development if they do not receive adequate support from Congress. In short, Congress needs to make funding the agencies regulating offshore oil and gas development a priority in order to ensure a safer and more environmentally responsible industry in the future.

BOEMRE currently receives a portion of its funding from offsetting collections from industry. In its Fiscal Year 2011 Budget Justification, it requested that just less than half of its budget—$174.9 million—come from these collections.[37] The oil and gas industry, however, should do significantly more and provide the funds necessary for regulation of offshore oil and gas operations and oil spill preparedness planning. The amount of funding needs to keep pace as industry moves into ever-more challenging depths and geologic formations because the related challenges of regulatory oversight likewise increase. This could be accomplished many different ways. Congress could, for instance, raise the inspection fees already imposed on facilities operating on the OCS—currently offsetting about three percent of BOEMRE's annual budget—or impose a differently based annual regulatory fee on new and existing leases. Or Congress could instruct the Department of the Interior to include lease provisions that require the imposition of regulatory fees. Interior already possesses broad authority to include in leases "such rental and other provisions as the Secretary may prescribe at the time of offering the area for lease."[38] No matter the precise mechanism, the oil and gas industry would be required to pay for its regulators, just as fees on the telecommunications industry support the Federal Communications Commission. Regulation of the oil and gas industry would no longer be funded by taxpayers but instead by the industry that is being permitted to have access to a publicly-owned resource. Future Congresses would therefore have less incentive to reduce agency funding.

Recommendation

G2: Congress should enact legislation creating a mechanism for offshore oil and gas operators to provide ongoing and regular funding of the agencies regulating offshore oil and gas development.

The President asked this Commission to recommend not only "improvements to Federal laws, regulations, and industry practices applicable to offshore drilling," but also "organizational or other reforms of Federal agencies or processes necessary to ensure such improvements are implemented and maintained." In carrying out this charge, the Commission has been mindful of the dangers of "fighting the last war": that is, addressing the specific failures revealed by the *Deepwater Horizon* disaster, but neglecting to anticipate future problems whose contours are yet unknown. Our recommendations—for a new approach to risk assessment and management; a new, independent agency responsible for safety and environmental review of offshore drilling; stronger environmental review and enforcement; a reorientation of spill response and containment planning; and a revision of liability rules to better protect victims and provide proper incentives to industry—aim to establish an oversight regime that is sufficiently strong, expert, well-resourced, and flexible to prevent the next disaster, not the last. The oil and gas industry—remarkable for its technological innovation and productivity—needs government oversight and regulation that can keep pace.

Chapter Ten

American Energy Policy and the Future of Offshore Drilling

Introduction

The BP *Deepwater Horizon* disaster undermined public faith in the oil and gas industry, in government regulators, and even in America's ability to respond to crises. The disaster raised serious questions about our nation's ability to manage and protect for current and future generations the invaluable natural resources of the outer continental shelf and the multiple uses they sustain—the patrimony of all Americans. Based on the Commission's thorough and vigorous accounting of this tragedy, the central lesson to be drawn from the catastrophe is that no less than an overhauling of both current industry practices and government oversight is now required. The changes necessary will be transformative in their depth and breadth, requiring an unbending commitment to safety by government and industry to displace a culture of complacency. Drilling in deepwater does not have to be abandoned. It can be done safely. That is one of the central messages of this report. The reforms proposed herein are intended to do for this industry what new policies and practices have done for other high-risk industries after their disasters.

It was clear sailing for a fleet of oil rigs off Louisiana in April 2009. The *Deepwater Horizon* disaster a year later was a tragic wake-up call. Moving forward, offshore drilling in the Gulf of Mexico or in new U.S. frontiers will require, in the words of the report, "unbending commitment to safety by government and industry."

< *Benjamin Lowy/VII Network/Associated Press*

The potential for such a transformation to ensure productive, safe, and responsible offshore drilling is significant, and provides reason for optimism even in the wake of a disaster.

The significance of the *Deepwater Horizon* disaster, however, is broader than just its relevance to the future of offshore drilling. The disaster signals the need to consider the broader context of the nation's patterns of energy production and use, now and in the future—the elements of America's energy policy. The explosion at the Macondo well and the ensuing enormous spill—particularly jarring events because of the belief they could never happen—force a reexamination of many widely held assumptions about how to reconcile the risks and benefits of offshore drilling, and a candid reassessment of the nation's policies for the development of a valuable resource. They also support a broader reexamination of the nation's overall energy policy.

Offshore oil and gas will continue to be an important part of the nation's domestic energy supply for many decades. Offshore wells yield one-third of current U.S. oil production,[1] and in recent decades helped offset declines in production elsewhere in the United States (U.S. production peaked in 1970).[2] That already-crucial role is likely to increase. The area of federal jurisdiction, the outer continental shelf, contains an estimated 85 billion barrels of oil in technically recoverable resources[3] —more than all onshore resources and those in the shallower state waters *combined*.[4] The future of domestic oil production will rely to a substantial extent on current outer continental shelf sources and further development of deposits there—in progressively deeper, more distant waters, and perhaps in such challenging environs as the Alaskan Arctic. Whether we explore for and produce oil and gas from those prospective reserves, and if so, under what conditions, depends crucially on taking to heart the lessons we learn from the *Deepwater Horizon* disaster and the energy policies we put in place.

Important decisions about whether, when, where, and how to engage in offshore drilling cannot be made wisely if they are made in a vacuum. Policies about offshore drilling should be powerfully shaped by economic, security, pace of technology, safety, and environmental concerns. Offshore drilling will certainly be an important part of any national energy policy. But it is only a part of the picture, and its relative importance today will not, and should not, be the same a half-century from now. The nation must begin a transition to a cleaner, more energy-efficient future. Nonrenewable oil and gas resources are just that—nonrenewable—which means any nation forging an energy policy for the future must develop the technologies that provide maximum energy efficiency and create renewable substitutes. Otherwise, the nation's security and well-being will be increasingly dependent on diminishing supplies of nonrenewable resources, and even more dependent on supplies from foreign sources.

Domestic consumption of oil has exceeded domestic production since the late 1940s, making the country increasingly dependent on imports, which now supply about 52 percent of U.S. needs compared to 42 percent in 1990. In the near term, oil from federal offshore lands helps moderate America's dependence on imported supplies, lessening the current trade deficit and contributing to national security.

The government also reaps significant revenues from the leasing of federal lands and the collection of royalties on production—typically, billions of dollars per year. The development of offshore energy resources contributes substantially to local economies, supporting businesses small and large and employing tens of thousands of workers. But any sensible energy policy must recognize the substantial risks that accompany these real benefits, in addition to the dangers of an economy and national security dependent on nonrenewable energy supplies. The impressive technologies developed for offshore drilling and production have not been accompanied by comparable improvements in safety and environmental protection. As Americans now know, three major companies failed to apply rigorous process safety measures to their drilling operations in the Gulf of Mexico: Halliburton and Transocean, which service drilling operations throughout the Gulf, along with BP —underscoring the systemic nature of the offshore industry's problems.

This Commission has documented and explained these tragic failures, and in this report has recommended a comprehensive, integrated set of reforms required to improve the performance of the offshore oil and gas industry, as appropriately overseen by an effective regulatory authority. A safe offshore oil and gas industry matters—both because the costs of needlessly risky behavior are so high, and because the nation is so dependent on offshore energy supplies. In light of present knowledge, inaction is a policy of dangerous default—of continuing to rely on chance and luck to avoid a "next time." American citizens will demand and will hold the oil and gas industry and government officials responsible for creating the conditions under which a robust offshore oil and gas industry can operate safely and co-exist with human health, environmental protection, and other economic activities.

Weighing National Security, the Economy, Human Safety, and the Environment

In contemporary America, petroleum is woven into every aspect of our lives. The continuous availability of oil products—gasoline, diesel, and jet fuel—powers the mobility that has become key to a strong economy. Military operations, the movement of food and other commercial products, and personal travel would all grind to a halt without oil—at least as our society is organized today. Yet growing demand for oil around the world, particularly in the huge and rapidly developing economies of Asia, ensures heightened competition for supplies, putting upward pressure on oil prices. That poses a long-term challenge for the United States, which is not and cannot be self-sufficient in oil supply. At the same time, scientific evidence has continued to mount on the interconnections among the use of all carbon-based fuels, including oil and natural gas, the growing concentrations of greenhouse gases, and global climate change.[5]   Energy policy thus embraces considerations of national security, the economy, environmental protection, the need to limit climate change, the pace of development of renewable energy sources and nonpetroleum dependent vehicles, human health and safety, and unique regional conditions.

Security and petroleum resources. The major American security risk derives from oil's predominant role in transportation: 72 percent of oil consumed in the United States in 2009 was used for transportation—and 94 percent of transportation relied on oil.[6]   As the National Academy of Sciences recently concluded, the nation "needs to lower its dependence on fragile supply chains for some energy sources, particularly petroleum at present and possibly natural gas in the future, and to avoid the impacts of this dependence on our nation's economy and national security."[7] The good news is that energy-efficient technologies exist today that can in the near term moderate the nation's demand for oil and change the mix of supplies of electricity and energy over time. But changing existing reliance on oil in general and oil imports in particular will require a major overhaul of our energy and transportation systems, a challenging shift that would require strong public leadership, and would take decades to effect even if we agreed on the course of action tomorrow.

Recent events have made clear the magnitude of the stakes. The United States has repeatedly been surprised by sudden interruptions in the oil supply from various unexpected events—underscoring the nation's potential vulnerability. These include politically motivated production cuts by oil-exporting countries (the oil embargo of 1973-1974); border wars between oil exporters (between Iraq and Iran in 1980-1988, and Iraq and Kuwait in 1990-1991); strife and unrest within several oil-exporting countries; and severe weather events affecting offshore oil production or coastal refineries (Hurricanes Katrina and Rita in 2005 and Ike in 2008—all in the Gulf of Mexico). Energy planners also worry about the possibility that the Straits of Hormuz—the only sea passage to the open ocean for the bulk of Persian Gulf petroleum exports—could be closed, or that a major oil pipeline somewhere in the world could be ruptured by accident or attack.

Even absent an actual interruption in supplies, our reliance on foreign oil is a national security concern. Hostile exporting nations can use the threat of interrupting supplies to pressure the United States. Money spent on foreign oil can also end up in the hands of terrorists or be used to build nuclear or develop biological weapons in nations flouting the international atomic and biological regulatory regimes. The ultimate nightmare would be an America depleted of petroleum, which has failed to make a sufficient transition to alternative sources, facing another Pearl Harbor or the aftershocks of 9/11.

Since "Colonel" Drake first struck oil at his Pennsylvania site in 1859, the United States has already extracted over 200 billion barrels of oil from its territory[8]—more than our estimated remaining reserves. The United States did not relinquish its position as the world's leading producer until 1974[9]—but now it finds itself credited with only 1.4 percent of the world's proved oil reserves, while consuming 22 percent of the global supply annually.[10] (The use of advanced extraction technologies and a relatively favorable investment climate have enabled the United States to remain the world's third-largest oil producer, despite its relatively meager reserves.)

Would the country's security interests be better served by developing domestic oil resources as rapidly as possible—or by reserving some for future generations? President Harry Truman argued that federal offshore oil resources should become part of the naval petroleum reserve system, leaving the oil in the ground for later development (see Chapter 3). In recent decades, the concept of the Naval Petroleum Reserve has been superseded by a more readily accessible Strategic Petroleum Reserve, which currently contains more than 700 million barrels of unrefined crude oil stored in Louisiana and Texas salt caverns along the Gulf coast where it is available for national emergencies (such as sudden disruptions of supply).[11] That provides some insurance—but only about 75 days of supply at the current rate of U.S. imports, and clearly not sufficient to displace any long-term decline in domestic production or respond to a spike in demand. The United States has kept some areas of the outer continental shelf off-limits for oil and gas production: to protect their unique and valuable environmental characteristics, to avoid incurring risks to major industries such as fishing and tourism, or to maintain open waters for testing of military armaments and training exercises over the Gulf. One way of viewing these areas where drilling is prohibited—Atlantic Coast, Eastern Gulf of Mexico and Florida coast and the coasts of Northern California, Oregon, and Washington—is as energy sources held in reserve.

National economic implications. The domestic oil and gas sector is a major employer, particularly in fuel-producing regions. Fluctuations in oil and gas prices generally pass quickly through to energy-intensive sectors of the economy: trucking, airlines, agriculture, and petrochemicals such as plastics. Although energy's share of the economy has diminished in recent decades, Americans paid $740 billion for oil and gas products in 2007,[12] and energy prices still have a major impact on inflation. Because oil and gas behave and are traded as commodities, their prices can undergo large changes even apart from immediate supply and demand factors. This volatility, from all sources, can make it difficult for businesses and individuals to plan and adhere to their budgets for energy costs. Price jolts stemming from undependable supplies can have major, adverse effects on the whole economy. Economists Hillard Huntington and Stephen Brown have found that "Historical experience shows that the Gross Domestic Product (GDP) losses associated with oil supply shocks can be considerable."[13] Most strikingly, they noted that 10 of the 11 U.S. recessions since World War II were preceded by sharply rising oil prices.

Given Americans' consumption of petroleum products in excess of domestic supply, the country runs a staggering trade imbalance. Between 2004 and 2009, the U.S. trade balance for oil and gas ranged between negative $186 billion and negative $414 billion per year—typically exceeding the much-publicized trade deficit with China.[14] Economic theories of comparative advantage may suggest that particular trade deficits are not worrisome—but the large, sustained trade deficit incurred to import petroleum, particularly, makes energy a significant factor in America's overall trade, deficit, and financing strategies and challenges.

Environmental and safety challenges. This report has documented in painful detail the far-reaching environmental consequences of catastrophic accidents involving the extraction of oil from offshore sources, and the associated risks to workers' safety from drilling, refinery operations, and the emergency clean-up of spills. Further environmental damage occurs when oil products are used as transportation fuels. Emissions released when fuel is burned are generally controlled under federal law, but can still (in combination with emissions from combustion to generate electricity) create conditions that can cause serious health consequences for the American public and serious ecological consequences for our natural systems, forests, and waters. And the combustion of all fossil-based carbon fuels (oil, gas, and coal) has long-term impacts on the increasing volume of greenhouse gases in the atmosphere and the warming climate. Transportation fuels contribute one-third of U.S.

carbon emissions, making them the nation's second-largest source contributing to climate change.

Criteria for balanced energy policy. Reconciling the multiple, sometimes conflicting aims that underlie any transportation-related American petroleum energy policy depends on six criteria:

- Maintaining a sufficient reserve of petroleum to protect American national security should access to foreign sources be lost or become unreliable;
- Requiring energy-efficient automobiles and other vehicles (among other sources of consumption) to reduce fuel use, and promoting energy-efficient transit alternatives;
- Promoting the development of clean and domestically produced alternative fuels or sources of power for transportation;
- Managing the inherent risks of domestic production of oil and gas—including from offshore areas—while considering the short- *and* long-term availability of these fuels;
- Requiring safe operations to protect human health; and
- Protecting the natural environment, including steps to limit climate change.

Reasonable people can disagree about the relative importance of these criteria—and have over time. President Truman ordered a postponement of mineral development on the outer continental shelf in order to ensure oil and gas would be there later for strategic purposes. During the 1970s, Congress adopted legislation to maximize environmental protection, and then to expand energy production (as discussed in Chapter 3)—but over the long term, none can be pursued to the exclusion of the others. It is notable, moreover, that various policies *have* had significant effects on U.S. energy use and production. For example, the country has achieved intermittent but sizable increases in automobiles' fuel efficiency; major reductions in tailpipe emissions from gasoline-fueled vehicles; and less reliance on oil to generate electricity.[15] At several points during the past four decades, consumption of oil in the United States actually *declined* for several years (in some cases reflecting adverse economic conditions, and in others successful public policies and adoption of technological advances).[16]

The United States today pursues many discrete policies bearing on all of these issues: vehicle-fuel efficiency standards, subsidies for ethanol production for fuel, research into alternative fuels, varying incentives for production of electricity by wind and solar power, and so on. In the aggregate, they are, de facto, the nation's energy policy. But they do not constitute a comprehensive, coherent strategy—such as recently called for by both the National Research Council[17] and the President's Council of Advisors on Science and Technology[18]—one that encompasses *all* of these elements, identifies tradeoffs and priorities, and implements them through incentives, investments in research and development, regulations, and tax policy. Difficult though it may be to arrive at such a consensus, it would provide guidance on balancing the risks and rewards of oil and gas development in especially challenging or sensitive locations, offshore or elsewhere. It is possible—and imperative—to manage that balance over time for offshore development of oil and gas as part of that overall policy.

Learning from the Macondo Disaster: The Gulf of Mexico

This report describes in great detail what went wrong on the *Deepwater Horizon* and in the drilling of the Macondo well, and the well blowout's staggering cost. As the nation considers exploring for and producing energy from offshore frontiers, we have a new opportunity to do things right. Some of those frontiers are in deeper waters or unexplored areas of the Gulf of Mexico. Others are at the far extreme of the country, in both distance and climate in Alaska.

Improving safety and environmental integrity immediately. It will take several years to fully implement the stringent new safety regime this Commission has recommended—essential changes from doing business as usual in the Gulf of Mexico. But it is not necessary to put deepwater drilling on hold until all the changes are in place. The national and regional energy and economic imperatives can be reconciled effectively with the equally urgent needs to assure human safety and environmental integrity in the Gulf context, now and in the long term.

Several benchmarks must be met for exploratory drilling to resume on existing leases, and for operations to begin on new ones. Operators must assure that better practices for maintaining well integrity and the isolation of hydrocarbons are used at all times. And they must insist upon heightened vigilance throughout all the steps from the inception of well design to the consideration of changes during drilling operations. Similarly, protocols for testing of blowout preventers must be put in place and enforced. The industry must also demonstrate that it is deploying readily available and effective systems for containment and response.

As the energy industry works to satisfy these requirements, the Department of the Interior must work promptly to reorganize its divisions, augment its regulatory staff, and enhance their skill. The American public has every reason to insist that Congress provide regulators with adequate resources to do their vital job—and that the industry apply its resources and expertise to improving practices. Both must focus on the substantial challenges of making offshore drilling safe, reliable, and productive. The circumstances demand a shared commitment by government and industry to work for immediate and long-term reforms that allow deepwater exploratory drilling to resume quickly and safely. And, to that end, industry should be ready to pay fees as part of their lease agreements in order to ensure that government overseers have the resources required to get the job done in a rigorous and timely fashion.

Emerging challenges from ultra-deepwater drilling. That shared commitment must extend beyond current conditions. While correcting the many problems revealed at the Macondo well, both industry and government must anticipate and adjust to new challenges arising in the Gulf. Current technology enables drilling in water *twice as deep* as Macondo. Drilling at such depths requires all parties to set their standards still higher for difficult issues such as remote containment systems in water depths with extreme pressures and very limited human access, as well as different geological pressures and formations and mixes of hydrocarbons. Desire to tap resources in deeper waters should be accompanied by equivalent investments in subsea equipment, operator training, research and development for containment and response technologies, demonstrated financial capacity, and continuous improvement in and communication of industry practices devoted to safety.

The emerging international challenge. Drilling for oil in the Gulf of Mexico is not solely a matter for U.S. consideration. Both Mexico and Cuba have expressed interest in deepwater drilling in the Gulf in the near future. Pemex, Mexico's state-owned petroleum company, and Cuba, through both the Spanish company Repsol and the large Russian oil and gas production company Gazprom, in which the Russian government maintains a controlling stake,[19] have either actually drilled exploratory and production wells or are likely soon to do so.[20] Potential drilling sites are close enough to waters and land within U.S. jurisdiction—Cuba's mainland lies only 90 miles from Florida's coast and the contemplated wells only 50 miles—that if an accident like the *Deepwater Horizon* spill occurs, fisheries, coastal tourism, and other valuable U.S. natural resources could be put at great risk.

It is in our country's national interest to negotiate now with these near neighbors to agree on a common, rigorous set of standards, a system for regulatory oversight, and the same operator adherence to the effective safety culture called for in this report, along with protocols to cooperate on containment and response strategies and preparedness in case of a spill. Though some precedent exists for a direct agreement between the United States and Cuba, Mexico may prove an important partner in developing such an agreement covering the entire Gulf of Mexico. In any event, the U.S. objectives should be to prevent drilling by companies unwilling or unprepared to meet the high safety standards essential to extracting oil and gas resources responsibly and to have a verification process to ensure compliance.

Beyond the Gulf of Mexico: Frontier Regions

The nation's demand for domestic oil production will push the boundaries of technology and geography. The industry will develop new exploration and extraction techniques and equipment in new areas in the decades ahead. Drilling safely in the Gulf of Mexico requires a new industry safety culture and significantly improved regulatory oversight. Those reforms, and further heightened vigilance, will be required for oil exploration and production in frontier offshore regions. When the Macondo blowout dumped enormous volumes of oil into the Gulf waters, scientists and policymakers realized how little was known about biological systems, environmental conditions, and even key aquatic and coastal species. Leasing of vast acreage combined with weak policies and limited funding had resulted in inadequate studies of unique habitats and sensitive environmental features where greater caution should be exercised. What information was available was often not shared, or was disregarded, in leasing and permitting decisions. And little, if any, research or policy existed to address human health impacts and the risks to responders from a major spill, or the far-reaching effects of such a disaster on other businesses dependent on the region's resources.

In addition to these challenges, each frontier area presents important differences in implementing any drilling program—different geologies, hydrocarbon formations, coastal communities and environments, and climate conditions, to mention some. Federal waters of the United States other than the central and western Gulf of Mexico, parts of

Southern California, and the Lower Cook Inlet in Alaska would be regarded as frontier territory. In the late 1970s, attention turned briefly to areas off of northern California and Massachusetts (Georges Banks), and in the early 1980s, the potential of the outer continental shelf off Alaska attracted considerable investment (see Chapter 2). In recent years, the focus has turned to exploring in the Atlantic Ocean off the state of Virginia; in the eastern Gulf of Mexico; and, most notably, to taking another serious look at offshore regions in the Alaskan Arctic. Drilling water depths of 10,000 feet or more anywhere in the Gulf of Mexico might also be considered opening a new frontier, given the new technologies required.

In March 2010, President Obama and Interior Secretary Ken Salazar announced a plan to open the eastern Gulf and parts of the Atlantic coast—including offshore Virginia—to oil and gas exploration (subject to studies of the suitability of doing so in each area, and to the lifting of a congressional moratorium restricting drilling in the eastern Gulf). But on December 1, in the wake of the *Deepwater Horizon* experience and the resulting broad restructuring of regulations and the federal oversight capabilities, Secretary Salazar announced that the Administration would not proceed with drilling in areas where there are "no active leases" during the next five-year leasing plan. As a result, exploration and production in certain frontier areas—the eastern Gulf and off of the Atlantic and Pacific coasts—are deferred. The Secretary also indicated that plans for 2011 drilling in Alaska's Beaufort Sea would be subjected to additional environmental assessments. There will consequently be a continuing examination of the various stages of drilling, if pursued, consistent with national energy policy and with a full awareness of the risks and of the values that must be balanced in each region, and with assurance that operators rigorously adhere to the best practices of a functioning safety culture.

By their very location and nature, these frontier areas differ from the Gulf of Mexico and in important respects from each other. Environmental and biological conditions are at least as well understood along the Atlantic coast as in the Gulf—and there are also important facilities, such as Coast Guard installations in place; in contrast, equivalently detailed geological and environmental information does not exist for the Arctic exploration areas of greatest interest for energy exploration—and industry and support infrastructures are least developed, or absent, there. In the near term, the Alaskan frontier is likely to attract the greatest attention, and to require the closest scrutiny, given the potential energy resources and the physical and environmental challenges of pursuing them safely.

Large prospects in offshore Alaska. The interest in offshore Alaska reflects the likelihood of finding significant new sources of oil:[21] the Chukchi and Beaufort Sea areas off Alaska's north coast rank behind only the Gulf of Mexico in estimated domestic resources.[22] The most recent federal lease sales for the Beaufort Sea, from 2003 to 2008, netted $98 million, reflecting high levels of industry interest. And despite its remoteness and harsh conditions, the Chukchi Sea—with vast potential resources—attracted over $2.6 billion in high bids for almost 2.8 million acres, including $2.1 billion from Shell Oil Company, during a 2008 lease sale.[23]

If deemed feasible, new offshore Alaskan oil production may be well-timed to offset the sustained decline in output elsewhere in Alaska. Oil production in the state (primarily from the onshore field at Prudhoe Bay) has decreased by more than two-thirds, from the 1988 peak of 2 million barrels per day to 645,000 barrels per day in 2009.[24] Depending on future prices, this decline could constitute a threat to the state's economy, which is highly dependent on oil and gas revenues and related employment. The Energy Information Administration projects that Alaska's production will continue to decline, to just 420,000 barrels per day by the end of this decade.[25] Such declines could threaten the viability of the Trans-Alaska Pipeline System, which transports oil from the North Slope to the port at Valdez.

Despite the Energy Information Administration's pessimism about long-term production trends in Alaska, other projections show a potential upswing[26] An optimistic scenario developed in 2009 study by Northern Economics for Shell Exploration and Development projects production from multiple Alaska outer continental shelf sites beginning in 2018 and eventually peaking at 1.8 million barrels of oil per day.[27] (New pipelines would need to be built to connect these reservoirs, if brought into production, to the Trans-Alaska Pipeline System.)

But finding and producing those potentially important supplies of oil offshore Arctic Alaska requires the utmost care, given the special challenges and risks associated with this frontier. Many of these challenges also arise elsewhere in the world, as Russia, Norway, Canada, and Denmark (Greenland) evaluate their Arctic oil and gas resources. The Alaskan Arctic is characterized by extreme cold, extended seasons of darkness, hurricane-strength storms, and pervasive fog—all affecting access and working conditions. The Chukchi and Beaufort Seas are covered by varying forms of ice for eight to nine months a year. These conditions limit exploratory drilling and many other activities to the summer months. The icy conditions during the rest of the year pose severe challenges for oil and gas operations and scientific research. And oil-spill response efforts are complicated year-round by the remote location and the presence of ice, at all phases of exploration and possible production.

The geological pressures in hydrocarbon deposits in shallow seas off Alaska are likely to be substantially below those encountered at Macondo, reducing some of the risks of a major blowout and challenges of containment. But oil spilled off Alaska (from blowouts, pipeline or tanker leaks, or other accidents) is likely to degrade more slowly than that found in the Gulf of Mexico because of lower water temperatures, reduced mixing of the oil into the water due to the presence of ice, and the shallower depths through which oil would travel from the wellhead to the surface. Some think the slow weathering could facilitate the skimming and in situ burning of escaped oil under ideal weather conditions, but the slow pace of natural dispersion means that oil would linger much longer in the marine environment. And serious questions remain about how to access spilled oil when the area is iced over or in seasonal slushy conditions.

The Arctic ecosystem, the need for scientific information and informed decision-making, and Alaska native peoples. The stakes for drilling in the U.S. Arctic are raised by the richness of its ecosystems. The marine mammals in the Chukchi and Beaufort are among the most diverse in the world, including seals, cetaceans, whales, walruses, and bears. The Chukchi Sea is home to roughly one-half of America's and one-tenth of the world's polar bears.[28] In November 2010, the U.S. Fish and Wildlife Service ruled that a large part of the polar bears' "critical habitat" included sea ice in the Beaufort and Chukchi Seas.[29] The Chukchi and Beaufort Seas also support millions of shorebirds, seabirds, and waterfowl, as well as abundant fish populations.

It is known that these are vibrant living systems, but scientific research on the ecosystems of the Arctic is difficult and expensive. Good information exists for only a few species, and even for those, just for certain times of the year or in certain areas. As a result, the Commission recommends an immediate, comprehensive federal research effort to provide a foundation of scientific information on the Arctic (with periodic review by the National Academy of Sciences), and annual stock assessments for marine mammals, fish, and birds that use the Beaufort and Chukchi Seas. This initiative should be coordinated with the state of Alaska, native organizations, academic institutions, non-governmental organizations, the private sector, and international partners. The information generated should be capable of informing decision-making related to oil and gas leasing, exploration, and development and production in the Arctic; measuring and monitoring impacts of oil and gas development on Arctic ecological resources; natural resource damage assessment should an oil spill occur and protocols in any treaty negotiated among the Arctic nations. The existing gaps in data also support an approach that distinguishes in leasing decisions between those areas where information exists and those where it does not, as well as where response capability may be less and the related environmental risks may therefore be greater. The need for additional research should not be used as a *de facto* moratorium on activity in the Arctic, but instead should be carried out with specific timeframes in mind in order to inform the decision-making process.

The Inupiat Eskimos of Alaska's remote arctic and subarctic communities rely heavily for their subsistence on resources from the marine environment, particularly bowhead whales. Bowhead whales can reach 60 feet in length and weigh more than 120,000 pounds. They migrate from Russian to Canadian waters and back through the Chukchi and Beaufort Seas.[30] They are the most important subsistence animal for the coastal communities of northwest and northern Alaska.[31] Whale hunting and the customs surrounding it are also an important part of their cultural heritage. Oil and gas development has the potential, directly or indirectly, to affect hunting success or the habitats of species important to subsistence. (Of course, offshore oil development could play a positive economic role in the native communities; some Inupiat whaling captains also work in the oil industry, for instance.) An Arctic Regional Citizens Council could help assure the active participation of the people who know this region the best in planning and response.

Arctic spill response and containment. The remoteness and weather of the Arctic frontier create special challenges in the event of an oil spill. Successful oil-spill response methods from the Gulf of Mexico, or anywhere else, cannot simply be transferred to the Arctic.

Industry and academic organizations are conducting research on response to oil on ice, but more needs to be done. A comprehensive interagency research program to address oil-spill containment and response issues in the Arctic should be developed, funded, and implemented within the federal government. Spill trajectory and weather models based on Arctic conditions must also be developed. This research should be funded promptly by the Oil Spill Liability Trust Fund, and the resulting analysis should inform when and where leasing occurs.

The National Contingency Plan requires the Coast Guard to oversee oil-spill planning and preparedness, and to supervise an oil-spill response in coastal waters. Current federal emergency response capabilities in the region are very limited: the Coast Guard operations base nearest to the Chukchi region is on Kodiak Island, approximately 1,000 miles from the leasing sites. The Coast Guard does not have sufficient ice-class vessels capable of responding to a spill under Arctic conditions: two of its three polar icebreakers have exceeded their service lives and are non-operational.[32] In addition to overseeing spill response, the Coast Guard provides search and rescue capabilities in other areas. Without a presence in the Arctic, it would be very difficult for the Coast Guard to conduct any emergency search and rescue operations.

To deal with these serious concerns about Arctic oil-spill response, containment, and search and rescue, the Commission recommends three approaches before the Department of the Interior makes a fully informed determination that drilling in a particular area is appropriate. First, the Department of the Interior should ensure that the containment and response plans proposed by industry are adequate for each stage of development and that the underlying financial and technical capabilities have been satisfactorily demonstrated in the Arctic. Second, the Coast Guard and the oil companies operating in the Arctic should carefully delineate their respective responsibilities in the event of an accident, including search and rescue, and then must build and deploy the necessary capabilities. Third, Congress should provide the resources to establish Coast Guard capabilities in the Arctic, based on the Coast Guard's review of current and projected gaps in its capacity.

International standards for Arctic oil and gas. The Arctic is shared by multiple countries, many of which are considering or conducting oil and gas exploration and development. The extreme weather conditions and infrastructure difficulties are not unique to the U.S. Arctic. The damages caused by an oil spill in one part of the Arctic may not be limited to the waters of the country where it occurred. As a result, the Commission recommends that strong international standards related to Arctic oil and gas activities be established among all the countries of the Arctic. Such standards would require cooperation and coordination of policies and resources. The Arctic Council[33] has begun work in this direction, updating its voluntary Arctic Offshore Oil and Gas Operation Guidelines in 2009. The International Standards Organization is also developing international standards for Arctic offshore structures that would apply to the activities of petroleum and natural gas industries in Arctic and cold regions. These guidelines are expected to specify requirements and provide recommendations and guidance for the design, construction, transportation, installation, and removal of offshore structures in the Arctic. Additional work is needed to strengthen these guidelines and standards, ensuring that they are both consistent and mandatory across the entire Arctic, and the United States could pay an important leadership role in securing these vital safeguards.

Bringing the potentially large oil resources of the Arctic outer continental shelf into production safely will require an especially delicate balancing of economic, human, environmental, and technological factors. Both industry and government will have to demonstrate standards and a level of performance higher than they have ever achieved before. One lesson from the *Deepwater Horizon* crisis is the compelling economic, environmental, and indeed human rationale for understanding and addressing the prospective risks comprehensively, before proceeding to drill in such challenging waters.

Conclusion
Creating and implementing a national energy policy will require enormous political effort and leadership—but it would do much to direct the nation toward a sounder economy and a safer and more sustainable environment in the decades to come. In the meantime, decisions about offshore drilling—one crucial element in any discussion of energy supply—remain controversial. The reaction to the December 1 decision to defer offshore exploration and production in the eastern Gulf of Mexico and along the Atlantic and Pacific coasts illustrates the polarization of opinion. Energy companies, seeking to pursue potential reserves in brand-new frontiers, criticized the announcement for closing off too many areas. Others, more concerned about environmental protection and national security, however, questioned why the Secretary was even considering allowing future drilling in these areas at all. And there were sharp differences in response among public officials in different regions, reflecting their local economies and sources of revenues.

These reactions echo the divided opinions presented to this Commission throughout its work. Though the Commission heard many ideas for improving safety and other aspects of offshore drilling, we also heard from Americans who advocate no future drilling whatsoever; they cited the adverse effects of fossil fuels on the climate, environmental damage, safety, and other factors.

Whether additional offshore drilling proceeds soon, in the longer term, or never depends on evolving public opinion. Given Americans' consumption of oil, finding and producing additional domestic supplies will be required in coming years, no matter what sensible and effective efforts are made to reduce demand—in response to economic, trade, and security considerations, and the rising challenge of climate change.

The extent to which offshore drilling contributes to augmenting that domestic supply depends importantly on rebuilding public faith in existing offshore energy exploration and production. That rebuilding begins with a clear, independent explanation of what happened at the Macondo well in April 2010, and of the reforms required in the wake of that terrible tragedy. That has been the work of this Commission, published in this report; the forthcoming separate report of the Commission's Chief Counsel; and background materials available on the Commission's website. Together, they present a clear, independent, unvarnished picture of what happened and why—and of the major reforms the nation must adopt.

This Commission proposes in this report a series of recommendations that will enable the country and the oil and gas industry to move forward on this one critical element of U.S. energy policy: continuing, safe, responsible offshore oil drilling to meet our nation's energy demands over the next decade and beyond. Our message is clear: both government and industry must make dramatic changes to establish the high level of safety in drilling operations on the outer continental shelf that the American public has the right to expect and to demand. It is now incumbent upon the Congress, the executive branch, and the oil and gas industry to take the necessary steps. Respect for the 11 lives lost on that tragic day last April requires no less.

ENDNOTES

The Commission has reviewed thousands of pages of documents from dozens of government agencies, private companies, and other entities, and interviewed hundreds of witnesses from these same agencies, companies, and entities. When possible, we include all pertinent details in the following endnote citations for those documents and interviews that have contributed to this report. Many documents and interviews, however, were disclosed or given to the Commission on a confidential basis. For these "non-public" sources, our citations include only as much detail as we can comfortably disclose while still respecting the privacy concerns of the source (e.g., "non-public BP document," "interview with government official," "interview with Coast Guard official").

The vast majority of non-public material that we cite in the endnotes below comes from documents and interviews provided by four government agencies—the Chemical Safety Board, the Coast Guard, the Department of Energy, and the Department of the Interior—and ten companies—BP, Cameron, Chevron, Dril-Quip, ExxonMobil, Halliburton, Schlumberger, Shell, Transocean, and Weatherford. In addition, the Commission participated in the Coast Guard's Incident Specific Preparedness Review of the BP Deepwater Horizon spill, through which dozens of officials from a variety of federal and state agencies, federal, state, and local elected officials, and executives and personnel from private companies and other spill response-related entities have been interviewed. All Coast Guard Incident Specific Preparedness Review interviews are also cited as non-public. Finally, the Commission has interviewed many Gulf Coast residents who wish to remain anonymous. These interviews are cited as non-public as well.

Chapter One

[1] Internal Halliburton document (HAL_0011208); Testimony of Nathaniel Chaisson, Hearing before the Deepwater Horizon Joint Investigation Team, August 24, 2010, 423. This report cites many "Internal documents" that the Commission received from companies, including BP, Halliburton, and Transocean. Those internal documents are identified by their document production serial numbers when available, which were assigned by the entity that provided them.

[2] Internal BP document (BP, presentation to Commission, August 9, 2010, slides 5 & 12).

[3] Testimony of Nathaniel Chaisson, 411; U.S. Department of Energy, *Well Configuration* (BP document made public by the Department of Energy), http://www.energy.gov/open/documents/3.1_Item_2_Macondo_Well_07_Jun_1900.pdf; Testimony of Natalie Roshto, Hearing before the Deepwater Horizon Joint Investigation Team, July 22, 2010, 15.

[4] Testimony of Michael Williams, Hearing before the Deepwater Horizon Joint Investigation Team, July 23, 2010, 35–36.

[5] Testimony of John Guide, Hearing before the Deepwater Horizon Joint Investigation Team, July 22, 2010, 260–266; Testimony of James Wilson, Hearing before the Deepwater Horizon Joint Investigation Team, October 6, 2010, 176.

[6] Brian Morel, e-mail message to Richard Miller and Mark Hafle, April 14, 2010, 13:31, http://energycommerce.house.gov/documents/20100614/BP-April14.Email.calling.Macondo.a.nightmare.well.pdf.

[7] BP, "GoM Exploration Wells: MC 252 #1—Macondo Prospect Well Information," September 2009, http://bpoilresponse.markimoore.com/blog/bp-media/docs/Macondo.Prospect.Well.Information.pdf.

[8] Testimony of Richard Tink, Hearing before the Deepwater Horizon Joint Investigation Team, May 26, 2010, 392; Deepwater Horizon Joint Investigation Team, *AFE Summary for the Macondo Well*, October 7, 2010, http://www.deepwaterinvestigation.com/external/content/document/3043/914919/1/AFE%20Summary%20for%20the%20Macondo%20Well.pdf.

[9] BP, Deepwater Horizon *Accident Investigation Report* (September 8, 2010), 17.

[10] Transocean, *Our Company*, http://www.deepwater.com/fw/main/Our-Company-2.html.

[11] Press Release, Transocean, Transocean Ltd. Reports Fourth Quarter and Full-Year 2009 Results, February 24, 2010.

[12] Press Release, Transocean, Transocean Inc. and GlobalSantaFe Corporation Agree to Combine, July 23, 2007.

[13] "Contractors ordering offshore rigs on speculation," *Drilling Contractor*, May/June 2002.

[14] "Global 500," CNNMoney.com, July 26, 2010, http://money.cnn.com/magazines/fortune/global500/2010/full_list/index.html.

[15] Internal Transocean documents (TRN-HCJ 93526, 93528).

[16] Internal BP document (BP-HZN-MBI 126338); Internal BP document (BP-HZN-OSC 5378).

[17] "Brazil Pins Hopes on Massive, untapped Oil Fields," NPR, December 1, 2009, http://www.npr.org/templates/story/story.php?storyId=120966523.

[18] Bureau of Ocean Energy Management, Regulation, and Enforcement, *Installations, Removals, and Cumulative Totals of Offshore Production Facilities in Federal Waters; 1959–2010*, February 2010, http://www.boemre.gov/stats/PDFs/OCSPlatformActivity.pdf.; Bureau of Ocean Energy Management, Regulation and Enforcement, *OCS Incidents/Spills by Category: 1996–2005*, October 19, 2007, http://www.boemre.gov/incidents/Incidents1996-2005.htm; Bureau of Ocean Energy Management, Regulation, and Enforcement, *OCS Incidents/Spills by Category: 2006–2010*, July 10, 2010, http://www.boemre.gov/incidents/IncidentStatisticsSummaries.htm.

19 Testimony of Ronald Sepulvado, Hearing before the Deepwater Horizon Joint Investigation Team, July 23, 2010, 7, 14, 34.

20 Testimony of John Guide, 23.

21 *Ibid.*, 43–44 and 189; Schlumberger, "Oilfield Glossary: cement bond log," accessed November 19, 2010, http://www.glossary.oilfield.slb.com/Display.cfm?Term=cement%20bond%20log.

22 Testimony of John Guide, 43–44, 189–191.

23 Testimony of Douglas Brown, Hearing before the Deepwater Horizon Joint Investigation Team, May 26, 2010, 88, 91.

24 Testimony of Jimmy Harrell, Hearing before the Deepwater Horizon Joint Investigation Team, May 27, 2010, 77; Internal Transocean document (TRN-HCDC 92).

25 Internal Transocean document (TRN-HCDC 92); BP, Deepwater Horizon *Accident Investigation Report*, 82.

26 Testimony of Ross Skidmore, Hearing before the Deepwater Horizon Joint Investigation Team, July 20, 2010, 264.

27 BP, Deepwater Horizon *Accident Investigation Report*, 24.

28 Testimony of Jimmy Harrell, 38, 113; Testimony of Curt Kuchta, Hearing before the Deepwater Horizon Joint Investigation Team, May 27, 2010, 166, 183, 184.

29 Testimony of Daun Winslow, Hearing before the Deepwater Horizon Joint Investigation Team, August 24, 2010, 188 and 191.

30 Testimony of Jimmy Harrell, 113; Testimony of Curt Kuchta, 184.

31 Testimony of David Sims, Hearing before the Deepwater Horizon Joint Investigation Team, August 26, 2010, 119.

32 Testimony of Daun Winslow, Hearing before the Deepwater Horizon Joint Investigation Team, August 23, 2010, 442.

33 Testimony of Stephen Bertone, Hearing before the Deepwater Horizon Joint Investigation Team, July 19, 2010, 29, 33; Testimony of Randy Ezell, Hearing before the Deepwater Horizon Joint Investigation Team, May 28, 2010, 279.

34 Testimony of Randy Ezell, 275.

35 BP, Deepwater Horizon *Accident Investigation Report*, 24.

36 Testimony of Stephen Bertone, 33.

37 *Ibid.*; Testimony of Randy Ezell, 280.

38 Testimony of Daun Winslow, August 23, 2010, 443.

39 Testimony of Stephen Bertone, 33–34; Testimony of Daun Winslow, August 23, 2010, 443.

40 Testimony of Randy Ezell, 281.

41 *Ibid.*

42 *Ibid.*

43 *Ibid.*

44 Testimony of Chris Pleasant, Hearing before the Deepwater Horizon Joint Investigation Team, May 28, 2010, 115, 281.

45 *Ibid.*, 116–118; Testimony of Jimmy Harrell, 117.

46 John R. Smith, *Review of Operational Data Preceding Explosion on Deepwater Horizon in MC252*, July 1, 2010, 11–12.

47 Testimony of Lee Lambert, Hearing before the Deepwater Horizon Joint Investigation Team, July 20, 2010, 291; Internal BP documents (BP-HZN-CEC 20347, 20178).

48 Internal BP documents (BP-HZN-CEC 20347, 20178).

49 Internal BP document (BP-HZN-MBI 21265).

50 Testimony of Patrick O'Bryan, Hearing before the Deepwater Horizon Joint Investigation Team, August 26, 2010, 364–365, 393.

51 Brian Morel, e-mail message to Richard Miller and Mark Hafle.

52 Testimony of Jimmy Harrell, 13.

53 BP, Deepwater Horizon *Follow Up Rig Audit, Marine Assurance Audit and Out of Service Period*, September 2009, 2, 18–48; Internal BP document (BP-HZN-MBI 136211).

54 Testimony of Patrick O'Bryan, 364.

55 Testimony of David Sims, Hearing before the Deepwater Horizon Joint Investigation Team, May 29, 2010, 172, 313.

56 BP, Deepwater Horizon *Accident Investigation Report*, 25; Internal BP document (BP-HZN-CEC 17621).

[57] BP, Deepwater Horizon *Accident Investigation Report*, 33.

[58] *Ibid.*, 25; Testimony of Chris Pleasant, 118–119.

[59] Testimony of John Gisclair, Hearing before the Deepwater Horizon Joint Investigation Team, October 8, 2010, 131–132.

[60] Testimony of Curt Kuchta, 185–186; Testimony of Jimmy Harrell, 12.

[61] Testimony of Yancy Keplinger, Hearing before the Deepwater Horizon Joint Investigation Team, October 5, 2010, 128–129.

[62] *Ibid.*; Testimony of Andrea Fleytas, Hearing before the Deepwater Horizon Joint Investigation Team, October 5, 2010, 16; Testimony of Daun Winslow, August 23, 2010, 296.

[63] Testimony of Daun Winslow, August 23, 2010, 295; Testimony of Pat O'Bryan, 366.

[64] Testimony of Daun Winslow, August 23, 2010, 295–296.

[65] Testimony of Randy Ezell, 281, 282, 294.

[66] *Ibid.*, 282.

[67] *Ibid.*, 281-282, 311.

[68] Testimony of Patrick O'Bryan, 219–220.

[69] Testimony of David Sims, August 26, 2010, 163.

[70] *Ibid.*, 317; Testimony of Patrick O'Bryan, 367.

[71] Testimony of David Sims, August 26, 2010, 174.

[72] *Ibid.*, 367.

[73] Testimony of Patrick O'Bryan, 367.

[74] Internal BP documents (BP-HZN-MBI 21418, 21420); BP, Deepwater Horizon *Accident Investigation Report*, 150.

[75] Testimony of Randy Ezell, 282, 283.

[76] *Ibid.*, 283.

[77] *Ibid.*, 283–284.

[78] Testimony of Micah Sandell, Hearing before the Deepwater Horizon Joint Investigation Team, May 29, 2010, 8, 10, 12.

[79] *Ibid.*, 11.

[80] Internal BP documents (*Deepwater Horizon* Schematic; BP August 9, 2010 presentation to Oil Spill Commission, slide 5).

[81] Testimony of Douglas Brown, 88–89, 92–93.

[82] Testimony of Paul Meinhart, Hearing before the Deepwater Horizon Joint Investigation Team, May 29, 2010, 28

[83] Testimony of Douglas Brown, 93–94.

[84] *Ibid.*, 94–95.

[85] Testimony of Steve Bertone, Hearing before the Deepwater Horizon Joint Investigation Team, July 19, 2010, 28, 34.

[86] Testimony of James Nicholas Wilson, Hearing before the Deepwater Horizon Joint Investigation Team, October 13, 2010, 10; Testimony of Steve Bertone, 35.

[87] Testimony of Steve Bertone, 35.

[88] Testimony of Gregory Meche, Hearing before the Deepwater Horizon Joint Investigation Team, May 28, 2010, 198.

[89] Testimony of Steve Bertone, 35–36.

[90] *Ibid.*

[91] Testimony of Andrea Fleytas, 14.

[92] Testimony of Gregory Meche, 235.

[93] Testimony of Andrea Fleytas, 14.

[94] Complaint at 2, Shivers v. BP Plc., No. 10-cv-381 (S.D. Ala. July 20, 2010).

[95] *Ibid.*

[96] *Ibid.*

[97] *Ibid.*

[98] *Ibid.*; Tracey Dalzell Walsh, "Forced To Become Emergency Workers, Fishermen Say BP Never Even Said Thanks," *Courthouse News Service*, July 22, 2010.

[99] Testimony of Steve Bertone, 37.

[100] *Ibid.*, 37–38.

[101] *Ibid.*, 38.

[102] *Ibid.*, 38–39.

[103] Testimony of Randy Ezell, 284–285.

[104] *Ibid.*, 285.

[105] Testimony of Yancy Keplinger, 165.

[106] Testimony of Randy Ezell, 285–286.

[107] *Ibid.*, 286.

[108] *Ibid.*

[109] *Ibid.*, 286–287.

[110] *Ibid.*, 287.

[111] Testimony of Yancy Keplinger, 152; Testimony of Tyrone Benton, Hearing before the Deepwater Horizon Joint Investigation Team, July 23, 2010, 250.

[112] Testimony of Gregory Meche, 209; Testimony of David Young, Hearing before the Deepwater Horizon Joint Investigation Team, May 27, 2010, 327; Testimony of Randy Ezell, 283; Testimony of Jimmy Harrell, 65; Testimony of Yancy Keplinger, 153.

[113] Testimony of Micah Sandell, 11–13.

[114] Testimony of Capt. Alwin Landry, Hearing before the Deepwater Horizon Joint Investigation Team, May 11, 2010, 98–100.

[115] Testimony of Paul Erickson, Hearing before the Deepwater Horizon Joint Investigation Team, May 11, 2010, 231–232.

[116] Testimony of Capt. Alwin Landry, 101–102.

[117] *Ibid.*, 104–105.

[118] Testimony of Gregory Meche, 202, 211, 223.

[119] Testimony of Anthony Gervasio, Hearing before the Deepwater Horizon Joint Investigation Team, May 11, 2010, 173, 187–188.

[120] *Ibid.*, 187; Testimony of Kevin Robb, Hearing before the Deepwater Horizon Joint Investigation Team, May 11, 2010, 42.

[121] Testimony of Anthony Gervasio, 189.

[122] *Ibid.*, 105, 190; Testimony of Gergory Meche, 223.

[123] Testimony of Daun Winslow, August 23, 2010, 447–448.

[124] *Ibid.*, 448–449, 452.

[125] Testimony of Mark Hay, Hearing before the Deepwater Horizon Joint Investigation Team, May 28, 2010, 225.

[126] Testimony of Daun Winslow, August 23, 2010, 452; Testimony of Randy Ezell, 287.

[127] Testimony of Daun Winslow, August 23, 2010, 452.

[128] *Ibid.*, 449–450, 452; Testimony of Randy Ezell, 289; Testimony of Anthony Gervasio, 190, 199.

[129] Testimony of Daun Winslow, August 23, 2010, 450; BP, Deepwater Horizon *Accident Investigation Report*, 123.

[130] Testimony of Daun Winslow, August 23, 2010, 450; Testimony of Steve Bertone, 39.

[131] Testimony of Steve Bertone, 39.

[132] *Ibid.*

[133] *Ibid.*

[134] Testimony of Daun Winslow, August 23, 2010, 451; Testimony of Steve Bertone, 39.

[135] Testimony of Steve Bertone, 39.

[136] *Ibid.*

[137] Testimony of Patrick O'Bryan, 368, 396.

[138] Testimony of Daun Winslow, August 23, 2010, 452.

[139] Internal BP Document (BP-HZN-MBI 21277).

[140] Testimony of Daun Winslow, August 23, 2010, 451–452.

[141] Internal BP Document (BP August 9, 2010 presentation to Oil Spill Commission, slide 13).

[142] Testimony of Daun Winslow, August 23, 2010, 454.

[143] Ibid., 454–455.

[144] Testimony of Yancy Keplinger, October 5, 2010, 157.

[145] Associated Press, "'The Real Deal': Survivors recall the Deepwater Horizon explosion," *Press-Register*, May 9, 2010.

[146] Ibid.; BP, Deepwater Horizon *Accident Investigation Report*, 103.

[147] Testimony of Steve Bertone, 39–40.

[148] Ibid., 40.

[149] Ibid., 40–41.

[150] Ibid., 41–43.

[151] Ibid., 43.

[152] Ibid.

[153] Testimony of Randy Ezell, 288.

[154] Testimony of Steve Bertone, 44.

[155] Ibid., 44–46.

[156] Ibid., 45–46.

[157] Ibid., 46–47.

[158] Ibid., 47–48.

[159] Testimony of Michael Williams, 26.

[160] Testimony of Steve Bertone, 48.

[161] Testimony of Andrea Fleytas, 15.

[162] Testimony of Steve Bertone, 48.

[163] Ibid.

[164] Ibid., 48–49.

[165] Ibid., 48.

[166] Testimony of Curt Kuchta, 219.

[167] Testimony of Daun Winslow, August 28, 2010, 467.

[168] Testimony of Steve Bertone, 50.

[169] Ibid.

[170] Testimony of Anthony Gervasio, 197.

[171] Testimony of Steve Bertone, 49.

[172] Internal Transocean document (TRN-USCG_MMS 30428).

[173] Testimony of Anthony Gervasio, 224.

[174] Testimony of Steve Bertone, 50.

[175] Testimony of Capt. Alwin Landry, 112.

[176] Testimony of Steve Bertone, 51.

[177] Testimony of Kevin Robb, Hearing before the Deepwater Horizon Joint Investigation Team, May 11, 2010, 44.

[178] Ian Urbina and Justin Gillis, "Workers On Oil Rig Recall a Terrible Night of Blasts," *New York Times*, May 7, 2010.

[179] Internal BP Document (BP-HZN-MBI 143366).

[180] Testimony of Alwin Landry, 115.

[181] Urbina and Gillis, "Workers On Oil Rig Recall a Terrible Night of Blasts."

[182] Walsh, "Forced to Become Emergency Workers, Fishermen Say BP Never Even Said Thanks."

[183] Testimony of Steve Bertone, 52; *Ibid.*, 48–53.

[184] Testimony of Randy Ezell, 330.

[185] Testimony of Alwin Landry, 120–121.

[186] Testimony of Daun Winslow, August 28, 2010, 44–45.

[187] Testimony of Capt. Alwin Landry , 121–122.

[188] *Ibid.*, 125–126.

[189] *Ibid.*, 126.

Chapter Two

[1] Joseph Pratt, Tyler Priest, and Christopher Castaneda, *Offshore Pioneers: Brown & Root and the History of Offshore Oil and Gas* (Houston: Gulf Publishing, 1997), 7–13; "First Well in Gulf of Mexico Was Drilling Just 25 Years Ago," *Offshore* (October 1963): 17–19.

[2] Quoted in Tom Zoellner, "Oil and Water: The Adventure of Getting One from Deep Beneath the Other," *Invention and Technology* (Fall 2000): 48.

[3] Daniel Yergin, *The Prize: The Epic Quest for Oil, Money, and Power* (New York: Simon and Schuster, 1992), 409.

[4] Pratt, Priest, and Castaneda, *Offshore Pioneers*, 15–52, 137–157.

[5] *Ibid.*, 21–25.

[6] Tyler Priest, "Extraction Not Creation: The History of Offshore Petroleum in the Gulf of Mexico," *Enterprise & Society* 8, no. 2 (June 2007): 240.

[7] Alden J. LaBorde, *My Life and Times* (New Orleans: LaBorde Printing Company, 1996), 174.

[8] James W. Calvert, "Gulf Offshore Activity Booming," *World Petroleum* (January 1957): 48.

[9] Ben C. Belt, "Louisiana and Texas Offshore Prospects," *Drilling* (March 1956): 119.

[10] "Special Offshore Report," *World Oil* (May 1957): 118; Calvert, "Gulf Offshore Activity Booming," 48.

[11] Pratt, Priest, and Castaneda, Offshore Pioneers, 36–48.

[12] Tyler Priest, *The Offshore Imperative: Shell Oil's Search for Petroleum in Postwar America* (College Station: Texas A&M Press, 2007), 81–91.

[13] *Ibid.*, 95–98.

[14] Tyler Priest, "Auctioning the Ocean: The Creation of the Federal Offshore Leasing Program, 1954-1962," *History of the Offshore Oil and Gas Industry in Southern Louisiana: Vol. 1: Papers on the Evolving Offshore Industry* (Minerals Management Service OCS Study 2004-049, 2008).

[15] U.S. Department of Interior, "Petroleum and Sulfur on the U.S. Continental Shelf," internal study, August 1969, box 134, Central Classified Files, 1969–1972, Record Group 48, Records of the Secretary of Interior, National Archives and Records Administration (NARA), College Park, MD.

[16] Priest, "Auctioning the Ocean," 113.

[17] On Project Mohole and JOIDES, see David K. van Keuren, "Breaking New Ground: The Origins of Scientific Ocean Drilling," in *The Machine in Neptune's Garden: Historical Perspectives on Technology and the Marine Environment*, eds. Helen M. Rozwadowski and David K. van Keuren (Sagamore Beach, MA: Science History Publications, 2004), 183–210. On Shell's *Eureka* project, see Priest, *The Offshore Imperative*, 97, 218.

[18] F. P. Dunn, "Deepwater Production: 1950-2000" (Offshore Technology Conference [OTC] Paper 7627, Houston, TX, May 1994).

[19] Priest, *The Offshore Imperative*, 127–130.

[20] *Ibid.*

[21] Cliff Hernandez, interview by Andrew Gardner, May 1, 2001, New Iberia, LA, *History of the Offshore Oil and Gas Industry in Southern Louisiana*, Houston History Archives, M.D. Anderson Library Special Collections, University of Houston, Houston, TX. This interview is one of approximately 450 oral histories conducted for *History of the Offshore Oil and Gas Industry in Southern Louisiana*, Minerals Management Service OCS Study 2004-049 (2008).

[22] Ken Arnold, interview with Tyler Priest, May 10, 2004, Houston, TX, *History of the Offshore Oil and Gas Industry in Southern Louisiana*, Houston History Archives, M.D. Anderson Library Special Collections, University of Houston, Houston, TX.

[23] Don E. Kash et al., *Energy Under the Oceans: A Technology Assessment of Outer Continental Shelf Oil and Gas Operations* (Norman: University of Oklahoma Press, 1973), 104.

[24] U.S. Geological Survey, *Monthly Engineering Reports* Vol. 128 (December 1958) and *Monthly Engineering Reports* Vol. 144 (February 1960), RG 57, Records of the U.S. Geological Survey, NARA.

[25] Kash et al., *Energy Under the Oceans*, 105.

[26] Neil R. Etson to President Nixon, March 18, 1970, Central Classified Files, 1968-1974, Box 71, RG 57, Records of the

U.S. Geological Survey, NARA.

[27] Kash et al., *Energy Under the Oceans*, 104.

[28] Robert E. Kallman and Eugene D. Wheeler, *Coastal Crude in a Sea of Conflict* (San Luis Obispo: Blake Printery and Publishing, 1984), 63.

[29] Riley E. Dunlap and Angela G. Mertig, *American Environmentalism: The U.S. Environmental Movement, 1970–1990* (Philadelphia: Taylor and Francis, 1992).

[30] Russell Wayland, "The New Federal OCS Regulations in the Light of Santa Barbara," (Society of Petroleum Engineers [SPE] Paper 2780, San Francisco, CA, November 1969); Richard B. Krahl and David W. Moody, "Gulf Coast Lease Management Inspection Program" (OTC Paper 1714, Houston, TX, May 1972), 846.

[31] M.D. Reifel, "Offshore Blowouts and Fires," in *The Technology of Offshore Drilling, Completion and Production*, ETA Offshore Seminars, Inc. (Tulsa: The Petroleum Publishing Company, 1976), 239–257; "The Wicked Witch is Dead," *Shell News* no. 2 (1978): 2–8; and R.C. Visser, "Offshore Platform Accidents, Regulations, and Industry Standards" (OTC Paper 7118, Houston, TX, May 1993).

[32] Krahl and Moody, "Gulf Coast Lease Management Program;" Donald Solanas, "Update—OCS Lease Management Program" (OTC Paper 1754, Houston, TX, April/May, 1973); E.W. Standley to Jack W. Boller, February 15, 1972, Central Classified Files, 1969–1972, Box 136, Part 13, RG 48, Records of the Secretary of Interior, NARA.

[33] K. E. Arnold, P. S. Koszela, and J. C. Viles, "Improving Safety of Production Operations in the U.S. OCS" (OTC Paper 6079, Houston, TX, May 1989).

[34] Peter Lovie, "Classification and Certification of Offshore Drilling Units," in *The Technology of Offshore Drilling, Completion and Production*, ETA Offshore Seminars, (Tulsa: The Petroleum Publishing Company, 1976), 389–413.

[35] Dunn, "Deepwater Production."

[36] See data in National Academy of Sciences, Committee on Assessment of Safety of OCS Activities, *Safety and Offshore Oil* (Washington D.C.: National Academy Press, 1981).

[37] E. P. Danenberger, "Outer Continental Shelf Drilling Blowouts, 1971-1991" (OTC Paper 7248, Houston, TX, May 1993).

[38] U.S. Energy Information Administration (EIA), "Petroleum," Table 5.13.c, in *Annual Energy Review 2009* (Washington, D.C.: U.S. EIA, 2010), http://www.eia.gov/emeu/aer/petro.html.

[39] "Bidders Snub Most Deepwater Tracts," *Oil and Gas Journal* (April 8, 1974): 36.

[40] Priest, *The Offshore Imperative*, 191–195.

[41] Stephen P.J. Cossey, "Celebrations Began with Cognac," *AAPG Explorer* (September 2004), http://www.aapg.org/explorer/2004/09sep/gom_history.cfm.

[42] Priest, *The Offshore Imperative*, 196–201.

[43] Pratt, Priest, and Castaneda, *Offshore Pioneers*, 83–90.

[44] "Gulf Lease Sale Shatters Two Records," *Oil & Gas Journal* (October 6, 1980): 34; Charlie Blackburn, quoted in Priest, *The Offshore Imperative*, 216; D.A. Holmes, "1970-1986 Lookback of Offshore Lease Sales in the Gulf of Mexico Cenozoic," interoffice memorandum, Shell Offshore Inc., August 24, 1987.

[45] Priest, *The Offshore Imperative*, 209–215.

[46] Juan Carlos Boué with Edgar Jones, *A Question of Rigs, of Rules, or of Rigging the Rules? Upstream Profits and Taxes in U.S. Gulf Offshore Oil and Gas* (Oxford: Oxford University Press, 2007), 17.

[47] Rich Sears, "A Brief History of Deepwater" (draft prepared for the National Commission, August 2010).

[48] Paul Voosen, "Gulf of Mexico's Deepwater Oil Industry Is Built on Pillars of Salt," *New York Times*, July 28, 2010; Gary Steffens and Neil Braunsdorf, "The Gulf of Mexico Deepwater Play: 50 Years from Concept to Commercial Reality" (AAPG Distinguished Lecture Series, 1997–1998).

[49] Priest, *The Offshore Imperative*, 218–220.

[50] Juan Carlos Boué and Gerardo Lyando, *U.S. Gulf Offshore Oil: Petroleum Leasing and Taxation and Their Impact on Industry Structure, Competition, Production, and Fiscal Revenues* (Oxford: Oxford Energy Institute, 2002).

[51] Bureau of Ocean Energy Management, Regulation, and Enforcement (BOEMRE), "Gulf of Mexico Oil and Gas Leasing Offerings," http://www.gomr.boemre.gov/homepg/lsesale/swiler/swiler.html.

[52] Priest, *The Offshore Imperative*, 221–222.

[53] "The Time to Start Looking is Now," *Shell News* no. 4 (1984): 16.

[54] By 1990, Americans consumed less gasoline on a per capita basis (437 gallons per year) than they did in 1979. U.S. Energy Information Administration (EIA), Annual Energy Review, Petroleum, Table 5.13.c, http://www.eia.gov/emeu/aer/petro.html.

[55] On the forgotten victory of energy conservation and efficiency, see Jay Hakes, *A Declaration of Energy Independence: How Freedom from Foreign Oil Can Improve National Security, Our Economy, and the Environment* (Hoboken: John Wiley & Sons, 2008), 41–71.

[56] Robert Gramling, *Oil on the Edge: Offshore Development, Conflict, Gridlock* (Albany, NY: SUNY Press, 1996), 118.

[57] "Bullwinkle Takes Shape," *Shell News* no. 6 (1987): 2–7; "Rising Above the Crowd," *Shell News* no. 6 (1988): 28–34.

[58] "How Conoco Developed the Tension-Leg Platform," *Ocean Industry*, August 1984, 35–46.

[59] Tom Curtis, "Lifestyles of the Rich and Bankrupt," *Texas Monthly*, March 1988, 90.

[60] Congress of the United States, Office of Technology Assessment, *Oil and Gas Technologies for the Arctic and Deepwater: Summary* (Washington: GPO, 1985), 22–23.

[61] On the struggle over Bristol Bay, see Charles Frederick Lester, "The Search for Dialogue in the Administrative State: The Politics, Policy, and Law of Offshore Development" (Ph.D. dissertation, University of California, Berkeley, 1992), 113–146.

[62] Priest, *The Offshore Imperative*, 209–215.

[63] Steffens and Braunsdorf, "The Gulf of Mexico Deepwater Play."

[64] BOEMRE, "Gulf of Mexico Oil and Gas Leasing Offerings," http://www.gomr.boemre.gov/homepg/lsesale/swiler/swiler.html.

[65] Priest, *The Offshore Imperative*, 237–251.

[66] *Ibid.*, 254–255.

[67] *Ibid.*, 253–261; "Launch Pad into the Deep," *Houston Chronicle*, August 17, 1997.

[68] Bob Horton quoted in Tom Bower, *Oil: Money, Politics, and Power in the 21st Century* (New York: Grand Central Publishing, 2009), 19.

[69] William A. Schneider, "3-D Seismic: A Historical Note," *The Leading Edge* (March 1998): 375; "Looking Ahead in Marine and Land Geophysics—A Conversation with Woody Nestvold and Ian Jack," *The Leading Edge* (October 1995): 1061–1067.

[70] "Exploring the Ocean's Frontiers," *Time*, December 17, 1990, 98; "Offshore Oil: How Deep Can They Go?" *Popular Science*, January 1992): 80–97.

[71] "Oil and Gas Technology Development," (Topic Paper #26, National Petroleum Council Global Oil & Gas Study, November 22, 2006), 16. This topic paper was one of 38 working documents used to produce the 2007 National Petroleum Council study, *Facing the Hard Truths About Energy* http://www.npchardtruthsreport.org/.

[72] Susanne S. Pagano, "Offshore Drilling, Production—New Waves of Technology," *Sea Technology* (April 1991): 19–21; "There's Oil Down There . . . Way Down There," *Texas Shores* 31, no. 1 (Spring 1998): 14–15.

[73] Priest, *The Offshore Imperative*, 243–251.

[74] "Shell Marks Progress in Deepwater Gulf," *Oil & Gas Journal 93*, no. 46 (November 13, 1995); "Debottlenecking Removes Auger Production Constraints," *Oil & Gas Journal 94*, no. 46 (November 11, 1996).

[75] Priest, *The Offshore Imperative*, 251–253.

[76] Press Release, Minerals Management Service, Shell to Pay $49 Million in Settlement Agreement with Minerals Management Service, August 5, 2003.

[77] Boué and Jones, *A Question of Rigs*, 130.

[78] F. Jay Schempf, "New Study Finds Port Fourchon 'Vital' to U.S. Economy," *Offshore* (March 1, 2008).

[79] D.G. Godfrey et al., "The Mars Project Overview" (OTC Paper 8368, Houston, TX, May 1997).

[80] *Ibid.*

[81] David Ernst and Andrew M.J. Steinhubl, "Alliances in Upstream Oil and Gas," *McKinsey Quarterly* 2 (1997).

[82] Jeff Ryser, "Hot Play in the Gulf," *Texas Business* (August 1995): 33.

[83] "The Cloning of Mars," *Shell News* 64, no. 1 (1996): 8–13; Michael Davis, "Shell Oil Goes Deep in Gulf," *Houston Chronicle*, April 9, 1999; Priest, *The Offshore Imperative*, 260–262.

[84] Mary Judice, "Out of the LOOP," *Times Picayune*, September 17, 1995; C.G. Steube, "Addressing Transportation Needs for Deepwater Gulf of Mexico" (OTC Paper 13169, Houston, TX, April/May 2001).

[85] Boué and Jones, *A Question of Rigs*, 17.

[86] Bureau of Ocean Energy Management, Regulation, and Enforcement (BOEMRE), "Installations, Removals, and Cumulative Totals of Offshore Production Facilities in Federal Waters: 1959-2010," www.boemre.gov/stats/PDFs/OCSPlatformActivity.pdf.

[87] Dolly Jorgenson, "An Oasis in a Watery Desert: Discourses on an Industrial Ecosystem in the Gulf of Mexico Rigs-to-Reefs Program," *History and Technology* 25, no. 4 (November 2009): 343–364.

[88] Press Release, Minerals Management Service, High Bids Total $307 Million in Central Gulf of Mexico Lease Sale 152, May 10, 1995, http://www.boemre.gov/ooc/press/1995/50037.txt.

[89] Voosen, "Gulf of Mexico's Deepwater Oil Industry Is Built on Pillars of Salt"; Helen Thorpe, "Oil and Water," *Texas*

Monthly (February 1996): 140–141.

[90] Scott L. Montgomery and Dwight Moore, "Subsalt Play, Gulf of Mexico: A Review," *AAPG Bulletin* 81, no. 6 (June 1997): 875–876.

[91] Rhonda Duey, "Pioneering a Global Play," *Hart's E&P* (July 1, 2009); Thorpe, "Oil and Water," 142.

[92] R.R. Israel et al., "Challenges Evolve for Directional Drilling Through Salt in Deepwater Gulf of Mexico," *Drilling Contractor* (May/June 2008), http://drillingcontractor.org/challenges-evolve-for-directional-drilling-through-salt-in-deepwater-gulf-of-mexico-1622.

[93] David Ivanovich, "Gulf is Heart of Deepwater Drilling," *Houston Chronicle*, May 4, 1997.

[94] Brian Knowlton, "Oil Growth Boomerangs on Houston," *International Herald Tribune*, April 1, 2002.

[95] David Townshend, "Golden Triangle Dominates," *Petroleum Economist*, October 2002.

[96] Tim Colton and LaVar Huntziner, *A Brief History of Shipbuilding in Recent Times* (Alexandria, VA: CNA Corporation, 2002); Mike Hunt and Lenny Gary, "Gulf of Mexico Fabrication Yards Built 5,500 Platforms Over 50 Years," *Offshore* (January 2000).

[97] Ronald W. Ferrier, *The History of the British Petroleum Company, Vol. 1: The Developing Years, 1901–1932* (Cambridge: Cambridge University Press, 1982); J.H. Bamberg, *The History of British Petroleum, Vol. 2: The Anglo-Iranian Years, 1928–1945* (Cambridge: Cambridge University Press, 1994); and James Bamberg, *British Petroleum and Global Oil, 1950–1975: The Challenge of Nationalism* (Cambridge: Cambridge University Press, 2000).

[98] Agis Salpukas, "BP Amoco's Leader Remakes An Oil Giant, Again," *New York Times*, April 1, 1999.

[99] Kathy Shirley, "Vision Led to Crazy Horse Find," *AAPG Explorer*, March 2002.

[100] *Ibid.*

[101] Kristen Hays, "After All of Thunder Horse's Problems, BP Looks Ahead To Seeing A Return On Its Enormous Investment In The Platform, Payoff Is A Long Time in Coming," *Houston Chronicle*, November 18, 2007.

[102] *Ibid.*

[103] Peter Lehner with Bob Deans, *In Deep Water: The Anatomy of a Disaster, the Fate of the Gulf, and Ending Our Oil Addiction* (New York: The Experiment, 2010), 63.

[104] "Deepwater GOM New Focus of BP Growth Strategy," *Oil & Gas Journal* 100, no. 33 (August 19, 2002): 36.

[105] Neela Banerjee, "This Oil's Domestic, but It's Deep and It's Risky," *New York Times*, August 11, 2002.

[106] "The Jack-2 Perspective," *Oil & Gas Journal* 104, no. 34 (September 11, 2006): 17.

[107] B.F. Thurmond, D.B.L. Walker, H.H. Banon, A.B. Luberski, M.W. Jones, and R.R. Peters, "Challenges and Decisions in Developing Multiple Deepwater Fields" (OTC Paper 16573, Houston, TX, May 2004).

[108] K.L. Marshall and G.H. Smith, "Inspection Management Experience for a Fleet of Spars in the Gulf of Mexico" (OTC Paper 17619, Houston, TX, May 2005); C. Jim Thibodeaux, R. Don Vardeman, and Charles E. Kindel, "Nansen/Boomvang Projects: Overview and Project Management" (OTC Paper 14089, Houston, TX, May 2002).

[109] Thurmond et al., "Challenges and Decisions in Developing Multiple Deepwater Fields."

[110] Bill Kirton, Gary Wulf, and Bill Henderson, "Thunder Horse Drilling Riser Break—The Road to Recovery" (SPE Paper 90628, 2004).

[111] Simon Todd and Dan Replogle, "Thunder Horse and Atlantis: The Development and Operation of Twin Giants in the Deepwater Gulf of Mexico" (OTC Paper 20395, Houston, TX, May 2010).

[112] *Ibid.*

[113] Laurel Brubacker Calkins, "BP Sued by Watchdog Group over Atlantis Platform," Bloomberg, September 13, 2010, http://www.bloomberg.com/news/2010-09-10/bp-sued-over-alleged-safety-gaps-at-atlantis-production-platform.html.

[114] Det Norske Veritas, *Pipeline Damage Assessment from Hurricane Ivan in the Gulf of Mexico*, (Minerals Management Service Report No. 440 38570, May 8, 2006). Includes data on damages from hurricanes through 2005.

[115] Lesley D. Nixon et al., *Deepwater Gulf of Mexico 2009: Interim Report of 2008 Highlights* (OCS Report, MMS 2009-016, 2009), https://www.gomr.mms.gov/homepg/espis/espisfront.asp.

[116] "BP Taps Vast Pool of Crude in Deepest Oil Well," *Associated Press*, September 2, 2009; Brett Clanton, "Shell's Perdido First to Produce in Key Deep Water Gulf Region," *Houston Chronicle*, March 31, 2010; Brett Clanton, "Chevron Plans New Floating City," Houston Chronicle Energy Watch blog, FuelFix, October 21, 2010, http://fuelfix.com/energywatch/2010/10/21/chevron-plans-new-floating-city/.

[117] Frank Close, Bob McCavitt, and Brian Smith, "Deepwater Gulf of Mexico Development Challenges Overview," (SPE Paper 113011, 2008), 2.

[118] Melvyn Whitby, "Design Evolution of a Subsea BOP: Blowout Preventer Requirements Get Tougher as Drilling Goes Ever Deeper," *Drilling Contractor* (May/June 2007).

[119] Mary C. Boatman and Jennifer Peterson, *Oceanic Gas Hydrate Research and Activities Review* (OCS Report MMS

2000-017, U.S. Department of Interior, Minerals Management Service, Gulf of Mexico OCS Region, 2000).

[120] Fergus Addison, Kevin Kennelley, and Fikry Botros, "Future Challenges for Deepwater Developments" (OTC Paper 20404, Houston, TX, May 2010).

[121] Center for Biological Diversity v. U.S. Department of the Interior, 563 F.3d 466 (D.C. Cir. 2009).

[122] The White House, Office of the Press Secretary, Remarks by the President in a Discussion on Jobs and the Economy in Charlotte, North Carolina, April 2, 2010, http://www.whitehouse.gov/the-press-office/remarks-president-a-discussion-jobs-and-economy-charlotte-north-carolina.

[123] Gabriel Garcia Marquez, *One Hundred Years of Solitude*, translated by Gregory Rambassa (New York: Avon Books, 1970), 212.

Chapter Three

[1] Press Release, U.S. Department of the Interior, Salazar Launches Safety and Environmental Protection Reforms to Toughen Oversight of Offshore Oil and Gas Operations, May 11, 2010, http://www.doi.gov/news/pressreleases/Salazar-Launches-Safety-and-Environmental-Protection-Reforms-to-Toughen-Oversight-of-Offshore-Oil-and-Gas-Operations.cfm.

[2] Press Release, U.S. Department of the Interior, Salazar Divides MMS's Three Conflicting Missions, May 19, 2010, http://www.doi.gov/news/pressreleases/Salazar-Divides-MMSs-Three-Conflicting-Missions.cfm; Secretary of the Interior, Establishment of the Bureau of Ocean Energy Management, the Bureau of Safety and Environmental Enforcement, and the Office of Natural Resources Revenue, No. 3299 (May 19, 2010), http://www.doi.gov/deepwaterhorizon/loader.cfm?csModule=security/getfile&PageID=32475.

[3] Secretary of the Interior, Change of the Name of the Minerals Management Service to the Bureau of Ocean Energy Management, Regulation, and Enforcement, No. 3302 (June 18, 2010), http://www.doi.gov/deepwaterhorizon/loader.cfm?csModule=security/getfile&PageID=35872.

[4] 42 U.S.C. § 4331(a).

[5] U.S. Department of the Interior, "Statement by Secretary of the Interior James Watt Instituting Changes in the Mineral Royalty Management Program – July 21, 1982," Commission on Fiscal Accountability of the Nation's Energy Resources: Subject Files, 1981–1982, RG 48, Entry 994, Box 1 (National Archives and Records Administration, Washington, DC).

6 U.S. Constitution, Art IV, § 3, cl. 2.

[7] Kleppe v. New Mexico, 426 U.S. 529, 539 (1976), quoting United States v. San Francisco, 310 U.S. 16, 29 (1940).

[8] Utah Power & Light Co. v. United States, 243 U.S. 389, 405 (1917); Kleppe v. New Mexico, 426 U.S. at 540 ("Congress exercises the powers of both a proprietor and of a legislature over the public domain.").

[9] United States v. Midwest Oil, 236 U.S. 459, 466–68, 474–83 (1915). (Upholding authority of the president to withdraw unilaterally from private disposition valuable energy resources located on public lands in order to protect those resources while Congress considers legislation for their retention in national ownership).

[10] Outer Continental Shelf Lands Act, 42 U.S.C. §§ 1331–1356a.

[11] E.R. Bartley, *The Tidelands Oil Controversy: A Legal and Historical Analysis* (Austin: University of Texas Press, 1953); Tyler Priest, "Claiming the Coastal Sea: The Battle for the Tidelands, 1937–1953," *History of the Offshore Oil and Gas Industry in Southern Louisiana: Vol. 1: Papers on the Evolving Offshore Industry*, MMS OCS Study 2004-049 (New Orleans: U.S. Department of the Interior, Minerals Management Service, 2008), 67–90, https://www.gomr.mms.gov/homepg/espis/espisfront.asp.

[12] See United States v. California, 332 U.S. 19, 35 (1947); United States v. Louisiana, 339 U.S. 699 (1950); United States v. Texas, 339 U.S. 707 (1950).

[13] Priest, "Claiming the Coastal Sea: The Battle for the Tidelands, 1937–1953."

[14] Other states petitioned for the 9-nautical-mile boundary in the federal courts, but failed to prevail.

[15] "Oil Shelf Bill Enacted; President Reaffirms U.S. Title to Outer Offshore Deposits," *New York Times*, August 8, 1953, 27.

[16] Richard Vietor, *Energy Policy in America since 1945: A Study of Business-Government Relations* (New York: Cambridge University Press, 1984), 19.

[17] E.R. Bartley, *The Tidelands Oil Controversy: A Legal and Historical Analysis*.

[18] "Interior Expects Big Things from . . . Offshore Lease Sale," *Oil and Gas Journal*, September 13, 1954, 96.

[19] Diane Austin et al., *History of the Offshore Oil and Gas Industry in Southern Louisiana, Volume 1: Papers on the Evolving Offshore Industry*, OCS Study MMS 2008-042 (New Orleans: U.S. Department of the Interior, Minerals Management Service, September 2008), 97–98, http://www.gomr.boemre.gov/PI/PDFImages/ESPIS/4/4530.pdf.

[20] 43 U.S.C § 1334.

[21] "Oil and Gas Leases Bow to Rare Wildlife Species," *New York Times*, December 9, 1955.

[22] John C. Whitaker, *Striking a Balance: Environment and Natural Resources Policy in the Nixon-Ford Years* (Washington, D.C.: American Enterprise Institute, 1976), 267–268; Russell Wayland, "The New Federal OCS Regulations in the Light of Santa Barbara" (Society of Petroleum Engineers [SPE] Paper 2780, San Francisco, CA, November 1969); Richard B. Krahl and David W. Moody, "Gulf Coast Lease Management Inspection Program," (Offshore Technology Conference [OTC] Paper 1714, 1972), 846.

[23] National Environmental Policy Act of 1969, 42 U.S.C. § 4321-4370h.

[24] Richard J. Lazarus, *The Making of Environmental Law*, (Chicago: University of Chicago Press, 2004), 70.

[25] 42 U.S.C. § 4332(c).

[26] Calvert Cliffs Coordinating Committee v. Atomic Energy Commission, 449 F.2d 1109 (D.C. Cir. 1971).

[27] National Research Council, *Assessment of the U.S. Outer Continental Shelf Environmental Studies Program: III. Social and Economic Studies* (The National Academies Press: Washington, DC, 1992), http://www.nap.edu/catalog.php?record_id=2062.

[28] U.S. Department of the Interior, *Leasing Oil and Natural Gas Resources: Outer Continental Shelf* (Washington, D.C.: U.S. Department of the Interior, 2005), 12, http://www.boemre.gov/ld/PDFs/GreenBook-LeasingDocument.pdf.

[29] Lazarus, *The Making of Environmental Law*, 70 (listing 18 statutes, and not including several such as the Magnuson Fishery Management and Conservation Act of 1976).

[30] The five laws included the Public Utility Regulatory Policies Act, Pub. L. No. 95-617, Energy Tax Act, Pub. L. No. 95-618, National Energy Conservation Policy Act, Pub. L. No. 95-619, Power Plant and Industrial Fuel Use Act, Pub. L. No. 95-620, and Natural Gas Policy Act, Pub. L. No. 95-621.

[31] Natural Resources Defense Council v. Morton, 458 F.2d 827 (D.C. Cir. 1972).

[32] Outer Continental Shelf Leasing Program: Hearings before the H. Comm. on Appropriations, 93rd Cong., 2d Sess. (1974).

[33] Outer Continental Shelf Lands Act, Pub. L. No. 95-372, 92 Stat. 629 (1978).

[34] 43 U.S.C. § 1801.

[35] 43 U.S.C. § 1802.

[36] 43 U.S.C. § 1344.

[37] 43 U.S.C. § 1340.

[38] 43 U.S.C. § 1351.

[39] 43 U.S.C. § 1344(a)(3).

[40] 43 U.S.C. § 1346.

[41] 43 U.S.C. § 1347(c).

[42] 43 U.S.C. § 1347(b).

[43] 43 U.S.C. § 1347(b)

[44] 43 U.S.C. § 1351.

[45] 43 U.S.C. § 1340.

[46] 43 U.S.C. § 1351(c)(3).

[47] 43 U.S.C. § 1351(e)(1).

[48] 43 U.S.C. § 1351(e)(1).

[49] 43 U.S.C. § 1531(l).

[50] See S. Rep. No. 95-285, at 154–5 (reprinting letter from Secretary of the Interior Cecil Andrus).

[51] See S. Rep. No. 95-285, at 50, 62, 82, 144–5.

[52] Robert Gramling, *Oil on the Edge: Offshore Development, Conflict, Gridlock* (Albany: SUNY Press, 1996), 121.

[53] Charles Babcock, "Watt Defies Critics of Plan for Oil Leases," *Washington Post*, July 7, 1981, A3.

[54] "Problems with Government," *Ocean Industry* (April 1982): 21.

[55] Commission on Fiscal Accountability of the Nation's Energy Resources, *Fiscal Accountability of the Nation's Energy Resources* (Washington, D.C.: January 1982), xv, http://www.onrr.gov/Laws_R_D/frnotices/PDFDocs/linowes-rpt1-5.pdf.

[56] Don E. Kash, *Lease Management Activities in the Geological Survey*, Commission on Fiscal Accountability of the Nation's Energy Resources: Technical Reports, 1981–1982, RG 48, Entry 998, Box 10, File 239, National Archives and Records Administration, 8, 9, 27.

[57] "Industry Warning Watt Against Transfer of BLM Leasing Functions to MMS," *Inside Energy/with Federal Lands*, November 1, 1982, 11.

[58] G. Kevin Jones, "Outer Continental Shelf Oil and Gas Development During the Reagan Administration—Part 1," *Western New England Law Review* 12, 1, (1990):8–13.

[59] "Interior Denies Oil Leasing Plan Will Cost $77 Billion," *Associated Press*, September 28, 1982.

[60] 43 U.S.C. § 1337.

[61] Charles Lester, "Contemporary Federalism and New Regimes of Ocean Governance: Lessons from the Case of Outer Continental Shelf Oil Development," *Ocean & Coastal Management* 23 (1994), 14.

[62] National Research Council Committee on Marine Area Governance and Management, *Striking a Balance: Improving Stewardship of Marine Areas* (Washington, D.C.: National Academy of Sciences, 1997), 37, http://www.nap.edu/openbook.php?record_id=5797&page=37.

[63] President George H.W. Bush, "Statement on Outer Continental Shelf Oil and Gas Development," (June 26, 1990), http://bushlibrary.tamu.edu/research/public_papers.php?id=2035&year=1990&month=6.

[64] 30 C.F.R. pt. 250.

[65] U.S. Department of the Interior, Documents pertaining to offshore inspection types and practices produced to the Oil Spill Commission, August 2010.

[66] Jan Erik Vinnem, *Offshore Risk Assessment: Principles, Modelling and Applications of QRA Studies*, 2nd ed. (London: Springer Studies in Reliability Engineering, 2007), 91, 100, 102.

[67] Petroleum Safety Authority of Norway, "From Prescription to Performance in Petroleum Supervision," March 12, 2010, http://www.ptil.no/news/from-prescription-to-performance-in-petroleum-supervision-article6696-79.html.

[68] Magne Ognedal, interview with Commission staff, November 10, 2010.

[69] E.P. Danenberger et al., *Investigation of March 19, 1989 Fire, South Pass Block 60 Platform B, Lease OCS-G 1608*, OCS Report MMS 90-0016 (New Orleans: U.S. Department of the Interior, Minerals Management Service, April 1990): 15, http://www.gomr.boemre.gov/PDFs/1990/90-0016.pdf.

[70] Marine Board of the National Research Council Committee on Alternatives for Inspection of Outer Continental Shelf Operations, *Alternatives for Inspecting Outer Continental Shelf Operations* (Washington: National Academy Press, 1990): 3, http://www.nap.edu/openbook.php?record_id=1517&page=1.

[71] Minerals Management Service, *Final Report, Findings and Recommendations, MMS Task Force on OCS Inspection and Enforcement* (Washington, D.C.: U.S. Department of the Interior, Minerals Management Service, February 1990), 1-3.

[72] Marine Board, *Alternatives for Inspecting Outer Continental Shelf Operations*, 80.

[73] *Ibid.*, 82.

[74] Exec. Order No. 12,777, 56 Fed. Reg. 54,757 (October 22, 1991).

[75] E.P. Danenberger, "Changes in the Minerals Management Service Offshore Regulatory Programs Resulting From the Oil Pollution Act of 1990" (Offshore Technology Conference [OTC] Paper 6823, May 1992), 150.

[76] Oil and Gas and Sulphur Operations in the Outer Continental Shelf, 56 Fed. Reg. 30,400 (July 2, 1991).

[77] *Ibid.*

[78] Salient differences were, as MMS noted, that "Platforms in the GOM are typically smaller, technically less sophisticated, produce fewer hydrocarbons, and operate in less severe environmental conditions [than North Sea platforms]. The number of personnel on OCS platforms is significantly smaller than on North Sea platforms. There is, however, a substantially greater number of OCS platforms in the GOM, over 3,800." Marshall Courtois, William Hauser, and Paul Schneider, "Minerals Management Service Safety and Environmental Management Program: Evolution of the Concept," (Offshore Technology Conference [OTC] Paper 6822, May 1992), 145.

[79] Oil and Gas and Sulphur Operations in the Outer Continental Shelf, 56 Fed. Reg. 30,400 (July 2, 1991).

[80] Former senior MMS officials, interviews with Commission staff, August and September 2010; Offshore Operators Committee, "Oil, Gas, and Sulphur Operations in the Outer Continental Shelf (OCS)—Safety and Environmental Management Systems," Public Comment (May 22, 2006), http://www.boemre.gov/federalregister/PDFs/AD15-OOCcomments5-22-06.pdf.

[81] T.A.F. Powell, "US Voluntary SEMP Initiative: Holy Grail or Poisoned Chalice?" (Offshore Technology Conference [OTC] Paper 8111, May 1996): 828.

[82] E.O. Redd, Jean Chevallier, and Ian Paterson, "Preparing a Safety Case: A Drilling Contractor's Experience" (Society of Petroleum Engineers [SPE] Paper 27293, January 1994): 799.

[83] L.D. Easley, J.E. Stark, and R.A. Bradford, "Implementing API RP 75 '*Recommended Practice for Development of a Safety and Environmental Program for Outer Continental Shelf (OCS) Operations and Facilities*'" (Offshore Technology Conference [OTC] Paper 7384, May 1994): 130.

[84] American Petroleum Institute, Recommended Practices for Development of a Safety and Environmental Management Program for Outer Continental Shelf (OCS) Operations and Facilities, Recommended Practice 75, 1st ed. (Dallas, TX: May 15, 1993).

[85] Oil and Gas and Sulphur Operations in the Outer Continental Shelf, 59 Fed. Reg. 33,779 (June 30, 1994).

[86] Safety and Environmental Management Program (SEMP) on the Outer Continental Shelf (OCS), 61 Fed. Reg. 37,493 (July 18, 1996).

[87] *Ibid.*

[88] Patrick Crow, "New slant on safety," *Oil & Gas Journal* (July 22, 1996): 23.

[89] TA.F Powell, "US Voluntary SEMP Initiative: Holy Grail or Poisoned Chalice?" (Offshore Technology Conference [OTC] Paper 8111, 1996).

[90] E.P. Danenberger, interview with Commission staff, September 2, 2010; E.P. Danenberger, e-mail message to Commission staff, October 25, 2010.

[91] Oil and Gas and Sulphur Operations in the Outer Continental Shelf–Incident Reporting Requirements, 68 Fed. Reg. 40,585 (July 8, 2003).

[92] E.P. Danenberger, interview with Commission staff, September 2, 2010; E.P. Danenberger, e-mail message to Commission staff, October 25, 2010.

[93] Oil and Gas and Sulphur Operations in the Outer Continental Shelf—Incident Reporting Requirements, 71 Fed. Reg. 19,640 (April 17, 2006).

[94] Commission staff analysis of Bureau of Ocean Energy Management, Regulation and Enforcement data. See http://www.boemre.gov/adm/budget.html.

[95] Jim Morris, "Lost at Sea/OFFSHORE RISKS/Safety concerns return with rise of oil, gas boom," *Houston Chronicle*, December 22, 1996, http://www.chron.com/CDA/archives/archive.mpl?id=1996_1384981.

[96] Commission staff analysis of Bureau of Ocean Energy Management, Regulation and Enforcement data. See http://www.gomr.boemre.gov/homepg/fastfacts/WaterDepth/wdmaster.asp.

[97] Commission staff analysis of Bureau of Ocean Energy Management, Regulation and Enforcement data; Minerals Management Service, *U.S. Offshore Milestones* (as of August 2006): 5. See http://www.boemre.gov/stats/PDFs/milestonesAUG2006.pdf.

[98] Commission staff analysis of Bureau of Ocean Energy Management, Regulation and Enforcement and U.S. Energy Information Administration data. See http://www.gomr.boemre.gov/PDFs/2009/2009-016.pdf, 71–72; http://www.eia.gov/oog/info/twip/twiparch/100526/twipprint.html.

[99] Commission staff analysis of MMS yearly budget request and enactments, by nominal and real (2005) dollars.

[100] Tetrahedron, Inc., *Reliability of Blowout Preventers Tested Under Fourteen and Seven Days Time Interval: Study Report, Submitted to Minerals Management Service, Department of the Interior*, MMS Technology Assessment & Research Project 253, "Blowout Preventer Study" (December 20, 1996), http://www.boemre.gov/tarprojects/253/AA.PDF.; Blowout Preventer (BOP) Testing Requirements for Drilling and Completion Operations, 63 Fed. Reg. 29,604 (June 1, 1998).

[101] Per Holand, *Reliability of Subsea BOP Systems for Deepwater Application, Phase II DW, SINTEF* Report STF38 A99426 (November 7, 1999); Per Holand, *Deepwater Kicks and BOP Performance*, SINTEF Report STF38 A01419 (July 24, 2001); WEST Engineering Services, Inc., *Mini Shear Study for U.S. Minerals Management Service*, Requisition No. 2-1011-1003 (December 2002); WEST Engineering Services, Inc., *Shear Ram Capabilities Study for U.S. Minerals Management Service*, Requisition No. 3-4025-1001 (September 2004).

[102] WEST Engineering Services, Inc., "Comments by WEST Engineering Services, Houston, Texas, to The National Commission on the BP Deepwater Horizon Oil Spill and Offshore Drilling" (November 12, 2010): 3.

[103] David Barstow and others, "Regulators Failed to Address Risks in Oil Rig Fail-Safe Device," *New York Times*, June 20, 2010, www.nytimes.com/2010/06/21/us/21blowout.html.

[104] U.S. Department of the Interior, Outer Continental Shelf Safety Oversight Board, *Report to the Secretary of the Interior* (September 1, 2010), 6.

[105] *Ibid.*

[106] *Ibid.*

[107] U.S. Department of the Interior, Office of Inspector General, *Survey Report: Offshore Civil Penalties Program, Minerals Management Service* (March 30, 1999), http://www.doioig.gov/images/stories/reports/pdf/99-I-374.pdf.

[108] Commission staff analysis of Bureau of Ocean Energy Management, Regulation and Enforcement data provided to the Commission by the Department of the Interior of unannounced MMS inspections of MODUs/drilling rigs, 1990 (1,985 inspections) to 2009 (85 inspections). The pivotal change occurs in 1998–1999, as the numbers drop from 864 to 41 in the span of one year.

[109] Yearly MMS Incident Summary Reports are available at http://www.boemre.gov/incidents/IncidentStatisticsSummaries.htm.

[110] "Deepwater Gulf of Mexico production rising," *Oil & Gas Journal* (November 1, 1999): 34 ("In 1999, 11 more deepwater development production projects in the gulf have already begun producing or are on the verge of doing so"); Michael Davis, "LEARNING THE DRILL/The oil patch rebound brought with it a need for drilling companies to find, train and keep people to work the rigs," *Houston Chronicle* (February 1, 1998): 1 ("A shortage of qualified personnel has been a nagging problem since the oil patch has come back in the past year. But over the next two years some 50 new offshore jack-up rigs, semi-submersibles and drill ships currently being built or converted will

go into operation. Finding qualified crews to operate these increasingly high tech drilling rigs is a major worry for drilling companies.").

[111] 33 C.F.R. § 140.1.

[112] 46 C.F.R. pt. 2.

[113] Curry L. Hagerty and Jonathan L. Ramseur, Deepwater Horizon *Oil Spill: Selected Issues for Congress*, (Washington, D.C.: Congressional Research Service, July 15, 2010): 37. The Coast Guard proposed new safety rules in 1999, which triggered significant industry opposition, and has not since made those rules final. Outer Continental Shelf Activities, Notice of Proposed Rulemaking, 64 Fed. Reg. 68,416 (December 7, 1999).

[114] Inspection Under, and Enforcement of, Coast Guard Regulations for Fixed Facilities on the Outer Continental Shelf by the Minerals Management Service, 67 Fed. Reg. 5912 (February 7, 2002).

[115] The MMS and the United States Coast Guard have signed three governing Memoranda of Understanding (in 1989, 1999, and 2004, with supporting Memoranda of Agreement) in order to clarify roles and responsibilities related to workplace safety and the approval of technical systems and equipment that are applicable to both drilling and marine systems on offshore oil and gas facilities. See http://www.boemre.gov/regcompliance/MOU/MOUindex.htm.

[116] S. Elizabeth Birnbaum, interview with Commission staff, August 2010; Randall B. Luthi, interview with Commission staff, August 2010; Thomas R. Kitsos, interview with Commission staff, August 2010.

[117] Deepwater Royalty Relief Act of 1995, Pub. L. 104-58, 109 Stat. 563 (1995).

[118] Press Release, U.S. Department of the Interior, Secretary Salazar Launches Ethics Reform Initiative in Meeting with Minerals Management Service Employees, January 29, 2009, http://www.doi.gov/news/pressreleases/2009_01_29_release.cfm.

[119] For example, in 2006, Congress responded to Gulf state demands for greater revenues by enacting the Gulf of Mexico Energy Security Act, which provides that Alabama, Louisiana, Mississippi, and Texas and the coastal political subdivisions will receive 37.5 percent of all revenue (bonus bids, rentals, and royalty production) for new leases in the 5 million acres in the Eastern Gulf and the 5.8 million acres in the Central Gulf. See http://www.boemre.gov/ooc/press/2008/FactSheet-MMSGOMSecurityActMARCH202008.htm. The Fiscal Year 2010 allocation to the four Gulf States and their political subdivisions was approximately $866 million. See http://www.boemre.gov/offshore/PDFs/GOMESAFY2010Final.pdf.

[120] U.S. Department of the Interior, Outer Continental Shelf Safety Oversight Board, *Report to the Secretary of the Interior* (September 1, 2010), 11.

[121] U.S. Department of the Interior, Office of the Inspector General, *MMS Oil Marketing Group–Lakewood*, September 10, 2008.

[122] U.S. Department of the Interior, Office of the Inspector General, *MMS Oil Marketing Group–Lakewood*, Report Transmittal Letter, September 9, 2008, 3, http://www.doioig.gov/images/stories/reports/pdf/RIKinvestigation.pdf.

[123] Department of the Interior Office of the Inspector General, Minerals Management Service, *Island Operating Company, et al.*, (May 25, 2010), 7, http://www.doioig.gov/images/stories/reports/pdf/IslandOperatingCo.pdf.

[124] *Ibid.*

[125] Press Release, U.S. Department of the Interior, Secretary Salazar Launches Ethics Reform Initiative in Meeting with Minerals Management Service Employees, January 29, 2009, http://www.doi.gov/news/pressreleases/2009_01_29_release.cfm.

[126] U.S. Department of the Interior, Outer Continental Shelf Safety Oversight Board, *Report to the Secretary of the Interior* (September 1, 2010), 8.

[127] *Ibid.*, 13.

[128] *Ibid.*, 8, 13.

[129] *Ibid.*, 13.

[130] *Ibid.*, 6.

[131] Don E. Kash, *Lease Management Activities in the Geological Survey*, Commission on Fiscal Accountability of the Nation's Energy Resources: Technical Reports, 1981–1982, RG 48, Entry 998, Box 10, File 239, National Archives and Records Administration, 27.

[132] U.S. Department of the Interior, Outer Continental Shelf Safety Oversight Board, *Report to the Secretary of the Interior* (September 1, 2010), 11–12.

[133] Ibid., 11.

[134] 43 U.S.C. § 1344.

[135] 43 U.S.C. § 1344.

[136] 43 U.S.C. § 1344(a)(3).

[137] 42 U.S.C. § 4332.

[138] 40 C.F.R. § 1508.8 ("Effects includes ecological . . ., aesthetic, historic, cultural, economic, social, or health, whether direct, indirect, or cumulative").

[139] 16 U.S.C. §§ 1801-1891d.

[140] 16 U.S.C. §§ 1531-1544.

[141] 16 U.S.C. §§ 1361-1423h.

[142] 16 U.S.C. §§ 1431-1445c-1.

[143] 33 U.S.C. §§ 1251-1387.

[144] 33 U.S.C. §§ 2701-2762.

[145] Exec. Order No. 12,777, 56 Fed. Reg. 54,757 (October 22, 1991).

[146] 43 U.S.C. §1344.

[147] 43 U.S.C. §1340(c)(1).

[148] It appears to be understood that the meaning of this language is that an environmental impact statement is not required for the Gulf of Mexico, but it should be pointed out that is not the compelled or obvious reading of the language. The provision can also be fairly read to say no more than at least one impact statement has to be prepared for areas outside the Gulf and not address the issue, one way or another, concerning the application of NEPA within the Gulf. That potentially significant nuance, however, is beyond the scope of this report's inquiry.

[149] National Environmental Policy Act; Revised Implementing Procedures, 45 Fed. Reg. 75336 (proposed Nov. 14, 1980) (proposed NEPA rules); National Environmental Policy Act; Revised Implementing Procedures, 46 Fed. Reg. 7485 (Jan. 23, 1981) (final NEPA rules); see 516 Departmental Manual, 2.3.A(2) (1980).

[150] 43 C.F.R. § 46.215

[151] U.S. Department of the Interior, Outer Continental Shelf Safety Oversight Board, *Report to the Secretary of the Interior* (September 1, 2010), 20.

[152] *Ibid.*

[153] 516 Departmental Manual 15.4.C (providing for exceptions from categorical exclusion in certain "extraordinary circumstances," including when there are highly uncertain and potentially significant environmental effects).

[154] 51 Fed. Reg. 15,624 (1986).

[155] NOAA Fisheries Service, Southeast Regional Office, letter to MMS dated July 1, 1999 (subsequently updated in 2006, 2007, and 2008).

[156] *Essential Fish Habitat Assessment for the Minerals Management Service Programmatic Consultation for Gulf of Mexico Outer Continental Shelf (OCS) Oil and Gas Activities* (June 4, 1999).

[157] NOAA Fisheries Service, Southeast Regional Office, letter to MMS dated July 1, 1999 (subsequently updated in 2006, 2007, and 2008).

[158] 30 C.F.R. § 254.21.

[159] 30 C.F.R. § 254.23.

[160] The Response Group on behalf of ExxonMobil, *Gulf of Mexico Regional Oil Spill Response Plan* (August 2009), Rev. 5; The Response Group on behalf of ConocoPhillips, *Gulf of Mexico Regional Oil Spill Response Plan* (April 2010), Rev. 6; The Response Group on behalf of Chevron, *Gulf of Mexico Regional Oil Spill Response Plan* (February 2010), Version 3; The Response Group on behalf of Shell Offshore Inc., *Gulf of Mexico Regional Oil Spill Response Plan*, (June 2010), Rev. 6.1.

[161] The Response Group on behalf of BP, *Regional Oil Spill Response Plan-Gulf of Mexico* (June 30, 2009), App. H: 5, 17, and 32.

Chapter Four

[1] John Guide (BP), interview with Commission staff, September 17, 2010.

[2] Internal Transocean document (TRN-HEC 90686). Internal documents are identified by their document production serial numbers when available, which were assigned by the entity that provided them.

[3] Internal BP document (BP-HZN-MBI 126338).

[4] Internal Transocean document (TRN-USCG-MMS 11597).

[5] Internal BP document (BP-HZN-MBI 126338).

[6] *Ibid.*

[7] *Ibid.* Three companies own the Macondo well. BP has a 65 percent share, Anadarko Petroleum Corporation has a 25 percent share, and MOEX Offshore has a 10 percent share. BP maintained regular contact with Anadarko and MOEX throughout the drilling of the well.

[8] Internal Transocean documents (TRN–USCG–MMS 11600, 11605, 11609, 11613, 11617, 11621, 11625).

[9] Brett Clanton, "New tactic might seal leaking well sooner, BP CEO says," *Houston Chronicle*, May 5, 2010.

[10] Gregory Walz (BP), interview with Commission staff, October 6, 2010.

[11] Testimony of Gregory Walz, Hearing before the Deepwater Horizon Joint Investigation Team, October 7, 2010, 157–59.

[12] Internal BP document (BP-HZN-MBI 143300) (emphasis added).

[13] Internal BP documents (BP-HZN-MBI 136937, 136941).

[14] Internal BP document (BP-HZN-CEC 8848-58).

[15] Internal BP document (BP-HZN-MBI 129238-39).

[16] Guide, interview. Indeed, just days before the running of the long string at Macondo, another well drilled by Transocean's DD3 suffered just such a complication. *Ibid.*

[17] Testimony of Jesse Gagliano, Hearing before the Deepwater Horizon Joint Investigation Team, August 24, 2010, 320.

[18] Internal BP document (BP-HZN-CEC 22433). Walz also noted that the flight carrying centralizers would not increase costs. *Ibid.*

[19] Guide, interview. BP had special one-piece bolt-on centralizers made for the Thunder Horse project. *Ibid.*

[20] Internal BP document (BP-HZN-MBI 128379).

[21] Internal BP document (BP-HZN-CEC 22669).

[22] Internal BP document (BP-HZN-CEC 22433).

[23] Testimony of Steve Lewis, Hearing before the National Commission, November 9, 2010, 93–94; Internal BP document (BP-HZN-MBI 129226). Prior to conversion, a small ball drops from the top of the float valves to block the main path through the auto-fill tube, leaving only two small holes on the side of the tube through which mud can flow. *Ibid.*

[24] The Well Site Leaders—Bob Kaluza and Don Vidrine—would normally have been on the rig. Morel, a relatively junior BP engineer, had flown to the rig out of a professional interest in learning more about the cementing process. Guide, interview.

[25] Bryan Clawson (Weatherford), interview with Commission staff, October 28, 2010; BP, Deepwater Horizon *Accident Investigation Report* (September 8, 2010), 70.

[26] Testimony of Steve Lewis, 96; Internal Transocean document (TRN-USCG_MMS 11638).

[27] Internal BP document (BP-HZN-MBI 137367).

[28] *Ibid.*; Testimony of Nathaniel Chaisson, Hearing before the Deepwater Horizon Joint Investigation Team, August 24, 2010, 432.

[29] Internal BP documents (BP-HZN-MBI 137367, 21304). Since the incident, BP has argued that the M-I SWACO models predicted an erroneously high circulation pressure, and that the readings the crew observed were proper. This may ultimately explain the readings, but it does not explain why the BP Macondo team dismissed them as the result of a broken pressure gauge.

[30] David Izon, E.P. Danenberger, and Melinda Mayes, "Absence of fatalities in blowouts encouraging in MMS study of OCS incidents 1992-2006," *Well Control* July/August (2007), 84.

[31] Testimony of John Guide, Hearing before the Deepwater Horizon Joint Investigation Team, July 22, 2010, 87.

[32] John Gisclair, Sperry Sun data, April 20, 2010 (annotations, September 20, 2010). Commission calculation based on internal Halliburton document (HAL_10994).

[33] Internal BP document (BP-HZN-MBI 127537-39); Internal Halliburton document (HAL_11196).

[34] 30 C.F.R. § 250.421.

[35] Internal BP document (BP-HZN-MBI 193549). BP's internal guidelines further specify that centralization should extend 100 feet above any such hydrocarbon-bearing zones. If either the top of cement or centralization requirements are not met, the guidelines require that the actual top of cement should be confirmed by a "proven cement evaluation technique." *Ibid.*

[36] Internal BP documents (BP-HZN-MBI 143295, BP-HZN-CEC 22663); BP, Deepwater Horizon *Accident Investigation Report*, 34.

[37] Document provided to the Commission by Halliburton entitled "Halliburton GoM Foam Jobs 2002–2010."

[38] S.L. Pickett and S.W. Cole, "Foamed Cementing Technique for Liners Yields Cost-Effective Results" (Society of Petroleum Engineers SPE Paper #27679, Midland, Texas, March 1994), 523–24.

[39] Halliburton had delivered the slurry blend to the *Deepwater Horizon* several months earlier. It had developed the blend to match the temperature and pressure profile of the well that *Deepwater Horizon* had drilled immediately prior to Macondo—another BP well called Kodiak. Jesse Gagliano (Halliburton), interview with Commission staff, September 10, 2010.

40 At this point, it appears that lab personnel replicated the dry blend recipe that was on the rig using off-the-shelf materials from their lab. For later tests, Halliburton sent samples of the cement that was actually on the *Horizon* back to the lab and directly tested those materials.

41 Internal BP document (BP-HZN-MBI 109218).

42 Internal Halliburton document (HAL_DOJ 68).

43 Internal Halliburton document (HAL_DOJ 36).

44 Internal Halliburton document (HAL_DOJ 43).

45 *Ibid.*

46 Internal BP document (BP-HZN-MBI 136946-47).

47 Internal BP document (BP-HZN-MBI 171151).

48 Internal BP document (BP-HZN-MBI 136946-47).

49 Internal BP document (BP-HZN-CEC 20234).

50 *Ibid.*

51 Testimony of Vincent Tabler, Hearing before the Deepwater Horizon Joint Investigation Team, August 25, 2010, 22–23, 36.

52 Internal Halliburton document (HAL_0011208).

53 Internal BP document (BP-HZN-MBI 137370).

54 Internal BP document (BP-HZN-MBI 129141).

55 Internal Transocean document (TRN–USCG_MMS 30422); Internal Schlumberger document (SLB-EC-2).

56 Testimony of John Guide, 44–45.

57 Internal BP document (BP-HZN-MBI 143304).

58 Testimony of John Guide, 298 (the cement plug was "deeper than normal"); Testimony of Ronald Sepulvado, Hearing before the Deepwater Horizon Joint Investigation Team, July 20, 2010, 145 ("the top of the surface plug is normally at 500 feet below the wellhead").

59 Internal BP document (BP-HZN-CEC 8574).

60 Testimony of Jimmy Harrell, Hearing before the Deepwater Horizon Joint Investigation Team, May 27, 2010, 118.

61 Internal BP document (BP-HZN-CEC 8574).

62 Internal BP document (BP-HZN-CEC 21260-279).

63 Internal BP document (BP-HZN-MBI 126928).

64 Internal BP document (BP-HZN-OSC 1438).

65 30 C.F.R. § 250.423.

66 The blind shear rams closed and sealed as expected during the positive-pressure test. This fact suggests that the rams were capable of sealing the well when the blowout occurred. But the evidence is inconclusive on its own; during the positive-pressure test the crew closed the blind shear rams using a low pressure hydraulic system, rather than the high pressure hydraulic system that would have activated the rams in the event of a blowout.

67 Internal Transocean document (TRN–HCEC 90).

68 Testimony of Patrick O'Bryan, Hearing before the Deepwater Horizon Joint Investigation Team, August 26, 2010, 360.

69 Testimony of David Sims, Hearing before the Deepwater Horizon Joint Investigation Team, August 26, 2010, 204. There were no regulations or industry standards guiding the conduct or interpretation of negative-pressure tests at the time of the Macondo blowout. The absence of any such guidance may have contributed to the failure to conduct and interpret the test correctly here.

70 This calculation is based on approximate values of the depths and mud weights involved.

71 Testimony of Leo Lindner, Hearing before the Deepwater Horizon Joint Investigation Team, July 19, 2010, 297; BP, Deepwater Horizon *Accident Investigation Report*, app. Q, 1.

72 BP, Deepwater Horizon *Accident Investigation Report*, 83.

73 Testimony of Leo Lindner, 308–11. The exclusion for "[d]rilling fluids, produced waters, and other wastes associated with the exploration, development, or production of crude oil, natural gas or geothermal energy" is found at 40 C.F.R. § 261.4.

74 Testimony of Leo Lindner, 276–79, 297, 359–60; Internal BP document (BP-HZN-BLY 47100).

75 Testimony of Randy Ezell, Hearing before the Deepwater Horizon Joint Investigation Team, May 28, 2010, 279–81.

76 Testimony of Daun Winslow, Hearing before the Deepwater Horizon Joint Investigation Team, August 24, 2010, 219;

Testimony of Randy Ezell, 279.

[77] Testimony of Randy Ezell, 279.

[78] Testimony of Lee Lambert, Hearing before the Deepwater Horizon Joint Investigation Team, July 20, 2010, 292. Transocean disputes these accounts. It points out that the only individuals who have stated that Anderson advanced the "bladder effect" theory are BP employees.

[79] Testimony of Lee Lambert, 292.

[80] Testimony of Jimmy Harrell, 117; Internal BP documents (BP-HZN-MBI 127909, BP-HZN-CEC 20189-90). While that may have been Mr. Vidrine's stated reason for running the test on the kill line, the Commission notes that the negative-pressure test performed at Macondo—whether on the drill pipe or kill line—was different from the negative-pressure test described in the Application for Permit to Modify. Testimony of Mark Bly, Hearing before the National Commission, November 8, 2010, 293–95.

[81] BP, Deepwater Horizon *Accident Investigation Report*, 86.

[82] There are several possible explanations for the inconsistent readings on the drill pipe and kill line. One possibility is that the viscous spacer that had leaked through the annular preventer migrated into and clogged the kill line. John Smith, *Review of Operational Data Preceding Explosion on Deepwater Horizon in MC252* (July 1, 2010), 20–21. Another possibility is that a valve was inadvertently closed that should have been open. BP, Deepwater Horizon *Accident Investigation Report*, 87. A third, more remote, possibility is that hydrocarbons coming up the well formed solid hydrates when they hit the cold seawater and those hydrates clogged the kill line. Guide, interview.

[83] Testimony of Christopher Haire, Hearing before the Deepwater Horizon Joint Investigation Team, May 28, 2010, 247.

[84] For example, a bubble of gas, under ideal conditions, would expand approximately 166-fold. This number differs under actual conditions based on fluid properties and flow.

[85] Mudloggers operate systems that collect and transmit real-time data from sensors on the rig. BP employed mudloggers from Sperry Drilling (a Halliburton subsidiary) on the Deepwater Horizon.

[86] The driller first sent mud to pits 9 and 10, then switched to pit 7, and then switched to pit 6. Sperry Sun data, April 20, 2010, 20:10–21:18.

[87] *Ibid.*, 20:28–20:36, 20:58–21:06.

[88] *Ibid.*, 20:20–21:01.

[89] *Ibid.*, 21:01.

[90] *Ibid.*, 21:01–21:08.

[91] The Commission believes, based on interviews of the mudloggers on the *Horizon*, that the Hitec system may have shown a more obvious trend because it displays numeric values as opposed to trend lines such as those seen in the Sperry data shown in the text. Joseph Keith (Sperry), interview with Commission staff, October 6, 2010; Cathleenia Willis (Sperry), interview with Commission staff, October 21, 2010.

[92] Testimony of Greg Meche, Hearing before the Deepwater Horizon Joint Investigation Team, May 28, 2010, 207–09.

[93] 40 C.F.R. §§ 261.4, 435.11.

[94] Testimony of Greg Meche, 207–09, 219.

[95] Keith, interview.

[96] Internal BP document (BP-HZN-MBI 21415).

[97] Keith, interview. Given what we now know, it is all but impossible that the well was not flowing as of 9:08 p.m. BP, Deepwater Horizon *Accident Investigation Report*, 25; Smith, *Review of Operational Data Preceding Explosion on Deepwater Horizon*, 22–23. Other than faulty memory, the only apparent explanations for Mr. Keith's statement are that the crew had already closed off the portion of the flow line Mr. Keith was watching or that Mr. Keith watched for an inadequate period of time. Keith, interview; Darryl Bourgoyne (LSU), interview with Commission staff, November 23, 2010.

[98] Testimony of Greg Meche, 207–09.

[99] *Ibid.*

[100] Internal BP document (BP-HZN-MBI 21415).

[101] Sperry Sun data, April 20, 2010, 21:08–21:14.

[102] *Ibid.*, 21:14–21:15.

[103] *Ibid.*, 2010, 21:17–21:18.

[104] Testimony of Chad Murray, Hearing before the Deepwater Horizon Joint Investigation Team, May 27, 2010, 335–36.

[105] *Ibid.*, 336.

[106] Testimony of Randy Ezell, 282.

[107] Testimony of Bill Ambrose, Hearing before the National Commission, November 8, 2010, 381.

[108] David Young (Transocean), interview with Commission staff, November 19, 2010.

[109] Testimony of David Young, Hearing before the Deepwater Horizon Joint Investigation Team, May 27, 2010, 259.

[110] Young, interview.

[111] Sperry Sun data, April 20, 2010, 21:08–21:14.

[112] Bill Ambrose (Transocean), interview with Commission staff, September 21, 2010.

[113] Sperry Sun data, April 20, 2010, 21:38.

[114] Young, interview.

[115] Sperry Sun data, April 20, 2010, 21:38–21:42.

[116] Testimony of Randy Ezell, 283; Young, interview.

[117] Testimony of Micah Sandell, Hearing before the Deepwater Horizon Joint Investigation Team, May 29, 2010, 10.

[118] Testimony of Christopher Pleasant, Hearing before the Deepwater Horizon Joint Investigation Team, May 28, 2010, 173.

[119] Testimony of Randy Ezell, 283.

[120] Testimony of Bill Ambrose, 244.

[121] Smith, *Review of Operational Data Preceding Explosion on Deepwater Horizon*, 14; Testimony of Bill Ambrose, 252–53; BP, Deepwater Horizon *Accident Investigation Report*, 28.

[122] Testimony of Christopher Pleasant, 165.

[123] *Ibid.*, 123.

[124] *Ibid.*

[125] Various parties have suggested other causes for the deadman's failure, including leaks, overdue equipment certification, and improper modifications.

[126] Interview with industry expert, September 24, 2010.

[127] After the blowout, some industry CEOs testified they would never have used a long string production casing, suggesting there was a causal connection between BP's choice of the long string and the blowout. Hearing Before the Subcomm. on Energy and Environment, 111th Cong. 104 (June 15, 2010) (statements of John Watson, Chairman and Chief Executive Officer, Chevron Corporation; and Rex Tillerson, Chairman and Chief Executive Officer, Exxon-Mobil).

[128] First, the long string required the cement to travel through a longer stretch of steel casing—roughly 12,000 feet longer—before reaching its final destination, potentially increasing the risk of cement contamination. Second, because it can require higher cement pumping pressure, a long string design can lead to the selection of lower cement volumes, lower densities, and lower pump rates. Third, the cement job at the bottom of a long string is more difficult to remediate than one at the bottom of a liner.

[129] Internal BP document (BP-HZN-MBI 128489); BP, Deepwater Horizon *Accident Investigation Report*, 64 ("the BP Macondo well team did not ask for the OptiCem model to be re-run"). This may have been because of Mr. Guide's distrust of the OptiCem model. Testimony of John Guide, 275 ("it's wrong a lot"). When Halliburton rig personnel eventually informed Gagliano of BP's decision themselves, he responded by e-mailing BP modeling data suggesting again that more centralizers would be needed to prevent channeling. Internal BP document (BP-HZN-MBI 128708).

[130] Testimony of Jesse Gagliano, 259; Testimony of Nathaniel Chaisson, 415.

[131] BP, Deepwater Horizon *Accident Investigation Report*, 35. Mr. Guide disagreed with the BP report's conclusion in an interview with Commission staff. Guide, interview.

[132] Internal BP document (BP-HZN-CEC 22670).

[133] Ronald Sepulvado (BP), interview with Commission staff, September 1, 2010.

[134] BP, Deepwater Horizon *Accident Investigation Report*, 66.

[135] Fred Bartlit, letter to the National Commission, October 28, 2010 (reporting the results of cement testing).

[136] If BP were looking, the one February test actually reported to BP could have prompted BP to question the design as well. BP argues that its failure to do so here is understandable given that it had hired one of the world's leading cementers specifically for purposes of designing and testing the cement slurry.

[137] To the contrary, Halliburton's selection of conditioning time appears to have been haphazard at best. Lab personnel used different conditioning times (ranging from zero conditioning time to three hours) in each of the four foam stability tests that they conducted.

[138] Internal Halliburton document (HAL_DOJ 43).

[139] Testimony of Daun Winslow, 209; Guide, interview.

[140] Moreover, once the BP Well Site Leaders and crew realized that the annular preventer was leaking, they should have circulated out any spacer that had migrated below the annular preventer prior to continuing with the test. Testi-

mony of John Smith, Hearing before the National Commission, November 9, 2010, 140–41.

[141] The Commission agrees with others that there is no such thing as a "bladder effect" that could account for the pressures the rig crew was observing. There was no apparent explanation for the 1400 psi on the drill pipe other than that the well was flowing.

[142] Transocean asserts that its personnel, including the driller and toolpusher, were not "in any way responsible for interpreting the negative pressure test or making the decision that the well was secure and work could properly proceed." Rachel Clingman, letter to Commission staff, November 16, 2010, 1. As the Commission's staff made clear at the November 8, 2010 hearing, the Commission is not tasked with deciding legal responsibility. Based on available evidence, however, Revette and Anderson agreed the negative-pressure test was a success and did not stop the job before moving on to the remaining temporary abandonment procedures. Testimony of Lee Lambert, 291; Internal BP documents (BP-HZN-CEC 20347, 20178).

[143] Guide, interview.

[144] Benjamin Powell, "BP Response to Presidential Commission's Preliminary Technical Conclusions," letter to Commission staff, November 22, 2010, att. 1, 3 (citing Hearing Before the Senate Comm. on Energy and Natural Resources, 111th Cong. (May 11, 2010) (statement of Testimony of Tim Probert, Halliburton President, Global Business Lines, Chief Health, Safety and Environmental Officer)).

[145] Testimony of Mark Bly, 213; Testimony of Charlie Williams, Hearing before the National Commission, November 9, 2010, 45.

[146] Testimony of Steve Lewis, 54, 124. BP argues that "[t]he use of additional mechanical plugs would have brought its own additional risks." Powell, letter, att. 1, 6 (citing API, *Recommended Practice 65—Part 2* (May 2010), § 3.1); Guide, interview. However, BP does not present any evidence that the Macondo team in fact evaluated those risks or compared them with the risks of setting a single surface cement plug in seawater 3,300 feet below the mud line.

[147] Merrick Kelley (BP), interview with Commission staff, October 22, 2010; Industry expert, interview.

[148] BP asserts that "[u]sing drill collars would have required unracking the drill pipe on the rig and then locating and re-racking drill collars—a set of additional operations with attendant risks." Powell, letter, att. 1, 5. BP does not provide any evidence to substantiate the extent of such "attendant risks" or whether they outweighed the risks of the procedure BP chose. Most significantly, BP offers no evidence that its Macondo team ever considered such risks or performed a rigorous comparative risk analysis.

[149] Internal BP document (BP-HZN-CEC 8574).

[150] Testimony of Mark Bly, 308. BP has suggested that the float valves provided an additional barrier to flow. BP, Deepwater Horizon Accident Investigation Report, 68. The Commission does not agree that float valves, even when converted, constitute a distinct physical barrier to flow, but instead reinforce the cement in the shoe track. Clawson, interview (indicating that Weatherford does not consider the float collar to be a barrier to hydrocarbons); API, *Recommended Practice 65—Part 2* (May 2010), §§ 3.4, 4.4.3 (float valves not included in the list of subsurface mechanical barriers; float equipment used to prevent cement from flowing back into the casing).

[151] Testimony of Darryl Bourgoyne, Hearing before the National Commission, November 9, 2010, 133.

[152] Testimony of Charlie Williams, 46–53.

[153] Testimony of Bill Ambrose, 380–84.

[154] Between 8:00 and 9:49 p.m., the crew was performing a number of other activities that may have further confounded the data or at least distracted the driller. The crew was emptying various tanks on the rig into the active pit system, including "trip tanks" and "sand traps," which may have masked increased flow out of the well into the active pit system. At 9:18 p.m., a valve on one of the pumps blew, and a number of crew members from the rig floor went to fix it. Finally, the crew was operating one or both of the cranes on the main deck, which could have affected flow-out and volume readings.

[155] Internal BP document (BP-HZN-OSC 5420).

[156] Guide, interview.

[157] *Ibid.*; Internal BP document (BP-HZN-MBI 193529-39).

[158] It appears that the chain of command and responsibilities at BP during the execute phase were not well-understood by the Macondo Engineering Team Leader. When asked during an interview who was responsible for designing or amending the temporary abandonment procedures, the Macondo Engineering Team Leader said he would need to look at the company's chart of roles and responsibilities. Walz, interview.

[159] Internal BP document (BP-HZN-MBI 117603).

[160] Internal BP document (BP-HZN-MBI 128542).

[161] Internal BP document (BP-HZN-OSC 6224).

[162] There is a dispute as to whether BP personnel called back to shore that evening to discuss the data observed during the negative-pressure test. The Commission staff has to date seen no direct evidence of such a call. The staff's investigation is ongoing.

[163] Internal BP document (BP-HZN-BLY 38354).

[164] Internal BP document (BP-HZN-BLY 38355).

[165] Internal BP document (BP-HZN-BLY 38354).

[166] Internal BP document (BP-HZN-BLY 38361).

[167] *Ibid.*

[168] Internal BP document (BP-HZN-BLY 38362).

[169] Internal Transocean document (TRN-PC 3227).

[170] Transocean states that on April 5, 2010, it posted a short, two-page version of this advisory to an internal electronic document platform, which supervisors on the *Deepwater Horizon* had access to. But the advisory was limited to completion operations, and, as of this writing, Transocean has not offered any evidence that anyone on the rig actually saw or reviewed the advisory.

[171] The industry and the international community also failed to adequately communicate lessons learned from the Montara blowout, which for ten weeks beginning on August 21, 2009 spewed between 400 and 1500 barrels per day of oil and gas into the Timor Sea approximately 150 miles off the northwest coast of Australia. David Borthwick, *Report of the Montara Commission of Inquiry* (The Montara Commission of Inquiry, Australia, June 2010), 5, 26. According to the *Report of the Montara Commission of Inquiry*, released on November 24, 2010, many of the technical and managerial causes of the Montara blowout track those at Macondo. For instance, the Commission of Inquiry concluded that the cement job in the "9 5/8" casing shoe failed, that there were numerous risk factors surrounding the cement job that went unheeded, and that the cement job was not properly pressure tested. *Ibid.*, 7. According to the Commission of Inquiry:

> The multiple problems in undertaking the cement job—such as the failure of the top and bottom plugs to create a seal after "bumping," the failure of the float valves and an unexpected rush of fluid—should have raised alarm bells. Those problems necessitated a careful evaluation of what happened, the instigation of pressure testing and, most likely, remedial action. No such careful evaluation was undertaken. The problems were not complicated or unsolvable, and the potential remedies were well known and not costly. This was a failure of "sensible oilfield practice 101."

Ibid. The Commission of Inquiry went on to conclude that while the "absence of tested barriers was a proximate cause of the Blowout," the deeper failure was a systemic failure of management on the part of the operator, PTTEP Australasia. *Ibid.*, 9.

[172] Testimony of Rex Tillerson, Hearing before the National Commission, November 9, 2010, 250–52; Testimony of Marvin Odum, Hearing before the National Commission, November 9, 2010, 278–79.

[173] 30 C.F.R. § 250.1721(d).

[174] 30 C.F.R. § 250.141(a).

[175] Internal BP document (BP-HZN-OSC 1436).

[176] Internal BP document (BP-HZN-MBI 127906). MMS approved a number of other requests by BP for deviations on the Macondo well. None of those other approvals appear to have contributed to the blowout. However, they do suggest that the MMS staff did not spend much time deciding whether to grant the requests, which may have been due to the severe funding and staffing shortages in the New Orleans office.

Chapter Five

[1] Brady Dennis and Shailagh Murray, "GOP Changes Tone on Financial Bill," *Washington Post*, April 21, 2010; Edward Wyatt and David M. Herszenhorn, "Bill on Finance Wins Approval of Senate Panel," *New York Times*, April 22, 2010; Jim Puzzanghera, "In N.Y., Obama to Push for Financial Overhaul," *Los Angeles Times*, April 22, 2010; Adam Liptak, "Justices Reject Ban on Depicting Animal Cruelty," *New York Times*, April 21, 2010; Joan Biskupic, "High Court Negates Animal Cruelty Law as Too Broad, 8-1" *USA Today*, April 21, 2010; Jess Bravin, "Court Voids Law on Animal Cruelty," *Wall Street Journal*, April 21, 2010; Bart Barnes, "A Movement's Matriarch," *Washington Post*, April 21, 2010; Andrew Zajac and Melissa Healy, "FDA Puts the Pinch on Salt," *Los Angeles Times*, April 21, 2010.

[2] Neil MacFarquhar, "Routine Flights Become Overland Odysseys, Minus Clean Socks," *New York Times*, April 22, 2010.

[3] Campbell Robertson, "11 Remain Missing After Oil Rig Explodes Off Louisiana," *New York Times*, April 22, 2010.

[4] Rick Jervis, "Gulf Blast Appears to be 'Blowout'," *USA Today*, April 22, 2010; Ben Casselman, Russell Gold, and Angel Gonzalez, "Blast Jolts Oil World," *Wall Street Journal*, April 22, 2010.

[5] Jervis, "Gulf Blast Appears to be 'Blowout.'"

[6] Richard Fausset, "Oil Rig Explodes; 11 Missing," *Los Angeles Times*, April 22, 2010.

[7] 40 C.F.R. § 300, Subpart D.

[8] Paul Purpura et al., "Search continues for 11 missing in rig blast," *Times-Picayune*, April 22, 2010.

[9] Paul Rioux and Chris Kirkham, "Search for 11 Workers Missing After Oil Rig Explosion Is Expected To Be Called Off Friday," *Times-Picayune*, April 22, 2010.

[10] Testimony of Captain James Hanzalik, Hearing Before the Deepwater Joint Investigation Team, October 4, 2010, 29-30.

[11] 40 C.F.R. § 300.305(c).

[12] Press Release, White House, Statement by the Press Secretary on the President's Oval Office Meeting to Discuss the Situation in the Gulf of Mexico, April 22, 2010.

[13] 40 C.F.R. § 300.175(b).

[14] Leslie Kaufman, "Search Ends for Missing Oil Rig Workers," *New York Times*, April 23, 2010.

[15] Press Release, Unified Command, Unified Command Continues to Respond to Deepwater Horizon, April 25, 2010.

[16] Interview with Coast Guard official, August 27, 2010.

[17] BP, *Initial Exploration Plan*, Mississippi Canyon Block 252 (February 23, 2009), § 2.6.

[18] Doug Suttles, interview with Commission staff, October 13, 2010; Interviews with Minerals Management Service officials, October 15, 2010; Interview with well control expert, October 14, 2010.

[19] Press Release, BP, Work Begins To Drill Relief Well To Stop Oil Spill, May 4, 2010; White House, Ongoing Response Timeline, May 17, 2010; David Hayes, memo to Commission staff, November 12, 2010.

[20] Joe Stephens and Mary Pat Flaherty, "Oil Industry Cleanup Organization Swamped by BP Spill," *Washington Post*, June 29, 2010.

[21] The Response Group on behalf of BP, *Regional Oil Spill Response Plan-Gulf of Mexico* (June 30, 2009), App. H: 40.

[22] Jonathan Ramseur, *Oil Spills in U.S. Coastal Waters: Background, Governance, and Issues for Congress* (Congressional Research Service, 2008), 2.

[23] Joint Industry Oil Spill Preparedness and Response Task Force, *Joint Industry Recommendations to Improve Oil Spill Preparedness and Response* (September 3, 2010), V-3, V-5; Henry Fountain, "Advances in Oil Spill Cleanup Lag Since Valdez," *New York Times*, June 24, 2010.

[24] Sarah L. Milton et al., "Obituary Peter L. Lutz," *Journal of Experimental Biology* 208 (2005): 2817–18; *Regional Oil Spill Response Plan-Gulf of Mexico* App. F:19, § 11:7, App. E.

[25] Opening Statement of Chairman Edward Markey, "Drilling Down on America's Energy Future: Safety, Security, and Clean Energy," Hearing Before the House Committee on Energy and Commerce, Subcommittee on Energy and Environment, 111th Congress (June 15, 2010).

[26] Interview with NOAA scientist, August 20, 2010; Interview with NOAA scientist, October 13, 2010.

[27] NOAA Scientist, *Estimation of the Oil Released from Deepwater Horizon Incident*, April 26, 2010; Mark Miller, e-mail to Martha Garcia, June 14, 2010.

[28] Interview with NOAA scientist, August 30, 2010; Interview with NOAA scientist, October 13, 2010.

[29] Press Conference, Admiral Mary Landry and Doug Suttles, New Orleans, LA, April 28, 2010.

[30] Press Release, Deepwater Horizon Incident Joint Information Center Update: The Ongoing Administration-Wide Response to the BP Deepwater Horizon Oil Spill, July 15, 2010.

[31] Paul Purpura, "Guard Troops Going Home," *Times-Picayune*, October 21, 2010.

[32] 40 C.F.R. § 300.322(b).

[33] 40 C.F.R. § 300.305(d).

[34] Clifford Krauss, "Oil Spill's Blow to BP's Image May Eclipse Its Cost," *New York Times*, April 29, 2010.

[35] Office of Science and Technology, *First Report of the President's Panel on Oil Spills* (1969), 9.

[36] Interview with well control expert, October 14, 2010.

[37] Transcript, Office of the Press Secretary, Press Briefing on the BP Oil Spill in the Gulf Coast, April 29, 2010.

[38] Transcript, State of the Union with Candy Crowley, CNN, May 2, 2010.

[39] 40 C.F.R. § 300.323; Campbell Robertson, "White House Takes a Bigger Role in the Oil Spill Cleanup," *New York Times*, April 29, 2010.

[40] 40 C.F.R. § 300.5.

[41] 40 C.F.R. § 300.323(c).

[42] Interview with Coast Guard official, November 12, 2010.

[43] Press Release, Deepwater Horizon Incident Joint Information Center, Coast Guard Commandant Admiral Thad Allen Designated National Incident Commandant For Continued Response To BP Oil Spill, May 1, 2010.

[44] Thom Shanker, "Commander Accustomed to Scrutiny and Crises," *New York Times*, September 10, 2005; Matthew L. Wald, "A New, Experienced Protector for Navy in Home Waters," *New York Times*, November 9, 2001; Elizabeth Bumiller, "Casualty of Firestorm: Outrage, Bush, and FEMA Chief," *New York Times*, September 10, 2005.

[45] Editorial, "Allen Candid About Recovery," *Advocate*, December 11, 2005.

[46] Jim Tankersley, "The Government's 'Rock Star' in Charge of the Oil Spill," *Los Angeles Times*, June 1, 2010.

[47] Testimony of Harry Thierens, Hearing before the Deepwater Horizon Joint Investigation Team, August 25, 2010, 104–5.

[48] Henry Fountain, "Notes from Wake of Blowout Outline Obstacles and Frustration," *New York Times*, June 21, 2010; Non-public BP document, May 6, 2010.

[49] Testimony of Harry Thierens, 106.

[50] Government science advisor, e-mail to Commission staff, October 7, 2010; Testimony of William Stringfellow, Hearing before the Deepwater Horizon Joint Investigation Team, August 25, 2010, 352.

[51] BP, Deepwater Horizon *Accident Investigation Report* (September 8, 2010), 150.

[52] Non-public BP document, May 7, 2010.

[53] David Barstow et al., "Regulators Failed to Address Risks in Oil Rig Fail-Safe Device," *New York Times*, June 20, 2010; Interview with senior administration official, November 8, 2010.

[54] FEMA, "Disasters Declared by Year or State," http://www.fema.gov/news/disaster_totals_annual.fema.

[55] 42 U.S.C. §§ 5121-5206.

[56] 40 C.F.R. § 300.105(c)(3).

[57] Interview with government official, August 24, 2010.

[58] Press Release, Office of the Governor, Governor Jindal Issues State Declaration of Emergency for Oil Leak, April 29, 2010.

[59] Press Release, Governor Barbour Issues State of Emergency for Mississippi Gulf Coast, April 30, 2010; Press Release, Gov. Riley Declares State of Emergency to Prepare for Oil Approaching Alabama Coast, April 30, 2010; State of Florida, Office of the Governor, Executive Order Number 10-99 (Emergency Management—Deepwater Horizon), April 30, 2010.

[60] Interview with government official, August 24, 2010; Interview with government official, September 13, 2010; Interview with government official, September 15, 2010.

[61] Interview with Coast Guard official, August 31, 2010.

[62] Interview with BP official, October 22, 2010; Interview with government official, October 5, 2010; Interview with government official, August 24, 2010; Interview with Coast Guard official, August 25, 2010.

[63] La. Rev. Stat. § 29: 727.

[64] Interview with government official, October 8, 2010.

[65] Interview with Coast Guard official, October 20, 2010.

[66] Interview with government official, October 8, 2010; Interview with government official, October 14, 2010.

[67] Testimony of Admiral Thad Allen, National Incident Commander, Hearing before the National Commission, September 27, 2010.

[68] Press Release, In Precautionary Move, LDWF and DHH Announce Closures Due to Oil Spill, April 30, 2010; Press Release, Alabama Department of Conservation and Natural Resources, Some State Waters Closed to Fishing, June 2, 2010; Press Release, Mississippi Department of Marine Resources, Revised Precautionary Closure: Portions of Mississippi Marine Waters Reopen to Commercial and Recreational Fishing, June 4, 2010; Florida Fish and Wildlife Conservation Commission, Order No. EO 10-29, Emergency Closure of State Waters of the Gulf of Mexico in response to the Deepwater Horizon Oil Spill, June 13, 2010.

[69] NOAA, Office of Response and Restoration, *Oil Forecast Outlook* (April 23, 2010).

[70] Fisheries of the Caribbean, Gulf of Mexico, and South Atlantic; Emergency Fisheries Closure in the Gulf of Mexico Due to the Deepwater Horizon Oil Spill, 75 Fed. Reg. 24,822 (May 6, 2010); NOAA Fisheries Service, *Deepwater Horizon/BP Oil Spill: Size and Percent Coverage of Fishing Closures Due to BP Oil Spill* (November 15, 2010), http://sero.nmfs.noaa.gov/ClosureSizeandPercentCoverage.htm.

[71] Fisheries of the Caribbean, Gulf of Mexico, and South Atlantic; Amendment to Emergency Fisheries Closure in the Gulf of Mexico Due to the Deepwater Horizon Oil Spill, 75 Fed. Reg. 26,679 (May 12, 2010); NOAA, Deepwater Horizon/BP Oil Spill: Size and Percent Coverage of Fishing Closures Due to BP Oil Spill.

[72] Fisheries of the Caribbean, Gulf of Mexico, and South Atlantic; Emergency Fisheries Closures in the Southeast Region Due to the Deepwater Horizon Oil Spill; Amendment 2, 75 Fed. Reg. 27,217 (May 14, 2010).

[73] NOAA, *Deepwater Horizon/BP Oil Spill: Size and Percent Coverage of Fishing Closures Due to BP Oil Spill*.

[74] Interview with government official, October 12, 2010.

[75] BP, "Factsheet on BP Vessels of Opportunity Program" (July 7, 2010), 4, http://www.bp.com/liveassets/bp_internet/globalbp/globalbp_uk_english/incident_response/STAGING/local_assets/downloads_pdfs/factsheet_bp_vessels_of_opportunity_program.pdf.

[76] National Incident Command, *National Incident Commander Strategy Implementation Plan Version 5.0* (2010), 474–75.

77 BP, Factsheet on BP Vessels of Opportunity Program, 2.

78 Bruce Nolan, "Many Vietnamese fishers isolated by language from oil spill aid," *Times-Picayune*, May 7, 2010; Mireya Navarro, "Spill Takes Toll on Gulf Workers' Psyches," *New York Times*, June 16, 2010; Jessica Ravitz, "Vietnamese Fishermen in Gulf Fight to Not Get Lost in Translation," CNN, June 25, 2010.

79 BP, Factsheet on BP Vessels of Opportunity Program 5.

80 Interview with BP official, October 22, 2010.

81 40 C.F.R. § 300.150.

82 Rebecca Bratspies et al., *From Ship to Shore: Reforming the National Contingency Plan to Improve Protections for Oil Spill Cleanup Workers* (Center for Progressive Reform, September 2010), 8–9.

83 Interview with responder, November 17, 2010; Bryan Walsh, "Assessing the Health Effects of the Oil Spill," *Time*, June 25, 2010.

84 Scott Deitchman, interview with Commission staff, November 29, 2010.

85 Nicole Lurie, interview with Commission staff, October 6, 2010.

86 *Ibid.*

87 Deitchman, interview; Lurie, interview; *Strategy Implementation Plan*, 252.

88 Molly Reid, "Only One Oil-slicked Bird Rescued so far from Gulf of Mexico Oil Spill," *Times-Picayune*, April 30, 2010.

89 U.S. Fish and Wildlife Service, "Cumulative Impacts to Wildlife and Actions to Protect Wildlife in the Gulf of Mexico" (November 25, 2010), http://www.fws.gov/home/dhoilspill/pdfs/CumulativeImpactsBP.pdf.

90 U.S. Fish and Wildlife Service, "Oil Spill Response" (May 2010), http://www.fws.gov/home/dhoilspill/pdfs/OilSpill-FactSheet.pdf.

91 Michele Wilson, "Oil Spill Update: Two More Birds Recovering, BP and Other Execs Point Fingers, and More," *Audubonmagazine.org*, May 12, 2010.

92 Interview with wildlife responder, October 26, 2010; Interview with representatives of wildlife organizations, October 15, 2010.

93 Craig Pittman, "Bird rescue experts kept on sideline after gulf oil spill," *St. Petersburg Times*, September 5, 2010; Interview with wildlife responder, October 26, 2010.

94 Testimony of Kevin Costner, "Deluge of Oil Highlights Research and Technology Needs for Effective Cleanup of Oil Spills," Hearing Before the House Committee on Science and Technology, 111th Congress (June 9, 2010); Fountain, "Advances in Oil Spill Cleanup Lag Since Valdez."

95 Press Release, Deepwater Horizon Joint Information Center, New Effort to Collect; Review Oil Spill Response Solutions Announced, June 4, 2010.

96 Commander Todd Offutt, e-mail to Commission staff, November 17, 2010.

97 Interview with Coast Guard official, September 2, 2010.

98 White House Office of the Press Secretary, Press Briefing by Press Secretary Robert Gibbs and National Incident Commander Thad Allen, July 1, 2010; U.S. Department of State, Deepwater Horizon Oil Spill Response: International Offers of Assistance from Governments and International Bodies Chart, June 18, 2010.

99 46 U.S.C. § 688.

100 Interview with Coast Guard officials, August 3, 2010; API Joint Oil Spill Preparedness and Response Task Force, interview with Commission staff, October 12, 2010; Scott Segal and Kevin Ewing, interview with Commission staff, October 14, 2010; H. Clayton Cook Jr., Letter to the Editor, "Don't Blame Delays on Jones Act," *Wall Street Journal*, July 20, 2010; U.S. Department of Homeland Security, Jones Act Fact Sheet (July 6, 2010), http://www.deepwaterhorizonresponse.com/external/content/document/2931/784459/1/USCG-Jones%20Act.pdf.

101 U.S. Department of Homeland Security, Jones Act Fact Sheet; Press Release, Deepwater Horizon Joint Information Center, Admiral Allen Provides Guidance to Ensure Expedited Jones Act Waiver Processing Should It Be Needed, June 15, 2010.

102 Non-public Coast Guard documents, June 29, 2010, June 30, 2010, and July 9, 2010.

103 Coastal Response Research Center, *Research & Development Needs for Making Decisions Regarding Dispersing Oil* (April 2006), 1.

104 Ramon Antonia Vargas, "Oil is Leaking from Well at Deepwater Horizon Explosion Site," *Times-Picayune*, April 24, 2010.

105 Interview with Coast Guard official, October 29, 2010.

106 National Research Council, Committee on Understanding Oil Spill Dispersants, *Oil Spill Dispersants: Efficacy and Effects* (2005), 2.

107 Coastal Response Research Center, 1.

108 National Research Council, *Oil Spill Dispersants*, 196, 274.

[109] Merv Fingas, *A Review of Literature Related to Oil Spill Dispersants, 1997-2008* (September 2008), 18 http://www.pwsrcac.org/docs/d0053000.pdf.

[110] *Ibid.*, 25.

[111] Non-public Coast Guard document, April 23, 2010.

[112] RRT-6, *FOSC Dispersant Pre-Approval Guidelines And Checklist* (2001), iii-iv, http://www.losco.state.la.us/pdf_docs/RRT6_Dispersant_Preapproval_2001.pdf; Region IV Regional Response Team Response and Technology Committee Dispersant Workgroup, *Use of Dispersants in Region IV* (1996), ii-1, http://www.nrt.org/production/NRT/RRTHome.nsf/Resources/DUP/$file/1-RRT4DISP.PDF.

[113] 40 C.F.R. § 300.910(a).

[114] S.L. Ross Environmental Research, Ltd., *Technology Assessment of the Use of Dispersants on Spills from Drilling and Production Facilities in the Gulf of Mexico Outer Continental Shelf* (December 2000), Summary-1; Robert J. Fiocco and Alun Lewis, "Oil Spill Dispersants," 1 *Pure Applied Chemistry* (1999): 31.

[115] 40 C.F.R. § 300.910(b).

[116] Figures on the volume of dispersant use are either taken directly from, or calculated based on data in, the Operations and Ongoing Response daily reports for the Deepwater Horizon Response, available at www.restorethegulf.gov.

[117] 40 C.F.R. § 300.915 (a)(8).

[118] David Biello, "Is Using Dispersants on the BP Gulf Oil Spill Fighting Pollution with Pollution?" *Scientific American*, June 18, 2010.

[119] 40 C.F.R. § 300.915; 40 C.F.R. Part 300 Appendix C.

[120] National Research Council, *Oil Spill Dispersants*, 68–69; Samuel K. Skinner and William K. Reilly, *The Exxon Valdez Oil Spill: A Report to the President* (May 1989), 17, App. A.

[121] David Hammer, "BP Clashes with Critics on Gulf of Mexico Oil Crisis Response," *Times-Picayune*, May 31, 2010.

[122] Elana Schor, "BP Continues to Use Surface Dispersants in Gulf Despite EPA Directive," *New York Times*, June 24, 2010.

[123] Ernest Scheyder, "Nalco CEO on Gulf Coast to Defend Dispersant," *Reuters*, June 3, 2010.

[124] Interview with NOAA scientist, October, 21, 2010; Testimony of Lisa Jackson, Hearing before the National Commission, September 27, 2010.

[125] Dana Tulis and Mathy Stanislaus, interview with Commission staff, October 1, 2010.

[126] Kenneth Meade, e-mail to Commission staff, September 27, 2010.

[127] Tim Webb, "BP Boss Tony Hayward Admits Job is on the Line Over Deepwater Oil Spill," *The Guardian*, May 14, 2010.

[128] Tulis and Stanislaus, interview.

[129] EPA, *Dispersant Monitoring and Assessment Directive for Subsurface Dispersant Application*, May 10, 2010; EPA, *Dispersant Monitoring and Assessment Directive for Subsurface Dispersant Application—Addendum 1*, May 14, 2010; EPA, *Dispersant Monitoring and Assessment Directive*, May 20, 2010; EPA, *Dispersant Monitoring and Assessment Directive—Addendum 3*, May 26, 2010.

[130] Testimony of Lisa Jackson, September 27, 2010.

[131] Richard Lynch, interview with Commission staff, October 13, 2010; Suttles, interview.

[132] Press Release, BP, Work Begins to Drill Relief Well to Stop Oil Spill, May 4, 2010.

[133] Press Release, White House, The Ongoing Administration-Wide Response to the Deepwater BP Oil Spill, May 6, 2010; "Deepwater Team Attempts To Put 100-Tonne Box over Blown-out Oil Well," *Associated Press*, May 7, 2010; Matthew Bigg, "Oil From Gulf Spill Creeps Ashore in Louisiana," *Reuters*, May 6, 2010.

[134] Ian Urbina, Justin Gillis, and Clifford Krauss, "On Defensive, BP Readies Dome to Contain Spill," *New York Times*, May 3, 2010.

[135] Suttles, interview; Lynch, interview.

[136] Non-public BP document, May 7, 2010.

[137] Interview with well control expert, October 14, 2010; Interview with drilling expert, October 1, 2010.

[138] Lynch, interview.

[139] Campbell Robertson, "New Setback in Attempt to Contain Gulf Oil Spill," *New York Times*, May 8, 2010.

[140] Lynch, interview.

[141] Clifford Krauss, Henry Fountain, and John M. Broder, "Acrimony Behind the Scenes of Gulf Oil Spill," *New York Times*, August 26, 2010.

[142] Interview with U.S. Geological Survey official, October 21, 2010.

[143] Suttles, interview.

[144] Interview with U.S. Geological Survey official, October 21, 2010; Interview with Minerals Management Service official, October 15, 2010; Interview with well control expert, October 14, 2010.

[145] Sam Dolnick and Henry Fountain, "Unable to Stanch Oil, BP Will Try To Gather It," *New York Times*, May 5, 2010.

[146] Clifford Krauss and Michael Cooper, "Cap Slows Gulf Oil Leak as Engineers Move Cautiously," *New York Times*, June 5, 2010.

[147] Lynch, interview.

[148] Jeremy Hsu, "Why Don't We Just Drop a Nuclear Bomb on the Gulf Oil Spill?" *Christian Science Monitor*, May 13, 2010.

[149] Testimony of Richard Camilli, "Sizing up the BP Oil Spill: Science and Engineering Measuring Methods," Briefing Before the Subcommittee on Energy and Environment of the House Committee on Energy and Commerce, 111th Congress (May 19, 2010).

[150] John Amos, "Gulf Oil Spill Rate Must Be Much Higher Than Stated—6 Million Gallons So Far?", Skytruth.org, April 27, 2010, http://blog.skytruth.org/2010/04/gulf-oil-spill-rate-must-be-much-higher.html; John Amos, "Gulf Oil Spill—Bigger Than Exxon Valdez," Skytruth.org, April 28, 2010, http://blog.skytruth.org/2010/04/gulf-oil-spill-bigger-than-exxon-valdez.html; John Amos, "Gulf Oil Spill—New Spill Calculation—Exxon Valdez Surpassed Today," Skytruth.org, May 1, 2010,http://blog.skytruth.org/2010/05/gulf-oil-spill-new-spill-rate.html.

151 Richard Harris, "Gulf Spill May Far Exceed Official Estimates," National Public Radio, May 14, 2010, http://www.npr.org/templates/story/story.php?storyId=126809525.

152 Testimony of Steven Wereley (Professor, Purdue University), "Sizing up the BP Oil Spill: Science and Engineering Measuring Methods," Briefing Before the Subcommittee on Energy and Environment of the House Committee on Energy and Commerce, 111th Congress (May 19, 2010).

[153] Harris, "Gulf Spill May Far Exceed Official Estimates."

[154] Transcript, Marcia McNutt, Deepwater Blowout Containment Conference, September 22, 2010.

[155] Press Release, Deepwater Horizon Incident Joint Information Center, Flow Rate Group Provides Preliminary Best Estimate of Oil Flowing From BP Oil Well, May 27, 2010.

[156] Marcia McNutt, *Summary Preliminary Report from the Flow Rate Technical Group* (June 2, 2010).

[157] Admiral Thad Allen, letter to Honorable Edward J. Markey, October 1, 2010, 12.

[158] Press Release, U.S Department of Energy, Secretary Salazar and Secretary Chu To Meet with Scientists and Engineers at BP Houston Command Center, May 11, 2010.

[159] Interview with U.S. Department of Energy official, November 8, 2010; Interview with government science advisor, October 5, 2010; Interview with government science advisor, October 6, 2010.

[160] Kenneth Chang and Andrew Revkin, "At a Sleek Bioenergy Lab, a Lens on a Cabinet Pick," *New York Times*, December 22, 2008.

[161] Paul Tooms, interview with Commission staff, October 13, 2010; Interviews with Minerals Management Service officials, October 15, 2010; Interview with Coast Guard official, October 18, 2010.

[162] Interview with U.S. Department of Energy official, November 8, 2010; Interview with Coast Guard official, October 18, 2010; Interview with government science advisor, October 5, 2010.

[163] Interview with government science advisor, October 1, 2010; Interview with U.S. Department of Energy scientist, October 26, 2010.

[164] "Leno: 'Junk Shot,'" *New York Times*, June 1, 2010.

[165] Campbell Robertson, Clifford Krauss, and John M. Broder, "Oil Hits Home, Spreading Arc of Frustration," *New York Times*, May 24, 2010.

[166] Lynch, interview.

[167] Non-public U.S. Department of Energy document, May 17, 2010; Non-public U.S. Department of Energy document, May 19, 2010.

[168] Tooms, interview.

[169] Interview with U.S. Department of the Interior official, October 21, 2010.

[170] Interview with government science advisor, October 6, 2010.

[171] Non-public BP document, May 31, 2010.

[172] Suttles, interview.

[173] Interview with government science advisor, October 6, 2010; Suttles, interview; Tooms, interview.

[174] Interview with Minerals Management Service official, October 15, 2010; Interview with well control expert, October 14, 2010.

[175] Robertson, Krauss, and Broder, "Oil Hits Home, Spreading Arc of Frustration."

[176] Mimi Hall, Rick Jervis, and Allen Levin, "Is Oil Spill Becoming Obama's Katrina?," *USA Today*, May 27, 2010.

[177] Matthew Daly, "Month After Oil Spill, Why Is BP Still in Charge?," ABC News, May 21, 2010, http://abcnews.go.com/Business/wireStory?id=10713257.

[178] Interview with Coast Guard official, November 12, 2010.

[179] Frank McCormack, "Privateer Perfection," *Plaquemines Gazette*, June 7, 2010.

[180] Paul Rioux, "President Barack Obama in Grand Isle after Touring Beach in Port Fourchon," *Times-Picayune*, May 28, 2010.

[181] Paul Rioux, "President Barack Obama Promises No Retreat from Gulf of Mexico Oil Spill Response," *Times-Picauyne*, May 28, 2010.

[182] Interview with Coast Guard official, August 26, 2010; Interview with Coast Guard official, September 2, 2010; Non-public Coast Guard document, June 14, 2010.

[183] Jeffrey Ball and Jonathan Weisman, "Slippery Start: U.S. Response to Spill Falters," *Wall Street Journal*, June 16, 2010.

[184] Interview with Coast Guard official, November 12, 2010.

[185] Executive Order No. 13543, National Commission on the BP Deepwater Horizon Oil Spill and Offshore Drilling, 75 Fed. Reg. 29,397, May 21, 2010.

[186] Peter Baker, "Obama Extends Moratorium; Agency Chief Resigns," *New York Times*, May 27, 2010.

[187] Gardner Harris, "Minerals Management Service Director Resigns Over Spill," *New York Times*, May 27, 2010.

[188] Mike Allen, "Gulf Commander to Begin Solo Briefings," *Politico*, May 31, 2010.

[189] Interview with government official, October 8, 2010.

[190] Interview with NOAA officials, November 18, 2010.

[191] Interview with Coast Guard official, August 24, 2010; Interview with Coast Guard official, August 30, 2010.

[192] Interview with Coast Guard official, August 24, 2010; Interview with Coast Guard official, August 31, 2010.

[193] Non-public Coast Guard document, October 12, 2010.

[194] Holbrook Mohr, Justin Pritchard, and Tamara Lush, "BP's Gulf Oil Spill Response Plan Lists the Walrus as a Local Species. Louisiana Gov. Bobby Jindal Is Furious.," *Christian Science Monitor*, June 9, 2010; Interview with Coast Guard official, Aug. 31, 2010.

[195] Campbell Robertson, "Louisiana Officials Threaten Action if Spill Response Proves Inadequate," *New York Times*, May 23, 2010.

[196] Craig Pittman and Rebecca Catalanello, "BP Plan to Protect Florida From Oil Spill Inadequate, Officials Say," *St. Petersburg Times*, May 3, 2010.

[197] Interview with government official, October 13, 2010.

[198] Non-public Coast Guard document, October 12, 2010.

[199] Interview with government official, October 12, 2010.

[200] Interview with Coast Guard official, August 30, 2010; Interview with government official, August 24, 2010.

[201] Liz Robbins and Campbell Robertson, "Tension Among Officials Grows as Storm Nears," *New York Times*, July 23, 2010.

[202] Angel Gonzalez, "Locals to BP: Don't Leave Town Yet," *Wall Street Journal*, Aug. 1, 2010; Interview with Coast Guard official, August 26, 2010.

[203] Interview with Coast Guard official, August 25, 2010; Interview with Coast Guard official, October 24, 2010; Non-public Coast Guard document, June 14, 2010.

[204] U.S. Department of Homeland Security, Summary of Ineligible PWs for Barrier Islands (November 11, 2010); Tod Wells, e-mail to Commission staff, November 8, 2010; Tim Padgett, "Dredge, Baby, Dredge: Can Sand Stop the Oil?," *Time*, June 1, 2010.

[205] Van Oord and Deltares, *Save the Delta, The Dutch Perspective*, May 6, 2010; Chris Kirkham, "Gov. Bobby Jindal and Plaquemines Officials Float Plan to Rebuild Barrier Islands to Stop Encroaching Oil," *Times-Picayune*, May 8, 2010.

[206] Interview with Coast Guard official, August 30, 2010; Mark Schleifstein, "Barrier Berm Advocates Not Deterred by Environmental Regulators' Misgivings," *Times-Picayune*, September 20, 2010.

[207] Kristi Cantu, letter to Pete J. Serio, May 11, 2010.

[208] Colonel Alvin Lee, interview with Commission staff, October 28, 2010.

[209] Colonel Lee, interview; Press Release, Governor's Office of Homeland Security and Emergency Preparedness, Governor Jindal & Coastal Parish Leaders Meet with Army Corps of Engineers to Stress Importance of Approving Dredg-

ing Plan, May 17, 2010.

[210] Senator Mary Landrieu et al., letter to Colonel Alvin Lee and Admiral Thad Allen, May 20, 2010.

[211] Senator David Vitter, letter to President Barack Obama, May 21, 2010.

[212] Press Release, Army Corps of Louisiana, Corps Decision on State's Emergency Permit Request, May 27, 2010; Army Corps of Engineers, "New Orleans District Emergency Permit Request Action," June 1, 2010, http://www.mvn. usace.army.mil/pao/MVNIPR1June2010Final.pdf.

[213] Agency comments were compiled by the Army Corps of Engineers at http://www.mvn.usace.army.mil/news/ Emergency%20Permit%20Documents%20Compressed%20FINAL.pdf.

[214] Transcript, Press Briefing by National Incident Commander, June 2, 2010.

[215] Press Release, Deepwater Horizon Incident Joint Information Center, Admiral Allen Approves One Section of Louisiana Barrier Island Project Proposal as Part of Federal Oil Spill Response, May 27, 2010.

[216] NIC Decision Support Document Regarding Barrier Island Proposal Based Upon Interagency Solutions Group Discussion and Army Corps of Engineers NOD 20 Permit Discussions, May 17, 2010; Draft, Berm Construction and Spill Response, U.S. Department of Homeland Security, May 19, 2010; Berm Construction and Spill Response, U.S. Department of Homeland Security, May 25, 2010.

[217] Admiral Thad Allen, e-mail to Captain Mike White, May 22, 2010.

[218] Mark Schleifstein, "Sand Berm to Protect Barataria Bay Wetlands Gets Federal OK," *Times-Picayune*, May 27, 2010.

[219] Interview with Coast Guard official, November 12, 2010.

[220] Press Release, Governor's Office of Homeland Security and Emergency Preparedness, Governor Jindal: President Promised Sand-Boom Plan Progress in Days, Need Swift Action, May 28, 2010.

[221] Transcript, Anderson Cooper 360 Degrees, "BP Cleanup Sham; President Obama Visits Louisiana; Oystermen in Jeopardy," CNN, May 28, 2010.

[222] Transcript, Press Briefing by National Incident Commander Admiral Thad Allen, June 2, 2010.

[223] Bigad Shaban, "Upset Nungesser Walks Out on Coast Guard Meeting," www.ltv.com, June 1, 2010.

[224] National Incident Command, Summary of NIC Barrier Island Berm Meeting, June 1, 2010.

[225] Admiral Thad Allen, interview with Commission staff, November 2, 2010; Denise Reed, interview with Commission staff, November 16, 2010; Interview with Coast Guard official, November 12, 2010.

[226] Glenn Thrush, "Carville Doesn't Regret Ripping W.H.," *Politico*, June 2, 2010.

[227] Press Release, National Incident Command, National Incident Commander Admiral Allen Directs BP to Pay for Five Additional Barrier Island Projects in Louisiana, June 2, 2010.

[228] Mark Kaufman, "BP Says More La. Barrier Island Berms Will Cost $360 Million," *Washington Post*, June 3, 2010.

[229] William Grawe, e-mail to Admiral Thad Allen, June 2, 2010.

[230] "Shaw Group Wins Contract to Build Barrier Island Temporary Berms," *Times-Picayune*, June 4, 2010; Jeffrey Ball, "Accusations Fly in Sand-Berm Project," *Wall Street Journal*, October 12, 2010.

[231] Shaw's Environmental & Infrastructure Group, *Shaw Barrier Berm Project—Daily Report Day 43*, July 14, 2010.

[232] Sean Smith, e-mail to Juliette Kayyem, Department of Homeland Security, May 27, 2010.

[233] Tooms, interview.

[234] Interview with Coast Guard official, October 18, 2010; Interview with Minerals Management Service official, October 15, 2010.

[235] Internal BP document (BP-HZN-MBI 143338-50).

[236] Tooms, interview; Non-public BP document, May 31, 2010.

[237] Non-public BP document, May 29, 2010.

[238] Tooms, interview.

[239] Interview with Coast Guard official, October 18, 2010; Interview with U.S. Geological Survey official, October 21, 2010.

[240] Interview with U.S. Geological Survey official, October 21, 2010; Non-public government document, June 1, 2010.

[241] Interview with U.S. Geological Survey official, October 21, 2010; Interview with U.S. Department of Energy official, September 17, 2010.

[242] Non-public BP document, May 23, 2010; Non-public BP document, May 25, 2010; Daniel Squire, letter to Commission staff, November 2, 2010, att. 1, 2.

[243] Non-public BP document, May 31, 2010; Non-public BP document, May 29, 2010.

[244] Non-public BP document, May 31, 2010; Non-public BP document, May 29, 2010.

[245] Lynch, interview.

[246] Deepwater Horizon Response Joint Information Center, Ongoing Administration-Wide Response to the Deepwater BP Oil Spill, May 29, 2010; Press Release, BP, Update on Gulf of Mexico Oil Spill, May 29, 2010.

[247] Helene Cooper and Peter Baker, "U.S. Opens Criminal Inquiry into Oil Spill," *New York Times*, June 1, 2010.

[248] "BP Chief Hopes Cap Will Capture Most of Gulf Oil," *Reuters*, June 6, 2010.

[249] Doug Suttles, letter to Admiral James Watson, June 9, 2010 (suggesting that with the *Clear Leader* attached to the kill line, BP could collect 5-10,000 barrels per day).

[250] Lisa Jackson, EPA Conference Call on Dispersant Use in the Gulf of Mexico with U.S. Coast Guard Rear Admiral Landry, May 24, 2010.

[251] EPA, *Dispersant Monitoring and Assessment Directive—Addendum 3*, May 26, 2010.

[252] Dana Tulis, e-mail to Admiral James Watson, June 7, 2010.

[253] Captain James Hanzalik, e-mail to Captain Anthony Lloyd, June 8, 2010.

[254] Admiral James Watson, e-mail to Dana Tulis, et al., June 7, 2010; Dana Tulis, e-mail to Admiral James Watson, June 7, 2010.

[255] Captain James Hanzalik, e-mail to Captain Anthony Lloyd, June 8, 2010.

[256] Dana Tulis, e-mail to Admiral James Watson, June 8, 2010.

[257] Mathy Stanislaus, e-mail to Admiral James Watson, July 9, 2010, att.

[258] Stanislaus, interview.

[259] Charles Huber, e-mail to Commander William Carter and Captain Roger Laferriere, July 13, 2010.

[260] Mathy Stanislaus, e-mail to Admiral Paul Zukunft, July 13, 2010.

[261] Admiral Paul Zukunft, e-mail to Mathy Stanislaus, July 14, 2010.

[262] EPA, "July 11-14 Dispersant Request Summary," (provided to Commission staff October 21, 2010).

[263] Matthew L. Wald, "Despite Directive, BP Used Dispersant Often, Panel Finds," *New York Times*, July 31, 2010; "Allen 'Satisfied' with Dispersant Use in Gulf Oil Disaster," CNN, August 2, 2010.

[264] Interview with U.S. Department of Energy official, October 25, 2010; Interview with Coast Guard official, October 18, 2010.

[265] Interview with U.S. Geological Survey official, October 21, 2010; Interview with U.S. Department of Energy official, October 25, 2010; Interview with U.S. Department of Energy official, October 26, 2010.

[266] Interview with U.S. Department of Energy official, November 8, 2010.

[267] Interview with U.S. Geological Survey official, October 21, 2010.

[268] Tooms, interview.

[269] Interview with U.S. Department of Energy official, November 8, 2010.

[270] Interview with industry expert, October 14, 2010.

[271] Interview with U.S. Geological Survey official, October 21, 2010.

[272] Secretary Steven Chu, e-mail to Arun Majumdar and others, June 18, 2010; Admiral James Watson, letter to Doug Suttles, June 19, 2010.

[273] Suttles, interview; Tooms, interview.

[274] Daniel Squire, letter to Commission staff, November 2, 2010, att. 3; Lynch, interview; Tooms, interview; Non-public U.S. Department of Energy document, July 6, 2010.

[275] Interview with U.S. Geological Survey official, October 20, 2010; Non-public government science advisor document, July 2, 2010; Interview with industry expert, October 14, 2010.

[276] Admiral Thad Allen, letter to Bob Dudley, July 9, 2010.

[277] Suttles, interview.

[278] Admiral Thad Allen, letter to Bob Dudley, July 12, 2010.

[279] Interview with U.S. Department of Energy official, October 26, 2010; Interview with industry expert, October 28, 2010.

[280] Interview with U.S. Department of Energy official, November 8, 2010; Non-public government science advisor document, July 13, 2010.

[281] Statement from National Incident Commander Admiral Thad Allen on Well Integrity Test, July 13, 2010.

[282] Interview with U.S. Department of Energy official, November 8, 2010.

[283] Admiral Thad Allen, letter to Bob Dudley, July 14, 2010.

[284] Interviews with U.S. Geological Survey official, October 20, 2010; Non-public U.S. Department of Energy document, July 11, 2010.

[285] Non-public government document, July 11, 2010; Interview with U.S. Department of Energy official, October 25, 2010.

[286] Campbell Robertson and Henry Fountain, "BP Says Oil Flow Has Stopped as Cap Is Tested," *New York Times*, July 15, 2010.

[287] Interview with U.S. Department of Energy official, November 8, 2010; Non-public U.S. Department of Energy document, July 16, 2010; Non-public government science advisor document, July 15, 2010.

[288] Interview with U.S. Department of Energy official, October 26, 2010; Interview with Minerals Management Service official, October 15, 2010; Interview with U.S. Department of Energy official, October 21, 2010; Non-public government science document, July 15, 2010.

[289] Interview with U.S. Department of Energy official, October 25, 2010; Interview with U.S. Department of Energy official, October 26, 2010; Interview with U.S. Geological Survey official, October 21, 2010.

[290] Interview with Coast Guard official, October, 18, 2010; Interview with U.S. Geological Survey official, October 21, 2010.

[291] Non-public U.S. Department of Energy document, June 30, 2010.

[292] Interview with U.S. Geological Survey official, October 21, 2010; Interview with U.S. Geological Survey official, October 21, 2010.

[293] Tooms, interview; Interview with U.S. Geological Survey official, October 21, 2010; Interview with U.S. Geological Survey official, October 21, 2010.

[294] Interview with U.S. Geological Survey official, October 21, 2010.

[295] Transcript, Press Briefing by National Incident Commander Admiral Thad Allen and NOAA Administrator Dr. Jane Lubchenco, July 24, 2010.

[296] Bob Dudley, letter to Admiral Thad Allen, July 19, 2010.

[297] Pat Campbell, letter to Richard Lynch, July 28, 2010; Henry Fountain, "Expert is Confident about Sealing Oil Well," *New York Times*, May 24, 2010; Interview with industry expert, October 14, 2010.

[298] Transcript, Press Briefing by National Incident Commander Admiral Thad Allen, August 2, 2010.

[299] Press Release, BP, Static Kill Injectivity Testing Commences on MC252 Well, August 3, 2010; Non-public U.S. Department of Energy document, August 3, 2010.

[300] Press Release, BP, MC252 Well Reaches Static Condition; Well Monitoring Underway, August 4, 2010.

[301] Statement by National Incident Commander Admiral Thad Allen, August, 4 2010.

[302] Face the Nation, CBS News, August 8, 2010.

[303] *Deepwaer Horizon MC252 Gulf Incident Oil Budget* (August 4, 2010); Jane Lubchenco et al., *BP Deepwater Horizon Oil Budget: What Happened to the Oil?* (August 4, 2010).

[304] *Deepwater Horizon MC252 Gulf Incident Oil Budget*, 1.

[305] Heather Zichal, e-mail to Jane Lubchenco, July 29, 2010.

[306] Jane Lubchenco, e-mail to Sean Smith and others, August 4, 2010.

[307] Margaret Spring, e-mail to Heather Zichal and others. July 30, 2010.

[308] Transcript, Press Briefing by Press Secretary Robert Gibbs, Admiral Thad Allen, Carol Browner, and Dr. Lubchenco, August 4, 2010.

[309] David A. Fahrenthold, "Scientists Question Government Team's Report of Shrinking Gulf Oil Spill," *Washington Post*, August 5, 2010; Katie Howell, "White House, Critics Reach Stalemate in Dispute Over Oil Budget in Gulf," *New York Times*, August 23, 2010.

[310] Editorial, "Do the Math on the Spill," *Times-Picayune*, August 6, 2010.

[311] Press Conference, Jane Lubchenco Discusses Federal Peer-Reviewed "Oil Budget" Technical Documentation, November 23, 2010.

[312] Press Release, NOAA, Federal Interagency Group Issues Peer-Reviewed 'Oil Budget' Technical Documentation, November 23, 2010.

[313] Federal Interagency Solutions Group, Oil Budget Science and Engineering Team, *Oil Budget Calculator Technical Documentation* (November 2010).

[314] Interview with Coast Guard official, October 24, 2010.

[315] Shaw's Environmental & Infrastructure Group, *Shaw Barrier Berm Project—Daily Report Day 44* (July 15, 2010).

[316] Padgett, "Dredge, Baby, Dredge: Can Sand Stop the Oil?"

[317] Press Release, Office of the Governor, Governor Jindal Announces Agreement with BP for Seafood Safety, Coastal Restoration & Tourism Funding, November 1, 2010.

[318] Cain Burdeau, "EPA: Louisiana's Sand Berms Not Stopping Much Oil," *Associated Press*, September 10, 2010; Mark Ballard, "EPA Opposes La. Berms," *Advocate*, September 9, 2010; John Maginnis, "Louisiana's Sand Berms Challenged," *Times-Picayune*, September 15, 2010; Interview with government official, September 22, 2010; Transcript, Meet the Press, November 21, 2010 (Governor Jindal stating "[w]e've collected thousands of pounds of oily debris off these berms"); *Oil Budget Technical Documentation*, 34 ("Based upon past spills, the oil content of collected debris mass is only a few percent.").

[319] Bobby Jindal, *Leadership and Crisis* 6 (Washington, D.C.: Regnery Publishing, Inc., 2010).

[320] Statement from Admiral Allen on the Successful Completion of the Relief Well, September 19, 2010.

[321] Press Release, NOAA, NOAA Reopens One-Third of Closed Gulf Fishing Area, July 22, 2010; Press Release, NOAA, NOAA Reopens More Than 8,000 Square Miles in the Gulf of Mexico to Fishing, November 15, 2010.

[322] Kim Murphy, "A Poor Appetite for Gulf Seafood," *Los Angeles Times*, August 26, 2010; Interview with government official, October 15, 2010.

[323] Krissah Thompson, "Waste from BP Oil Spill Cleanup Has Gulf Residents Near Landfills Concerned," *Washington Post*, August 16, 2010.

[324] 40 C.F.R. § 261.4(b)(5).

[325] Admiral James Watson and Al Armendariz, *Recovered Oil, Contaminated Materials and Liquid and Solid Wastes Management Directive* (June 29, 2010).

[326] Elana Schor, "How Has BP's Oily Waste Escaped 'Hazardous' Label?," *New York Times*, July 20, 2010.

[327] Admiral Paul Zukunft, letter to Doug Suttles, July 24, 2010; BP, "Waste and Recoverable Material Tracking," http://www.bp.com/genericarticle.do?categoryId=9034343&contentId=7063466.

[328] Schor, "How Has BP's Oily Waste Escaped 'Hazardous' Label?"; EPA, "Waste Sampling Strategy and Results," http://www.epa.gov/bpspill/waste.html#sampling_strategy; Stanislaus, interview.

[329] EPA, "Waste Management on the Gulf Coastline," http://www.epa.gov/bpspill/waste.html.

[330] Robert Bullard and Al Huang, "Oil's Toxic Legacy Not Erased," *Politico*, August 13, 2010.

[331] Lesley Clark and Fred Tasker, "Oil-Soaked Waste Worries Gulf Coast Landfills' Neighbors," *McClatchy Newspapers*, July 30, 2010; Robert Bullard, "Government Allows BP to Dump Oil-Spill Waste on Black Communities," *OpEdNews.com*, July 22, 2010.

[332] Stanislaus, interview.

[333] Admiral Paul Zukunft, letter to Mike Utsler, August 9, 2010; Stanislaus, interview.

[334] "Statement from Admiral Allen on the Transfer of Oversight Responsibilities, October 1, 2010.

Chapter Six

[1] President Barack Obama, "Remarks by the President to the Nation on the BP Oil Spill" (June 15, 2010) http://www.whitehouse.gov/the-press-office/remarks-president-nation-bp-oil-spill].

[2] Campbell Robertson and Clifford Krauss, "Gulf Spill Is the Largest of Its Kind, Scientists Say," *New York Times*, August 2, 2010.

[3] EPA, *Government Response to the BP Oil Spill: Odors from the BP Spill* (June 2010), http://www.epa.gov/bpspill/reports/odorfactsheet.pdf (announcing help line for residents experiencing oil-related odors); Press Release, NOAA, Administration Launches Dockside Chats to Promote Gulf Seafood Safety Awareness, August 25, 2010, http://www.restorethegulf.gov/release/2010/08/25/administration-launches-dockside-chats-promote-gulf-seafood-safety-awareness; BP, *Claims and Government Payments Gulf of Mexico Oil Spill Public Report* (November 18, 2010).

[4] Testimony of Timothy Ragen, Executive Director of the U.S. Marine Mammal Commission, "The Short and Long-Term Impacts of the Deepwater Horizon Oil Spill," Hearing Before the House Subcommittee on Insular Affairs, Oceans, and Wildlife, 111th Congress (June 10, 2010); Kim B. Ritchie and Brian D. Keller, eds., *A Scientific Forum on the Gulf of Mexico: The Islands in the Stream Concept* (NOAA, January 23, 2008), 6–8; Elliott A. Norse and John Amos, "Impacts, Perception, and Policy Implications of the Deepwater Horizon Oil and Gas Disaster," *Environmental Law Reporter* 40, no. 11 (2010): 11071; *Deepwater Horizon Oil Spill: Scientific Symposium Meeting Summary* (Consortium for Ocean Leadership, June 23, 2010), 15–16.

[5] Federal Interagency Solutions Group, Oil Budget Science and Engineering Team, *Oil Budget Calculator Technical Documentation* (November 2010).

[6] Curtis Morgan, "Another sign of oil spill recovery in the Gulf: Oil in the Gulf has dissipated and degraded into barely detectable concentrations, although federal scientists say it's too soon to say the threat is over," *Miami Herald*,

September 8, 2010.

[7] Brian Hamacher, "Wind Keeps Oil From Loop Current & Away From Florida Shores," *Associated Press*, July 19, 2010.

[8] Richard Camilli et al., "Tracking Hydrocarbon Plume Transport and Biodegradation at Deepwater Horizon," *Science* 330, no. 6001 (2010): 201–204; David Valentine et al., "Propane Respiration Jump-Starts Microbial Response to a Deep Oil Spill," *Science* 330, no. 6001 (2010): 204–208; Terry Hazen et al., "Deep-Sea Oil Plume Enriches Indigenous Oil-Degrading Bacteria", *Science* 330, no. 6001 (2010): 208–211.

[9] Alan Krupnick et al., "A Framework for Understanding the Costs and Benefits of Deepwater Drilling Regulation" (DRAFT) (Resources for the Future, 2010).

[10] Leslie Kaufman and Shaila Dewan, "Gulf May Avoid Direst Predictions After Oil Spill," *New York Times*, September 13, 2010.

[11] NOAA, *Other Significant Oil Spills in the Gulf of Mexico*, http://sero.nmfs.noaa.gov/sf/deepwater_horizon/1890_HistoricalSpillsGulfofMexico.pdf.

[12] Darryl L. Felder and David K. Camp, *Gulf of Mexico Origin, Waters, and Biota: Volume I, Biodiversity* (Corpus Christi, TX: Texas A&M University Press, 2009).

[13] *Ibid.*

[14] Christine Ribic et al., "Distribution of Seabirds in the Northern Gulf of Mexico in Relation to Mesoscale Features: Initial Observations," *ICES Journal of Marine Science* 54 (1997): 545–551.

[15] S. Heileman and N. Rabalais, *Gulf of Mexico: Large Marine Ecosystem Brief #5* (NOAA, 2009), http://www.lme.noaa.gov/index.php?option=com_content&view=article&id=51:lme5&catid=41:briefs&Itemid=72.

[16] David Biello, "The BP Spill's Growing Toll on the Sea Life of the Gulf," *Yale Environment* 360, June 9, 2010, http://e360.yale.edu/content/feature.msp?id=2284.

[17] Holly K. Ober, Effects of Oil Spills on Marine and Coastal Wildlife (University of Florida, May 2010).

[18] International Bird Rescue Research Center, *How Oil Affects Birds: Just a little bit of oil can be deadly* (2010), http://www.ibrrc.org/pdfs/IBRRC-How-oil-affects-birds.pdf.

[19] Camilli et al., "Tracking Hydrocarbon Plume Transport," 201–204.

[20] *Oil Budget Calculator Technical Documentation.*

[21] White House, Ongoing Administration-Wide Response to the Deepwater BP Oil Spill: By the Numbers to Date (August 23, 2010), http://www.restorethegulf.gov/release/2010/08/23/ongoing-administration-wide-response-deepwater-bp-oil-spill.

[22] Unified Area Command, *Shoreline Clean-up and Assessment Technique (SCAT) Map -- Maximum Oiling by Zone: Florida*, November 11, 2010.

[23] Audubon Society, *Oil and Birds: Too Close for Comfort. Louisiana's Coast Six Months into the BP Disaster* (October 2010).

[24] Dr. Holly Bik (University of New Hampshire), interview with Commission staff, October 28, 2010.

[25] NOAA, *Environmental Sensitivity Index: Alabama* (August 2007), 1, http://response.restoration.noaa.gov/book_shelf/1458_SampleESI_AL2007.pdf.

[26] Joseph Dineen, *Tidal Flat Habitats* (Smithsonian Institution, 2010), http://www.sms.si.edu/irlspec/Tidal_Flats.htm.

[27] V. Grossi et al., "Burial, Exportation and Degradation of Acyclic Petroleum Hydrocarbons Following a Simulated Oil Spill in Bioturbated Mediterranean Coastal Sediments," *Chemosphere* 48, no. 9 (2002): 947–954.

[28] Qianxin Lin and Irving Mendelssohn, "Evaluation of Tolerance Limits for Restoration and Phytoremediation with *Spartina Alterniflora* in Crude Oil-Contaminated Coastal Salt Marshes," in *Proceedings of the 2008 International Oil Spill Conference* (Washington, D.C.: American Petroleum Institute, 2008), 869-874, http://www.iosc.org/papers/2008%20148.pdf.

[29] Jeffrey Ball, "Storm-Tossed Boom Complicates Spill Cleanup," *Wall Street Journal*, July 27, 2010.

[30] Dr. Eugene Turner (Professor, Louisiana State University), e-mail to Commission staff, November 24, 2010.

[31] Dr. Eugene Turner (Professor, Louisiana State University), interview with Commission staff, November 4, 2010.

[32] Bob Marshall, "Oysters are uniquely sensitive to Gulf of Mexico oil spill," *Times-Picayune*, May 25, 2010.

[33] NOAA, *MC252 Shoreline Current Oiling Situation Map – LA: As of 8/03/2010*; Louisiana Department of Wildlife and Fisheries, *Oil Spill Response: Closure Maps*, http://www.wlf.louisiana.gov/oilspill.

[34] Nicole Santa Cruz and P.J. Huffstutter, "Effort to Keep Oil Spill at Bay Tips Ecological Balance," *Los Angeles Times*, August 3, 2010.

[35] L. Scott Mills, Michael E. Soule and Daniel F. Doak, "The keystone-species concept in ecology and conservation," *BioScience* 43, no. 4 (1993): 219–224.

[36] Mississippi Department of Marine Resources, *Rebuilding Mississippi's Oyster Reefs* (Fall 2009).

[37] Scott McMillion, *The Reef Makers* (Nature Conservancy, 2010).

[38] "The effect of the oil spill on Gulf fisheries: An Interview with Harriet Perry," Mississippi Public Broadcasting, August 17, 2010.

[39] Harriet Perry, interview with Commission staff, October 28, 2010.

[40] *Ibid.*

[41] 16 U.S.C. § 1802(10).

[42] NOAA, *Affected Gulf Resources* (2010), http://www.gulfspillrestoration.noaa.gov/oil-spill/affected-gulf-resources/.

[43] NOAA, *Bioaccumulation of Oil Chemicals in Seafood* (May 2010).

[44] *Ibid.*

[45] Biello, "The BP Spill's Growing Toll On the Sea Life of the Gulf."

[46] NOAA, *Affected Gulf Resources*; National Incident Command Joint Analysis Group, *Review of Preliminary Data to Examine Oxygen Levels In the Vicinity of MC252#1: May 8 to August 9, 2010* (August 16, 2010).

[47] NOAA, *Mississippi Canyon 252 Incident: Work Plan for the Collection of Data to Determine Impacts of the Deepwater Horizon Mississippi Canyon 252 Incident on Endangered and Protected Marine Mammals in the Northern Gulf* (June 14, 2010); NOAA, *Mississippi Canyon 252 Incident: Preassessment Plan to Determine Potential Exposure and Injuries of Nesting and Hatchling Loggerhead Sea Turtles* (July 28, 2010); NOAA, *Mississippi Canyon 252: Preassessment plan to Determine Potential Exposure and Injuries of Nesting and Hatchling Kemp's Ridley Turtles* (August 31, 2010; Testimony of Steve Murawski (NOAA Director of Scientific Programs), Hearing before the National Commission, September 28, 2010.

[48] "Bluefin Tuna Hit Hard by 'Deepwater Horizon' Disaster," *European Space Agency News*, October 18, 2010, http://www.esa.int/esaCP/SEM1K4WO1FG_index_0.html.

[49] Mike Soraghan, "As Spill Drifts Toward Gulf Shores, Oil Companies Brace for Political Whirlwind," *New York Times*, April 29, 2010.

[50] Unified Area Command, *Deepwater Horizon Response Consolidated Fish and Wildlife Collection Report* (November 1, 2010).

[51] Steve Hampton, *Estimating Bird Mortality* (California Department of Fish and Game, November 2004).

[52] Testimony of Jane Lyder, Deputy Assistant Secretary Fish and Wildlife and Parks, Hearing before the National Commission, September 28, 2010.

[53] Our Natural Resources at Risk: The Short and Long-Term Impacts of the Deepwater Horizon Oil Spill, Before the House Subcommittee on Insular Affairs, Oceans, and Wildlife, 111th Cong. (June 10, 2010) (Statement of Timothy Ragen, Executive Director of the U.S. Marine Mammal Commission).

[54] NOAA, *Affected Gulf Resources*.

[55] Unified Area Command, *Deepwater Horizon Response Consolidated Fish and Wildlife Collection Report*.

[56] NOAA, *Sea Turtles, Dolphins, and Whales and the Gulf of Mexico Oil Spill* (2010), http://www.nmfs.noaa.gov/pr/health/oilspill.htm.

[57] Joseph Schuman, "Dead Sperm Whale Found Near BP Oil Spill," *AOL News*, June 17, 2010.

[58] NOAA, *Sea Turtles, Dolphins, and Whales and the Gulf of Mexico Oil Spill*.

[59] Camilli et al., "Tracking Hydrocarbon Plume Transport"; Valentine et al., "Propane Respiration Jump-Starts Microbial Response to a Deep Oil Spill"; Hazen et al., "Deep-Sea Oil Plume Enriches Indigenous Oil-Degrading Bacteria."

[60] National Incident Command Joint Analysis Group, *Review of Preliminary Data to Examine Oxygen Levels In the Vicinity of MC252#1: May 8 to August 9, 2010* (August 16, 2010).

[61] *Ibid.*

[62] *Ibid.*

[63] A. Diercks et al., "Characterization of Subsurface Polycyclic Aromatic Hydrocarbons at the Deepwater Horizon Site," *Geophysical Research Letters* 37 (2010).

[64] *Oil Budget Calculator Technical Documentation.*

[65] Cain Burdeau and Seth Borenstein, "Where's the oil? On the Gulf floor, scientists say," *Associated Press*, September 13, 2010; Steve Newborn, "Oil Found Deep in Gulf is Toxic to Tiny Marine Life," *WUSF News*, August 17, 2010, http://www.wusf.usf.edu/news/2010/08/17/oil_found_deep_in_gulf_is_toxic_to_tiny_marine_life.

[66] Mark Schrope, "Oil spill cruise finds field of dead coral: Scientific Expedition Assesses Deep-Sea Damage in the Gulf of Mexico," *Nature News*, November 5, 2010, http://www.nature.com/news/2010/101105/full/news.2010.589.html.

[67] NOAA, "10 Famous Spills" (NOAA Incident News), http://www.incidentnews.gov/famous.

[68] Kim B. Ritchie and Brian D. Keller, eds., *A Scientific Forum on the Gulf of Mexico: The Islands in the Stream Concept* (NOAA, January 23, 2008), 6–8; John Farrington and Judith McDowell, "Mixing Oil and Water: Tracking the Sources and Impacts of Oil Pollution in the Marine Environment," *Oceanus Magazine* 42, no. 3 (2004): 1–4, http://www.

whoi.edu/cms/files/dfino/2005/4/v42n3-farrington_2285.pdf; Elliott A. Norse and John Amos, "Impacts, Perception, and Policy Implications of the Deepwater Horizon Oil and Gas Disaster," *Environmental Law Reporter* 40, no. 11 (2010): 11071; *Deepwater Horizon Oil Spill: Scientific Symposium Meeting Summary* (Consortium for Ocean Leadership, June 23, 2010), 15–16.

[69] 33 U.S.C. § 2706.

[70] 15 C.F.R. § 990.30; NOAA, *Injury Assessment: Guidance Document for Natural Resource Damage Assessment Under the Oil Pollution Act of 1990* (August 1996).

[71] NOAA, *Gulf Spill Restoration: Co-Trustees* (2010), http://www.gulfspillrestoration.noaa.gov/about-us/co-trustees/.

[72] Discharge of Oil From Deepwater Horizon/Macondo Well, Gulf of Mexico; Intent to Conduct Restoration Planning, 75 Fed. Reg. 60,800 (Oct. 1, 2010).

[73] NOAA, *Gulf Spill Restoration: Co-Trustees.*

[74] 15 C.F.R. § 990.10.

[75] 15 C.F.R. § 990.30.

[76] Ritchie and Keller, eds., *A Scientific Forum on the Gulf of Mexico: The Islands in the Stream Concept*, 6–8.

[77] 15 C.F.R. § 990.30; NOAA, *Injury Assessment: Guidance Document for Natural Resource Damage Assessment Under the Oil Pollution Act of 1990.*

[78] S.M. Gagliano, "Canals, Dredging, and Land Reclamation in the Louisiana Coastal Zone" in *Hydrologic and Geologic Studies of Coastal Louisiana*, Report no. 14 (Center for Wetland Studies, Louisiana State University, 1973); Robert A. Morton et al., *Rapid Subsidence and Historical Wetland Loss in the Mississippi Delta Plain: Likely Causes and Future Implications* (U.S. Geological Survey, 2005); Testimony of Senator Mary Landrieu, Louisiana, Hearing before the National Commission, September 28, 2010.

[79] NOAA, *Deepwater BP Oil Spill, Natural Resource Damage Assessment: NRDA by the Numbers*, November 1, 2010, http://www.gulfspillrestoration.noaa.gov/wp-content/uploads/2010/11/FINAL-NRDA_by_the_Numbers_11.03.pdf.pdf.

[80] NOAA, *Mississippi Canyon 252 Incident: Work Plan for the Collection of Data to Determine Impacts of the Deepwater Horizon*; NOAA, *Mississippi Canyon 252 Incident on Endangered and Protected Marine Mammals in the Northern Gulf*; NOAA, *Mississippi Canyon 252 Incident: Preassessment Plan to Determine Potential Exposure and Injuries of Nesting and Hatchling Loggerhead Sea Turtles*; NOAA, *Mississippi Canyon 252: Preassessment plan to Determine Potential Exposure and Injuries of Nesting and Hatchling Kemp's Ridley Turtles*; Testimony of Steve Murawski, September 28, 2010.

[81] Shaila Dewan, "The Oil Spill's Money Squeeze," *New York Times*, September 12, 2010.

[82] Press Release, National Science Foundation, Gulf Oil Spill: NSF Awards Grant to Study Effects of Oil and Dispersants on Louisiana Salt Marsh Ecosystem, August 16, 2010.

[83] Phil Taylor (Head, Oceans Section, Division of Ocean Sciences, National Science Foundation), e-mail to Commission staff, December 9, 2010.

[84] Dewan, "The Oil Spill's Money Squeeze."

[85] Press Release, BP, BP and the Gulf of Mexico Alliance Announce Implementation of BP's $500 Million Independent Research Initiative, September 29, 2010, http://www.bp.com/genericarticle.do?categoryId=2012968&contentId=7065262.

[86] Sea Grant, *Oil Spill in the Gulf of Mexico: Deepwater Horizon Oil Spill Research and Monitoring Activities Database* (2010), http://gulfseagrant.tamu.edu/oilspill/database.htm.

[87] "Gulf Seafood Industry Works to Wipe Oil Off Image," National Public Radio, August 20, 2010; Louisiana Office of Tourism, *Regional Effects on Perception/BP Oil Spill Survey Wave 1 Results* (June 30, 2010); University of Minnesota Food Industry Center, "Continuous Consumer Confidence in Food Safety/Defense Tracking" (presentation, FDA Symposium, September 16, 2010).

[88] U.S. Census Bureau: 2007 Economic Census, *2007 Summary Tables: Selected Statistics by Economic Sector.*

[89] NOAA, *Deepwater Horizon/BP Oil Spill: Federal Fisheries Closure and Other Information* (2010), http://sero.nmfs.noaa.gov/deepwater_horizon_oil_spill.htm.

[90] Testimony of Timothy Fitzgerald, Environmental Defense Fund, Hearing before the National Commission, September 28, 2010.

[91] Testimony of Lt. Gov. Scott Angelle, Louisiana, Hearing before the National Commission, September 28, 2010.

[92] Campbell Robertson, "As Claims for Spill Losses Shift to Administrator, Queries Follow," *New York Times*, August 23, 2010.

[93] Rob Shaw, "Clearwater BP Office Shells out for Claims," *Tampa Bay Online*, August 8, 2010, http://www2.tbo.com/content/2010/aug/08/na-clearwater-bp-office-shells-out-for-claims/.

[94] David Fahrenthold and Kimberly Kindy, "Six Months After the Spill, BP's Money is Changing the Gulf as Much as the Oil," *Washington Post*, October 20, 2010.

[95] *Inter-Agency Economic Report: Estimating the Economic Effects of the Deepwater Drilling Moratorium on the Gulf*

Coast Economy (September 16, 2010), http://www.esa.doc.gov/drilling_moratorium.pdf.

[96] Press Release, BP, BP Establishes $20 Billion Claims Fund for Deepwater Horizon Spill and Outlines Dividend Decisions, June 16, 2010, http://www.bp.com/genericarticle.do?categoryId=2012968&contentId=7062966; Steven Mufson, "BP Details Plan for $20 Billion Claim Fund for Oil Spill in the Gulf of Mexico," *Washington Post*," June 17, 2010.

[97] Gulf Coast Claims Facility, *GCCF Program Statistics - Overall Summary*, November 23, 2010.

[98] Kenneth Feinberg, *Final Report of the Special Master for the September 11th Victim Compensation Fund of 2001, Volume 1* (2010).

[99] 33 U.S.C. § 2702(b)(2)(E). The Oil Pollution Act recognizes the following categories of damages: (1) injury to natural resources (recoverable by federal or state trustees); (2) loss of real or personal property and any resultant economic losses (recoverable by an owner of that property); (3) loss of subsistence use of natural resources (recoverable by a subsistence user); (4) loss of revenues resulting from destruction of property or natural resource injury (recoverable by a government claimant); (5) loss of profits or impairment of earning capacity resulting from property loss or natural resource injury (recoverable by any claimant); and (6) costs of providing extra public services during or after spill response (recoverable by a government claimant); 33 U.S.C. § 2702(b)(2).

[100] David Segal, "Should BP's Money Go Where the Oil Didn't?," *New York Times*, October 23, 2010 (noting that Kenneth Feinberg has "hired one of the country's foremost scholars on torts . . . to write a memorandum about the validity and value of proximity claims.").

[101] John Flesher, "Gold Rush On The Gulf: Researchers Clamor For Cash," ABC News, September 29, 2010.

[102] Mary Rickard, "Gulf Coast oil spill chills seafood industry," *Reuters*, May 12, 2010; Kat Kinsman and Sarah LeTrent, "Gulf Coast Chefs, Fishermen Fight Tide of Misinformation," CNN, May 12, 2010.

[103] NOAA, *NOAA's Oil Spill Response: Fish Stocks in the Gulf of Mexico* (May 12, 2010), http://www.response.restoration.noaa.gov/book_shelf/1886_Fish-Stocks-Gulf-fact-sheetv2.pdf.

[104] U.S. Energy Information Administration, *Gulf of Mexico Fact Sheet* (October 2010), http://www.eia.doe.gov/special/gulf_of_mexico/index.cfm.

[105] EPA, *General Facts about the Gulf of Mexico*, http://www.epa.gov/gmpo/about/facts.html#resources.

[106] NOAA, *The Gulf of Mexico at a Glance: A Tool for the Gulf of Mexico Alliance and the American Public* (June 2008), http://gulfofmexicoalliance.org/pdfs/gulf_glance_1008.pdf.

[107] U.S. Census Bureau: 2007 Economic Census, *Statistics by Economic Sector*. Compiled data from Gulf coast counties using the following industry codes: 451110, 487210, 713990, 114210, 721214, 532292, 721110, 721120, 712190, 721199, 114111, 114112, 114119, 311711, 311712, 424490, 445220, 424420, 424460.

[108] NOAA, *NOAA's Oil Spill Response: Fish Stocks in the Gulf of Mexico* (May 12, 2010), http://www.response.restoration.noaa.gov/book_shelf/1886_Fish-Stocks-Gulf-fact-sheetv2.pdf.

[109] *Ibid.*

[110] NOAA, *Deepwater Horizon/BP Oil Spill: Size and Percent Coverage of Fishing Area Closures Due to BP Oil Spill* (2010), http://sero.nmfs.noaa.gov/ClosureSizeandPercentCoverage.htm.

[111] NOAA, *Protocol for Interpretation and Use of Sensory Testing and Analytical Chemistry Results for Re-Opening Oil-Impacted Areas Closed to Seafood Harvesting* (June 18, 2010).

[112] NOAA, *Deepwater Horizon/BP Oil Spill: Size and Percent Coverage of Fishing Area Closures Due to BP Oil Spill.*

[113] Rob Holbert, "Spreading the Word about Gulf Seafood," *Lagniappe* 215, October 5, 2010.

[114] Testimony of William Walker, Executive Director Mississippi Department of Marine Resources, Hearing before the National Commission, September 28, 2010.

[115] Remarks of Jane Lubchenco, NOAA Administrator, American Bar Association's Section of Environment, Energy, and Resources Law Summit, New Orleans, September 30, 2010, http://www.noaanews.noaa.gov/stories2010/20101001_lubchenco_seer.html.

[116] Brad Jacobson, "Is Gulf Seafood Really Safe to Eat? Government Withholding Key Data on Seafood Testing, Scientists Say," AlterNet, October 7, 2010, http://www.alternet.org/food/148433/is_gulf_seafood_really_safe_to_eat_government_withholding_key_data_on_seafood_testing,_scientists_say.

[117] Travis Pillow, "Low Ball Spill Estimates May Have Hurt Florida Tourism," *The Florida Independent*, October 7, 2010.

[118] Testimony of Timothy Fitzgerald, Environmental Defense Fund, Hearing before the National Commission, September 28, 2010.

[119] Jean R. Kinsey et al., "Index of Consumer Confidence in the Safety of the Food System," *American Journal of Agricultural Economics* 91, No. 5 (2009): 1470–1476 (citing H.G. Zucker, "The Variable Nature of News Media Influence," in *Communication Yearbook* 2, ed. B.D. Ruben [New Brunswick, NJ: Transaction Books, 1978], 225–40).

[120] Holbert, "Spreading the Word about Gulf Seafood."

[121] Wendy Kaufman, "Gulf Seafood Industry Works to Wipe Oil Off Image," National Public Radio, August 20, 2010.

[122] Press Release, NOAA, NOAA and FDA Announce Chemical Test for Dispersant in Gulf Seafood; All Samples Test Within Safety Threshold, October 29, 2010, http://www.noaanews.noaa.gov/stories2010/20101029_seafood.html.

[123] Press Release, BP, Seafood Safety, Tourism and Coastal Restoration Funding Announced, November 1, 2010, http://www.louisianagulfresponse.com/go/doc/3047/940587/; Press Release, Florida Department of Agriculture and Consumer Services, Bronson Announces That BP Will Pay $20 Million To Fund Seafood Inspections, Marketing Efforts In Wake Of Oil Spill, October 25, 2010. http://www.doacs.state.fl.us/press/2010/10252010_2.html.

[124] Paul Quinlan, "Gulf Spill: Ala., La. fighting over potential billions in BP penalties," *Energy & Environment Daily*, November 23, 2010.

[125] U.S. Census Bureau: 2007 Economic Census, *Statistics by Economic Sector*. Compiled data from Gulf coast counties using the following industry codes: 451110, 487210, 713990, 114210, 721214, 532292, 721110, 721120, 712190, 721199.

[126] *Ibid.*

[127] Testimony of Keith Overton, Louisiana Shrimp Association, Hearing before the National Commission, July 12, 2010.

[128] Testimony of Michael Hecht, President Greater New Orleans Inc., Hearing before the National Commission, July 12, 2010.

[129] Louisiana Office of Tourism, *Effects on Perception/BP Oil Spill Survey Wave 2 Results* (August 16, 2010), http://crt.louisiana.gov/tourism/research/Documents/2010-11/NationalOilSpillReport20100816.pdf.

[130] Matthew R. Lee and Troy C. Blanchard, *Health Impacts of Deepwater Horizon Oil Disaster on Coastal Louisiana Residents* (Louisiana State University, July 2010), http://www.lsu.edu/pa/mediacenter/tipsheets/spill/publichealthreport_2.pdf.

[131] *Ibid.*

[132] Brian Skoloff, "Final Well Sealing Small Comfort to Gulf Residents," ABC News, Sept. 16, 2010.

[133] Testimony of Grace Scire, Gulf Coast Regional Director, Boat People SOS, Hearing before the National Commission, July 13, 2010.

[134] Administration health officials (Department of Human Health Services, National Institute of Health, National Institute of Environmental Health Sciences, and Occupational Safety and Health Administration), interviews with Commission staff, October 5, 2010.

[135] Dan Witters, "Gulf Coast Residents Worse Off Emotionally after BP Oil Spill," Gallup, September 28, 2010, http://www.gallup.com/poll/143240/gulf-coast-residents-worse-off-emotionally-oil-spill.aspx.

[136] Jonathan White (Program policy Analyst, Administration for Children & Families), e-mail to Commission staff, November 16, 2010.

[137] David Abramson et al., *Impact on Children and Families of the Deepwater Horizon Oil Spill: Preliminary Findings of the Coastal Population Impact Study* (National Center for Disaster Preparedness, August 3, 2010).

[138] Matthew Lee et al., *Health Impacts of Deepwater Horizon Oil Disaster on Coastal Louisiana Residents*, (Louisiana State University, July 2010).

[139] Abramson et al., *Impact on Children and Families of the Deepwater Horizon Oil Spill*.

[140] *Ibid.*,9.

[141] *Ibid.*

[142] Testimony of Grace Scire.

[143] Sharon Cohen, "Vietnamese 'Lost' as Gulf Oil Spill Hits Community Hard," *Associated Press*, July 11, 2010.

[144] Hearing on Ensuring Justice for Victims of the Gulf Coast Oil Disaster, Before the Committee on the Judiciary, 111th Cong. (2010) (statement of Kenneth Feinberg, Administrator, Gulf Coast Claims Facility).

[145] Hearing before the National Commission, Panel 5: Community and Ecological Impacts, July 13, 2010.

[146] Brenda Robichaux (Houma Nation), interview with Commission staff, October 2010.

[147] Lawrence Palinkas et al., "Community Patterns of Psychiatric Disorders after the Exxon Valdez Oil Spill," *American Journal of Psychiatry* 150 (1993): 1517-1523.

[148] *Ibid.*

[149] Catalina Arata et al., "Coping with Technological Disaster: An Application of the Conservation of Resources Model to the Exxon Valdez Oil Spill," *International Society for Traumatic Stress* 13, no. 1 (2000): 23–39.

[150] Stephen Braud and Jack Kruse, eds., *Synthesis: Three Decades of Research on Socioeconomic Effects Related to Offshore Petroleum Development in Coastal Alaska* (Minerals Management Service, May 2009), 306.

[151] Gina Solomon and Sarah Janssen, "Health Effects of the Gulf Oil Spill," *Journal of the American Medical Association* 304, no. 10 (2010): 1118–1119.

[152] Hearing on Ensuring Justice for Victims of the Gulf Coast Oil Disaster, Before the Committee on the Judiciary, 111th Cong. (2010) (statement of Kenneth Feinberg, Administrator, Gulf Coast Claims Facility).

[153] SAMSA, "Gulf States Receive $52 Million from BP for Behavioral Health," *SAMSA News* 18, no. 4 (July/August 2010), http://www.samhsa.gov/samhsanewsletter/Volume_18_Number_4/GulfStates.aspx.

[154] National Institutes of Health officials, interviews with Commission staff, October 2010.

[155] Louisiana Office of Public Health, *State Narrative for Louisiana: Maternal and Child Health Title V Block Grant, Application for 2008/Annual Report for 2006* (October 4, 2007); See also "Agenda, Interagency Meeting – Gulf Oil Spill Workers' Study" (NIH Campus, Bethesda, Maryland, August 19, 2010), http://www.niehs.nih.gov/about/od/programs/docs/agenda-aug19-2010.pdf.

[156] Editorial, "Ruling in Charity Hospital case is a significant victory: An editorial," *Times-Picayune*, April 4, 2010.

[157] Robin Rudowitz, Diane Rowland, and Adele Shartzer, "Health Care In New Orleans Before and After Hurricane Katrina," *Health Affairs* 25, no. 5 (2006): 393–406.

[158] *Ibid.*

[159] Louisiana Office of Public Health, *State Narrative for Louisiana: Maternal and Child Health Title V Block Grant.*

[160] U.S. Government Accountability Office, *Hurricane Katrina: Federal Grants Have Helped Health Care Organizations Provide Primary Care, but Challenges Remain* (July 2009).

[161] Karen B. DeSalvo, "Community Health Clinics: Bringing Quality Care Closer to New Orleanians," in *The New Orleans Index at Five*, Amy Liu and Allison Plyer, eds. (Brookings Institution, August 2010).

Chapter Seven

[1] Louisiana Coastal Protection and Restoration Authority, *Fiscal Year 2011 Annual Plan: Integrated Ecosystem Restoration and Hurricane Protection in Coastal Louisiana* (April 2010), 2–3.

[2] U.S. Environmental Protection Agency, Mississippi River Gulf of Mexico Watershed Nutrient Task Force, *Hypoxia 101*, http://www.epa.gov/owow_keep/msbasin/hypoxia101.htm.

[3] Complaint at ¶ 28, Louisiana v. Triton Asset Leasing GmBH al., No. 2:10-cv-03059 (E.D. La. September 14, 2010).

[4] Ray Mabus, *America's Gulf Coast: A Long Term Recovery Plan after the Deepwater Horizon Oil Spill* (September 28, 2010).

[5] Charles Simenstad et al., "When is Restoration Not? Incorporating Landscape-Scale Processes to Restore Self-Sustaining Ecosystems in Coastal Wetland Restoration," *Ecological Engineering* 26, no. 1 (2006): 28, 31.

[6] For background about "resiliency," see C.S. Holling, "Resilience and Stability of Ecological Systems," *Annual Review of Ecology and Systematics* 24 (1973): 1–23.

[7] Mabus, *America's Gulf Coast: A Long Term Recovery Plan after the Deepwater Horizon Oil Spill*, 26.

[8] U.S. Geological Survey, *The Gulf of Mexico Hypoxic Zone*, http://toxics.usgs.gov/hypoxia/hypoxic_zone.html.

[9] Mississippi River/Gulf of Mexico Watershed Nutrient Task Force, *Gulf Hypoxia Action Plan 2008—For Reducing, Mitigating, and Controlling Hypoxia in the Northern Gulf of Mexico and Improving Water Quality in the Mississippi River Basin* (2008).

[10] Bureau of Ocean Energy Management, Regulation and Enforcement, *Leasing*, http://www.gomr.boemre.gov/homepg/lsesale/lsesale.html.

[11] Executive Order 13547, Stewardship of the Ocean, Our Coasts, and the Great Lakes, 75 Fed. Reg. 43023, July 22, 2010.

[12] White House Council on Environmental Quality, *Final Recommendations of the Interagency Ocean Policy Task Force* (July 19, 2010).

[13] For an overview of issues in Gulf of Mexico marine policy, see Linwood Pendleton, Larry Crowder, Daniel Dunn, Clare Fieseler, Morgan Gopnik, Catherine Latanich, Mike Orbach, Steve Roady, Mary Turnipseed, Cindy van Dover, "Marine Protection in the Gulf of Mexico: Current Policy, Future Options, and Ecosystem Outcomes," *Policy Brief*, Nicholas Institute for Environmental Policy Solutions, Duke University (October 2010). Elliott Norse (Marine Conservation Biology Institute), interview with Commission staff, October 18, 2010; Larry McKinney (Harte Institute for Gulf of Mexico Studies), interview with Commission staff, October 18; 2010 Sandra Whitehouse (Ocean Conservancy), interview with Commission staff, October 20, 2010; Deerin Babb-Brott (Massachusetts Office of Coastal Zone Management), interview with Commission staff, October 21, 2010; Barry Gold (Moore Foundation), interview with Commission staff, Sept. 13, 2010.

[14] NOAA, *Coastal and Marine Spatial Planning Examples*, http://www.msp.noaa.gov/examples/index.html.

[15] United Nations Educational, Scientific and Cultural Organization (UNESCO), *Marine Spatial Planning Initiative: Norway*, http://www.unesco-ioc-marinesp.be/spatial_management_practice/norway.

[16] Bureau of Ocean Energy Management, Regulation and Enforcement, Outer Continental Shelf Lands Act, http://www.gomr.boemre.gov/homepg/regulate/regs/laws/ocslasht.html.

[17] For geospatial maps on uses of Gulf resources, see NOAA, *Multipurpose Marine Cadastre*, http://csc-s-web-p.csc.noaa.gov/MMC.

[18] Cornelius Hammer et al., "Framework of stock-recovery strategies: analyses of factors affecting success and failure,"

ICES Journal of Marine Science 67 (2010): 1849–1855.

[19] For background overview of deltaic science described in this section, see, e.g., Committee on the Restoration and Protection of Coastal Louisiana, *Drawing Louisiana's New Map: Addressing Land Loss in Coastal Louisiana* (National Research Council, 2006), 29–42; James M. Coleman, Harry H. Roberts, and Gregory W. Stone, "Mississippi River Delta: An Overview," *Journal of Coastal Research* 14, no. 3 (1998): 698–716; John W. Day Jr. et al., "Restoration of the Mississippi Delta: Lessons from Hurricanes Katrina and Rita," *Science* 315, no. 5819 (2007): 1679–1684.

[20] "Storm Death Toll at 31 as Floodwaters Recede," CNN, May 6, 2010; Paul Kemp, "Use the Mississippi River to stop the oil," CNN, June 13, 2010. The approximate travel time of water along the Ohio and then Mississippi Rivers can be estimated by noting the sequence of peak water levels along the river, in the National Weather Service's Lower Mississippi River Forecast Center, particularly the summary data for weeks ending in May 5, 2010, and May 12, 2010. River Summary Archives for these dates and the rest of 2010 can be found here: http://www.srh.noaa.gov/lmrfc/?n=riversummaryarchive.

[21] For description of Atchafalaya diversion, see, e.g., Martin Reuss, *Designing the Bayous: The Control of Water in the Atchafalaya Basin, 1800-1995* (Alexandria, VA: Texas A&M University Press, 2004).

[22] U.S. Geological Survey, *Northern Gulf of Mexico (NGOM) Ecosystem Change and Hazard Susceptibility Project—Overview* (2010), http://ngom.usgs.gov/overview/intro.html.

[23] Kevin Kosar, *Disaster Response and Appointment of a Recovery Czar: The Executive Branch's Response to the Flood of 1927* (Congressional Research Service, 2005).

[24] 33 U.S.C. § 702c (1928).

[25] U.S. Army Corps of Engineers, *The Mississippi River & Tributaries (Mr&T) Project* (2010), http://www.mvn.usace.army.mil/bcarre/missproj.asp.

[26] Testimony of Senator Mary Landrieu, Louisiana, Hearing before the National Commission, September 28, 2010.

[27] *Coastal Wetlands Planning, Protection, And Restoration Act: Summary of Wetland Benefits for Priority List Projects* (2010), http://www.lacoast.gov/reports/wva/CWPPRA%20project%20benefits%202010-06-18.pdf; U.S. Army Corps of Engineers, *Louisiana Coastal Area Ecosystem Restoration Plan* (2010), http://www.lca.gov/.

[28] Robert H. Meade and John A. Moody. "Causes for the decline of suspended-sediment discharge in the Mississippi River system, 1940-2007," *Hydrological Process* 24 (2010): 35–49; Robert B. Jacobson, Dale W. Blevins and Chance J. Bitner, "Sediment Regime Constraints on River Restoration—an Example from the Lower Missouri River," *Geological Society of America Special Papers* 451 (2009): 1–22.

[29] Day et al., "Restoration of the Mississippi Delta: Lessons from Hurricanes Katrina and Rita," 1682.

[30] Robert Morton et al., *Rapid Subsidence and Historical Wetland Loss in the Mississippi Delta Plain: Likely Causes and Future Implications*, (U.S. Geological Survey, 2005).

[31] John Barras et al., *Land Area Change in Coastal Louisiana—a Multidecadal Perspective (from 1956 to 2006)* (U.S. Geological Survey, 2008).

[32] Torbjorn Tornqvist et al., "Mississippi Delta Subsidence Primarily Caused by Compaction of Holocene Strata," *Nature Geoscience* 1 (2008): 173–176.

[33] Roy Dokka, "Modern-Day Tectonic Subsidence in Coastal Louisiana," *Geology* 34, no. 4 (2006): 281–84.

[34] Robert Morton, "Evidence of Regional Subsidence and Associated Interior Wetland Loss Induced by Hydrocarbon Production, Gulf Coast Region, USA," *Environmental Geology* 50 (2006): 261–74.

[35] Committee on the Restoration and Protection of Coastal Louisiana, *Drawing Louisiana's New Map: Addressing Land Loss in Coastal Louisiana* (National Research Council, 2006), 48.

[36] James G. Gosselink, "Comments on 'Wetland Loss in the Northern Gulf of Mexico: Multiple Hardworking Hypotheses,'" *Estuaries* 24, no. 4 (August 2001), 636–651.

[37] James B. Johnston, Donald R. Cahoon and Megan K. La Peyre, *Outer Continental Shelf (OCS)-Related Pipelines and Navigation Canals in the Western and Central Gulf of Mexico: Relative Impacts on Wetland Habitats and Effectiveness of Mitigation* (Minerals Management Service, 2009), 157.

[38] Richard Campanella, *Time and Place in New Orleans: Past Geographies in the Present Day* (Gretna, LA: Pelican Publishing Company, Inc., 2002), 78; Panama Canal Authority, *Frequently asked questions*, http://www.pancanal.com/eng/general/canal-faqs/index.html.

[39] U.S. Army Corps of Engineers, *Integrated Final Report to Congress and Legislative Environmental Impact Statement for the Mississippi River—Gulf Outlet Deep-Draft De-Authorization Study* (June 2008), 6.

[40] Gary P. Shaffer et al., "The MRGO Navigation Project: A Massive Human-Induced Environmental, Economic, and Storm Disaster," *Journal of Coastal Research*, Special Issue 54 (2009): 206–224; R.H. Caffey and B. Leblanc, *'Closing' the Mississippi River Gulf Outlet: Environmental and Economic Considerations* (LACoast.gov, 2002).

[41] Day et al., "Restoration of the Mississippi Delta: Lessons from Hurricanes Katrina and Rita," 1679–1684.

[42] U.S. Army Corps of Engineers, *MRGO Navigation Channel Closure* (2010), http://www.mrgo.gov/MRGO_Closure.aspx.

[43] James Coleman, "James P. Morgan: Scientific Contributions," *Journal of Coastal Research* 14, no. 3 (1998): 868–69.

[44] Avenal v. United States, 33 Fed. Cl. 778 (1995).

[45] National Research Council, Panel on River Basin and Coastal Systems Planning, Committee to Assess the U.S. Army Corps of Engineers Methods of Analysis and Peer Review for Water Resources Project Planning, *River Basins and Coastal Systems Planning Within the U.S. Army Corps of Engineers* (2004): 104.

[46] S.M. Gagliano, "Canals, Dredging, and Land Reclamation in the Louisiana Coastal Zone" in *Hydrologic and Geologic Studies of Coastal Louisiana*, Report no. 14 (Center for Wetland Studies, Louisiana State University, 1973).

[47] N.J. Craig, R.E. Turner, and J.W. Day Jr., "Land Loss in Coastal Louisiana (U.S.A.)" *Environmental Management* 3, no. 2 (1979): 133–144.

[48] Paul Kemp, Vice-President, National Audobon Society, interview with Commission staff, October 7, 2010.

[49] Denise Reed, "Seeing the Future of the Louisiana Coast," in *After the Storm: Restoring America's Gulf Coast Wetlands, A Special Report of the National Wetlands Newsletter* (Washington, D.C.: Environmental Law Institute, 2006), 45.

[50] Michael Blum and Harry Roberts, "Drowning of the Mississippi Delta due to Insufficient Sediment Supply and Global Sea-Level Rise," *Nature Geoscience* (June 28, 2009): 489–490.

[51] U.S. General Accountability Office, *Coastal Wetlands: Lessons Learned from Past Efforts in Louisiana Could Help Guide Future Restoration and Protection* (December 14, 2007), 10.

[52] U.S. Army Corps of Engineers, *Coastal Wetlands Planning, Protection & Restoration Act* (2010), http://www.mvn.usace.army.mil/pd/cwppra_mission.htm.

[53] Mark Schleifstein, "Breaux Act Anniversary Marks 20 Years of Coastal Restoration Progress," *Times-Picayune*, April 8, 2010; *Caring for Coastal Wetlands: The Coastal Wetlands Planning, Protection and Restoration Act* (LaCoast.gov, November 2007), http://lacoast.gov/new/Pubs/Report_data/Caring.aspx.

[54] Louisiana Wetlands Conservation and Restoration Task Force and the Wetlands Conservation and Restoration Authority, *Coast 2050: Toward a Sustainable Coastal Louisiana, an Executive Summary* (Louisiana Department of Natural Resources, 1998).

[55] Joel Bourne, "Gone with the Water," *National Geographic*, October 2004; Water Resources Development Act of 2007, Pub. L. No. 110-114, Title VII, 121 Stat. 1041, 1270–1283 (2007).

[56] State of Louisiana, *Coastal Protection & Restoration: Funding Sources*, http://www.coastal.la.gov/index.cfm?md=pagebuilder&tmp=home&nid=123&pnid=79&pid=82&catid=0&elid=0.

[57] Donald T. Resio and Joannes J. Westerink, "Modeling the physics of storm surges," *Physics Today* 61, no. 9 (September 2008): 32–38.

[58] Louisiana Office of Coastal Protection and Restoration, Library, *Coastal Initiatives & Programs*, "http://coastal.la.gov/index.cfm?md=pagebuilder&tmp=home&nid=82&pnid=76&pid=77&catid=0&elid=0 ("Donaldsonville to the Gulf Panel" and "Morganza to the Gulf Project").

[59] U.S. Army Corps of Engineers, *Mississippi Coastal Improvement Program (MsCIP) Interim Report* (2006).

[60] Supplemental Appropriations Act of 2009, H.R. 2346, Title IV.

[61] U.S. Army Corps of Engineers, *Louisiana Coastal Protection and Restoration (LACPR): Final Technical Report* (June 2009).

[62] Louisiana Coastal Protection and Restoration Authority, *Fiscal Year 2008 Annual Plan: Ecosystem Restoration and Hurricane Protection in Coastal Louisiana* (April 2007); Coastal Protection and Restoration Authority of Louisiana, *Fiscal Year 2011 Annual Plan: Integrated Ecosystem Restoration and Hurricane Protection in Coastal Louisiana*, (Baton Rouge, 2010): xiii.

[63] Bureau of Ocean Energy Management, Regulation and Enforcement, *Coastal Impact Assistance Program (CIAP)*, http://www.boemre.gov/offshore/ciapmain.htm.

[64] Bureau of Ocean Energy Management, Regulation and Enforcement, Gulf of Mexico Energy Security Act (GOMESA), http://www.boemre.gov/offshore/GOMESARevenueSharing.htm.

[65] White House Council on Environmental Quality, *Gulf Coast Ecosystem Restoration*, http://www.whitehouse.gov/administration/eop/ceq/initiatives/gulfcoast.

[66] Louisiana-Mississippi Gulf Coast Ecosystem Restoration Working Group, *Roadmap for Restoring Ecosystem Resiliency and Sustainability* (March 2010).

[67] Mabus, *America's Gulf Coast: A Long Term Recovery Plan after the Deepwater Horizon Oil Spill*.

[68] Executive Order 13554: Establishing the Gulf Coast Ecosystem Restoration Task Force, 75 Fed. Reg. 62313, October 5, 2010.

[69] Frank Donze, "Gulf Coast Restoration Chief Ray Mabus has no Oil Spill Answers Just Yet," *Times-Picayune*, June 29, 2010.

[70] Estimate based on John Barras, *Land Area Change in Coastal Louisiana—a Multidecadal Perspective (from 1956 to 2006)* (U.S.Geological Survey, 2008).

[71] Louisiana-Mississippi Gulf Coast Ecosystem Restoration Working Group, *Roadmap for Restoring Ecosystem Resiliency and Sustainability*, 2–3.

[72] Testimony of Brian McPeek, Regional Managing Director for North America, The Nature Conservancy, Hearing before the National Commission, September 28, 2010.

[73] Testimony of James T.B. Tripp, Senior Counsel, Environmental Defense Fund, Hearing before the National Commission, Sept 28, 2010; Testimony of Brian McPeek.

[74] Gulf of Mexico Energy Security Act of 2006, Pub. L. 109-432.

[75] 33 U.S.C. § 2706(e).

[76] 33 U.S.C. § 1321(b)(7); 40 C.F.R. § 19.4. According to the current official government estimate, the Macondo well released approximately 4.9 million barrels of oil over the course of the spill (±10 percent), roughly 830,000 barrels of which were captured at the wellhead using the top hat and other devices. *Deepwater Horizon MC252 Gulf Incident Oil Budget* (August 1, 2010), http://www.noaanews.noaa.gov/stories2010/PDFs/DeepwaterHorizonOilBudget20100801.pdf); Joel Achenbach and David Fahrenthold, "Oil spill dumped 4.9 million barrels into Gulf of Mexico, latest measure shows," *Washington Post*, August 3, 2010 (range is $4.5 billion to $18 billion, based on estimated 4.1 million barrels discharged); Jonathan Tilove, "BP disputes government estimates of volume of Gulf of Mexico oil spill;" *Times-Picayune*, December 3, 2010 (penalties could be as high as $21 billion, based on estimate of 4.9 million barrels discharged). BP has not released its own estimate for the total release from the well, but it disputes the government's figures on the grounds that, among other things, they fail to take into account "significant flow impediments" and "rely on incomplete or inaccurate information, rest in large part on assumptions that have not been validated, and are subject to far greater uncertainties than have been acknowledged." BP, letter to the National Commission, October 21, 2010, 1, 4.

[77] Testimony of Richard Stewart, New York University School of Law, Hearing before the National Commission, September 28, 2010.

[78] 33 U.S.C. § 1319(c)(1).

[79] 33 U.S.C. § 1319(c)(2).

[80] 26 U.S.C. § 9509.

[81] Ray Mabus, *America's Gulf Coast: A Long Term Recovery Plan after the Deepwater Horizon Oil Spill*.

[82] Exxon Valdez Oil Spill Trustee Council, *Science Panel*, http://www.evostc.state.ak.us/people/sp.cfm.

[83] Joe Hunt, *Mission Without a Map: The Politics and Policies of Restoration Following the Exxon Valdez Oil Spill: 1989-2002*, Exxon Valdez Oil Spill Trustee Council (Anchorage, 2009): 156-157.

[84] See, e.g., Testimony of Stanley Senner, Director of Conservation Science, Ocean Conservancy, Hearing before the National Commission, September 28, 2010.

[85] President Barack Obama, "Remarks by the President to the Nation on the BP Oil Spill" (June 15, 2010), http://www.whitehouse.gov/the-press-office/remarks-president-nation-bp-oil-spill.

[86] Press Release, Office of the Governor, Gov. Jindal Announces "Agenda For Revitalizing Coastal Louisiana," July 15, 2010, http://wwwprd.doa.louisiana.gov/LaNews/PublicPages/Dsp_PressRelease_Display.cfm?PressReleaseID=2550&Rec_ID=1.

[87] NOAA, Damage Assessment, *Remediation, and Restoration Program: Glossary*, http://www.darrp.noaa.gov/glossary/index.htm.

[88] Testimony of Stanley Senner.

Chapter Eight

1 Magne Ognedal, "Thirty years since Kielland – why are major accidents still happening?" (speech, Petroleum Safety Authority of Norway, August 27, 2010) 3, http://www.ptil.no/major-accidents/safety-lunch-at-ons-risk-of-a-major-accident-is-always-present-article7202-144.html.

[2] BP, *Sustainability Review* (2009), 20–21. http://www.bp.com/assets/bp_internet/globalbp/STAGING/global_assets/e_s_assets/e_s_assets_2009/downloads_pdfs/bp_sustainability_review_2009.pdf

[3] Health and Safety Executive, *Major Incident Investigation Report, BP Grangemouth Scotland (29th May – 10th June 2000)* (August 18, 2003), 7, http://www.hse.gov.uk/comah/bpgrange/images/bprgrangemouth.pdf.

[4] *Ibid.*

[5] *Ibid.*

[6] Health and Safety Executive, *BP Grangemouth Executive Summary—Findings and Recommendations*, http://www.hse.gov.uk/comah/bpgrange/execsumm/findings.htm.

[7] Andrew B. Wilson, "BP's Disaster: No Surprise to Folks in the Know," CBS, June 22, 2010, http://www.cbsnews.com/stories/2010/06/22/opinion/main6605248.shtml.

[8] Jan Erik Vinnem, *Offshore Risk Assessment: Principles, Modelling and Applications of QRA Studies*, Second Edition (London: Springer Studies in Reliability Engineering, 2007), 91, 100, 102.

[9] Andrew B. Wilson, "BP's Disaster: No Surprise to Folks in the Know," CBS, June 22, 2010, http://www.cbsnews.com/stories/2010/06/22/opinion/main6605248.shtml.

[10] Oberon Houston, email message to Commission staff.

[11] *The Report of the BP US Refineries Independent Safety Review Panel*, (January 2007).

[12] U.S. Chemical Safety and Hazard Investigation Board, *Investigation Report: Refinery Explosion and Fire* (March 2007),145, http://www.csb.gov/assets/document/CSBFinalReportBP.pdf.

[13] Testimony of Carolyn W. Merritt, Chairman and Chief Executive Officer, U.S. Chemical Safety Board, before the U.S. Senate Committee on Environment and Public Works, Subcommittee on Transportation Safety, Infrastructure Security, and Water Quality, July 10, 2007.

[14] *Ibid.*

[15] U.S. Chemical Safety and Hazard Investigation Board, *Investigation Report: Refinery Explosion and Fire*, 19-20.

[16] *Ibid.*

[17] *Ibid.*

[18] *The Report of the BP US Refineries Independent Safety Review Panel.*

[19] *Ibid.*

[20] *Ibid.*, 224.

[21] *Ibid.*, 165

[22] "BP's Alaskan Oil Spill Triggers Lawsuit," 815 *TCE: The Chemical Engineer* (May 2009): 9.

[23] *Ibid.*

[24] *Ibid.*

[25] "BP Faces Lawsuits for 2006 Spills," 32 *Oil Spill Intelligence Report*, no. 17 (April 16, 2009); "BP Settles with Royalty Trust," 32 *Oil Spill Intelligence Report*, no. 22 (May 21, 2009).

[26] *The Report of the BP US Refineries Independent Safety Review Panel*, 1.

[27] *Ibid.*, XVII.

[28] L. Duane Wilson, *Independent Expert Third Annual Report, 2001 covering January–December 2009* (March 2010): 4.

[29] Ibid., 25–26.

[30] Elmer Danenberger, interview with Commission staff, December 9, 2010.

[31] BP, Deepwater Horizon *Accident Investigation Report* (September 8, 2010).

[32] "BP Report Attacked," *New Scientist*, 2 October, 2010, 4.

[33] Richard Sears, e-mail message to Commission staff, November 23, 2010.

[34] Consulting Services Lloyd's Register EMEA Aberdeen Energy, *North American Division Summary Report* (March 2010).

[35] *Ibid.*, App. C, 6.

[36] *Ibid.*, App. C, 8, 11.

[37] *Ibid.*, 10-11.

[38] *Ibid.*, 29.

[39] Halliburton, *History of Halliburton*, http://www.halliburton.com/AboutUs/default.aspx?navid=970&pageid=2312.

[40] *Ibid.*

[41] Russell Gold and Ben Casselman, "Drilling Process Attracts Scrutiny in Rig Explosion," *Wall Street Journal*, April 30, 2010.

[42] Montara Commission of Inquiry, *Report of the Montara Commission of Inquiry*, (June 17, 2010), http://www.ret.gov.au/Department/Documents/MIR/Montara-Report.pdf.

[43] *Ibid.*, 63.

[44] *Ibid.*

[45] Commission staff created this map and associated table using loss of well control data available on BOEMRE's Incident Statistics and Summary webpage. Although efforts were made to accurately capture and illustrate every loss of well control from 1996-2009 in the U.S. Gulf of Mexico, the data presented does not purport to be comprehensive, but instead illustrative of the fact that losses of well control, blowouts, potential catastrophes, and near misses are more frequent than commonly reported and publicized.

[46] Commission staff analysis of International Regulators Forum International Association of Drilling Contractors and International Association of Oil and Gas Producers data. See http://www.irfoffshoresafety.com/country/performance/, http://www.iadc.org/asp.htm, and http://www.ogp.org.uk/index.asp?main=publications/main.asp.

[47] Testimony of Eric Milito, Upstream Director, American Petroleum Institute, "The Deepwater Horizon Incident: Are The Minerals Management Service Regulations Doing The Job?" Hearing Before the Subcommittee on Energy and Mineral Resources of the House Committee on Natural Resources, 111th Congress (2010) ("Since 1924, API has developed industry standards and practices that promote reliability and safety through the use of proven engineering practices. . . . API standards are developed through a collaborative effort among industry experts, technical experts from government, and other interested stakeholders. The industry has helped create more than 500 standards, including some 240 exploration and production standards that address offshore operations.")

[48] American Petroleum Institute, API 2010 Publics Programs and Services Catalog (March 2010), http://www.api.org/Standards/upload/2010_Catalog_web.pdf.

[49] American Petroleum Institute, "Certifications recognized around the world," *Training and Certifications Program brochure* (August 9, 2009), http://www.api.org/certifications/upload/ENGLISH_SUMMARY_BROCH.pdf.

[50] Testimony of Eric Milito ("Seventy-eight of these standards are referenced in Minerals Management Service regulations."). For MMS rulemakings that incorporate industry standards into regulations over time, see Oil and Gas and Sulphur Operations in the Outer Continental Shelf, 61 Fed. Reg. 60,019 (November 26, 1996); Oil and Gas and Sulphur Operations in the Outer Continental Shelf—Pipelines and Pipeline Rights-of-Way, 72 Fed. Reg. 56,442 (October 3, 2007); Press Release, Minerals Management Service, Minerals Management Service to Adopt the Latest Edition of Industry Standard on Fixed Offshore Production Platforms, April 21, 2003, http://www.boemre.gov/ooc/press/2003/press4-21.htm.

[51] Letter from Allen Verret, Offshore Operators Committee, and Tim Sampson, American Petroleum Institute, to the U.S. Minerals Management Service (September 15, 2009), http://www.scribd.com/doc/30588089/Joint-API-OOC-Letter-to-MMS; American Petroleum Institute and Offshore Operators Committee, "Safety and Environmental Management Systems for Outer Continental Shelf Oil and Gas Operations," Public Comment (September 15, 2009), http://www.boemre.gov/federalregister/PublicComments/AD15SafetyEnvMgmtSysforOCSOilGasOperations/OOCAPICommentLetter9-15-09.pdf; American Petroleum Institute, "Postlease Operations Safety," Public Comment (July 1, 1998), http://www.boemre.gov/federalregister/PublicComments/Sub_A_Comments/prorule.pdf, http://www.boemre.gov/federalregister/PublicComments/Sub_A_Comments/subacomm.pdf.

[52] Commission staff held several meetings during August and September 2010 with representatives of major oil and gas companies during which the role of API in standard setting processing, including the impact of API's broader advocacy role on those standards, was discussed.

[53] T.A.F. Powell, "US Voluntary SEMP Initiative: Holy Grail or Poisoned Chalice?" (Offshore Technology Conference [OTC] Paper 8111, May 1996).

[54] Letter from Allen Verret, Offshore Operators Committee, and Tim Sampson, American Petroleum Institute, to the U.S. Minerals Management Service (September 15, 2009), http://www.scribd.com/doc/30588089/Joint-API-OOC-Letter-to-MMS; Offshore Operators Committee and American Petroleum Institute, "Oil, Gas, and Sulphur Operations in the Outer Continental Shelf (OCS)—Safety and Environmental Management Systems," Public Comment (May 22, 2006).

[55] T.A.F. Powell, "US Voluntary SEMP Initiative: Holy Grail or Poisoned Chalice?"

[56] Oil and Gas and Sulphur Operations in the Outer Continental Shelf—Safety and Environmental Management Systems, 75 Fed. Reg. 199 (October 15, 2010).

[57] T.A.F. Powell, "US Voluntary SEMP Initiative: Holy Grail or Poisoned Chalice?"

[58] Elmer Danenberger, interview with Commission staff, December 9, 2010.

[59] Testimony of Tad W. Patzek, "Beneath the Surface of the BP Spill: What's Happening Now, What's Needed Next," Briefing Before the Subcommittee on Energy and Environment of the House Committee on Energy and Commerce, 111th Congress (2010): 4.

[60] Ibid.

[61] Ibid.

[62] Testimony of James Ellis, Institute of Nuclear Power Operations, Hearing before the National Commission, August 25, 2010.

[63] Federal Aviation Administration, "Mission," http://www.faa.gov/about/mission/.

[64] Federal Aviation Administration, "Delegation and Designee Background," http://www.faa.gov/about/history/deldes_background/.

[65] Federal Aviation Administration, "Designees and Delegations: Designated Engineering Representative (DER)," http://www.faa.gov/other_visit/aviation_industry/designees_delegations/designee_types/der/; Nancy Leveson (MIT), interview with Commission staff, October 13, 2010.

[66] Federal Aviation Administration, "Delegation and Designee Background," http://www.faa.gov/about/history/deldes_background/.

[67] Leveson, interview.

[68] Ibid.
[69] Nancy Leveson, *Safeware: System Safety and Computers* 556 (Boston: Addison-Wesley, 1995).

[70] Ibid.

[71] Nancy Leveson, *Engineering A Safer World: Systems Thinking Applied To Safety* 376-77 (Cambridge, MA: MIT Press, forthcoming in 2011), http://sunnyday.mit.edu/safer-world.

[72] *Ibid.*, 375.

[73] *Ibid.*, 376.

[74] *Ibid.*, 376, 378.

[75] *Ibid.*, 375–6.

[76] *Ibid.*, 375–6.

[77] *Ibid.*, 378.

[78] *Ibid.*, 378.

[79] *Ibid.*, 379.

[80] *Ibid.*, 380–1.

[81] *Ibid.*, 380.

[82] *Ibid.*, 380.

[83] *Ibid.*, 380.

[84] *Ibid.*, 381–2.

[85] *Ibid.*, 385.

[86] *Ibid.*, 385–6.

[87] *Ibid.*, 388.

[88] Alaska Oil Spill Commission, *Spill: The Wreck of the Exxon Valdez* (Final Report) (February 1990), 1.

[89] Samuel K. Skinner and William K. Reilly, *The Exxon Valdez Oil Spill: A Report to the President* (May 1989), 1.

[90] *Ibid.*, 27–8.

[91] National Transportation Safety Board, *Safety Recommendation* (September 18, 1990), http://www.ntsb.gov/recs/letters/1990/M90_26_31A.pdf.

[92] Exxon Valdez Oil Spill Trustee Council, "Settlement," http://www.evostc.state.ak.us/facts/settlement.cfm; Exxon Valdez Oil Spill Trustee Council, "Questions and Answers," http://www.evostc.state.ak.us/facts/qanda.cfm.

[93] Exxon Mobil, *2009 Corporate Citizenship Report*, 15.

[94] Testimony of Rex Tillerson, CEO of Exxon Mobil, Hearing before the National Commission, November 9, 2010.

[95] *Ibid.*

[96] *Ibid.*

[97] Exxon Mobil, *2009 Corporate Citizenship Report*, 14.

[98] *Ibid.*,13, 19.

[99] "Shell 'Ignored Accident Warning,'" BBC online, June 14, 2006, http://news.bbc.co.uk/2/hi/5077886.stm; Terry Macalister, "Shell Accused Over Oil Rig Safety," *The Guardian*, June 23, 2006.

[100] "Shell 'Ignored Accident Warning.'"

[101] Shell, *Sustainability Report 2009*, 16–17, http://sustainabilityreport.shell.com/2009/servicepages/downloads/files/all_shell_sr09.pdf.

[102] Testimony of Marvin Odum, Shell, Hearing before the National Commission, November 9, 2010.

[103] *Ibid.*

[104] *Ibid.*

[105] *Ibid.*

[106] *Ibid.*

[107] Responsible Care, Who We Are, http://www.responsiblecare.org/page.asp?p=6406.

[108] *Ibid.*

[109] Jody Freeman, "Private Parties, Public Functions and the New Administrative Law" in *Recrafting the Rule of Law: The Limits of Legal Order*, ed. David Dyzenhaus (Toronto: Hart Publishing, 1999), 21.

[110] *Ibid.*, 33.

[111] Press Release, Securities and Exchange Commission, Chairman Cox Announces End of Consolidated Supervised Entities Program, September 26, 2008; Stephen Labaton, "Agency's '04 Rule Let Banks Pile Up New Debt," *New York Times*, October 3, 2008.

[112] Press Release, Securities and Exchange Commission, Chairman Cox Announces End of Consolidated Supervised Entities Program.

[113] Edward J. Balleisen and Marc Eisner, "The Promise and Pitfalls of Co-Regulation: How Governments Can Draw on Private Governance for Public Purpose," in *New Perspectives on Regulation*, ed. David Moss and John Cisternino, (Cambridge, UK: Cambridge University Press, 2009), 31.

[114] *Ibid.*, 130.

[115] *Ibid.*

[116] *Ibid.*

[117] Testimony of Marvin Fertel, President and CEO of Nuclear Energy Institute, "Three Mile Island—Looking Back on Thirty Years of Lessons Learned," Before the Subcommittee on Clean Air and Nuclear Safety, 111th Congress (2009).

[118] Testimony of James Ellis, Institute of Nuclear Power Operations, Hearing before the National Commission, August 25, 2010.

[119] John G. Kemeny, *Report of The President's Commission on the Accident at Three Mile Island: The Need for Change: The Legacy of TMI* (1979), 68. The full subsection of the recommendation reads, "The industry should establish a program that specifies appropriate safety standards including those for management, quality assurance, and operating procedures and practices, and that conducts independent evaluations. The recently created Institute of Nuclear Power Operations, or some similar organization, may be an appropriate vehicle for establishing and implementing this program."

[120] Institute of Nuclear Power Operations, "About Us," http://www.inpo.info/AboutUs.htm.

[121] Joseph V. Rees, *Hostages of Each Other: The Transformation of Nuclear Safety Since Three Mile Island* (Chicago: University of Chicago Press, 1996), 50–51.

[122] Lee Gard, interview with Commission staff, November 8, 2010.

[123] Rees, *Hostages of Each Other: The Transformation of Nuclear Safety Since Three Mile Island*, 57–58.

[124] Rees, *Hostages of Each Other: The Transformation of Nuclear Safety Since Three Mile Island*, 143.

[125] Lee Gard, interview.

[126] *Ibid.*

[127] *Ibid.*

[128] *Ibid.*

[129] *Ibid.*

[130] *Ibid.*

[131] Lee Gard, e-mail message to Commission Staff, December 6, 2010.

[132] Lee Gard, interview.

[133] Testimony of A. C. Tollison Jr., Executive Vice President, Institute of Nuclear Power Operations, "National Energy Policy: Nuclear Energy," Before the Subcommittee on Energy and Air Quality, 107th Congress (2001).

[134] *Ibid.*

[135] Rees, *Hostages of Each Other: The Transformation of Nuclear Safety Since Three Mile Island*, 76.

[136] Alice Camp, "Nuclear: In Pursuit of a Renaissance," *EPRI Journal* (Summer 2007): 20.

[137] Rees, *Hostages of Each Other: The Transformation of Nuclear Safety Since Three Mile Island*, 81.

[138] *Ibid.*, 53.

[139] *Ibid.*, 53

[140] *Ibid.*, 53–54.

[141] Lee Gard, e-mail message to Commission Staff, December 1, 2010.

[142] Rees, *Hostages of Each Other: The Transformation of Nuclear Safety Since Three Mile Island*, 104.

[143] Lee Gard, interview.

[144] Michael Golay (MIT), interview with Commission Staff, October 27, 2010.

[145] Lee Gard, e-mail message to Commission Staff, December 1, 2010.

[146] Michael Rencheck (AREVA Inc.), interview with Commission staff, November 1, 2010.

[147] Rees, *Hostages of Each Other: The Transformation of Nuclear Safety Since Three Mile Island*, 104.

[148] Michael Golay, interview.

[149] 33 U.S.C. § 2210.

[150] Lee Gard, e-mail message to Commission Staff, December 1, 2010.

[151] Lee Gard, e-mail message to Commission Staff, November 15, 2010.

[152] Lee Gard, e-mail message to Commission Staff, December 13, 2010.

[153] "Oil Industry Needs Self-Regulation, Says Alternate Energy Holdings Inc. CEO," *Forbes Magazine*, August 26, 2010.

[154] Lee Gard, interview.

[155] Rees, *Hostages of Each Other: The Transformation of Nuclear Safety Since Three Mile Island*, 57.

[156] Lee Gard, interview.

[157] *Ibid.*

[158] Rees, *Hostages of Each Other: The Transformation of Nuclear Safety Since Three Mile Island*, 96–97.

[159] *Ibid.*, 116.

[160] *Ibid.*, 111–117.

[161] Testimony of James Ellis, Institute of Nuclear Power Operations, Hearing before the National Commission, August 25, 2010; Institute of Nuclear Power Operations, *2009 Annual Report*; Institute of Nuclear Power Operations, *1994 Annual Report*.

[162] Testimony of James Ellis, Institute of Nuclear Power Operations, Hearing before the National Commission, August 25, 2010.

[163] Institute of Nuclear Power Operations, *Performance Objectives and Criteria* (May 2005); Institute of Nuclear Power Operations, *Principles for Nuclear Safety Culture* (November 2004).

[164] Rees, *Hostages of Each Other: The Transformation of Nuclear Safety Since Three Mile Island*, 44.

[165] *Ibid.*, 64.

[166] U.S. Department of the Interior, Outer Continental Shelf Safety Oversight Board, *Report to the Secretary of the Interior* (September 1, 2010), 11–13.

[167] *Ibid.*, 13–14.

[168] 10 C.F.R. Parts 1–171.

[169] Testimony of Rex Tillerson, Exxon Mobil, Hearing before the National Commission, November 9, 2010.

[170] *Ibid.*

[171] Testimony of Michael Bromwich, Director, Bureau of Ocean Energy Management, Regulation and Enforcement, Department of the Interior, Hearing before the National Commission, November 9, 2010, 228.

[172] Oil and Gas and Sulphur Operations in the Outer Continental Shelf – Safety and Environmental Management Systems, 75 Fed. Reg. 199 (October 15, 2010).

[173] National Commission Staff, "Response/Clean-Up Technology Research & Development and the Deepwater Horizon Oil Spill," (staff working paper, 2010)

[174] Angel Gonzalez, "Oil Firms Plan Rapid-Response Force," *Wall Street Journal*, July 22, 2010; Daniel Squire, e-mail message to Commission staff, December 1, 2010.

[175] Marine Well Containment Company, "Industry Initiatives to Ensure Safe, Protective Drilling Practices in the Deepwater Gulf of Mexico: The Marine Well Containment System" (presentation, Washington, D.C., September 2010).

[176] Marine Well Containment Company, "About Us," http://www.marinewellcontainment.com/index.php.

[177] Helix Energy Solutions Group, "Spill Containment: Fast Response to GOM Subsea Oil Spills" (unpublished document provided to Commission staff by Helix Energy Solutions Group).

[178] Independent Deepwater Exploration Coalition, meeting with Commission staff, November, 29, 2010.

[179] "Moody's Offshore drilling insurance rates to jump," *BusinessWeek*, June 4, 2010.

[180] Julia Kollewe, "Oil industry Set for Surge in Insurance Premiums after Deepwater Disaster," *The Guardian*, September 20, 2010, http://www.guardian.co.uk/business/2010/sep/20/deepwater-oil-rigs-insurance-costs.

[181] Aspen Re interview with Commission staff, October 19, 2010; Testimony of Dr. Robert Hartwig, President and Economist, Insurance Information Institute, "Liability and Financial Responsibility for Oil Spills under the Oil Pollution Act of 1990 and Related Statutes," Hearing Before the House Committee on Transportation and Infrastructure, 111th Congress (2010).

[182] 33 U.S.C. § 2702.

[183] *Ibid.*

[184] 33 U.S.C. § 2704.

[185] 33 U.S.C. § 2704; 33 U.S.C § 1321 (Clean Water Act civil and criminal penalties); Jonathan Ramseur, *Oil Spills in U.S. Coastal Waters: Background, Governance, and Issues for Congress* (Congressional Research Service, updated September 2, 2008), 26 ("A 2003 study identified 16 states that impose unlimited liability for oil spills.").

[186] CLEAR Act, H.R. 3534, 111th Cong. § 702 (2010) (as passed by House); S. 3663, 111th Cong. §102 (2010)("Reid Clean Energy bill"); RESPOND Act, S. 3763, 111th Cong. § 6 (2010)("Landrieu bill"); Big Oil Bailout Prevention Act, H.R. 5214, 111th Cong. § 2 (2010).

[187] Testimony of Charles Anderson, SKULD North America, "Liability and Financial Responsibility for Oil Spills under the Oil Pollution Act of 1990 and Related Statutes," Hearing Before the House Committee on Transportation and Infrastructure, 111th Congress (2010), 9.

[188] Graeme Wearden, "BP oil spill costs to hit $40bn," *The Guardian*, November 2, 2010 ($39.9 billion estimated costs); 33 U.S.C. §2716 (maximum required financial responsibility for offshore facilities is $150 million).

[189] Rawle King, *Deepwater Horizon Oil Spill Disaster: Risk, Recovery, and Insurance Implications* (Congressional Research Service, July 12, 2010), 16–18.

[190] Press Release, Munich Re, Munich Re Develops New Insurance Solution for Oil Catastrophes, September 12, 2010, http://www.munichre.com/en/media_relations/press_releases/2010/2010_09_12_press_release.aspx; Munich Re executives, telephone interview with Commission staff, September 17, 2010.

[191] RESPOND Act, S. 3763, 111th Cong. § 7 (2010).

[192] Graeme Wearden, "BP oil spill costs to hit $40bn," *The Guardian*, November 2, 2010.

Chapter Nine

[1] Exec. Order No. 13543, 75 Fed. Reg. 29,397 (May 21, 2010).

[2] See 43 U.S.C. § 1337(b)(6) ("An oil and gas lease issued pursuant to this section shall . . . contain such rental and other provisions as the Secretary may prescribe at the time of offering the area for lease.").

[3] These terms are taken directly from the Council on Environmental Quality (CEQ) NEPA implementing regulations. 40 C.F.R. § 1508.28.

[4] 40 C.F.R. §1508.4.

[5] A "Development Operations Coordination Document" in the Gulf of Mexico is functionally the same as a "Development and Production Plan" in other LES regions.

[6] Press Release, Department of the Interior, Categorical Exclusions for Gulf Offshore Activity to be Limited While Interior Reviews NEPA Process and Develops Revised Policy, August 16, 2010,

[7] Minerals Management Service, *MMS 2007-018 Gulf of Mexico OSC Oil and Gas Lease Sales: 2007-2010 Final Environmental Impact Statement* (April 2007), Volume I, 2-3 to 2-5.

[8] Minerals Management Service, *MMS 2007-026 Chukchi Sea Planning Area Oil and Gas Lease Sale 193 and Seismic Surveying Activities in the Chukchi Sea Final Environmental Impact Statement* (May 2007), Volume I, 1.

[9] Department of Interior, *Department Manual Part 516: National Environmental Policy Act of 1969* (September 2009), 3.4.

[10] Government Accountability Office, *GAO-10-276 Offshore Oil and Gas Development: Additional Guidance Would Help Strengthen the Minerals Management Service's Assessment of Environmental Impacts in the North Aleutian Basin* (March 2010), 21.

[11] Council on Environmental Quality, *Final Recommendations of the Interagency Ocean Policy Task Force* (July 19, 2010), 41.

[12] 43 U.S.C. § 1346.

[13] Commission staff analysis of MMS yearly budget request and enactments, by nominal and real (2005) dollars. Bureau of Ocean Energy Management, *Office of Administration and Budget: Budget Division*, http://www.boemre.gov/adm/budget.html; Herbert Kaufman and Cheryl Anderson, Department of the Interior, *OCS Environmental Studies Contract Projects—Fiscals Years 1973 through 1983* (DOI Minerals Management Service Branch of Environmental Studies, December 1983), II-8.

[14] 33 U.S.C. § 1321(j)(5)(D)(i); 40 C.F.R. § 300.211.

[15] 30 C.F.R. § 254.2(a).

[16] 30 C.F.R. § 254.126

[17] 40 C.F.R. § 300.322

[18] 23 U.S.C. § 125.

[19] Pub. L. No. 107-171, § 2701,116 Stat. 134, 278–279 (2002).

[20] Department of the Interior, National Notice to Lessees and Operators of Federal Oil and Gas Leases, Outer Continental Shelf No. 2010-N10 (November 8, 2010), http://www.gomr.boemre.gov/homepg/regulate/regs/ntls/2010NTLs/10-n10.pdf.

[21] 30 C.F.R. §§ 250.410–418.

[22] 30 C.F.R. § 250.418(j).

[23] Transcript, Deepwater Blowout Containment Conference (September 22, 2010), http://www.doi.gov/news/video/Deepwater-Blowout-Containment-Conference.cfm.

[24] Doug Suttles, interview with Commission staff, October 13, 2010.

[25] Response workers generally must be trained pursuant to the Hazardous Waste Operations and Emergency Response ("HAZWOPER") regulation administered by the Occupational Safety and Health Administration. 29 C.F.R. § 1910.120. This regulation requires specific training and medical surveillance and monitoring for workers dealing with hazardous materials. While this regulation presumably applied to formal response contractors after the Deepwater Horizon spill, it was not applied consistently to citizen responders who also require its protections.

[26] Public information should further be provided in languages and formats that are understandable to individuals with limited English proficiency and individuals with disabilities. ESF #8—Public Health and Medical Services Annex at 7.

[27] Indeed, the Public Health and Medical Services Annex provides for long-term monitoring of potentially exposed individuals, requiring the Department of Health and Human Services to "assist[] State, tribal, and local officials in establishing a registry of potentially exposed individuals . . . and conducting long-term monitoring of this population for potential long-term health effects." ESF #8 – Public Health and Medical Services Annex at 9–10; Rebecca Bratspies, et al., *From Ship to Shore: Reforming the National Contingency Plan to Improve Protections for Oil Spill Cleanup Workers* (Center for Progressive Reform, September 2010).

[28] Whether or not respirators should be required for cleanup workers emerged as a major controversy in the response.

[29] Ray Mabus, *America's Gulf Coast: A Long Term Recovery Plan after the Deepwater Horizon Oil Spill* (September 2010); Exec. Order No. 13554, 75 Fed. Reg. 62313–62317 (October 8, 2010).

[30] Federal liability for damages is not the only potential liability that could result from an offshore drilling incident. Under the Oil Pollution Act, drillers are strictly liable for removal costs. Companies can also be subject to federal civil and criminal penalties as well as unlimited liability for damages under some state laws. These liabilities presumably drive business to internalize risk and mitigate safety, though not as fully as they might if damages liability were not capped.

[31] Gulf Coast Claims Facility, *Frequently Asked Questions*, http://www.restorethegulf.gov/sites/default/files/imported_pdfs/library/assets/gccf-faqs.pdf.

[32] Gulf Coast Claims Facility, *Frequently Asked Questions*, http://www.gulfcoastclaimsfacility.com/faq#Q9. Government claims for loss of revenue are being handled by BP: http://www.bp.com/governmentclaims. A $60 million BP fund is in place for real estate claims across the five Gulf states and is being administered by National Catastrophe Adjusters, a claims adjustment firm: www.gulfreclaims.com; Kathy Jumper, "Realtors Tap National Catastrophe Adjusters To Administer Oil Spill Claims," *Press-Register*, August 24, 2010, http://blog.al.com/live/2010/08/realtors_oil_claims.html. BP has set aside $100 million for rig workers who experience hardship due to the moratorium, to be administered by the Gulf Coast Restoration and Protection Foundation: http://www.gcrpf.org/. Claims for repairs or damage to vessels involved in the Vessel of Opportunity program are being handled by BP.

[33] Letter from Thomas J. Perrelli, Associate Attorney General, Department of Justice, to Kenneth Feinberg, September 17, 2010.

[34] "Leader on BP Claims Blames Fraud for Slow Payouts", *Associated Press*, October 5, 2010.

[35] Press Release, Gulf Coast Claims Facility, Feinberg Announces Faster and More Generous Payments from GCCF, September 25, 2010, http://www.gulfcoastclaimsfacility.com/press6.php; Press Release, Gulf Coast Claims Facility, Feinberg Announces Clarification Regarding Geographic Proximity, October 4, 2010, http://www.gulfcoastclaimsfacility.com/press7.php; Editorial, "Are Victims of the Gulf Oil Spill Getting What They Deserve?," *Washington Post*, November 25, 2010, http://www.gulfcoastclaimsfacility.com/pressA.php; Siobhan Hughes and Ryan December, "Feinberg Softens His Stance on Claims From Spill," *Wall Street Journal*, November 26, 2010.

[36] Gulf Coast Claims Facility, GCCF Program Statistics—Overall Summary, Gulf Coast Claims Facility, December 11, 2010, http://www.gulfcoastclaimsfacility.com/GCCF_Overall_Status_Report.pdf.

[37] Minerals Management Service, Budget Justifications and Performance Information Fiscal Year 2011.

[38] 43 U.S.C. § 1337(b)(6).

Chapter Ten

[1] Energy Information Administration, *Annual Energy Review 2009* (August 19, 2010), Table 5.2, 131, http://www.eia.doe.gov/emeu/aer/pdf/pages/sec5_7.pdf.

[2] Energy Information Administration, *Annual Energy Outlook 2010* (April, 2010), 75, http://www.eia.doe.gov/oiaf/aeo/pdf/0383(2010).pdf.

[3] Technically recoverable reserves, however, are very different from proven reserves, because the former unlike the latter includes reserves that may well be as a practical manner be too expensive to recover.

[4] Energy Information Administration, *Annual Energy Review 2008* (June 26, 2009), Table 4.1, 99, http://www.eia.

gov/FTPROOT/multifuel/038408.pdf.

[5] National Academy of Sciences, *Advancing the Science of Climate Change* (Washington, D.C.: The National Academies Press, 2010).

[6] Energy Information Administration, *Annual Energy Review 2009* (August 19, 2010), Figure 2.0, 37, http://www.eia. gov/emeu/aer/pdf/pages/sec2.pdf. (Most of the remaining transportation fuels came from ethanol and natural gas.)

[7] National Academy of Sciences, *America's Energy Future: Technology and Transformation* (Washington, D.C.: The National Academies Press, 2010), xi.

[8] Energy Information Administration, *Annual Energy Review 2009*, Tables 4.2, 5.1, 101, 129 (calculated from tables) http://www.eia.doe.gov/aer/pdf/aer.pdf.

[9] *Ibid.*, Table 11.5, 315.

[10] *Ibid.*, Tables 11.4, 11.10, 313, 325 (calculated based on tables). "Proved reserves" represent only a small part of can be ultimately recovered and are estimated by different standards around the world.

[11] *Ibid.*, Table 5.17, 167, http://www.eia.gov/emeu/aer/pdf/pages/sec5_43.pdf.

[12] *Ibid.*, Table 3.5, 77. http://www.eia.gov/emeu/aer/pdf/pages/sec3_11.pdf

[13] Stephen Brown and Hillard Huntington, "Estimating U.S. Oil Security Premiums: EMF OP 68," September 2009.

[14] Census Bureau, "Trade in Goods (Imports, Exports and Trade Balance) with China 1985-2010," http://www.census. gov/foreign-trade/balance/c5700.html#2010.

[15] Light-Duty Vehicle Greenhouse Gas Emission Standards and Corporate Average Fuel Economy Standards, 75 Fed. Reg. 25,324 (May 7, 2010). The joint rulemaking in 2010 by the Department of Transportation and EPA establishing light duty vehicle greenhouse gas emission standards and corporate average fuel economy standards promises to significantly increase fuel efficiency and reduce greenhouse gas emissions.

[16] Jay Hakes, *A Declaration of Energy Independence: How Freedom from Foreign Oil Can Improve National Security, Our Economy, and the Environment* (Hoboken, New Jersey: John Wiley & Sons, 1978), 68-70, 87-88; Energy Information Administration, *Annual Energy Review 2009* (August 19, 2010), Figure 5.1, 129, http://www.eia.gov/emeu/aer/pdf/pages/sec5_5.pdf.

[17] National Research Council, *America's Energy Future: Technology and Transformation* (Washington D.C.: National Academies Press, 2009); National Research Council, *Limiting the Magnitude of Future Climate Change* (Washington D.C.: National Academies Press, 2010).

[18] President's Council of Advisors on Science and Technology, *Report to the President on Accelerating the Pace of Change in Energy Technologies through an Integrated Federal Energy Policy* (Washington D.C.: Executive Office of the President, 2010).

[19] "Shares," Gazprom, http://www.gazprom.com/investors/stock/.

[20] "The Other Way Out," *Economist*, November 19, 2010; Energy Information Administration, "Country Analysis Briefs: Mexico," June 2010.

[21] There are also massive natural gas resources in and off Alaska, but until a pipeline is built to the lower 48 states, the gas cannot be brought to market and used.

[22] Department of the Interior, "Estimated Undiscovered, Economically Recoverable Resources," http://www.doi.gov/whatwedo/energy/ocs/upload/UERR-map-2012-2017-80-NoYear-Note.pdf.

[23] Bureau of Ocean Energy Management, "Lease Sales," December 2, 2010, http://alaska.boemre.gov/lease/hlease/LeasingTables/lease_sales.pdf; Minerals Management Service, "Summary of Company Bids," February 7, 2008, http://alaska.boemre.gov/cproject/Chukchi193/193Saleday/Sale%20193%20Sum%20of%20Co%20Bids%20by%20Co%20Code.pdf.

[24] *Energy Information Administration, Annual Energy Review 2009*, Table 5.2, 131.

[25] Energy Information Administration, Annual Energy Outlook 2011, Table A14.

[26] Unpublished information provided to the Commission by the Energy Information Administration.

[27] Northern Economics, *Economic Analysis of Future Offshore Oil and Gas Development: Beaufort Sea, Chukchi Sea, North Aleutian Basin* (March 2009), ES-7, 9.

[28] Audobon Alaska, "Chukchi Sea," http://ak.audubon.org/issues-action/chukchi-sea.

[29] Press Release, Department of the Interior, U.S. Fish and Wildlife Service Announces Final Designation of Polar Bear Critical Habitat, November 24, 2010.

[30] Lori Quakenbush, "Bowhead Whale," Alaska Department of Fish & Game, September 22, 2010.

[31] *Ibid.*

[32] Ronald O'Rourke, *Changes in the Arctic: Background and Issues for Congress* (Congressional Research Service, October 15, 2010), 31 ("On June 25, 2010, the Coast Guard announced that Polar Sea had suffered an unexpected engine casualty and consequently will likely be unavailable for operation until at least January 2011.").

[33] The Arctic Council is a multinational and intergovernmental group. Members include the governments of Canada,

Denmark (including the Faroe Islands and Greenland), Finland, Iceland, Norway, the Russian Federation, Sweden, and the United States of America. The Permanent Participants of the Arctic Council are: Aleut International Association (AIA), Arctic Athabaskan Council (AAC), Gwich'in Council International (GCI), Inuit Circumpolar Council (ICC), Russian Association of Indigenous Peoples of the North (RAIPON), and the Saami Council.

Appendix A

Commission Members

SENATOR BOB GRAHAM, Co-Chair, is the former two-term governor of Florida and served for 18 years in the United States Senate. After retiring from public life in January 2005, Senator Graham served for a year as a senior fellow at the Harvard Kennedy School of Government. There he commenced writing *America, the Owner's Manual*, published in 2009 as a guide to participatory citizenship. From May 2008 to February 2010, he served as chairman of the Commission on the Prevention of Weapons of Mass Destruction Proliferation and Terrorism, and currently serves as a member of the Financial Crisis Inquiry Commission and the CIA's Executive Advisory Board.

WILLIAM K. REILLY, Co-Chair, is a founding partner of Aqua International Partners, LP, a private equity fund dedicated to investing in companies engaged in water and renewable energy, and a senior advisor to TPG Capital, LP, an international investment partnership. He co-chaired the National Commission on Energy Policy. Mr. Reilly served as Administrator of the U.S. Environmental Protection Agency (1989-1993) and president of World Wildlife Fund (1985-1989). He also served as the head of the U.S. delegation to the United Nations Earth Summit at Rio in 1992.

Mandel Ngan/AFP/Getty Images

FRANCES G. BEINECKE, Member, is the President of the Natural Resources Defense Council (NRDC), a non-profit corporation that works to advance environmental policy in the United States and across the world. In addition, Ms. Beinecke currently serves on the Board of the World Resources Institute and the steering committees of the U.S. Climate Action Partnership. She is a member of the Aspen Institute's Commission on Arctic Climate Change, and on the advisory boards of the Yale School of Management and the Yale School of Forestry and Environmental Science.

DONALD F. BOESCH, Member, is President of the University of Maryland Center for Environmental Science, where he is also a Professor of Marine Science and Vice Chancellor for Environmental Sustainability for the University System of Maryland. He is a biological oceanographer who has conducted research on coastal ecosystems along the Atlantic Coast, the Gulf of Mexico, Australia and the East China Sea. A native of Louisiana, he has assessed the long-term environmental effects of offshore oil and gas development and multiple environmental problems of the Gulf Coast.

TERRY D. GARCIA, Member, is currently Executive Vice President for Mission Programs for the National Geographic Society, responsible for the Society's core programs that manage more than 400 scientific field research, conservation and exploration projects annually. From 1994 to 1996, he was General Counsel at NOAA and led the implementation of the Exxon Valdez Oil Spill Restoration Plan for Prince William Sound and the Gulf of Alaska. From 1997 to 1999, he was Assistant Secretary of Commerce for Oceans and Atmosphere and Deputy Administrator of NOAA.

CHERRY A. MURRAY, Member, is Dean of the Harvard School of Engineering and Applied Sciences and John A. and Elizabeth S. Armstrong Professor of Engineering and Applied Sciences. She is currently the Past President of the American Physical Society. She was formerly Senior Vice President of Physical Science & Wireless Research at Bell Labs and past Principal Associate Director for Science & Technology at Lawrence Livermore National Laboratory. A member of the National Academy of Engineering and the National Academy of Sciences, she has served on more than 80 national and international scientific advisory committees, governing boards, and National Research Council panels, including chairing the Council's Division of Engineering and Physical Science.

FRAN ULMER, Member, is Chancellor of the University of Alaska Anchorage, Alaska's largest public university. Ms. Ulmer has served as Mayor of Juneau and Lieutenant Governor of Alaska. As a state legislator, she served on the Special Committee on the Exxon Valdez Oil Spill Claims Settlement. She has been a member of the North Pacific Anadromous Fish Commission, the Alaska Coastal Policy Council, the Alaska Nature Conservancy, the National Parks Conservation Association, the Aspen Institute's Commission on Arctic Climate Change, among many others.

Appendix B

List of Acronyms

API   American Petroleum Institute
BOEMRE Bureau of Ocean Energy Management, Regulation and Enforcement
CWA   Clean Water Act
DOI   Department of the Interior
EA   Environmental Assessment
EIS   Environmental Impact Statement
FDA   Food and Drug Administration
HPSA   Health Professional Shortage Area
IADC   International Association of Drilling Contractors
INPO   Institute of Nuclear Power Operations
MMS   Minerals Management Service
NASA   National Aeronautics and Space Administration
NEPA   National Environmental Policy Act
NOAA   National Oceanic and Atmospheric Administration
NRC   Nuclear Regulatory Commission
NRDA   Natural Resource Damage Assessment
OPA   Oil Pollution Act of 1990
OPEC   Organization of Petroleum Exporting Countries
OCS   Outer Continental Shelf
OCSLA   Outer Continental Shelf Lands Act
SEMP   Safety and Environmental Management Program
SEMS   Safety and Environmental Management Systems

Appendix C

Executive Order-- National Commission on the BP Deepwater Horizon Oil Spill and Offshore Drilling

By the authority vested in me as President by the Constitution and the laws of the United States of America, it is hereby ordered as follows:

Section 1. Establishment. There is established the National Commission on the BP Deepwater Horizon Oil Spill and Offshore Drilling (the "Commission").

Sec. 2. Membership. (a) The Commission shall be composed of not more than 7 members who shall be appointed by the President. The members shall be drawn from among distinguished individuals, and may include those with experience in or representing the scientific, engineering, and environmental communities, the oil and gas industry, or any other area determined by the President to be of value to the Commission in carrying out its duties.

(b) The President shall designate from among the Commission members two members to serve as Co Chairs.

Sec. 3. Mission. The Commission shall:

(a) examine the relevant facts and circumstances concerning the root causes of the Deepwater Horizon oil disaster;

(b) develop options for guarding against, and mitigating the impact of, oil spills associated with offshore drilling, taking into consideration the environmental, public health, and economic effects of such options, including options involving:

    (1) improvements to Federal laws, regulations, and industry practices applicable to offshore drilling that would ensure effective oversight, monitoring, and response capabilities; protect public health and safety, occupational health and safety, and the environment and natural resources; and address affected communities; and

    (2) organizational or other reforms of Federal agencies or processes necessary to ensure such improvements are implemented and maintained.

(c) submit a final public report to the President with its findings and options for consideration within 6 months of the date of the Commission's first meeting.

Sec. 4. Administration. (a) The Commission shall hold public hearings and shall request information including relevant documents from Federal, State, and local officials, nongovernmental organizations, private entities, scientific institutions, industry and workforce representatives, communities, and others affected by the Deepwater Horizon oil disaster, as necessary to carry out its mission.

(b) The heads of executive departments and agencies, to the extent permitted by law and consistent with their ongoing activities in response to the oil spill, shall provide the Commission such information and cooperation as it may require for purposes of carrying out its mission.

(c) In carrying out its mission, the Commission shall be informed by, and shall strive to avoid duplicating, the analyses and investigations undertaken by other governmental, nongovernmental, and independent entities.

(d) The Commission shall ensure that it does not interfere with or disrupt any ongoing or anticipated civil or criminal investigation or law enforcement activities or any effort to recover response costs or damages arising out of the Deepwater Horizon explosion, fire, and oil spill. The Commission shall consult with the Department of Justice concerning the Commission's activities to avoid any risk of such interference or disruption.

(e) The Commission shall have a staff, headed by an Executive Director.

(f) The Commission shall terminate 60 days after submitting its final report.

Sec. 5. General Provisions. (a) To the extent permitted by law, and subject to the availability of appropriations, the Secretary of Energy shall provide the Commission with such administrative services, funds, facilities, staff, and other support services as may be necessary to carry out its mission.

(b) Insofar as the Federal Advisory Committee Act, as amended (5 U.S.C. App.) (the "Act"), may apply to the Commission, any functions of the President under that Act, except for those in section 6 of the Act, shall be performed by the Secretary of Energy in accordance with guidelines issued by the Administrator of General Services.

(c) Members of the Commission shall serve without any additional compensation for their work on the Commission, but shall be allowed travel expenses, including per diem in lieu of subsistence, to the extent permitted by law for persons serving intermittently in the Government service (5 U.S.C. 5701-5707).

(d) Nothing in this order shall be construed to impair or otherwise affect:

   (1) authority granted by law to a department, agency, or the head thereof; or

   (2) functions of the Director of the Office of Management and Budget relating to budgetary, administrative, or legislative proposals.

(e) This order is not intended to, and does not, create any right or benefit, substantive or procedural, enforceable at law or in equity by any party against the United States, its departments, agencies, or entities, its officers, employees, or agents, or any other person.

BARACK OBAMA

THE WHITE HOUSE,
   May 21, 2010.

Appendix D

Commission Staff and Consultants

Richard Lazarus, *Executive Director*

Tracy Terry, *Deputy Director*

Fred Bartlit, *Chief Counsel*   Jay Hakes, *Director of Policy & Research*

Priya Aiyar
Deputy Chief Counsel

Felicia Barnes
Analyst

Adam Benthem
Analyst

Gordon Binder
Senior Policy Advisor

Paul Bledsoe
Senior Policy Advisor

Jed J. Borghei
Counsel

C. Hobson Bryan
Analyst

Edwin H. Clark, II
Director of Operations

Kate Clark
Senior Analyst

Dave Cohen
Press Secretary

Cindy Drucker
Director of Public Engagement

Katherine Duncan
Analyst

J. Jackson Eaton
Counsel

Michelle Farmer
Executive Legal Assistant

Sean Grimsley
Deputy Chief Counsel

David Greenberg
Senior Policy Advisor

Brent Harris
Counsel

Lisa K. Hemmer
Senior Legal Advisor

Joe Hernandez
Analyst

Joel Hewett
Analyst

Christiana James
Staff Assistant

Jill Jonnes
Senior Researcher

Nancy Kete
Senior Analyst

Caitlin Klevorick
Policy Advisor

Emily Lindow
Senior Analyst

Claire Luby
Assistant to the Executive Director

Bethany Mabee
Communications Coordinator

Scott McKee
Analyst

Claudia A. McMurray
Senior Counsel for Congressional and State Relations

Louise Milkman
Chief of Staff to the Executive Director

Jon Monger
Counsel

Shirley Neff
Senior Analyst

Pete Nelson
Director of Communications

Elena Nikolova
Analyst

Jessica O'Neill
Counsel

Paul Ortiz
Senior Legal Advisor

Tony Padilla
Analyst

Tyler Priest
Senior Analyst

Sarah Randle
Analyst

Irwin Redlener
Senior Public Health Advisor

John S. Rosenberg
Chief Editor

Eric Roston
Senior Analyst

Sara Rubin
Analyst

Sambhav N. Sankar
Deputy Chief Counsel

Nicole A. Sarrine
Staff Assistant

Richard Sears
Senior Science & Engineering Advisor

Steven Siger
Counsel

Robert Spies
Senior Environmental Science Advisor

Danielle Stewart
Staff Assistant

Marika Tatsutani
Editor

Johnny Tenorio
Information Technology Officer

Saritha Komatireddy Tice
Counsel

Lloyd Timberlake
Senior Researcher

Clara Vondrich
Counsel

Jason Weil
Analyst

David Weiss
Counsel

Stephen M. Willie
Administrative Officer

Andrea J. Yank
Assistant to Co-Chair William K. Reilly

Senior Consultants

The Commission would like to thank the following individuals for their contributions to the Commission's work.

Albert Bolea, University of Alaska, *University of Houston*
Darryl A. Bourgoyne, *Louisiana State University*
Robert L. Booth, *National Geographic*
Margaret Caldwell, *Stanford University*
Elmer Peter Danenberger III, *Independent Consultant*
Joann Donnellan, *JD MEDIA, LLC*
Daniel A. Farber, *University of California, Berkley*
Jody Freeman, *Harvard Law School*
Jed Horne, *Freelance Writer*
Mary E. Laur, *University of Chicago Press*
Nancy G. Leveson, *MIT*
Igor Linkov, *US Army Engineer Research and Development Center*
Stephen K. Lewis, *Seldovia Marine Services*
Thomas W. Merrill, *Columbia Law School*
Ishan Nath, *Stanford University*
J.B. Ruhl, *Florida State University College of Law*
John Rogers Smith, *Louisiana State University*
Estes C. Thomas, *Bayou Petrophysics*
Mayank Tyagi, *Louisiana State University*

Organizational Consultants

The Commission would like to thank the following organizations as well as individuals for their contributions to the Commission's work.

Bipartisan Policy Center: Jason Grumet, Nate Gorence, Lourdes Long, David Rosner

Booz Allen Hamilton: Ken Saenz, Walton Smith, Nader Kalifa Betsy Christie, Randolph Sta. Ana, Bob Murray, Dana Ayers, John Papa, Tom Davis, Elizabeth Chervenak, Andrew Gumbiner, Tom Matta, Carrie Bittman, Bob Blaylock, Barbara McKinnon, Roxanne Bromiley, Gary Leatherman, Daniel Gregoire, Ted Perez, Linna Manomaitis, Marianne Martin, Kersley Joseph, James Lee, Christina Ashcraft, Joshua Guenther

Merdian Institute: John Ehrmann, Laura Cantral, Shawn Walker

Nicholas Institute for Environmental Policy Solutions, Duke University: Larry Crowder, Daniel Dunn, Clare Fieseler, Morgan Gopnik, Catherine Latanich, Mike Orbach, Tim Profetta, Linwood Pendleton, Steve Roady, Mary Turnipseed, Cindy van Dover

Resources for the Future: Bob Anderson, Sarah Campbell, Mark A. Cohen, Roger M. Cooke, Art Fraas, Todd Gerarden, Madeline Gottlieb, Carolyn Kousky, Alan Krupnick, Joshua Linn, Molly Macauley, Richard Morgenstern, Lucija Muehlenbachs, Tim Murphy, Ian Parry, Nathan Richardson, Heather L. Ross, Lynn Scarlett, Adam Stern

TrialGraphix: Megan O'Leary, William Lane, Devin Price

Appendix E

List of Commission Meetings

1st Meeting: New Orleans, LA
July 12-13, 2010: Gulf Region Perspectives

2nd Meeting: Washington, DC
August 25, 2010: Regulatory Oversight of Offshore Drilling

3rd Meeting: Washington, DC
September 27-28, 2010: Response & Restoration

4th Meeting: Washington, DC
October 13, 2010: Commission Deliberations

5th Meeting: Washington, DC
November 8-9, 2010: Causes of Macondo Well Blowout & Drilling Safety

6th Meeting: Washington, DC
December 2-3, 2010: Commission Deliberations

Appendix F

List of Staff Working Papers

Over the past several months, Commission staff prepared a number of working papers for use by Commission members to inform their work and deliberations. Listed below are all of the staff working papers completed as of the date of this report. The Staff Working Papers can be found at www.oilspillcommission.gov.

A Brief History of Offshore Drilling (No. 1)

Decision-Making Within the Unified Command (No. 2)

The Amount and Fate of the Oil (No. 3)

The Use of Surface and Subsea Dispersants During the BP Deepwater Horizon Oil Spill (No. 4)

The Challenges of Oil Spill Response in the Arctic (No. 5)

Stopping the Spill: The Five- Month Effort to Kill the Macondo Well (No. 6)

Response/Clean-Up Technology Research & Development and the BP Deepwater Horizon Oil Spill (No. 7)

The Story of the Louisiana Berms Project (No. 8)

Industry's Role in Supporting Health, Safety, and Environmental Standards: Options and Models for the Offshore Oil and Gas Sector (No. 9)

Liability and Compensation Requirements under the Oil Pollution Act (No. 10)

Scientific Research to Support Oil and Gas Decision Making: Evolution of the Department of the Interior's Environmental Studies Program (No. 11)

The National Environmental Policy Act and Outer Continental Shelf Oil and Gas Activities (No. 12)

Offshore Drilling in the Arctic: Background and Issues for the Future Consideration of Oil and Gas Activities (No. 13)

Unlawful Discharges of Oil: Legal Authorities for Civil and Criminal Enforcement and Damage Recovery (No. 14)

Long-Term Regional Restoration in the Gulf: Funding Sources and Governance Structures (No. 15)

Rebuilding an Appetite for Gulf Seafood after Deepwater Horizon (No. 16)

Natural Resource Damage Assessment: Evolution, Current Practice, and Preliminary Findings Related to the Deepwater Horizon Oil Spill (No. 17)

Continuous Improvement Is Essential: Leveraging Global Data and Consistent Standards for Safe Offshore Operations (No. 18)

A Competent and Nimble Regulator: A New Approach to Risk Assessment and Management (No. 19)

Demonstrating a Comprehensive, Rigorous Management Approach for Deepwater Drilling (No. 20)

Federal Environmental Review of Oil and Gas Activities in the Gulf of Mexico: Environmental Consultations, Permits, and Authorizations (No. 21)

INDEX

Page numbers in italics refer to figures and illustrations.